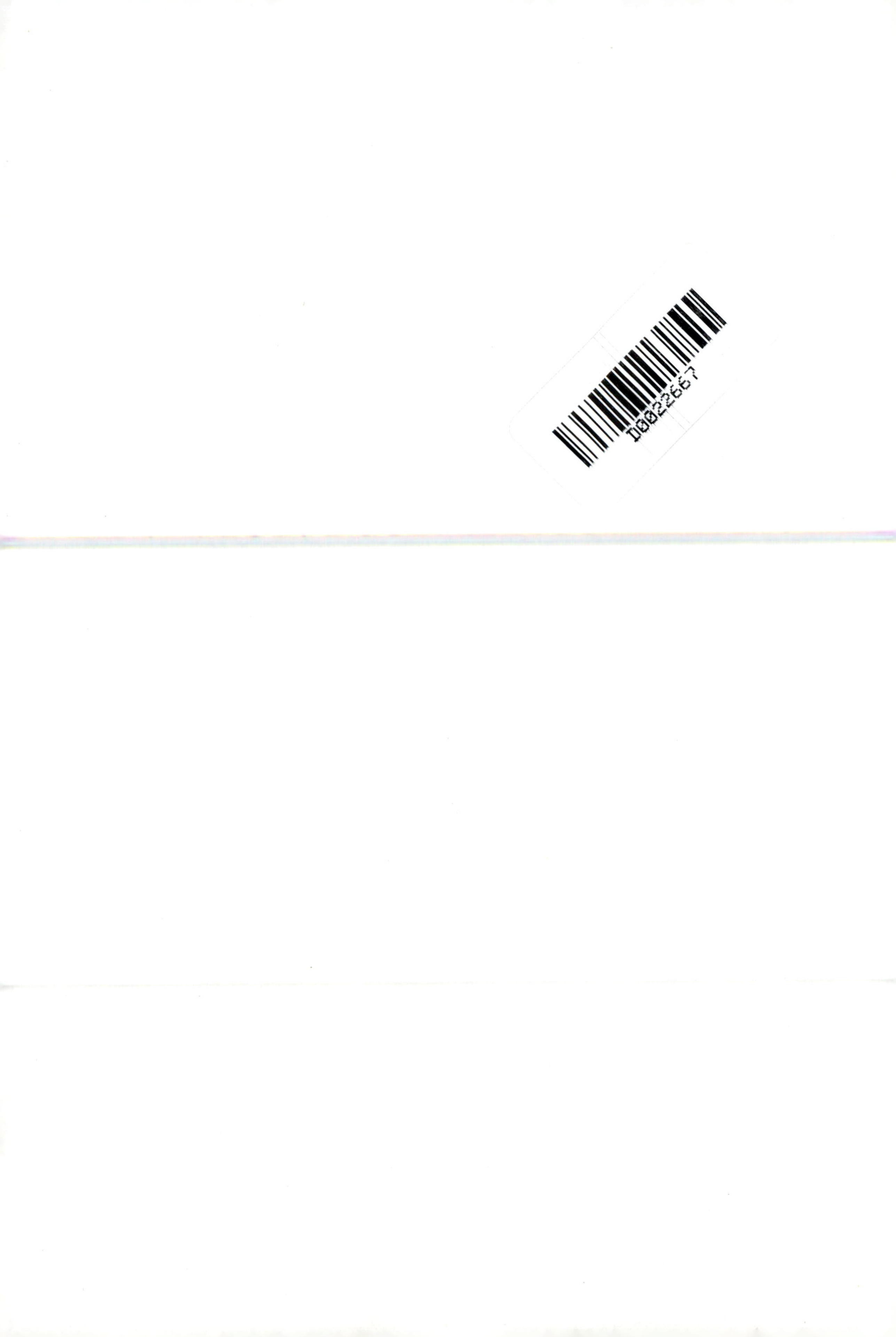

Modern British Women Writers

Modern British Women Writers

An A-to-Z Guide

Edited by Vicki K. Janik and Del Ivan Janik

Emmanuel S. Nelson, Advisory Editor

Greenwood Press
Westport, Connecticut • London

Library of Congress Cataloging-in-Publication Data

Modern British women writers : an A-to-Z guide / edited by Vicki K. Janik and Del Ivan Janik ; Emmanuel S. Nelson, advisory editor.
p. cm.
Includes bibliographical references and index.
ISBN 0–313–31030–0 (alk. paper)
1. English literature—Women authors—History and criticism. 2. Women and literature—Great Britain—History—20th century. 3. English literature—Irish authors—History and criticism. 4. Women and literature—Ireland—History—20th century. 5. Postmodernism (Literature)—Great Britain. 6. Modernism (Literature)—Great Britain. 7. Postmodernism (Literature)—Ireland. 8. Modernism (Literature)—Ireland. I. Janik, Vicki K. II. Janik, Del Ivan, 1945– III. Nelson, Emmanuel S. (Emmanuel Sampath), 1954–
PR116.M63 2002
820.9′9287′0904—dc21 2002016630

British Library Cataloguing in Publication Data is available.

Library of Congress Catalog Card Number: 2002016630
ISBN: 0–313–31030–0

First published in 2002

Greenwood Press, 88 Post Road West, Westport, CT 06881
An imprint of Greenwood Publishing Group, Inc.
www.greenwood.com

Printed in the United States of America

The paper used in this book complies with the Permanent Paper Standard issued by the National Information Standards Organization (Z39.48–1984).

10 9 8 7 6 5 4 3 2 1

For
Victor, Kathleen, Tyra, David, Mary, and Carolyn

Contents

Acknowledgments ix

Introduction xi

Fleur Adcock 1
Roberta M. Schreyer

Beryl Bainbridge 9
André L. DeCuir

Pat Barker 16
Laura Frost

Sybille Bedford 21
Mitchell R. Lewis

Elizabeth Bowen 27
Stella Deen

Vera Brittain 35
Britta Zangen

Anita Brookner 41
Del Ivan Janik

Brigid Brophy 47
Karl L. Stenger

A.S. Byatt 56
Maria Koundoura

Angela Carter 63
Anna Katsavos

Agatha Christie 72
Alan Lutkus

Caryl Churchill 81
Joel Shatzky

Ivy Compton-Burnett 88
Jonathan Bolton

Anne Devlin 93
Susanna Hoeness-Krupsaw

Margaret Drabble 99
Joseph Zeppetello

Maureen Duffy 106
Regina M. Buccola

Buchi Emecheta 113
Jerilyn Fisher

Penelope Fitzgerald 123
Douglas Clayton

Pam Gems 129
José Ramón Prado Pérez

Susan Elizabeth Hill 136
Mary Louise Hill

Winifred Holtby 142
Patricia Rae

Attia Hosain 148
Ashok Bery

Elizabeth Jane Howard 153
Heike Elisabeth Jüngst

P.D. James 159
Tony Giffone

Storm Jameson 166
Phyllis Lassner

Ann Jellicoe 174
Neil Novelli

Pamela Hansford Johnson 180
Chris Hopkins

Charlotte Keatley 187
Regina M. Buccola

Rosamond Lehmann 191
Jonathan Bolton

Doris Lessing 196
Del Ivan Janik

Penelope Lively 207
Jacqueline L. Gmuca

Katherine Mansfield 215
Karla Alwes

Kamala Markandaya 221
Hena Ahmad

Pauline Melville 230
John Thieme

Charlotte Mew 236
Gina Wisker

Penelope Mortimer 247
Jana L. French

Iris Murdoch 253
John Louis DiGaetani

Grace Nichols 257
Suzanne Scafe

Barbara Pym 262
Marlene San Miguel Groner

Jean Rhys 267
Joy Castro

Dorothy Richardson 273
Laura Frost

Vita Sackville-West 280
Peter F. Naccarato

Dorothy L. Sayers 285
Edmund Miller

May Sinclair 296
Melinda Harvey

Edith Sitwell 302
Gina Wisker

Stevie Smith 309
Julie Sims Steward

Muriel Spark 315
Frank Kelly

Lisa St. Aubin de Terán 321
Elizabeth Hoffman Nelson

Elizabeth Coles Taylor 327
Robert Ellis Hosmer, Jr.

Angela Thirkell 335
Mitchell R. Lewis

Sylvia Townsend Warner 341
Chris Hopkins

Fay Weldon 349
Kathleen Ellis

Timberlake Wertenbaker 358
John H. Lutterbie

Mary Wesley 367
Beverly E. Schneller

Rebecca West 372
Sarah Miles Watts

Jeanette Winterson 379
Maria Koundoura

Virginia Woolf 385
Peter F. Naccarato

E.H. Young 396
Stella Deen

Selected Bibliography 403

Index 411

About the Editors and Contributors 423

Acknowledgments

We wish to thank Dr. Emmanuel Nelson for proposing this project to us, and Dr. George Butler for his help in seeing it to completion. We are, obviously, indebted to our many contributors for their cooperation, care, and patience. Part of the editorial work was supported by a summer 1999 PDQWL (Professional Development and Quality of Working Life) Grant from the Joint Labor/Management Committee of United University Professions and the State University of New York and by a sabbatical leave from the State University of New York College at Cortland.

Introduction

Modern British Women Writers: each phrase within the title of this reference work implicitly calls for clarification or at least discussion. We can now look at, if not yet see, the twentieth century as a whole, recognizing that in literary terms—or indeed any terms other than the purely statistical—the isolation of a one-hundred-year period bounded by double zeros is artificial and arbitrary. Nevertheless, as a field for literary commentary, the period from (roughly) 1900 through 1999 seems to offer more than the usual justification for such an exercise. For one thing, the early decades of the century coincided with the rise of what we now call "modernism," not only in literature but also in painting, sculpture, architecture, music, and dance. An early observer of modernist art might well have described it with terms such as haziness, distortion, fragmentation, and dislocation, but from the perspective of later decades the movement seems far less disturbing. One of the most persuasive and least polemical definitions of modernism is David Lodge's in *Working with Structuralism* (1981):

> Modernism turned its back on the traditional idea of art as imitation and substituted the idea of art as an autonomous activity. . . . The writer's . . . style, however sordid and banal the experience it is supposed to be mediating, is so highly and lovingly polished that it ceases to be transparent but calls attention to itself by the brilliant reflections glancing from its surfaces. (5–6)

Lodge writes about fiction in particular, but his comments apply to modernist drama and poetry as well:

> In pursuing reality out of the daylight world of empirical common sense into the individual's consciousness, or subconscious, and ultimately the collective unconscious, discarding the traditional narrative structures of chronological succession and logical cause-and-effect, as being false to the essentially chaotic and problematic nature of subjective experience, the [modern] novelist finds himself relying more and more on literary strategies that belong to poetry, and specifically to Symbolist poetry, rather than to prose. (6)

Modernism, then, offers a more internal and self-reflexive, and therefore potentially more comprehensive, window on the human condition than the approaches to art that preceded it. But Lodge warns against equating "the modern" with the art of the twentieth century. He points out that throughout the period "modernism" coexisted with what he calls "anti-modernism," an anachronistic but more inclusive characterization than "realism" or "traditionalism." Lodge's definition of "anti-modernism" is simple enough:

> This is writing that continues the tradition modernism reacted against. It believes that traditional realism, suitably modified to take account of changes in human knowledge and material circumstances, is still viable and valuable. Anti-modernist art does not [like modernist art] aspire to the condition of music; rather it aspires to the condition of history. (6)

Of postmodernism, a third, later-appearing strain in twentieth-century writing that is also relevant to the subject at hand, Lodge observes,

> Postmodernism continues the modernist critique of traditional realism, but it tries to go beyond or around or underneath modernism, which for all its formal experiment and complexity held out to the reader the promise of meaning. . . . A lot of postmodernist writing implies that . . . whatever meaningful patterns we discern in [experience] are wholly illusory, comforting fictions. (12)

As Lodge, himself a late-twentieth-century novelist and professed antimodernist, asserts, among twentieth-century writers there was no clear chronological progression from one of these broad approaches to writing to another. This is true regardless of gender. T.S. Eliot, James Joyce, Dorothy Richardson, Edith Sitwell, and Virginia Woolf, for example, may all be identified as pioneering modernists. Indeed, Woolf wrote one of the most famous and evocative definitions of modernism in prose (and, for that matter, in poetry and drama):

> Life is not a series of gig-lamps symmetrically arranged; life is a luminous halo, a semi-transparent envelope surrounding us from the beginning of consciousness to the end. Is it not the task of the novelist to convey this varying, this unknown and uncircumscribed spirit, whatever aberration or complexity it may display, with as little mixture of the alien and external as possible? ("Modern Fiction," 106)

Any reader of *Mrs Dalloway* or *To the Lighthouse* soon recognizes the ways in which Woolf practiced the imperatives implied in this statement. The almost seamless interweavings of perspectives and modes of perception in *Mrs Dalloway* and the shifting focuses and asymmetricality of the three "chapters" of *To the Lighthouse* are applications, conscious or not, of the principles outlined in "Modern Fiction." In the ensuing three-quarters of the century Woolf's example was perhaps followed less often in terms of structure or point of view than in sensibility. Elizabeth Bowen and Penelope Fitzgerald, for example, constructed their novels fairly conventionally, but gave their characters the kind of subtlety or indeterminacy of thought that we find in Woolf's.

The antimodernist or realist approach to writing also flourished throughout the century, among women writers as well as men. It is most obviously to be seen in the mystery fiction of Agatha Christie, Dorothy Sayers, and P.D. James, where tightly constructed plots and traditional characterizations are essential to the genre. But it is equally apparent in the work of writers as different as Barbara Pym and Iris Murdoch. Postmodernism is generally considered a phenomenon of the final quarter of the century, but Woolf's *Between the Acts*, with its multiple focus on the playwright, the production of her play, and the play-behind-the-play, as well as its attention to the intersection of history and the immediate present, was postmodernist work from the pen of a "modernist" back in 1941. Other more recent examples include Ann Jellicoe's *The Knack* (1964), Penelope Lively's *Moon Tiger* (1987), and of course A.S. Byatt's *Possession* (1990), with its vertiginously entertaining and highly literate interweaving of the antics of contemporary critics with the lives and works of nineteenth-century poets and lovers. To write of twentieth-century literature, then, is not to pinpoint a particular manner or style. It includes the modernism of Woolf or Sitwell, the traditionalism or antimodernism of Pym and Sayers, and the postmodernism of Byatt or Caryl Churchill.

Furthermore, not all of the events of the twentieth century that affected the lives, works, and livelihoods of British women writers were literary. That is, they were not necessarily matters of writers reading other writers and adapting, modifying, or reacting against their techniques and ideas. The achievement of women's suffrage, the continuing pace of urbanization, the movement of women (in Britain, very gradual) into stereotypically "male" occupations, the redefinitions of class, power, and prestige that were effected, at least in part, by two world wars, the loss of Britain's international dominance, and the shifts of the political spectrum over both the short and long terms—all of these were at least equally important. In the more immediately artistic sense, the possibilities offered to women writers by the proliferation of small and specialized journals, presses, and fringe theaters—and most notably, the reemergence and growth in the final quarter of the century of the political and cultural feminist movements—contributed to the emergence of an identifiable "women's" literature. It gradually became easier for women writers to get their work published and performed: consider the distance between Woolf's lament in *A Room of One's Own* that Jane Austen had found it necessary to hide her manuscript of *Pride and Prejudice* at the approach of visitors (67) and that as late as 1928 one could read in the *New Criterion* that "female novelists should only aspire to excellence by courageously acknowledging the limitations of their sex" (75) and the founding in 1973 of Virago Press, a female and feminist publisher of reprints of "lost" works by writers like Vera Brittain and Rosamond Lehmann as well as new books by Angela Carter, Pat Barker, and Molly Keane and pertinent nonfiction such as Amrit Wilson's *Finding a Voice: Asian Women in Britain* (1978) and *The Heart of the Race: Black Women's Lives in Britain* by Beverley Brian, Stella Dadzie, and Suzanne Scafe (1985). Virago's success undoubtedly contributed to the interest of "mainstream" publishers in contemporary women's writing. Whether or not Woolf's wish for her fellow women writers—an income of £500 a year and a lock on the door—had come true, by the end of the century their chances for professional respect and public success had improved immeasurably.

The writers showcased by Virago Press have not been exclusively British, for they include Irish women like Molly Keane, Canadians like Margaret Atwood, and Americans from Willa Cather to Marilyn French. The scope of the present reference volume is more restricted. Because one volume could not possibly begin to do justice to the literature written by women in the twentieth century in both the United Kingdom and Ireland, it consciously excludes Irish writers except for those who, like Elizabeth Bowen, made their reputations or lived for substantial portions of their lives in the United Kingdom other than Northern Ireland. Not by design, most of the writers treated here are English rather than Scottish or Welsh. Not a few were, or are, émigrés from countries of the former British Empire or Commonwealth, like Katherine Mansfield, Fleur Adcock, and Doris Lessing, and, more recently, women of color like Kamala Markandaya from India and Buchi Emecheta from Nigeria. The increase in ethnic diversity is a trend that of course reflects the United Kingdom's accelerating evolution toward a multiethnic society; we can already recognize in Britain the beginnings of a proliferation of the kind of literature of immigration and assimilation that flourished in the United States a century earlier. It is significant that the most admired and most widely discussed new British novelist of the first year of the twenty-first century was Zadie Smith, a then twenty-four-year-old London-born writer of Jamaican and English parentage.

The final terms of this reference book's title, "women writers," probably raise the most difficult issue: to what extent is writing by women a distinguishable subset of the writing of any period or nation? One could finesse the question by asserting that women writers are, after all, writers who happen to be women, and that like their male counterparts they have written in a wide variety of genres and styles on a wide variety of subjects. But such an attempt at declassification would ignore the many critics who have made valuable observations in defining "women's" writing—British, twentieth-century, or otherwise. Perhaps more important, it would run counter to the judgments of readers of both sexes who are aware—sometimes painfully aware—of the historic and contemporary contrasts and inequities between female and male experience, and who see intimations and reflections of them in fiction, poetry, and drama by women.

As might be expected, there is not much agreement about the nature of "women's" writing. Elaine Showalter, in her 1977 study *A Literature of Their Own: British Women Novelists from Brontë to Lessing*, sees women as a "subculture" who have had to make a special effort at self-definition and self-assertion, much like any other "minority group" (11). Showalter describes a three-part historical development: the first, "Feminine," stage, which she identifies with Jane Austen, George Eliot, and the Brontës, was marked by the internalization of the dominant (male) tradition's standards. In the second, "Feminist," stage, lasting roughly from 1880 to 1920, women writers protested against these standards, often in the context of the movement for women's suffrage. The third, "Female" stage, which Showalter identifies with Dorothy Richardson, Virginia Woolf, and their twentieth-century successors, has involved an inward-turning process of identity seeking and self-discovery (20). According to Showalter, Richardson, Mansfield, and Woolf "created a deliberate female aesthetic, which transformed the feminine code of self-sacrifice into an annihilation of the narrative self, and applied the cultural analysis of the feminists to words, sentences, and structures of language in the novel" (33). Woolf and her contemporaries "tried to create a power base in inner space, an aesthetic that championed the feminine consciousness and asserted its superiority to the public, rationalist, masculine world" (298).

Two years earlier, Sydney Janet Kaplan had offered a definition of such a feminine consciousness:

> [Dorothy Richardson's] discoveries are concerned with state of being and not with state of doing. Miriam [Henderson, Richardson's protagonist] is aware of "life itself"; of the atmosphere of the table rather than of the table; of the silence rather than the sound. Therefore she adds an element to her perception of things which has not been noticed before or, if noticed, has been guiltily suppressed. (79)

Kaplan sees in Woolf's narrative style, too, an expression of a uniquely feminine perceptivity that recognizes the unity of things: "The kind of movement from self to the object of perception, to past and immediate past and present, the movement from perception to reflection and back again is characteristic of these sentences which illustrate the movements of the mind" (82). Maggie Humm points to Doris Lessing as a later exemplar of "feminine consciousness," noting that her novels "never have one simple and overarching structure" (520). Furthermore, Lessing herself insists that women's very thought processes simply differ from men's: "[T]hat's how women see things. Everything is a sort of continuous creative stream" (qtd. in Humm 52).

While many early attempts to define women's writing focused on psychology and language, Humm and other critics of the

1980s and 1990s began to put increasing emphasis on social and political factors. Humm refers to "borders" of genre, history, sexual preference, politics, and race, noting the emergence and importance of Asian and black women "writing in tandem about racism and sexism . . . [in] protest about the experience of Black women in Britain" (57). Flora Alexander writes, "Gender must be placed alongside, for example, social class and cultural background, as one of a set of interesting factors that produce a woman's use of language" (8). Furthermore, Alexander is apparently unconcerned by the acknowledged or recognized influences of male writers on their female counterparts, like Henry James's on Byatt or William Wordsworth's on Drabble: " 'You are what you eat,' says Angela Carter, referring to the formation of her imagination, and the same is surely true of use of language. Some feminists would regard this as colonization of the female by the male, but such analysis proceeds from an unsatisfactorily narrow view of literary value" (9). Anthea Trodd reminds us that writing by British women—even in the half-century most closely associated with modernism—was exceedingly diverse, and asserts that characterizations of "female consciousness" like Kaplan's based on the styles of Woolf and Richardson are simply inadequate:

> As modernism became more self-conscious and exclusive . . . the writers who distinguished themselves as modernists saw their literary activity as entirely distinct from that of other women writers; two sometimes antagonistic groups emerged from the intensive Edwardian engagement with women's issues: the modernists and those [like E. H. Young, Storm Jameson, and Winifred Holtby] who foregrounded content rather than formal innovation. (57)

Olga Kenyon, writing in a more international context, notes the "plurality of voices" in women's writing today: "Writers like Angela Carter and Bessie Head consider the central conflict to be that between men and women. Others, like Margaret Atwood, consider patriarchy a force equal to, and intertwined with capitalism" (9). Even Showalter, more than two decades earlier, had expressed the opinion that already by the 1950s the difference between English female and English male writers was less dramatic than the contrasts between English writers generally and "their more ambitious, explosive American counterparts" (301).

It seems clear that while analyses like Showalter's, Kaplan's, and Lessing's can help to illuminate twentieth-century texts and can suggest further psychological and sociological inquiries, the range and diversity of writing by British women in the twentieth century is too great to be pigeonholed and neatly categorized. We recommend, rather, that our readers explore the more specific biographical, critical, and bibliographical discussions that follow and, best of all, the poems, plays, novels, and stories themselves. Each entry in this reference work includes an overview of the writer's background, an analysis of the writer's work, an assessment of the critical reception of her writings, and primary and secondary bibliographies. The entries are arranged alphabetically to facilitate access, and the volume concludes with a selected bibliography and an extensive index.

WORKS CITED AND CONSULTED

Alexander, Flora. *Contemporary Women Novelists*. London: Edward Arnold, 1989.

Hanscombe, Gillian, and Virginia L. Smyers. *Writing for Their Lives: The Modernist Women 1910–1940*. London: Women's Press, 1987.

Humm, Maggie. *Border Traffic: Strategies of Contemporary Women Writers*. Manchester and New York: Manchester UP, 1991.

Kaplan, Sydney Janet. *Feminine Consciousness in the Modern British Novel*. Urbana: U of Illinois P, 1975.

Kenyon, Olga. *Writing Women: Contemporary Women Novelists*. London and Concord, MA: Pluto, 1991.

Lodge, David. *Working with Structuralism*. London: Routledge, 1981.

Scott, Bonnie Kime, ed. *The Gender of Modernism*. Bloomington: Indiana UP, 1990.

Showalter, Elaine. *A Literature of Their Own: British Women Novelists from Brontë to Lessing*. Princeton: Princeton UP, 1977.

Trodd, Anthea. *Women's Writing in English: Britain, 1900–1945*. London and New York: Longman, 1998.

Woolf, Virginia. "Modern Fiction." In *Collected Essays*, vol. 2. London: Hogarth, 1966.

———. *A Room of One's Own*. 1929. New York: Harcourt, 1981.

Fleur Adcock
1934–

Roberta M. Schreyer

As a poet, Fleur Adcock is keenly attuned to the particular regional imagery surrounding her, as the names of her various books of poetry attest. But her voyages out from New Zealand, first as a five-year-old child who spent the years 1939 to 1947 in London, and later as an adult who in 1963 settled permanently in Britain, embody both a trajectory of migration within the Commonwealth and of unflinching inner exploration when Adcock re-creates her journeys in poetry. In 1975 one of Adcock's most sensitive readers, Judith Moffett, described Adcock's volume of poems *The Scenic Route* as the product of "an authentic talent," one, I would add, whose technical expertise and emotional honesty deserve far more recognition from American readers than has yet been given to her. A poet able to capture the intricacies of ordinary life, Fleur Adcock skillfully celebrates the wonders of everyday emotions.

BACKGROUND

Born in Papakura, New Zealand, to Cyril John and Irene Robinson Adcock, Karen Fleur Adcock spent the most crucial years of World War II and of her childhood in England, where her father pursued a Ph.D. in psychology at the University of London. Both parents participated in the war effort as part of the Civil Defense First Aid Post. The war years spent abroad marked Adcock with great affection for England. Three of her grandparents had immigrated to New Zealand from Manchester, England. In 1914 Sam and Eva Adcock with their ten-year-old son, Cyril John (Fleur Adcock's father), left for New Zealand. About 1904 Alfred Robinson, Fleur's maternal grandfather, left Manchester for New Zealand, where he married Jane Brooks, who was technically a New Zealander, but one who was conceived on the voyage from Northern Ireland to New Zealand.

All of these ancestors are formative influences in Adcock's thinking about Commonwealth identity and the immigrant experience, particularly because much of her life has become a reverse migration back to the country of ancestral origin. In an autobiographical essay Adcock wrote for the *Contemporary Authors* series, she extols her ancestors' pioneer spirit: "to emigrate at all presupposes an adventurous nature, but they also had, or acquired, the versatility and practical skills necessary for survival" ("Autobiographical Essay" 7). In several of her books more than one poem attempts to imagine the hardships and rigors of sailing to a new world, as well as the painful nostalgia for the Old World in those who ventured away from the familiar.

In another autobiographical essay, "Rural Blitz: Fleur Adcock's English Childhood," the poet describes her sojourns in more than seven different schools during the war years spent in England, its German bombardment during the war, and her near-simultaneous discoveries of boys, terror, and poetry. During her first stay with relatives at a farm in Scalford when her parents were in London working for the war effort, boys at her school discovered that the seven-year-old Adcock was terrified of being tickled. "To avoid this I lurked in the playground shed and wrote poetry" ("Rural Blitz" 6). In secondary school she found herself captivated by Tennyson's "The Lady of Shalott" as her notebooks full of youthful poems grew and grew.

When Adcock was thirteen, her family returned to New Zealand, where her father assumed a post as lecturer at the university in Wellington. Having felt thoroughly at home in the English landscape, Adcock experienced a sense of cultural displacement in New Zealand that lasted another sixteen years, until she was able to return to England. In a retrospective view she wrote of the special insights being "an outsider" afforded her: "It is no bad thing to be an outsider, if one wants to see places and events clearly enough to write about them" ("Rural Blitz" 12).

Adcock found departure from England in 1947 heartbreaking, but the sights and sounds of New Zealand, very different from the stringencies of wartime rationing and the threat of bombing in England, all but overwhelmed the young traveler. Grandparents, uncles, cousins, and other relatives greeted Adcock and her family. Even the look of New Zealand stood in marked contrast to that of England:

> There were the unlikely-looking towns, with their sunbaked wooden houses, brightly coloured tin roofs and Wild West–style verandah fronted shops; there were the quaint accents, the casualness of manner, the untroubled prosperity; meals oozed richly with cream, butter, and meat, and the war seemed never to have happened. ("Autobiographical Essay" 11)

Adcock enrolled at Katherine Mansfield's old school, and her English accent incited laughter and ridicule in the local youngsters. Adcock wrote of her 1947 transition back to the land of her birth: "Thirteen is not a good age at which to undergo culture shock: it has shocks enough of its own built into the machinery of puberty" ("Autobiographical Essay" 11). Adcock deeply loved the English countryside, but woods and wildflowers were scarce in New Zealand. Not until she was fifteen did she make close friends who shared her passion for literature. Her poems written during adolescence were modeled after T.S. Eliot's *The Waste Land*, and were full of teenage angst and cosmic despair. But at the same time Adcock was opening her eyes to the incredible physical beauty and seascapes around her in New Zealand.

Almost by accident, Adcock developed a passion for languages: French, Latin, German, and Greek at the university level reflected her "enduring fascination with language itself" ("Autobiographical Essay" 12). Concentrating in the Classics Department at Victoria University proved to Adcock that translating and intensive study of other languages are the best ways to learn one's native language. The facility she gained in Latin was to prove useful in translating medieval verse later in Adcock's career.

Precipitous romantic involvements also began to characterize the poet's life at this time. At eighteen years of age she became engaged to another poet, Alistair Campbell, and married him six months later. A year later, in March 1954, a son, Gregory, was born. Three years later another son, Andrew, was born, and Adcock completed her master's degree. She admitted that she was "young, romantic, and ignorant" when she entered the marriage, and its end was not a surprise ("Autobiographical Essay" 12). Adcock also acknowledged that Campbell was a very good father and that she felt it wrong to remove both sons from his custody. In an arrangement highly unusual for 1960, Fleur left Gregory with his father and his new wife and became Andrew's sole parent.

Writing of the younger woman who made such an unusual maternal choice to surrender one of her children almost completely, Adcock describes a "constant tingling pain" under the scar tissue when she describes that decision. Today she says that she neither understands nor forgives her younger self for leaving Gregory. "I missed most of Gregory's childhood; he grew up without me, and my two sons without each other" ("Autobiographical Essay" 13). Remorse for the loss of Gregory did not fade as Adcock initially thought it would.

To support herself and Andrew, Adcock became a librarian at the university. During the next three years she read voraciously as she formally began her apprenticeship as a writer, experimenting with different styles and techniques once her workday in the library ended. The luxury of having time to write and a setting conducive to writing led to several poems in print. An added discovery was her need for and pleasure in solitude, a solitude that enabled her growth as a poet to occur.

But precipitous romance beckoned again in 1962. At twenty-eight she met and married Barry Crump, a best-selling author who, according to Adcock's article for *Contemporary Authors*, was also physically violent ("Autobiographical Essay" 14). After a year of marriage Adcock filed for separation and booked passage for herself and Andrew to England. Another twelve years passed before Adcock saw New Zealand again.

Her first job in London was in the civil service in the Colonial Office. With her genius for languages, Adcock found herself immersed in learning Italian and traveling with her son on holidays to Florence, Urbino, Siena, Venice, and Ravenna. Subsequent obsessions included the study of medieval Latin literature, twelfth-century history, Romania, and genealogy. In 1983 she was able to publish translations of medieval Latin poetry in *The Virgin and the Nightingale* that were the culmination of interests begun in the 1960s. In 1991 translations of a Romanian poet, Daniela Crasnaru, appeared in *Letters from Darkness: Poems*. The appeal of history and exotic locales is strong in Adcock's work. Adcock's interest in genealogy informs many of the poems in *Looking Back* (1997). *Looking Back* offers its readers an appreciative and often-phantasmagoric view of Adcock's ancestors going as far back as 1327; in the poem "Traitors" she supplies a dramatic poetic account of an ancestor who may have traitorously participated in the assassination of King Edward II and wonders if the blood of traitors runs in her own veins.

But in the year 1963 Adcock was struggling with her own outsider status in the cosmopolitan London scene; she felt sheltered and ignorant of political and social realities that were absent from the more provincial New Zealand. In Britain marches and demonstrations and the solid editorial comments contained in the British press only underscored how insular and isolated her life in New Zealand had been. For a time her efforts to write poetry were paralyzed as she adjusted to culture shock.

During the 1960s most of Adcock's associates in the world of poetry were men; "to be a woman poet [then] was still slightly freaky," she wrote ("Autobiographical Essay" 15). The male poets she met in London were called "The Group" and included George MacBeth, Peter Porter, Anthony Thwaite, Alan Brownjohn, and others. In 1967, as a result of their encouragement, Adcock published her first poetry collection in Britain, *Tigers*, with Oxford University Press. *Tigers* included new poems as well as some of the poems published in her earlier book, *The Eye of the Hurricane* (1964), distributed only in New Zealand.

In the same month as the publication of *Tigers*, Adcock bought her first house, in the suburb of East Finchley, a base she has kept for decades, perhaps as a reaction to the turbulence of her nomadic childhood. In 1975 she made a two-month visit to New Zealand and described her feelings toward the country as, at the very least, "ambivalent." After her "escape" from New Zealand in 1963 she experienced "recurrent nightmares of finding myself back there, trapped, with no return ticket and a weight of smothering guilt. In my waking life the guilt persisted, but so did something of the panic" ("Autobiographical Essay" 15).

In New Zealand she was reintroduced to her grown-up son Gregory; the visit itself she thought of as a "pilgrimage" and a "sacred duty." Abroad she felt herself homesick and exiled from all she loved and identified with England: newspapers; the BBC; medieval churches; varied regional accents; snow, spring, autumn, and fog. Adcock describes herself as possessing exquisite sensitivity to places, and the sensations created in her by traveling have often resulted in poems. In 1979 she left her civil service post permanently in order to dedicate herself to her craft. A two-year fellowship at the Universities of Newcastle upon Tyne and Durham took her to the north of England. At Newcastle she met another New Zealander, Gillian Whitehead, a composer. Adcock and Whitehead began to collaborate, first on a ballad, *Hotspur: A Ballad for Music*, with Adcock writing lyrics to be sung by Harry Percy's wife, Elizabeth Mortimer. The second collaboration, set in the twelfth century, is in a full-length opera libretto about Eleanor of Aquitaine.

In 1983 Oxford University Press released Adcock's *Selected Poems*, a distillation of what Adcock describes as the best of her work. In the 1980s both of Adcock's sons were living in New Zealand, and she found herself editing a collection of contemporary New Zealand poetry. In 1987 she edited a controversial anthology, *The Faber Book of Twentieth Century Women's Poetry*. In describing her personal life, Adcock admits to having had several lovers and to a preference for married men. In forming relationships consciously designed not to be long lasting, she preserves the solitude necessary for her writing life. Adcock seems thankful for the friendships and sense of community created because of poetry when she meets other enthusiasts. Admitting that writing poetry for a living may well be a "selfish" activity, Adcock knows that for her it is also an inescapable one.

ANALYSIS

While several critics note Adcock's fine eye for recording places in her poetry, many think that her poetry is best when she turns her attention to domestic detail and to intimate human relationships. In the poem "For a Five Year Old" in *Tigers*, her disciplined verse about the mother-child relationship avoids both sentimentalizing and romanticizing an essential human bond. Critic Howard Sergeant praises Adcock's "deft command of language" in this and other poems (*Review* 30). An unexpected view of what may be an essential harsh truth in parenting emerges in "For a Five Year Old," as it does in another poem about a son, "For Andrew." In "For Andrew" a child asks, "Will I die?" The poet/parent is forced to circumnavigate the harsh facts of life by couching them in consoling thoughts about his inevitable end. The child meets the parent's euphemisms with flat denial, but the poet sees the child's view as "optimism" that the adult longs to share.

Death intrigues Adcock and calls forth some of her most significant and affecting poems. The Festival of Wellington Poetry Award went to an early poem, "Flight, with Mountains" (*Selected Poems* 3), an elegiac tribute to the poet's friend, David Herron, who was killed in a murderous avalanche. The poem evokes his character, his habits, and his successful raconteur's personality. All are memorably etched into the poet's tribute to Herron, whose remembered presence is as enduring as the sight of the mountains to the poet. When the poem concludes with the assertion that David Herron is departed forever, the powerful evocation of him in the poet's memories shows that the dead friend lives on as a continuing presence in the poet's consciousness, or ego structure, and in her craft.

A remarkable poem to her first husband, "Letter to Alistair Campbell" (*Selected Poems* 101), displays her poetic discursive style at its best. Her life and the lives of her friends and relatives offer the subject matter of Adcock's art, but not with the intent to shock the reader, as in confessional poetry. Julian Stannard writes of a different atmosphere in Adcock's poetic world, where "an abiding impression that one is left with after reading Adcock's work as a whole is a willingness to welcome the reader into an almost familiar, sometimes intimate, world of mood and place and people" (34). Her book *The Scenic Route* is dedicated "in memory to Mother and those others" who endured the hardships of migration from England to New Zealand. In this collection of poems some, like Adcock's grandmother, Martha, are given poetic voice for the first time. A fascination with family history continues in Adcock's work twelve years later in "The Chiffonier" from *The Incident Book* (5).

Another sort of skill emerges in "Beauty Abroad" (*Selected Poems* 4) that reflects Adcock's disciplined use of meter and rhyme to retell the classic French fairy tale by Madame de Beaumont, "Beauty and the Beast." Beauty here is less a feminist than a satiric target to show how easily naïveté and innocence may be gulled and seduced.

Adcock's poetry in the 1960s and 1970s introduced more discordant and unsettling images than did her previous work. Critic John Mole finds a parallel to Adcock's achievement in the work of Robert Graves, "whose combination of fastidious classicism and violent phantasmagoric effect has served her as a model" (Mole 48). Mole adds that just as her mind is never fully at home in the places to which she travels and that she vividly describes in her poems, her imagination also shimmers between waking and sleeping states, luminously dwelling in various states of illusion. "Exile is the condition of her art," Mole adds (48). Among the pleasures of her poetry Mole counts her detailed observations of nature, the erotic candor of the often-anthologized "Against Coupling," and the elegant humor in her views of the literary and social scene. But it is the capacity within her work for a "terrible strangeness" that makes her poetry appealing to Mole and other readers. Adcock admitted in *The Faber Book of Twentieth Century Women's Poetry* that what attracts her in women's poetry is the unexpected detail that renders life's familiar phenomena in a startling and unfamiliar light.

Andrew Motion, writing in the *Times Literary Supplement*, argued that "Fleur Adcock's best poems have something to do with bed: she writes well about sex, very well about illness, and very well indeed about dreaming" ("Under" 922). Her poem "Mornings After" explores the nature of negative and disruptive dreams, an inquiry that challenges the decorum of her waking self, but that also energizes her poetry. At the end of "Mornings After" the poet concludes, as if her consciousness was a book she had read during her lurid dreams, "I do not care to know. Replace the cover" (*Selected Poems* 36). Motion argues that bed is central to her poetic discoveries because in sleep, in sexual passion, and in illness the barriers and inhibitions surrounding the self are temporarily breached. Dreams reveal a more complicated and tortuous self resistant to the artful decorum of conscious, waking life.

The tensions of another life lying latent beneath the daily manifest one have informed Adcock's work since its early days. In "Miss Hamilton in London," one of the first poems in *Selected Poems*, Adcock paints a vivid portrait reminiscent of W. H. Auden's biting satire in his poem "Miss Gee." Adcock's Miss Hamilton is another complacent spinster whose violent and turbulent dream life gives the lie to the ordered pieties of her waking life. In Adcock's poetry Motion sees the irruption of otherness into the placid surface of everyday existence as reminiscent of Movement poetry in general and Philip Larkin's influence in particular.

Julian Stannard's book *Fleur Adcock in Context: From Movement to Martians* (1997) offers an indispensable history of developments in British poetry after World War II. Movement poetry arose in 1950s Britain as part of an antiromantic and antimodernist position in order to foreground "a set of poetic qualities—rationality, economy, orderliness, craftsmanship, and restraint" (7) not bound to a particular historical period. After World War II a reaction against the poet-as-hero or poet-as-protagonist set in, with the example of poet Ezra Pound incarcerated in St. Elizabeth's Hospital warning others of the dangers of mixing poetry with ideology. Philip Larkin's *The Less Deceived* (1955) steadfastly refused the romantic evocations of childhood characteristic of Dylan Thomas's "Fern Hill," emphasizing instead the grim dullness of his Midlands childhood. Emotions are restrained in Larkin's work and in Movement poetry in general. Adcock's *The Incident Book* contains many poems referring to her childhood, an area of experience she often invokes nostalgically.

A. Alvarez's introduction to *The New Poetry* (1962) inaugurated "post-Movement" poetry where truth telling displaces restraint, and a new tone of confessional verse as seen in the work of Anne Sexton and Sylvia Plath usurps some of the restrained decorum of Movement verse. Julian Stannard identifies "truth to experience" and "representational honesty" as watchwords of post-Movement poetry (20). Adcock breaks new ground, according to Stannard, "by taking seriously playful and potentially subversive sidelong glances at a troubled pluralistic society" (20). The avoidance of pomposity and romantic excess characteristic of Movement poetry in favor of a sort of mannered modesty is also part of Adcock's work. What came to be known as post-Movement poetry expressed greater freedoms than Movement verse, and Stannard sees Adcock as strongly influenced by both Movement and post-Movement poetry.

Stannard writes: "To a large extent Adcock's poetry can be seen as a halfway house: she has taken on board and tempered a post-Movement language with its robust onus on clarity, sense, and immediacy, even as she moves into that 'postmodernist' world which resists the imposition of a restrictive logic" (2). Her declarative sentence structure and ordinary speech rhythms evoke the familiar, the everyday, as the domain of her poetry. Adcock's "laconic style," both open and unaffected, seems hardly to be a poetic style at all. Her capacity to express both surprise and consternation, to restrain the murky affects of the unconscious, but also to give them tantalizingly measured expression, makes poems like "An Ex-Queen among the Astronomers" among her best work. In that poem theme is secondary to erotic narrative, and its intensity seems to derive from its reluctance to declare its meaning.

ASSESSMENT

Peter Bland, citing Robert Frost's remark about "a genuine metaphysical tremor," finds Adcock a significant poetic talent. More than one reviewer has remarked on what seems to be a tension between objectivity and expressivity in her work. Qualities of complexity, irony and maturity and the degree of insight in Adcock's poetry would have made her the darling of academic New Critics if they still prevailed in universities. Many of Adcock's poems approximate the standards Cleanth Brooks announced in *The Well Wrought Urn*.

Another way of phrasing the tensions in Adcock's work is advanced by Julian Stannard when he identifies the opposing impulses of "restraint and liberation" that animate her poetry. Stannard argues that "a dynamic of displacement, cultural diversity,

[and] examination of self through distance" characterize Adcock's best work (123). Her poems about family practically invite the reader into a homely matrix, filled with emotion. Adcock's "My Father" (*Time-Zones* 4) compresses deep grief within understated details of a man's hard life of "factory smoke" and "malnutrition." A cruel irony surrounded the composition of the poem: Adcock's father lay dying in New Zealand as she visited Manchester, England, to discover his roots. In "My Father" the attraction of a human presence, the father's lived reality, is magnified by the poet's sense of a vanished community as she struggles to recover the details of his hometown. A keen but understated sense of loss pervades "My Father" as the magnitude of the poet's unfortunately timed quest for ancestors collides with the pain of her father's death.

Always aware of her poetic craft and with a sharp awareness of her own and her readers' intelligence, Fleur Adcock has transformed a "conservative model of poetry," Stannard declares, "into a compelling medium" (123). Restraint, craft, and a finely tuned eye and ear for life's nuances become enduring gifts in Fleur Adcock's versatile verse.

BIBLIOGRAPHY

Primary Sources

The Eye of the Hurricane. Wellington, New Zealand: Reed, 1964.

Tigers. London: Oxford UP, 1967.

High Tide in the Garden. London: Oxford UP, 1971.

The Scenic Route. London: Oxford UP, 1974.

New Poetry Four. Ed. with Anthony Thwaite. London: Hutchinson, 1974.

Below Loughrigg (pamphlet). Newcastle upon Tyne: Bloodaxe, 1979.

The Inner Harbour. Oxford: Oxford UP, 1979.

The Oxford Book of Contemporary New Zealand Poetry. Ed. Fleur Adcock. Auckland: Oxford UP, 1982.

Selected Poems. Oxford: Oxford UP, 1983.

The Virgin and the Nightingale: Medieval Latin Poems. Trans. Fleur Adcock. Newcastle upon Tyne: Bloodaxe, 1983.

"Rural Blitz: Fleur Adcock's English Childhood." *Poetry Review* 74. 2 (June 1984): 4–12.

Four-Pack, One: Four from Northern Women. With Maura Dooley, S. J. Litherland, and Jill Maugham. Newcastle upon Tyne: Bloodaxe, 1986.

Hotspur: A Ballad for Music (pamphlet). Newcastle upon Tyne: Bloodaxe, 1986.

The Incident Book. Oxford: Oxford UP, 1986.

The Faber Book of Twentieth Century Women's Poetry. Ed. Fleur Adcock. London: Faber, 1987.

Meeting the Comet (pamphlet). Newcastle upon Tyne: Bloodaxe, 1988.

Orient Express. By Grete Tartler. Trans. Fleur Adcock. Oxford: Oxford UP, 1989.

Letters from Darkness: Poems. By Daniela Crasnaru. Trans. Fleur Adcock. Oxford: Oxford UP, 1991.

Time-Zones. Oxford. Oxford UP, 1991.

Hugh Primas and the Archpoet. Trans. and ed. Fleur Adcock. New York: Cambridge UP, 1994.

The Oxford Book of Creatures. Ed. with Jacqueline Simms. Oxford: Oxford UP, 1995.

Looking Back. Oxford: Oxford UP, 1997.

"Autobiographical Essay." *Contemporary Authors* 182. Detroit: Gale, 2000. 6–19.

Poems, 1960–2000. Newcastle-upon-Tyne: Bloodaxe Books, 2000.

Secondary Sources

Alvarez, A. *The New Poetry*. Harmondsworth: Penguin, 1962.

Bland, Peter. "Slight Chill." *London Magazine* 25 (October 1985): 82–84.

Edmond, Lauris. "Fleur Adcock." *Landfall* 36 (1982): 320–326.

Moffett, Judith. "Life More and Less Abundantly." *Poetry* 127 (December 1975): 164–175.

Mole, John. "The Reflecting Glass." *Encounter* 62 (March 1984): 46–52.

Motion, Andrew. "Flogged." *New Statesman* 97 (8 June 1979): 833.

———. "Under the Covers." *TLS* 2 September 1983: 922.

Ruddick, Bill. " 'A Clear Channel Flowing': The Poetry of Fleur Adcock." *Critical Quarterly* 26.4 (1984): 61–66.

Sergeant, Howard. "British Poetry, 1952–1977." *Contemporary Review* 231 (October 1977): 196–201.

———. "Poetry in the New Decade." *Contemporary Review* 236 (June 1980): 323–328.

———. Rev. of *Tigers*. *English* 97 (Spring 1968): 30.

Stannard, Julian. *Fleur Adcock in Context: From Movement to Martians*. Lewiston, NY: E. Mellen, 1997.

Stevenson, Anne. "The Recognition of the Savage God: Poetry in Britain Today." *New England Review* 2 (1979): 315–326.

Waller, Gary. "I and Ideology: De-Mystifying the Self in Contemporary Poetry." *Denver Quarterly* 18.3 (Autumn 1983): 123–138.

Williams, Mary C. "The Aesthetics of Accessibility: Contemporary Poetry and Its Audience." *South Carolina Review* 16.1 (Fall 1983): 58–65.

Wood, Michael. "We All Hate Home: English Poetry since World War II." *Contemporary Literature* 18 (Summer 1977): 305–318.

Beryl Bainbridge
1933–

André L. DeCuir

Reading through reviews of Beryl Bainbridge's novels as well as the scholarly articles on her work that are beginning to sprout, one encounters adjectives such as "gothic," "absurdist" ("Beryl Bainbridge," *CLC* 21), "quirky" ("Beryl Bainbridge," *Feminist Companion* 51), and even "comic" (Zimmerman 81). All are applicable to the novels, which can be roughly divided into three "movements": those set in wartime England, those that deal with present-day domestic situations, and her latest novels, which are set around the time of historical events such as the Crimean War and the sinking of the *Titanic*. Her style has been described as "dead-pan" (Richter 171), "impersonal" (Richter 168), and "laconic" (Jefferson 75), but it is precisely this economical style, particularly in descriptions of settings that loom over and intensify the already-diseased psychological states of her characters, that consistently characterizes, throughout all of her fiction, a bleak, unbuffered view of individual human potential.

BACKGROUND

Beryl Bainbridge was born in depression-era Liverpool. She left school at sixteen to become an actress and toured with theater companies throughout the United Kingdom; her novel *An Awfully Big Adventure* is perhaps based upon her experiences and observations during this period of her life. In 1954 she married artist Austin Davis; they had three children and divorced in 1959. Bainbridge seriously turned to writing as a way to support herself, and in 1967 her first novel, *A Weekend with Claude*, was published by Hutchinson's New Authors (it was later rewritten and published in 1981 by Duckworth). As her career as a novelist began, she turned out a novel nearly every year and was eventually nominated for the Booker Prize five times. She won the Guardian Fiction Award in 1974 for *The Bottle Factory Outing*, the Whitbread Award in 1977 and 1996 for *Injury Time* and *Every Man for Himself*, and the W.H. Smith Fiction Prize in 1999 for *Master Georgie*. Her early novels draw upon her life in wartime England; her characters are often cold and hungry due to poverty made worse by rationing. She later turned to historical fiction, but she has also written short stories, articles, screenplays, and travel literature. She lives in London.

ANALYSIS

Novels such as *Harriet Said* (1972), *The Dressmaker* (1973; published in the United States as *The Secret Glass*), *A Quiet Life*

(1976), and *An Awfully Big Adventure* (1989) are perhaps the best examples of Bainbridge's "wartime Gothic" period because of atmospheres of "deprivation, disintegration and pervasive violence" (Richter 159). *Harriet Said* is a psychological portrait of the unnamed thirteen-year-old narrator, easily manipulated by her free-spirited friend, Harriet. While there are implications that the narrator harbors secret erotic desires for Harriet, the focus of the novel is the narrator's crush on a married man, Mr. Biggs, also known as the Tsar. Harriet encourages the narrator to pursue the man, and if the narrator is to be believed, they kiss on occasion and eventually have sex. One evening, when Mrs. Biggs is away, the girls visit the Tsar at his home. When he leaves the girls alone to go out and buy cigarettes, Mrs. Biggs returns unexpectedly. Harriet hands the narrator a walking stick and tells her to hit Mrs. Biggs. The narrator complies, killing Mrs. Biggs, and then the girls calmly plan to tell the authorities that Mr. Biggs attacked and murdered his wife.

The action of the novel takes place in post–World War II Formby, a small seaside town amid the profuseness of summer gardens and fragrances, representative of the adolescent girls' burgeoning sexuality, but a sexuality that must be kept in check according to society's norms. The tragedy, however, initiated by the tension between the girls' desire to express these new feelings and the subconscious awareness of society's attempts to suppress them, is foreshadowed by the still-present remnants of the war. Bainbridge, for example, ingeniously places the narrator's sexual encounter with the Tsar on a part of the beach that is still used as a rifle range, off limits to civilians and posted with warning signs.

A similar scene appears in *A Quiet Life*, which focuses upon the implosion of a lower-middle-class family. Because the war is over, the father has lost his sense of importance; he was an air-raid warden, and now he has become bitter and impatient. Finding her husband's demeanor intolerable, the mother spends her evenings reading at the railway station. The adolescent son, Alan, tries to hold his family together, while Madge, the teenage daughter, has trysts with a German POW, sometimes on the beach where active mines still lie. As in *Harriet Said*, a landscape of still-deadly remainders of past wide-scale destruction prepares for the individual emotional destruction of some of the novel's characters.

An Awfully Big Adventure, while focusing mainly on a "family" of actors in a Liverpool theater troupe, employs many of the elements of earlier novels. Stella Bradshaw is the theater company's newest and youngest member. Raised by her aunt and uncle after being abandoned by her mother, the love-starved Stella becomes infatuated with the troupe's leader, Meredith Potter. When he does not recognize her in the way she would like, she hopes to make him jealous by allowing herself to be seduced by an aging actor, P.L. O'Hara. She learns later that Potter is attracted to men, and in a twist that Richter says "links Bainbridge directly to the Gothic tradition: the motif of incest" (164), the reader learns that O'Hara is Stella's father. His mind reeling from this realization, O'Hara is killed in an accident. When Stella learns of his death, she appears to phone and speak to her mother from a phone booth, but with a final stroke of pathos, Bainbridge shows us that she is crying to the time and temperature recording. As in earlier novels, occasional descriptions of the physical remains of the war such as blasted churches and other buildings foreshadow the personal emotional devastation of characters such as Stella and O'Hara.

Perhaps the novel that best applies the traditional Gothic style to a study of physical and psychological landscapes in World War II Liverpool is *The Dressmaker*. Young Rita lives with her two aunts, Nellie and Margo. Nellie, the dressmaker of the novel's title, seems to be a throwback to the Victorian era, always dressed in black, concerned with what is and what is not proper, and almost tyrannical in her rule of the household. Margo is a more "modern" woman who works in a factory and appears to be more permissive and fun-loving. Rita falls in love with a rude, illiterate American soldier named Ira, who seduces Margo. Nellie "catches" them when they are finished, but when she finds that Ira has scratched her mother's table with the buttons of his coat as he dresses, she stabs him with scissors and kills him. She calmly sews a "body bag" for Ira's corpse, cleans the crime scene, and calls her brother Jack, who will transport the body to the river in his van.

This sudden violence springing from a long repression of feelings, a staple of the Gothic narrative, is foreshadowed by descriptions of bombed out sections of the city and many references to the cramped, cold, dark homes of the main characters and their neighbors. Virginia Richter relates these settings to the ruined monasteries of the Gothic novel, but while Phyllis Lassner in "Fiction as Historical Critique: The Retrospective World War II Novels of Beryl Bainbridge and Maureen Duffy," acknowledges the Gothic theme of the release of the repressed, she downplays the effect of the wartime landscape and implicates the industrial landscape as linked to the characters' aberrant psychological states. I would emphasize the importance of Bainbridge's war-torn landscapes, however, in an attempt to understand better her view of the individual, a view that she seems to put to the test in novels that take place long after and before the war. In the wartime novels, while the collective violence has ceased or is about to cease, individual apathy, pettiness, and brutishness are alive and well. In novels such as *Sweet William* (1975) and *Injury Time* (1977) the war is long over and the physical debris has been swept away, but the psychological malaise of the characters persists, perhaps as a legacy of the war; but more disturbingly, as put forth in Bainbridge's later novels, perhaps it has always existed in every era of human history, and it has worsened, with no means of relief in sight.

Sweet William is a convincing study of how an individual, Ann, can become totally dependent on a lover, William, who is deemed repellent by those observing the relationship, but also, at times, by the dependent party. William is a playwright who has been married at least twice and has lovers, both female and male. He maintains contact with them and even provides financial support for some of them and any children he may have sired. At no time does he judge the morality of his behavior, and he adds Ann to his list of liaisons. Ann knows that William is bad for her, but she cannot bring herself to break away from him. She becomes as morally numb as William and his circle of wives and lovers as she breaks off her engagement to a fiancé in America, quits her job, and has a child out of wedlock, a child that turns out to be Gerald's, her ex-fiancé's, and not that of "Sweet William."

In *Injury Time* a group of middle-aged friends with middle-class occupations is invited to a dinner party thrown by Binny, who happens to be having an affair with a married man, one of the guests. In the novel Bainbridge introduces other characters who show the turbulence beneath the seemingly quiet suburban facade, such as an abused wife and the mad Mrs. Papastavrou, who attacks the meals-on-wheels delivery woman and who wails on the balcony of her apartment building every night for about half an hour. The most obvious intrusion of the violence of the world into the seemingly immune suburban realms occurs when four escaping bank robbers break into Binny's home and hold her guests hostage. Bainbridge's usual matter-of-fact style of narration underscores the jaded natures of her characters as they seem to accept passively the intrusion, their captivity, and their humiliation as "part of the structure of [their] existence" (Richter 160).

When Bainbridge sets her novels in the past (the nineteenth and early twentieth centuries), such as *The Birthday Boys* (1991),

Every Man for Himself (1996), and *Master Georgie* (1998), she seems to explore a different facet of humanity; the apathy inherent in her characters from the post–World War II novels, according to Bainbridge's vision, has always existed and has perhaps contributed to (and still can contribute to) examples of humanity's inability to achieve "greatness" except through chance or through participation in disaster, initiated by human fallibility. This string of historical novels begins with *Young Adolf* (1978) and *Watson's Apology* (1984), the former a fictional account of Adolf Hitler's visit to Liverpool in 1912, and the latter a novel based upon an actual Victorian murder case.

In *Young Adolf* the twenty-three-year-old Adolf Hitler visits his brother, Alois, and sister-in-law in Liverpool. The "shock" for the reader in this novel perhaps depends on the reader's knowledge of Hitler as Führer rather than on a sudden act of violence committed by a character, for the young Hitler is portrayed, like many of Bainbridge's characters, as sullen, weary, perhaps more unambitious, but prone to hallucinations and fits—a depiction far removed from history's charismatic figure. He spends much of his time lying on his relatives' couch until he finally gets a job as an errand boy at a posh hotel. Because of Bainbridge's usual distanced narrative style, the reader experiences neither sympathy for nor revulsion toward young Adolf. While no clear reason is given for young Adolf's transformation into the Hitler of history, small, superficial trademark details are explained. For example, Hitler's first brown shirt is made by his sister-in-law, Bridget, and it is she who suggests that he comb his hair down and to the side in order to hide bruises received in an attempt to rescue poor children from a future of hard labor. These homely details, plus a character's comment at the end of the novel, "It is a pity he will never amount to anything," suggest that for Bainbridge human greatness or infamy may only be achieved by chance.

Human "ordinariness" is overcome through violence in *Watson's Apology*, a novel based upon an actual Victorian murder case. Bainbridge fashions her narrative into a series of journal entries, court documents, and newspaper reports in order to relate the case of John Selby Watson, a clergyman/headmaster/writer who beats his wife, Anne, to death, presumably because of her irritable personality. Ingeniously, "[p]oor dull" Watson's "mundane murder case" (Stasio 7), on Bainbridge's pages, results from the pressures of the "dull," "mundane" existence of Victorian women (Anne, at one point, describes her demeanor as the result of being left alone with nothing to do), and the novel becomes a part of the body of cultural criticism of that era.

Given Bainbridge's questioning of the individual's ability to aspire to greatness, it should be no surprise that her three most recent novels are considered "an ambitious trilogy of novels that dissect great examples of human folly" (Gleick 122). The facts behind *The Birthday Boys*, for example, seem most appropriate for a study of the vision versus the reality of human ambition. The novel is based upon Robert Scott's early-twentieth-century expedition to the South Pole, the disappointment at finding that the Norwegians had reached the pole at least a month before, and the deaths of the men on the way home. The novel is narrated by five members of the expedition, and Bainbridge grants each of them the ability to describe poetically their magnificent but deadly surroundings and to recognize, despite life-threatening hardships, greatness in each other.

Every Man for Himself has as its historical backdrop the sinking of the *Titanic*, that "unsinkable" ship designed and put together, of course, by human minds and hands. The novel is narrated by young, upper-class Morgan, but he is different from the other characters of this class because of his somewhat sketchy origins. His mother was the "half-sister" of the wealthy Morgan of New York who, after eloping to Europe, was deserted by her husband and died of influenza three years after young Morgan's birth. He was then placed in an orphanage in London until he was "found" by the Morgan family. Perhaps it is this background that is responsible for young Morgan's belief that men should be treated equally and that makes him an appropriate narrator to relate the vanity, pettiness, and utter cruelty, even in the face of imminent disaster, of the other upper-class passengers. Despite Bainbridge's usual distanced narrative stance, Morgan becomes one of her most sympathetic characters, and her prose is at its most lyrical, especially in the descriptions of parts of the wreckage swirling in the sea and the ice.

Bainbridge's 1996 novel, *Master Georgie*, perhaps most clearly addresses the problem of human beings' inability to achieve greatness even when they are placed in circumstances that could easily lead to it (heroism in war). The exploration of such a predicament begins with the novel's title. Master Georgie is George Hardy of the upper classes, a surgeon who decides to offer his services on the Crimean battlefield, but by the end of the novel the reader still does not know very much about George Hardy, as he is never given a "voice" that could at least exaggerate the significance of his exploits. Instead, the novel is narrated by three characters, Myrtle, a house servant of the Hardy family who is in love with George, Pompey Jones, a streetwise photographer's assistant, and Dr. Potter, George Hardy's brother-in-law, all of whom reveal more about themselves than about Master Georgie. At the novel's end, right after a bloody skirmish, George is shot and killed by a wounded Russian soldier, not while heroically trying to save the lives of the wounded, but while stopping to attend to Myrtle, who has twisted her ankle. George's corpse is then dragged to a group of surviving soldiers and "posed" with them for a photographer who believes that the shot of the "survivors" will be a good one "to show the folks back home."

ASSESSMENT

Those who study Bainbridge's work agree that her novels have yet to achieve a substantial readership in the United States, and Bainbridge herself is often grouped with British novelists such as Jean Rhys, Muriel Spark, Iris Murdoch, Harold Pinter, and Henry Green. Diane Johnson believes that the reason for this neglect on the part of the American readership is rooted in the classic American psyche itself:

> Perhaps Americans are surprised that the characters do not exert themselves more mightily than this against outrages of poverty and inconvenience; although exigency is certainly a fact of American life, it has little place in American fiction. . . . Except for some Depression literature about cutting out shoe soles from cereal boxes, our stories are all about escape and change. In an American story, if you start out poor, you are bound to end up rich or disillusioned. (98)

Johnson's assessment of American literature seems to be based mainly upon nineteenth-century sentimental fiction and ignores elements that could make Bainbridge's novels just as palatable as those of American writers who share her gloomy view of humanity—a minimalist narrative style fashioned from that of writers such as Hemingway and Carver and the grotesque, violent twists of a Flannery O'Connor. Her reporter's narrative style that intensifies her naturalistic view of humanity makes her narrative voice seem a compassionless one, but then, with a few well-chosen and carefully placed words, a repulsive character can begin to elicit some sympathy from the reader. Krystyna Stamirowska, for example, believes that Nellie, who viciously kills Ira in *The Dressmaker*, is made to seem less like a "monster" when Bainbridge allows us to read her concern for her niece, Rita, if she and Margo should be taken into custody. Similarly, at the conclusion of *An Awfully Big Adventure* a few lines exposing Stella crying to the time and temperature recording somewhat lessen a view of Stella as a conniving opportunist.

American readers might also find similarities between Bainbridge's fiction and that of Flannery O'Connor, especially in the element of violence that becomes farcical and absurd on their pages. Perhaps Bainbridge's finest example of this dark humor can be found in *The Bottle Factory Outing* (1974). The novel is centered around two roommates, the flamboyant Freda and the withdrawn Brenda, Englishwomen who work at an Italian wine-bottling factory. On an outing to a park with coworkers, Freda is accidentally killed while trying to resist the advances of one of the workers. Her death moves into the realm of the absurd because of the reaction of the group. Rather than call the police, Freda's coworkers decide that her death should not prevent them from enjoying the rest of their holiday, so they seat her body in a car and go on to the zoo. Back in the city, Freda's body is taken back to the bottle factory, where the workers lay it out in a white gown and surround it with plastic flowers. Her death moves completely onto the absurdist plane when her coworkers decide to place her body in an empty wine barrel and ship it to Spain. They will label the barrel as containing bad wine, for one of the bottle-factory workers knows that the practice of those men unloading the barrels, upon seeing the warning labels, is to throw such barrels into the sea.

Brenda and Freda form part of a long cast of female characters created by Bainbridge, but occasionally her novels are centered on male protagonists or are told from the perspectives of male characters. While her novels, according to Virginia Richter, "do not profess an explicitly feminist message" (163), they do address, sometimes directly, sometimes subtly, issues that women writers have addressed throughout time, such as the repression and fear of female sexuality in *Harriet Said*, *The Dressmaker*, and *A Quiet Life* and the limited choices available to women, both socially and professionally, in *The Bottle Factory Outing*, *Sweet William*, and *Injury Time*. Even in a novel such as *The Birthday Boys*, which is told from the points of view of five men on a voyage to the South Pole in 1912, Captain Robert Scott's memories of his wife, Kathleen, form a portrait of a good-natured, unconventional woman. She "wears her hair down indoors and goes barefoot," slept outside in the garden when she was pregnant because she believed that her "child needed to lie under the stars," and sends photographs of her friend, Isadora Duncan, to her husband—a far cry from Conrad's angel in the house "Intended" in *Heart of Darkness*.

American readers may indeed find the subject matter of Bainbridge's early novels (post–World War II England, the lives of Britain's lower-middle classes) too unfamiliar to capture and hold interest, but perhaps her later ones, particularly *Every Man for Himself*, about the sinking of the *Titanic*, may finally establish a following. Bainbridge comments on the strong sales of the book in a 1998 *Publishers Weekly* interview: "The film didn't hurt, of course" (Baker 53). Even a reader discovering Bainbridge by reading her later novels will still be treated to her consistent yet compact narrative style that allows for keen psychological portraiture and sweeping historical epics under two hundred pages.

BIBLIOGRAPHY

Primary Sources

A Weekend with Claude. London: Hutchinson, 1967. Rev. ed. London: Duckworth, 1981; New York: Braziller, 1982.

Another Part of the Wood. London: Hutchinson, 1968. Rev. ed. London: Duckworth, 1979; New York: Braziller, 1980.

Harriet Said. London: Duckworth, 1972; New York: Braziller, 1973.

The Dressmaker. London: Duckworth, 1973. Published in the United States as *The Secret Glass*. New York: Braziller, 1974.

The Bottle Factory Outing. London: Duckworth, 1974; New York: Braziller, 1975.

Sweet William. London: Duckworth, 1975; New York: Braziller, 1975.

A Quiet Life. London: Duckworth, 1976; New York: Braziller, 1977.

Injury Time. London: Duckworth, 1977; New York: Braziller, 1977.

Young Adolf. London: Duckworth, 1978; New York: Braziller, 1979.

Winter Garden. London: Duckworth, 1980; New York: Braziller, 1981.

English Journey (nonfiction). London: Duckworth, 1984; New York: Braziller, 1984.

Watson's Apology. London: Duckworth, 1984; New York: McGraw, 1985.

Mum and Mr. Armitage. London: Duckworth, 1985; New York: McGraw, 1987.

Filthy Lucre: or, The Tragedy of Ernest Ledwhistle and Richard Soleway. London: Duckworth, 1986.

Forever England: North and South (nonfiction). London: Duckworth, 1987.

An Awfully Big Adventure. London: Duckworth, 1989; New York: Harper, 1991.

The Birthday Boys. London: Duckworth, 1991.

Something Happened Yesterday (nonfiction). London: Duckworth, 1993.

Every Man for Himself. London: Duckworth, 1996.

Master Georgie. London: Duckworth, 1998.

According to Queeney. London: Little, Brown and New York: Carroll, 2001.

Secondary Sources

Baker, John F. "Beryl Bainbridge: Total Immersion in the Past." *Publishers Weekly* 9 November 1998: 52–53.

"Beryl Bainbridge." In *Contemporary Literary Criticism*. Vol. 62. Detroit: Gale, 1991.

"Beryl Bainbridge." In *The Feminist Companion to Literature in English*. Ed. Virginia Blain, Patricia Clements, and Isobel Grundy. New Haven: Yale UP, 1990.

"Beryl (Margaret) Bainbridge." In *Contemporary Authors: New Revision Series*. Vol. 75. Detroit: Gale, 1999.

Gleick, Elizabeth. "Mistress of Her Domain." *Time* 30 November 1998: 122.

Jefferson, Margo. "Violence under Glass." *Newsweek* 12 August 1974: 75–76.

Johnson, Diane. "Young Adolf Goes to Beryl Bainbridge's England." In *Terrorists and Novelists*. New York: Knopf, 1982. 97–104.

Lassner, Phyllis. "Fiction as Historical Critique: The Retrospective World War II Novels of Beryl Bainbridge and Maureen Duffy." *Phoebe* 3.2 (1991): 12–24.

Millard, Barbara C. "Beryl Bainbridge." In *British Novelists since 1960*. Vol. 14. *Dictionary of Literary Biography*. Detroit: Gale, 1983.

Punter, David. *The Hidden Script: Writing and the Unconscious*. London: Routledge, 1985.

Richter, Virginia. "Grey Gothic: The Novels of Beryl Bainbridge." *Anglistik und Englischunterricht* 60 (1997): 159–171.

Stamirowska, Krystyna. "The Bustle and the Crudity of Life: The Novels of Beryl Bainbridge." *Kwartalnik Neofilologiczny* 35 (1988): 445–456.

Stasio, Marilyn. "He Hid, She Howled." *New York Times Book Review* 20 October 1985: 7, 9.

Wennö, Elisabeth. *Ironic Formula in the Novels of Beryl Bainbridge*. Göteborg, Sweden: Acta Universitatis Gothoburgensis, 1993.

Yakovleva, Valentina. "On Reading Beryl Bainbridge." *Soviet Literature* 11 (1984): 141–149.

Zimmerman, Paul D. "Man for No Seasons." *New York Times Book Review* 17 May 1976: 81.

Pat Barker
1943–

Laura Frost

In 1995 Pat Barker won Britain's most prestigious literary award, the Booker Prize, for her novel *The Ghost Road.* The competition, which pitted Barker against authors as formidable as Salman Rushdie (*The Moor's Last Sigh*), signaled Barker's centrality to contemporary British literature. Readers of Barker's historically based trilogy about World War I—*Regeneration* (1991), *The Eye in the Door* (1993), and *The Ghost Road*—will be familiar with the unerring dialogue, compellingly complex characters, and masterful interweaving of fiction and history that earned Barker the Booker. However, prior to the trilogy Barker had published four regional novels about diverse working-class British lives that address many of the same themes—psychic trauma, conflicts of identity and moral choices, violence (in many forms), and the haunting of the past. Barker's intimate portraits of tightly circumscribed working-class lives are as captivating and convincing as her elegant historical fiction. Above all, Barker is a writer of remarkable range and intellectual depth whose contributions have revitalized the contemporary British novel.

BACKGROUND

Barker was brought up in a very poor working-class home in the Northeast of England. An illegitimate child (Barker says that she has still not discovered the identity of her father, a soldier), Barker was raised by women—a background that was formative for her deep concern with questions of class and sexuality, and her search for a feminism that is not exclusive or dogmatic. Barker's education took her out of the working-class world: she attended the London School of Economics, where she studied social sciences and became a specialist in diplomatic history, and she went on to teach history and politics. In 1970, after the birth of her son, she started to pursue creative writing. It was none other than Angela Carter, Barker's writing teacher, who encouraged Barker to write about her working-class background and who took the manuscript of *Union Street* to Virago Press, where it was eventually published. *Union Street* won the Fawcett Society Book Prize and was a runner-up for the *Guardian* Fiction Prize: Barker had "arrived." With this auspicious launching, Barker wrote three more novels about working-class characters (*Blow Your House Down, The Century's Daughter*, and *The Man Who Wasn't There*). Although these texts have often been viewed in the tradition of regional novelists of the 1960s (including Alan Sillitoe and John Osborne), Barker has said that she feels more literary affinity with African American women novelists such as Gloria Naylor and

Toni Morrison than she does with other British novelists, past or present. Indeed, Barker's explorations of gender, sexuality, and trauma set her well apart from her predecessors in the genre of the regional novel.

With the World War I trilogy Barker moved into new generic territory: the historical novel and the war novel, both of which have been primarily male-authored genres. Barker brings her historian's background and her sure touch for psychological portraits to the historical novel. The trilogy gives life to sociological and literary studies of war such as Paul Fussell's *The Great War and Modern Memory* and, conversely, gives a strong historical grounding to contemporary fiction that looks back on the wars. Although literary devices such as flashbacks and memories result in technical disruptions of strictly chronological narrative, Barker's work to date cannot be accurately classified as "postmodern," as it follows more in the tradition of linear, strongly plotted novels with a main narrator and conflicted but clearly delineated characters.

In postwar Britain there have been several periods in which the novel was declared "dead" as a genre. Barker is one of the most innovative among a generation of writers who have revitalized and increased the scope of the contemporary British novel. Many, including A.S. Byatt, Kazuo Ishiguro, and Jeanette Winterson, have turned to narratives of the past in structuring their novels; Barker joins these authors in their explorations of the function of history and memory in relation to the novel.

ANALYSIS

Barker's first novel, *Union Street* (1982), is comprised of seven separate but tangentially related sections about seven working-class women who live along one street. Their lives are rough, gritty, and mainly sad. The stories subtly reflect the progressive stages of a woman's life, from childhood through adolescence, marriage, motherhood, and old age, but this scheme is subordinated to the vivid realist style (the first story has echoes of early Joyce) in which the women's stories are told and the relish with which Barker renders dead-on colloquial dialogue and dark humor.

Even on Union Street, where many women raise children alone and struggle for money to feed them, there is a place that is worse: Wharfe Street. This dilapidated strip of broken-down houses, drug addicts, and prostitutes hovers in the background of several of the Union Street stories, and Barker uses this site to mark intraclass distinctions invisible to most other writers. Iris King, for example, who has pulled herself up from Wharfe Street, is driven back to her old neighborhood to arrange an illegal abortion for her daughter in order to protect the margin of class mobility she has achieved for her children. Domestic violence and sexual trauma are recurring themes in the novel, and Barker suggests that a woman's sexual experiences shape her life as profoundly as any other element. The women's stories are mainly joyless and depressing (the first section is about a young girl who is raped and "forces" her assailant to take her out for fish and chips afterward), but they are narrated with an intensity that is itself exhilarating even when the lives are not.

The penultimate section in *Union Street*, about an aging prostitute, led to Barker's next novel, *Blow Your House Down* (1984). This harrowing portrait (almost a psychological thriller) about a group of prostitutes in Yorkshire who are threatened by a serial murderer was a response to the real Yorkshire Ripper killings. Barker remarked in an interview, "Nobody paid any attention to the Ripper killings until a middle class girl was killed" (Perry 242). By shifting the focus to the primary victims, Barker's novel reveals the insidious class prejudices of the case. She begins by describing a warm domestic scene with a woman putting her children to bed; only in the following chapters does the reader learn that the woman is a prostitute. Barker portrays these women's whole lives (including first-person narration and scenes of pub camaraderie), rather than emphasizing their professions (as the newspaper coverage of the Yorkshire Ripper did). But *Blow Your House Down* does not whitewash the violence of the Ripper killings: it includes some very raw descriptions of the murders. One horrifying passage shows a killing from the murderer's perspective, the physical detail of which (including an association with a chicken-butchering factory) is very hard to read.

Characterizing her work at this point, Barker remarked in an interview, "[I]t's regional, it's working class, it's female, for God's sake" (Smith 99). She seemed to be frustrated with the critical reception that praised her narrative skill but constantly qualified that praise by emphasizing the author's gender and the class and regional settings of her work: for example, "a working-class masterpiece" instead of simply a masterpiece. Her subsequent novels strove for a larger scope.

The Century's Daughter (1986) takes a step back from the visceral horror and the almost unrelentingly bleak visions of Barker's first two novels. The novel entails more radical experiments with temporality, shifting between two characters in the present and a century's worth of memories from a woman born precisely at the turn of the century. *The Century's Daughter* involves a chronological sweep and historical background that Barker would later refine in the World War I trilogy. In a sense the novel marks a transition between the close focus of Barker's first two novels and the subsequent work. While it is skillfully executed, it does not have the riveting quality of Barker's previous or later novels. Barker's next novel, *The Man Who Wasn't There* (1988), can be similarly read as an early exploration of themes Barker would more fully articulate in the trilogy. The protagonist of *The Man Who Wasn't There* is a twelve-year-old boy, Colin, whose father died in World War II and who is brought up by women. Colin is fascinated by movies about the war, and the scenes of violence, treachery, and conspiracy surface in Colin's vivid fantasy life, in which a shadowy figure is Colin's double.

At this point Barker left Virago, the women's-collective press that had published her first four novels, for the larger Viking Penguin. Her subsequent novels adopted a cooler, less intense tone than her first novels. *Regeneration* (1991) is a stunning, carefully crafted work—perhaps Barker's best to date. She does not bring her reader quite so close to the explicit violence of *Union Street* and *Blow Your House Down*, but this increased distance allows for more tonal range and more subtle characterization. The whole trilogy takes place in under two years and centers on W. H. Rivers, a physician who has specialized in the treatment of "shell-shock": war-related psychic disorders. *Regeneration* focuses on Rivers's attempt to evaluate the mental condition of a conscientious objector (a "conchie"), the eminent poet and decorated second lieutenant Siegfried Sassoon. If Sassoon is found mentally unbalanced, the political implications of his public declaration that "the war is very deliberately prolonged by those who have the power to end it" will be undercut. Sassoon is clearly not insane, but his divided impulses—he objects to the war but wants to go back to the front to help his men survive—test Rivers's own ambivalent feelings about his contribution to "the war effort." Drawing on a number of medical texts from the period, Barker explores how shell-shock affected concepts of masculinity and sketches the correspondences between women's peacetime hysteria and men's wartime strain and enforced helplessness. Unlike the end games of *Union Street* and *Blow Your House Down*, *Regeneration* ends with increased knowledge and bitter hope for the future.

The Eye in the Door (1993) picks up with Billy Prior, a patient of Rivers's in *Regeneration* who was treated for disorders stemming from a particularly traumatic event: he was catapulted headfirst into the open, rotting body cavity of a corpse. Although Prior longs to return to the front, he has been assigned to the Home Office Intelligence Unit in London. Early in the novel Prior (who is engaged to a girl in Scotland who works in an ammunition factory) has a sexual encounter with another officer, Charles Manning. The "eye in the door" is a metaphor for the policing of two scapegoats that emerged in civilian society during the war: homosexuals and pacifists. Both Manning and Prior are living double lives as closeted homosexuals, and rumors of a German Black Book containing the names of 47,000 gay men and lesbians in Britain threaten them. A high-profile trial (the Pemberton Billing affair) is under way: an actress in Wilde's *Salomé* has been "libeled" by the suggestion that attendants of the play and the actress herself belong in the Black Book. Meanwhile, Prior has been ordered by the Home Office to obtain information on a close childhood acquaintance, a woman who has been accused of plotting to kill Lloyd George in order to put an end to the war. Almost all of the characters here are subject to a "Jekyll and Hyde" complex by leading double lives. Even Rivers emerges as a man divided from himself. In this precarious state of wartime, Barker suggests, "Perhaps, contrary to what was usually supposed, duality was the stable state; the attempt at integration, dangerous" (Perry 235).

The final installment in the trilogy, *The Ghost Road* (1995), continues to trace the progress of Billy Prior, who is still trying to rejoin the army. The novel is a bit more diffuse than the other two in the series, as Barker briefly introduces Lewis Carroll as a childhood acquaintance of Rivers and includes a number of flashbacks to the period Rivers spent living in Melanesia among "witch doctors." Billy does finally succeed in enlisting, and the last part of the novel features his journal entries from the front, describing the carnage of war. It is interesting to note how Barker unfolds her characters over the course of three books, holding back and disclosing details. Ultimately, however, *The Ghost Road* lacks the immediacy and brilliance of *Regeneration*. Indeed, when Barker won the Booker for *The Ghost Road*, there were some naysayers. David Gates (*Newsweek*) questions the choice of *The Ghost Road* for the Booker Prize, arguing that Barker falls prey to "the predictable pitfalls of the historical novel: overwrought design and underdeveloped character" (72). Ben Shephard (*Times Literary Supplement*) argues that Barker's observations here are "grounded in postfeminist pieties and the chic abstractions of modern historians, not in solid historical origins" (13).

Barker's novel *Another World* (1998) can be read as a synthesis of her earlier works in that she combines contemporary characters with aging soldiers who are haunted by the experiences of her war trilogy. Nick and Fran are a married couple struggling with two children from previous marriages, a baby, and a new home. Within the first few chapters there is a dramatic scene in which Nick and Fran try to involve their children in a family project of stripping the old wallpaper. They uncover a detailed drawing of the Victorian family that used to own the house, but this is no ordinary family portrait: the father's erect penis and the mother's breasts are exposed. "Patches of wallpaper still cling to the painting like scabs of chicken pox, but even so its power is clear. Victorian paterfamilias, wife and children: two sons, a daughter. Pinned out, exhibited. Even without the exposed penis, the meticulously delineated and hated breasts, you have sensed the tension in this family." The portrait reveals the conflicts simmering in Nick's and Fran's family, and this imbrication of the past and the present also describes how Nick's father Geordie, a 101-year-old war veteran who is dying of cancer (shades of *The Century's Daughter*), keeps reliving his combat memories. At the end of *Another World* Barker gives a complex formula for understanding memory: "It's easy to let oneself be dazzled by false analogies—the past never threatens anything as simple, or as avoidable, as repetition." As with Barker's earlier novels, the past inevitably encroaches on, and is even alive in, the present; the challenge is to face these haunting traumas but to not be ruled by them.

ASSESSMENT

Barker is one of the most important British novelists writing today. Her novels have an exceptional immediacy and clarity, with direct plotting and remarkably authentic dialogue. Barker regularly broaches complicated themes of trauma in a straightforward and often brutally explicit manner: this and her preoccupation with history and memory make her very much a novelist for our time. While several critics have expressed an interest in seeing her move into new thematic territory and experiment more with her literary techniques, there is no shortage of applause for her outstanding execution of what she has set out to do. It will be fascinating to see what direction and form Barker's work takes in the future.

BIBLIOGRAPHY

Primary Sources

Union Street. London: Virago, 1982.

Blow Your House Down. London: Virago, 1984.

The Century's Daughter. London: Virago, 1986.

The Man Who Wasn't There. London: Virago, 1988.

Regeneration. 1991. New York: Plume, 1993.

The Eye in the Door. 1993. New York: Dutton, 1994.

The Ghost Road. London: Viking, 1995.

Another World. London: Viking, 1998; New York: Farrar, Straus, 1999.

Border Crossing. London: Viking; New York: Farrar, Straus, 2001.

Secondary Sources

Becker, Alida. "Old War Wounds." Interview with Pat Barker. *New York Times Book Review* 16 May 1999: 6+.

Gates, David. "Woman's Eye on No Man's Land." *Newsweek* 18 December 1995: 72.

Harris, Greg. "Compulsory Masculinity, Britain, and the Great War: The Literary-Historical Work of Pat Barker." *Critique* 39.4 (Summer 1998): 290–304.

Morrison, Blake. Rev. of Barker's trilogy. *New Yorker* 22 January 1996: 78–80+.

Nixon, Rob. "Soldiers of Misfortune: In the Trenches with Pat Barker." *Village Voice* 14 July 1992: 91.

Perry, Donna. "Going Home Again: An Interview with Pat Barker." *Literary Review* 34 (Winter 1991): 235–44.

Pykett, Lyn. "The Century's Daughters: Recent Women's Fiction and History." *Critical Quarterly* 29 (Fall 1987): 71–77.

Shephard, Ben. "Digging Up the Past." *TLS* 22 March 1996: 12–13.

Sinker, Mark. "Temporary Gentlemen: Interview with P. Barker." *Sight and Sound* 7 December 1997: 22–24.

Smith, Amanda. "PW Interviews Pat Barker." *Publishers Weekly* 21 September 1984: 98–99.

Whitehead, Anne. "Open to Suggestion: Hypnosis and History in Pat Barker's *Regeneration*." *Modern Fiction Studies* 44.3 (Fall 1998): 674–694.

Sybille Bedford
1911–

Mitchell R. Lewis

Sybille Bedford is a distinguished literary journalist, travel writer, biographer, and novelist. In her most respected work of nonfiction she has written about wine, food, recently published books, famous court trials in England and the United States, and legal issues and procedures. She has also written a vivid and witty travelogue about Mexico and an authorized biography of the English writer and critic Aldous Huxley. Her work as a whole is personal in nature, often having the tone and feel of a memoir, and yet it is also characterized by a distinctly cosmopolitan European sensibility. The same is also true of her fiction. In her novels and short stories Bedford combines a concern with domesticity, family history, and individual ethics with an equally important preoccupation with European social and political history. Typically written in the first person, her work is deeply autobiographical, usually dwelling on the inherent difficulties of remembering and making sense of personal history, but it is also frequently punctuated with descriptions of the significance and impact of world events in the first half of the twentieth century, such as World War I, the 1920s depression, and the rise of socialism and fascism. In particular, Bedford tends to focus on the social rituals and declining fortunes of the European aristocratic class from which she descends. The result is often an effective combination of personal and sociopolitical history.

BACKGROUND

Bedford, the daughter of Elizabeth (Bernard) and Maximilian von Schoenebeck, was born on March 16, 1911, in Charlottenburg, Germany. Her mother was an Englishwoman of Jewish descent, and her father was an impoverished German aristocrat. At an early age, soon after her parents' marriage failed, she left her birthplace, joining her mother in Italy and then in France. She grew up mainly in Sanary, the quiet unfashionable end of the French Mediterranean coast. Like many of the semiautobiographical characters in her fiction, Bedford was educated privately, not only in France and Italy, but also in England. By 1926 she was reading voraciously and frequenting law courts. She considered studying law at the Sorbonne and at Oxford University, but she finally abandoned such ideas, choosing to write essays and novels instead. Like Virginia Woolf, she managed to acquire a remarkable education on her own. In 1935 she married one Walter Bedford, about whom nothing is known. The nature of the marriage remains a mystery, although critic Roger Kimball has suggested that some light may be shed on this matter in Bedford's third novel, *A Compass Error* (1968), in which "we are told that Flavia, this novel's version of the author, 'contracted what was looked on as a wasteful if not scandalous marriage to a man twice her age, a homosexual, of undoubted brilliance and initial talent, who drank too much and was then already an established failure' " (Kimball 13).

At sixteen Bedford began writing literary essays and fiction, eventually falling under the intellectual and literary influence of Aldous Huxley. After discovering Huxley's novels, she produced three novels of her own that were circulated among various publishers but never published, probably because of their novicelike attempt to imitate Huxley. In 1930, while living in southern France with her mother, she met Huxley and his wife Maria. They became fast friends. As a result, Huxley himself became even more of an intellectual inspiration for Bedford, who has referred to him as a "moral idol" and "universal genius" (qtd. in Kimball 11). Later, after Huxley's death, Bedford accepted the invitation of his family to write his authorized biography. Given the opportunity to express fully and publicly her admiration for Huxley's life and work, she wrote the monumental two-volume work *Aldous Huxley: A Biography* (1973–1974).

In the 1950s Bedford enjoyed her first successes as a writer. Her debut book-length publication was the critically acclaimed travelogue *The Sudden View: A Mexican Journey* (1953); in this work Bedford chronicles her one-year trip to Mexico with Esther Murphy Arthur, the daughter of the American president Chester A. Arthur. Soon after the publication of *The Sudden View* Bedford published her first novel, *A Legacy* (1956), an elegantly written domestic comedy about two pre–World War I German families, one Jewish and one Catholic. The novel received mixed reviews, but Bedford received enthusiastic praise from Nancy Mitford and Evelyn Waugh, among others. The novel eventually became Bedford's most popular and commercially successful work, so much so that it was televised in 1975.

During the 1950s and 1960s, while working for various British and American newspapers and magazines, Bedford also achieved success as a literary journalist. She wrote numerous articles on wine, food, travel, and books, many of the best pieces of which have been collected in *As It Was: Pleasures, Landscapes, and Justice* (1990). She also worked as a legal reporter for the London *Observer*, the *Saturday Evening Post*, and *Life*, covering the Auschwitz trial in Frankfurt, the trial of Jack Ruby in Dallas, and the *Lady Chatterley* and Stephen Ward trials in London, among others. Her most substantial and best-known work of legal journalism is *The Best We Can Do* (1958), a day-by-day account of the infamous trial of Dr. John Bodkin Adams, who was accused of murdering several of his elderly patients in order to collect their promised legacies. Ultimately, Bedford's abiding curiosity about the law prompted her to write *The Faces of Justice* (1961), a comparative study of legal systems and judicial procedures in Austria, England, France, Germany, and Switzerland. This work was especially well received by British critics, who found it useful for understanding legal systems different from their own, and it has been used as a textbook in comparative law in both the United States and Germany.

After seven years Bedford published her next novel, *A Favourite of the Gods* (1963), which was followed six years later by a sequel, *A Compass Error* (1968). These two novels, which take place during the first four decades of the twentieth century, focus on three generations of women: a puritan New England woman, her sexually liberated daughter, and her studious but equally unconventional granddaughter. After the publication of *A Favourite of the Gods* and *A Compass Error* Bedford ceased to publish fiction for nearly two decades. Finally, in 1989 she published the short story "Une Vie de Chateau" and the long novel *Jigsaw: An Unsentimental Education: A Biographical Novel.*

As the title of the latter work suggests, both were largely biographical in nature, the first returning to her family's history in Germany, the second focusing on her own life and immediate family up until the start of World War II. Critically acclaimed, Bedford's *Jigsaw* was ultimately shortlisted for the Booker Prize for Fiction along with Margaret Atwood's *Cat's Eye*, John Banville's *The Book of Evidence*, James Kelman's *A Disaffection*, and Rose Tremain's *Restoration*, the prize itself going to Kazuo Ishiguro's *The Remains of the Day*. In 1993 it was rumored that Bedford was working on a continuation of *Jigsaw* (Evans, "Paradise" 25).

In general recognition of her various literary accomplishments Bedford has been made a fellow of the Royal Society of Literature (1964); a vice president of Poets, Playwrights, Editors, Essayists, and Novelists (1980), an international writers' organization also known as PEN; and an officer of the Order of the British Empire (1981). The Royal Society of Literature has also recognized Bedford as a writer of conspicuous attainment, conferring on her the distinguished honor Companion of Literature (1991).

ANALYSIS

Much of Bedford's work, as many critics have noted, is grounded in memory, especially her novels, which have been appropriately described as "imaginative reorderings of the past—of [Bedford's] own past—efforts to extract some human truth from the specific dramas that life has presented her" (Kimball 13). In general, Bedford reflects on her early years before World War II. With an acute ethical sense she typically broods on her own motivations and those of the significant people she has known, trying to piece together a coherent account of her life. In doing so she not only raises more questions than she can ever possibly answer, but often suggests that fact and fiction are difficult if not impossible to separate. To this concern with remembering personal history Bedford also adds a concern with recalling some of the larger social and political developments of the early twentieth century, particularly as they relate to the fate of the European aristocracy. As one critic has aptly put it, Bedford is "an historian, not only in her grasp of events and movements but, more important for a novelist, of the *mores*, the nuances of vanished classes, their codes and passwords, their élites, their scents and dresses, their style, their singular households, private trains, pleasure-domes and spas" (Vansittart, *Compass* vii). In this regard Bedford shows herself to be concerned with both sociopolitical and personal history.

This concern is clearly evident in most of Bedford's major works of nonfiction. In her various legal writings, for instance, such as *The Best We Can Do* and *The Faces of Justice*, she demonstrates an interest in both comparative law and individual ethics, focusing on the study of different legal systems as well as particular cases. In examining the process of judgment as it plays out in institutional and personal contexts, Bedford shows herself to be concerned with the sociopolitical and the personal. In her travelogue of Mexico, *The Sudden View*, Bedford reveals a similar twofold preoccupation. In this case she writes a personal narrative filled with individual observations and opinions, but she also focuses on a bankrupt feudal landowner, Don Otavio, who lives in a dilapidated hacienda near Guadalajara, providing Bedford with ample opportunity to reflect on Mexico's social and political history. In her biography of Huxley, finally, Bedford downplays her concern with sociopolitical history, but she heightens all the more her concern with personal history as she is primarily concerned with recalling her own memories of Huxley. The biography as a whole, as Roger Sale notes, "takes its shape from reminiscence" (285), often to the point of Bedford becoming an intrusive narrator. In fact, it may be more precise to say that the two-volume work is not so much a biography as a personal memoir that happens to be, in this case, about Aldous Huxley.

Based on her own life, Bedford's fiction also reads very much like a memoir. In *A Legacy* the author tells a story about two German families at the turn of the century, the Catholic von Feldens and the Jewish Merzes, but she does so from the first-person perspective of Francesca, the daughter of Julius von Felden. Beginning with her birth in Charlottenburg, the narrator chronicles the early years of her life, eventually weaving together a complex set of plot lines about various family members, the most important one being about Johannes von Felden's problems with a Prussian military school and his eventual suicide. The novel, in other words, is a personal narrative about Francesca's memories of the two families between whom she divides her time. To this first-person account, however, Bedford's narrator also brings a concern with the social history of Germany. Describing this particular aspect of *A Legacy*, critic Roger Kimball has noted that the novel is a "story of collisions: between the decaying Catholic aristocracy of Southern Germany and the rich Jewish mercantile establishment of Berlin; between Bismarck's militantly nationalistic Prussia and the Francophilic culture of the South; between the old world in which duty and social position define one's compass and the fast, new society that seemed bent on dissolving everything" (14). In this regard *A Legacy* is as much a sociopolitical novel as a personal narrative. In fact, one critic has suggested that the novel deals with "the making of the modern Germany which three times plunged Europe and the world into war" (Evans, "Most" 210).

A similar combination of the personal and sociopolitical prevails in *A Favourite of the Gods* and its sequel, *A Compass Error*. In these two novels Bedford tells a story about three generations of women—Anna Howland, her daughter Constanza, and her granddaughter Flavia—but once again she does so from the perspective of a first-person narrator, in this case Flavia. The first novel begins with Flavia trying to recall how she and her mother Constanza once left Italy by train bound for the British Consulate in Brussels, where Constanza was to marry a man named Lewis Crane, only to end up instead in the French fishing port of St-Jean-le-Sauveur (a fictional version of Sanary). As Flavia recalls, Constanza decides to settle down in the small French town and, against her mother's wishes, to postpone and finally call off what would have been her second wedding. This memory leads Flavia to think about the nature of marriage and of mother-daughter relationships, as well as of sexuality, as her mother is a sexually liberated person who must have a *mariage de raison* if she is going to accept anyone's hand in marriage. What follows is a personal narrative that reaches back into the past to depict the problems of Anna's marriage as well as the education of Constanza, including her many experiences with men and her first marriage. Throughout, the narrative is guided by the memories of Flavia and her preoccupation with understanding maternal and sexual relationships—two leading issues of *A Favourite of the Gods* and *A Compass Error*. The reason for Flavia's preoccupation becomes especially clear in the second novel, which focuses on the seventeen-year-old Flavia's own education, her first sexual experiences with two women, and her inadvertent betrayal of her mother (Flavia reveals the hiding place of Constanza and her new lover Michel Devaux to one of her own lovers, who, unbeknownst to Flavia, happens to be Michel's wife). Here Flavia makes it clear that what prompts her personal narrative is a concern not only with recovering family history, but also with understanding the ethics of relationships and assuaging her own sense of guilt. Like Bedford, Flavia is concerned with judging the actions of herself and others, both in the past and in the present.

Just like the narrator in *A Legacy*, however, Flavia also demonstrates a persistent concern with sociopolitical history, an area of inquiry also requiring an act of judgment. In *A Favourite of the Gods*, which takes place in Italy, France, and England during the first thirty years of the twentieth century, periodic digressions mainly take note of the politics of England, touching on such events as the suffragette movement, the curtailing of the power of the House of Lords, the passage of the National Insurance Act, the movements for Irish Home Rule and prison reform, and the various doings of such politicians as Herbert Asquith, Winston Churchill, and David Lloyd George. The most extensively treated historical events of the novel are World War I and the rise of fascism in Italy, both of which are discussed extensively by narrator and characters alike. The second novel focuses less on sociopolitical history, but it takes the action up to 1940, until the Nazi invasion of France, during which Constanza is gunned down by strafing German airplanes.

Like *A Compass Error*, *Jigsaw* also focuses less on sociopolitical history than the first two novels, but it is the most accomplished example of Bedford's use of personal narrative. In this novel, which also uses first-person narration, Bedford gives up the pretense of the narrator being fictional. Although this autobiographical narrator is never named, she makes her identity known by confessing that she has written novels like *A Legacy*, which is, she notes, based on her family. Again focusing mainly on the 1920s and 1930s, Bedford proceeds to "piece" together the story of her early years, one that naturally overlaps with much of her previous novels and with much of her actual life. She discusses familiar people such as the Huxleys and revisits the usual locations in Germany, Italy, France, and England, dwelling principally on her mother and her harrowing descent into drug abuse (hence the subtitle *An Unsentimental Education*). While admitting the openly autobiographical nature of *Jigsaw*, Bedford still classifies the work as a "biographical novel." Her great theme here, as in all her works, is the necessarily fictional nature of biography. She indicates as much in the author's note of the novel, which tellingly comments on the various "characters" in *Jigsaw*: "These, and everyone and everything else, are what they seemed—at various times—to me" (Author's Note). Such might be said of much of Bedford's work.

ASSESSMENT

Bedford, as Roger Kimball has aptly put it, is "something more than a name one has heard, [but] something rather less than a literary celebrity" (11). Her most remarkable achievements are the result of her ability to weave together the personal and the sociopolitical. Bedford's greatest accomplishment in this regard, as most critics agree, is *A Legacy*. The fictional works that follow her first novel succeed in some respects, but they tend to be of varying quality. They are often loose and breezy in structure, with little focus. What contributes to this effect in part is Bedford's nearly obsessive concern with what characters eat and drink. A connoisseur of food and wine, Bedford never misses an opportunity to minutely describe all aspects of a meal. Another and similar contributing factor to the varying quality of her later works is their overreliance on random travelogue-like effects: long stretches of text describing details of place are often provided for their own sake. Over time, moreover, Bedford seems to withdraw more and more into the bygone aristocratic world of her family and friends, to such a point that many critics have been unable to relate sympathetically to her work. In spite of these common criticisms, Bedford's later work is still valuable, particularly for its honest effort to explore the ethics of interpersonal relationships and the fine line between fact and fiction in autobiography; in fact, in terms of substance and style, numerous passages of *A Favourite of the Gods*, *A Compass Error*, and especially *Jigsaw* can be favorably compared with *A Legacy*. Bedford may not be the most celebrated woman writer of the twentieth century, but she has written a thoughtful body of work worthy of attention.

BIBLIOGRAPHY

Primary Sources

The Sudden View: A Mexican Journey. London: Gollancz; New York: Harper, 1953. Also published as *A Visit to Don Otavio: A Traveler's Tale from Mexico.* London: Collins, 1960.

A Legacy. London: Weidenfeld, 1956; New York: Simon & Schuster, 1957.

The Best We Can Do: An Account of the Trial of John Bodkin Adams. London: Collins, 1958. As *The Trial of Dr. Adams.* New York: Simon & Schuster, 1959.

The Faces of Justice. London: Collins; New York: Simon & Schuster, 1961.

A Favourite of the Gods. London: Collins; New York: Simon & Schuster, 1963.

"Her Majesty's Incorruptible, Imperturbable, Incomparable Judges." *Esquire* October 1965: 78–82, 150–152.

A Compass Error. London: Collins, 1968; New York: Knopf, 1969.

Aldous Huxley: A Biography. 2 vols. London: Chatto, 1973–1974. 1 vol. New York: Knopf, 1974.

"The Last Trial of Lady Chatterley." *Esquire* October 1973: 228–237, 448–460.

Jigsaw: An Unsentimental Education: A Biographical Novel. London: Hamilton; New York: Knopf, 1989.

"Une Vie de Chateau." *New Yorker* 20 February 1989: 38–48.

As It Was: Pleasures, Landscapes, and Justice. London: Sinclair-Stevenson, 1990.

Secondary Sources

Evans, Robert Owen. "Sybille Bedford: A Paradise of Dainty Devices." In *Contemporary British Women Writers.* Ed. Robert E. Hosmer, Jr. Basingstoke: Macmillan, 1993. 1–25.

———. "Sybille Bedford: Most Reticent, Most Modest, Best." In *British Novelists since 1900.* Ed. Jack I. Biles. New York: AMS, 1987. 207–220.

Kimball, Roger. "Without Rancor: Sybille Bedford's Achievement. *New Criterion* 12.8 (1994): 11–18.

Olney, James. " 'Most Extraordinary': Sybille Bedford and Aldous Huxley." *South Atlantic Quarterly* 74 (1975): 376–386.

Sale, Roger. "Huxley and Bennett, Bedford and Drabble." *Hudson Review* 28 (1975): 285–293.

Vansittart, Peter. Introduction to *A Compass Error.* London: Virago, 1984.

———. Introduction to *A Favourite of the Gods.* London: Virago, 1984.

Elizabeth Bowen
1899–1973

Stella Deen

Elizabeth Bowen wrote short fiction and novels in which narrative detachment and controlled form shape stories of twentieth-century personal and cultural dispossession. Bowen bridges two traditions: in some works this dispossession reflects the isolation of the Anglo-Irish people and their loss of a vital outlet in Ireland; in others it functions as a critique of the English middle classes. Bowen's visionary intensity, a hallmark of her writing, lent itself especially to the evocation of place, which invariably engages with characters in the action of the story.

BACKGROUND

Elizabeth Bowen was born in Dublin on June 7, 1899, to Protestant Anglo-Irish parents, Henry and Florence Colley Bowen. The first Henry Bowen, a Welshman, fought under Oliver Cromwell and in 1653 was deeded an eight-hundred-acre piece of land in County Cork; the third Henry Bowen built Bowen's Court, completing it in 1776. Elizabeth's parents had expected to have a son, but Elizabeth was born instead, later becoming the first female heir to Bowen's Court. The Anglo-Irish, whose privileged position in Ireland was based on "an inherent wrong" (*Bowen's Court* [hereafter *BC*] 452), were separated from the native Catholic Irish by "nationality, religion, position, and finally by symbolic and protective walls" (Kenney 20). Their power, steadily whittled away throughout the nineteenth century, came to a formal close with the establishment of the Irish Free State in 1921. The Anglo-Irish are often said to exist in the "hyphen" between "Anglo" and "Irish," not belonging fully to either culture. Perhaps more than most Anglo-Irish writers, Elizabeth Bowen was shaped by an existence divided between Ireland and England. Until she was seven, the family spent summers at Bowen's Court and winters in Dublin, where her father was a barrister. This pattern changed abruptly when he suffered a psychiatric illness, and doctors advised that for Henry's good, Florence and Elizabeth should leave him for a time. They traveled to England, moving for the next five years among several villages on the Kentish coast and being taken in hand by "a grapevine of powerful Anglo-Irish relatives" (*Pictures and Conversations* [hereafter *PC*] 13). Although her father recovered, Elizabeth, at age thirteen, lost her mother to cancer. From this period of loss Bowen developed a stammer that she kept throughout her life. The personal losses marking Bowen's childhood were echoed in her adolescence and adulthood by the historical events of the Troubles in Ireland and the two world wars; in her writing personal turmoil often stands as a microcosm of loss and destruction on a grand scale.

In 1914 Bowen began a three-year term at Downe House School in Kent, under the shadow of World War I: "The world seemed to be bound up in a tragic attack of adolescence and there seemed no reason why we should ever grow up, since moderation in behaviour became impossible" (*The Mulberry Tree* 17). The grim comedy of a world with indistinct boundaries between children and adults became a characteristic element in Bowen's writing.

Bowen published the first of seven volumes of stories, *Encounters*, in 1923. In the same year she married Alan Cameron. Their marriage was a lasting and companionable one, though observers agree that it was not a passionate relationship. Alan's appointment to secretary for education of the city of Oxford led the Camerons to Oxford in 1925. There Bowen was appreciated for her "original, amusing, trenchant" conversation (Glendinning 76) and thrived on the friendship of a growing literary circle that included David Cecil, Maurice Bowra, and Isaiah Berlin. She also began a friendship with Virginia Woolf that lasted until Woolf's death in 1941.

When Alan took a post with the BBC in 1935, the Camerons moved to London. In addition to fiction, Bowen began to write articles on literature, film, and contemporary culture for the *New Statesman* and the *Tatler*. In these articles Bowen delineates the qualities of the writers who most influenced her. Her ghost stories reflect a debt to Anglo-Irish writers like Sheridan Le Fanu, for whose *Uncle Silas* Bowen wrote an introduction. The continuity of out-of-doors and "psychological" weather in Le Fanu's tale and his awakening of the childish fears we can never rationalize away are ingredients in Bowen's own fiction. Bowen admired impersonality in the work of writers like Flaubert and Joyce, arguing that only when the work of art has detached itself from its author can it become its own "new, whole, pure, iridescent world" (Preface to *Collected Stories* 128). In this statement one can also see Bowen's emphasis on the importance of appropriate form, an emphasis shared by Henry James. Along with James, Austen and Forster have been cited as influences on Bowen's novels, which portray characters' "complicated interaction of motives" (Stevenson 85) and dramatize the readjustment of a young heroine's moral vision (Heath 16). Finally, one sees at work in Bowen's fiction, especially in *The Little Girls* and *Eva Trout*, Proust's ideas about the relation between time, memory, and the imagination (Lee, Preface 3).

The Camerons' Regents Park house was hit several times during the blitzes of World War II, yet Bowen felt that the London war years were "the most interesting period of my life" (qtd. in Glendinning 158). Bowen's war work as an air-raid-precaution warden and her compilation of a report for the Ministry of Information about Irish attitudes toward the war generated some of her best short stories and a war novel, *The Heat of the Day*.

Throughout her adult life Bowen spent time at the beloved Bowen's Court, which she inherited upon the death of her father in 1930. She often entertained friends there, including Virginia Woolf, Rosamond Lehmann, and May Sarton. Cameron died in 1952. During this period Bowen lectured in the United States and accepted several writer-in-residence positions, notably at the American Academy in Rome. In 1960, despite her commissions with well-paying American magazines, she was forced to sell the ancestral home (Glendinning 255). Although she had expected the new owners to live in Bowen's Court, they tore it down. Bowen then moved among some of the places that had been important earlier in her life—including Hythe and Old Headington—before settling again in London, where she died of cancer in 1973.

Apart from ten novels, more than eighty short stories, several autobiographical works, and many radio talks, Bowen wrote numerous articles, reviews, and prefaces, some of which are collected in *Afterthought* and *Collected Impressions*. Her achievement was recognized in numerous ways during her lifetime, including honorary degrees from both Trinity College, Dublin, and Oxford University.

ANALYSIS

Elizabeth Bowen perfected the story of personal and historical dislocation. Her acute sense of her own time and place led her to adopt a condensed, suggestive language allowing poetic "radiation of meaning" (O'Faolain 203). The stories also reveal Bowen's commitment to formal discipline ensuring the "tautness and clearness" (Preface to *Faber* 43) of their emotional center.

In articles and reviews Bowen wrote frequently about the short story, claiming for it a unique ability to register twentieth-century life. She was especially interested in innovators who brought prestige to the story: Chekhov, who had "opened up for the writer tracts of emotional landscape"; Maupassant, who "stands for astringency, iron relevance" and who "transcribed passions in the only terms possible—dispassionate understatement" (Preface to *Faber* 39); and Mansfield, who evolved "a marvellous sensory notation hitherto undreamed of outside of poetry" (*Mulberry Tree* 75).

What Bowen called the "free" story does not attempt a synthesis of experience and is exempt from the novel's "too often forced and false" conclusiveness (Preface to *Faber* 38, 43). (The free story, however, does not lack controlled form, to which Bowen tied the story's "aesthetic and moral truth" [Preface to *Faber* 43].) Growing up with the cinema, the free story was well suited to capture the discontinuity of modern life, including the extreme experiences and disorientation of Ireland's civil war and two world wars. *The Demon Lover and Other Stories*, which many consider Bowen's finest volume of stories, captures the climate of war in ghost stories depicting a collective state of "lucid abnormality." In stories such as "Ivy Gripped the Steps" and "The Demon Lover," the "uncertain 'I' " is exposed when convention and routine are dissolved, while in stories like "Pink May" personal life puts up resistance to the annihilation threatening it (Postscript to *The Demon Lover* 95, 98, 97).

It is impossible not to notice the powerful elements of light, weather, and atmosphere in the stories of Elizabeth Bowen. For Bowen, the evocation of place meant revealing "the forceful mystery of inner being" (*BC* 20). Indeed, in some stories, including "Attractive Modern Homes," "Look at All Those Roses," and "A Walk in the Woods," the effect of places "*is* the story" (Lee, *Elizabeth Bowen* 132). Houses, city squares, or Irish landscapes are never merely the setting of action, but engage in a dynamic relation with characters. In the history of her ancestral home Bowen wrote that she knew of no house in which "the past is not pervadingly felt" (*BC* 19). Indeed, houses in stories like "The Last Night in the Old Home," "Foothold," and "The Shadowy Third" reverberate with the gender and family relations through which the past haunts the present. This is a moral relationship between place and plot, raising questions of inheritance and continuity, notes Lee (*Elizabeth Bowen* 132). *Bowen's Court* makes a similar point by generalizing the family lesson of what happens when the "outsize will" is deprived of "its outsize outlet, its big task" (455). Says Bowen at the conclusion of that history: "We have everything to dread from the dispossessed" (455). In Bowen's stories, whether or not she is writing about the Anglo-Irish, houses often expose aimless and diminished lives—as Lord Thingummy's mansion does in "The Disinherited"—and provide commentary on characters too apathetic or disillusioned to articulate their predicament.

Some readers of Bowen's long stories, "Mysterious Kor," "A Summer Night," "Ivy Gripped the Steps," and "The Disinherited," have found them to be a "unique release" for her talents (Bloom 148). In "A Summer Night," first published in the 1941 collection *Look at All Those Roses*, form and content mesh: characters "drift against each other" (Bloom 148) as Bowen juxtaposes scenes without any connective material. But the reader makes subtle connections between characters—for example, between Queenie and Fran, two "superfluous" women dealing differently with their positions at the margin of society—and can thus make a diagnosis unavailable to the characters. "A Summer Night" is set during World War II, and Irish neutrality forms a haunting background for the characters' personal isolation. Both the child Vivie and her mother Emma try to flee the isolated house from which the "human order seemed to have lapsed" (*Collected Stories* 596); the quest of each is squelched or flickers out. For Justin Cavey, war reestablishes a painful exclusion from the monuments of European culture around which he has reinvented himself. His sister Queenie, with her penetrating smiles, pulls him back into the "underwater, weedy region of memory" (*Collected Stories* 587) of his old home. Only Queenie, partially shielded from reality by her deafness, experiences a more-than-flickering happiness. As Julian Moynahan points out, her gift of imaginative fantasy is perhaps the only power "that could save modern Ireland from itself by binding the present to the past in a spirit of loving kindness" (81).

While Bowen's stories focus on the drama within the individual—the private fantasy that is her escape from fact—the novels dramatize the "overlooked and dwarfed" individual's contact with the world of manners (Preface to *Faber* 44). Central to three of the first four novels, *The Hotel, The Last September*, and *To the North*, is a young heroine pitted against an adult world of insensibility, cynicism, or malice. But Bowen's comment that "it is not only our fate but our business to lose innocence" (*Mulberry Tree* 50) suggests that her heroines' situation is not tragic. Indeed, Bowen successfully combines moral seriousness—the symptoms of a diminished society and its legacy to younger generations—with social comedy. *The Last September*, set during the Troubles of 1920, depicts Anglo-Irish gentry ensconced in their big houses and intent on ignoring the signs around them of violent civil conflict. The dialogue between the wife of an English soldier serving in the Black and Tans brought in to reinforce the Royal Irish Constabulary and the Anglo-Irish Mrs. Carey captures the comic discrepancy between two cultural notions of manners while it illustrates, more urgently, the dangerous Anglo-Irish refusal to acknowledge the Irish rebellion and their own dangerous position:

> "Well, I hope you are pleased with us now you have come," said Mrs. Carey hospitably. "I expect you have all been enjoying this lovely weather?"
>
> "Oh, *well*,—you see, we didn't come over to enjoy ourselves, did we? We came to take care of all of you—and of course, we are ever so glad to be able to do it. Not that I don't like the country; it's so picturesque. . . . But, you see, one can't help worrying all the time about Timmie—my husband—and all the boys: out all night sometimes with the patrols or else off in the mountains."
>
> "Terrible. And do you find this a tiring climate?" (47)

Looking at one season in the life of the Anglo-Irish and choosing one of the most violent years in Irish history, Bowen positions herself to underscore the irony of a way of life whose vital center has eroded. The 1800 Act of Union with Britain ended the era of Anglo-Irish "maturity" (*BC* 166), characterized by their "wish to add something to life" (*Mulberry Tree* 27) (and indeed the Anglo-Irish in the novel, like the adolescent protagonist Lois, seem to be suspended between childhood and adulthood). *The Last September* depicts the effects of this dying civilization on the Naylors' nineteen-year-old orphaned niece. Lois struggles to escape the "cocoon" of her Anglo-Irish destiny, wishing for "violent realness" (49). She wants "to be in a pattern" (98), but instinctively shrinks from the predetermined form held out to her by elders. Throughout the novel the completion of pattern is deathlike. Lois claps her hands over her ears when she overhears a houseguest about to describe her: "knowledge of this would stop, seal, finish one" (60). The burning of the Naylors' big house at the end of the novel releases Lois from the fear and inexperience characterizing her life at Danielstown (Kiberd 372).

Acting as an outlet for truths inadmissible in the house, the countryside in *The Last September* reflects the danger from which the Naylors turn their gaze: "The house seemed to be pressing down low in apprehension, hiding its face, as though it had her vision of where it was. It seemed to gather its trees close in fright and amazement at the wide, light, lovely unloving country, the unwilling bosom whereon it was set" (66). Again and again in articles and autobiographical writing Bowen emphasized the importance of place, arguing in "Notes on Writing a Novel," for example, that "[s]cene is only justified in the novel where it can be shown, or at least felt, to act upon action or character" (*Mulberry Tree* 40). This belief explains why, in Bowen's novels, places resonate with what the characters do not know, either because they lack experience or because they repress their feelings in obedience to social convention.

In *The House in Paris* Bowen shows the effect of environment in part through the use of contrasts, for example, the contrast between the house in Paris and the house in London, each with its set of cultural and social practices. These differences are accentuated by the characters' journeys across borders, journeys that Bowen felt enhanced what was within characters and sharpened the impact of change on them (*PC* 41–42). Travel in *The House in Paris* reflects its broader concerns with belonging and with alienation. Readers and characters are also subject to the dislocations of time. The importance of time is reflected both formally, in the tripartite structure of the novel, whose sections are named "The Present," "The Past," and "The Present," and in the characters' thoughts about time and about its shaping of their experience. From the nine-year-old Leopold to the elderly Madame Fisher, the characters take on time as an antagonist. The positioning of the past between two parts of one day in the present suggests that the past is woven into the present and is inescapable. A.S. Byatt and Hermione Lee, among others, have considered the complex effects of this sandwiching of the past between two moments of the present.

Bowen devises not only distinct forms for individual novels, as in *The House in Paris*, but networks of imagery and sentence structures to render the increasingly "cracked" surface of civilization. For example, in *The Heat of the Day* the contorted syntax of sentences is "an exact vehicle for the expression of awkward speech or twisted thought" (Bloom 98). Meaning also arises from parallels between characters in the main plot and subplots. Thus Bowen's best-known and perhaps best novel, *The Death of the Heart*, establishes connections between a set of experienced characters and a set of innocent ones to pose the central question of whether the young protagonist, Portia, and indeed anyone, can manage the passage from youth to maturity without the death of the heart (Bloom 14). In *The House in Paris* parallels between the children in the first and third sections and the young adults of the second section suggest both the childish core within the adults and the adult experiences that await the children.

In articles and autobiography Bowen insisted on the "overlapping and haunting of life by fiction" ("Out of a Book" 48), the writer's experience since childhood. She claimed, moreover, that the writer's imposition of an aesthetic shape on life met a fundamental human need in readers (*Mulberry Tree* 224). Thus the narrator of *The Heat of the Day*, referring to "the rules of fiction, with which life to be credible must comply" (140), suggests that fiction is necessary to the apprehension of reality. Bowen's allusion to literary conventions within the frameworks of her novels has led some readers, such as William Heath, to liken Bowen to other modern writers dramatizing the difficulty of finding an appropriate form for experience. Other critics have pointed to her postmodern querying of language itself, which does not reflect reality so much as constitute it (see Hoogland and Watson). Bowen's fictional references to aesthetic practice prove a flexible device. In *The House in Paris* Bowen draws an analogy between realism and the upper-middle-class life of the Michaelis family. Thus when Karen diagnoses the limitations of her parents' mode of perception as a problem of realism, Bowen likens this literary practice to bourgeois social convention that "stunned your imagination by *being* exact" (118). In all the novels allusions to the conventions of fiction, fairy tale, or melodrama illustrate that literary conventions may become internalized as norms (or, conversely, may misleadingly divide experience into polar extremes) that are as oppressive as any cultural or class code of behavior. Phyllis Lassner has focused on Bowen's interrogation of these literary conventions as they shape female identity.

The Heat of the Day, considered by many to be Bowen's most difficult novel, works this concern with language into the portrayed breakdown of civilization culminating in World War II. Bowen did not abandon realism but used its association with ordinary life to portray ironically civilian life during the blitz on London: "Bowen has devised a form capable of enclosing grotesque aberration within an ordinary realistic narrative" (Bloom 82). The main plot of the novel concerns Stella Roderick's attempt to uncover the truth behind an accusation that her lover, Robert Kelway, is an enemy spy. Bowen's use of realism and its settings, notably Robert's middle-class home, also suggests that ordinary life—the something wrong at the heart of middle-class life in many of her novels—is the source of Robert's treasonous motives. Since both the subject and the style of the novel render the breakdown of language and the pervasive uncertainty of life during the war, the reader must rely on imagery and on suggestive parallels between characters in the main plot and subplots to understand how the novel diagnoses the sources of the war and offers possibilities for rootedness and survival.

Bowen returned in *A World of Love* to themes of earlier novels: the past's continuing hold on the present, the innocent girl on the verge of love. While Jane concludes the novel with the experience of love still before her, her contact with middle-aged adults in a run-down Irish house positions that love among passions in "a darkened mirror" (qtd. in Glendinning 252). In her last two novels, *The Little Girls* and *Eva Trout*, Bowen began to work with new fictional methods, ones better suited, she felt, to capture the nature of memory and fantasy and to express her concern about the inadequacy of language as a vehicle for self-expression. These novels directly portray the "danger, despair and passion" (Glendinning 273) beneath the civilized surface maintained in most of the novels, what Bowen called the cracked surface of life.

ASSESSMENT

Elizabeth Bowen has been called one of the masters of modern fiction (Corn 159) and "one of very few great writers of prose fiction at work in Ireland and England between the end of the First World War and the end of the 1960s" (Moynahan 68). Best known for her novels and short stories, Bowen also produced a body of work, impressive in scope and quality, consisting of reviews, articles, prefaces, radio talks, and autobiography.

Bowen's fiction is marked by visionary intensity, particularly in her apprehension of the connection between places and people. Her acute perceptions take in both social transactions and the private, nebulous workings of the mind and heart. Her portrayal of the sensations and perceptions of children is unparalleled. Bowen's own memories led her to locate her writerly origins in childhood and to look for a core of childhood in others. Characteristically, her fiction dramatizes a conflict between the states of innocence and disenchantment. Her characters' experiences, particularly of loss, inexperience, and the transition to maturity, are grounded in a cultural and historical context of dispossession; they benefit from the strong historical instinct evidenced in *Bowen's Court*.

Bowen deplored "self-expression" in art at the same time that she acknowledged that any fiction was bound to be "transposed autobiography" (Preface to *Collected Stories* 129). She saw writing as a way to bridge the gulf between self and others. As the writer turns personal experience into art, she detaches it from herself and enables others to apprehend it. Bowen's fiction shows "scrupulous attachment to the highest Modernist standards of organic form and answerable style" (Moynahan 69). While her novels retain some traditional elements, such as omniscient narration, they also draw on the innovations of modernism in their use of interior monologue and cinematic juxtaposition of scenes. Over one hundred years after her birth, Elizabeth Bowen's distinctive, remarkable, and prolific literary oeuvre must place her among the very best writers of the century.

BIBLIOGRAPHY

Primary Sources

The Hotel. London: Constable, 1927; New York: Dial, 1928; New York: Penguin, 1943.

Encounters. 1923. Rpt. as *Encounters: Early Stories*. London: Sidgwick, 1949.

The Last September. London: Constable; New York: Dial, 1929; New York: Penguin, 1942.

Friends and Relations. London: Constable; New York: Dial, 1931; New York: Penguin, 1985.

To the North. London: Gollancz, 1932; New York: Knopf, 1933; New York: Penguin, 1987.

The House in Paris. London: Gollancz, 1935; New York: Knopf, 1936; New York: Penguin, 1987.

"Preface." *The Faber Book of Modern Short Stories*. London: Faber, 1936.

The Death of the Heart. London: Gollancz, 1938; New York: Knopf, 1939; New York: Penguin, 1962.

Look at All Those Roses. London: Gollancz; New York: Knopf, 1941.

Bowen's Court. London: Longmans; New York: Knopf, 1942.

Seven Winters. Dublin: Cuala, 1942; London and New York: Longmans, 1943.

"Novelists." 1944. In *The Heritage of British Literature*. By Elizabeth Bowen, Anthony Burgess, Lord David Cecil, Graham Greene, and Kate O'Brien. London: Thames, 1983.

The Demon Lover and Other Stories. London: Cape, 1945.

The Heat of the Day. London: Cape; New York: Knopf, 1949; New York: Penguin, 1962.

Collected Impressions. London: Longmans; New York: Knopf, 1950.

The Shelbourne. London: Harrap, 1951. As *The Shelbourne Hotel*. New York: Knopf, 1951.

A World of Love. London: Cape; New York: Knopf, 1955.

Afterthought: Pieces about Writing. London: Longmans, 1962.

The Little Girls. London: Cape; New York: Knopf, 1964; New York: Penguin, 1985.

Eva Trout; or, Changing Scenes. New York: Knopf, 1968; London: Cape, 1969; New York: Avon, 1978.

Pictures and Conversations. New York: Knopf, 1975.

The Collected Stories of Elizabeth Bowen. Introd. Angus Wilson. 1981. New York: Ecco, 1989.

The Mulberry Tree: Writings of Elizabeth Bowen. Ed. Hermione Lee. London: Virago, 1986; San Diego: Harcourt, 1987.

Secondary Sources

Austin, Allan E. *Elizabeth Bowen*. Rev. ed. Boston: Twayne, 1989.

Bloom, Harold, ed. *Elizabeth Bowen*. Modern Critical Views. New York: Chelsea, 1987.

Brooke, Jocelyn. *Elizabeth Bowen*. Bibliographical Series of Supplements to *British Book News*. London: Longmans, 1952.

Byatt, A.S. Introduction to *The House in Paris*. By Elizabeth Bowen. 1976. New York: Penguin, 1987. 7–16.

Corn, Alfred. "An Anglo-Irish Novelist." In *The Metamorphoses of Metaphor: Essays in Poetry and Fiction*. New York: Viking, 1987. Rpt. in Bloom 153–159.

Coughlan, Patricia. "Women and Desire in the Work of Elizabeth Bowen." In *Sex, Nation, and Dissent in Irish Writing*. Ed. Éibhear Walshe. New York: St. Martin's, 1997. 103–134.

Glendinning, Victoria. *Elizabeth Bowen*. 1977. New York: Knopf, 1978.

Hanson, Clare. "The Free Story." In *Short Stories and Short Fictions, 1880–1980*. London: Macmillan, 1985. Rpt. in Bloom 139–151.

Heath, William. *Elizabeth Bowen: An Introduction to Her Novels*. Madison: U of Wisconsin P, 1961.

Hoogland, Renée C. *Elizabeth Bowen: A Reputation in Writing*. New York: New York UP, 1994.

Jordan, Heather Bryant. *How Will the Heart Endure? Elizabeth Bowen and the Landscape of War*. Ann Arbor: U of Michigan P, 1992.

Kenney, Edwin J. *Elizabeth Bowen*. Lewisburg, PA: Bucknell UP; London: Associated, 1975.

Kiberd, Declan. *Inventing Ireland*. London: Cape, 1995; Cambridge, MA: Harvard UP, 1996.

Lassner, Phyllis. *Elizabeth Bowen*. Women Writers. Basingstoke: Macmillan, 1990.

———. *Elizabeth Bowen: A Study of the Short Fiction*. Twayne's Studies in Short Fiction 27. New York: Twayne, 1991.

Lee, Hermione. *Elizabeth Bowen: An Estimation*. London: Vision; Totowa, NJ: Barnes, 1981.

———. Preface to *The Mulberry Tree: Writings of Elizabeth Bowen*. Ed. Hermione Lee. London: Virago, 1986; San Diego: Harcourt, 1987. 1–7.

Moynahan, Julian. "Elizabeth Bowen: Anglo-Irish Postmortem." *Raritan* 9.2 (Fall 1989): 68–88.

O'Faolain, Sean. *The Short Story*. London: Collins, 1948.

Sellery, J'Nan M., and William O. Harris. *Elizabeth Bowen: A Bibliography*. Austin: U of Texas at Austin, 1981.

Stevenson, Randall. *The British Novel since the Thirties: An Introduction*. Athens: U of Georgia P, 1986.

Van Duyn, Mona. "Pattern and Pilgrimage: A Reading of *The Death of the Heart*." *Critique: Studies in Modern Fiction* 4.2 (Spring/Summer 1961). Rpt. in Bloom 13–25.

Watson, Barbara Bellow. "Variations on an Enigma: Elizabeth Bowen's War Novel." *Southern Humanities Review* 15.2 (Spring 1981). Rpt. in Bloom 81–101.

Weekes, Ann Owens. *Irish Women Writers: An Uncharted Tradition*. Lexington: UP of Kentucky, 1990.

Vera Brittain
1893–1970

Britta Zangen

Vera Brittain, author of the famous and best-selling *Testament of Youth*, has still not lost any of her fascination to the modern reader and scholar alike, because neither of the two causes for which she ardently fought most of her life—pacifism and feminism—have reached their goals yet, and because she consciously lived a feminist life in trying to unite marriage and motherhood with a career and a family with a close woman friend in the same house. A person of great energy and stamina and of an astounding integrity and sincerity, Brittain can still serve as a role model to modern women.

BACKGROUND

The two movements by which Brittain was influenced were the women's movement in the 1920s and 1930s and the pacifist one from the late 1930s onwards. Her childhood in a household with unshakable notions of male superiority laid the foundation stone for her vehement feminism. She saw her generation of feminists in direct succession to the suffragettes who had won political equality for women, leaving economic and social equality to be fought for. Refuting most of the traditional Victorian assumptions made about women, she supported companionate marriage and demanded the communal reorganization of child care and domestic work and a married woman's right to paid work.

With a husband, two children, and aging parents, the attempt to live out her feminist ideals proved a lifelong struggle. Although she succeeded in this on the whole, the difficulties were greater than she ever publicly admitted, and without the support of Winifred Holtby, her friend and living companion for thirteen years, she would probably have failed.

Her pacifism was essentially brought about by the losses of her brother and her fiancé and by her nursing experience during World War I. Speaking for the League of Nations and writing political articles, she realized early what German fascism was leading to and therefore joined the Peace Pledge Union in 1936. During World War II she never tired of speaking and writing against the war, which led to the total loss of the reputation she had gained with *Testament of Youth* in 1933.

ANALYSIS

Brittain's twenty-nine books, published between 1918 and 1968, cover a wide range of genres: novels, collections of poetry and letters, autobiographies, biographies, travel accounts, and sociohistorical studies. Apart from these she published about a thousand articles—mostly on feminist and pacifist issues—in nearly all the national newspapers and magazines. Sandra Gilbert justly calls her "a severely political writer" (436).

There is no disagreement among scholars that the documentary autobiography *Testament of Youth* is by far her best book, that it is "the most famous women's book of the Great War" (Tylee 209), and that it is still worth reading. It was intended by Brittain as a woman's answer to "the War Books" by Erich Maria Remarque, Siegfried Sassoon, Robert Graves, and others published to great success in the late 1920s, and it was to work out what was typical for the women of "the lost generation."

Most scholars also agree that for Brittain "her feminism was an integral part of her pacifism, and vice versa" (Bennett, "Peace" 194) and that this shows in *Testament of Youth*. The book "is both a vivid presentation of the war from a woman's point of view and a passionate feminist statement" (Gorham, "Vera Brittain, Flora" 140) and "a powerful attack on the false values of nationalism and militarism and on their roots in patriarchy" (Kennard 125). Deborah Gorham stresses its "intellectual and analytic quality" (*Vera Brittain* 232), but Claire Tylee blames it for not "elucidat[ing]" why the war "should ever have been believed to be glamorous, or glorious, or purposeful" (211) and maintains that it "veiled women's share in the moral responsibility for the waste of men's lives" (223). Alison Light holds against this that "[i]t was perfectly possible . . . for those who had lost their loved ones to learn to hate war and yet keep the romantic image of the heroic sacrifice of individuals untarnished" (200), while Marilyn Chandler explains that "Brittain wanted her readers to understand war not as an idea . . . but as the most intense kind of personal suffering multiplied a millionfold" (12). Maroula Joannou alone argues "that it can no longer be accepted as a feminist text" because it cannot possibly "address concerns shared by all feminists" (48). Jean Pickering and Jean E. Kennard see the claims of both the private and the public life to be another vital concern of the book (77; 135), while I have stressed that in writing it, Brittain "had to finally sort out the dichotomy between patriotism and compassion for the adversary" ("Above All" 12). Dale Spender summarizes—speaking about Brittain's pacifist writings in general—that "her ideas about the necessity for peace—and her notions of how peace might be achieved—are [still] entirely relevant" ("Women" 111).

Brittain's novels—*The Dark Tide* (1923), *Not without Honour* (1924), *Honourable Estate* (1936), *Account Rendered* (1945), and *Born 1925* (1948)—are not generally found to be good, though they are interesting "in that they record some of the major events and ideas of the time" (Mellown, "Reflections" 216). Janet Todd detects an "uncomfortably melodramatic" element in them and a "tendency [to] overdramatize and to stereotype lesser characters" (91). Like Kennard and me, Lynne Layton points to "a semireligious discourse of sacrifice and suffering" (80). Kennard addresses Brittain's "emphasis on heterosexual experience as healthy, liberating, and 'normal' " (4). Kennard, Susan Leonardi, and I stress the ambivalences in Brittain's novels: her "own continued ambivalence over the conflict between conventional female values and intellectual independence" (Kennard 48); the fact "that Brittain herself, as well as her fiction, wants and does not want to put women at the centre, wants and does not want to explore the possibilities of women alone or women with other women" (Leonardi, *Dangerous* 220); that "Brittain keeps undoing [her] positive portraits [of the successful New Women]" by making a man "the condition without which happiness for a woman is not to be attained" (Zangen, *A Life* 122–23). Kennard is alone in seeing female self-empowerment in Brittain's novels.

Brittain has been called "the best of the women war poets" (Crawford 28) because in her poetry "one can find the groping for meaning that critics have praised in the war poetry of [the male poets]" (141). Nosheen Khan finds her poems "primarily elegiac and documentary in character" (134). Diana Knight, in an unpublished paper, analyzes the poems as "absorbed in abstraction; poems replete with romantic mythologizing; poems of deflection and disengagement . . . exercises in psychological self-preservation . . . an escape and a sanctuary from the chaos and horror of her war-time present." This is further enlightened by Judith Kazantzis: "[T]he duty of the woman, bereaved and despairing, becomes clear. She will live her life as the dead one bequeathed it to her. She will immortalise him in her obedience to the values for which he died. To question those values is to question the Sacrifice itself—impossible. For then his death must become not only horrible but also meaningless" (xix).

It is regrettable that Brittain's journalism is so inaccessible. Barely twenty of her articles have been reissued in *Testament of a Generation*, although almost eight hundred have been gathered as photocopies in the Vera Brittain Archive at the McMaster University Library in Hamilton, Ontario. It is "her journalistic efforts (which were, in my opinion, far superior to all her literary efforts, barring *Testament of Youth*) [that] show off Brittain's punchy style to good advantage" (Bennett, "Peace" 195); it is here that "her feminism is often more explicitly stated and defended than it is in much of her literary work" (Spender, *Women* 105); it is their "characteristic combination of meticulous documentation, firmly logical development, and forceful . . . opinion" (Bishop, "Battle" 134) that still makes them as instructive as they are enjoyable to read.

ASSESSMENT

For the student of history who is interested in twentieth-century pacifism, Brittain's writings of all genres still provide an immensely instructive and powerfully moving experience. For those working on feminism, her texts are an endless source as much for the subject matters of the British "equality feminists" of the 1920s and 1930s as for still-relevant thoughts about the reasons for the inequality of the sexes. In unison with her own autobiographical materials, the recent biographical books on her offer absorbing information about one woman's ceaseless and difficult struggle for her own private equality and independence against the limitations of a family and, at the same time, for a public acceptance of pacifist ideals against a nation at war.

BIBLIOGRAPHY

Primary Sources

Verses of a V.A.D. and Other War Poems. 1918. London: Imperial War Museum, 1995.
The Dark Tide. London: Richards, 1923.
Not without Honour. London: Richards, 1924.
Women's Work in Modern England. London: Douglas, 1928.
Halcyon; or, The Future of Monogamy. London: Kegan Paul, 1929.
Testament of Youth: An Autobiographical Study of the Years 1900–1925. 1933. London: Virago, 1978.
Poems of the War and After. London: Gollancz, 1934.
Honourable Estate: A Novel of Transition. London: Gollancz, 1936.
"Authors Take Sides on the Spanish Civil War." *Left Review* December 1937.
Thrice a Stranger: New Chapters of Autobiography. London: Gollancz, 1938.
Testament of Friendship: The Story of Winifred Holtby. 1940. London: Virago, 1980.
England's Hour. 1941. London: Futura, 1981.
Humiliation with Honour. London: Dakers, 1942.
"One of These Little Ones . . .": A Plea to Parents and Others for Europe's Children. London: Dakers, 1943.
Seed of Chaos: What Mass Bombing Really Means. London: New Vision, 1944.
Above All Nations: An Anthology. Comp. George Catlin, Vera Brittain, and Sheila Hodges. London: Gollancz, 1945.
Account Rendered. 1945. London: Virago, 1982.
On Becoming a Writer. London: Hutchinson, 1947.
Born 1925: A Novel of Youth. 1948. London: Virago, 1982.

In the Steps of John Bunyan: An Excursion into Puritan England. London: Rich, 1950.
Search after Sunrise. London: Macmillan, 1951.
The Story of St. Martin's: An Epic of London. London: Pitkin, 1951.
Lady into Woman: A History of Women from Victoria to Elizabeth II. London: Dakers, 1953.
Testament of Experience: An Autobiographical Story of the Years 1925–1950. 1957. London: Virago, 1979.
Selected Letters of Winifred Holtby and Vera Brittain, 1920–1935. Ed. Vera Brittain and Geoffrey Handley-Taylor. London: Brown, 1960.
The Women at Oxford: A Fragment of History. London: Harrap, 1960.
Pethick-Lawrence: A Portrait. London: Allen, 1963.
The Rebel Passion: A Short History of Some Pioneer Peacemakers. London: Allen, 1964.
Envoy Extraordinary: A Study of Vijaya Lakshmi Pandit and Her Contribution to Modern India. London: Allen, 1965.
Radclyffe Hall: A Case of Obscenity? London: Femina, 1968.
"War Service in Perspective." In *Promise of Greatness: The War of 1914–1918.* Ed. George A. Panichas. New York: Day, 1968. 363–376.
Chronicle of Youth: War Diary, 1913–1917. Ed. Alan Bishop. London: Gollancz, 1981.
Testament of a Generation: The Journalism of Vera Brittain and Winifred Holtby. Ed. Paul Berry and Alan Bishop. London: Virago, 1985.
Chronicle of Friendship: Diary of the Thirties, 1932–1939. Ed. Alan Bishop. London: Gollancz, 1986.
Testament of a Peace Lover: Letters from Vera Brittain. Ed. Winifred Eden-Green and Alan Eden-Green. London: Virago, 1988.
Wartime Chronicle: Diary, 1939–1945. Ed. Alan Bishop and Y. Aleksandra Bennett. London: Gollancz, 1989.
Letters from a Lost Generation: First World War Letters of Vera Brittain and Four Friends. Ed. Alan Bishop and Mark Bostridge. London: Little, 1998.
"A Honeymoon in Two Worlds." Unpublished manuscript.

Secondary Sources

Bailey, Hilary. *Vera Brittain.* New York: Penguin, 1987; Oxford: Isis, 1988.
Beauman, Nicola. *A Very Great Profession: The Woman's Novel, 1914–39.* London: Virago, 1983.
Bennett, Yvonne Aleksandra. "Vera Brittain and the Peace Pledge Union: Women and Peace." In *Women and Peace: Theoretical, Historical, and Practical Perspectives.* Ed. Ruth Roach Pierson. London: Croom Helm, 1987. 192–213.
———. "Vera Brittain: Feminism, Pacifism, and Problem of Class, 1900–1953." *Atlantis: Canada* 12.2 (1987): 18–23.
Berkman, Joyce Avrech. " 'I Am Myself It': Comparative National Identity Formation in the Lives of Vera Brittain and Edith Stein." *Women's History Review* 6.1 (1997): 47–73.
Berry, Paul, and Mark Bostridge. *Vera Brittain: A Life.* London: Chatto, 1995.
Bishop, Alan. "The Battle of the Somme and Vera Brittain." In *English Literature of the Great War Revisited: Proceedings of the Symposium on the British Literature of the First World War.* Ed. Michel Roucoux. U of Picardy, 1986. 125–42.
———. " 'With Suffering and through Time': Olive Schreiner, Vera Brittain, and the Great War." In *Olive Schreiner and After: Essays on Southern African Literature in Honour of Guy Butler.* Ed. Malvern van Wyk Smith and Don Maclennan. Cape Town: Philip, 1983. 80–92.
Catlin, John. *Family Quartet.* London: Hamish Hamilton, 1987.
Chandler, Marilyn R. *A Healing Art: Regeneration through Autobiography.* New York: Garland, 1990.
Crawford, Fred D. *British Poets of the Great War.* Selinsgrove, PA: Susquehanna UP, 1988.
Faderman, Lillian. *Surpassing the Love of Men: Romantic Friendship and Love between Women from the Renaissance to the Present.* 1981. London: Women's Press, 1985.
Gilbert, Sandra M. "Soldier's Heart: Literary Men, Literary Women, and the Great War." *Signs* 8.3 (1983): 422–450.
Gorham, Deborah. "The Education of Vera and Edward Brittain: Class and Gender in an Upper-Middle-Class Family in Late Victorian and Edwardian England." *History of Education Review* 20.1 (1991): 22–38.
———. " 'The Friendships of Women': Friendship, Feminism, and Achievement in Vera Brittain's Life and Work in the Interwar Decades." *Journal of Women's History* 3.3 (1992): 44–69.
———. " 'Have We Really Rounded Seraglio Point?': Vera Brittain and Inter-war Feminism." In *British Feminism in the Twentieth Century.* Ed. Harold L. Smith. London: Elgar, 1990. 84–103.
———. *Vera Brittain: A Feminist Life.* Oxford: Blackwell, 1996.
———. "Vera Brittain, Flora Macdonald Denison, and the Great War: The Failure of Non-violence." In *Women and Peace: Theoretical, Historical, and Practical Perspectives.* Ed. Ruth Roach Pierson. London: Croom Helm, 1987. 137–149.
———. "A Woman at Oxford: Vera Brittain's Somerville Experience." *Historical Studies in Edu-*

cation/Revue d'Histoire de l'Education 3.1 (1991): 1–19.

Heilbrun, Carolyn G. *Hamlet's Mother and Other Women*. New York: Columbia UP, 1990.

———. *Writing a Woman's Life*. London: Women's Press, 1989.

Holtby, Winifred. *Letters to a Friend*. Ed. Alice Holtby and Jean McWilliam. 1937. Bath: Chivers, 1971.

Joannou, Maroula. "Vera Brittain's *Testament of Youth* Revisited." *Literature and History* 3rd ser. 2.2 (1993): 46–72.

Kazantzis, Judith. Preface to *Scars upon My Heart: Women's Poetry and Verse of the First World War*. Ed. Catherine W. Reilly. London: Virago, 1981.

Kennard, Jean E. *Vera Brittain and Winifred Holtby: A Working Partnership*. Hanover, NH: UP of New England, 1989.

Khan, Nosheen. *Women's Poetry of the First World War*. New York: Harvester, 1988.

Knight, Diana. "Vera Brittain's Poetry." Unpublished paper presented at the Centenary Conference, 15–16 October 1993, McMaster University, Hamilton, ON.

Layton, Lynne. "Vera Brittain's Testament(s)." In *Behind the Lines: Gender and the Two World Wars*. Ed. Margaret Randolph Higonnet et al. New Haven: Yale UP, 1987. 70–83.

Leonardi, Susan J. "Brittain's Beard: Transsexual Panic in *Testament of Youth*." *Literature Interpretation Theory* 2 (1990): 77–84.

———. *Dangerous by Degrees: Women at Oxford and the Somerville College Novelists*. New Brunswick, NJ: Rutgers UP, 1989.

Lesbian History Group. *Not a Passing Phase: Reclaiming Lesbians in History, 1840–1985*. London: Women's Press, 1989.

Light, Alison. *Forever England: Femininity, Literature, and Conservatism between the Wars*. London: Routledge, 1991.

Mellown, Muriel. "One Woman's Way to Peace: The Development of Vera Brittain's Pacifism." *Frontiers* 8.2 (1985): 1–6.

———. "Reflections on Feminism and Pacifism in the Novels of Vera Brittain." *Tulsa Studies in Women's Literature* 2.2 (Fall 1983): 214–228.

———. "Vera Brittain: Feminist in a New Age." In *Feminist Theorists: Three Centuries of Women's Intellectual Traditions*. Ed. Dale Spender. London: Women's Press, 1983. 314–334.

Minogue, Sally. "Prescriptions and Proscriptions: Feminist Criticisms and Contemporary Poetry." In *Problems for Feminist Criticism*. Ed. Sally Minogue. London: Routledge, 1990. 179–236.

Mister, Harry. "Vera Brittain." In *Peace Is the Way: A Guide to Pacifist Views and Actions*. Ed. Cyril Wright and Tony Augarde. Cambridge: Lutterworth, 1990.

Montefiore, Janet. " 'Shining Pins and Wailing Shells': Women Poets and the Great War." In *Women and World War I: The Written Response*. Ed. Dorothy Goldman. Basingstoke: Macmillan, 1993. 51–69.

Paul, Elizabeth L. "Women's Psychosocial Development: The Role of Marriage and Friendship in Two Lives." In *Perspectives in Personality: Approaches to Understanding Lives*. Ed. A.J. Stewart, J.M. Healy, Jr., and D. Ozer. London: Kingsley, 1991. 197–232.

Peterson, Bill E., and Abigail J. Stewart. "Using Personal and Fictional Documents to Assess Psychosocial Development: A Case Study of Vera Brittain's Generativity." *Psychology and Aging* 5.3 (1990): 400–411.

Pickering, Jean. "On the Battlefield: Vera Brittain's *Testament of Youth*." *Women's Studies* 13 (1986): 75–85.

Rintala, Marvin. "Chronicle of a Generation: Vera Brittain's Testament." *Journal of Political and Military Sociology* 12 (1984): 23–35.

Shaw, Marion. " 'A Noble Relationship': Friendship, Biography, and Autobiography in the Writings of Vera Brittain and Winifred Holtby." In *The Representation of the Self in Women's Autobiography*. Ed. Vita Fortunati and Gabriella Morisco. Bologna: U of Bologna, 1994.

Spender, Dale. *Time and Tide Wait for No Man*. London: Pandora, 1984.

———. *Women of Ideas and What Men Have Done to Them: From Aphra Behn to Adrienne Rich*. London: Routledge, 1982.

Stewart, Abigail J. "Toward a Feminist Strategy for Studying Women's Lives." In *Women Creating Lives: Identities, Resilience, and Resistance*. Ed. Carol E. Franz and Abigail J. Stewart. Boulder, CO: Westview, 1994. 11–35.

Stewart, Abigail J., Carol Franz, and Lynne Layton. "The Changing Self: Using Personal Documents to Study Lives." *Journal of Personality* 56.1 (1988): 41–74.

Stewart, Abigail J., and Joseph M. Healy, Jr. "The Role of Personality Development and Experience in Shaping Political Commitment: An Illustrative Case." *Journal of Social Issues* 42.2 (1986): 11–31.

Todd, Janet, ed. *Dictionary of British Women Writers*. London: Routledge, 1989.

Tylee, Claire M. *The Great War and Women's Consciousness: Images of Militarism and Womanhood in Women's Writings, 1914–64*. Basingstoke: Macmillan, 1990.

"The Vera Brittain Archive: Parts I–III." *McMaster University Library Research News* 4.3–5 (1977–1979).

Zangen, Britta. " 'Above All Nations Is Humanity': Vera Brittain's Painful Path to Radical Humanism." *Women's History Notebooks* 6.1 (1999): 10–17.

———. *A Life of Her Own: Feminism in Vera Brittain's Theory, Fiction, and Biography.* Frankfurt: Lang, 1996.

———. "A Lionized Best-Selling Authoress: Vera Brittain Lectures in the United States." In *Literaturimport transatlantisch.* Ed. Uwe Baumann. Tübingen: Narr, 1997. 153–165.

Anita Brookner
1928–

Del Ivan Janik

Since 1980, when she changed the focus of her writing from art history to fiction, Anita Brookner has been among the most prolific of literary novelists not only in Britain, but in the English-speaking world, publishing a new novel virtually every year. Her scope is not particularly broad; most of her novels center on the problems of middle-aged or elderly women who find themselves marginalized by or alienated from the society around them. But her works examine that subject from a variety of perspectives, and they include at least one acknowledged masterwork, the Booker Prize–winning *Hotel du Lac* (1984).

BACKGROUND

Anita Brookner was born in London in 1928 to Newson and and Maude Schiska Brookner. Her father, a Polish Jew who emigrated to England before the Great War and served in the British army, changed his name from Bruckner when he married Maude, whose family were less recent immigrants of similar background. Anita Brookner's interest in the arts was probably fostered by the atmosphere at home: her mother had been a professional singer before her marriage. That atmosphere was also characterized, however, by a degree of instability and melancholy. The Brookner house in the south London suburb of Herne Hill, besides harboring an extended family and a number of servants, welcomed a stream of Jewish refugees throughout the 1930s and the years of World War II (Fullbrook, *DLB* 40). According to Lynn Veach Sadler, the Dorn family in *Family and Friends* (1985) and the Livingstones in *A Friend from England* (1987) are fairly closely modeled on the Brookners. The circumstances of her childhood seem to have had a lasting effect on Brookner's sense of her relationship with her native country: "I think my parents' lives were blighted—and in some sense mine is too—largely by this fact of being outside of the natural order, being strangers in England. . . . I've never been at home here" (Haffenden 65). Brookner studied at James Allen's Girls School in Dulwich, read history and studied French at King's College, London, and completed a doctoral degree at the Courtauld Institute of Art. She lectured at the University of Reading from 1959 to 1964 and at the Courtauld from 1964 until her retirement in 1988, so that she actually wrote her first eight novels during her summer holidays. Brookner never married or developed a long-lasting intimate relationship, and in an interview with Olga Kenyon she left the impression that the lives—or at least the feelings—of her protagonists often reflect her own: "Mine was a dreary Victorian story: I nursed my parents till they died. I write out of a sense of injustice, because I felt invisible and passive. Life is so badly plotted" (Kenyon, *Women Writers* 12).

ANALYSIS

A number of reviewers and critics have noted the "formulaic" character of Brookner's novels, and some have, less justifiably, compared them to the popular romances of the Mills and Boon or Harlequin variety (see Skinner 7 for a summary of such critiques). That the outlines of Brookner's novels form what becomes a recognizable pattern is undeniable: a female protagonist, often an academic, who has experienced a difficult childhood in an eccentric family builds a successful but unglamorous career and finds herself lonely and alienated from her surroundings. She attempts a new approach to life, encounters female foils who share some of her characteristics but seem to place others in a negative light, meets an outgoing and superficially attractive man or, often, a sparkling couple somewhat in the mold of latter-day Scott Fitzgeralds or Gerald Murphys who take her under their wing but turn out to be self-absorbed opportunists: the Dixons of *A Start in Life* (1981) are the prime example. She may become involved with the man of the pair or with their unattached friend—either of whom proves a disappointment—and she settles, in the end, for a return to her original, unrewarding circumstances. This is, of course, an oversimplification, and not all of its elements appear in every novel, but it does serve to undermine the characterization of Brookner as a writer of romances, which, as she pointed out in an interview with Shusha Guppy, depend on happy endings, however achieved; furthermore, according to Brookner, "In the genuine Romantic novel there is a confrontation with truth and in the 'romance' novel a similar confrontation with a surrogate, plastic version of the truth" (161).

Brookner's novels, superficially traditionalist in form, on closer inspection reveal their ties to other late-twentieth-century fiction, not least in their use of intertextuality; they are often tied to a work of literature—Balzac's *Eugénie Grandet* in the case of her premiere novel *A Start in Life*, Benjamin Constant's *Adolphe* in her second, *Providence* (1982), and so on. Even Edith Hope of *Hotel du Lac*, ironically a writer of romance novels, is described as physically resembling Virginia Woolf. These traits of intertextuality and referentiality have led Patricia Waugh, among others, to classify Brookner as a postmodernist, but on the other hand, her emphasis on social criticism and her psychological observation link her to a tradition that includes Charles Dickens, Henry James, and Edith Wharton and, some argue, Barbara Pym (Sadler 5–6). Aspects of Brookner's novels also reflect the influence of her first career, as an art historian. The life of Goya is a subtext of *Look at Me* (1983); Titian's *Bacchus and Ariadne* is an important touchstone in *A Misalliance* (1986); and similar functions are performed by paintings by Giorgione in *A Friend from England* (1987), Turner in *A Closed Eye* (1991), and Rubens, Tintoretto, Redon, and Walter Sickert in *A Private View* (1994).

Hotel du Lac, besides being Brookner's most prominently honored novel, is also a conveniently typical example of her early fiction. Edith Hope (pen name Vanessa Wilde—the surnames are unsubtly significant), who has been carrying on a passionate but apparently doomed affair with a married man, David Simmonds, has left her fiancé Geoffrey Long standing at the altar (actually the Registry Office) and to escape the ensuing scandal has gone on holiday in Switzerland at the staid Hotel du Lac. The hotel is inhabited this autumn only by Mrs. Pusey and her daughter Jennifer, ardent shoppers whose apparent ages advance roughly a decade each time Edith observes them; Monica, the stunning but censorious lady-with-a-dog whose husband is seeking an heir or alternatively a divorce; Mme de Bonneuil, an aristocrat whose son and daughter-in-law have deposited her in the hotel as in a nursing home; and Philip Neville, a middle-aged gentleman-scoundrel who pursues a relationship with Edith. There is relatively little action but a great deal of observation and introspection, which come to a head when Edith, having agreed to marry Philip, sees him leaving Jennifer's bedroom in the middle of the night. Reluctantly recognizing her kinship with the other women of the Hotel du Lac, she decides to return to London, David, and her marginal existence. She is, as she writes in the telegram she sends David, not exactly "coming home"—the phrase implies a sense of place and a degree of warmth that will always elude her—but simply "returning" (*Hotel du Lac* 184).

Brookner presented similar patterns in *A Misalliance* (1986), *A Friend from England* (1987), and *Brief Lives* (1990). One departure was *Family and Friends* (1985), which focused not on one heroine but on the Dorns, a German-Jewish immigrant family resembling the Brookners, chronicling their lives from the beginning of the twentieth century to nearly its end. However, the contrasts between relatively passive characters and their more colorful and often-unscrupulous counterparts that form the basis of many of her other novels are represented here by the younger Dorns, Mimi and Alfred in the first instance, Betty and Frederick in the second. A similar contrast is evident in *Latecomers* (1988), which uncharacteristically centers on two men, Holocaust survivors Thomas Hartmann and Thomas Fibich. Hartmann fits successfully into British society, but Fibich remains an outsider, haunted by the terrors of the 1930s and the loss of his parents. A trip to Berlin gives him a respite, during which he is able to write a book of memories to pass on to his son. In *Lewis Percy* (1989) the protagonist is again male, but his life resembles those of Brookner's early heroines. Lewis, a completely unheroic librarian who has written a thesis on heroism in the nineteenth-century novel, is abandoned by his feminist wife after she becomes pregnant. Unlike Edith Hope, however, he responds to disillusionment with action rather than acquiescence, publishing his book, quitting his job, and leaving for Paris with a new lover. A third male protagonist, George Bland (another significant surname), is at the center of *A Private View*: Grieving for his old friend Michael, George, who is sixty-five years old and has never married, makes a lonely pilgrimage to Nice, and on returning to London he comes under the spell of Katy Gibb, a flamboyant young neighbor who has until recently been living in the United States. In one of Brookner's few hopeful endings, George eventually recognizes Katy as an opportunist and dismisses her from his life, reviving an old relationship with a former lover.

Europe, particularly France, figures significantly in many of Brookner's novels in addition to those already mentioned; perhaps this is a reflection of her own sense of "foreignness" in Britain. John Skinner pointed out in his 1992 study that "Brookner has repeatedly emphasized her own sense of marginality and alienation in England. Her predominantly female protagonists are also mentally, if not actually ethnically, outsiders" (50). Nice, for example, is a setting again in *The Bay of Angels* (2001), where it seems to offer new possibilities of life for the sheltered protagonist Zoe and her widowed mother. In *Brief Lives* (1990) Owen, the husband of Fay Langdon, a singer who had given up her career for him, dies in an automobile accident on the Riviera. *A Closed Eye* (1991), like *Hotel du Lac* a revelation of and a reflection on a middle-aged woman's lonely life, is, like that earlier novel, set in Switzerland. Anna Durant of *Fraud* (1992), after a protected, uneventful, and frustrating life, suddenly leaves for Paris and a career as a fashion designer. *Incidents in the Rue Laugier* (1995) reverses the direction of movement but not the geographical symbolism: it begins in Dijon, where Maud Gonthier is seduced by an Englishman named David Tyler, who then abandons her. His friend Edward "rescues" the pregnant girl by marrying her and taking her to England, where they live out a comfortable, placid, and passionless life that contrasts with the brief excitement of her affair with David.

Whatever their settings, however, Brookner's novels taken as a whole are characterized by variety of invention and detail in the context of consistency of thematic focus. Brookner's subject is an almost Manichaean division between innocence, goodness, and haplessness and the opposing values of opportunism, worldly success, and, if not evil, blithe self-absorption. Both her early protagonists, like Ruth Weiss in *A Start in Life* and Edith Hope in *Hotel du Lac*, and their later counterparts, like Maud Gonthier in *Incidents in the Rue Laugier*, Miriam Sharpe of *Falling Slowly* (1998), and Claire Pitt in *Undue Influence* (1999), are quiet, sheltered, and marginal individuals who are drawn for a time into the mainstream of life with disquieting and usually damaging results, only to return to their decent but unexciting lives.

ASSESSMENT

As John Skinner summarizes, early reactions to Brookner's novels, while recognizing their intelligence and erudition, generally related them to the fiction of Barbara Pym and, less flatteringly, to popular romances of the Victoria Holt, Barbara Cartland, Mills and Boon, and Harlequin varieties (6–7). The publication of *Hotel du Lac* and its recognition via the 1984 Booker Prize (in the face of outstanding competition that included Julian Barnes's *Flaubert's Parrot* and Penelope Lively's *According to Mark*) won Brookner a degree of both material security and critical respect as a novelist. Writing in 1990 about Brookner's first seven novels, Lynn Veach Sadler emphasizes their focus on "moral choice" and how they "remind us of the novel's genuine legacy as a purveyor of values" (140). Sadler observes that "we come away from them in internal debate"; Brookner takes us "across hecatombs . . . of human reach—pagan, Christian (though she is Jewish), female, male, principled, unprincipled" (141). Patricia Waugh (in 1989) interestingly reads Brookner in the context of contemporary feminism, pointing out that in spite of her conscious repudiation of "adversarial positions" (Haffenden 75), she depicts characters like Edith Hope as at least seeking satisfying identities outside the stereotypes that seem on the surface to define feminine success (142, 149). Although it dates from 1992 and addresses fewer than half of Brookner's novels, the most stimulating full-length study to date is Skinner's *The Fictions of Anita Brookner*. Skinner agrees with Waugh that Brookner addresses feminist issues in spite of herself, noting her tendency "to separate feminine intelligence from female sexuality—an insistence on mutual exclusivity which bears an ironic resemblance to reactionary male stereotypes" (81). He subjects the opening paragraph of *Hotel du Lac* to a close reading that he says linguistically reveals a "double tension" in Edith Hope and perhaps in Brookner herself between "the simultaneous desire for economic independence and need for psychic relief" while "she nevertheless faces a world where woman is defined in socio-economic terms *by* and *through* men, and where her imaginings can only be articulated in a patriarchal or phallocentric discourse" (82), which might be taken as more evidence of Brookner's belief, voiced in her interview with Olga Kenyon, that "life is so badly plotted" (12). Skinner's recognition of "Brookner's common concern to provide, in her fiction, the kind of moral order that she finds so conspicuously absent in life" (170)—not, I would add, an anachronistic moralism but a genuine exploration of what "morality" can mean in a rapidly changing society—applies not only to the nine novels he examines but to her work of the 1990s and of the new century. It may be what finally accounts for her continuing appeal to readers and critics.

BIBLIOGRAPHY

Primary Sources

J.A. Dominique Ingres. Paulton, UK: Purnell, 1965.

Jacques-Louis David. Paulton, UK: Purnell, 1967.

Watteau. London: Hamlyn, 1968.

The Genius of the Future: Studies in French Art Criticism. London and New York: Phaidon, 1971.

Greuze: The Rise and Fall of an Eighteenth-Century Phenomenon. London: Elek, 1972.

Jacques-Louis David, A Personal Interpretation. London: Oxford UP, 1974.

Jacques-Louis David. London: Chatto; New York: Harper, 1980.

A Start in Life. London: Cape, 1981. As *The Debut*. New York: Linden, 1981.

Providence. London: Cape, 1982; New York: Pantheon, 1984.

Look at Me. London: Cape; New York: Pantheon, 1983.

Hotel du Lac. London: Cape; New York: Pantheon, 1984.

Family and Friends. London: Cape: New York: Pantheon, 1985.

A Misalliance. London: Cape, 1986. As *The Misalliance*. New York: Pantheon, 1986.

A Friend from England. London: Cape; New York: Pantheon, 1987.

Latecomers. London: Cape; New York: Pantheon, 1988.

Lewis Percy. London: Cape; New York: Pantheon, 1989.

Brief Lives. London: Cape; New York: Random House, 1990.

A Closed Eye. London: Cape; New York: Random House, 1991.

Fraud. London: Cape; New York: Random House, 1992.

A Family Romance. London: Cape, 1993. As *Dolly*. New York: Random House, 1993.

A Private View. London: Cape; New York: Random House, 1994.

Incidents in the Rue Laugier. London: Cape, 1995; New York: Random House, 1996.

Altered States. London: Cape; New York: Random House, 1996.

Soundings. London: Harvill, 1997.

Visitors. London: Cape, 1997; New York: Random House, 1997.

Falling Slowly. London: Viking, 1998; New York: Random House, 1998.

Undue Influence. London: Viking, 1999; New York: Random House, 2000.

Romanticism and Its Discontents. London: Viking; New York: Farrar, 2000.

The Bay of Angels. London: Viking; New York: Random House, 2001.

Secondary Sources

Baxter, Giselle Marie. "Clothes, Men, and Books: Cultural Experiences and Identity in the Early Novels of Anita Brookner." *English* 42 (Summer 1993): 125–139.

Fisher-Wirth, Anne. " 'Hunger Art:' The Novels of Anita Brookner." *Twentieth Century Literature* 41 (Spring 1995): 1–15.

Fullbrook, Kate. "Anita Brookner." In *British Novelists since 1960, Second Series*. Ed. Merritt Moseley. Vol. 195 of *Dictionary of Literary Biography*. Detroit: Gale, 1998. 38–48.

———. "Anita Brookner: On Reaching for the Sun." In *British Women Writing Fiction*. Ed. Abby H.P. Werlock. Tuscaloosa: U of Alabama P, 2000.

Grover, Jan Zita. "Small Expectations." *Women's Review of Books* 11 (July 1994): 38–40.

Guppy, Shusha. "The Art of Fiction XCVIII: Anita Brookner." Interview. *Paris Review* 104 (Fall 1987): 147–169.

Haffenden, John. "Anita Brookner." Interview. In *Novelists in Interview*. Ed. John Haffenden. London and New York: Methuen, 1985. 57–75.

Hosmer, Robert E., Jr. "Anita Brookner." In *Dictionary of Literary Biography Yearbook 1987*. Detroit: Gale, 1988. 293–308.

———. "Paradigm and Passage: The Fiction of Anita Brookner." In *Contemporary British Women Writers*. Ed. Robert E. Hosmer, Jr. Basingstoke: Macmillan, 1993. 26–54.

Kenyon, Olga. "Anita Brookner." In *Women Novelists Today: A Survey of English Writing in the Seventies and Eighties*. Ed. Olga Kenyon. Brighton: Harvester, 1988. 144–165.

———. "Anita Brookner." Interview. In *Women Writers Talk: Interviews with 10 Women Writers*. Ed. Olga Kenyon. Oxford: Lennard, 1989. 7–24.

May, Gita. "Anita Brookner." In *British Writers: Supplement IV*. Ed. George Stade and Carol Howard. London: Simon & Schuster; New York: Scribner's, 1997.

Sadler, Lynn Veach. *Anita Brookner*. Boston: Twayne, 1990.

Skinner, John. *The Fictions of Anita Brookner: Illu-*

sions of Romance. Basingstoke: Macmillan; New York: St. Martin's, 1992.

Stetz, Margaret Diane. "Anita Brookner: Woman Writer as Reluctant Feminist." In *Writing the Woman Artist*. Ed. Suzanne W. Jones. Philadelphia: U of Pennsylvania P, 1991. 96–112.

Waugh, Patricia. *Feminine Fictions: Revisiting the Postmodern*. London and New York: Routledge, 1989.

Wyatt-Brown, Anne M. "Creativity in Midlife: The Novels of Anita Brookner." *Journal of Aging Studies* 3.2 (1989): 175–181.

Brigid Brophy
1929–1995

Karl L. Stenger

"His . . . life can be read as a fable: propounding the problem of a man born into the wrong time and place." Brigid Brophy's portrait of Ambrose Bierce in her collection *The Adventures of God in His Search for the Black Girl* (20) as the artist as outsider applies to her life and work as well. She was one of the most outspoken and polemic literary figures of the 1960s, and her vociferous support of such issues as feminism, gay rights, the protection of animals, vegetarianism, atheism, pacifism, and the protection of authors' rights led to her image as an iconoclast and enfant terrible. Brophy used her writing to crusade for the issues close to her heart and to depict twentieth-century people's alienation from their environment and from themselves. To her consternation, she was frequently misunderstood as a controversialist, polemicist, shrew, and heckler, and the literary importance of her works was often overshadowed by their "message." Recent studies, however, have fully revealed Brophy as a maverick and innovator and her masterpiece *In Transit* as "a locus classicus for today's gender critics and advocates of experimental fiction" (Moore 9).

BACKGROUND

Brigid Antonia Brophy was born on June 12, 1929, in London into a literary family. Her father, John Brophy, was the prolific author of highly entertaining war novels as well as nonfiction, and her mother, Charis Weare (Grundy), was a schoolteacher who published a novel in her twenties. Having a father who was of Irish descent but who was born and who spent his life in England was seminal to Brigid Brophy's lifelong sense of alienation. She states in her essay "Am I An Irishwoman?" published in the collection *Don't Never Forget*: "I feel a foreigner there [in Ireland]: but I feel a foreigner in England, too. I was brought up to do so" (317). From her father Brophy inherited a sense of religious nonconformism. Whereas her mother and her maternal grandparents were members of the now-defunct apocalyptic sect of the Irvingites or the Catholic Apostolic Church, Brophy and her father were "natural, logical and happy atheist[s]" (Afterword, *The King of a Rainy Country* 276). A precocious girl, Brophy started reading Shakespeare, Milton, Bernard Shaw, Ronald Firbank, and Evelyn Waugh at the age of five as well as composing poetic dramas. The disruptions caused by World War II adversely affected her education, and Brophy was moved from school to school twelve times. When she was eighteen, Brigid Brophy was admitted to St. Hugh's College, Oxford, and as an exceptionally promising candidate she was awarded a scholarship. She studied

Greek and Latin, but was expelled for unspecified misconduct after four semesters. It has been surmised that her offenses included appearing drunk in chapel and advocating lesbianism, but Brophy was reluctant to discuss the incident in later life because it had traumatized her so deeply: "I shall never describe, because I won't risk re-living, the distress I suffered" (Newman 139).

Brigid Brophy returned to London and eked out a meager living as a part-time shorthand typist while writing short fiction. Her first collection of short stories was published in 1953 as *The Crown Princess* to positive notices, and her satirical novel *Hackenfeller's Ape*, which is based on her lifelong advocacy of animals' rights and her opposition to experiments with animals, was awarded first prize by the Cheltenham Literary Festival the same year. Brophy's second novel, *The King of a Rainy Country*, which appeared in 1956, is her only work of fiction to contain autobiographical elements. Brophy stressed on several occasions that her temperament is antiautobiographical: "I do not dislike or despise autobiographical novelists. . . . I cannot, however, be one of them" (*Reads* 75). Susan, the main protagonist of *The King of a Rainy Country*, however, represents a "cut-down version" or "stunted self portrait" of the author, whose baptismal name was Susan (Afterword 273f.). Neale, the man Susan is in love with, is a "tolerably accurate portrait" of John, a man Brophy had met while she was at Oxford and with whom she had undertaken a trip to Italy. When John fell in love with and married a woman Brigid Brophy had never met, she was free to marry Michael Levey, an art historian and assistant keeper at the National Gallery, in 1954. While their marriage was ostensibly a happy and successful one, Brigid Brophy's provocative public statements concerning the "immorality of marriage," the unreasonableness of society to "impose monogamy on the ones who have not chosen it" (*Don't Never Forget* 29), and her support of gay marriage contributed to her image as an enfant terrible and iconoclast.

In 1957 Brophy's only child, Kate, was born, and motherhood together with a serious personal crisis caused a six-year-long gap in Brophy's creative output. In the preface to her play *The Burglar* Brophy describes the disintegration of her personality she experienced as follows: "In a dark crisis of my personal life, the constituents of my personality were broken down, like the constituents of a caterpillar inside the chrysalis-case." It was not until 1962 that *Flesh: A Novel of Indolent Passion*, one of her numerous perceptive portrayals of an unconventional marriage/relationship, was published. *The Finishing Touch*, a hilarious "lesbian fantasy," followed in 1963 and *The Snow Ball*, a sophisticated comedy of manners, in 1964. The last two novels, which were published in the United States appropriately together in one volume, were deeply influenced by two of Brigid Brophy's idols, Ronald Firbank and Wolfgang Amadeus Mozart. *The Finishing Touch* has justly been called "the most concentrated single example of Firbank's influence, really a posthumous monument to him" (Newman 141), and references to Mozart's opera *Don Giovanni* pervade *The Snow Ball*. Brigid Brophy also paid tribute to her idols in two detailed, well-researched, and perceptive studies. In *Mozart the Dramatist: A New View of Mozart, His Operas, and His Age* (1964) she applied Freud's theories to the composer's work. While some reviewers praised her originality, others objected vociferously to her methodology. Joseph Kerman, for example, claimed in the *Hudson Review*: "I do not think that Miss Brophy knows quite what she is up to. . . . Criticism is not psychoanalysis" (309). In her monumental study *Prancing Novelist: A Defence of Fiction in the Form of a Critical Biography in Praise of Ronald Firbank* (1973) Brophy rescued this innovative and original writer from oblivion, and by documenting his role as a pioneer of twentieth-century literature she was at the forefront of a Firbank revival.

Brophy's acquaintance with Charles Osborne, the assistant editor of *London Magazine*, led to numerous magazine and newspaper articles as well as television and radio appearances in the 1960s and 1970s. Brophy not only praised and condemned writers and their works in her articles and broadcasts (pro: Firbank, Shaw, Henry James, John Horne Burns, Jean Genet, Katherine Mansfield, Colette; anti: Henry Miller, Simone de Beauvoir, Virginia Woolf, Evelyn Waugh), but she also used her pulpit to preach against vivisection, censorship, marriage, and monogamy and for the rights of women, gays, authors, and animals. Several of her distinctive essays were collected in *Don't Never Forget* (1966), *Baroque-'n'-Roll* (1987), and *Reads* (1989). Her outspokenness, coupled with her public persona, which came across as strident and abrasive (while in reality she was rather shy and retiring), cemented the general perception of Brophy as an opinionated, mischievous enfant terrible. Brophy poured oil on the fire when she published the polemical *Fifty Works of English and American Literature We Could Do Without* (1967), written in collaboration with her husband and with her friend Charles Osborne. The book caused a firestorm of outrage, and its authors were savaged by reviewers. Anthony Burgess, for example, chastised them as naughty little children: "Like children, they have shown off, and the showing-off has provoked attention. . . . They're still in the nursery, cut off from the big world" (71). Brophy and her coauthors had clearly touched a sore spot, and no matter whether one agreed with their assessment of individual authors or works, their questioning of the literary canon paved the way toward the reassessment of a fossilized value system.

Brophy's uneasy relationship with her critics deteriorated even further when her play *The Burglar* (1968), a mildly amusing bedroom farce in which the author skewered middle-class mores, "met an instant and virtually unanimous critical cannonade" that sank the play within three weeks of opening night at the Vaudeville Theatre in London (9). Brophy did not take her defeat lying down but came out swinging, defending her work and herself in a forty-seven-page combative preface. The conventional character of *The Burglar* did not prepare Brophy's reading audience for what was in store next, namely, the highly experimental *In Transit* (1969), "an heroi-cyclic novel." While it contained many themes and concerns depicted in her previous works, *In Transit* was a radical stylistic departure for Brophy. The novel was so avant-garde that it nonplussed and exasperated readers and reviewers alike. Joyce Carol Oates, for example, lamented, "[T]he reader feels a kind of desperation in his desire to come upon something good in all these pages—something intelligent, something original and striking—something" (4). Posterity has been kinder to this challenging work, and several recent studies have documented its innovative character. There can be no doubt that *In Transit* is Brophy's most original and enduring creation.

It is not surprising that Brophy was unable to repeat the originality of *In Transit*. Her subsequent writing is more conventional and resembles her earlier works. Among her later works are a collection of short stories entitled *The Adventures of God in His Search for the Black Girl* (1973) and *Palace without Chairs* (1978), a satirical, "baroque" novel set in an imaginary kingdom. One of the reasons for Brophy's gradual retreat from fiction writing was her increased political activism. She joined the Labour Party and campaigned for animal rights as vice president of the British Anti-Vivisection Society. Together with the distinguished lesbian writer Maureen Duffy, Brophy founded the Writers' Action Group with the goal of providing writers with a fee every time their books are lent by public libraries, an idea her father had originated as "the Brophy penny." After lengthy and intense lobbying by the Writers' Action Group the Public Lending Right Bill was passed by Parliament in 1979. Another reason for Brophy's increasing abstinence from writing was her health. Having been in excellent health throughout her life, she developed disconcerting floating sensations and difficulties walking in 1982 and was diagnosed with multiple sclerosis two years later, an event she decribed movingly in "A Case-Historical Fragment of Autobiography," which was included in the collection *Baroque-'n'-Roll*. She was housebound, confined to a wheelchair, and cared for by nurses, friends, and her husband, who quit his job as director of the National Gallery in 1987 to devote himself to her full-time. Eventually, Brophy's worsening condition necessitated her move to a nursing home in Lincolnshire, where she died on August 7, 1995, at the age of sixty-six.

ANALYSIS

"She was a moated castle, a royal castle, with draw-bridge and ramparts; and there was nothing inside. . . . She had no self. She had no character" (*The Crown Princess* 26). Teresa, the protagonist in the title story of Brophy's first collection *The Crown Princess and Other Stories*, is, like most of Brophy's characters, an outsider. She feels incapable of following the path prescribed by tradition; instead of marrying a cousin she does not know and ascending the throne, she feels the urge to become a painter. Her upbringing has alienated her from the common folk, and her naïve attempts to learn about real life through films and actors are doomed to failure. She realizes that "her idols were dolls" (30) and that she cannot escape her destiny. Standing on the palace's balcony and acknowledging the crowd's wishes for her twenty-first birthday, the unhappy princess screams inside, "GO AWAY, she shouted—THERE'S NOBODY HERE!" (40).

The fatalism of "The Crown Princess" gives way to satire in Brophy's first novel, *Hackenfeller's Ape*. It combines the author's opposition to the use of animals in experimentation with her "first attempt at a type she draws expertly: the delicate, ineffectual male" (Newman 140). Professor Clement Darrelhyde, an introverted scientist who spends his days watching the mating habits of two apes in the London Zoo, is obsessed with Mozart to such a degree that he frequently breaks into opera arias in public. On one occasion he is transformed into one of Mozart's female characters: "[H]e . . . was transported into another era, another sex. He became the middle-aged Countess, tragically and with dignity calling on Love to restore her treasure—the affections of her Count" (12). When Darrelhyde learns that the apes are scheduled to be used in a scientific experiment, he and Gloria, a young criminal he befriends, make several unsuccessful attempts at saving the animals. When they facilitate the male ape's escape from the zoo, he is shot to death. The novel, however, ends on a hopeful note. Edwina, the female ape, gives birth, and her baby takes after its father: "It woke all the other animals and set them gibbering as it let out its roar of wrath" (177). Brophy considered *Hackenfeller's Ape* her best work since the novel "displays at its most intense the violently romantic feeling in a precisely classical form to which most of my fiction aspires" (Newman 139).

In a candid 1975 interview with Leslie Dock, Brophy expounded the intricate musical form of her works as follows: "Everything . . . I have written . . . is structured on the concerto, in three movements, with a one, two-A structure within each movement" ("Interview" 169). This tripartite structure is clearly evident in Brophy's second novel, *The King of a Rainy Country*, her only partially autobiographical work. The first part of the novel depicts the unconventional, chaste, and at times uneasy relationship between two bohemians and incurable romantics in postwar London. Neale, a young intellectual, works as a dishwasher in a grungy restaurant and struggles with his sexual identity. There are numerous indications that he is bisexual or homosexual. One day he brings François, a young gay Frenchman, back from the restaurant and lets him stay at his apartment. Neale constantly wonders whether other men are "queer," his favorite saying is "bugger me backwards" (15), and on one occasion he makes a revealing pun: "What does okay mean? . . . Gay? I doubt if I'm okay" (128). Susan works as a typist for a sleazy bookseller whose principal income derives from pornography. Her past catches up with her when she discovers the nude photo of her former friend Cynthia Bewly in one of the books. Susan had shared a passionate love affair with Cynthia while attending an all-girls school, and the discovery of the photo sets in motion a search for the object of her affection. When Neale's and Susan's detective work uncovers Cynthia's attendance at an upcoming film festival in Venice, they decide to follow her there. The second part of the novel consists of a hilarious, picaresque travelogue. For financial reasons Neale and Susan are forced to accompany a motley group of American tourists from Nice to Venice. This trip gives Brophy an opportunity to lampoon organized tourism in general and American tourists in particular. The third part takes place in Venice and resembles the last act of a Mozart opera. Susan and Neale meet Cynthia and her acquaintance, the famous opera singer Helena Buchan. Eventually, they couple off. Neale decides to marry Cynthia, not because he is in love with her but because he has appropriated Susan's past ("Your past, my past—what's the difference? . . . You and I are practically the same person" [91]). Susan begins a relationship with Helena Buchan only to lose her to terminal illness. The end of the novel implies symbolically that Susan might find happiness with a future (female?) partner. Analyzing the shifts from one master narrative to another in Brophy's "slippage-ridden text," Patricia Juliana Smith has demonstrated convincingly in her study of *The King of a Rainy Country* that the novel should be regarded as "an example of early post-modernity, a metafiction that tries on and discards a variety of conventional generic plots which, because of their deeply ingrained heterosexual narrative ideologies, offer no viable solutions or means of closure to the protagonists" ("Desperately" 23).

Brophy's next novel, *Flesh*, is a contemporary version of the Pygmalion and Galatea theme. Marcus, a young Jew, is, like many of Brophy's male characters, an outsider. He is unattractive, overly sensitive, shy, and socially inept and cannot find a job that holds his interest. When he meets Nancy at a party, she decides to transform him into a competent lover, husband, father, and breadwinner. Marcus, who is painfully thin at the beginning of the novel, is transformed at the end into his favorite painter's best-known image: he becomes a fleshy Rubens woman. It is not clear how the reader should interpret this transformation, because the third-person narrator presents the characters and story with clinical detachment and neutrality. Chris Hopkins has shown in his perceptive analysis of the novel that this ambiguity is a sign of modernity: "[T]he building up of clues that are never pushed into an interpretation easily available to the reader does seem a distinctive and perhaps particularly modern quality" (14).

Transformation is also the theme of *The Finishing Touch*, this time from a closeted to an out and proud lesbian existence. The novel, whose original title *Antonia* was changed to the appropriately ambiguous one by Brophy's publishers (one of its meanings refers to masturbation), is set in an all-girls boarding school in the south of France. Hetty Braid and Antonia Mount, the finishing school's mistresses, clearly have feelings for some of the girls in their care as well as for each other, but they suppress them. The arrival of royalty disturbs the uneasy equilibrium, and an ensuing scandal opens the lesbian closet. Her Royal Highness is stung by a wasp, and when Miss Mount sucks the venom from the royal bosom, paparazzi document the supposedly scandalous act. The headmistress is outed in the press, and as a result, her school becomes a haven for openly lesbian students. Brophy's "comic masterpiece of girls' school homo-eroticism" (Blackmer 32) was clearly influenced by the writings of Ronald Firbank and Colette, and though it parodies preceding works of this genre, it "represents an important milestone in the history of lesbian and, more broadly, antihomophobic literature" (Blackmer 38).

Brophy's subsequent novel, *The Snow Ball*, is, next to *In Transit*, her most enigmatic and challenging work. The author confessed in the preface to her play *The Burglar* that "the complexity of *The Snow Ball*'s design defies even my own intellectual analysis" (30). While her previous novels were modeled on the classical concerto form, *The Snow Ball* resembles a Mozart opera. The novel is set during a New Year's Eve costume ball in an eighteenth-century town house, and allusions to Mozart's *Don Giovanni* and *Nozze di Figaro* abound. Whereas Mozart left it ambiguous whether or not Don Giovanni succeeded in seducing Donna Anna before the opera opens, Brophy solves the mystery and gives the episode a feminist twist. "Donna" Anna in *The Snow Ball* is not a helpless victim but rather is in full control. She chooses her persona deliberately, pursues "Don Giovanni," and enthusiastically participates in their sexual encounter, insisting on anonymity. As in *Flesh*, the narrative stance impedes the unambiguous interpretation of the events. The third-person narrator is clinically detached, resembling at times a film camera (12, 16), and leaves the reader to draw his/her own conclusions. Chris Hopkins's assessment of *Flesh* can be applied to *The Snow Ball* as well: "[A]t the end of the novel, we cannot readily interpret the significance of the events of which we (apparently) know so much" (14).

The deliberate anonymity of the protagonists in *The Snow Ball* (they are masks and have neither past nor future) is pushed to the extreme in Brophy's masterwork *In Transit*. Evelyn Hilary "Pat" O'Rooley, the ambiguously named first-person narrator, finds him/herself in an airport transit lounge ("a suitable symbol of the dislocations of modernity" [Hopkins 16]), having deliberately missed his/her connecting flight. S/he is not only devoid of a past (we only learn that her/his parents died in a plane crash), but has also no defined identity. S/he tries unsuccessfully to discover his/her gender thoughout the novel and after a series of increasingly bizarre and surrealistic adventures splits into Patrick and Patricia. Concomitant with the loss of gender identity, the disintegration of language occurs. Pat suffers both from "linguistics leprosy" (11) and "sexual amnesia" (76). Brophy brilliantly demonstrates the disintegration of language by using Joyce-inspired puns, portmanteau words, and typographical games and by parodying the fairy tale, the detective novel, the pornographic novel, and opera (Maack 41). Och, the heroine of the interpolated mock-pornographic novel, reveals the author's basic intention when she states: "To be absolutely frank, what I should most like to resemble is a small but powerful and concentrated bomb. My ambition is to explode and shatter the rules" (193). Brophy used similar words when she stated in her interview with Leslie Dock that "*In Transit* is about a series of disintegrations of rulebooks" and "of accepted routines" ("Interview" 167). She revealed in the same interview that she based the structure of the novel on symphonies by Brahms since she sensed in them self-doubt and lost faith. As Annegret Maack has shown, *In Transit* "breaks with every convention of the traditional novel" (40) and "illustrates that the genre of the novel is in an intermediate and, for her [Brophy], revolutionary state" (45).

After the unique and innovative *In Transit*, Brophy's last novel is somewhat of a return to her beginnings. *Palace without Chairs*, a "baroque" novel that is partly Firbankian, partly Kafkaesque, is set, like her early short story "The Crown Princess," in an imaginary kingdom and depicts, like the short story, the conflict between monarchy and a modern world. When the king of Evarchia falls ill and dies, the monarchy disintegrates. Three of the royal children meet with premature and bizarre deaths, while Crown Prince Ulrich and his sister Heather renounce their right to the throne. Whereas the fate of the crown princess in Brophy's early story looked bleak, Ulrich and Heather are able to adjust to the outside world and to lead happy lives: Ulrich moves to Sweden and works in a bank, while Heather is able to pursue an openly lesbian lifestyle in London. Despite Brophy's recycling of themes and motifs, *Palace without Chairs* is not devoid of innovative elements. Chris Hopkins has shown that the novel "draws on aspects of modernism in unexpected ways (given its comic aspects and apparent genre)," for example, by displaying "a great interest in language itself . . . and the capacity or incapacity of language to render the self" (16). We can only surmise what kind of unique creations Brigid Brophy would still have had in store if her voice had not been silenced by her illness when she was in her fifties.

ASSESSMENT

Considering Brophy's reputation in the 1960s and 1970s and her unique, innovative artistic vision, it is astonishing, perhaps even "scandalous" (Moore 10), that almost all of her works are out of print and that only a few courageous members of the academy have delved into her fascinating oeuvre. Much of the early reception of her works, both fiction and nonfiction, consisted of reviews in which the discussion of controversial subject matter frequently overshadowed the appreciation of her artistic achievement. Two of Brophy's early champions were S.J. Newman and Leslie Dock. Newman's comprehensive overview of Brophy's life and work in the *Dictionary of Literary Biography* included much useful information. However, it also contained some questionable assessments, such as the description of *In Transit* as Brophy's "most self-exacerbated book" (144), which is "less a novel than a cross between a neurotic essay in criticism and a farcical nightmare" (146). Dock analyzed Brophy's work in her unpublished 1976 dissertation and published an extensive and candid interview with the author the same year. The recent explosion of gender studies, coupled with the exploration of modernism and postmodernism, has led the way to a long-overdue reassessment of Brophy's work. In 1991 Sheryl Stevenson demonstrated Brophy's connection with modernist writing: "By suggesting that individual identity is tied to language and by presenting both in an unstable condition, *In Transit* draws attention to a juncture between feminist studies of gender and Mikhail Bakhtin's theory of language" (181). In 1995, the year of Brophy's death, the *Review of Contemporary Fiction* dedicated part of the fall issue to her work (the other writers featured were Robert Creeley and Osman Lins). Several insightful articles dealt with the innovative quality of her fiction, while others traced influences found in her work (Firbank, Mozart) or discussed lesbian themes. However, these studies were only able to scratch the surface, and much needs to be done before the unique and innovative character of Brigid Brophy's work can fully be appreciated. There can be no doubt that "there is nobody like her, no one who sees the world quite in her original way" (Byatt 269).

BIBLIOGRAPHY

Primary Sources

The Crown Princess and Other Stories. London: Collins, 1953; New York: Viking, 1953.

Hackenfeller's Ape. London: Hart-Davis, 1953; New York: Random House, 1954.

The King of a Rainy Country. London: Secker, 1956; New York: Knopf, 1957.

Black Ship to Hell. London: Secker, 1962; New York: Harcourt, 1962.

Flesh: A Novel of Indolent Passion. London: Secker, 1962; Cleveland: World, 1963.

The Finishing Touch. London: Secker, 1963; London: GMP, 1987.

*Mozart the Dramatist: A New View of Mozart, His

Operas, and His Age. London: Faber, 1964; New York: Harcourt, 1964. Rev. ed. *Mozart the Dramatist: The Value of His Operas to Him, to His Age, and to Us*. London: Libris, 1988; New York: Da Capo, 1990.

The Snow Ball. London: Secker, 1964; London: Allison & Busby, 1979.

The Snow Ball. The Finishing Touch. Cleveland: World, 1964.

The Rights of Animals. London: Animal Defence & Anti-Vivisection Society, 1965.

Don't Never Forget: Collected Views and Reviews. London: Cape, 1966; New York: Holt, 1967.

Fifty Works of English and American Literature We Could Do Without. With Michael Levey and Charles Osborne. London: Rapp & Carroll, 1967; New York: Stein & Day, 1968.

Religious Education in State Schools. London: Fabian Society, 1967.

Black and White: A Portrait of Aubrey Beardsley. London: Cape, 1968; New York: Stein & Day, 1969.

The Burglar: A Play and a Preface. London: Cape, 1968; New York: Holt, 1968.

"The Waste-Disposal Unit." In *Best Short Plays of the World Theatre, 1958–67*. New York: Crown, 1968.

In Transit: An Heroi-cyclic Novel. London: Macdonald, 1969; New York: Putnam's Sons, 1970; London: GMP, 1989.

The Longford Threat to Freedom. London: National Secular Society, 1972.

The Adventures of God in His Search for the Black Girl: A Novel and Some Fables. London: Macmillan, 1973; New York: Atlantic Monthly, 1974.

Prancing Novelist: A Defence of Fiction in the Form of a Critical Biography in Praise of Ronald Firbank. London: Macmillan, 1973; New York: Barnes & Noble, 1973.

Beardsley and His World. London: Thames & Hudson, 1976; New York: Harmony, 1976.

Pussy Owl: Superbeast. London: BBC Publications, 1976.

Palace without Chairs: A Baroque Novel. London: Hamish Hamilton, 1978; New York: Atheneum, 1978.

A Guide to Public Lending Rights. Aldershot, Hampshire: Gower, 1983.

The Prince and the Wild Geese. London: Hamish Hamilton, 1983; New York: St. Martin's, 1983.

Baroque-'n'-Roll and Other Essays. London: Hamish Hamilton, 1987; New York: David & Charles, 1987.

Reads: A Collection of Essays. London: Cardinal, 1989.

Secondary Sources

Axelrod, Mark. "Mozart, Moonshots, and Monkey Business in Brigid Brophy's *Hackenfeller's Ape*." *Review of Contemporary Fiction* 15.3 (Fall 1995): 18–22.

Blackmer, Corinne E. "*The Finishing Touch* and the Tradition of Homoerotic Girls' School Fictions." *Review of Contemporary Fiction* 15.3 (Fall 1995): 32–39.

Burgess, Anthony. "The Democracy of Prejudice." *Encounter* 29.2 (August 1967): 71–75.

Byatt, A.S. "An Explosive Embrace." *TLS* 13 January 1987: 269.

Dock, Leslie A. "Brigid Brophy: Artist in the Baroque." Diss. U of Wisconsin at Madison, 1976.

———. "An Interview with Brigid Brophy." *Contemporary Literature* 17 (Spring 1976): 151–170.

Hoepffner, Bernard. "Translating *In Transit*: Writing By Proxy." *Review of Contemporary Fiction* 15.3 (Fall 1995): 54–61.

Hopkins, Chris. "The Neglect of Brigid Brophy." *Review of Contemporary Fiction* 15.3 (Fall 1995): 12–17.

Horvath, Brooke. "Brigid Brophy's It's-All-Right-I'm-Only-Dying Comedy of Modern Manners: Notes on *In Transit*." *Review of Contemporary Fiction* 15.3 (Fall 1995): 46–53.

Kerman, Joseph. "Opera Misconstrued." *Hudson Review* 18.3 (Summer 1965): 309–312.

Lee, Patricia. "Communication Breakdown and the 'Twin Genius' of Brophy's *In Transit*." *Review of Contemporary Fiction* 15.3 (Fall 1995): 62–67.

Lyall, Sarah. "Brigid Brophy Is Dead at 66: Novelist, Critic, and Crusader." *New York Times* 9 August 1995: D20.

Maack, Annegret. "Concordia Discors: Brigid Brophy's *In Transit*." *Review of Contemporary Fiction* 15.3 (Fall 1995): 40–45.

Miller, Mark. "Brigid Brophy: A Memoir." *Raritan* 15 (Spring 1996): 38–52.

Moore, Steven. "Brigid Brophy: An Introduction and Checklist." *Review of Contemporary Fiction* 15.3 (Fall 1995): 7–11.

Newman, S.J. "Brigid Brophy." In *British Novelists since 1960: Part One: A–G*. Vol. 14 of *Dictionary of Literary Biography*. Detroit: Gale, 1983. 137–147.

Oates, Joyce Carol. "Miss Brophy's Probing Pen." *Washington Post* 25 January 1970: 4–5.

Parker, Peter. " 'Aggressive, Witty, and Unrelenting' ": Brigid Brophy and Ronald Firbank." *Review of Contemporary Fiction* 15.3 (Fall 1995): 68–78.

Smith, Patricia Juliana. "Brophy, Brigid." In *The Gay and Lesbian Literary Heritage*. Ed. Claude J. Summers. New York:Holt, 1995. 115.

———. "Desperately Seeking Susan[na]: Closeted Quests and Mozartean Gender Bending in Brigid Brophy's *The King of a Rainy Country*." *Review of Contemporary Fiction* 15.3 (Fall 1995): 23–31.

Stevenson, Sheryl. "Language and Gender in Transit: Feminist Extensions of Bakhtin." In *Feminism, Bakhtin, and the Dialogic*. Ed. Dale M. Bauer and Susan Jaret McKinstry. Albany: State U of New York P, 1991. 181–198.

A.S. Byatt
1936–

Maria Koundoura

A.S. Byatt uses nineteenth-century form in much the same way that she uses nineteenth-century content or history: not nostalgically, as most postmodern writers do of the styles of the past, but as the tenuous referent of a present that is itself contingent. She sees writing as that which produces but also that which derails this contingency. Her work is thus concerned with the artistic process—not only with its methods but with its uses and abuses as exorcism, manipulation, self-projection, self-forgetfulness, rescue, and paradigm.

BACKGROUND

Antonia Susan (Drabble) Byatt was born in Sheffield, England, on August 24, 1936. She is the sister of Margaret Drabble, another noted novelist. Byatt earned a B.A. from Newnham College, Cambridge (1957), and did her graduate work at Bryn Mawr College (1957–1958) and at Somerville College, Oxford (1958–1959). She has taught at the University of London, the Central School of Art and Design, Newnham College, and University College London and as a British Council lecturer in Spain, India, Australia, Hong Kong, China, Korea, and Germany. She has been a member of the panel of judges for the Booker Prize and the Hawthornden Prize, among others. Also, she is a member of the British Broadcasting Corporation (BBC) Social Effects of Television Advisory Committee, a member of the Communications and Cultural Studies Board of the Council for National Academic Awards, and a member of the Kingman Committee on the Teaching of English. She has won numerous awards, among them the Silver Pen Award for *Still Life* and the Booker Prize for *Possession*.

ANALYSIS

"I'm a political feminist. I think women's lives need quite a lot of improving, some of which has now happened. I'm interested in feminist themes, women's freedom," declared Byatt in a 1999 *Salon* interview with Laura Miller, distinguishing her kind of feminism from the "literary feminism" of Monique Wittig. She takes issue with the latter's singularity of focus, not looking at "anything else that might have contributed to a woman's life or writing other than women." "It's because I'm a feminist," she explains, "that I can't stand women limiting other women's imagination" by focusing only on what "they think are female styles" or "women's themes" (*Salon* interview). "If you want to teach women to be great writers," she concludes, "you should show them the best, and the best was often done by men." Clearly, feminism is a major background to Byatt's work. As this interchange indicates, however, there is not one feminism but feminisms. Unlike the French feminism of Wittig, Byatt's is the more traditional kind: she wants to represent women's lives so that her reader can be aware of the problems they face, see those problems in her life, and improve them. In *Ways of Seeing* John Berger, Marxist art critic, screenwriter, and novelist, has discussed the way in which the display of women in the visual arts (a field in which Byatt immerses herself) results in "a woman's being split into two. A woman must continually watch herself. She is continually accompanied by her own image of herself. While she is walking across the room or whilst she is weeping at the death of her father, she can scarcely avoid envisaging herself walking and weeping" (46). "From earliest childhood," he explains, "she has been taught and persuaded to survey herself continually" (46). Byatt wants to intervene in this watching, hence the duality of her representation of the women Morph, Eugenia, and Matty in *Angels and Insects*, and the self-consciousness of her fiction. She is not interested in arguing for a different sphere for the "feminine"; rather, she represents women in the world as it is. French feminists like Wittig, Julia Kristeva, Luce Irigaray, and Hélène Cixous, whose work came out in the mid- to late 1970s, believe that Western thought has been based on the systematic repression of women's experience. As Ann Rosalind Jones has argued in "Writing the Body," they assert the existence of a bedrock female nature (*féminité*) from which to deconstruct language, philosophy, psychoanalysis, and the social practices (86). Furthermore, they argue that if women are to discover and to express who they are, to bring to the surface what masculine history has repressed in them, they must begin with their sexuality (Jones 91), and their sexuality begins with their bodies. The immediacy with which the body is experienced, according to them, promises a clarity of perception and a vitality that can bring down mountains of phallocentric delusion. Finally, to the extent that the female body is seen as a direct source of female writing, a powerful alternative discourse seems possible: to write from the body is to re-create the world. "Féminité" and "feminine writing" are problematic as well as powerful concepts. They have been criticized as idealist and essentialist, bound up in the very system they claim to undermine (Marks and Courtivron 212–230). They have also been attacked, as was seen in Byatt's comments, as fatal to constructive political action. Nevertheless, they have influenced contemporary women's writing. Byatt herself admits in the Miller interview that she did "cannibalize" Wittig's *The Lesbian Body* for *Babel Tower* because "it fits into all the Norman O. Brown theories of polymorphous perversity being the true and proper and right form of sex."

One of the means through which Byatt intervenes politically in the lives of her readers is through her use of realism. As the Marxist feminist critic Catherine Belsey has argued, using the work of French critics Roland Barthes and Louis Althusser, realism is a code that is characterized by "illusionism," a narrative that leads to "closure," and a "hierarchy of discourses" that establishes the "truth" of the story ("Constructing the Subject" 53). The classic realist text, she explains, and by this she means primarily the Victorian novel and its subsequent inheritors, "turns on the creation of an enigma through the precipitation of disorder." Disorder's commonest sources at the level of plot, she points out, are "murder, war, a journey, or love" (53). But the story moves inevitably toward closure, "which is also disclosure, the dissolution of enigma through the re-establishment of order" (53). The moment of closure is the point at which events become intelligible to the reader, but a "high degree of intelligibility is sustained throughout the narrative as a result of the hierarchy of discourses in the text" (53). This hierarchy is most evident in the use of quotation marks (real or imaginary) and the fact that every utterance or idea that is in them is subordinated to the narrative that is out of them. "By these means," Belsey concludes, "classic realism offers the reader a position of knowingness which is also a position of identification with the narrative voice" (53). To the extent that the story first constructs and then depends on this knowingness, it confirms both the universality of the reader's intelligence and the obviousness of the shared truths in question. This is why Byatt's texts are so appealing to readers, and it is also how she hopes to change their lives.

Although she uses the code of realism, Byatt has also been read as a postmodern writer. One of the reasons for such a characterization is the fact that she is a contemporary writer in what is, according to quite a few literary critics, our postmodern age. The other is that her novels and stories are characterized by the self-consciousness characteristic of postmodern metafiction. In metafiction, according to Linda Hutcheon, "the most radical boundaries crossed . . . have been those between fiction and nonfiction and—by extension—between art and life" (*Poetics of Postmodernism* 10). Metafiction is a fictional form that is culturally relevant and comprehensible to contemporary readers. In showing us how literary fiction creates its imaginary worlds, metafiction helps us to understand how the reality we live day by day is similarly constructed, similarly written. Women's postmodern texts often employ metafiction on the personal level; the truth they are questioning, for example, is often related to the microcosmic rather than the macrocosmic. Similarly, the metahistoriography they undertake may have as much to do with personal events and multiple stories as with official records and global history. George Eliot, one of Byatt's favorite authors and a huge influence on her work, offers a good, although not postmodern, example of this kind of historicism in *Middlemarch*. For her there is no "universal" past, but a past that continually changes based on individual perspective. History in *Middlemarch* maintains a fidelity to documented events (for example, the local political agitations leading to the first Reform Bill of 1832), but Eliot's true focus is on those unhistorical acts that shape the public record in subtle and usually unnoticed ways. Similarly, history in *Possession*, for example, is not seen as "hard facts" that are knowable—given enough patience and research—but as something that is continuously evolving with the interventions of the present. *Possession* consistently works, through the use of the parodic self-reflexiveness characteristic of metafiction, to undermine its characters' assumption that given enough access to enough documents, the scholar can attain complete knowledge of his or her subject. "Parodic self-reflexiveness," Hutcheon argues, "paradoxically leads [in postmodern historical novels like *Possession*] to the possibility of a literature which, while asserting its modernist autonomy as art, also manages simultaneously to investigate its intricate and intimate relations to the social world in which it is written and read" (19).

Because of Byatt's wide experience as a critic, novelist, editor, and lecturer, she "offers in her work an intellectual kaleidoscope of our contemporary world" (Musil). "Both an awareness of the dangers of academic introspection, and an instinctive longing to unify intellect and intuition," writes Gail Davey in "Still Life and the Rounding of Consciousness," "seem to have contributed to Byatt's convincing grasp of such a broad range of disciplines" (1544). In her novels and stories she is as comfortable writing about fractal theory as she is about fine art, and about photosynthesis as about a tense family Sunday brunch. In her first novel, *The Shadow of the Sun*, she struggles to combine the role of critic with that of novelist, and the role of mother with that of visionary. Her second novel, *The Game*, established her reputation as a novelist in England. It is a study of the artistic process. The novelist in the text is the artist as consumer, attacking her human subjects with what Byatt (speaking of *The Game*) has described as "the sharp teeth and the gaping jaws" of her imagination (*Sugar* 22). *The Virgin in the Garden* (the first volume of her projected tetralogy) is set in 1953, the year of the coronation of Queen Elizabeth II; its theme is growing up, coming of age, tasting knowledge. The book's central symbol is Queen Elizabeth I, a monarch Byatt sees as surviving because she used her mind and thought things out, unlike her rival Mary, Queen of Scots, who "was driven by sex and made a lot of very silly choices" (Miller interview). *Still Life* (the second volume of her tetralogy) is an example of what Byatt terms the "rounding of consciousness." In this book she explores Ludwig Wittgenstein's view of the mathematics of color, the demystification of the church, Vincent van Gogh's struggle with metaphor in painting, and theories on the acquisition of language. Still-life representations, Alexander Wedderburn, the playwright character in the novel tells us, are a "version of the golden age—a world without desire and division." A still life, in other words, is an attempt to capture a perfect, timeless moment within the ravages and strivings of living. Byatt uses this discussion and the highly vivid tableaux that she creates throughout the novel to heighten the contrast with what she, in *Passions of the Mind*, calls "self-conscious realism"—a realism that "leaves space for thinking minds as well as feeling bodies" (46). The inadequacy of words in describing the "real" has haunted Byatt for much of her writing life; the still-life contrasts in *Still Life* are her dialogic attempt at exorcising this ghost. In her short-story collection *Sugar and Other Stories* Byatt extends her exploration of art and reality. The line between realism and postmodernist metafiction gets blurred in this collection, which is about real life and about the art that tries to capture it. Taken as a sequence, the stories move from the more realistic to the more metafictional end of the scale. "The confecting process," writes Jane Campbell, "the imagination's shaping activity, itself emerges gradually as a subject; and, simultaneously, the reader, warily addressed in 'Racine' [the first story], is invoked more confidingly in 'Sugar' [the last story]" (106).

The 1990 publication of *Possession* brought the greatest attention to Byatt as a novelist. The novel tells the story of Maud and Roland, two contemporary literary scholars whose paths cross during their research. Roland is an expert on the famous fictional Victorian poet Randolph Henry Ash, and Maud is interested in the obscure Christabel LaMotte. They discover that the two Victorians were linked in a passionate relationship; their joint investigation, meanwhile, leads to an affair of their own. *Possession* won critical acclaim for its "true" representation of the two fictional Victorians, its use of self-reflexive parody, and its critique of fact-driven knowledge. So did Byatt's *Angels and Insects*, with its two novellas, both set in the Victorian age. The first, "Morpho Eugenia," concerns a biologist who becomes part of a wealthy family with an ugly secret. The second, "The Conjugal Angel," revolves around the Victorian fascination with spiritualism. In *The Matisse Stories* Byatt adopted a more concrete style. The stories in the book all make reference to the French impressionist painter Henri Matisse. The third of the stories in the book, "The Chinese Lobster," Byatt told Lewis Frumkes in an interview in the *Writer*, "is one of my favorites of anything I've ever written" (15). As is usual in all her fiction, these stories are self-conscious about the act of writing. She renders her own prose after Matisse, creating stylized settings and interpersonal dialogues. In places she directly ponders questions of aesthetics, as in the instance of the story about the neorealist painter who is forced to ask himself, "Why make representations of anything at all?" *The Djinn in the Nightingale's Eye*, a collection of contemporary self-reflexive fairy tales, continues Byatt's dialogue with herself as writer and critic. The title story dramatizes literary theories of the fairy tale through the story of a middle-aged narratologist who encounters a djinn, or genie, with the power to grant her the three traditional wishes. Being the scholar, she knows all the pitfalls, so her wishes are anything but traditional. Byatt relies on her readers' expectations of the plot and themes of fairy tales to experiment with the form's and the readers' boundaries.

Babel Tower (the third volume of her tetralogy) has Frederica Potter (the heroine also of *The Virgin in the Garden* and *Still Life*) trying to overcome a soured marriage and make it on her own as a single mother in 1960s London. The novel is centered on two trials: an obscenity prosecution against Frederica's employer for publishing "Babbletower," an overripe fairy tale of a utopia gone bad, and the heroine's own battle for custody of her son. Byatt tells us that she based "Babbletower" on the Marquis de Sade's *120 Nights of Sodom* and on the work of the utopian social philosopher Charles Fourier. In her latest collection, *Elementals: Stories of Fire and Ice*, she mixes reality with folktales and fairy tales and again draws on her love of fine arts to put together a series of contrasting stories to explore the alienation that most of us feel in the world. Her narrative practice, blending fact and fabrication, demonstrates the duplicitous relationship of the imagination to its materials.

ASSESSMENT

In her essay "People in Paper Houses" in *Passions of the Mind*, Byatt observed that Julian Mitchell's novel *The New Satyricon* provides a criticism of "the relation of the novel, the writer, and his world." She continues: "It plays games with truth, lies and the reader, teasing him with the knowledge that he cannot tell where veracity ends and games begin. It is the game all novelists played anyway, raised on the structural principle" (180). She is describing her own practice here and also echoing her work's critical reception. It is a reception that has been enthusiastic, for, as Gail Davey says, her work is "particularly pleasing for any frustrated polymath." Most academic criticism of her focuses on her use of realism and metafiction. Jane Campbell, for example, argues that Byatt's fiction is a rare example where "intertextuality"—a key element of metafiction —"works organically: her probing of the processes of narrative illuminates, and is inseparable from, the stories she tells" (105). Juliet Dusinberre has observed that Byatt knows that "what is real in terms of specific moments of experience is without shape or order until the mind has placed it in time and so given it form" (58). Byatt's fiction, however, also calls narrative patterning and plotting into question. It fits into the category that Patricia Waugh places at the center of metafiction: "[T]hose texts that manifest the symptoms of formal and ontological insecurity but allow their deconstructions to be finally recontextualized or 'naturalized' and given a total interpretation" (19). This is how, as Catherine Belsey points out, realist fiction builds and confirms the "knowingness" of the reader and "interpellates" the reader/subject, that is, makes her willingly entangle herself in the ideology represented by the text (52–53).

Clearly, this kind of willing entanglement also happens with metafiction. Byatt's fiction successfully blends the self-reflexive (metafictional) and the mimetic (realist). She does this through her use of history as a referent for a "real" whose truth we can never know but are always willing to speculate on (and hence confirm the author's view of it). *Possession* is an excellent example of this use of history in which the historian/author/reader's view of the past is continually augmented and revised by present knowledge. It calls into question how completely we can know the past from its textual traces. It is full of mysteries that resist the very notion of solution while, at the same time, it illuminates (and pokes fun at) the insatiable curiosity of its scholar-detectives, who come to learn that collecting the artifacts of dead poets and scrutinizing their marginalia does not itself produce knowledge and that attention must be paid to what is left out of the standard biographies. Like Ellen in *Possession*, Byatt despairs of language's capacity for conveying "the truth of the way it had been, of the silences in the telling, the silences that extended before and after it, always the silences" (492). Like the narrator in "Sugar" and its central question—the exploration of the dividing line between lived events and mythmaking—she is aware of "the long black shadows of the things left unsaid" (241). Like Matty from "Morpho Eugenia," however, she also knows how to manipulate forms. This is why she stretches the realist form to its limits until it shatters; she then uses its relics as the referent of the real of her metafiction. In other words, she uses earlier literary forms and styles to reveal the tenuous foundations of the present. She is also committed to enacting the ambiguities and confusions of these foundations so that her characters (and her readers) can achieve "moral freedom" in the present. Byatt defines moral freedom, using the words of Iris Murdoch, as "knowing and understanding and respecting things quite other than ourselves" (quoted in *Iris Murdoch* 8).

BIBLIOGRAPHY

Primary Sources

The Shadow of the Sun. New York: Harcourt, 1964.

Degrees of Freedom: The Novels of Iris Murdoch. New York: Barnes & Noble, 1965.

The Game. London: Chatto, 1967; New York: Scribner's, 1968.

(Contributor) *The Major Victorian Poets: Reconsiderations*. Ed. Isobel Armstrong. London: Routledge, 1969.

Wordsworth and Coleridge in Their Time. London: Nelson, 1970. As *Unruly Times*. London: Hogarth, 1989.

Iris Murdoch. London: Longman, 1976.

The Virgin in the Garden. London: Chatto, 1978; New York: Knopf, 1979.

The Mill on the Floss. By George Eliot. Ed. and introduction by A.S. Byatt. London: Penguin, 1979.

Still Life. London: Chatto; New York: Scribner, 1985.

Sugar and Other Stories. New York: Scribner's, 1987.

Possession: A Romance. London: Chatto, 1990; New York: Vintage, 1991.

Selected Essays, Poems, and Other Writings. By George Eliot. Ed. A.S. Byatt and Nicholas Warren. London: Penguin, 1990.

Dramatic Monologues. By Robert Browning. Ed. A.S. Byatt. London: Folio Society, 1991.

Passions of the Mind. London: Chatto, 1991.

Angels and Insects: Two Novellas. London: Chatto, 1992.

The Matisse Stories. London: Chatto, 1993; New York: Random, 1995.

The Djinn in the Nightingale's Eye: Five Fairy Stories. London: Chatto, 1994.

Babel Tower. New York: Random, 1996.

Imagining Characters: Conversations about Women Writers: Jane Austen, Charlotte Brontë, George Eliot, Willa Cather, Iris Murdoch, and Toni Morrison. With Ignés Sodré. New York: Vintage, 1997.

The Oxford Book of English Short Stories. Ed. A.S. Byatt. Oxford: Oxford UP, 1998.

Elementals: Stories of Fire and Ice. New York: Random, 1999.

Secondary Sources

Belsey, Catherine. "Constructing the Subject: Deconstructing the Text." In *Feminist Criticism and Social Change*. Ed. Judith Newton and Deborah Rosenfelt. London: Methuen, 1985. 45–64.

Berger, John. *Ways of Seeing*. New York: Viking, 1973.

Campbell, Jane. "Confecting 'Sugar': Narrative Theory and Practice in A.S. Byatt's Short Stories." *Critique* 38.2 (Winter 1997): 105–122.

Davey, Gail. "Still Life and the Rounding of Consciousness." *Lancet* 7 November 1998.

Dusinberre, Juliet. "Forms of Reality in A.S. Byatt's *The Virgin in the Garden*." *Critique* 24 (1982): 55–62.

Frumkes, Lewis. "A Conversation with A.S. Byatt." *Writer* 110 (May 1997).

Hutcheon, Linda. *A Poetics of Postmodernism: History, Theory, Fiction*. London: Routledge, 1988.

Jones, Ann Rosalind. "Writing the Body: Toward an Understanding of *l'écriture femininé*." In *Feminist Criticism and Social Change*. Ed. Judith Newton and Deborah Rosenfelt. London: Methuen, 1985. 86–101.

Marks, Elaine, and Isabelle de Courtivron, eds. *New French Feminisms: An Anthology*. Amherst: U of Massachusetts P, 1980.

Miller, Laura. Interview with A.S. Byatt. <www.salon1999.com/weekly/interview 2960617. html/>.

Musil, Caryn McTighe. "A.S. Byatt." In *British Novelists since 1960*. Vol. 14 of *Dictionary of Literary Biography*. Detroit: Gale, 1980.

Waugh, Patricia. *Metafiction: The Theory and Practice of Self-Conscious Fiction*. London: Methuen, 1984.

Angela Carter
1940–1992

Anna Katsavos

Angela Carter, one of Britain's most original, provocative contemporary writers, was a cultural subversive who was fascinated and disturbed by the impact of popular culture on gender politics. Her work treats issues of female sexuality, eroticism, and violence with a transgressive humor that stuns and unnerves, leaving readers uncertain whether to laugh, scream, or cry.

A novelist, short-story writer, journalist, and scriptwriter, Carter received little scholarly attention, especially in the United States. She confounded critics by crossing and fusing genre boundaries with unpredictability and ease. Employing a pastiche of traditional literary forms, Carter conflated romance with realism and infused the picaresque with the pornographic, the Gothic with the grotesque, and the fairy tale with the fantastic. Although she was noted for her lush imaginative prose, Carter's profane themes, wicked wit, irreverent tone, and radical leftist/feminist politics contributed to her wildly variable literary reception.

Carter's early novels, *Shadow Dance* (1966), *The Magic Toyshop* (1967), *Several Perceptions* (1968), and *Love* (1971), written in the social realist tradition, were well received in England and established the author as a promising new writer. *The Magic Toyshop* received the 1967 John Llewellyn Rhys Memorial Prize; *Several Perceptions* won the 1968 Somerset Maugham Award. Her reputation shifted, however, as Carter moved from the mimetic to the speculative and her fiction began more forcefully to rebuke patriarchal assumptions about femininity and female sexuality. Following the publication of *Heroes and Villains* (1969), *The Infernal Desire Machines of Doctor Hoffman* (1972), and *The Passion of New Eve* (1977), reviewers became increasingly alarmed that Carter's literary fireworks were a bit too explosive. What is more, her 1979 feminist polemic on the ideology of pornography, *The Sadeian Woman*, and her eroticized fairy tales collected in *The Bloody Chamber* (published that same year), baffled or annoyed critics, especially feminists, and served further to alienate Carter from the inner circle of the literati.

In the mid-1980s Carter once again shifted artistic gears, and her critical acclaim began to flourish. Her fanciful comic novel *Nights at the Circus* (1984), winner of Britain's James Tait Black Memorial Prize, and her short-story collection *Black Venus* (1985) (U.S. title *Saints and Strangers*, 1986), hailed in the *New York Times Book Review* as "one of the Best Books of 1986," made her a literary outsider no longer. Carter's last novel, *Wise Children* (1991), praised as her best, deservedly secured her a place in the modern British canon.

BACKGROUND

Born in 1940 in Eastbourne, England, Angela Carter was the overprotected daughter of middle-class parents. Her father was a Scottish journalist, her mother a would-be scholar who, Carter lamented, dropped out of school to work as a salesclerk. Practically at birth (Carter was born the week that Dunkirk fell), the infant Angela and her twelve-year-old brother were evacuated from London to escape the blitz and what seemed an imminent German invasion. They were sent to live with their maternal grandmother in Wath-upon-Dearne, a mining village in South Yorkshire. "Gran," a working-class chambermaid who had marched in support of the 1870 miners' strikes and, years later, prominently displayed her "Votes for Women" badge, was Carter's strongest feminist model.

Carter's pubescent years were painful, due in part to a troubled relationship with her mother, whom Angela considered simultaneously trapped by the demands of domesticity and complicit with prevailing attitudes about women. Ironically, Angela, eager to leave her parental home, married Paul Carter at twenty. She apprenticed for two years as a junior reporter for the *Croydon Advertiser* until she and her husband settled in Bristol, where she studied English and medieval literature at Bristol University.

The intellectual climate and relaxed sexual mores of the 1960s shaped Carter's development as a writer and cultural theorist. By the time she was twenty-five, Carter had written her first novel, *Shadow Dance*, and by the end of the decade she had completed *The Magic Toyshop*, *Several Perceptions*, and *Love*. Presenting female characters as visitors in their own flesh, Carter exposed socially prescribed notions about femininity, sexuality, and family as debilitating to women.

ANALYSIS

Shadow Dance examines the restrictive boundaries of marriage as well as the consequences of a powerful, unchecked female sexuality. Carter's treatment of three female characters—Ghislaine, Edna, and Emily—points to the physical and emotional abuse confronting women whose sexual activities are for pleasure, not procreation.

The Magic Toyshop, which reads like a Freudian fairy tale about Oedipal relationships, blends puppets and toys with magic and psychoanalysis. It charts the maturation of young Melanie, who, while living with her ogre Uncle Philip and his mute wife Margaret, grapples with pubescent anxieties about sexuality and marriage. With often-biting sarcasm Carter dismisses notions of male sexuality as aggressive, all-consuming, and destructive.

Like Carter's first novel, *Several Perceptions* is not feminist friendly. Women do not figure prominently and serve primarily as stereotypes. Depicted as objects, they are referred to derisively as "birds," "bitches," "whores," or "old cows" who get "screwed" or "poked" by men. Nevertheless, though they remain peripheral to the male protagonist, three of Carter's female characters are noteworthy prototypes. Charlotte, Anne Blossom, and Mrs. Boulder are representative of Carter's evolving tendency to portray independent, unattached women characters who in part escape male violence. As does *The Magic Toyshop*, this novel ends up attacking traditional notions of marriage and family. It works best as a novel of ideas that exposes paternity as a matter of semantics and motherhood as an arduous, thankless job.

Carter continued to undermine romanticized notions of love and marriage in subsequent novels. *Love*, ironically entitled, looks at the flimsy, sometimes-bizarre connections that hold people together in their desperate search for attention. Probing the complex interrelationships of three characters who serve more as metaphors than as individuals, *Love* charts a sexual triangle comprised of the fragile, eighteen-year-old Annabel, her hippie husband, and his crazy half brother. The trio plays out a grotesque scenario through which Carter exposes human perversities, sending the frightening message that "the only place for a woman in the kind of male-dominated world that the novel depicts is either the loony bin or the grave" (*Love*, 1987 ed., Afterword). Ultimately, the female characters in Carter's early novels are depicted not as individuals, but as icons. Their behavior reflects their basic allegiance to the domestic sphere, as well as to the universally accepted premise that women are defined as a function of their bodies.

In 1969 Carter received the Somerset Maugham Travel Award—prize money that enabled her to flee a failing marriage that ended in 1972. She went first to America and then to Japan, where she found a strengthened political consciousness and a stronger voice to protest the sexual objectification of women. During her two years in Japan she wrote a number of articles for the British magazine *New Society* (collected in 1982 as *Nothing Sacred*), as well as many of the stories collected in *Fireworks: Nine Profane Pieces* (1974), some of which have an autobiographical quality. Reflecting her sharpened sensitivity to feminist issues, three of these stories, "A Souvenir of Japan," "The Smile of Winter," and "Flesh and the Mirror," resonate with misgivings about a culture that she experienced as blatantly hostile toward women.

The novels written after Carter's experience in Japan, *Heroes and Villains*, *The Infernal Desire Machines of Doctor Hoffman*, and *The Passion of New Eve*, attempt to imagine the world differently. Influenced by the works of J. G. Ballard and Michael Moorcock, Carter began to dabble in speculative writing, explaining that she desired an alternative to naturalism—a revolutionary fiction of the imagination that tapped into the domain of the unconscious, what she called "inner space."

In *Heroes and Villains*, using elements of the fantastic and the surreal, Carter probes the possibilities and consequences of a civilization not bound by inherited social order. With parody and exaggeration she stretches human relationships almost to the grotesque, depicting a speculative situation that, as the title suggests, insists upon a symbolic reading of the characters. Set in a post-Armageddon world, the novel presents two domains: the steel and concrete villages of the Professors (Heroes) and the surrounding jungles of the tribal Barbarians (Villains). Marianne, a Professor's daughter, learns to renegotiate her position in the hostile Barbarian environment, vacillating between hunter and prey to survive. At the end of the novel, though she seems the idealized icon of domesticity—in the kitchen, pregnant, stirring stew—she is, in fact, self-assured, more a powerful witch at her cauldron. Ultimately, the novel's surreal landscape enables Carter to assault accepted ideologies of gender politics by presenting Marianne as one who must be reckoned with, perhaps feared.

Carter's next venture into speculative fiction resulted in *The Infernal Desire Machines of Doctor Hoffman* (published in the United States as *The War of Dreams*). Lengthy and overwritten (sounding much like a literary psychedelic trip), the novel runs amok, and many of the passages are prosaic speculations on language and dream theory. Nevertheless, this work exemplifies Carter's continued experimentation with magic realism and her further exploration of what she called the "artificiality" of gender. Two characters in particular, Desiderio and Albertina, pave the way for the creation of the "New Eve" in Carter's subsequent novel, *The Passion of New Eve*, written five years later.

With this 1977 work Carter assumes a more radical approach to the "feminization" of Evelyn, the male narrator obsessed with Tristessa, the beautiful, "artificially constructed" queen of celluloid. Carter stretches gender boundaries to unprecedented limits as Evelyn, transgendered into Eve, experiences pleasure in her sexual awakening as a female. As Carter's "man-made masterpiece of skin and bone" (146), the new Eve no longer feels like a visitor in her own flesh. She understands, instead, that flesh can be "a function of enchantment" (148) separate from the masks of masculinity and femininity that we choose to wear.

By the late 1970s Carter was exploring many of these same gender issues in her nonfiction. In *The Sadeian Woman* (1979), a feminist tract appropriating the Marquis de Sade as a feminist ally, Carter claims the importance of Sade's "refusal to see female sexuality in relation to its reproductive function" (1). To Carter, because women have been defined solely as childbearers and nurturers, female sexuality traditionally has been ignored. Carter insists that Sade exposed culturally determined myths about female sexuality, femininity, and motherhood as "consolatory nonsense" used to justify and continue women's subservient and acquiescent social positions.

During this same period Carter was working on *The Bloody Chamber*, her revised variations of traditional fairy tales such as "Beauty and the Beast," "Snow White," and "Little Red Riding Hood." Moving toward fictional landscapes wherein female desire could be expressed without harm or restraint, Carter unabashedly injected her own radical reworking of the tales with a double shot of the erotic and the pornographic. These adult tales, often distorted versions of the classic originals, focus on the perversely human attraction to that which is most feared. With language at once provocative and unsettling, Carter portrays women as victims and agents of violence. Exploring erotic possibilities for women, she ventures into territory where nothing is sacred and everything is taboo. In addition to her own writing, Carter translated the stories of Charles Perrault and Madame de Beaumont (collected in *Sleeping Beauty and Other Favourite Fairy Tales*) and edited *The Virago Book of Fairy Tales*, an anthology of international tales demonstrating the diversity of female response to the common predicament of being born a woman. Carter's fascination with the fairy-tale form continued until her last days. Working from her hospital bed on *The Second Virago Book of Fairy Tales* (published posthumously in 1992), she was determined to bequeath something to "the girls"—the women of future generations. Presenting some of Carter's favorite themes, including erotic violence and women's feral nature, this volume also features the quick-witted women found in popular tales from around the world.

As expressed in Carter's nonfiction of this period, she very much admired the work of Colette, Charlotte Brontë, Christina Stead, Louise Erdrich, and Grace Paley. In her 1980 essay "The Language of Sisterhood" Carter discussed the role of the woman writer, maintaining that the so-called language of sisterhood, which relies on the instinctive camaraderie all women share, is a potentially subversive tool that can be used by women writers to find a place for themselves in history. Three years later, in "Notes from the Front Line," Carter discussed how writing is the vehicle with which women writers can accelerate "the slow process of decolonializing our language and our basic habits of thought" (75). Women writers, Carter believed, have a responsibility to create a language for expressing "an infinitely greater variety of experience than has been possible heretofore, to say things for which no language previously existed" (75).

In 1986 Carter edited *Wayward Girls and Wicked Women*, an anthology of short stories by women writers, featuring female characters who represent a "new kind of being unburdened with a past" ("Notes from the Front Line" 74), women who "know about life," who even in defeat "are not defeated" (*Wayward* xii). Carter's last two novels, *Nights at the Circus* (1984) and *Wise Children* (1991), are populated by just such women. In these works Carter first introduced female characters who ignore all socially imposed restrictions. These "liberated" heroines shed their history and often their clothes. Neither domestic nor domesticated, they are perfectly equipped for survival: they are in control of their lives, their money, their bodies, their pleasures, their language. They do anything and everything except fit traditional molds of female domesticity.

With these novels Carter again moved in a new direction, away from the speculative and fairy-tale forms. She employed conventional devices of the carnivalesque and the fantastic narrative to blur reality and fantasy. She lured her readers into worlds of surreal logic and metaphysical impossibilities to subvert notions of Western culture that traditionally romanticize marriage and sanctify motherhood. To the female protagonists of Carter's last two novels, neither hearth nor home is sacred. Enterprising, inventive, qualified by experience, they could easily rule the roost, but they choose instead to call the shots. They flee the private, familial sphere of the kitchen and head for the public domain of the brothel, the stage, the circus, television—landscapes that evoke a Bakhtinian sense of the carnivalesque.

Characters like Fevvers (*Nights at the Circus*) and the Chance twins (*Wise Children*) free themselves from the confines of a preexisting social order. By shifting her gaze away from the domestic, Carter has empowered Fevvers (a trapeze artist with wings) and Nora and Dora Chance (vaudeville dancers) to operate within territories where they can behave by self-generated rules. Whether they tap-dance into the night or, with wings, swing on a trapeze, they take on (sometimes only out of necessity) unconventional professions.

Especially in *Wise Children* the nuclear family, as idealized by Western culture, vanishes. Carter's "wise children" of this novel know that although marriage, domesticity, and motherhood exist as desirable ideals, being a wife, homemaker, and mother often leads to negation of self. For Carter's later female characters, not having a husband increases rather than precludes happiness. Though for Carter, nurturing and fertility remained necessary goals, the romantic notions associated with motherhood and fatherhood have been blown to pieces.

Ultimately, the real magic of Carter's fiction is a surreal logic that forces us to envision new possibilities. At the close of *Nights at the Circus* Walser and Fevvers's relationship suggests that theirs is a true companionship between the sexes, a mute understanding of their shared responsibilities. At the end of *Wise Children* Dora and Nora, though septuagenarian spinsters, are still kicking, perhaps because they are single. They are last seen dressed to kill in spandex miniskirts, pushing a pram (with two babies), and singing "I Can't Give You Anything but Love, Baby." Carter, the master conjurer, created a fantastic world where love outside of matrimony is not only plausible but desirable.

ASSESSMENT

"For Angela Carter, a very good wizard and a very dear friend"—so reads the dedication of Salman Rushdie's monograph on *The Wizard of Oz*, one of Carter's favorite films. Rushdie reiterates the compliment in his obituary tribute to Carter, whom he further acclaims as the "high sorceress" and "benevolent witch-queen" of English literature.

Carter would have appreciated the plaudits, especially since during her lifetime she never enjoyed the recognition that she desired and deserved. Regrettably, this literary wizard's reputation suffered because, unlike the fraudulent Wizard of Oz who uttered empty rhetoric, Carter dazzled her readers with verbal pyrotechnics. A public intellectual, she set out to expose all shamans who hide behind the curtain of cultural myths, unaware that artificial constructs are not universal truths. In the end, however, the author's literary and linguistic acrobatics proved too risky; many reviewers, though impressed by individual works, never figured out quite how to classify Carter.

Unlike her British contemporaries Doris Lessing, Muriel Spark, Iris Murdoch, and Margaret Drabble, Carter did not make it into *A Literature of Their Own*, Elaine Showalter's 1977 study of British women novelists. Nor was she included in Patricia Meyer Spacks's *Contemporary Women Novelists*, published that same year. It is distressing that it took two decades after the publication of her first novel for Carter's fiction to find its way into collections, such as *The Norton Anthology of Literature by Women* (1985) edited by Sandra Gilbert and Susan Gubar—the same amount of time that it took for Carter's name to appear in the *International Who's Who*.

Fortunately, Carter's literary popularity is on the upswing. Not only is Carter included in Robert Hosmer's 1993 *Contemporary British Women Writers*, but contemporary novelists Jeanette Winterson and Michelle Roberts, among others, have acknowledged Carter's influence on their work. Furthermore, as the progressively increasing volume of current Carter scholarship indicates, she is commanding a secure, if yet not specifically determined, place in the contemporary canon of English literature.

In both her fiction and her nonfiction Carter imaginatively examined the construction and deconstruction of fixed gender roles. Most notably through her use of the fairy tale and the fantastic modes, she artfully protested the repression of female sexuality and desire by debunking culturally constructed ideologies, specifically myths about femininity, marriage, and motherhood. She redefined the sexual politics of desire as separate from romantic love and procreation, suggesting too that sexual impulses are potentially dangerous and in no way gender specific. Particularly in her later works Carter created a gallery of spirited, wayward women characters; young and old, these lovable "bad girls"—prostitutes, circus performers, and music-hall dancers—parley their feminine wiles into pleasure and profit. Angela Carter is a notable literary figure of our postmodern era who deserves recognition for her innovative narrative strategies as well as for her representation of strong female characters whose smarts and sexuality she celebrated without restraint.

BIBLIOGRAPHY

Primary Sources

Shadow Dance. London: Heinemann, 1966. As *Honeybuzzard*. New York: Simon & Schuster, 1967.

Unicorn (poems). Leeds: Location, 1966.

The Magic Toyshop. London: Heinemann, 1967; New York: Simon & Schuster, 1968.

Several Perceptions. London: Heinemann; New York: Simon & Schuster, 1968.

Heroes and Villains. London: Heinemann; New York: Simon & Schuster, 1969.

Miss Z, the Dark Young Lady. New York: Simon & Schuster, 1970.

Love. London: Rupert Hart-Davis, 1969. Rev. ed. London: Chatto, 1987; New York: Viking Penguin, 1988.

The Infernal Desire Machines of Doctor Hoffman. London: Rupert Hart-Davis, 1972. As *The War of Dreams*. New York: Bard/Avon, 1977.

Fireworks: Nine Profane Pieces. London: Quartet, 1974. As *Nine Stories in Various Disguises*. New York: Harper, 1981. Rev. ed. London: Chatto, 1987.

The Passion of New Eve. London: Gollancz; New York: Harcourt, 1977.

The Bloody Chamber and Other Stories. London: Gollancz, 1979; New York: Harper, 1981.

The Sadeian Woman: An Exercise in Cultural History. London: Virago, 1979. As *The Sadeian Woman and the Ideology of Pornography*. New York: Pantheon, 1979.

"The Language of Sisterhood." In *The State of the Language*. Ed. Leonard Michaels and Christopher Ricks. Berkeley: U of California P, 1980. 226–234.

Moonshadow. With Justin Todd. London: Gollancz, 1982.

"Notes from the Front Line." In *On Gender and Writing*. Ed. Michelene Wandor. London: Pandora, 1983. 69–77.

Nothing Sacred: Selected Writings. London: Virago, 1982. Rev. ed. London: Virago, 1992.

Nights at the Circus. London: Chatto, 1984; New York: Viking, 1985.

Black Venus. London: Chatto, 1985. As *Saints and Strangers*. New York: Viking, 1986.

Come unto These Yellow Sands. Newcastle upon Tyne: Bloodaxe, 1985.

Wayward Girls and Wicked Women. Ed. Angela Carter. London: Virago, 1986.

The Virago Book of Fairy Tales. Ed. Angela Carter. London: Virago, 1990. As *Old Wives' Fairy Tale Book*. New York: Pantheon, 1990.

Sleeping Beauty and Other Favourite Fairy Tales. Boston: Otter, 1991; London: Gollancz, 1982.

Wise Children. London: Chatto, 1991; New York: Farrar, Straus, 1992.

Expletives Deleted. London: Chatto, 1992.

The Second Virago Book of Fairy Tales. Ed. Angela Carter. London: Virago, 1992. As *Strange Things Sometimes Still Happen: Fairy Tales from around the World*. Boston: Faber, 1993.

American Ghosts and Old World Wonders. London: Chatto, 1993.

Burning Your Boats: Stories. London: Chatto, 1995; New York: Holt, 1996.

Shaking a Leg: Journalism and Writings. London: Chatto, 1997. As *Shaking a Leg: Collected Writings*. New York: Penguin, 1998.

Secondary Sources

Altevers, Nanette. "Gender Matters in *The Sadeian Woman*." *Review of Contemporary Fiction* 14.3 (1994): 18–23.

Bayley, John. "Fighting for the Crown." *New York Review of Books* 23 April 1992: 9–11.

Blodgett, Harriet. "Fresh Iconography: Subversive Fantasy by Angela Carter." *Review of Contemporary Fiction* 14.3 (1994): 49–55.

Boehm, Beth A. "Feminist Metafiction and Androcentric Reading Strategies: Angela Carter's Reconstructed Reader in *Nights at the Circus*." *Critique* 37.1 (1995): 35–50.

———. "*Wise Children*: Angela Carter's Swan Song." *Review of Contemporary Fiction* 14.3 (1994): 84–89.

Bonca, Cornel. "In Despair of the Old Adams: Angela Carter's *The Infernal Desire Machines of Dr. Hoffman*." *Review of Contemporary Fiction* 14.3 (1994): 56–62.

Brown, Richard. "Postmodern Americas in the Fiction of Angela Carter, Martin Amis, and Ian McEwan." In *Forked Tongues? Comparing Twentieth-Century British and American Literature*. Ed. Ann Massa and Alistair Stead. London: Longman, 1994. 92–110.

Bryant, Sylvia. "Re-constructing Oedipus through 'Beauty and the Beast.' " *Criticism* 31.4 (1989): 439–453.

Christensen, Peter. "The Hoffmann Connection: Demystification in Angela Carter's *The Infernal Desire Machines of Dr. Hoffmann*." *Review of Contemporary Fiction* 14.3 (1994): 63–70.

Clark, Robert. "Angela Carter's Desire Machine." *Women's Studies* 14 (1987): 147–161.

Coover, Robert. "A Passionate Remembrance." *Review of Contemporary Fiction* 14.3 (1994): 9–10.

Ducornet, Rikki. "A Scatological and Cannibal Clock: Angela Carter's 'The Fall River Axe Murders.' " *Review of Contemporary Fiction* 14.3 (1994): 37–42.

Duncker, Patricia. "Re-imagining the Fairy Tales: Angela Carter's Bloody Chambers." *Literature and History* 10.1 (1984): 3–14.

Fowl, Melinda. "Angela Carter's *The Bloody Chamber* Revisited." *Critical Survey* 3.1 (1991): 71–79.

Garrett, George. "Technics and Pyrotechnics." *Sewanee Review* 88.3 (1980): 412–423.

Gass, Joanne M. "Angela Carter: An Introduction." *Review of Contemporary Fiction* 14.3 (1994): 7–8.

———. "Panopticism in *Nights at the Circus*." *Review of Contemporary Fiction* 14.3 (1994): 71–76.

———. "Written on the Body: The Materiality of Myth in Angela Carter's *Heroes and Villains*." *Arkansas Review* 4.1 (1995): 12–30.

Hanson, Clare. "Each Other: Images of Otherness in the Short Fiction of Doris Lessing, Jean Rhys, and Angela Carter." *Journal of the Short Story in English* 10 (Spring 1988): 67–82.

Hardin, Michael. "The Other Other: Self-Definition outside Patriarchal Institutions in Angela Carter's *Wise Children*." *Review of Contemporary Fiction* 14.3 (1994): 77–83.

Johnson, Heather. "Textualizing the Double-gendered Body: Forms of the Grotesque in *The Passion of New Eve*." *Review of Contemporary Fiction* 14.3 (1994): 43–48.

Jordan, Elaine. "The Dangers of Angela Carter." In *New Feminist Discourses: Critical Essays on Theories and Texts*. Ed. Isobel Armstrong. London: Routledge, 1992. 119–131.

———. "Down the Road; or, History Rehearsed." In *Postmodernism and the Re-reading of Modernity*. Ed. Francis Barker, Peter Hulme, and Margaret Iversen. Manchester: Manchester UP, 1992. 159–179.

———. "Enthralment: Angela Carter's Speculative Fictions." In *Plotting Change: Contemporary Women's Fiction*. Ed. Linda Anderson. London: Edward Arnold, 1990. 18–40.

Kaiser, Mary. "Fairy Tale as Sexual Allegory: Intertextuality in Angela Carter's *The Bloody Chamber*." *Review of Contemporary Fiction* 14.3 (1994): 30–36.

Katsavos, Anna. "An Interview with Angela Carter." *Review of Contemporary Fiction* 14.3 (1994): 11–17.

———. "Using the Fantastic to Disrupt the Domestic: An Examination of Marriage and Family in Angela Carter's *Nights at the Circus* and *Wise Children*." In *Trajectories of the Fantastic*. Ed. Michael A. Morrison. Westport, CT: Greenwood, 1997. 27–37.

Kendrick, William. "The Real Magic of Angela Carter." In *Contemporary British Women Writers: Narrative Strategies*. Ed. Robert E. Hosmer, Jr. New York: St. Martin's, 1993. 66–84.

Landon, Brooks. "Eve at the End of the World: Sexuality and the Reversal of Expectations in Novels by Joanna Russ, Angela Carter, and Thomas Berger." In *Erotic Universe: Sexuality and Fantastic Literature*. Ed. Donald Palumbo. New York: Greenwood, 1986.

Ledwon, Lenora. "The Passion of the Phallus and Angela Carter's *The Passion of New Eve*." *Journal of the Fantastic in the Arts* 5.4 (1993): 26–41.

Lewallen, Avis. "Wayward Girls but Wicked Women? Female Sexuality in Angela Carter's 'The Bloody Chamber.'" *Perspectives on Pornography*. Ed. Gary Day and Clive Bloom. New York: St. Martin's, 1988. 144–157.

Linkin, Harriet Kramer. "Isn't It Romantic? Angela Carter's Bloody Revision of the Romantic Aesthetic in 'The Erl-King.'" *Contemporary Literature* 35.2 (1994): 305–323.

Lokke, Kari. "*Bluebeard* and *The Bloody Chamber*: The Grotesque of Self-Parody and Self-Assertion." *Frontiers* 10.1 (1988): 7–12.

Manlove, Colin. "'In the Demythologising Business': Angela Carter's *The Infernal Desire Machines of Dr. Hoffman* (1972)." In *Twentieth-Century Fantasists: Essays on Culture, Society, and Belief in Twentieth-Century Mythopoeic Literature*. Ed. Kath Filmer. New York: St. Martin's, 1992. 148–160.

Matus, Jill. "Blonde, Black, and Hottentot Venus: Context and Critique in Angela Carter's 'Black Venus.'" *Studies in Short Fiction* 28.4 (1991): 467–476.

Michael, Magali Cornier. "Angela Carter's *Nights at the Circus*: An Engaged Feminism via Subversive Postmodern Strategies." *Contemporary Literature* 35.3 (1994): 492–521.

———. *Feminism and the Postmodern Impulse*. Albany: State U of New York P, 1996.

Palmer, Paulina. "From 'Coded Mannequin' to Bird Woman: Angela Carter's Magic Flight." In *Women Reading Women's Writing*. Ed. Sue Roe. New York: St. Martin's, 1987. 179–205.

Punter, David. "Angela Carter: Supersessions of the Masculine." *Critique* 25 (1984): 209–222.

———. "Essential Imaginings: The Novels of Angela Carter and Russell Hoban." In *The British and Irish Novel since 1960*. Ed. James Acheson. New York: St. Martin's, 1991. 142–158.

Rose, Ellen Cronan. "Through the Looking Glass: When Women Tell Fairy Tales." In *The Voyage In: Fictions of Female Development*. Ed. Elizabeth Abel, Marianne Hirsch, and Elizabeth Langland. Hanover: UP of New England, 1983. 209–227.

Rubenstein, Roberta. "Intersexions: Gender Metamorphosis in Angela Carter's *The Passion of New Eve* and Lois Gould's *A Sea-Change*." *Tulsa Studies in Women's Literature* 12.1 (1993): 103–118.

Rushdie, Salman. "Angela Carter, 1940–92: A Very Good Wizard, a Very Dear Friend." *New York Times Book Review* 8 March 1992: 5.

Sage, Lorna. *Angela Carter*. Plymouth, UK: Northcote, 1994.

———. "Death of an Author." *Granta* 41 (1992): 235–254.

———, ed. *Flesh and the Mirror: Essays on the Art of Angela Carter*. London: Virago, 1994.

Schmidt, Ricarda. "The Journey of the Subject in Angela Carter's Fiction." *Textual Practice* 3.1 (1989): 56–75.

Sears, John. *Angela Carter's Monstrous Women*. Sheffield: Pavic, 1992.

Sheets, Robin Ann. "Pornography, Fairy Tales, and Feminism: Angela Carter's 'The Bloody Chamber.'" *Journal of the History of Sexuality* 1.4 (1991): 633–657.

Shulman, Polly. "Sex and Violence: Angela Carter's Body Politics." *Voice Literary Supplement* April 1993: 17–18.

Siegel, Carol. "Postmodern Women Novelists Review Victorian Male Masochism." *Genders* 11 (1991): 1–16.

Smith, Patricia Juliana. "All You Need Is *Love*: Angela Carter's Novel of Sixties Sex and Sensibility." *Review of Contemporary Fiction* 14.3 (1994): 24–29.

Snitow, Ann. "Angela Carter, Wild Thing: Conversation with a Necromancer." *Voice Literary Supplement* June 1989: 14+.

Turner, Rory P.B. "Subjects and Symbols: Transformations of Identity in *Nights at the Circus*." *Folklore Forum* 20.1–2 (1987): 39–60.

Vallorani, Nicoletta. "The Body of the City: Angela Carter's *The Passion of the New Eve*." *Science Fiction Studies* 21 (1994): 365–379.

Wilson, Robert Rawdon. "SLIP PAGE: Angela Carter, in/out/in the Postmodern Nexus." In *Past the Last Post: Theorizing Post-colonialism and Postmodernism*. Ed. Ian Adam and Helen Tiffin. Calgary: U of Calgary P, 1990. 109–123.

Agatha Christie
1890–1976

Alan Lutkus

With her estate-reported sales beyond two billion—third to the Bible and Shakespeare—more of you have likely read Agatha Christie than anyone else in this volume, and early commentary could hardly explain why you would. Why bother with this "trivial, dated, classbound, intellectually and socially dead" writer (Barnard 7)?

BACKGROUND

Commentators needed to re-create Agatha Christie to appreciate her, and commendably some did even before Janet Morgan's estate-assisted 1984 biography supplied gaps in the posthumous 1977 *An Autobiography* (henceforth AA) and Gwen Robyns's 1978 life. Where once her women characters were "a depressing cast of thousands" (Peters and Krouse 150), more attentive reading reveals accurate 1920s–1960s portraits—passivity but also independence (Vipond 123) or sympathetically portrayed patriarchal victims balancing assertive spirits (Knepper 406). Her accuracy extends elsewhere, to labor questions and more (Lathen 90–91), dispelling impressions made by somewhat antiquated characters like her main detectives Hercule Poirot and Jane Marple, both coming from a generation before Christie herself, or stereotypes like a brusque stiff-upper-lip British major actually named "Blunt" in her most important work, *The Murder of Roger Ackroyd* (1926). Her novels' anti-Semitism has upset even admirers (Osborne 17, 57, 61, 66, 70), but at least at times derives from characters' insecurity with talented and creative Jewish newcomers (Gill 93–94), her fictions perhaps anticipating recent explications like J. Mordaunt Crook's of early-twentieth-century British anti-Semitism.

Central to revaluing Christie is her favorite setting, the Edwardian/Victorian country house (Bargainnier 28), derided by 1940s detective-fiction rival Raymond Chandler as too aristocratic: "Cheesecake Manor" (231). The country house surely commemorates Ashfield in Devonshire, home of the young Agatha Miller (born on September 15, 1890), but as a goal of a woman trying to restore her place in English society (Gill 18), largely taken from her as Ashfield almost was on the 1901 death of her father Frederick. Ashfield stood for sacrifices from her mother Clara, whose property it was, and who retained it—and educated Agatha—with help from Agatha's grandmothers and older sister Madge—life-shaping "dominant female images" (Maida and Spornick 13, prefiguring Morgan [9] on "forceful women"). Agatha went to Paris in 1906 to further her considerable musical talent, and she had a 1910 debut season—though in Cairo, not expensive England. From Ashfield's female sanctuary Clara arranged for popular novelist Eden Philpotts to see Agatha's early writing (his thorough commentary survives) (Morgan 51–53); partly in that sanctuary older sister Madge both introduced Agatha to popular literature and challenged her in early World War I years to write her own detective piece, seconded by Clara, who "always thought her daughters could do anything" (AA 5.3 [pt. 5, chap. 3]).

Agatha—Christie now, married since 1914 to aviator Captain Archibald Christie—prepared herself better than she knew for detective fiction with World War I dispensary training in medicine, drugs, and poisons, her hundreds of fictional uses of which are all discussed medically by Michael C. Gerald. Poison dominates her first novel, *The Mysterious Affair at Styles*, finished by midwar, published later; but it is its country-house Styles Court that elliptically summarizes Christie's own story, a matriarchy under attack, with indolent but perhaps deceptive men a contrast with its hardworking women, as Gill views it (59–61); and while it is no woman but detective Poirot who reestablishes order, as a Belgian, he is certainly an "other" and does partly embody the "feminine" (Munt 8).

Immediately following *Styles*, little suggested Christie's impending trauma, partly from Archie. True, he did suggest selling Ashfield after Clara's further financial reverses on one grandmother's death (Morgan 82). But as an alternate financial solution, he also encouraged Christie's continuing writing, and 1922's thriller *The Secret Adversary* arguably idealizes a Christies-like male-female pair in Tommy and Tuppence, portrayed as adventurous equals—a departure from detective fiction's usual female-subordinate duos (Gill 73–74, Klein 198–199). The Christies also adventured, despite their one child, Rosalind (born in 1919), taking a ten-month world tour (underwritten by Britain's Empire Exhibition, which Archie promoted). Agatha, with a new, more remunerative publisher (Collins) and magazine royalties, bought the Christies' first car and house, even if the latter's name—"Styles," given by Archie—had ominous associations, while its proximity to a golf course catered to Archie's, not Agatha's, interests. In 1926, Agatha published *Ackroyd*, whose unreliable narrator briefly tossed the detective subgenre up into mainstream discussion about fair play for readers (she had played fair). But in 1926 also, Clara died, with Agatha absent at her death; Archie asked for a divorce to marry golfing companion Nancy Neele; and, in a case sensationalized in the press, Agatha disappeared on December 3, her car was found abandoned on the road, and Agatha herself then somehow turned up in London, then in Harrowgate as "Teresa Neele," her registered name at the Hydropathic Hotel.

Agatha never discussed specifics of her "memory loss," the official explanation for what Jared Cade recently demonstrated as a clever but unsuccessful plot to shame Archie, whom Agatha knew was visiting friends on December 3, with Nancy Neele, near the abandoned-car site. A 1927 divorce helped precipitate Agatha's psychological depression but very probably also new professional (and perhaps wish-fulfilling) directions in the 1928 (magazine date) tales of supernaturally acute Harley Quin and 1934's Parker Pyne, more mender of broken lives than detective, and, beginning in 1930, certainly in the non-detective novels of "Mary Westmacott," where Agatha developed themes of marital breakup and overpossessive love (Gill 156, Maida and Spornick 121, Morgan 168–169, Shaw and Vanacker 37–38). Perhaps more important than any of these, the divorce put her among the class of "surplus women," as Marion Shaw and Sabine Vanacker show (38)—trapped her there textually, since she remained "Christie" on her publishers' advice, though she would marry again, happily, becoming archaeologist Max Mallowan's wife in 1930. Ultimately, the years as marginalized woman contributed to the creation of her second great detective, the spinster—and so also marginalized—Miss Marple of St. Mary Mead, first appearing in a 1928 magazine and embodying at once stereotypical limitations and new-realized potentialities of a single woman (Shaw and Vanacker 42–43).

Outside biography, with larger literary and social influence, commentary always met Christie's anti-intellectual pose—1971's "One up for the lowbrows!" on becoming Dame Agatha is representative (Gill 23), the pose even covering detective-fiction writing because of her claim for Marple and to a great extent Poirot as original creations (AA 5.3, 9.2). Christie, however, demonstrated genre expertise early, with 1929's parodies of detective-story practitioners (herself included) in *Partners in Crime*; and critics have long proposed sources for Poirot's detective, theatrical, and comic aspects (Thomson 194–198, 209; Maida and Spornick 87–88; Munt 8 reads "Poirot" as "clown," but the name is closer to "pear," referring to his shape), though none ever determines his relationship to fictional contemporary Hercules Popeau. While critics rightly allow Christie's basing Miss Marple on one grandmother, to her may be added infinitely wise Father Brown and, probably, investigator Amelia Butterworth (Maida and Spornick 106–107; Shaw and Vanacker 35; Gill 32, 217n; Roberts 6–10). Christie educated readers in twentieth-century music (see Weaver or music historian Osborne passim); in other areas, at least in later years she read widely, as is demonstrated in Morgan, who unfortunately rarely discusses titles listed (360, 363). Christie's work easily enough aligns with nineteenth- and twentieth-century literary ruralism and other daughter/spinster novels, but recent critics (Shaw and Vanacker 23, 32–33, 39–43; Gill 187–188) largely ignore her report on home schooling (AA 1.2, 1.4)—her only conventional education—which emphasizes only the Bible and Dickens.

These and other influences qualify as requisite Christie "areas for further study." Shaw and Vanacker (42), for instance, provide only Radclyffe Hall's 1928 *Well of Loneliness* as important to Agatha's homosexual portraits, though Hall seems an unlikely source for a gay couple integrated with their community (*A Murder Is Announced*) and outrageously irrelevant to the dissolution of a female same-sex relationship on arrival of Mister Right (*Nemesis*). How Christie's tolerance toward homosexuality fits her well-known conservatism goes begging critically; she makes no mention even of draconian British law toward gays, though Gill (197–198) begins a relevant dialogue.

ANALYSIS

Genre innovator from 1926's *Ackroyd* on, then from about 1949 self-imitator or imposter—"less predictably able" then, in "decline" or "collapse" (Wagoner 76, Symons 34, Barnard 91): this is the still-dominant critical short form of Christie's long career. Recently awakened interest in her dramas has helped her later reputation, Morgan calling the 1950s her decade of plays (327); and certainly a 1954 Londoner could choose among three concurrent Christie hits—*Spider's Web; The Mousetrap*, already two years into the consecutive-run record it still sets at this writing; and *Witness for the Prosecution*, also the New York Drama Critics' best 1954 foreign play (Osborne 166–169, 172–177). Interest in the Marple works of Christie's later period has only started to confront the dominant Poirot-weighted critical model, eight of her twelve novels appearing after 1949 but only ten of his thirty-three then (numbers reflect World War II–composed dates for Poirot and Marple finales *Curtain* and *Sleeping Murder*).

Christie quickly shed her 1931 title "paragon of orthodoxy" (Thomson 193), mostly awarded for replicating the Sherlock Holmes–Dr. Watson, detective–"idiot friend" pairing in Poirot with narrator Captain Hastings and for adhering to "least-likely-suspect" villains. But Hastings had already disappeared in *Ackroyd*, and there, rather than repeat easy formulae, Christie showed that others used *lesser* likely suspects while she had found—with some advice (AA 7.3)—a *more* least likely. Christie exiled Hastings permanently by 1936 (1975's *Curtain* excepted), replacing him either with third-person narration or an ordinary but not stupid first-person narrating associate. Christie meanwhile enlarged the form with, in one work, multiple most likely suspects, four known murderers, one new killing, and four detectives in the bargain; with another work's whodunit question answered "everybody" and a third work's "nobody," at least by investigators; and with her own closed suspect gatherings transported from country house to railroad (*Murder on the Orient Express*), water (*Death on the Nile*), and air (*Death in the Clouds*). Wagoner (47) finds formal experimentation paralleled thematically, Christie's first five 1930s detective novels considering perfect alibis, the next five disguise, followed by five on power hunger, with questions raised about the efficacy of justice. The wartime Christie retreated from thematic excursions, patriotically allowing British justice to prevail (Wagoner 69), but inventing elsewhere, *The Body in the Library* parodying while reusing the hoariest detective clichés; *Five Little Pigs* juggling several oral and written accounts of events, a kind of prose *Citizen Kane* with, for Osborne (129), characters unusually complex for Christie; *Towards Zero* rejecting a frequent Christie norm of cover-up killings following an initial murder; and *One, Two, Buckle My Shoe* conventional but so perfectly so that John Cawelti (111–118) chooses it to illustrate exemplary genre construction.

This is Christie's great era for Symons (35), who calls *Ackroyd, The A.B.C. Murders*, and *Ten Little Niggers* her best outings, slightly above *Orient Express, Peril at End House*, and *Curtain*—no Marples, five Poirots. But even while writing some of these, Christie had decried Poirot's superannuation (Morgan 222), disenchantment probably helping prompt new postwar directions—already suggested by her near-obsessive work on the Westmacott *Absent in the Spring* (entirely done in three days) and by her turn toward memoir in *Come, Tell Me How You Live* (emphasizing 1930s trips to Max's Middle East archaeological digs), toward ancient Egypt as setting in *Death Comes as the End*, and against Poirot's presence in the novel *The Hollow* (AA 9.5). Gill imagines Christie's 1951 satisfaction in excising Poirot from the play *The Hollow*—a possible springboard, together with the 1944–1945 success for *Ten Little Niggers* on stage, to the theater, Poirot never taken "from page to stage" (Wagoner 129). Morgan (270) notes Christie's 1950 renewed Marple interest coming specifically at the expense of "insufferable Poirot."

The Poirot work *Taken at the Flood* of 1948 certainly showed Christiean recycling, with postwar loss of national identity filtered through her theme of disguise (Wagoner 76); and the Marple novels generally accommodated some form of disguise to the loss of an older England. Rural villagers in 1950's *A Murder Is Announced* failed any more to recognize one another. Housing developments in 1957's *4:50 from Paddington* disrupted family in the shadow of old Rutherford Hall. Marple in 1965's *At Bertram's Hotel* saw through more than the nostalgia of the artificial Edwardian setting itself, perhaps a "least likely location" and certainly a demonstration, if a late one, that Christie hardly believed unequivocally in the old-world stereotypes inhabiting her fictions.

Such recycling joins nicely, even innovatively, with a supposed Marple flaw, her un-Poirot-like predilection for keeping clues to herself (Osborne 205, Wagoner 81). Christie's readership knew and appreciated her old strategies, enough so that every postwar Christie work could be counted on to be an automatic best-seller (Osborne 137); Marple novels then let readers test themselves on old strategies reapplied, without a Poirot mediator. This view extends Shaw and Vanacker's discussion of Christie's "democratization" of detection beyond Marple's ordinariness, where their argument restrains it (34), to include the reader as a working detective and nears Stephen Knight's argument (131) on Christie's favoring "individualistic detective authority," Knight noting that two of Christie's own three favorite works (1949's *Crooked House* and 1958's *Ordeal by Innocence*; see AA 11.3) had no true detective, while the other, 1942's *The Moving Finger*, has Marple only at the end. The view is consistent with Christie's 1962 onstage experiment in "The Patient," originally ending solutionless with her recorded voice informing playgoers simply that they now had all necessary clues (Osborne 199).

The democratization does stand uneasily against the human limitation echoing through much late Christie, from Poirot's semiderision of youth culture in 1966's *Third Girl* (Osborne 209) through general full despair over self-destructive political impulses in 1970's thriller *Passenger to Frankfurt* to, most pronouncedly, Marple's belief in genetic propensity for evil in 1971's *Nemesis*. Such biological determinism had developed from earlier Marple novels, particularly *4:50* and 1953's *A Pocket Full of Rye*, and suggests how much Christie herself was influenced by the one postwar (probable) innovation Wagoner (77) grants her, the serial-killer prototype of *Crooked House*. But democratization allies well with Christie's celebrating in her last-written works the capacities of the aged, indicated even in the title of the Poirot *Elephants Can Remember* and found also in *Nemesis* and the last Tommy-Tuppence, *Postern of Fate*. In these, however, the detectives investigate crimes of the distant past—perhaps Christie's admission that they could no longer deal with the modern world.

ASSESSMENT

Christie's major achievement surely resides in democratizing the detective form. Most strongly put, any later detective arising from any marginalized group—Mary Wings's lesbian Emma Victor or, Christiean anti-Semitism notwithstanding, Howard Engel's Jewish Benny Cooperman—owes an indirect debt to Poirot as other and particularly to Marple as overlooked spinster.

The democratization process also extends further within the genre than suggested earlier, to her choice of method and clues. Knight (54–55, 72, 81) makes much of Christie's predecessors' overintellectualizing the form through textual emphases, most notably in the prolonged bouts of reading undertaken by Edgar Allan Poe's C. Auguste Dupin, but present too in Holmes's involvement with watermarks and Petrarch (see also Carey 8–9 on less intellectual text); textuality in early detection also finds support from academe's dean of literacy studies, Walter J. Ong (149–51). Though Poirot arrives in literature conventionally textual enough, worrying over will fragments, spelling conventions, and letter formation (*Styles* chaps. 4, 5, 10), he soon enough contents himself with far simpler textual matters, the alphabet (*The A.B.C. Murders*) and nursery rhyme (*One, Two, Buckle My Shoe*), eventually claiming speech as his milieu—"I am a gossip. . . . I like to hear all about people" (*Dead Man's Folly* chap. 13). Poirot, however, ultimately never leaves the printed word, the late *Clocks* surrounding him with books for his own monograph (chap. 14), published by the start of *Third Girl*—though his work itself is on detective fiction, the textual form folding in on itself. Marple does move more definitively away from textuality, even if she too sometimes considers a nursery rhyme (*A Pocket Full of Rye*), as Hanna Charney notes (1–2). Marple nonetheless shines in the verbal sphere, as in her properly understanding conversational stress on "She" (*A Murder Is Announced*, chaps. 19, 23). That humblest of linguistic pursuits, gossip or small talk, is a Marple strength, as many have noted (Barnard 90, Maida and Spornick 109, Wagoner 79, Shaw and Vanacker 64–68), but never with reference to the historical development of the genre. But Christie's focus on the spoken word allows wider scope for later genre figures, even such non-Christiean detectives as Chandleresque Lew Archer, whose prime characteristic is deft listening: "I've always known about voyeurs," says one Archer friend, "but you're an auditeur, aren't you?" (Macdonald chap. 20).

Christie also contributes to, perhaps initiates, redirection of a genre-relevant new model of knowledge. Carlo Ginzburg (81–83, 92, 102–103, 109) argues that the late nineteenth century sees the emergence of a "conjectural or semiotic paradigm" opposed to the mathematical model of reasoning refined since Galileo's time, with reading of clues in the Holmes works as definitively expressing the alternative paradigm's procedures as (pseudonymous) Giovanni Morelli, Freud, and Darwin do in reading features from art, medical symptoms, and landscape. But Christie's work increasingly rejects such Holmesean concrete evidence. Thomson (200) notes clues lessening after *Styles* even in her 1920s work; Symons (31–34) outlines her 1930s–1940s preference for intangible clues, not only the verbal but the deceptively visual—a trouser stain in *Death on the Nile* both helps and deceives readers—and Gill (194) suggests more later, Christie having further "decided to prune her clues" in 1950. Poirot even implicitly warns convention-driven readers in *The A.B.C. Murders* (chap. 35), revealing that he had manufactured one visual clue because dense Hastings expected it; Marple goes further, forgoing normal clues in dismissing one murder suspect on the grounds of character alone—he simply "wasn't that kind of person" (*A Murder Is Announced* chap. 8). This growing Christiean disdain for clues falls somewhere between simple increased emphasis on mental processes—for Poirot particularly, with his interest in "little grey cells" and "the psychology" of suspects that he values—to near-god(dess)like judgment upon guilt or innocence, however well versed Marple may be with her universal template, the character traits of St. Mary Mead inhabitants that serve as a model of all other human behavior. Christie here perhaps democratizes too much with a procedure allowing anyone's biases to flourish, and she certainly diverges from the path to which Ginzburg's paradigm logically leads, forensic detection, but again provides scope for different later detectives like Thomas Harris's Will Graham, the psychic FBI agent who is horrific Hannibal Lecter's first antagonist.

BIBLIOGRAPHY

Primary Sources

Excepting the final Poirot work and the final Marple novel, works appear by date of composition or production rather than of publication. U.S. titles, when different from those in the United Kingdom, are listed second.

The Mysterious Affair at Styles. London: Bodley Head, 1920.

The Secret Adversary. London: Bodley Head, 1922.

Murder on the Links. London: Bodley Head, 1923.

The Man in the Brown Suit. London: Bodley Head, 1924.

Poirot Investigates (stories). London: Bodley Head, 1924.

The Road of Dreams (poetry). London: Geoffrey Bles, 1924.

The Secret of Chimneys. London: Bodley Head, 1925.

The Murder of Roger Ackroyd. London: Collins; New York: Dodd, Mead, 1926.

The Big Four. London: Collins; New York: Dodd, Mead, 1927.

The Mystery of the Blue Train. London: Collins; New York: Dodd, Mead, 1928.

Partners in Crime. London: Collins; New York: Dodd, Mead, 1929.

The Seven Dials Mystery. London: Collins; New York: Dodd, Mead, 1929.

Behind the Screen (radio script). 1930.

Black Coffee (play, novelized 1998 by Charles Osborne). 1930.

Giant's Bread. As Mary Westmacott. London: Collins; New York: Dodd, Mead, 1930.
The Murder at the Vicarage. London: Collins; New York: Dodd, Mead, 1930.
The Mysterious Mr. Quin (stories). London: Collins; New York: Dodd, Mead, 1930.
The Floating Admiral (with other writers). London: Doubleday, 1931.
The Scoop (radio script). 1931.
The Sittaford Mystery. London: Collins, 1931. As *Murder at Hazelmoor*. New York: Dodd, Mead, 1931.
Peril at End House. London: Collins; New York: Dodd, Mead, 1932.
The Thirteen Problems. London: Collins, 1932. As *The Tuesday Club Murders*. New York: Dodd, Mead, 1932.
The Hound of Death and Other Stories. London: Collins; New York, Dodd, Mead, 1933.
Lord Edgware Dies. London: Collins, 1933. As *Thirteen at Dinner*. New York: Dodd, Mead, 1933.
The Listerdale Mystery (stories). London: Collins; New York: Dodd, Mead, 1934.
Murder on the Orient Express. London: Collins, 1934. As *Murder in the Calais Coach*. New York: Dodd, Mead, 1934.
Parker Pyne Investigates (stories). London: Collins; New York: Dodd, Mead, 1934.
Unfinished Portrait. As Mary Westmacott. London: Collins; Garden City, N.Y.: Doubleday, 1934.
Why Didn't They Ask Evans? London: Collins, 1934. As *The Boomerang Clue*. New York: Dodd, Mead, 1934.
Death in the Clouds. London: Collins, 1935. As *Death in the Air*. New York: Dodd, Mead, 1935.
Three-Act Tragedy. London: Collins, 1935. As *Murder in Three Acts*. New York: Dodd, Mead, 1935.
The A.B.C. Murders. London: Collins; New York: Dodd, Mead, 1936.
Cards on the Table. London: Collins; New York: Dodd, Mead, 1936.
Murder in Mesopotamia. London: Collins; New York: Dodd, Mead, 1936.
Akhnaton (play). Written in 1937. London: Collins; New York: Dodd, Mead, 1973.
Death on the Nile. London: Collins; New York: Dodd, Mead, 1937.
Dumb Witness. London: Collins, 1937. As *Poirot Loses a Client*. New York: Dodd, Mead, 1937.
Murder on the Mews. London: Collins, 1937. As *Dead Man's Mirror*. New York: Dodd, Mead, 1937.
Appointment with Death. London: Collins; New York: Dodd, Mead, 1938.
Hercule Poirot's Christmas. London: Collins, 1938. As *Murder for Christmas*. New York: Dodd, Mead, 1938.
Murder Is Easy. London: Collins, 1939. As *Easy to Kill*. New York: Dodd, Mead, 1939.
The Regatta Mystery and Other Stories. New York: Dodd, Mead, 1939.
Ten Little Niggers. London: Collins, 1939. As *And Then There Were None*. New York: Dodd, Mead, 1939. Also known as *Ten Little Indians*.
One, Two, Buckle My Shoe. London: Collins, 1940. As *The Patriotic Murders*. New York: Dodd, Mead, 1940. Also known as *An Overdose of Death*.
Sad Cypress. London: Collins; New York: Dodd, Mead, 1940.
Evil under the Sun. London: Collins; New York: Dodd, Mead, 1941.
N or M? London: Collins; New York: Dodd, Mead, 1941.
The Body in the Library. London: Collins; New York: Dodd, Mead, 1942.
Five Little Pigs. London: Collins, 1942. As *Murder in Retrospect*. New York: Dodd, Mead, 1942.
The Moving Finger. London: Collins; New York: Dodd, Mead, 1942.
And Then There Were None (play). London: French, 1943.
Absent in the Spring. As Mary Westmacott. London: Collins; New York: Farrar, 1944.
Towards Zero. London: Collins, 1944. As *Come and Be Hanged*. New York: Dodd, Mead, 1944.
Appointment with Death (play). Written in 1945. London: French, 1956.
Death Comes as the End. London: Collins; New York: Dodd, Mead, 1945.
Sparkling Cyanide. London: Collins, 1945. As *Remembered Death*. New York: Dodd, Mead, 1945.
Ten Little Niggers (play). London: French, 1945.
Come, Tell Me How You Live. As Agatha Christie Mallowan. London: Collins; New York: Dodd, Mead, 1946.
The Hollow. London: Collins; New York: Dodd, Mead, 1946.
Murder on the Nile (play). London: Collins; New York: Dodd, Mead, 1946.
The Labours of Hercules (stories). London: Collins; New York: Dodd, Mead, 1947.
Three Blind Mice (radio script). 1947.
The Rose and the Yew Tree. As Mary Westmacott. London: Heinemann; New York: Rinehart, 1948.

Taken at the Flood. London: Collins, 1948. As *There Is a Tide*. New York: Dodd, Mead, 1948.
Witness for the Prosecution and Other Stories. London: Collins; New York: Dodd, Mead, 1948.
Crooked House. London: Collins; New York: Dodd, Mead, 1949.
A Murder Is Announced. London: Collins; New York: Dodd, Mead, 1950.
Three Blind Mice and Other Stories. New York: Dodd, Mead, 1950.
The Hollow (play). London: French, 1951.
They Came to Baghdad. London: Collins; New York: Dodd, Mead, 1951.
The Under Dog and Other Stories. New York: Dodd, Mead, 1951.
A Daughter's a Daughter. As Mary Westmacott. London: Heinemann, 1952; New York: Dell, 1963.
The Mousetrap (play). Written in 1952. New York: Dodd, Mead, 1978.
Mrs. McGinty's Dead. London: Collins, 1952. As *Blood Will Tell*. New York: Dodd, Mead, 1952.
They Do It with Mirrors. London: Collins, 1952. As *Murder with Mirrors*. New York: Dodd, Mead, 1952.
After the Funeral. London: Collins, 1953. As *Funerals Are Fatal*. New York: Dodd, Mead, 1953.
A Pocket Full of Rye. London: Collins; New York: Dodd, Mead, 1953.
Witness for the Prosecution (play). London and New York: French, 1953.
Destination Unknown. London: Collins, 1954. As *So Many Steps to Death*. New York: Dodd, Mead, 1954.
Spider's Web (play). Written in 1954. London: French, 1957.
Hickory, Dickory Dock. London: Collins, 1955. As *Hickory, Dickory Death*. New York: Dodd, Mead, 1955.
The Burden. As Mary Westmacott. London: Heinemann, 1956; New York: Dell, 1963.
Dead Man's Folly. London: Collins; New York: Dodd, Mead, 1956.
Towards Zero (play). With Gerald Verner. Written in 1956. New York: Dramatists Play Service, 1957; London: French, 1958.
4:50 from Paddington. London: Collins, 1957. As *What Mrs. McGillicuddy Saw!* New York: Dodd, Mead, 1957.
Ordeal by Innocence. London: Collins; New York: Dodd, Mead, 1958.
The Unexpected Guest (play). London: French, 1958.
Verdict (play). London: French, 1958.
Cat among the Pigeons. London: Collins; New York: Dodd, Mead, 1959.
The Adventure of the Christmas Pudding and a Selection of Entrees (stories). London: Collins, 1960.
Go Back for Murder (play). London: French, 1960.
Double Sin and Other Stories. New York: Dodd, Mead, 1961.
The Pale Horse. London: Collins; New York: Dodd, Mead, 1961.
The Mirror Crack'd from Side to Side. London: Collins, 1962. As *The Mirror Crack'd*. New York: Dodd, Mead, 1962.
Rule of Three (plays; includes "The Rats," "Afternoon at the Seaside," and "The Patient"). London: French, 1962.
The Clocks. London: Collins; New York: Dodd, Mead, 1963.
A Caribbean Mystery. London: Collins; New York: Dodd, Mead, 1964.
At Bertram's Hotel. London: Collins; New York: Dodd, Mead, 1965.
Star over Bethlehem (a children's book). As Agatha Christie Mallowan. London: Collins; New York: Dodd, Mead, 1965.
Third Girl. London: Collins; New York: Dodd, Mead, 1966.
Endless Night. London: Collins; New York: Dodd, Mead, 1967.
By the Pricking of My Thumbs. London: Collins; New York: Dodd, Mead, 1968.
Hallowe'en Party. London: Collins; New York: Dodd, Mead, 1969.
Passenger to Frankfurt: An Extravaganza. London: Collins; New York: Dodd, Mead, 1970.
Nemesis. London: Collins; New York: Dodd, Mead, 1971.
The Golden Ball and Other Stories. New York: Dodd, Mead, 1971.
Elephants Can Remember. London: Collins; New York: Dodd, Mead, 1972.
Fiddlers Three (play). 1972.
Poems. London: Collins; New York: Dodd, Mead, 1973.
Postern of Fate. London: Collins; New York: Dodd, Mead, 1973.
Poirot's Early Cases (stories). London: Collins, 1974. As *Hercule Poirot's Early Cases*. New York: Dodd, Mead, 1974.
Curtain. London: Collins; New York: Dodd, Mead, 1975.
Sleeping Murder. London: Collins; New York: Dodd, Mead, 1976.
An Autobiography. London: Collins; New York: Dodd, Mead, 1977.
A Murder Is Announced (play). 1977.

The Harlequin Tea Set and Other Stories. New York: G.P. Putnam, 1997.

Secondary Sources

Bargainnier, Earl F. *The Gentle Art of Murder: The Detective Fiction of Agatha Christie*. Bowling Green, OH: Bowling Green U Popular P, 1980.

Barnard, Robert. *A Talent to Deceive*. New York: Dodd, Mead, 1980.

Cade, Jared. *Agatha Christie and the Eleven Missing Days*. London: Peter Owen, 1998.

Carey, John. *The Intellectuals and the Masses: Pride and Prejudice among the Literary Intelligentsia, 1880–1939*. London: Faber, 1992; New York: St. Martin's, 1993.

Cawelti, John. *Adventure, Mystery, and Romance*. Chicago: U of Chicago P, 1976.

Chandler, Raymond. "The Simple Art of Murder." In *The Art of the Mystery Story: A Collection of Critical Essays*. Ed. Howard Haycraft. New York: Simon & Schuster, 1946. 222–237.

Charney, Hanna. *The Detective Novel of Manners: Hedonism, Morality, and the Life of Reason*. Rutherford, NJ: Fairleigh Dickinson UP, 1980.

Crook, J. Mordaunt. *The Rise of the Nouveaux Riches: Style and Status in Victorian and Edwardian Architecture*. London: John Murray, 1999.

Gerald, Michael C. *The Poisonous Pen of Agatha Christie*. Austin: U of Texas P, 1993.

Gill, Gillian. *Agatha Christie: The Woman and Her Mysteries*. New York: Free Press, 1990.

Ginzburg, Carlo. "Clues: Morelli, Freud, and Sherlock Holmes." In *The Sign of Three: Dupin, Holmes, Peirce*. Ed. Umberto Eco and Thomas A. Sebeok. Bloomington: Indiana UP, 1983. 81–118.

Gregg, Hubert. *Agatha Christie and All That Mousetrap*. London: Kimber, 1980.

Harris, Thomas. *Red Dragon*. New York: Dell, 1990.

Hart, Anne. *The Life and Times of Hercule Poirot*. New York: Putnam's, 1990.

———. *The Life and Times of Miss Jane Marple*. New York: Dodd, Mead, 1985.

Keating, H.R.F., ed. *Agatha Christie: First Lady of Crime*. New York: Holt, 1977.

Klein, Kathleen Gregory. *The Woman Detective: Gender and Genre*. 2nd ed. Urbana: U of Illinois P, 1995.

Knepper, Marty S. "Agatha Christie: Feminist." *Armchair Detective* 16 (1983): 398–406.

Knight, Stephen. *Form and Ideology in Crime Fiction*. Bloomington: Indiana UP, 1980.

Lathen, Emma. "Cornwallis's Revenge." In Keating 79–94.

Macdonald, Ross. *The Underground Man*. New York: Bantam, 1972.

Maida, Patricia D., and Nicholas B. Spornick. *Murder She Wrote: A Study of Agatha Christie's Detective Fiction*. Bowling Green, OH: Bowling Green State U Popular P, 1982.

Mallowan, Max. *Mallowan's Memoirs*. London: Collins, 1977.

Morgan, Janet. *Agatha Christie: A Biography*. London: Collins, 1984; New York: Knopf, 1985.

Munt, Sally R. *Murder by the Book? Feminism and the Crime Novel*. New York: Routledge, 1994.

Ong, Walter J. *Orality and Literacy*. New York: Methuen, 1982.

Osborne, Charles. *The Life and Crimes of Agatha Christie*. London: Collins, 1982; New York: Holt, 1983.

Peters, Margot, and Agate N. Krouse. "Women and Crime: Sexism in Allingham, Sayers, and Christie." *Southwest Review* 59 (1974): 144–152.

Roberts, Joan Warthling. "Amelia Butterworth: The Spinster Detective." In *Feminism in Women's Detective Fiction*. Ed. Glenwood Irons. Toronto: U of Toronto P, 1995. 3–11.

Robyns, Gwen. *The Mystery of Agatha Christie*. Garden City, NY: Doubleday, 1978.

Shaw, Marion, and Sabine Vanacker. *Reflecting on Miss Marple*. New York: Routledge, 1991.

Sova, Dawn B. *Agatha Christie A to Z: The Essential Reference to Her Life and Writings*. New York: Facts on File, 1996.

Symons, Julian. "The Mistress of Complication." In Keating 25–38.

Thomson, H. Douglas. *Masters of Mystery: A Study of the Detective Story*. London: Collins, 1931.

Vipond, M. "Agatha Christie's Women." *International Fiction Review* [Canada] 8 (1981): 119–123.

Wagoner, Mary S. *Agatha Christie*. Boston: Twayne, 1986.

Weaver, William. "Music and Mystery." In Keating 183–192.

Caryl Churchill
1938–

Joel Shatzky

BACKGROUND

Caryl Churchill was born on September 3, 1938, in London, England. She began her education in Canada during World War II and after the war returned to England, where she studied at Oxford University, taking a B.A. in 1960. The following year she married David Harter. They have three sons.

Churchill wrote her first produced play, *Downstairs*, at the age of twenty while she was at Oxford; it was also staged in London in 1959. Another London-produced play, *Having a Wonderful Time*, followed in 1960. *Early Death* was produced at Oxford in 1962, marking the end of the first phase of Churchill's career. During the late 1960s and early 1970s she wrote a series of radio plays including *Lovesick* (1967), *Identical Twins* (1968), *Abortive* (1971), *Schreber's Nervous Illness* (1972), and *Perfect Happiness* (1973). In 1972, with *Owners*, she began her association with the Royal Court Theatre, noted as a pioneering company in experimental drama from the beginning of the century with Bernard Shaw's plays. In the last twenty-five years the Royal Court has produced ten of Churchill's works including her best known, *Cloud Nine* (1979) and *Top Girls* (1982).

In the late 1960s the dramatist began studying radical politics, and her plays since that time have taken a decidedly leftist turn. This is reflected in her work from the mid-1970s on when she began to collaborate with the first of two feminist theater companies, Monstrous Regiment, with which she wrote *Vinegar Tom* (1976), in Churchill's words, "a play about witches with no witches in it" (preface, rpt., in Worthen 845). Incidentally, the Monstrous Regiment got its name from a quote by John Knox, referring to his diatribe against Queen Mary of England in "The First Blast of the Trumpet against the Monstrous Regiment of Women" (qtd. in Worthen 844).

The most productive years of Churchill's collaborative efforts were when she began working with Joint Stock, another feminist acting group. It was through this collaboration that Churchill produced her two most noted plays about feminism and role stereotyping, *Cloud Nine* and *Top Girls*, which were shortly followed by *Fen* (1983). Two other plays reflect her collaborative tendencies: *A Mouthful of Birds* (1986) was written with David Lan and *Lives of the Great Poisoners* (1991) with Orlando Gough and Ian Spink.

Among her more recent works are *Mad Forest* (1990) about the Romanian revolution and *The Skriker* (1994), which was produced in London at the National Theatre. In a career that has spanned more than thirty years, Churchill has been given as yet limited recognition. She won an Obie in 1982–1983 for *Top Girls* and the Susan Smith Blackburn Prize in 1984 for *Fen* and in 1987 for *Serious Money*. The latter play was also recognized with an Olivier Award as best play of the 1987 season as well as a *London Evening Standard* award for best comedy. Although she is known for her unconventional and arresting dramaturgy as well as her ideology, Churchill's most produced and anthologized plays are the two she wrote almost twenty years ago: *Cloud Nine* and *Top Girls*.

ANALYSIS

The influence of Bertolt Brecht, the great German playwright, can be clearly seen in Churchill's work from the mid-1970s on. Like Brecht, she intersperses her dramas with "distancing" devices such as songs, very much a Brechtian technique, as in *Vinegar Tom*, with the added anachronism of actors performing these songs in modern dress, considering that the play takes place in the seventeenth century. As one of the participants in the production of *Vinegar Tom*, Sue Beardon, said: "We didn't want to allow the audience to ever get completely immersed in the stories. . . . We wanted to make them continually aware of our presence, of our relationship to the material which was combative, anguished" (qtd. in Neblett 2 from Itzin 276).

Another Brechtian technique Churchill uses can be found in her choice of subject matter, deliberately putting a historical or geographical distance between her audience and the milieu of the play. *Vinegar Tom* takes place in a period remote from our century, as does *Light Shining in Buckinghamshire*; the first part of *Cloud Nine* is set in colonial nineteenth-century Africa; and although *Top Girls* has many scenes of contemporary London, it begins with an ahistorical reunion of women both historic and mythic from Dull Gret and Pope Joan to Isabella Bird, a nineteenth-century world traveler. Like Brecht as well, Churchill uses satire to make a critique on modern capitalism, particularly skewering the Thatcher era in her plays of the late 1970s and 1980s.

Where Churchill appears to be more on her own is in her feminist critique of contemporary society, which is evident in *Vinegar Tom* and virulent in *Top Girls*. The device of cross-dressing which is ingeniously employed in *Cloud Nine*, is found in Brecht's own brilliant take on gender roles, *The Good Person of Szechwan*. While Brecht contributed a great deal to the theories of theater in his *Messingkauf Dialogues* and his development of the "V-effekt," the "making strange" of the content of the play to the audience so that it can look at the questions it raises rather than the emotions it engenders, Churchill developed a number of her own devices in "making" her plays "strange." Of particular note was her manipulation of time. In *Cloud Nine* the second act takes place one hundred years after act one, yet "for the characters it is twenty-five years later" (*Cloud Nine* n.p.) The modern dress of the singers in *Vinegar Tom* is also a deliberate anachronism; and in *Top Girls* the last act occurs a year earlier than the second act. The doubling of characters in both *Cloud Nine* and *Top Girls* also serves as a commentary on the nature of their roles, particularly in the former, where some male and female roles are played by the opposite sex.

Another innovation of Churchill is found in *Top Girls* in her "unique language" that "links her with other contemporary playwrights rarely viewed positively in feminist criticism: Harold Pinter and David Mamet" (Price 1). The most striking aspect of this language is the use of the / and * to indicate to the actor where a speech is interrupted with another speech. Churchill notes this directorial-like process in the prefatory note to *Top Girls*:

> A speech usually follows the one immediately before it BUT: 1: when one character starts speaking before the other has finished, the point of interruption is marked /. eg.
>
> ISABELLA: This is the Emperor of Japan? / I once met the Emperor of Morocco.
>
> NIJO: In fact it was the ex-Emperor.
>
> 2: a character sometimes speaking right through another's speech: eg.
>
> ISABELLA: When I was forty I thought my life was over. / Oh I was pitiful. I was
>
> NIJO: I didn't say I felt it for twenty years. Not every minute.
>
> ISABELLA: sent on a cruise for my health and I felt even worse. Pains in my bones, pins and needles . . . etc.
>
> 3: sometimes a speech follows on from a speech earlier than the one immediately before it, and continuity is marked *. eg.
>
> GRISELDA: I'd seen him riding by, we all had. And he'd seen me in the fields with the sheep*.
>
> ISABELLA: I would have been well suited to minding sheep.
>
> NIJO: And Mr Nugent riding by.
>
> ISABELLA: Of course not, Nijo, I mean a healthy life in the open air.
>
> JOAN: *He just rode up while you were minding the sheep and asked you to marry him?
>
> where "in the fields with the sheep" is the cue to both "I would have been" and "He just rode up." (*Cloud Nine* Note on characters n.p).

Obviously, it is impossible for the audience to make out more than fragments of words and sentences when two speeches are spoken simultaneously, but this is exactly the effect Churchill wishes to create. It both forces the audience to listen more carefully and makes them choose which speech to focus on in order to understand the context. This device of overlapping dialogue, the very opposite of Pinter's "silences," was also employed in the play following *Top Girls*, *Fen*. It is a brilliant device that could be considered truly Brechtian in its effect. It was also through her experience in working with feminist theater companies that Churchill was able to develop and perfect these techniques. Here again she resembles Brecht, who was always finding material through various collaborators such as Elisabeth Hauptmann.

Although she has written over two dozen plays, it is in the three primarily discussed here, *Vinegar Tom*, *Cloud Nine*, and *Top Girls*, that Churchill has written her most powerful and innovative work. As John A. Price observes in his critique of "The Language of Caryl Churchill": "The songs [in *Vinegar Tom*] serve to emphasize the post-modern feminism of Churchill's 'sign-systems'; the structural placement of the songs emphasizes the feminist position against traditional male dramatic structures, while simultaneously criticizing traditional patriarchal mistreatment of women" (5).

Paradoxically, in a 1997 interview in the *New Yorker*, Churchill also reveals the influence of David Mamet:

> Out of the muck of ordinary speech—the curses, interruptions, asides, midsentence breaks, and sudden accelerations—Mamet carefully weaves a tapestry of motifs which he sees as a "counterpoint." . . . Mamet says he doesn't picture the characters on stage he hears them "The rhythms don't just unlock something in the character. . . . They *are* what's happening." (qtd. in Price 9)

But Churchill's interest in language delves into the social and political elements of class and gender oppression. "Churchill successfully stages 'democratic history,' socialist commentary, and the lives of the Fen women—all through linking actor to character through her rhythmic Mamet-like, yet duplicitously unique, language" (Price 10).

Vinegar Tom, as already stated, is "a play about witches with no witches in it." Churchill observes that in doing research into the play, "One of the things that struck me reading the detailed accounts of witch trials in Essex . . . was how petty and everyday the witches' offences were, and how different the atmosphere of actual English witch hunts seemed to be from my received idea, based on slight knowledge of the European witch-hunts and films and fiction, of burnings, hysteria and sexual orgies" (preface in Worthen 845). This attitude toward the nature of the social response to witchcraft faintly echoes Arthur Miller's premise in *The Crucible* that much of the Salem Witch Trials was about a minister's envy and a greedy neighbor's desire for a piece of land. But Churchill's play, although in some respects resembling Miller's in structure, is more clearly a feminist critique. The innocent Alice Noakes is ultimately condemned to be hanged through the false accusations of a neighbor and the machinations of a professional witchhunter. The content of the songs clearly reveals the political nature of the play:

> Where have the witches gone?
> Who are the witches now?
> Here we are.
>
> All the gentle witches' spell
> blast the doctors' sleeping pills.
> The witches hanging in the sky
> haunt the courts where lawyers lie.
> Here we are.
>
> (Worthen 860)

The last song, which concludes the play, ironically titled "Evil Women," ends with the kind of question worthy of a Brecht play:

> Evil women
> Is that what you want?
> Is that what you want to see?
> In your movie dream
> Do they scream and scream?
> Evil women
> Evil women
> Women.
>
> (Worthen 861)

In *Cloud Nine*, written three years later, Churchill uses the device of cross-dressing to reveal her view of gender and racial stereotypes. The play begins in the colonial Africa of the British Empire at the height of Victorianism. The plot is in the style of Victorian melodrama with a Great White Hunter, an apparently compliant native servant, the "typical" British family, and a Gilbertian plot with assignations and twists galore. Churchill's view of the characters, however, is anything but Victorian:

> There were no black members of the company and this led me to the idea of Joshua being so alienated from himself and so much aspiring to be what white men want him to be that he is played by a white. Similarly, Betty [the wife], who has no more respect for women than Joshua has for blacks, and wants to be what men want her to be, is played by a man. For Edward [the son] to be played by a woman is within the English tradition of women playing boys (e.g. PETER PAN); for Cathy [a four-year-old girl] to be played by a man is a simple reversal of this. Of course, for both that reversal highlights how much they have to be taught to be society's idea of a little boy and girl. (*Cloud Nine* viii)

In this play the second act has a naturalistic texture, with some of the characters in this act commenting in their more unconventional and open behavior (Edward, the effeminate son in act 1, is now openly gay) on their stereotypical characteristics in the first act. This, too, is a distancing device that leads us to become more critical of gender roles.

In *Top Girls* Churchill critiques some aspects of feminism itself. In an interview with Emily Mann she says:

> What I was intending to do was make it first look as though it was celebrating the achievements of women then—by showing the main character Marlene, being successful in a very competitive, destructive, capitalist way—ask, what kind of achievement is that? The idea was that it would start out looking like a feminist play and turn into a socialist one, as well. (qtd. in Price 8)

The play begins with a fantasy dinner attended by five embodiments of different aspects of feminism in history and literature: Isabella Bird, a world traveler, Lady Nijo, an imperial courtesan who later became a Buddhist nun, Dull Gret, a subject in a Brueghel painting who leads a crowd of women through hell, fighting the demons, Pope Joan, who was thought to be Pope from 854 to 856 in a man's disguise, and the fictional Patient Griselda from Chaucer's "Clerk's Tale" in *The Canterbury Tales*. They all are there to pay tribute to Marlene, the central character in the play, who has just gotten a promotion at her company. In the course of the dinner conversation various aspects of feminist issues and issues of male chauvinism are raised.

The second and third acts, done in reverse chronological order, concern Marlene's relationship with her office coworkers and, later, her treatment of her "niece" Angie (really her biological daughter who has been raised by Marlene's sister, Joyce) and the family she has abandoned. In this last act Churchill's political sentiments are clearly expressed in the words of Joyce, Marlene's working-class sister who gets into an argument with her about the "Thatcher Revolution."

> MARLENE. . . . I don't believe in class. Anyone can do anything if they've got what it takes.
>
> JOYCE. And if they haven't?
>
> MARLENE. If they're stupid or lazy or frightened, I'm not going to help them get a job, why should I? (III 86)

The consequences of a tunnel-vision feminism in which women make the same kind of mistakes as men in the way they vie for jobs and lose sight of more humane values is brilliantly critiqued in a play that seems to be a celebration of a woman who has "made it" and ends with questioning at what cost. It is with these plays that Caryl Churchill has established herself as one of the most significant playwrights of the last twenty years. It is both through her theatrical innovations and her incisive and controversial subject matter that she deserves more attention from the American theater than she has received in the past two decades.

ASSESSMENT

Churchill was hailed as a major playwright from the time *Cloud Nine* was produced. The play traveled across the Atlantic and opened Off-Broadway at the Theatre de Lys in May 1981. Frank Rich's review in the *New York Times* notes, "[N]ot only does [Churchill] examine a cornucopia of sexual permutations—from heterosexual adultery right up to bisexual incest, but she does so with a wild array of dramatic styles and tricks" (qtd. in "Caryl Churchill" 70). Clive Barnes in the *New York Post* views favorably Churchill's openmindedness and insistence that any relationships between people "if genuine have their validity." He also regards it as "fundamentally a play about love relationships to which the fading Empire merely provides the backcloth" (qtd. in "Caryl Churchill" 70).

Benedict Nightingale assessed *Cloud Nine* along with *Top Girls*: "[T]aken together [they] show that [Churchill] has evolved into a playwright of genuine audacity and assurance, able to use her considerable wit and intelligence in ways at once unusual, resonant and dramatically riveting" (qtd. in "Caryl Churchill" 70). Rich's evaluation of *Top Girls* indicates that it is "far more simplistic and obvious than the fervent pansexuality of *Cloud Nine*," but it is also "one of the few plays [of the 1983] season that allows its audience to watch a truly original theatrical mind at work" (qtd. in "Caryl Churchill" 70).

Fen also received favorable reviews from the critics. Nightingale in a *New York Times* review observes that the lives of these figures of the still-peasant class in Britain are not easily understood in the United States: "[N]either in the Middle West nor anywhere else in America will you find people quite so paralyzed by class and tradition, so stuck in the roles that birth and geography have thrust upon them, as . . . Churchill's villagers. . . . The feeling runs through the play that as long as the economic system is what it is these people will be what they are" (qtd. in "Caryl Churchill" 71).

Serious Money (1987), Churchill's next major effort, delves into the London Stock Exchange and its financial scandals as well as those well-known figures of corporate manipulation in the United States, Ivan Boesky and Michael Milken. In his review of the play Frank Rich states: "If *Serious Money* is an angry, leftist political work about ruthlessness and venality, about plunderings and piggishness, it is also vivid entertainment" (qtd. in "Caryl Churchill" 71). It has been Churchill's skill, as it was Brecht's, to take a controversial stand on a vital issue and entertain the audience while bringing home her ideological position, often quite explicitly. A more recent effort, *Mad Forest*, which is about the overthrow of the Nicolae Ceauşescu regime in Romania, has elements of surrealism as well as monologues taken from the words of actual survivors of the uprising. Writing in the *London Times*, Jeremy Kingston observes: "The style is theatre-verite, rich in the absurd or homely details people do remember at such times" (qtd. in "Caryl Churchill" 72). Churchill's work, witty and brilliantly theatrical, continues to both entice and confront audiences more than forty years after her earliest efforts at Oxford. The range, quantity, and excellence of her work make her one of the most important playwrights of our times.

BIBLIOGRAPHY

Primary Sources

Downstairs. Prod. Oxford, 1958; London, 1959.

Having a Wonderful Time. Prod. London, 1960.

Early Death. Prod. Oxford, 1962.

The Ants (radio play; broadcast 1962). In *New English Dramatists 12*. London: Penguin, 1968.

Lovesick (radio play), 1967.

Identical Twins (radio play), 1968.

Abortive (radio play), 1971.

Owners. Prod. London, 1972. London: Eyre Methuen, 1973.

Perfect Happiness. Broadcast on radio, 1973; prod. London, 1974.

Schreber's Nervous Illness. Broadcast on radio, 1973; prod. London, 1974.

Moving Clocks Go Slow. Prod. London, 1975.

Objections to Sex and Violence. Prod. London, 1975; London: Margaret Ramsey, 1975.

Light Shining in Buckinghamshire. Prod. Edinburgh, 1976. London: Pluto, 1978.

Vinegar Tom. Prod. Hull, England, 1976. London: TQ, 1978.

Floorshow. With David Bradford, Bryony Lavery, and Michelene Wandor. Prod. London, 1977.

Traps. Prod. London, 1977. London: Pluto, 1978.

Cloud Nine. Prod. London, 1979. London: Pluto, 1979. Rev. ed. New York: Routledge, 1988.

Three More Sleepless Nights. Prod. London, 1980.

Top Girls. Prod. London, 1982. New York: Samuel French, 1982. Fully revised ed., London: Methuen, 1984.

Fen. Prod. London, 1983. London: Methuen, 1983.

Midday Sun. With Geraldine Pilgrim, Pete Brooks, and John Ashford. Prod. London, 1984.

Softcops. Prod. London, 1984. London: Methuen, 1984.

Churchill: Plays One (includes *Owners*, *Light Shining in Buckinghamshire*, *Vinegar Tom*, *Traps*, and *Cloud Nine*). London: Methuen, 1985.

A Mouthful of Birds. With David Lan. Prod. London, 1986; London: Methuen, 1986.

Softcops and Fen. London: Methuen, 1986.

Serious Money. Prod. London, 1987. London: Heinemann Educational, 1987.

Ice Cream. Prod. London, 1989. London: Hern, 1989.

Churchill Shorts (includes *The Hospital at the Time of the Revolution; Seagulls; Lovesick; Abortive; Not, Not, Not, Not, Not Enough Oxygen; Schreber's Nervous Illness; The Judge's Wife; The After-Dinner Joke; Three More Sleepless Nights*; and *Hot Fudge*). London: Hern, 1990.

Ice Cream with Hot Fudge (contains *Ice Cream* and *Hot Fudge*). Prod. New York, 1990. New York: Samuel French, 1990.

Mad Forest. Prod. London, 1990. London: Hern, 1990.

Plays 2 (includes *Softcops*, *Top Girls*, *Fen*, and *Serious Money*). London: Methuen, 1990.

Lives of the Great Poisoners. With Orlando Gough and Ian Spink. Prod. London, 1991. London: Methuen, 1993.

The Skriker. Prod. London, National Theatre, 1994; London: Hern, 1994.

Secondary Sources

Aston, Elaine. *Caryl Churchill*. Plymouth, UK: Northcote, 1997.

"Caryl Churchill." In *Contemporary Authors*. New Revision Series. Vol. 46. Detroit: Gale, 1995. 68–73.

Cohn, Ruby. *Anglo-American Interplay in Recent Drama*. Cambridge: Cambridge UP, 1995.

Diamond, Elin. "Refusing the Romanticism of Identity: Narrative Intervention in Churchill, Benmussa, Duras." *Theatre Journal* 37 (October 1985): 273–286.

Domvros, Panayotis. " 'Alice Doesn't': Refusing the Seduction of the Narrative in Caryl Churchill's *Vinegar Tom*." *Gramma: Journal of Theory and Criticism* (1994): 47–60.

Gray, Frances. "Mirrors of Utopia: Caryl Churchill and Joint Stock." In *British and Irish Drama since 1950*. Ed. James Acheson. Basingstoke: Macmillan, 1993.

Henderson, Liza. "*Serious Money* and Critical Cost: Language in the Material World." *Theater* 19 (Summer–Fall 1988): 87–88.

Itzin, Catherine. *Stages in the Revolution: Political Theatre in Britain since 1968*. London: Methuen, 1986.

Keyssar, Helene. "The Dramas of Caryl Churchill: The Politics of Possibility." *Massachusetts Review* 24 (Spring 1983): 198–216.

Marohl, Joseph. "De-realised Women: Performance and Identity in *Top Girls*." *Modern Drama* (September 1987): 376–388.

———. "Caryl Churchill's *Mad Forest*: Polyphonic Representations of Southeastern Europe." *Modern Drama* 36 (December 1993): 499–511.

Neblett, Robert. " 'Nobody Sings About It': In Defense of the Songs in Caryl Churchill's *Vinegar Tom*." Paper presented at Central New York Conference on Literature and Language, SUNY Cortland, NY, October 1998.

Price, John A. "The Language of Caryl Churchill: The Rhythms of Feminist Theory, Acting Theory, and Gender Politics." Paper presented at Central New York Conference on Literature and Language, SUNY Cortland, NY, October 1998.

Quigley, Austin E. "Stereotype and Prototype: Character in the Plays of Caryl Churchill." In *Feminine Focus: The New Women Playwrights*. Ed. Enoch Brater. Oxford: Oxford UP, 1989. 25–52.

Randall, Phyllis, ed. *Caryl Churchill: A Casebook*. New York: Garland, 1988.

Reinelt, Janelle. "Beyond Brecht: Britain's New Feminist Drama." In *Feminist Theatre and Theory*. Ed. Helene Keyssar. New York: St. Martin's Press, 1996. 35–48.

———. "Feminist Theory and the Problem of Performance." *Modern Drama* 32 (March 1989): 48–57.

Solomon, Alisa. "Witches, Ranters, and the Middle Class: The Plays of Caryl Churchill." *Theater* 12 (Spring 1981): 49–55.

Swanson, Michael. "Mother/Daughter Relationships in Three Plays by Caryl Churchill." *Theatre Studies* 31–32 (1984–1985): 49–66.

Worthen, W.B., ed. *The HBJ Anthology of Drama*. New York: Harcourt, 1993.

Ivy Compton-Burnett
1884–1969

Jonathan Bolton

Readers of Ivy Compton-Burnett's fiction have been sharply divided in their response, finding her work either gruesome or hilarious, disturbing or delightful, artificial and stilted or subtly penetrating. Such disparate reactions account for both her critical neglect (especially in the United States) and her ardent following (especially in the United Kingdom). The retrospective settings and classical influence on her work, moreover, have made it difficult for critics to place her as either a modernist or a late Victorian. She was writing during the heyday of Virginia Woolf, James Joyce, and D.H. Lawrence, yet one is never admitted directly to the interior lives of her characters. She wrote much of her best work in the 1930s and 1940s, yet in her novels one gets no direct sense of that era's political upheaval, economic depression, and war. In many ways Compton-Burnett's reputation has suffered most from the uncontemporaneousness of her material, her extensive use of dialogue, her novels' plotlessness, and the narrow social milieu of her fiction, which typically centers on domestic crises related to marriage, death, inheritance, and sibling rivalries in upper-middle-class families living on a provincial estate during late Victorian England. While such factors help account for Compton-Burnett's relatively minor status, they also serve to diminish unfairly the significance of her achievement. Her exacting investigation of domestic conflicts and economies, her development of the dialogue novel, and her innovative blend of tragedy and black comedy constitute a valuable contribution to the modern novel.

BACKGROUND

When asked why she always set in her fiction in the past, Ivy Compton-Burnett replied: "I do not feel that I have any real organic knowledge of life later than about 1910. I should not write of later times with enough grasp or confidence. When an age is ended you see it as it is. And I have a dislike, which I cannot explain, of dealing with modern machinery and inventions. When war casts its shadow, I find I recoil" (Sprigge 115). There is, in fact, a quite logical explanation for Compton-Burnett's aversion to post-Edwardian life, and her "dislike" for later periods may be traced back to a series of family tragedies that destroyed the relative harmony of her early life.

Because of the domestic settings and preoccupation with family relations in her fiction, Compton-Burnett's family life is of special interest. She was the eldest child of Dr. James Compton-Burnett, a specialist in homeopathic medicine, and his second wife, Katherine Rees. Unlike the hostile, quarreling, or coldly detached families in her novels, the Compton-Burnett household was generally a happy one. The father was often away on medical calls, but was attentive and adoring toward his children when he was at home, and Katherine was a lively woman who loved to play charades with her children. The domestic harmony was completed by a kind governess, Minnie Smith, a likely prototype for what Marlon Ross has called "the educating spinster—especially the governess—[who is] a crucial figure in Compton-Burnett's fiction" (39). Compton-Burnett was encouraged in her scholarly endeavors. She was sent to Royal Holloway College, a women's college annexed by the University of London in 1900, where she studied classical literature. It was during this time, as Compton-Burnett's interest in Greek tragedy deepened, that family misfortune began. Her father died in 1902, and in 1904 her brother Guy succumbed to pneumonia, leaving Katherine, as biographer Elizabeth Sprigge puts it, "increasingly difficult and critical" (34). After taking a second in classics at Royal Holloway in 1906, Ivy was made tutor to her younger sisters, Stephanie and Topsy, and returned home to a mournful, tension-fraught home environment. Her mother died in 1911, leaving Ivy as legal guardian of her sisters. In 1916 her closest sibling, Noel, was killed in the war, and his death was succeeded by the double suicide, by overdose of veronal, of Stephanie and Topsy. In 1919 Compton-Burnett began a relationship, which she described as sexually "neuter," with Margaret Jourdain, an accomplished writer, first of poetry and then of books on interior decoration, with whom she cohabited for thirty-two years.

ANALYSIS

One of the earliest proponents of Compton-Burnett's fiction, Frederick Karl, has suggested that perhaps her foremost achievement was to have "taken the Victorian family novel and turned it inside out, revealing the dirt behind the romantic exterior" (177). Indeed, Compton-Burnett seems to have revived the Victorian family novel to expose the seamier side of Victorian family life, introducing features of classical tragedy—incest, patricide, infanticide, suicide, and illegitimacy—in order to reveal how numb and indifferent human beings are inclined to be toward the tragic events of life, and to disclose the self-interest, jealousy, hypocrisy, and insincerity inherent in human nature. This incongruity between the awfulness of what happens and her characters' indifferent response to the tragic is a common source of her disturbing comedy. The words of Justine, from *A Family and a Fortune*, seem to come straight from Compton-Burnett: "Oh, why are we laughing? Why cannot we take a serious view of what is serious and even tragic in itself?" (262). Her art also reverses the unrealistic moral imperatives of Victorian fiction so that vice is rewarded, and virtue very often is punished. Compton-Burnett's families are typically ruled by tyrannical patriarchs who, among other abuses of their power, neglect or insult their dependents, disinherit male heirs, marry too hastily after becoming widowers, and humiliate servants. As Andrzej Gasiorek has observed, "in her pessimistic worldview social structures encourage tyrannical behavior but do not create it; rather they allow egotism to flourish because they grant certain individuals outrageous latitude in their exercise of power" (27). In this view, human beings are intrinsically corrupt and predisposed to act out of self-interest. Therefore, social and economic institutions—marriage, class, primogeniture—exist to support and sanction the cutthroat instinct. In *A Father and His Fate*, for example, Miles Mowbray remarries after receiving news that his wife is presumed dead in a shipwreck, and then refuses to give up his new bride when the first wife returns; and Sir Godfrey Haslem, in *Men and Wives*, considers proposing to Camilla Bellamy upon the death of his wife, whose fortune he had been squandering during her hospitalization.

Although critics have been inclined to focus on Compton-Burnett's patriarchal despots, other members of her fictional families are equally unappealing and are typically engaged in some form of backbiting, selfish intention, manipulation, deceit, or violence. In many ways Compton-Burnett appears to have viewed human nature much the same way as her character Mrs. Jekyll from *A House and Its Head*: "She seems to impute evil to everyone she sees. I hate to look into her hard, old eyes" (223). Indeed, most all human motivation in her fiction can be traced back to self-interest, greed, or malice, and all claims to altruistic feeling are shown to be false and feigned. That is, in Compton-Burnett's fiction there are few characters capable of doing good, only characters bent on appearing to be good, and thus even self-sacrificial acts can be ascribed to self-interest and malice. For example, in *A Family and a Fortune*, altruistic deeds are clearly performed only to make other characters feel inadequate and self-centered, whereas those who stand to benefit from such acts encourage but do not imitate them. Early in the novel Dudley remarks: "It is a pity we have to be human. . . . Human failings, human vanity, human weakness! We don't hear the word applied to anything good. Even human nature seems derogatory." His niece, Justine, counters by saying, "Human charity, human kindness. . . . I think that gives us to think, Uncle." Dudley replies, "People are always so pleased about people's sacrifices. . . . I mean other people's. It is not very nice of them. I suppose it is only human" (30). As Dudley's remark suggests, the very encouragement of acts of charity and self-sacrifice is part of human indignity, for self-sacrifice in others is likely to benefit them personally. Justine, on the other hand, persists in acting, or claiming to act, in a self-sacrificial manner only to acquire the power or claim to goodness it bestows. Her selflessness, therefore, is a pose designed to conceal selfishness. In Compton-Burnett's fictional cosmology even kind acts stem from base intentions.

However, as a number of critics have noted, Compton-Burnett is not entirely misanthropic. Rather, in her view the flaws in human nature are more deeply rooted in economic and social structures outside the realm of individual human influence. Given her concern with hostility and rivalries within the family, her satirical targets are mainly the codes governing the inheritance of fortunes and management of estates and the corrupting influence of autocratic authority. Kathy Gentile has applied the proverb "To know all is to forgive all" to much of Compton-Burnett's work and argues that extrinsic social and economic factors are largely to blame for the corruption of Compton-Burnett's characters. As Justine remarks in *A Family and a Fortune*, "Dear, dear, money, money, money . . . directly it comes in, away fly dignity, decency, everything" (128). Indeed, for Compton-Burnett, to know and understand human nature and the social and economic structures that we create and are created by is to expect little in the way of "dignity" and "decency."

ASSESSMENT

Compton-Burnett's major technical achievement is perhaps her development of the dialogue novel. Her novels contain minimal description, and such detail is usually limited to introducing a character's dress and physical features, so that plot is advanced and character is revealed almost entirely through conversation. Compton-Burnett's characters, moreover, speak often in long, precisely formed, and artificially polished lines, and they often say things that one ordinarily keeps hidden—frank confessions of failure or villainy, claims to superior goodness or morality, cruel insults, and curious forms of self-revelation. Such odd dialogue certainly contributes to what many term the "eccentricity" of her fiction, but, as Nathalie Sarraute has pointed out, one must not take

Compton-Burnett's dialogue for realistic presentation. Rather, as Sarraute notes, her dialogue novels exist on two separate planes: the conversation level, which includes ordinary small talk, platitudes, and observations on the weather; and "sub-conversations," which constitute a verbalization or open articulation of what is thought, felt, and perceived but rarely spoken. Sarraute also includes as "sub-conversation" the precisely expressed, perfectly formed, "long, stilted sentences . . . [that] do not recall any conversations we have ever had" (155). In this sense Compton-Burnett has created, by forgoing any attempt at realistic representation of human intercourse, a dialogue that reveals sides to character that are normally concealed by politeness and manners. Robert Liddell describes the quality of her dialogue aptly when he writes, "[H]er idiom sometimes approximates to what one might actually say if one were in the character's skin and situation, but also to what one might think of saying and bite back; to what one might afterwards wish one had said" (99). Her characters, then, are able to express themselves perfectly, had they time to get it right, and are free to flatter themselves, insult others, and generally speak their mind with relative impunity. Clearly, critics who have complained of the lack of depth to her characters have not paid sufficient attention to her innovative use of dialogue, much of which should be read as the exterior expression of interior states of consciousness—what is often thought but rarely said.

The overall consistency and obsessive concerns of Compton-Burnett's twenty novels make it difficult to single out any one as being her masterpiece, and many critics have remarked on their inability to distinguish one novel from another. Compton-Burnett herself disowned *Dolores* (1911), her first novel, which is uncharacteristic but by no means unaccomplished. Her work of the mid- to late 1930s, including *A House and Its Head* (1935) and *A Family and a Fortune* (1939), are generally regarded as her most outstanding achievements, the latter representing a gentler take on human failings. Dissenting views of note include those of Charles Burkhart, who regards *Manservant and Maidservant* (1947) as the pinnacle of her career (*The Art* 158). Compton-Burnett herself felt that *Manservant and Maidservant* and the first two-thirds of *A Family and a Fortune* were probably her most accomplished works (Millgate 42).

BIBLIOGRAPHY

Primary Sources

Dolores. Edinburgh: Blackwood, 1911.
Pastors and Masters. London: Heath Cranton, 1925.
Brothers and Sisters. London: Heath Cranton, 1929.
Men and Wives. London: Heinemann, 1931.
More Women than Men. London: Heinemann, 1933.
A House and Its Head. London: Heinemann, 1935.
Daughters and Sons. London: Gollancz, 1937.
A Family and a Fortune. London: Gollancz, 1939.
Parents and Children. London: Gollancz, 1941.
Elders and Betters. London: Gollancz, 1944.
Manservant and Maidservant. London: Gollancz, 1947; New York: Knopf, 1949.
Two Worlds and Their Ways. London: Gollancz, 1949.
Darkness and Day. London: Gollancz, 1951; New York: Knopf, 1951.
The Present and the Past. London: Gollancz, 1953.
Mother and Son. London: Gollancz, 1955.
A Father and His Fate. London: Gollancz, 1957.
A Heritage and Its History. London: Gollancz, 1959.
The Mighty and Their Fall. London: Gollancz, 1961.
A God and His Gifts. London: Gollancz, 1963.
The Last and the First. London: Gollancz, 1971.

Secondary Sources

Baldanza, Frank. *Ivy Compton-Burnett*. New York: Twayne, 1964.
Burkhart, Charles, ed. *The Art of I. Compton-Burnett: A Collection of Critical Essays*. London: Gollancz, 1972.
———. *I. Compton-Burnett*. London: Gollancz, 1965.
———, ed. *Twentieth Century Literature* [Ivy Compton-Burnett issue] 25.2 (1979).
Dick, Kay. *Ivy and Stevie: Ivy Compton-Burnett and

Stevie Smith, Conversations and Reflections. London: Duckworth, 1971.
Gasiorek, Andrez. *Post-War British Fiction: Realism and After*. London: Edward Arnold, 1995.
Gentile, Kathy Justice. *Ivy Compton-Burnett*. New York: St. Martin's, 1991.
Grylls, R. Glynn. *I. Compton-Burnett*. Harlow, England: Longman, 1971.
Johnson, Pamela Hansford. *I. Compton-Burnett*. London: Longman, 1951.
Karl, Frederick R. *A Reader's Guide to the Contemporary English Novel*. New York: Farrar, Straus, 1972.
Liddell, Robert. *The Novels of I. Compton-Burnett*. London: Gollancz, 1955.
Millgate, Michael. "Interview with Ms. Compton-Burnett." In Burkhart, ed., *The Art of I. Compton-Burnett*.
Nevius, Blake. *Ivy Compton-Burnett*. New York: Columbia UP, 1970.
Sarraute, Nathalie. "Conversation and Sub-Conversation." In Burkhart, ed. *The Art of I. Compton-Burnett*.
Ross, Marlon. *Contented Spinsters Governessing and the Limits of Discursive Desire in the Fiction of Ivy Compton-Burnett*. Urbana: U of Illinois P, 1991.
Sprigge, Elizabeth. *The Life of Ivy Compton-Burnett*. New York: Braziller, 1973.
Spurling, Hilary. *Ivy: The Life of Ivy Compton-Burnett*. New York: Knopf, 1984.

Anne Devlin
1951–

Susanna Hoeness-Krupsaw

Like her namesake, the patriot Anne Devlin, who participated in Robert Emmet's rebellion of 1803, the writer Anne Devlin is concerned with the political situation in Ireland. Unlike her rebel namesake, however, she hopes for more peaceful means of reconciliation. Furthermore, as Christina Hunt Mahony points out in *Contemporary Irish Literature: Transforming Tradition*, Devlin investigates political issues that are often overlooked by other writers, such as "women's contribution to revolutionary situations in contemporary Ulster" (174).

BACKGROUND

Anne Devlin, Northern Irish playwright, screenwriter, and author of short stories and radio plays, was born in Belfast in 1951. Her father, Paddy Devlin (1923–1999), a trade unionist opposed to violence, was a member of the Social Democratic and Labour Party (SDLP) and a 1969 member of Parliament representing the Falls. Devlin was raised a Catholic and participated in the civil rights movement. She read English at the University of Ulster, Coleraine. Between 1974 and 1976 she taught English and drama at Dunluce Comprehensive School in Bushmills, County Antrim, and then lived in Freiburg, Germany, where she started writing fiction. She served as writer associate at the Royal Court Theatre (1985–1986), visiting tutor in playwriting at Birmingham University (1987 and 1989), and writer-in-residence at the University of Lund, Sweden (1990). Devlin now resides in Birmingham. She is married to the English producer Chris Parr and has one son.

Devlin has received many awards, including the Hennessy Literary Award in 1982 for her short stories, the Samuel Beckett Award for Television Drama in 1984 for *The Long March* and in 1988 for *A Woman Calling*, as well as the Susan Smith Blackburn Prize and the George Devine Award for *Ourselves Alone*.

ANALYSIS

Having published several short stories, Anne Devlin made her drama debut in 1982 with the broadcast of her first radio play. Two television dramas soon followed, *A Woman Calling* and *The Long March* (1984). She also contributed *Five Notes after a Visit* to the Thought Crimes Festival at the Barbican. Her publishing career continued with a collection of short stories entitled *The Way-Paver* (1986). One of the stories in this collection, "Naming the Names," was also made into a BBC television special in 1987, directed by Stuart Burge. This story anticipates many of Devlin's most important concerns: women's issues, relationships, the clash between Northern Irish and English, and the resulting violence affecting both public and private lives.

In "Naming the Names" a young Irish woman falls in love with the son of an English judge and lures him into an Irish Republican Army (IRA) trap. Police and friends are incredulous at her deed, but during police interrogation her memory flashbacks reveal her long initiation into violent and destructive behavior. Hugo Williams in a review for the *New Statesman* praised the story as "a frightening geography lesson calling a whole century's empire building into the witness box" ("Hooked" 27). He also noted that history is a very personal matter for Devlin, made by people rather than armies.

Devlin's first success on stage came with the play *Ourselves Alone*, coproduced in 1985 at the Liverpool Playhouse and at the Royal Court Theatre. In the foreword Devlin indicated that she "wanted to write about the women who lived in the Catholic ghetto in West Belfast" where she herself had grown up. She thought of the three main characters as a "trinity of women: the mother (Donna), the mistress (Josie), and the career woman (Frieda)." Devlin also points out that over the years she has found herself in all three roles.

The title of the play is a loose translation of the Gaelic term *sinn fein* (we ourselves), the name of the militant political branch of the Irish Republican Army. Yet in the foreword Devlin draws attention to her own journey "toward the maternal." Since she became a mother, her politics have changed, and death has no part in this play. It is set in Andersonstown, West Belfast, where Frieda pursues a career as a singer, but struggles to sing "her own songs" (234) and to cut herself loose from her family's nationalistic politics. Her sister Josie is politically active, but ends up pregnant with an English informer's child, while her sister-in-law Donna bears the burden of awaiting their brother Liam's return from prison and caring for his daughter Catherine.

Devlin's is a drama of ideas, not of action. Conflicts and characters are carefully developed through long conversations that some reviewers have found to be tedious, even rambling, monologues. Mel Gussow's review of the play's opening at the Kreeger Theatre/Arena Stage in Washington, D.C., although generally favorable to Devlin's handling of the three sisters' "death in life" in often-lyrical fashion, points up a shortcoming that others have also found, the one-dimensional, perhaps even stereotypical fashioning of the male characters (Lojek 66). Upon its return to the Theatre Upstairs, Benedict Nightingale observed more of the play's subtle nuances, such as the paralleling of the power relations between Irish and British and between Greta and her father and mother. The "mocking, antinationalistic, revisionist spirit" of Sean O'Casey's *The Plough and the Stars* (1926) also exists in Devlin's play (Sternlicht 138).

Published in the same volume as *Ourselves Alone* are the two television screenplays *The Long March* and *A Woman Calling*. *The Long March* deals with Helen's return to Belfast after a long stay in England. Almost immediately she becomes embroiled in political activities surrounding the hunger strike of IRA members in the Maze prison in 1979–1980. She observes that IRA violence is frequently directed against the innocent, like her father, an ardent union supporter. Helen concludes, "Sometimes I get so tired of the weight of being Irish" (154).

A Woman Calling deals with a young woman's recollection of a murder she witnessed as a girl. Emphasis on the past and on psychoanalysis as a means of coping anticipates many of Devlin's current interests. The Gothic atmosphere of this play anticipates her work on the film script for *Wuthering Heights*.

In *Heartlanders*, a cooperative effort by Devlin, Stephen Bill, and David Edgar for the City of Birmingham's centennial celebrations in 1989, issues of alienation and community come to the fore again. In this piece Devlin has joined her creative efforts to a project that highlights the possibilities that arise when people come together rather than being separated by matters of age, gender, class, and ethnicity. For this purpose, the authors used a large cast of more than one hundred diverse characters, Welsh, Afro-Caribbean, Indian, Polish, and English, who all converge upon the City of Birmingham. Initially struggling to communicate and "find" each other, they eventually form lasting bonds, and in the process of finding friends and family, they also find out something about their own identities.

Devlin's play *After Easter* premiered simultaneously at the Other Place in Stratford and at the Lyric Players Theatre in Belfast (1994). Devlin insisted that Irish actors be hired for the cast of the Royal Shakespeare Company (Headrick 1). Like *Ourselves Alone*, the play features a group of three sisters and their responses to the continued political upheavals in Belfast. While Aoife remained in Toomebridge, a town in Ulster, to raise a family much as her mother had done before her, Helen left home in order to become a successful commercial artist in London. The third sister, Greta, has also left Ireland for England, but her departure has caused serious mental and emotional consequences. By living abroad, she has lost her identity. This main character underscores a persistent question in Devlin's fiction and drama: what happens when people are treated like strangers in their own country? Devlin herself considers this play a "gift" in which she depicts women who illustrate facets of herself. Greta's insanity speaks to the Northern Irish troubles; her healing reveals Devlin's hopes for the future (Headrick 192). According to Clare Baylay's review, the play illustrates "a personal and spiritual exploration which evades simple explanation" (28).

While the play opened to excellent reviews in Stratford-upon-Avon, Irish critics at the Belfast Theatre Festival in 1994 were clearly less enthusiastic, criticizing Devlin's depiction of British soldiers as well as the formlessness of her play (Headrick). Even though the three women's relations appear at times strained, Devlin alludes to the idea that women's salvation may lie in their strengthening of small communities of women. If all else around them fails, this is the security network that may catch them, as indeed happens in Greta's case, as her sisters' care allows her to leave the English sanitarium. Greta in the end has been reconciled to both her sisters and, as Carol Headrick's astute interpretation indicates, in Greta's healing, the play's audience may see a symbol of Devlin's hope for a healing of the rift between English and Irish. Indeed, in an interview with Jane Coyle for the *Irish Times* Devlin affirmed these hopes (Headrick 193). Like Stewart Parker's *Pentecost*, this is a play about "reconciliation" (Murray 220), and like other Irish dramatists, Devlin does not just observe "cultural conditions" but "generates fresh possibilities" (Murray 247).

More recently Devlin has focused her efforts on screenplays for both television and big-screen movies. She appears to specialize in the transformation of (sometimes classical English) novels into successful adaptations. She prepared yet another version of Emily Brontë's *Wuthering Heights* for Paramount Pictures in 1991. Reviewers referred to the choice of cast as somewhat unfortunate; however, Devlin's version of the story includes Brontë herself (Sinead O'Connor), who arrives at the Heights wondering what her imagination might reveal about the ancient dwelling. The brevity of the film required many cuts in the action, making some of the scene changes and time passages a little awkward, but reviewer John Leonard lauded the inclusion of Cathy's daughter in Devlin's "scrupulous TV screenplay" (121).

A television adaptation of D.H. Lawrence's famous novel *The Rainbow* gave Devlin another chance at examining male-female relationships in the early part of the twentieth century. Her screenplay for *Titanic Town* is based on the autobiographical novel by Belfast writer Mary Costello, whose mother Tess worked toward a peace settlement in the 1970s. *Vigo* is a tragic love story inspired by the passionate relationship of the young cinematographer Jean Vigo and his wife Lydu. Devlin is currently preparing a screenplay, *Mrs. Jordan's Profession*, based on the biography of Claire Tomalin.

ASSESSMENT

Devlin's short stories do not elaborate visual details but emphasize dialogue. One reviewer praised them as "skillfully constructed" (Radin 31), while another considered them mere sketches with "one-dimensional characters" (Wesley 18). Both agreed, however, on Devlin's ear for dialogue, one reason perhaps why she has found her true métier in writing for stage, movies, and television. While the terseness of the exchanges she creates is reminiscent of Hemingway, she deftly interweaves deep psychological concerns into her stories.

Since Yeats's Irish Literary Revival, the Irish theater has flourished both in Dublin and in Belfast. Devlin concerns herself with the typical literary themes cited in Sanford Sternlicht's *Reader's Guide to Modern Irish Drama*: nationalism, Anglo-Irish conflict and its effect on intermarriages, family ties, and individuals, poverty, exile, and church power (31) all occur in her work coupled with a feminist touch. Fused in her work are also the two paths, the expressionist and the realist/naturalist, that Sternlicht thinks Irish drama has taken since Yeats and Lady Gregory (37).

Greta's biography in *After Easter*, for instance, following a realistic pattern established by other Devlin pieces, appears to parallel Devlin's own career. Greta's marriage to a Protestant Englishman alienated her from her family, country, and faith; consequently, she had to subdue her female identity and her Irish identity all at once. This silencing, a kind of Freudian repression, has inflicted serious psychological scars on the already-fragile character. Consequently, she has difficulty coping with marriage and motherhood and is periodically institutionalized to adjust her responses to an insane situation. Devlin handles Greta's mental problems in expressionistic manner when past and present intertwine in a conversation between Greta and her deceased father. Devlin questions whether, as Emily Dickinson put it, "much madness is divinest sense." Greta's sister Aoife puts a more chauvinistic spin on the issue when she says, "You are normal—it's the English who have a problem" (6).

But it is not only the Anglo-Irish relations that come under close scrutiny in Devlin's plays; male-female relationships are also examined. Greta has her share of marital troubles. The same is apparent in her younger sister's more traditional marriage. The older sister on the career path, however, has relinquished her traditional female role for frequently changing partners and a great deal of heartbreak and instability. Looking back at their childhood, Greta and her sisters come to question their parents' reasons for marriage. These two, the atheist political rebel and the devoutly Catholic homemaker and business owner, share nothing in common.

In his study of contemporary Irish drama Anthony Roche explains that Northern Ireland experiences the kind of political conflict that supplies the subject matter of which the best dramas are made. The unstable political structures affect the way dramas are written. As a matter of fact, Devlin's work exemplifies most of the features mentioned by Roche as "marked dramatic features that may collectively constitute a new genre" (216). She employs the "linguistic dissonances" Roche describes; that is, her characters often observe that their Irish accents alone turn them into exiles. For instance, Helen in *After Easter* prefers to sport an American accent while she visits Belfast in order to avoid the

English bureaucrats' scrutiny and prejudice. Oftentimes language fails to reveal adequately the experiences characters wish to describe.

Her plays are also "anti-hierarchical," highlighting the experiences of individuals within communities rather than of individualistic protagonists. Devlin seems to reject the notion of the well-made play. She defies notions of classical unity; action is often fragmented and discontinuous. Headrick underscores that female dramatists often reject earlier Aristotelian models of playwriting, opting purposely for looser structures that depict the "complexities of women's lives" more adequately. Catriona Clutterbuck's comparative study of Devlin's play and Brian Friel's *Dancing in Lughnasa* praises Devlin for her creation of the Greta character who finally realizes what Friel's play intended (118). Devlin succeeds in presenting a female character who finds her own voice, thus alluding to the fact that lack of speech underscores the effects of imperialism (103, 110).

C.L. Innes observes that Ireland is often depicted as Erin, mother or Virgin Mary. She easily falls prey to British imperialist assaults. Consequently, "the contestation of patriarchal authority is marked by a struggle to claim authority over Ireland." A trace of this pattern may be seen in Josie's preferring an Englishman over her Irish admirers. Despite the difficulty of her situation, she is also willing to carry his baby. Generally, it seems, however, that Devlin's women find English rule as oppressive as native Irish patriarchy: police raids and father Malachy occur in the same scene.

Anthony Roche reminds us that Northern Irish women writers may actually benefit from English politics. While Irish theaters have sometimes been reluctant to accept female playwrights at all, the Royal Court Theatre encourages feminist playwrights like Caryl Churchill, and it may well have become a "testing ground" even for Devlin's works (229).

Irish drama has always been interested in examining issues of memory and the past. "The best contemporary Irish playwrights," writes Roche, "are engaged in a search for dramatic means to reinterpret by reimagining that past. All offer alternative narratives whose aim is liberation, a setting free of ghosts" (12). This is exactly one of the motivations that drives the protagonist in "Passages" (later called *A Woman Calling*) to reveal her recurrent dream of a murder she overheard during her childhood to a psychologist whom she believes to be the murderer.

In several of *The Way-Paver*'s short stories dream and imagination are contrasted with everyday realities. One of Devlin's noteworthy storytelling techniques involves her counterpointing of current narrative with characters' memories. Oftentimes actions will parallel each other, and one character, the woman in "The Journey to Somewhere Else," wonders whether "the future was already a part of what I was becoming, and if I stopped this vacuum, there would be no future, only an endless repetition of moments from the past which I will be compelled to relive" (75). An interesting coincidence of scenes occurs in *Wuthering Heights* and in "Naming the Names." Just as Cathy attempts to stick her arm through the window in her old room, frightening both Lockwood and Heathcliffe, so Granny's outstretched arm tries to pull the protagonist of "Naming the Names" back into the past. Reviewer John Leonard refers to Brontë's work as a novel "about inheritance," and this must be, in the end, what attracted Devlin to the material, for she continues to demonstrate her interest in the power of memory and the imagination.

Devlin's characters' strong sense of fatedness or their fear of having provoked a bad turn of events, itself creating feelings of guilt and shame, may be a strong reminder of Devlin's Catholic Irish upbringing. While several characters, like Josie, for instance, make feeble attempts at breaking out of unhealthy situations, their Irishness or their femaleness eventually leads to a kind of paralysis. One is here reminded of Joyce's notion of the Irish paralysis that befalls the characters in *Dubliners* who forever wish to get away from Ireland, only to become more deeply immersed in its issues.

BIBLIOGRAPHY

Primary Sources

Ourselves Alone with A Woman Calling and The Long March. London: Faber, 1986.

The Way-Paver. London and Boston: Faber, 1986.

The Venus de Milo Instead (screenplay). Dir. Danny Boyle. BBC, 1987.

The Rainbow (screenplay). Dir. Stuart Burge. BBC1, 1988.

Heartlanders. With Stephen Bill and David Edgar. London: Nick Hern, 1989.

Wuthering Heights (screenplay). Dir. Peter Kosminsky. Paramount Films, 1992.

After Easter. London and Boston: Faber, 1994.

Titanic Town (screenplay). Dir. Roger Michell. 1998.

Vigo: A Passion for Life (screenplay). With Peter Ettedigue. Dir. Julien Temple. GB/France, 1999.

Secondary Sources

Anderson, Lisa M. "Anne Devlin." In *Irish Playwrights: 1880–1995: A Research and Production Sourcebook*. Ed. Bernice Schrank and William Demastes. Westport, CT: Greenwood, 1997.

Baylay, Clare. "A Passion for the Theatre of Ecstasy." Rev. of *After Easter*. *Independent* 25 March 1995: 28.

Bowden, Bryony. Rev. of *Wuthering Heights*. *TLS* 23 October 1992: 17.

Casey, Daniel J., and Linda M. Casey, eds. *Stories by Contemporary Irish Women*. Syracuse, NY: Syracuse UP, 1990.

Clutterbuck, Catriona. "*Lughnasa* after *Easter*: Treatments of Narrative Imperialism in Friel and Devlin." *Irish University Review: A Journal of Irish Studies* 29.1 (Spring and Summer 1999): 101–118.

Goodman, Walter. Rev. of *The Rainbow*. *New York Times* 4 August 1989: C26.

Gussow, Mel. Rev. of *Ourselves Alone*. *New York Times* 5 April 1987: 61:1.

Headrick, Charlotte. "Anne Devlin's *After Easter*: Towards Reconciliation." In *Contemporary Northern Irish Drama: Anne Devlin and John Boyd*. By Charlotte Headrick and John Countryman. *Working Papers in Irish Studies*. Ft. Lauderdale, FL: Department of Liberal Arts, Nova Southeastern University, 1996.

Innes, C.L *Woman and Nation in Irish Literature and Society, 1880–1935*. Athens: U of Georgia P, 1993.

Leonard, John. "Puberty Gone Awry." Rev. of *Wuthering Heights*. *New York* 5 December 1994: 121.

Lojek, Helen. "Difference without Indifference: The Drama of Frank McGuinness and Anne Devlin." *Eire-Ireland* 25.2 (1990): 56–68.

Mahony, Christina Hunt. *Contemporary Irish Literature: Transforming Tradition*. New York: St. Martin's, 1998.

Murray, Christopher. *Twentieth-Century Irish Drama: Mirror up to Nation*. Manchester and New York: Manchester UP, 1997.

Nightingale, Benedict. "Home Truth." Rev. of *Ourselves Alone*. *New Statesman* 24 January 1986: 31.

Radin, Victoria. "On the Map." Rev. of *The Way-Paver*. *New Statesman* 27 February 1987: 31.

Roche, Anthony. *Contemporary Irish Drama: From Beckett to McGuinness*. Dublin: Gill and Macmillan, 1994.

Solomon, Alisa. "Challenging Rhetoric." Rev. of *Ourselves Alone*. *Village Voice* 13 May 1997: 92.

Sternlicht, Sanford. *A Reader's Guide to Modern Irish Drama*. Syracuse, NY: Syracuse UP, 1998.

Wesley, Valerie Wilson. N.T. *New York Times Book Review* 31 July 1988: 18.

Williams, Hugo. "Hooked." Rev. of *Naming Names*. *New Statesman* 27 February 1987: 27.

———. "Poetry and Prose." Rev. of *A Woman Calling*. *New Statesman* 27 April 1984: 26.

Margaret Drabble
1939–

Joseph Zeppetello

One word that comes to mind when one thinks of the writing of Margaret Drabble is "boundless." She has written thirteen novels, numerous short stories, two biographies, three book-length works of nonfiction, plays, and essays in literary criticism and has edited two major revisions of *The Oxford Companion to English Literature*. She is a writer who seems to take no notice of the academic barriers between literary writing and academic writing. Her novels are full of literary and philosophical references, and the plot of her *The Witch of Exmoor* (1996) begins with the characters asking what type of society they would create if they were starting from scratch. We get a hint of Drabble's thoughts on this from the chapter title "The Veil of Ignorance," which comes from John Rawls's *Theory of Justice*. Drabble lives out her social concerns. In spite of the amount of time she spends on writing, she is well known for devoting time and resources to political causes that are in keeping with her Quaker-inspired social conscience.

Breaking into the literary scene in 1962 with her first novel, *A Summer Bird-Cage*, she was dismissed by some critics as a "girls' writer" and after publishing seven more novels was labeled a "Hampstead writer." In spite of dismissive criticism, Drabble studies have become a solid area for both the English and American literary academies. She is the subject of numerous book-length works of interpretation and criticism and dozens of doctoral dissertations. She continues to satisfy her reading public with thoughtful, somewhat dark, novels whose characters ask the big questions and listen pensively for the answers.

BACKGROUND

Margaret Drabble was born on June 5, 1939, in Sheffield, Yorkshire, England, to John Frederic Drabble, a barrister and county-court judge, and Marie Bloor Drabble, a Cambridge-educated schoolteacher. John Drabble's parents owned a sweets factory, and he worked his way to Cambridge University. Marie Bloor was a daughter of the "Methodist working class" and was the first member of her family to go to university. Both parents, however, shared a strong left-leaning political vision, and Margaret herself was a member of the Labour Party. Author A.S. Byatt is Margaret Drabble's older sister. She has another sister and a brother. All the Drabble girls went to the Mount, a Quaker boarding school, although it is not clear that the Drabbles were Quakers themselves. Joanne V. Creighton in *Margaret Drabble* claims that the Drabbles were sympathetic to Quaker values and beliefs, but Marie was an atheist, and John attended the Anglican church (19). Valerie Grosvenor Myer in *Margaret Drabble: A Reader's Guide* mentions that the Drabbles converted to the Quaker religion (16). In any case, the inherently egalitarian and hopeful values and beliefs of the Quakers, especially the belief in "the Light of God" in everyone, have a strong influence on Drabble's novels, as do the contrary Calvinist beliefs in a determined universe in which all are predestined, and free will is an illusion. Many of Drabble's characters puzzle over the themes of free will and determinism. Both Margaret Drabble and her sister A.S. Byatt went to Newnham College, Cambridge, their mother's alma mater, on scholarships.

Drabble married her first husband, the actor Clive Swift, soon after graduation in 1960, and both were members of the Royal Shakespeare Company. Although she enjoyed being an actress and was an understudy to famous women of the theater such as Judi Dench and Vanessa Redgrave, an early pregnancy changed the course of her professional life. Since she could play few parts and spent most of her time alone while her husband was at rehearsal or performing, Drabble began to write to fill her time. Her first novel, *A Summer Bird-cage*—the title is derived from a bittersweet comment by John Webster about marriage—was accepted for publication by Weidenfeld and Nicolson in 1962 after arriving unsolicited. The novel was an immediate popular success, but received mixed critical reviews. Some critics regarded the work as a "girls' book," while others thought of it as a "work of genius" (Hattersley). *A Summer Bird-Cage* is about the rivalry between two sisters. More than one critic has looked for parallels in the book between Margaret Drabble and her older sister, A. S. Byatt, and literary connections with the Brontës. Byatt published her own novel about the rivalry between two sisters, entitled *The Game*, in 1967.

By the mid-1980s Margaret Drabble had produced nine novels and had received critical acclaim as one of England's major writers. Her writing had gone through several major shifts of point of view and subject matter. *A Summer Bird-cage* (1962), *The Garrick Year* (1964), and *The Millstone* (1965), her first three novels, are all narrated in the first person by the main character and deal with the subjective and personal experiences of well-educated women coming of age in a new world where gender rules had gone through profound changes. Her next two novels, *Jerusalem the Golden* (1967) and *The Waterfall* (1969), both employ the third person; the former is entirely in the third person, and the latter alternates between third and first. They also show a departure from the feminine themes of the first three novels and take up issues of social mobility. In *The Needle's Eye* (1972), which is considered a breakthrough novel, Drabble introduces two protagonists, one male, Simon Camish, and one female, Rose Vassiliou, who reappears as a cameo in other novels. Her son, Konstantin, a child in *The Needle's Eye*, reappears as an adult supporting character in *The Gates of Ivory* (1991). Drabble employs a large cast of characters in what has been called the "Trilogy of the Thatcher Years"—*The Radiant Way* (1987), *A Natural Curiosity* (1989), and *The Gates of Ivory* (1991). *The Needle's Eye* marks the beginning of her middle novels, which include *The Realms of Gold* (1975), *The Ice Age* (1977), and *The Middle Ground* (1980), and reveals a change in the landscape and characters of Drabble's work. Simon is a trades lawyer, and Rose is an heiress struggling with her sense of social justice. Characters appear in this and subsequent novels from many layers of British society and explore larger emotional, sexual, and religious themes.

Feminists have always had an interest in Drabble, but she does not rest easily with many branches of feminism and can be called at best a moderate or "cautious" feminist (Moran 10). One thing that does bring Drab-

ble in line with more radical feminists is her exploration of the injustices suffered by women, especially well-educated, talented, and ambitious women who choose to have children and are suddenly limited in their possibilities to a world of diapers, car seats, and warmed-over oatmeal. She also addresses the problem of career women who in spite of long workdays are also expected to continue with traditional homemaking duties of raising children, cooking meals, and running households. These themes recur in many of her novels. In many ways Drabble resists being defined as a feminist writer; on the other hand, she is very much concerned with matters of equity and fairness between the sexes. However, she does not feel, as do some radical feminists, that there is something inherently wrong with the traditional aspects of the female role, except when those traditional aspects become unduly limiting because of an unequal sharing of the burden of those roles; and she is "eloquent in her denunciation of households in which both men and women work but the woman is expected to stop at noon and prepare lunch" (Hattersley).

In 1975 Drabble divorced Clive Swift and by this time had become a person of independent means. She has since continued to write, supporting herself through her novels, biographies, and articles and by editing *The Oxford Companion to English Literature*, which she describes as an "investment in my pension" (Hattersley). In the early 1980s Drabble married the biographer Michael Holroyd, but continued to live in Hampstead while he lived in west London. In 1996 she moved to join Michael Holroyd after twelve years of marriage. After twenty-nine years the "Hampstead writer" left Hampstead. The name stuck even though two recent novels, *The Gates of Ivory* (1991) and *The Witch of Exmoor* (1996), never even mention Hampstead; the former is set partly in Cambodia.

Drabble is a writer who had early success, winning the John Llewellyn Rhys Memorial Prize for *The Millstone* (1965), the James Tait Black and E.M. Forster awards, and the CBE in 1980. She continues to write critically acclaimed novels and to work steadily as an author and editor.

ANALYSIS

In "Spots of Joy in the Midst of Darkness: The Universe of Margaret Drabble," Mary H. Moran writes, "Margaret Drabble's fiction portrays a bleak, often menacing universe, ruled over by a harsh deity who allows human beings very little free will" (32). Many of Drabble's characters struggle with the internal constraints of personality type and the external constraints of money, power, and social position. In many cases Drabble seems to be a Freudian determinist when it comes to the personalities of her characters. In *The Realms of Gold* Francis Wingate, an archaeologist, Drabble's first strong, successful, professional female character and a late-twentieth-century role model for the liberated woman, is not quite able to accept Freud's views of women, but becomes "more and more convinced that what every woman wanted was a man, and that what every man wanted was a woman, and if they didn't want that they ought to" (*Realms* 185). While Francis Wingate finds a successful conclusion with a heterosexual marriage, Rose Vassiliou in *The Needle's Eye* returns to her abusive husband.

These two characters in the middle Drabble novels underscore a recurring paradox in her work. While her characters live in a darkly determined universe where free will is almost nonexistent, they seem at the same time to have Nietzschean origins. Rose Vassiliou creates her own existential and moral space from which she views and interprets the world. Her act of renouncing her wealth and choosing to live in poverty shows a level of existential choosing that more often than not baffles Simon Camish. But, if anything, Rose is an ironic Nietzschean heroine, and

Drabble makes a point of this in the last paragraph:

> She [Rose] looked at a wall: one of the lions had been broken, . . . the lion: shabby, weathered, crudely cast in a cheap mould . . . was hollow inside. . . . She remembered the beasts on the gateposts at Branston [her childhood home] elevated, distinguished, aristocratic . . . the shabby mass-produced creature before her was one with the houses. . . . Half its head was gone. It was one of many. Somebody had written on it, years ago, in red paint: SPURS [A reference to a work by Nietzsche] . . . it was a beast of the people. (*Needle's Eye* 368–369)

Other philosophical issues are explored in Drabble's novels, including the ethical ideas of Kant, where actions are judged to be good only in and of themselves, and Mill, who argued that the opposite was true—that the goodness or badness of an action needs to be determined only by consequential good or evil. In *The Witch of Exmoor* the main characters, a privileged group of the upper class, play a parlor game called the Veil of Ignorance, which comes from the work of the twentieth-century philosopher John Rawls, where the participants are asked to imagine a "just society" that they would accept if they had no foreknowledge of their own place in it. The fact that they cannot seem to arrive at a new social arrangement, and their eventual return to their real reason for gathering—to discuss what is to be done about Frieda, their very eccentric mother, who is endangering the family fortune with her erratic behavior—shows the humor and irony of Drabble. It would be a difficult thing indeed for the privileged to see the world through the eyes of the less fortunate, and impossible for them not to be myopic regarding the fate of their personal fortunes. This is the basic irony of the well-educated, socially responsible, upper-middle class that Drabble knows so well. Nietzsche, however, and his concepts of socially constructed good and evil, recur in much of her writing as she continually explores the tension between a deterministic universe and the human need for self-creation. The mystical concept of good and evil being one and the same are part of her "festering subplots," especially in *The Radiant Way* and *A Natural Curiosity*.

Drabble, however, is not a philosopher. She is a novelist and interweaves webs of images by bringing ideas together from various disciplines that are historically separated in the academic world. References to literary and theological works such as *The Pilgrim's Progress*, the Koran, and the Bible are juxtaposed with images from classical painting and allusions to Shakespeare, Milton, and other canonical writers, along with references to Freud and Marx, as well as Enlightenment, Renaissance, Christian, and ancient Greek philosophers. Some of her novels come complete with bibliographies, and as Valerie Grosvenor Myer puts it, "It is always unwise not to check Drabble's references, integral to her webs of imagery; it does not do to under-estimate her learning" (149).

Two common criticisms of Drabble are (1) that she is a "Hampstead writer" who is preoccupied with the world from the point of view of the privileged and comfortable middle class, and (2) that she is essentially a "women's writer," in the very negative sense of the word—that she is a "lightweight." While it is true that even *The Witch of Exmoor* deals with a prosperous family wrestling with the idea of inherent social injustice, and that her characters can be absolutely self-absorbed, like Simon Camish, and wrapped in their own personalities, like Francis Wingate, there is always room in their lives for them to integrate with the outside world in a progressive and high-minded way. Simon helps Rose Vassiliou keep her estranged husband from kidnapping her children and in turn gets a glimpse of her personal moral vision. While Drabble's novels are peopled with comfortably middle-class characters, the juxtaposition of the intuitive and the rational, the ever-present social consciousness, the rich philosophical and literary imagery,

Ivory." *Twentieth Century Literature* 45 (Fall 1999): 278–298.

Brownley, Martine Watson. *Deferrals of Domain: Contemporary Women Novelists and the State*. New York: St. Martin's, 2000.

Creighton, Joanne V. *Margaret Drabble*. London: Methuen, 1985.

Hannay, John. *The Intertextuality of Fate: A Study of Margaret Drabble*. Columbia: U of Missouri P, 1986.

Hattersley, Roy. "The Guardian Profile: The Darling of Hampstead." *Guardian* 26 June 1999; n.p. Online. Proquest. 20 June 2000.

Kenyon, Olga. *Women Novelists Today: A Survey of English Writing in the Seventies and Eighties*. Brighton: Harvester, 1988.

Moran, Mary Hurley. *Margaret Drabble: Existing within Structures*. Carbondale: Southern Illinois UP, 1983.

Myer, Valerie Grosvenor. *Margaret Drabble: A Reader's Guide*. London: Vision, 1991; New York: St. Martin's, 1991.

———. *Margaret Drabble: Puritanism and Permissiveness*. London: Vision, 1974; New York: Barnes & Noble, 1974.

Rose, Ellen Cronan, ed. *Critical Essays on Margaret Drabble*. Boston: G.K. Hall, 1985.

———. *The Novels of Margaret Drabble: Equivocal Figures*. London: Macmillan, 1980. Tocown, NJ: Barnes and Noble, 1980.

Roxman, Susanna. *Guilt and Glory: Studies in Margaret Drabble's Novels, 1963–80*. Stockholm: Almqvist, 1984.

Rubenstein, Roberta. "Fragmented Bodies/Selves/Narratives: Margaret Drabble's Postmodern Turn." *Contemporary Literature* 35.1 (Spring 1994): 136–155.

Sadler, Lynn Veach. *Margaret Drabble*. Boston: Twayne, 1986.

Schmidt, Dorey, ed. *Margaret Drabble: Golden Realms*. Living Author Series 4. Edinburg, TX: Pan American University, School of Humanities, 1982.

Seale, Jan and Dorey Schmidt. "Spots of Joy in the Midst of Darkness: The Universe of Margaret Drabble." In *Margaret Drabble: Golden Realms*. Ed. Jan Seale. Edinburg, TX: Pan American U, 1982.

Skoller, Eleanor Honig. *The In-between of Writing: Experience and Experiment in Drabble, Duras, and Arendt*. Ann Arbor: U of Michigan P, 1993.

Soule, George. *Four British Women Novelists: Anita Brookner, Margaret Drabble, Iris Murdoch, and Barbara Pym*. Pasadena, CA: Salem, 1998.

Stovel, Nora Foster. *Margaret Drabble: Symbolic Moralist*. Mercer Island, WA: Starmont House, 1989.

Wojcik-Andrews, Ian. *Margaret Drabble's Female Bildungsromane: Theory, Genre, and Gender*. New York: Lang, 1995.

Maureen Duffy
1933–

Regina M. Buccola

Maureen Duffy is a prolific writer who lacks the recognition her impressive corpus seems by right to command and who enjoys what critical acclaim she has secured to date primarily for her work in fiction, a genre to which she had to be lured from her first literary loves, poetry and playwriting. The call to the novel came when Duffy was teaching for the South London school system in 1961. Determined "to take the make or break chance and try to live as a professional writer," Duffy had been reducing her teaching load and "had written three full-length stage plays and joined, in so far as there was a semi-official membership, the Royal Court writers' group which included at that time John Arden, Edward Bond, Ann Jellicoe and Arnold Wesker" (*That's How It Was*, Preface v). A publisher and friend suggested that she attempt a novel. Duffy agreed to try, and the experiment produced *That's How It Was*, a tender memoir of growing up half Irish and fatherless in World War II–era Britain, a relentless examination of the brutal realities of lives lived out in abject poverty, and a subtle exploration of the forces that combined to create Maureen Duffy, lesbian feminist poet, playwright, novelist, social historian, literary scholar, and animal rights activist.

Duffy relied on her experience as a playwright to produce much of the novel's gritty realism: "I had tried in my plays to deal with working-class life in language as concrete and evocative as I could write it, to create a kind of neo-Jacobethan that was based on precise observation and this was the style I carried over into the novel" (Preface vi). This style and these aesthetic and sociocultural considerations have continued to mark Duffy's work over the past four decades. Duffy has produced an impressive body of work that includes fourteen plays for stage, radio, and television; fifteen novels; six collections of poetry, culminating with her *Collected Poems*; and numerous works of literary criticism, including one of the earliest successful efforts to incorporate the work of seventeenth-century playwright and novelist Aphra Behn into the literary canon. Duffy has also twice forayed into nonfiction prose with sociohistorical works in which her thorough research is embellished by her imaginative hypothetical reconstructions of the periods with which she is concerned. Duffy's socialist political sensibilities emerge in her persistent confrontation in all genres with the social tensions generated by class conflict, patriarchal power structures, castigation of homosexuality, and racism, ethnocentrism, and speciesism. Her work is feminist in the fully politicized sense of the word. In the mid-1980s and early 1990s she put her activist spirit to work on behalf of British writers by serving as president of the Writers' Guild of Great Britain and chairing the Authors' Lending and Copyright Society. In the latter position Duffy proposed unique publishing agreements and copyright legislation greatly beneficial to British writers (Fritz 24).

BACKGROUND

Maureen Duffy was born on October 21, 1933, in Worthing, Sussex, England. Her father, Cahia Patrick Duffy, was an Irishman who abandoned Duffy and her mother, Grace Rose Wright, when Duffy was an infant. The two scavenged their way across England during the difficult years leading up to and following World War II, Duffy's tubercular mother managing always to keep her daughter in school. Duffy memorializes Wright and the dramatic impact her mother's commitment to education had upon her in *That's How It Was*.

The intensely autobiographical novel paints a viscerally realistic portrait of the grim realities of poverty tempered by the tender exuberance that marks the devoted love between mother and daughter. The novel includes examples of Duffy's poetic juvenalia, overtly charting her adolescent determination to "follow in the penprints of my hero Keats" (Preface x), and implicitly reveals her ideological debt to Sartre, Kierkegaard, and Freud. Duffy also describes her first visit to the theater in the novel, an outing to a production of *Hamlet* arranged by her teacher and love object. Her account of this experience is revelatory of Duffy's attitudes toward the dramatic arts and their potential social influence:

> Listening to the conversations around me I realized that other people regarded the whole thing as a diversion, as nothing to do with the reality of work and home, yet to me what was happening down there was more real than they were. . . . The last act was terrible in its implications . . . I knew now the meaning of catharsis. The applause seemed sacriligious. (200)

Relentlessly forthright and frank in her portrayals of life as it is lived on society's margins, Duffy consistently forces those who read her poems and novels or who experience her plays to look straight on at those members of society typically relegated to a peripheral position. Art is not a diversion to her but a potent form of social critique and catalyst for change.

However, Duffy is keenly aware that even her chosen mode of drawing attention to society's marginal members is itself marginalized. *Memorials of the Quick and the Dead* begins with several witty poems about being a poet, about society's simultaneous need for the "culture" that a poet provides and its disregard for the people who produce the work that constitutes the material of that culture. As Duffy wryly notes in "A Letter to Whom It Doesn't Concern," England does not care "if Shakespeare's child's children beg" as long as tourists to Stratford-upon-Avon continue to pour money into the national coffers (9).

Duffy's *Collected Poems* opens with an epigram to her hero, Keats, and poems throughout the collection offer homage to her literary influences. The poems from *The Venus Touch*, like the sonnet sequences of Duffy's lesbian feminist poet contemporary Adrienne Rich, offer images in which lesbians can find themselves. Duffy offers playful, woman-centered tribute to a number of her literary forefathers, including Andrew Marvell and T.S. Eliot (deflected through Shakespeare's *The Tempest*), in *Evesong*, but it is in *Memorials of the Quick and the Dead* that she most directly addresses both her own poetic sensibilities and those of other writers. Duffy writes her own versions of many of Elizabeth Barrett Browning's *Sonnets from the Portugese* and in "Song of Ignorance" revisits nursery rhyme from a Blakean perspective focused on the interconnection of all elements of the natural world and indicative of Duffy's own commitment to animal rights. The collection also includes a series of poems directly addressed to her poet peers, including John Berryman and Seamus Heaney as well as her poet hero, Keats. Though Duffy has a positive relationship with her poetic forefather Keats, she has a much more complicated, antagonistic relationship to Freud, whose psychoanalytic theories emerge in both her creative work and her literary criticism. *A Nightingale in Bloomsbury Square* is Duffy's theatrical attempt to confront both her frustration with the failure of another of her literary influences, Virginia Woolf, to pursue her feminist inclinations as fully as she might have and her resentment of the heterosexist bias of Freud's psychoanalytic methodology. In her examination of the occurrence of fairy lore in literature from classical times to the twentieth century, *The Erotic World of Faery*, Duffy identifies Freud as second only to the Christian church in the repressive force he exerted upon the homosexual and bisexual tendencies that Duffy identifies as utterly natural. It is her premise in this thorough literary-critical and sociohistorical analysis that fairy figures in both popular lore and its invocation in literature of all periods and places serve as outlets for erotic impulses that are suppressed by dominant social forces, such as the church, as well as Freudian theories of psychosexual development. The depth and breadth of Duffy's literary and cultural knowledge are immediately apparent in this impressive work, in which the intellectualism that at times disrupts the flow of her fiction is set to best advantage.

ANALYSIS

Critics have been stymied by both the style and content of much of Duffy's work, particularly her fiction and drama. Critics lauded her first novel, *That's How It Was*, perhaps in part because the autobiographical tenor of the work produced a straightforward narrative line that is not characteristic of the rest of her fiction. Duffy frequently adopts a stream-of-consciousness narrative style to present a pastiche of characters and their personal stories; often the interconnections between and among these plot strands are not obvious. Duffy shares these attributes with another of her literary predecessors, James Joyce, but is often castigated for mere mimicry of her modernist forefather by critics who fail to see the unique use that she makes of Joycean techniques.

In *The Microcosm*, for example, Duffy relies on a certain amount of authorial obfuscation to make the reader feel as much an outsider as the lesbian women inhabiting the subsociety suggested by the novel's title. The fragments that make up the novel's narrative include such diverse elements as interior monologues strongly phonetically marked with regional and period-specific dialect by characters to whom the reader is never formally "introduced"; a lengthy, unpunctuated, uncapitalized passage reminiscent of the Molly Bloom chapter in Joyce's *Ulysses*; and the story of the warrior queen Boadicea provided by Matt, the character whose thoughts the reader most closely follows.

While most critics are free with their praise of Duffy's easy portrayal of lesbian sexuality and the vivid detail with which she depicts both character and scene in *The Microcosm*, many are frustrated with the novel's complexity. As one reviewer put it, "[I]t takes Matt over 300 pages to discover the obvious: deviants are not like most people, and to live solely in the Lesbian world—a subculture Matt once viewed as a microcosm of the rest of society—is actually to remove oneself from life" (Dienstag 21). However, this assessment misses Duffy's central point: rather than emphasizing the differences between social deviants and the dominant members of society, she seems instead to be demonstrating how very similar the struggle to live and love is for people of all social classes, sexual preferences, and time periods (hence Boadicea).

Duffy pursued the same narrative style in

her loose trilogy of novels, *Wounds*, *Capital*, and *Londoners*. The trio focuses on the lives of lesbian women in Duffy's beloved London, paying it the sort of homage Joyce sought to pay Dublin in *Ulysses* and employing a similar narrative strategy to do so (Werson 279). Offered similar material in a similar form, critics had much the same response to these works as they had to *The Microcosm*. Of *Wounds* Clive Jordan asserted, "Such structural links as there are hardly offer themselves easily and the extreme discontinuity of the narrative makes for difficult reading which does not always yield its own reward" (22). On a more positive note, however, Sara Blackburn defends Duffy's work in *Wounds*, noting that "Duffy's failures are always in reaching too far, never in being content with accomplishing too little" (8). Like *The Microcosm*, all three of the novels in this trilogy sweep through time (e.g., Al, the central character in *Londoners*, blurs the lines between the 1960s London she inhabits and the medieval Paris of François Villon, whose poetry she is translating).

Duffy offers similar intellectual and chronological breadth in another of her early novels, *Love Child*, set in late 1960s Italy but reliant on classical Greek myth as well as early-twentieth-century Freudian theory for much of its content. Though many critics again balked at the hyperintellectual character of the novel—particularly because the narrator is an extremely precocious child—James R. Frakes perceived the attribute that marks not only this novel, but much of Duffy's work when he noted that the child-narrator's sexual ambiguity serves as "an effective metaphor in which Unisex represents the rarefied atmosphere of a class" (2).

In two of her best-known plays, *Rites* and *A Nightingale in Bloomsbury Square*, Duffy also conflates sex and class while performing in divergent ways the disruptions of chronology that mark her fiction. *Rites* contemporizes Euripides' *The Bacchae*, setting a similarly impotent brand of violently destructive rage in a public women's restroom in London. As Victoria Sullivan and James Hatch note in their introduction to the play, the lower-class women who serve as the central characters of *Rites* "are neither educated nor consciously liberated, yet they possess a gut-level recognition of the inequities of the [capitalist, patriarchal] system" (xiii). Acutely aware of her precarious position in the sexual marketplace, the character who dominates the action in *Rites*, the washroom matron Ada, pauses in her cosmetic ministrations before the mirror to observe the necessity of "making the best of what you've got. It's not much and you've got to tart it up a bit to sell it high. After all the goods are all the same when they get the wrapping off. You've got to make them pay for the wrapping off. It's the first law of finance" (355). A voice for the play's castigation of social oppression predicated on gender and class, Ada also instigates the orgy of man-hating violence that concludes the play, in which a murderous group assaults a sexually ambiguous figure whom they discover too late is actually a woman. In her own introductory comment on the play Duffy observes that Ada "is society's product if not victim. All reduction of people to objects, all imposition of labels and patterns to which they must conform, all segregation can lead only to destruction" (351). Despite the violence of the play's conclusion, Michelene Wandor finds *Rites* emancipatory for women insofar as it enables "the power that women have as social beings to be theatrically explored" (100). In her dramatic work Duffy not only tends to foreground women's issues, but also strives to offer more and better roles for female performers (Fritz 24). The only men who appear on stage in *Rites* are the silent, uniformed figures who construct the set, suggesting the way in which male power circumscribes and contains both women and female space (Wandor 98), and the young son of one of the women who enters the washroom, portrayed by "a lifesize toddler boy doll" that should, according to Duffy's stage directions, "be as realistic as possible" (367).

A Nightingale in Bloomsbury Square involves three performers, but the vast majority of the text is put into the mouth of the central character, Virginia Woolf. In *Nightingale* Duffy imaginatively re-creates the day of Woolf's suicide, conveniently resurrecting Freud to serve as an external sounding board for her final reflections and self-analyses. Standing in stark opposition to the wild dancing and frenzied gang murder of *Rites*, *Nightingale* earned criticism when it was staged in 1973 for the marked lack of dramatic conflict and action (Sizemore, "Virginia Woolf" 130 n. 12). Duffy has written plays for radio performance, and *Nightingale* is perhaps best presented in that forum. A simultaneous study of and assault upon psychoanalysis, the play is completely driven by dialogue. At times the hyperintellectual banter between Woolf and Freud becomes tedious, yet there are moments when Duffy's imaginative reconstructions of Woolf's aesthetic, intellectual, and personal motivations are quite brilliant. Expressing her restlessness with the insularity of the celebrated Bloomsbury group, Duffy has Woolf exclaim, "I liked to go out and crack people's bones at parties to taste the pith of them, gulp and cannibalize an evening of all its oddity and excitement and salt every experience away till I need to take it out and unfurl it" (176). Duffy cannibalized Woolf's own diaries to produce this remarkable passage (Sizemore, "Virginia Woolf" 125); *Nightingale* is, in essence, a patchwork quilt of Woolf's and Freud's writings, including both their published work and unpublished documents such as letters and diaries. Duffy thoroughly researches her creative work and exercises her considerable imaginative creativity in her scholarly work. In 1994 she published a biography of the seventeenth-century British composer Henry Purcell. The work was well received critically, largely because of Duffy's success in combining "a formidable amount of scholarship" with "a very welcome inclination to dramatize wherever possible" (Rev. of *Henry Purcell*, *Publishers Weekly* 70). Duffy's success in the many genres she has attempted stems from her unique ability to inject drama into her scholarship, poetry into her prose, and narrative into her verse.

ASSESSMENT

Maureen Duffy's work embodies the feminist mantra "The personal is political" by virtue of her persistent use of art to stimulate critical thought about issues of class, gender, sexual orientation and animal rights. At times, particularly in her poetry, her politicization can overwhelm her aesthetics. While many critics have found Duffy's fiction no more moving than an equally well researched political treatise, such a response fails to consider the care that Duffy takes in bringing her characters to life. She personalizes social issues by creating vivid characterizations of the people who live through them. Brought to care about the characters, the reader is inevitably drawn to care about the social pressures they face. As Leah Fritz notes, "One is moved not so much by the characters' reactions to events as by the introspection these reactions and events evoke" (25).

Duffy's drama and fiction in particular have begun to gain a new audience among lesbian feminists; *The Microcosm* was republished in a Virago Modern Classics edition. Persistent in her social criticism and in her optimism about the possibilities for change, Duffy is, perhaps, a writer ahead of her time. Willfully committed to pursuing nontraditional narrative strategies devoted to people and issues that range from unpopular to vilified, Duffy has forgone critical acclaim in favor of pointed social criticism. Duffy is a thinking woman's writer, and her works offer rich rewards to those willing to work for them.

BIBLIOGRAPHY

Primary Sources

The Lay-Off (play). Prod. London, 1961.
That's How It Was. London: Hutchinson, 1962.

A Blush of Shame. By Domenico Rea. Trans. Maureen Duffy. London: Barrie & Rockliff, 1963.
The Single Eye. London: Hutchinson, 1964.
The Microcosm. 1966. London: Virago, 1989.
The Paradox Players. London: Hutchinson, 1967.
The Silk Room (play). Prod. Watford, 1966.
Lyrics for the Dog Hour. London: Hutchinson, 1968.
Wounds. New York: Knopf, 1969.
Olde Tyme (play). Prod. Cambridge, 1970.
Love Child. New York: Knopf, 1971.
The Venus Touch (poems). London: Weidenfeld, 1971.
The Erotic World of Faery. London: Hodder, 1972.
Actaeon (poems). Rushden, Northamptonshire: Sceptre, 1973.
All Heaven in a Rage. New York: Knopf, 1973.
A Nightingale in Bloomsbury Square (play). In *Factions*. Ed. Giles Gordon and Alex Hamilton. London: Michael Joseph, 1974.
Rites. In *Plays by and about Women*. Ed. Victoria Sullivan and James Hatch. New York: Vintage, 1974. 353–377.
Capital: A Fiction. London: Cape, 1975.
Evesong (poems). London: Sappho, 1975.
Housespy. London: Hamilton, 1978.
Memorials of the Quick and the Dead (poems). London: Hamilton, 1979.
Inherit the Earth: A Social History. London: H. Hamilton, 1980.
Gor Saga. London: Methuen, 1981.
Scarborough Fear. London: Macdonald, 1982.
Londoners: An Elegy. London: Methuen, 1983.
Men and Beasts: An Animal Rights Handbook. London: Paladin, 1984.
Collected Poems. London: Hamilton, 1985.
Oroonoko and Other Stories. By Aphra Behn. Ed. Maureen Duffy. London: Methuen, 1986.
Change. London: Methuen, 1987.
Five Plays. By Aphra Behn. Ed. Maureen Duffy. London: Methuen, 1990.
Illuminations: A Fable. London: Sinclair-Stevenson, 1991.
Occam's Razor. London: Flamingo, 1993.
Henry Purcell. London: Fourth Estate, 1994.

Secondary Sources

Barron, Janet. "Kindly Light." *New Statesman and Society* 17 May 1991: 36–37.
Blackburn, Sara. "The World Beyond." *Washington Post Book World* 31 August 1969: 8.
Brimstone, Lyndie. " 'Keepers of History': The Novels of Maureen Duffy." In *Lesbian and Gay Writing: An Anthology of Critical Essays*. Ed. Mark Lilly. Basingstoke: Macmillan, 1990. 23–46.
Dienstag, Eleanor. "Members of the Club." *New York Times Book Review* 11 August 1968: 20–21.
Frakes, James R. "Privileged Monster." *Washington Post Book World* 11 April 1971: 2.
Fritz, Leah. "In a Class by Herself." *Women's Review of Books* 5.2 (November 1987): 24–25.
Jordan, Clive. "Dangerous Doodles." *New Statesman and Society* 78 (4 July 1969): 21–22.
Lassner, Phyllis. "Fiction as Historical Critique: The Retrospective World War II Novels of Beryl Bainbridge and Maureen Duffy." *Phoebe* 3.2 (Fall 1991): 12–24.
Marowski, Daniel G., ed. "Maureen Duffy." In *Contemporary Literary Criticism* 37. Detroit: Gale, 1986.
Newman, Jenny. "Mary and the Monster: Mary Shelley's *Frankenstein* and Maureen Duffy's *Gor Saga*." In Where No Man Has Gone Before: Women and Science Fiction. Ed. Lucie Armitt. London: Routledge, 1991. 85–96.
Partnow, Elaine T. "Maureen Duffy." In *The Female Dramatist: Profiles of Women Playwrights from the Middle Ages to Contemporary Times*. New York: Facts on File, 1988. 63–64.
Rev. of *Henry Purcell*, by Maureen Duffy. *Publishers Weekly* 13 May 1996: 70.
Rev. of *The Paradox Players*, by Maureen Duffy. *Books and Bookmen* 13.1 (October 1967).
Rev. of *The Paradox Players*, by Maureen Duffy. *New Yorker* 5 October 1968: 181–182.
Rule, Jane. *Lesbian Images*. London: Peter Davies, 1976.
Scott, Mary. "Over the Edge." *New Statesman and Society* 16 July 1993: 40.
Sizemore, Christine. *A Female Vision of the City: London in the Novels of Five British Women*. Knoxville: U of Tennessee P, 1989.
———. "Virginia Woolf as Modernist Foremother in Maureen Duffy's Play *A Nightingale in Bloomsbury Square*." In *Unmanning Modernism: Gendered Re-readings*. Ed. Elizabeth Jane Harrison and Shirley Peterson. Knoxville: U of Tennessee P, 1997. 117–132.
Smith, Patricia Juliana. "Maureen Duffy." In *The Gay and Lesbian Literary Heritage: A Reader's Companion to the Writers and Their Works, from Antiquity to the Present*. Ed. Claude J. Summers. New York: Holt, 1995. 208–209.
Sullivan, Victoria, and James Hatch, eds. Introduction to *Plays by and about Women*. New York: Vintage, 1974.

Wandor, Michelene. "Transitional Pioneers: *Vagina Rex and the Gas Oven* by Jane Arden and *Rites* by Maureen Duffy." In *Look Back in Gender: Sexuality and the Family in Post-war British Drama*. New York: Methuen, 1987. 95–100.

Werson, Gerard. "Maureen Duffy." In *British Novelists since 1960: Part 1:* A–G. Vol. 14 of *Dictionary of Literary Biography*. Detroit: Gale, 1983. 273–282.

Winkler, Elizabeth Hale. "Three Recent Versions of *The Bacchae*." In *Madness in Drama*. Themes in Drama 15. New York: Cambridge UP, 1993.

Buchi Emecheta
1944–

Jerilyn Fisher

> All I ever wanted was to tell stories from my home, just like my big mother Nwakwaluzo used to tell her stories in her very own compound with her back leaning against the *ukwa* tree.
>
> (*Head above Water* 227)

At home in both England and Nigeria, Buchi Emecheta claims an ever-widening circle of diverse readers and critics who are intrigued by her tales of girls and women stymied by oppressive double standards that entrap and sometimes kill them. Emecheta's protagonists are caught between their deep connection to tribal customs and their attraction to cultural modernity. Female characters in Emecheta's books attempt, with limited success, to negotiate this conflict between the old and the new. Both readers and characters become painfully aware that each way of life—traditional and Western—exacts from women particularly high costs. Yet Emecheta's literary and social concerns span a broader range than the complexities of changing gender relations: she also writes of the imposition of white, Western values on indigenous people, of African history, and of the ravages of war. Her stories are set in postcolonial Ibuza and Lagos and in contemporary London, where she has lived with her children for almost forty years.

Emecheta has been inspired by the traditional Igbo oral narrative mode called *ifo*, in which the Big Mother, in her role as *griotte*, tells stories that flow from the matrix of women's traditional lives. These stories often counsel girls to accept male privilege in exchange for the rewards of female compliance and offer descriptions of consequences faced by disrespectful wives, sisters, or daughters who challenge their men's rights (Arndt 40–41, 43). Emecheta liberally uses literary devices such as irony, proverb, and song that she imbibed with lasting pleasure from her Big Mother. But the contemporary Nigerian-British writer actively reinterprets aspects of this ancestral oral genre by writing stories that question long-held cultural perceptions of women's roles and talents. Susan Arndt provides an example of what she describes as Emecheta "writing back" to *ifo*. *The Bride Price* does not reverse but rather reworks the myth and cautionary image of the marriageable girl who dares to choose her own life partner. While the disobedient sixteen-year-old Aku-nna dies by her lover's side, in childbirth, Emecheta makes abundantly clear that this girl was neither strong nor old enough to survive the throes of labor. The real conditions of her life thus overrule superstition: Emecheta "writes back" by emphasizing that Aku-nna's fate was not sealed because she defied her father's rule. Instead, this young girl fell victim because she lacked sufficient support or knowledge to guide her through her self-propelled emancipation (Arndt 46–48).

BACKGROUND

Buchi Emecheta's bicultural experiences seemingly provide her with illimitable tales to tell, several of them based on her own trials and eventual triumphs, first as a young girl in Nigeria and later as a single mother in London. In her first two novels, *In the Ditch* (1972) and *Second-Class Citizen* (1975), Emecheta narrates stories that mirror but do not wholly represent direct, personal experience. More than ten years later she published *Head above Water*, her first purely autobiographical work. But generally her books blend fiction and lore and are peopled with amalgams of family and community members from the two different cultures she has known intimately. Throughout her oeuvre—including fifteen novels, a memoir, several television plays, and children's stories—Emecheta writes audaciously, stirring social criticism and consciousness raising into the mix of myth, bildungsroman, ironically developed plots, and humor that mark her fiction.

Born in the Ibuza village of Umuezeokolo Odanta, Emecheta lost a secure, loving home at age nine when her father, a railway worker and soldier in the Burmese army, died. As Igbo tradition dictates, his death occasioned the immediate fracture of their nuclear family life, leaving her mother to be claimed as an inheritance by her deceased father's brother. Her younger brother, Adolpho, privileged by gender, was allowed to live with their father's brother, but Buchi was sent to her mother's cousin's home, where she was treated not like family, but like the family servant. This irreparable disruption in Emecheta's early life impelled her turning inward for comfort and counsel. In two of her fictional works, *The Slave Girl* (1977) and *The Joys of Motherhood* (1979), and in her autobiography, *Head above Water* (1986), Emecheta reflects on this guiding force within, alternately referring to it as "The Presence" and with the Igbo term *chi*. One's *chi* can be understood as an individual's personal deity, often the spirit of a dead person, reincarnated inside the living, a voice that directs the living person's fortunes (Arndt 53, n. 26; Stratton 107).

Even in her youth, Emecheta's inner voice directed her to take daring actions that a more submissive, conformist Igbo girl would not consider, let alone attempt. From the time she was quite small, she found courage to resist inferior conditions for daughters and sisters that were etched into the hallowed beliefs of her people. While the young Emecheta was kept at home, Adolpho was sent to school. Seeing her brother enjoying his studies, Emecheta listened closely to that small voice inside that encouraged her to realize her desire for advancement. Without her relatives' knowledge she walked bravely, by herself, to the local school in Lagos, where she inquired about enrolling. Learning of their daughter's boldness, Emecheta's parents understood that this was a girl who would not remain passive, accepting secondary status. They consented to registering her in school, and there she saw firsthand how important it is for girls, like boys, to have the lifelong benefits of a good education. Later, when financial limits dimmed her scholastic prospects once again, Emecheta slyly took money from the family funds so that she could apply for a scholarship at the prestigious Methodist Girls' High School. The high value Emecheta places on education for a woman resounds thematically in her fiction. Access to formal study means the possibility of attaining economic independence; this avenue for self-sufficiency provides the most effective channel for her female characters to traverse as they attempt to move beyond oppressive domestic conditions.

From the time she was young, Emecheta has defied patriarchal constraints that have thwarted her desire for personal and professional growth. The most hazardous obstacle to her professional development surfaced in her marriage. In 1960, when she was sixteen years of age, Emecheta wed a fellow student to whom she had been engaged since she was eleven. Emecheta remained in Nigeria until 1962, when she left Lagos to join her husband in London. When she arrived, she had two small children still in diapers, and it was not long before she found her marriage stultifying, both financially and emotionally. Not only was her husband unwilling to work to support their growing family, he also was severely threatened by his wife's determination to attain a university degree and become a writer.

Emecheta knew that she would have to find the strength to leave her husband when, in 1964, he burned the entire typed manuscript of her first novel, *The Bride Price*. While she never was able to recover the original (she worked without carbon paper or duplicate copies), Emecheta did eventually return to the idea behind this inaugural work. Twelve years later she rewrote the story completely, publishing it under the title she had given it in 1964. While the book was recovered, the marriage was not: the memory of the burnt manuscript fueled Emecheta's courage, and she separated from her husband, though she understood well that such an action would make her a pariah in London's community of Nigerian émigrés. Two years following their separation Emecheta effected a divorce and took the couple's children with her to government-provided housing.

To support her four youngsters and a baby on the way, Emecheta began employment in the library of the British Museum. Within several weeks of her new job she delivered a baby daughter. After a period of recovery from giving birth Emecheta initiated evening studies toward a degree in sociology from the University of London. During this same period she wrote fiction while her children were in school or while they slept.

ANALYSIS

In 1972, eight years after seeing her original literary creation destroyed, Buchi Emecheta witnessed the publication of her first book, *In the Ditch*. Adah Obi, the author's fictional representative, begins this narrative looking back on her overseas trip to join Francis, her Nigerian husband, carrying two small children in tow and another on the way. In London Adah, like Emecheta, soon separates from her irresponsible husband and begins the challenge of raising five children while completing her university degree. The novel depicts the narrator's struggles to survive and emphasizes the common suffering she shares with coarser, less well educated women on the dole who help her. *In the Ditch*—part memoir, part novel—explores Emecheta's experiences as a single mother within the British welfare system.

Subsequent to *In the Ditch* Emecheta has written prolifically, reworking ancestral stories of her people and exploring customs, myths, and rituals that flow from Igbo world views. Emecheta's books repeatedly protest patriarchal privileges that subjugate Nigerian women, such as widow inheritance (to which her mother had to succumb), preclusion from career-directed schooling, valorization of childbearing, and the system of polygamy that casts off older wives or those who bear no sons. In general, she exposes the traditions that demand women's self-sacrifice in Nigeria as well as those conditions abroad that hurt women émigrés like herself. Through her fiction Emecheta rails against colonial intrusions that rob men of their honor, and cultural requirements that have relentlessly compromised women's independence and empowerment.

Reading Emecheta's oeuvre, one hears a defiant cry for both male and female voices to resist systems or traditions that delimit human potential. Emecheta receives praise for giving voice to the "hidden feelings of African women and she voices them as perhaps no one has done before . . . insisting that female complacency and the unquestioning acceptance of male domination do not constitute the quintessence of femininity" (Ngcobo 10). While her literary success has been supported by Western women's movements, Emecheta pointedly describes herself as "an African feminist with a small 'f,' " emphasizing her lived sense that female subordination takes place within stubborn and corrupted systems of social injustice (Nnaemeka 147). In doing so, she calls attention to women's second-class status globally, connecting women's greater equality with an improvement in living conditions for all humanity (Umeh, "Introduction" xxxi, xxxv).

As an artistic influence, the work of Nigerian author Flora Nwapa must be cited. Emecheta's *The Joys of Motherhood*, her best-known and most widely celebrated novel, indisputably reaches back to and extends Nwapa's *Efuru* (1966), the first internationally recognized novel by an African woman. Efuru is a virtuous, traditional Igbo woman who, in the early 1930s, has the misfortune of having only one baby that dies soon after its birth. Condemned to childlessness in a culture that affords no family honor to women without children, Efuru nevertheless achieves a life of dignity. In *The Joys of Motherhood* Emecheta presents the paradoxical tragedy of Nnu Ego, a traditional wife who gives up everything for her many children. Yet her two sons, who become successful, do not honor her in her old age, as she expected they would, for having made a lifetime of sacrifices as a good Igbo mother. Emecheta's ironic title draws directly from one of Nwapa's final lines. Moreover, Nwapa's influence can be felt in the latter book through the intertextual reference Emecheta makes to the Igbo Women's War of 1920, an event that *Efuru* preserves.

Like that of Nwapa before her, Emecheta's imagination is fed by the imperialist tragedy of this political stripping of Igbo women's traditional power. During November and December of that year many thousands of Igbo women protested women's taxation and the British system of justice imposed in the provinces of Calabar and Owerri. These Igbo women made their displeasure known by invoking a traditional, sanctioned form of female power and protest. Through their market network they sent the message to women throughout the provinces to "make war on" or "sit on" the corrupt male warrant chiefs by demonstrating near the native courts where the warrant chiefs, put in place by the British, ruled. Although the rebellion was conducted according to women's traditional ways of exercising power in the villages, it was squelched violently by the British. Both Nwapa's *Efuru* and Emecheta's *The Joys of Motherhood* take place only several years after this rebellion, and each novelist makes reference to the Women's War as emblematic of the impossible place in which women found themselves in the crunch of imperialism against indigenous African culture.

Florence Stratton also shows that in *Second-Class Citizen* Emecheta uses Flora Nwapa herself as inspiration for her courageous protagonist (*Contemporary* 119). This strong artistic relationship between these two Nigerian writers has been cited as the beginning of Igbo women's literary history (Andrade 95; Nnaemeka 145). In addition to her literary foremother's significance and the inspirational stories of her "Big Mother," Emecheta acknowledges that her work has been influenced by her education in the English university system and by the ideas of European and American feminist writers of the early 1970s. Speaking of the literary acclaim she has earned, Emecheta believes that she owes its wide scope to the attention she has received from women all over the globe who have brought not only her work but also books by other African women into their countries' public and scholarly conversations (Umeh, "Introduction" xxx).

Emecheta weaves several related motifs into the intricate texture of her fiction. With women's thwarted lives and status in the author's foreground, she writes to document social, economic, and domestic arrangements that have crippled women's choices and potential. In *The Bride Price* young Aku-nna fearfully but joyously elopes with Chike, the man she loves, forbidden to her by her father and tribal law because his ancestor was a slave. When Aku-nna soon dies, her story seems to fulfill Ibo customary beliefs that warn that any woman whose family refuses to pay her bride price will not survive childbirth. Indeed, in the final paragraph of *The Bride Price* the narrative voice claims that in the future Aku-nna's fate will warn young girls against the consequences of disobedience. Yet the author's compassion for the protagonist throughout the story serves to criticize roundly the rigid legal and social customs that ultimately crush Aku-nna. Moreover, Emecheta's ironic ending shows the oral tradition, for its own conservative purposes, promulgating a distorted version of Aku-nna's story, retelling it as a moral tale about the heavy hand of fate that took the young girl's life instead of a story about the insurmountable social and physical conditions that befell her. As critic Tuzyline Jita Allan writes of *The Bride Price*, "[T]he novel captures in unforgettable close-ups the shattering impact of gender oppression on a young girl" (211).

Providing strong evidence of the terrible costs patriarchal imposition incurs for girls and women, Emecheta exposes sexist double standards in a postcolonial Nigeria marching toward modernity. In *Double Yoke* Nko, a beautiful and brilliant young woman attending university in Nigeria, must choose between prostituting herself to her professor or having him make good on his vengeful threat to fail her final project, which she needs to pass for graduation. Although Nko loses her boyfriend, Ete Kamba, when he learns of her affair, Nko cannot oppose Professor Ikot's authoritative will; his power over her future gives her no means for resisting his "flattering" offer to "supervise" her final project. Professor Ikot's open, deceptive expression of special interest in Nko's work transparently displays the "double yoke" women carry and the double standard for males and females seeking career success. Says another student in the novel:

> "I wonder how beautiful female students always manage to come up with projects so interesting that they require the dean of a faculty to supervise." Nko had never felt so cheap. . . . She had wanted her degree, she could work hard for her degree, but now everybody seemed to be insinuating that she would get it without having to work for it. . . . Was such a degree worth her losing her good name, and maybe Ete? Then what was left for her to do when people were now telling her that she could not have both? She must either have her degree and be a bad, loose, feminist, shameless, career woman who would have to fight men all her life; or do without her degree and be a good loving wife and Christian woman. (134–135)

Needless to say, there is no male character who faces the same impossible dilemma. However unfair the double standard Emecheta exposes, critic Ezenwa-Ohaeto finds that the author's opposition to male chauvinism results in the novel being flawed by the intrusion of her politics. Judging her characters to be unconvincing and the plot melodramatic, Ezenwa-Ohaeto believes Emecheta to be representative of recent African female writers, who, influenced by women's liberationists, attempt without literary success to rewrite dominant masculine myths. Reading *Double Yoke*, Lloyd Brown concurs, observing that Emecheta's "criticisms of African men are often marred by generalizations that are too shrill and transparently overstated to be altogether convincing" (36).

In *The Joys of Motherhood*, her most widely read book, Emecheta exposes two other double standards plaguing women in Nigerian culture: that sexual pleasure is for men only, and that educational opportunities are important for boys and not girls. Ona, a beautiful, flamboyant, intriguing woman, boldly refuses to marry Chief Agbadi. Instead, she prefers to be his lover so that she can continue to live "for pleasure and power over her man" (Sengupta 233), a posture unacceptable in a wife. With an adoring father teaching her self-respect and self-determination, Ona, like no other woman in this Igbo village, seems to understand that "pleasure in sexual intercourse was natural and meant for both women and men to enjoy" (Stratton 196). In contrast, Agunwa, Agbadi's senior wife, suffers her jealousy silently and later becomes ill after overhearing Ona cry out with the pleasure Agunwa is denied when her husband favors his younger mistress.

On her deathbed Ona pleads with Agbadi to ensure that Nnu Ego, their beautiful daughter, is allowed "a life of her own" (28). But Agbadi marries the passive Nnu Ego to a man she has never seen, a physically repulsive man whom the young girl cannot hope to control with her sexual power. Soon this husband, Nnaife, takes a new wife who, like Ona, moans shamelessly when their husband comes to her bed. Nnu Ego wonders, "Did she [the junior wife] think Nnaife was her lover and not her husband, to show her enjoyment so?" (125). In an article that examines female sexual experience in *Joys*, Marie Umeh writes: "[L]egitimate wives rarely achieve sexual gratification because of the culture's moral code: chastity and sexual demure is the measure of a good woman's moral character. This code does not apply to men" (*Emerging Perspectives* 194). Noting Emecheta's depiction of two wives in *Joys*—Agbadi and Nnu Ego, both of whom experience sexual neglect and express desire for sexual pleasure with their husbands—Umeh maintains that "most Igbo women want a fulfilling sex life as much as they want sons" (195).

In *Joys* Adaku, the junior wife, refuses to accept second-class status. With a clear vision of her own worth, she claims her daughters equal to Nnu Ego's sons and leaves the security of Nnaife's patriarchal abode, valiantly and iconoclastically setting out on her own to ensure that her girls become educated. Critic Obioma Nnaemeka wonders why writers like Nwapa and Emecheta, committed to questioning women's subordination, consistently give literary center stage to the traditionalist female character and marginalize the defiant women, like Adaku and Ona, who refuse domestic conformity for the sake of acceptance (Nnaemeka 151).

Nnu Ego is slow to realize fully the double standard inherent in beliefs that declare that bearing sons is the most important contribution a woman can make in her lifetime. Tradition-bound Nnu Ego unquestioningly complies with patriarchal authority, hushing her young daughters' protest against having to stay at home so that their brothers can go to school. "But you are girls!" she tells them. "They are boys. You have to put them in a good position in life, so that they will be able to look after the family. When your husbands are nasty to you they will defend you" (176). However, toward the end of the novel Nnu Ego finally begins to see the inequities, writ large, that, without knowing, she herself has been trying to escape all her life:

> God, when will you create a woman who will be fulfilled in herself, a full human being, not anybody's appendage? . . . When I lost my first son I wanted to die, because I failed to live up to the standard expected of me by the males in my life, my father and my husband—and now I have to include my sons. But who made the law that we should not hope in our daughters? We women subscribe to that law more than anyone. Until we change all this, it is still a man's world, which women will always help to build. (186–187)

This is Emecheta's voice of lived experience, speaking from what life has taught her. Before her career as a writer earned her a living wage, Emecheta herself worked hard to secure an education so that she would not be dependent on any man to provide for her and her children. *Second-Class Citizen* chronicles Emecheta's early life in England, reintroducing Adah, from *In the Ditch*, as the author's fictional persona. When Adah gets a job in the public library and wants to attend night classes at London University, her husband Francis asks, "Who is going to look after your children for you?" Adah remembers then that in Nigeria, "when children were good, they were the father's, they took after him, but when they were bad, they were the mother's, taking after her and her old mother" (45). Through portraits of defiant women like Adah who reject male domination and survive on their own resourcefulness, Emecheta shows that such hardships can make women stronger if they exert intelligence, initiative, and belief in their own worth. Critics have responded variously to this novel: Abioseh Michael Porter says that Emecheta successfully depicts Adah's growth from dependence to selfhood, but that in her descriptions of Francis, the narrator "pour[s] what looks like personal venom into the text" (274). While Emecheta shows patriarchal culture choking women's potential, she sees the patriarchal system as the problem, not the individual men who are fighting for a place within the structure that rewards them for oppressing women. In a 1994 interview with Oladipo Joseph Ogundele the author responded to criticism, like Porter's, of her male characters by saying that men in her novels "don't possess any type of weakness . . . [they] need to reeducate themselves or reexamine their actions" (453).

Amid her chronicles of sexism and women's oppression Emecheta presents another related motif: the young girl condemned to slavery. Notably, in *The Slave Girl* the newly orphaned Ojebeta is sold by her adolescent brother so that he can pay for fancy clothes to impress his peers during a coming-of-age ritual. He sells his sister to a powerful woman who shrewdly exploits her and other girls her age, becoming richer by the day from their labors. In this novel Emecheta examines the economic factors that would lead one woman to enslave another. When Ojebeta, the adult, finally leaves Ma Palagada's house, she asserts her freedom by choosing her own marriage partner, but realizes quickly that in fact she has simply been granted the freedom to choose one master over another.

In both *The Slave Girl* and *The Joys of Motherhood* Emecheta inserts the story of a young slave girl who resists being buried alive alongside her mistress, a custom believed to ensure that the dead woman will continue to be served in the afterlife. Refusing to be silenced forever, the slave girl rises in spirit and brings vengeance to the lives of female children born after her, symbolically depicting how "female human potential . . . is more often than not, buried in a narrow definition of sex" (Umeh, "Introduction" xxxvi). In these two novels Emecheta creates the image of helpless women—dead and alive—existing in bondage to men. Ojebeta and Nnu Ego are *ogbanje*, "the Igbo term for spirit-children, children believed to be destined to die and be reborn repeatedly to the same mother unless a means can be found to break the cycle" (Stratton, "Shallow Grave" 101) and defined by Emecheta in *The Bride Price* as "a 'living dead.' " Ojebeta becomes such a living corpse because she must endure life without ever voicing aloud her own concerns, without ever experiencing freedom or agency. In *The Joys of Motherhood* Nnu Ego is born with her head misshapen precisely where the recently buried slave woman was struck into fatal submission; thus the infant girl is assumed to be the reincarnation of the unfortunate slave woman. For most of Nnu Ego's story she, like the slave girl, remains trapped inside the male order, incapable of lifting herself from the depths of submission during her lifetime.

Rape appears as a third motif in Emecheta's work. In cultures where women are enslaved, rape becomes a means and a metaphor through which men express dominion. In many of Emecheta's novels a woman is forced or beaten into sexual compliance. Husbands demand marital rights, and in *The Family* (first published as *Gwendolen*), a father rapes his daughter. In later works Emecheta parallels the forcible overtaking of individual Nigerian women and Europe's political, cultural rape of the African continent. Debbie's rape experience during wartime, the cruel climax in *Destination Biafra*, cannot be read except alongside the country's ravishment and the depravity of soldiers on both sides. In *The Rape of Shavi* Princess Ayoko and the entire country of Shavi are concomitantly raped by morally deficient, culturally insensitive "albino aliens" looking for sexual and materialistic opportunity. But justice prevails: the older women of Shavi protect the princess from the worst repercussions, and the allegory concludes with the African survivors agreeing that Shavi "has been raped once [but] we must never allow her to be raped again" (178).

ASSESSMENT

When it was first published, Emecheta's work met with criticism mostly held by men, scholars, who valorize the traditional, submissive women in her books, who do not appreciate as realistic or morally respectable rebellious female characters like Adah, Ona, Adaku, Debbie, and the women of Shavi, and who see her male characters as caricatures in their villainy (Frank, "Feminist Criticism" 34–48; Emenyonu, "Technique" 253). Today Emecheta's work generates a range of acclamation, interrogation, and dissension. Among disputant readers are those who feel that this author wields too heavy a hand in her characters' proclamations about gender inequities (Barthelemy 565), or that in spite of other redeeming literary features, Emecheta's male characters remain "greedy," "selfish" men in cutting and unconvincing one-dimensional portraits that overplay her political message (Porter 272). Yet her adherents far outnumber her detractors, and Emecheta enjoys the distinction of having been called "both a disruptive and a cohesive force within the contemporary African literary tradition" (Stratton 112). Known best for her pointed social criticism, Emecheta receives further praise for deftly blending African oral elements within her aesthetic, for her gifted use of figurative language, and for her dynamic storytelling. She has also gained attention for her ability to depict the complexities of women's experiences under patriarchal control. Her use of multifarious voices in her novels has also gained her critical acclaim (Ezeigbo 5–7, 22–23). In *Destination Biafra*, the novel that is seen as largest in its scope, Porter credits Emecheta with having made a major contribution to literature depicting war in this century ("They were There" 313–315); moreover, Nwachukwu-Agbada notes her apt portrayal in this novel of women's leadership potential during times of national crisis (394).

Emecheta writes of survival and resistance. She writes with one eye toward the complex, promising world of tomorrow and the other glancing back at the simpler indigenous past. She tells life stories, myth, and history; she gives voice to Igbo traditional people and, as John Hawley suggests, continually struggles to tell stories that will convey her "on-going birth" (qtd. in Umeh, "Introduction" xxxviii). Throughout her varied collection of autobiographical and imaginative fiction Emecheta sharply criticizes any institution—national or domestic—that sees itself as morally superior and therefore rightful in imposing one particular way of life. She captures the thoughts, fears, and dreams of women and men torn between loyalties to ancient custom and imminent cultural change.

Buchi Emecheta is an enormously important Igbo-Nigerian, British writer, notable for the transcultural stories that she tells, the particular and universal abuses she exposes, the human potential she explores, and the empowerment she inspires. In an interview that marked her fiftieth birthday celebration, Emecheta said: "I like to tell the world our part of the story while using the voices of women. Women in our area are silenced a lot" ("Ogundele" 449). Despite the odds she herself has faced—as a daughter, as a wife, as a mother, and as a writer—Emecheta, the prolific writer and *griotte*, succeeds in ensuring that no longer will African women's voices be stifled or buried. Resurrecting women's stories from the crypts of historical silence, Emecheta gives them new life—not in spirit alone, but in substance and in aesthetically and culturally meaningful forms that wholly and fully sustain them.

BIBLIOGRAPHY

Primary Sources

In the Ditch. London: Barrie & Jenkins, 1972.
Second-Class Citizen. New York: Braziller, 1975.
The Bride Price. New York: Braziller, 1976.
The Slave Girl. New York: Braziller, 1977.
The Joys of Motherhood. New York: Braziller, 1979.
Destination Biafra. London and New York: Schocken, 1982.
Naira Power. London: Macmillan: 1982.
Adah's Story. London: Allison & Busby, 1983.
Double Yoke. 1988. New York: Braziller, 1983.
The Rape of Shavi. London: Ogwugwo Afo, 1983; New York: Braziller, 1985.
Head above Water. London: Ogwugwo Afo, 1986.
A Kind of Marriage. London: Macmillan, 1986.
Gwendolen. London: Collins, 1989. As *The Family*. New York: Braziller, 1990.
Kehinde. Oxford and Portsmouth, NH: Heinemann, 1994.
The Bride Price. London: Heinemann, 1995.

Secondary Sources

Allan, Tuzyline Jita. *Womanist and Feminist Aesthetics*. Athens: Ohio UP, 1995.
Andrade, Susan Z. "Rewriting History, Motherhood, and Rebellion: Naming an African Women's Literary Tradition." *Research in African Literatures* 21 (1990): 91–110.
Arndt, Susan, and Elizabeth Cole. *African Women's Literature, Orature, and Intertextuality*. Bayreuth: Bayreuth, U, 1998.
Barthelemy, Anthony. "Western Time, African Lives: Time in the Novels of Buchi Emecheta." *Callaloo* 12.3 (1989): 559–574.
Brown, Lloyd. "Buchi Emecheta." In *Women Writers in Black Africa*. Westport, CT: Greenwood, 1981.
Emenyonu, Ernest. "Technique and Language in Buchi Emecheta's *The Bride Price*, *The Slave Girl*, and *The Joys of Motherhood*." In Umeh, *Emerging Perspectives* 251–265.
———. "Who Does Flora Nwapa Write For?" *African Literature Today* 7 (1975): 28–33.
Ezeigbo, Theodora Akachi. "Tradition and the African Female Writer: The Example of Buchi Emecheta." In Umeh, *Emerging Perspectives* 5–25.
Ezenwa-Ohaeta. "Replacing Myth with Myth: The Feminist Streak in Buchi Emecheta's *Double Yoke*." In Umeh, *Emerging Perspectives* 155–168.
Fishburn, Katherine. *Reading Buchi Emecheta: Cross-Cultural Conversations*. Westport, CT: Greenwood, 1995.
Frank, Katherine. "The Death of the Slave Girl: African Womanhood in the Novels of Buchi Emecheta." *World Literature Written in English* 21 (1982): 476–497.
———. "Feminist Criticism and the African Novel." *African Literature Today* 14 (1984): 34–48.
Hawley, John C. "Coming to Terms: Buchi Emecheta's *Kehinde* and the Birth of a Nation." In Umeh, *Emerging Perspective* 333–348.
Ngcobo, Lauretta. "The African Woman Writer." *Kunapipi* 7.2–3 (1985).
Nnaemeka, Obioma. "From Orality to Writing: African Women Writers and the (Re)Inscription of Womanhood." *Research in African Literatures* 21 (1990): 137–157.
Nwachukwu, Agbada, J.O.J. "Buchi Emecheta: Politics, War, and Feminism in *Destination Biafra*." In Umeh, *Emerging Perspectives* 387–394.
Ogundele, Oladipo Joseph. "A Conversation with Dr. Buchi Emecheta." In Umeh, *Emerging Perspectives* 445–456.
Ojo-Ade, Femi. "Female Writers, Male Critics." *African Literature Today* 13 (1983): 158–179.
Palmer, Eustace. "The Feminine Point of View: Buchi Emecheta's *The Joys of Motherhood*." *African Literature Today* 13 (1983): 38–55.
Porter, Abioseh Michael. "*Second Class Citizen*: The Point of Departure for Understanding Buchi Emecheta's Major Fiction." In Umeh, *Emerging Perspectives* 267–275.
———. "They Were There, Too: Women and the Civil War(s) in *Destination Biafra*." In Umeh, *Emerging Perspectives* 313–332.
Sengupta, Shivaji. "Desire and the Politics of Control in *The Joys of Motherhood* and *The Family*." In Umeh, *Emerging Perspectives* 227–246.

Stratton, Florence. *Contemporary African Literature and the Politics of Gender*. London: Routledge, 1994.

Umeh, Marie, ed. *Emerging Perspectives on Buchi Emecheta*. Trenton, NJ: African World Press, 1996.

———. "Introduction: (En)Gendering African Womanhood: Locating Sexual Politics in Igbo Society and across Boundaries." In Umeh, *Emerging Perspectives* xxiii–xlii.

Ward, Cynthia. "What They Told Buchi Emecheta: Oral Subjectivity and the Joys of Otherhood." *PMLA* 105 (1990): 83–97.

Penelope Fitzgerald
1916–2000

Douglas Clayton

Penelope Fitzgerald was a writer of seemingly modest aims who aptly described herself as one of the "understatement people" (Cole 302). Yet she emerged in recent decades as an uncommonly original and intriguing novelist, winning acclaim and awards on both sides of the Atlantic. She was, moreover, a rare late bloomer. Her first novel, a mystery titled *The Golden Child*, was published in England in 1977, when Fitzgerald was sixty-one years old. Her third novel, *Offshore* (1979), won the Booker Prize, Great Britain's most prestigious literary award. Three other novels—*The Bookshop* (1978), *The Beginning of Spring* (1988), and *The Gate of Angels* (1990)—were shortlisted for the Booker. *The Blue Flower* (1995) won the National Book Critics Circle Award for fiction in the United States; it also received extraordinary praise—probably greater than for any of her preceding novels—in Britain. Published when Fitzgerald was nearly eighty years old, *The Blue Flower* is a testament to the growing intellectual and literary powers of a writer who continued to surprise and delight her ever-widening circle of admirers.

While her productivity and excellence are widely acknowledged, the precise nature of her achievement is more difficult to pinpoint. Her books, which are written in a readily accessible, straightforward fashion, tend to focus on the daily, uneventful lives of small communities or groups of people. They avoid climactic moments, portentous atmosphere, and revelatory conclusions. Rather, they acknowledge only the most commonplace moments in persistently quotidian lives. In this respect her novels can be seen as latecomers to the long, staunchly middlebrow tradition of the British novel of manners.

Nonetheless, there are recurring elements within Fitzgerald's novels that mark them as unmistakably contemporary, inventive works. The presence of these modern elements, combined with indisputably traditional features of her writings, makes for a unique, unpredictable mix of convention and innovation. Robert Plunket points toward this combination in a review of *The Beginning of Spring*, in which he describes Fitzgerald as "that refreshing rarity, a writer who is very modern but not the least bit hip" (15). Thus her focus tends to be on people at the margins of society—women (often elderly women), young girls, and eccentric outcasts—as they struggle to attain the humblest measures of success and happiness in an inhospitable world. This interest in outsiders and the powerless allies Fitzgerald in the most general way to numerous other contemporary novelists, but she parts company with many of these (younger) novelists by steadfastly resisting any specific ideological themes or interpretations in her work. Moreover, Fitzgerald developed (particularly in her last four novels) an interest in past settings and historical figures—an interest that plainly contributes to the traditional character of her writings. Yet this ostensibly conventional interest in the past leads, in unexpected ways, to thoroughly up-to-date explorations of the relationship between reality, fiction, and the literary imagination.

BACKGROUND

Penelope Fitzgerald was born on December 17, 1916, in Lincoln, England. Her father, Edmund Valpy Knox, was later the editor of *Punch*, the British humor magazine; her mother, Christina Hicks Knox, was the daughter of an Anglican pastor. Fitzgerald tells much about her parents—their marriage, backgrounds, and literary and intellectual enthusiasms—in *The Knox Brothers*, her 1977 account of Edmund and his three brothers, Dillwyn, Wilfred, and Ronald. In 1939 Fitzgerald graduated from Somerville College, Oxford, with first-class honors in English. Two years later she married Desmond Fitzgerald. In the following decades she held various jobs, working occasionally as a teacher, as a clerk in a bookstore, and as a program assistant at the BBC. She also devoted many years to raising her three children. "I would have liked to have [written] all my life," she told Nicholas Basbanes in 1998, "but that just wasn't possible in my case. I had a family to raise" (10).

As Fitzgerald explained to Basbanes, her initial decision to write books was inspired by pressing financial worries in the early 1970s, when her husband was incapacitated by illness. Her first book, published in 1975, was a biography of the Pre-Raphaelite artist Edward Burne-Jones. Her second, *The Knox Brothers*, was a "biography" of an altogether different sort, a group portrait of her remarkable father and his three equally notable brothers. She then turned to fiction for the first time, writing her mystery novel, *The Golden Child*, for the entertainment of her ailing husband.

While *The Golden Child* was to be her sole mystery, it plainly awakened her ambitions as a writer of fiction. She followed it a year later (1978) with *The Bookshop* and then with seven more novels in the next seventeen years. Only one further work of nonfiction—*Charlotte Mew and Her Friends*, a life and times of the British poet—appeared, published in Britain in 1984 and in the United States in 1988. It was with *The Bookshop*, in 1978, that Fitzgerald emerged decisively as a writer of fiction and as a literary talent to be reckoned with. She died in the year 2000.

ANALYSIS

Fitzgerald's first novel, *The Golden Child*, is part mystery, part novel of manners. A tale of multiple murders and intrigue in the midst of a fraudulent special exhibit at a leading museum in London, *The Golden Child* is interesting less for its creation of suspense than for its droll delineation of the odd habits and relationships of the sundry museum employees. As Fitzgerald remarked in her interview with Basbanes, her "publisher thought it wasn't thrilling enough to call a thriller, so they cut the last eight chapters and called it a mystery" (10). Despite this emphatic editorial effort to heighten the book's identity as a mystery, however, Fitzgerald seems primarily interested in personalities, character development, and social milieu. It was something of a false start in her career as a novelist—she never attempted another mystery in the two-plus decades following the publication of *The Golden Child*—but Fitzgerald remarked that at least "the story did amuse my husband, for which I am grateful. It seems old-fashioned now, but there you are" (Basbanes 10).

Her next novel, *The Bookshop*, represented a giant leap forward. A penetrating, even caustic portrait of provincial life in a tiny seaside town in Sussex, Britain, *The Bookshop* recounts Florence Green's efforts to open and operate a modest bookstore in the face of spiteful opposition from the town's denizens (natural and supernatural). Fitzgerald displays here an incisive, thoroughgoing insight into human mediocrity, mendacity, and malevolence. Her unsentimental, evenhanded attention to her characters identifies her at once as belonging, if only in a general way, to that eclectic satiric tradition of the British novel advancing from Jane Austen to Evelyn Waugh and extending on to such diverse recent stalwarts as A.S. Byatt and Ian McEwan. There is a pitiless humor in her portrait of an older, inexperienced woman under siege by her vindictive neighbors—humor that was imperfectly forecast by Fitzgerald's performance in *The Golden Child*, but that is managed in *The Bookshop* with precision and conspicuous flair.

Offshore (1979) also exemplifies this talent for social realism and satire, yet it is a perceptibly gentler novel than its predecessor, peopled by residents of barges moored at Battersea Reach, on the Thames, in London. At the novel's center is Nenna, a young woman with two daughters. Her hapless efforts to salvage her marriage with Edward take place amid this loose-knit community of oddballs on these rotting houseboats (at least one of which sinks, with little discernible provocation, in the course of the novel). Fitzgerald is again the pitiless observer of human frailties and self-deceptions, yet in *Offshore* she seems more kindly disposed to her subjects—particularly to Nenna and her resilient young girls—and more likely to discover incompetence than wickedness among them.

Human Voices (1980) draws on Fitzgerald's experience as an employee at the BBC during World War II. Like its predecessors, it reveals her exceptional ability to conjure up a time and place with rare, quirky vividness and in relatively few words. The novel's account of intrigue and rivalry among senior employees at the wartime BBC—and the innocent love of a sixteen-year-old girl for an appallingly indifferent middle-aged scoundrel—makes for what A.S. Byatt, in the *Times Literary Supplement*, called "a wonderful combination of deadpan English comedy and surreal farce" (1057). Fitzgerald's next novel, *At Freddie's* (1982), transports readers to the early 1960s and the Temple Stage School, or Freddie's, as it is familiarly called in honor of its long-standing proprietress. There children are prepared for careers on the London stage. Like her earlier books, *At Freddie's* concentrates on adult eccentrics and irrepressibly hardy children as they are jostled about in a fragile, endangered institution. It is evident by now that Fitzgerald has settled into a characteristic tone—one that mixes an uncompromising, highly localized realism with an unsentimental, yet resolutely compassionate, view of human affairs.

In her next pair of novels Fitzgerald preserved this tone and approach while adding a penchant for faraway locales. Italy in the decade after World War II is the setting for *Innocence* (1986), the tale of a long-since-decayed noble family and the young, passionate woman in its midst, Chiara Ridolfi, whose impulsive stratagems for marrying Doctor Salvatore Rossi lead to unhappiness for all concerned. The novel that followed two years later, *The Beginning of Spring* (1988), goes even farther afield, being set among English residents of Moscow in the years just before the Russian Revolution of 1917. Fitzgerald's meticulous research—in the one case into postwar Italy and in the other into prerevolutionary Russia—results in uncanny evocations of other worlds, yet it is always the ordinariness of these worlds, not their exotic nature or momentous times, that prevails. This is especially apparent in *The Beginning of Spring*, where it is the prosaic travails of the Reid family that take center stage: as the book opens, the mother has just left her husband and returned temporarily to Britain, while her husband, Frank, struggles haplessly in Moscow to raise his three young children and preserve his chaotic printing business. Fitzgerald's evocation of Moscow in the early 1910s is preternaturally precise; and yet one would scarcely imagine that Lenin and revolution are in the offing. (The echo of Reid with Reed—as in John Reed, the American left-wing reporter who pictured the Russian Revolution in his *Ten Days That Shook the World*—is particularly telling in this regard, since John Reed was a foreigner with an unqualified preoccupation with Russia's political turmoil, whereas Frank Reid and his family are foreigners who, despite their many years in Moscow, seem quite oblivious to the momentous changes under way.)

Fitzgerald's talents as a researcher are also very much on display in *The Gate of Angels* (1990), even if she does return to Britain for her locale. Set at Cambridge University in 1913, the story captures the collision between two incompatible worlds. We first meet a young scientist, Fred Fairly, who has abandoned his father's religious faith in favor of the new rationalist, scientific dogma. While riding his bicycle one evening, Fred collides, quite literally, with Daisy Saunders, a young working-class woman from London. When he finds himself convalescing beside her in a rural home in the countryside outside Cambridge, his sudden and irrevocable infatuation with her (indeed, he resolves at once to marry her) seems to rattle all his complacent faith in science and reason. A tale that mixes whimsy with keen insights into class and gender inequalities, *The Gate of Angels* is an idiosyncratic work that resists sentimentalization even as it explores the uncomfortable, comic facts of romantic love.

A version of that theme—the inexplicable nature of love—takes center stage in Fitzgerald's last book, *The Blue Flower* (1995). In many ways her most audacious novel, *The Blue Flower* polishes and perfects many of the tendencies at work in her earlier books. Set in late-eighteenth-century Germany, amid the rising enthusiasm for romantic poetry and philosophy, *The Blue Flower* is a vivid portrait of daily, domestic life in Germany at a particularly momentous time in its intellectual and cultural history (in part, Fitzgerald infuses the book with German atmosphere by toying with words and syntax in the subtlest of ways, coaxing Germanic sounds and sense from her language in a subterranean fashion that largely escapes the reader's consciousness even as it transforms her or his experience of the novel). Like other Fitzgerald novels, *The Blue Flower* is an absorbing, if also ironic, study of love, focusing on the young poet Friedrich von Hardenberg (who soon thereafter adopted the pen name Novalis) and his inexplicable adoration of a plain twelve-year-old girl named Sophie von Kühn. A novel that wears its research lightly, even as it juggles philosophy with the torments of love, *The Blue Flower* is in every way a virtuoso achievement. At just over two hundred pages, it is startlingly brief (though longer than most of Fitzgerald's other books), yet it is indisputably the work of a bold, accomplished author. It is not surprising that it won the highest praise from critics throughout the English-speaking world: the *New York Times*, like many other newspapers in the United States and Britain, named it one of the best books of 1997, extolling it as "a wholly convincing evocation of that notoriously difficult matter, genius" ("Best Books" 12). It was, significantly, the first non-American book to be awarded the National Book Critics Circle Award in the United States.

Unlike Fitzgerald's other novels, *The Blue Flower* is centrally concerned with the mind and character of an artist, Friedrich von Hardenberg. As such, the novel is a shrewd consideration of the literary imagination and its problematic relation to the world. Hardenberg's love for Sophie is difficult to grasp, and its origins are still more mysterious. He regards Sophie with unremitting gentleness and adoration and speaks of her in the most exalted, if indecipherable, terms. The dignity and honor of his love are granted full credence by Sophie and her parents, even if they fail to fathom it. Yet there is something impersonal and domineering about Hardenberg's tender adoration of Sophie. In his insistence that she is his "spirit's guide," Hardenberg dominates her even as he ennobles her. Undoubtedly his love for Sophie is associated with his poetic calling—she is clearly his muse—and so Fitzgerald's ambiguous portrait of Hardenberg's love for Sophie becomes an uneasy meditation on art and the world. In Hardenberg imagination seems to disregard the prerogatives, and indeed the reality, of the world (in this case, Sophie's plain, innocent girlhood) even as it exalts and transfigures it. The conduct of other women in the novel—practical, self-sacrificing figures such as the poet's loving sister, Sidonie; Karoline Just, who also loves Hardenberg but is confined to a life of drudgery and scant opportunities; and Sophie's older sister, Friederike, who selflessly cares for Sophie in the months before the girl dies, horribly, of tuberculosis—presents a worldly, dignified context within which Hardenberg's radical idealization of Sophie begins to seem frivolous, untenable, and even cruel.

ASSESSMENT

Fitzgerald's career was an unconventional one, almost as idiosyncratic as her sundry novels and characters. Beginning at age sixty-one with a literary genre (the mystery novel) that she was to abandon at once, Fitzgerald soon won a devoted following in Britain (and some years later in the United States) for her short, perfectly rendered novels about small, unusual communities, described, as in the early *Bookshop* and *Offshore*, with a telling mix of realism, satire, and saving compassion. In these early successes her acute interests in struggling women, eccentric elderly people, and cast-off children were evident. What became apparent more gradually was her interest in the vicissitudes, redemptive possibilities, and hidden injustices of romantic love. In fact, in her last four novels—*Innocence, The Beginning of Spring, The Gate of Angels*, and *The Blue Flower*—that complex attention to love came unmistakably to the fore. In all these novels, but especially in *The Blue Flower*, Fitzgerald increasingly suggested the mystery and stubborn reality—if also the perverseness and occasional tyranny—of love.

Penelope Fitzgerald sometimes described herself as a literary traditionalist, or conservative, and in fact these descriptions seem to fit her well. Her novels are told in an accessible fashion, with emphasis on character and local detail, and are governed by a strong authorial point of view. (She also wrote all of her novels by hand—"in pen and ink, and I labor over every word," as she told Basbanes [10].) Yet one should beware of overemphasizing the traditional nature of her books. In their indefatigable research and surprising combinations of fact and invention, Fitzgerald's novels are identifiably works of their own era—postmodern works, after a fashion, that challenge our complacent assumptions about fiction and reality. In their stubborn evocations of the most mundane aspects of our lives, combined with their sudden flashes of light upon the mysteries of human experience, her novels begin to reveal their truest scope, ambition, and originality.

Yet that mix of the mundane and miraculous is no matter for simple celebration, as Fitzgerald's deeply ambivalent portrayal of Friedrich von Hardenberg's love for Sophie von Kühn in *The Blue Flower* demonstrates. Hardenberg's transformative imaginative powers and impulses are regarded with a complex mixture of admiration and skepticism by Fitzgerald. The determined, daily realism that informs all her books (including *The Blue Flower*) seems to reflect a suspicion of the unfettered imagination and a heightened respect for the quotidian world. If Fitzgerald's subject in *The Blue Flower* and other books is the mystery of love and human imagination, it is just as surely the persistent, irreducible facts of the world itself. In this respect Fitzgerald was a highly individual, yet not atypical, writer of her own era: a novelist whose traditional predilections could not altogether mask a lively, subversive suspicion of art and the romantic imagination.

BIBLIOGRAPHY

Primary Sources

Edward Burne-Jones: A Biography. London: Joseph, 1975.

The Golden Child. London: Duckworth; New York: Scribner's, 1977.

The Knox Brothers. London: Macmillan; New York: Coward, McCann, 1977.

The Bookshop. London: Duckworth, 1978; Boston: Houghton, 1997.

Offshore. London: Collins, 1979; Boston: Houghton, 1998.

Human Voices. London: Collins, 1980; Boston: Houghton, 1999.

At Freddie's. London: Collins, 1982; Boston: Godine, 1985.

Charlotte Mew and Her Friends. London: Collins, 1984; North Reading, MA: Addison-Wesley, 1988.

Innocence. London: Collins, 1986; Boston: Houghton, 1998.

The Beginning of Spring. London: Collins, 1988; New York: Holt, 1989.

The Gate of Angels. London: Collins, 1990; Boston: Houghton, 1998.

The Blue Flower. London: Flamingo, 1995; Boston: Houghton, 1997.

Secondary Sources

Basbanes, Nicholas. "The Traditionalist and the Revolutionary." Interviews with Penelope Fitzgerald and Robert Coover. *Biblio* September 1998: 10.

"Best Books of 1997." *New York Times Book Review* 7 December 1997: 12.

Byatt, A.S. "The Isle Full of Noises." Rev. of *Human Voices*. *TLS* 26 September 1980: 1057.

Christensen, Philip Harlan. "Penelope Fitzgerald." In *British Novelists since 1960, Second Series*. Vol. 194 of *Dictionary of Literary Biography*. Detroit: Gale, 1998. 120–127.

Cole, Catherine Wells. "Penelope Fitzgerald." In *British Novelists since 1960, Part 1*. Vol. 14 of *Dictionary of Literary Biography*. Detroit: Gale, 1982. 302–308.

Plunket, Robert. "Dear, Slovenly Mother Moscow." Rev. of *The Beginning of Spring*. *New York Times Book Review* 7 May 1989: 15.

Pam Gems
1925–

José Ramón Prado Pérez

BACKGROUND

Born in Bransgore, Dorset, Pam Gems graduated in psychology in 1949 from Manchester University. She served in the Women's Royal Naval Service from 1944 to 1946. She is married and has four children (two sons and two daughters). She worked as a research assistant for the BBC from 1950 to 1953. In 1970 she moved to London and began writing for fringe/alternative theater. A writer for the feminist group the Women's Company and Women's Theatre Group and a member of the Women's Playhouse Trust and of the board of the Soho Theatre, she embraces the idea that theater should be dominated by women if a genuine women's theater is to be developed. Her feminism is not so much academic as the result of her personal life experience and her necessity to affirm a set of values that she firmly believes in.

ANALYSIS

Pam Gems's dramatic production is informed by the dynamic social context in Great Britain around the eve of the 1968 events that gave rise to the feminist movement and the emergence and later consolidation of the phenomenon of alternative theater. Her early work in the 1960s was associated with the small-scale productions of the incipient touring companies and small independent theater buildings or other alternative spaces not constructed specifically for theatrical performance. It was after her first successes, especially with the play *Dusa, Fish, Stas, and Vi* in 1976–1977, which was transferred to the West End commercial theater (Mayfair Theatre), that she established a fruitful and lasting collaboration with the Royal Shakespeare Company in the second part of the 1970s. From this point onward her work became institutionalized, though remaining provocative, in a contradictory process that has tended to canonize her as an intellectual writer with a message to voice in her plays, while, on the other hand, her works have been incorporated into the mainstream of a middle-class educated audience, opening up new possibilities in her dramatic approach. In fact, her mastery and control of the textual nature of drama might have helped her to enter the mainstream of the institutional theaters more easily than others of her women colleagues.

The evolution in her work can be explained in historical, theatrical, and social and cultural terms, with each play a step further in her development as a dramatist, as well as a development in her exploration of women's and feminist issues. Thus her apprenticeship started in the field of radio and television drama, more suitable for women who had to raise children, since it could be done privately at home. The next stage saw her involvement in the fringe with the emergent feminist groups the Women's Theatre Group and The Women's Company and her participation in the first Women's Theatre Festival in 1973 and the one following in 1975. Progressively, Gems's work, though still collaborative, moved away from the fringe and alternative circuit and toward the institutional theaters, especially the Royal Shakespeare Company (R.C.), developing a very personal and distinct dramatic voice.

In any case, Gems's case is paradigmatic of the difficulties that women encountered in the theatrical establishment. *Piaf*, written earlier than *Dusa, Fish, Stas, and Vi*, had to wait for the appropriate time to be staged or even taken into consideration, 1978. The R.C. did not take a risk with Gems, but adopted her once she had made an impact in the fringe and at the Edinburgh Festival with the production of *Dusa, Fish, Stas, and Vi*.

Gems's plays are strongly related to the emergence of the feminist movement and the women's liberation movement around 1969–1970. However, she did not achieve prominence until a substantial change in the alternative-movement trends took place, moving away from agitprop, street performance, and purely collective forms of theater toward hybrid forms of collaboration, in which the playwright as author recovered some of her former status. She also benefited, as did other women writers, from a certain democratization of the theatrical establishment, as well as the appearance of a new audience with specific interests. Thus the collective of women, which had not been fully represented in the theater, began to find a place in the medium with the production of plays written by, for, and about women, from their own perspective.

Pam Gems's apprenticeship in the fringe, in collaboration with the Almost Free Theatre, provided her with a special gift for handling theatrical space in a practical and economical way, which has become a distinctive characteristic of her plays. Equally, her treatment of space has been determined by her willingness to experiment with form and her adoption of narrative and spatial techniques from the cinematic spectrum. Among these we could list the use of ellipsis, simultaneity of action, collapse of temporal frames, and conflation of character representation, thus disrupting the psychologist approach to character and the use of the unities, endorsed by theatrical naturalism.

Her fascination with film surfaces in the various plays in which Gems sets out to revise the role given by the film industry to heroines such as Greta Garbo in *Queen Christina* or Marlene Dietrich in *The Blue Angel* and *Marlene*. The use of these cinematic icons serves the author to illustrate the indissoluble nature of the private and the public domains. Gems focuses on the private sphere by reclaiming the realm of emotions and inner lives of these actresses/characters while stripping them of the false glamor attached to them by the consumerist Hollywood industry. Her reinterpretations of these popular icons emphasize the role of the woman heroine, recovering their humanity and providing a feminist critique of the appropriation and manipulation to which they have been subjected by the patriarchal ideology. Additionally, Gems unveils the ideological project behind film that attempts to perpetuate the subordination of women through stereotype.

In rewriting the histories of popular women icons such as Garbo and Dietrich or the singer Edith Piaf or the nineteenth-century fictional character Camille, the recurrent link among these various women is the fact that they had become outcast problematic female figures who would transgress and subvert their given role in society by using their positions of fame, never to conform to the established rule. Moreover, these women show a deviant sexual conduct that amounts for a great deal of their transgressive nature: Greta Garbo in the role of Queen Christina, a character who had to assume a male role and identity as a state imposition; or Marlene Dietrich, impersonating a prostitute in *The Blue Angel*. Garbo and Dietrich had allegedly had lesbian relationships while having been worshipped as beauty icons by the film industry. Lesbian relationships also appear overtly in *Stanley*, where Patricia and Dorothy are lovers. On the other hand, Camille and Piaf belong to the group of sexually liberated and promiscuous women who use sex not only to survive, but also to achieve higher aims.

Gems explains her interest in, as well as the power of, these famous iconic women when she describes Marlene Dietrich:

> Yet our icon did not console. She kept herself to herself. She judged us. She accepted our worship . . . demanded it, turned it over for worth. And bowed acceptance. This icon was Aphrodite and Diana, Juno and Demeter in one . . . A modern icon. A made woman. A stayer. Tough, hard to please, alluring, comforting . . . and there for us. The working Madonna. (Introduction to *Marlene* 9)

These popular heroines are portrayed in a dual way, similar to the ambivalence emanating from any popular genre, with contradictory features that provide the necessary distance in order to present a revision of the mythical figure without falling into the trap of romanticizing it. As Gems puts it, they share the complementary features of the "working Madonna" even when, for society, such a combination might be antithetical. With these characters it is the antithesis that provides for their difference, complexity, and greatness. In *Piaf* the freshness and spontaneity of the character make her a woman able to overcome any difficulty thanks to her almost carnivalesque personality. It is the combination of her hedonistic attitude toward life, her hardworking nature, and the preservation of her feelings and concern for other people that enriches her personality, superseding the received image of the fallen idol. In the case of *Marlene*, we also see the human side of this woman at the end of her career. It is in the portrayal of the human side of these heroines that their greatness emerges unscathed. These women are described as complex characters in constant interaction with their social milieu, sharing positive and negative traits upon which they act in order to survive, as well as to avoid the roles imposed on them by society. This fight against conventionalism is painful but desirable, and eventually this act of rebellion becomes a truly political stand.

The feminist approach in Gems's plays could be considered a romantic one, toeing a fine line between the bourgeois, the socialist, and the radical. There are instances where Gems's plays are focused more prominently on individual women characters and their internal conflicts, although not in the classical masculine way of the psychological portrait; at other times, the forces of society acquire a relevance that makes them conspicuous, almost an additional character, but, unlike in tragedy, there is no hint of the inevitability of events or the intromission of fate. Both the individual and social elements stand in a relation of tension that provides the conflictual pattern in the plays. It is just a matter of degree as to which becomes more prominent in the resolution of each particular piece.

Formal experimentation in Gems serves the purpose of rejecting classical and accepted modes of representation associated with a masculine and patriarchal point of view. She presents such a perspective, which has been naturalized as the universal commonsense view, as the ideological construct that it is, and she confronts it with a genuine female perspective, presented as a valid alternative. For that reason, her plays attempt, and successfully accomplish, the subversion of the Aristotelian model of climactic structure and final resolution of the conflict. In fact, conflicts often remain unresolved or postponed at the closing of her pieces. Experiment also focuses on the self-reflexive nature of the play, showing it as a performance in progress rather than a naturalistic slice of life. The departure from illusionism aims at barring the easy identification and empathy of the audience with the main characters or the narrative events. As such, the plays reveal the contradictions arising from the patriarchal structures of power and thought when they are contrasted with the actual circumstances in the lives of the women characters. In terms of their construction, Gems's plays rely on a discursive structure and the idea of reversal (a typical technique associated with comedy) rather than climax, thus refusing any tragic sense openly.

Some of her plays adopt the Brechtian format, which had become a point of reference for committed or aspiring political productions in the late 1960s and 1970s. In the case of Gems, the Brechtian structure is put to the service of the feminist ideology with ample success while she reinterprets and adapts the form to the specificity of her message. *Piaf* constitutes an example of the combination of Brechtian techniques and the form of the musical. In terms of style, the arrangement of scenes and the use of the songs follow the Brechtian maxim of providing an explanation or a commentary to the narrative, while the adoption of a double frame for the play breaks the illusionist effect. Regarding the theme, certain distinctive elements of the musical are retained: the topical story line of the newcomer who achieves easy and sudden success and subsequently falls; or the happy ending, which is retained so as to avoid the morality of the tale, thus subverting the idea of any moral retribution for the excesses committed by Piaf in her life. However, these features from the classic musical are challenged by putting on stage a number of eschatological elements of Piaf's life, in order to shock the audience and to discard the glamor and the stereotypical nature of the musical form.

Marlene includes a similar use of songs, which appear integrated into the logic of the plot, although there is a conscious avoidance, as in *Piaf*, of the idea of spectacle and glamor associated with the musical. Gems's exploitation of music could be observed already in *Dusa, Fish, Stas, and Vi*, where it served as an element to punctuate the action and provide commentary and audience guidance in a similar way as the cinema does (indicating emotion, atmosphere, suspense, or transition).

The conditions that appeared in society and the theater during the Thatcher government, with the gradual withdrawal of state subsidy for the arts in favor of private sponsoring and the retreat into conservative social and cultural codes, helped the further development of the feminist slogan "The personal is political," under which women's drama continued its successful growth until it acquired its maturity and recognition in the British scene. Feminist drama provided a critique of Thatcherite politics from the sphere of the private rather than the public field that was to be followed by a wide group of committed and political playwrights. It was in this context that Gems's play *Loving Women* (1984) has conceived, uniting the concerns of a disillusioned Left with the problems of living together in an increasingly more individualistic society. It is the male character, Frank, who had served as an inspiration for his comrades and especially his lover/partner, Susannah, who betrays the ideals for which both had worked in the 1970s. The betrayal of ideas and convictions is paralleled by the physical betrayal of his relationship with Susannah, thus making the personal and the political conflate graphically. The ending of the play is hopeful and positive in presenting the possibility of developing feelings and the sense of a community of women as an alternative to the dehumanization and disintegration undergone by the male character. The final rejection of Frank by the two women who had been involved with him sentimentally, followed by their union, makes Susannah and

Crystal complementary sides of the spectrum of the female microcosm: the progressive left-wing committed woman, Susannah, and the bourgeois, uncommitted woman, Crystal, who are brought together by their common experiences. The play could be said to embrace a socialist-feminist dynamics due to the suggestion that it offers of a future where women share forces, united as a community. In that sense *Loving Women* is a development from *Dusa, Fish, Stas, and Vi*. The latter, in fact, was criticized by certain sectors of the feminist movement for its pessimism and the absence of a future alternative for the women in the play: Fish commits suicide after progressively degenerating into madness because she cannot get over the fact that her partner has run away with another woman. Since Fish is the only character with an overt political attitude, working for the Labour movement, this ending would provide an intellectual closure to the play that would place it nearer to the bourgeois individualist positions of feminism. However, the hints presented in the play as to the survival of the rest of the characters, after going through negative experiences related to their condition as women, help us think of possibilities of change and survival despite Fish's end, as in the case of Fish's friend, Dusa, who recovers her children, or the sketched commonality that Stas shows at the end of the play and her liberality with money earned through prostitution. In her case, as well as with the rest of Gems's prostitutes, she reverses the exploitative nature of prostitution to her own advantage in order to achieve personal freedom.

Loving Women and, to a certain extent, *Dusa, Fish, Stas, and Vi* are paradigmatic of Gems's use of the theatrical love triangle. This classic semiotic structure in the presentation of the characters' relationships is a constant thematic preoccupation with the author, who inverts and subverts the roles of hero, object, and opponent in order to denounce the situation of women. The resolution of the conflict posed by the love triangle is almost always obliteration for one of the women involved in it, with the exception of *Loving Women*, where the male axis of the triangle is suppressed at the end. In the other plays where there is a love triangle, one of the women suffers physical or psychological destruction, or both. With the manipulation of the triangle roles, it is this destroyed woman, always a common woman, naïve in her assumptions and ready to sacrifice for love, who emerges as the heroine, as opposed to the sophistication and inauthenticity of the rest of the triangle.

Stanley conforms to this pattern. Patricia convinces Stanley to marry her and divorce his wife Hilda, who will become the victim. Patricia is just a dilettante who only wants Stanley for the position that he holds both in the social and artistic milieu. The arrangement is that Hilda will satisfy his sexual appetite, while Patricia will be the legally entitled wife. Hilda's sacrifice for love at the beginning of the relationship and her economic dependence in raising the children later perpetuate this unjust situation, encouraged by Stanley's egocentric, narcissistic, and chauvinistic nature. Here the male figure, Stanley, is clearly reminiscent of Frank in *Loving Women*. In *Stanley* art becomes the metaphor for political and social commitment, embodied in the historical figure of Stanley Spencer, a working-class painter, totally opposed to the elitism of the avant-gardists of the 1910s and 1920s. The betrayal of his own class and origin, illustrated in the exchange of Hilda for Patricia, destroys Hilda and reveals the dislocation between his social and private personae.

Another thematic concern dealt with by Gems is the portrayal of society as mostly hypocritical and Manichaean toward women when it is not frontally opposed to them. The end result of such a social behavior is the final destruction of the women involved, or when they do survive, their answer to such social rejection is the development of an utter cynicism in order to protect themselves. Cynicism and suffering are combined with a genuine and truthful attitude toward life, which serves these women to transform their predicament and destruction into their victory, since they are able to achieve the independence and freedom that other women are effectively denied. Piaf defies the utilitarian and moralist restrictive rules of society with her hedonistic lifestyle, which makes her a heroine from the lower classes who is able to transcend her origins while remaining a successful barrier breaker. She is satisfied with herself and her actions up to the last minute, in contrast with the official story, which emphasizes the exemplary nature of this tale of destruction, making Piaf a victim of her own success and excess. Similarly, the development of plot in *Camille*, based on *La Dame aux Camélias*, rejects the victimization of the main character and presents her as a tenacious fighter, thus avoiding her possible demonization by society.

ASSESSMENT

Gems's works explore a number of women's issues that become recurrent in all her plays. Among others, we may list the analysis of women's independence and freedom, very closely related to economic and emotional freedom; the questioning of sexual and gender roles and stereotype by presenting different angles in the lives of theoretically liberated women; and the examination of sexual relationships between the male and the female in connection with the conflicts that appear between the social public sphere and the private one.

In her evolution as a playwright Pam Gems progressively shows how the private is or becomes political, even when the endings of various of her plays may have negative consequences for the women who endorse the private alone. However, this could be regarded as the ultimate political act: the denunciation of the destruction that women suffer for reaffirming the private as a positive alternative to the established values in society. Gems's words may summarize her theatrical practice and vital attitude toward art and life:

> Only if you know what you want to say, and need passionately to say it, does the courage come to stick it out. Which is as it should be. Art is of necessity. Which is why we need women playwrights just now very badly. We have our own history to create, and to write. Personally, I think there will be brilliant women playwrights. I think the form suits us. Women are very funny, coarse, subversive. All good qualities for drama, and for the achievement of progress by the deployment, not of violence, but of subtlety, love and imagination. (Afterword to *Dusa, Fish, Stas, and Vi*, in Wandor, *Plays by Women 1* 72–73)

BIBLIOGRAPHY

Primary Sources

A Builder by Trade (television play). 1961.

Betty's Wonderful Christmas. Prod. London, 1972.

After Birthday. Prod. London, 1973; revised as *Sandra*, 1979.

The Amiable Courtship of Miz Venus and Wild Bill. Prod. London, 1973.

My Warren. Prod. London, 1973.

Sarah B. Divine! Collaboration with Tom Eyen, music by Jonathan Kramer. Prod. 1973.

Go West, Young Woman. Prod. London, 1974.

Up in Sweden. Prod. Leicester, 1975.

Dusa, Fish, Stas, and Vi. Previously titled *Dead Fish*, prod. Kundry's Theatre, Edinburgh Festival, 1976; as *Dusa, Fish, Stas, and Vi*, Hampstead Theatre Club, 1976; Mayfair Theatre, 1977.

Guinevere. Prod. Edinburgh, 1976.

My Name Is Rosa Luxemburg (adaptation of Marianne Auricoste). Prod. London, 1976.

The Project. Prod. London, 1976; revised as *Loving Women*, 1984.

The Rivers and Forests (adaptation of Marguerite Duras). Prod. London, 1976.

Franz into April. Prod. 1977.

Queen Christina (based on the film directed by Rouben Mamoulian, 1933). Prod. Stratford, 1977; revised 1982.

Piaf. Prod. Stratford, 1978.

Ladybird, Ladybird. Prod. 1979.

Sandra. Prod. 1979.

Uncle Vanya (adaptation of Anton Chekhov). Prod. London, 1979. London: Eyre Methuen, 1979.

We Never Do What They Want (television play). 1979.

A Doll's House (adaptation of Henrik Ibsen). Prod. Tyne/Wear, 1980.

Aunt Mary. Prod. Stratford, 1982.

The Treat. Prod. 1982; film version, dir. Jonathan Gems, 1998.

Variety Night (collaboration). Prod. 1982.

Camille (adaptation of Alexander Dumas fils). Prod. Stratford, 1984.

The Cherry Orchard (adaptation of Anton Chekhov). Prod. 1984. Cambridge: Cambridge UP, 1996.

Loving Women. Prod. London, 1984.

Pasionaria. Lyrics by Gems and Paul Sand; music by Sand. Prod. 1985.

Three Plays (*Piaf*, *Camille*, and *Loving Women*). London: Penguin, 1985.

The Danton Affair (adaptation of Stanislawa Przybyszewska). Prod. 1986.

Mrs. Frampton (novel). 1989.

Bon Voyage, Mrs. Frampton (novel). 1990.

The Blue Angel (adaptation of novel by Heinrich Mann, film directed by Josef von Sternberg, 1930). Prod. Stratford, 1991.

Ghosts (adaptation of Henrik Ibsen). Prod. 1993.

Yerma (adaptation of Federico García Lorca). Prod. 1993.

Deborah's Daughter. Prod. Manchester, 1994.

The Seagull (adaptation of Anton Chekhov). Prod. London, 1994. London: Hern, 1994.

Marlene. Prod. Oldham, 1996. London: Oberon, 1998.

Stanley. Prod. London, 1996.

The Snow Palace (adaptation of Stanisława Przybyszewska). Prod. London, 1997.

Secondary Sources

Aston, Elaine. "Pam Gems: Body Politics and Biography." In *The Cambridge Companion to Modern British Women Playwrights*. Ed. Elaine Aston and Janelle Reinelt. Cambridge: Cambridge UP, 2000.

Baccolini, Raffaella. "L'identità femminile nel teatro contemporaneo in lingua inglese." In *Il teatro e le donne: Forme drammatiche e tradizione al femminile nel teatro inglese*. Ed. R. Baccolini, Vita Fortunati, Romana Zacchi. Urbino: Quattroventi, 1991. 183–196.

Burkman, Katherine H. "The Plays of Pam Gems." In *British and Irish Drama since 1960*. Ed. James Acheson. Basingstoke: Macmillan, 1993. 190–201.

Galeotti, Rossella. "Pam Gems e Caryl Churchill: Due figure femminili nel teatro inglese contemporaneo." *Quaderni del Dipartimento di Lingue e Letterature Straniere Moderne* [Genova: Università di Genova], 5 (1992): 167–177.

Innes, Christopher. "Pam Gems." In *Contemporary Women Dramatists*. Ed. K.A. Berney. London: St. James, 1994. 87–90, 308–309.

———. "Pam Gems: Reinterpreting the stereotype." In *Modern British Drama, 1890–1990*. Cambridge: Cambridge UP, 1996. 453–459.

Keyssar, Helene. *Feminist Theatre: An Introduction to Plays of Contemporary British and American Women*. Basingstoke: Macmillan, 1984.

Neumeier, Beate. "Past Lives in Present Drama: Feminist Theatre and Intertextuality." In *Frauen und Frauendarstellung in der englischen und amerikanischen Literatur*. Ed. Therese Fischer-Seidel. Tübingen: Narr, 1991. 181–198.

Omasreiter Blaicher, Ria. "Die gescheiterte Emanzipation der Frauen in feministischen Drama der Gegenwart." *Anglia* 112: 3–4 (1994): 390–410.

Rudolph, Sarah J. "Pam Gems." In *British Playwrights, 1956–1995: A Research and Production Sourcebook*. Ed. William W. Demastes. Westport, CT: Greenwood, 1996. 158–168.

Stephenson, Heide, and Natasha Langridge, eds. *Rage and Reason: Women Playwrights on Playwriting*. London: Methuen, 1997.

Wandor, Michelene. "Pam Gems." In *Carry On, Understudies: Theatre and Sexual Politics*. London: Routledge, 1986. 161–166.

———, ed. *Plays by Women 1*. London: Methuen, 1982.

———, ed. *Plays by Women 3*. London: Methuen, 1984.

———. "Sexuality and Gender: Lowe, Sherman, Gay Sweatshop, Churchill, O'Malley, Gems, Dunn, Page." In *Drama Today: A Critical Guide to British Drama, 1970–1990*. Harlow: Longman and British Council, 1993.

Susan Elizabeth Hill
1942–

Mary Louise Hill

BACKGROUND

Born in Scarborough, Yorkshire, England, as the only child of older parents, Susan Hill produced her first novel, *The Enclosure*, in 1961, just as she was completing grammar school. Her second novel appeared in 1963, the same year she received her B.A. degree in English from King's College at the University of London. The bulk of what she has called her "serious" work appeared between 1968 and 1974, including *I'm the King of the Castle* (1970), which was awarded the 1971 Somerset Maugham Award, *Strange Meeting* (1971), *The Bird of Night* (1972), which received the 1972 Whitbread Literary Award for Fiction, and *In the Springtime of the Year* (1974). Her 1971 collection of short stories, *The Albatross*, received the 1972 John Llewellyn Rhys Memorial Prize. In 1977 she began writing her own column, "The World of Books," for the *London Daily Telegraph*; here, in 1981, she announced, "I have done with novels, I gave them up seven years ago and have absolutely no intention of returning to them, and no more desire to do so than I have of smoking a cigarette again" (qtd. in Hofer 143). One would hope that her resolve over cigarettes has been stronger than that against novel writing: *The Woman in Black* appeared in 1983, followed by several more novels and a collection of short stories. Her most recent novel, *The Service of Clouds*, was published in 1998. She has never stopped writing; during her hiatus from fiction (in which she married Shakespearean scholar Stanley Wells and had two daughters), Hill produced children's books, gardening books, and books about the English countryside.

Perhaps Hill's radio plays offer the most intense experience of her narrative technique. Donald A. Low has commented, "The formula she adopts . . . in her radio plays is essentially a simple one. Something which begins by being low key and apparently trivial gradually gathers pace, is felt to be thoroughly ominous, and moves towards a desperate and painful ending" (112). "Apparently trivial" is not quite appropriate for the outset of *The Cold Country*, a radio play about four men trapped in a blizzard somewhere near the South Pole. The beginning displays a neat economy of detail that immediately points toward the ominous: a ghostlike countertenor sings of what will happen "[W]hen thou from hence doest pass away," fading into the sound of a lone harmonica and a card game. All is suddenly interrupted by the command "Here . . . here listen" (*The Cold Country* 73–74). What are they listening for? A crackle, a connection—on a radio. These details immediately set a tone of loneliness and expectation while demanding that the radio listener also hearken. In listening, the audience is drawn into these men's realization that they are facing death. In a less threatening manner the radio play *Strange Meeting* (also a novel) begins with a man's arrival into a gentle, bird-filled, rural atmosphere. However, the listener soon learns that this man, Hilliard, is returning to a World War I war zone, where he meets the dynamic young soldier Barton. The play traces the development of their friendship as they approach the front, where they, too, must ultimately encounter death.

In a personal letter written in 1995, Hill mused, "Interestingly, although I no longer write for radio, I still always hear everything that I write as a novelist in my head as I put it down, rather as if I were listening to a radio play." This comment intimates that her fictional structure has its roots in oral storytelling. Her 1983 *The Woman in Black* displays the oral roots of her style: the entire story is framed by a narrator who has a tale that "should be exorcised" (22). Similarly, her primary forms—Gothic tales of mystery and doom, ghost stories, and children's stories—all rely on a suspenseful buildup such as that described by Low. But even her children's stories move toward a confrontation with death. *Lanterns across the Snow* evolves toward a Christmas day on which a young girl encounters her first human corpse. The cold, dead grouse that the child picks up as she and her father walk to the dead man's home becomes emblematic of the child's unanswered query: "Why does God make people die?" (46). That question and a probing into the often-lonely life that precedes death lie at the center of much of Hill's work.

ANALYSIS

Hill's well-constructed narrative structure, coupled with the fact that most of her works are in the third person, results in a dispassionate distancing and coldness. In addition, her characters are emotionally freakish, suffering from a fundamental inability to express or explore themselves. Notably, too, until fairly recently, most of her primary characters have been men, resulting in statements such as this, from the *Times Literary Supplement*: "[S]he seems happier . . . inside the skin of male characters" (qtd. in Campbell). Rosemary Jackson takes the expected feminist step in her criticism of this male-dominated world:

> Instead of clarifying or confronting difficult ideological issues, about the role of the artist within contemporary culture, and the problem of women's oppression within patriarchy, Susan Hill's work evades them. Her art is trapped within a tradition of humanism. . . . Her women are trapped in their ignorance of the political roots of their misery. Attempts to resolve these questions on an apolitical, metaphysical level prove both unsatisfactory and, as Hill's fiction illustrates, impossible. It is no accident that Susan Hill's work has been so well received by a liberal literary tradition, for it ends by silencing its own timorous interrogation of some of the fatal and crippling effects of a patriarchal, "male" culture and retreats into a familiar "female" enclosure of defeatism. (103)

Working from Jackson's cue, one might say that Hill's work offers fuel to the argument that the liberal patriarchal hegemony (which has used standard narrative as a means of shaping experience) has indeed refused women a significant space to develop their own authorial voice. Yet even though Hill's work provides ample material for such an analysis, the "enclosures" that she depicts do not merely limit women. In its tendency to present male voices, Hill's work also exposes the restrictions that the patriarchal hegemony places upon men.

Several of Hill's works indeed include women who suffer a mild case of gender confusion. The young girl in *Lanterns across the Snow* early admits, "I am a disappointment to them, because I am not a son" (12). In the novel *Strange Meeting* the narrator's much-loved sister Beth really seems to be a man in disguise: "Beth had inherited their father's long bony face, the high, narrow bridge to a nose that, in age, would become beak-like. Her hair grew far back from a very high forehead. Only her eyes, flint coloured and thickly lashed, made her seem beautiful sometimes, because of their stillness" (27). Hilliard opts not to introduce his sister to his friend Barton because she is "plain." Barton becomes a replacement for her when she asserts her womanliness by announcing her engagement. If Hill's women are not plagued by the fact that those around them would prefer that they be men, they are merely one-dimensional, like Helena Kingshaw in *I'm the King of the Castle*, who in her quest to get married despite her own son's needs proves to be "the most incompetent of all incompetent mothers in Susan Hill's fiction" (Schubert). These characters are, at best, the shadows of women, and they reach their apogee in *The Woman in Black*, where the primary female character is a ghost.

Cast alongside these wispy characters, Hill's men assume a fullness that is almost fleshy. For purposes of brevity, I will here focus upon *I'm the King of the Castle* and *Strange Meeting* (the novel), both of which foreground male relationships and expose the limitations placed upon these men by society.

In *I'm the King of the Castle* Charles Kingshaw accompanies his mother, who has gained the position of "informal housekeeper" in the home of Joseph Hooper and his son Edmund. While Helena and Joseph begin courting each other, Charles is left to his own means against the evil plotting of Edmund. "We cannot fathom the minds of young children," his father muses (53); indeed, this novel exposes how evil these minds might be. Greeted by a note that reads "I DIDN'T WANT YOU TO COME HERE," and the claim "This isn't your place," Kingshaw is immediately cast into a feeling of isolation that only compounds as the book progresses. In the house Edmund Hooper dominates; if Kingshaw finds a hiding place, the other boy quickly discovers it. Possessing keys to the various rooms, Hooper has the power to lock Kingshaw into the places he most fears, which he does. When Kingshaw tries to escape to the nearby Hang Woods, Hooper follows him. Away from "the forbidding house where the boys are 'enclosed' " (Hofer 134), Kingshaw can practice some power, only to be cut short when Hooper reminds him, "Anybody who hasn't got a father is useless" (128).

As Jackson points out, this is a novel about "survival in an adult world whose rules are patriarchal" (89). But it also poses the question: what happens when there is a problem with the patriarch? Overshadowed by his own father, who was a famous lepidopterist, Joseph Hooper "knew himself to be an ineffectual man, without any strength or imposing qualities, a man who was liked and honoured but little regarded, a man who had failed—but not dramatically, as one falling from a great height, who attracts attention. He was a dull man, a man who got by" (12). Further, he refuses to assert himself with his son: "Perhaps I should strike him, Joseph Hooper thought. . . . I do not like his supercilious expression. I should assert myself. But he knew that he would not" (28). His vengeful son assumes a silent power in the house, while the elder Hooper merely occupies the position required of him by society. Thus *I'm the King of the Castle* could be seen as an indictment of an inept patriarchy. Despite his mediocrity, Joseph Hooper is still the head of the house, the man whom Helena knows she needs for security, the father that Charles desperately wants, and the decision maker. The elder Hooper refuses to acknowledge that young Kingshaw could be suffering abuse by Edmund, and it is ultimately Hooper's decision to send him to Edmund's boarding school that causes the tormented child to commit suicide.

The elder's unfocused leadership is contrasted with his son's meticulous tyranny. On the boy's wall hangs the map of a battleground, to which Joseph responds:

> "But that is not what any battlefield ever was, that . . ." He made a gesture—for he wanted to talk . . . more than anything, it angered

> him to see his son's careful map, he wanted to say, this is *nothing*, nothing, this tight, neat, careful little plan, he wanted to tell the truth of the matter, to impart a vision of men and blood and horses, the boom and stench of gunfire and the noise of pain, the terrible confusion of it all. But he could not begin. (26)

Clearly, Joseph Hooper knows the truth of war—the ultimate patriarchal power game. If he could impart this to his son, could he curb that child's plotting? The map and some toy soldiers reappear at various points in the book, suggesting that Edmund Hooper has carefully plotted his assault on Kingshaw. Indeed, the younger Hooper has the cold-blooded mind of a military strategist, as is chillingly revealed: "When he saw Kingshaw's body, upside down in the water, Hooper thought suddenly, . . . I did that, *it was because of me*, and a spurt of triumph went through him" (252).

Strange Meeting (written the year after *I'm the King of the Castle*) examines what happens when such strategists grow up and begin playing real war games. As Ernest H. Hofer describes, "[T]wo young men [are] forced into one another's company by virtue of their army assignment. Hilliard could not be a more cramped, stereotypical English upper middle-class product: he is the senior lieutenant, son of non-communicating parents. He cannot meet people, or indeed even talk to his parents, except in the most level, conventional way. Then Barton arrives in his billet, a newly assigned junior lieutenant, a doctor's son, with none of the built-in hang-ups of class that strangle Hilliard" (136). Upon first meeting the gregarious Barton, Hilliard feels "a wave of relief, coupled with an instinctive suspicion" (*Strange Meeting* 57). Gradually, though, Hilliard becomes fascinated by the other man. In a provocative early scene that features the two men lying together in a field, Barton seduces Hilliard into sharing his past. The two men's increasing intimacy is marked by a scene in which Barton inspects the shrapnel wound on Hilliard's leg: "The only people to look at it until now had been doctors. . . . He himself had examined it, peering at it closely as he used to peer at scabs and bruises on arms and knees when he was a small boy. . . . He touched this shrapnel wound with the pads of his fingers . . . and now Barton was looking at it with the same kind of curiosity" (70).

Several critics have commented upon the homosexual overtones in this and other Hill works, but she successfully avoids anything too overt. Her true intent is to reveal the horrors of war. Hilliard has seen these horrors, and his scars stand as testimony to that. The shrapnel penetrated him, destroying whatever innocence was left in him. This innocence is what Hilliard wants to keep intact with Barton. When he is faced with orders for Barton to go to the front on a map-drawing mission, Hilliard offers to take his place, but he cannot stop the inevitable. Barton goes, experiences trench warfare, and returns altered. In Hill's wartime environment where men learn to love each other without physical intimacy, war becomes sex, but it is more like rape. Each man encounters it alone, and if he returns, he returns with a new physical and emotional knowledge.

That knowledge is gained due to the misguided wishes of a war-loving patriarchy. Truly, the "strangeness" of this meeting comes from the fact that because of their contrasting social status, Hilliard would never have met Barton in "normal" society, would never have discovered that he could "love him, as he had loved no other person in his life" (130). Indeed, social class and sexual repression are two more cruel jokes of the patriarchy. Thrust into the chaos of wartime, the two men meet. Inevitably Barton disappears and is presumed dead. One wonders if these men's lives can ever be their own as long as they must serve the whims of their leaders, who strategize with the same aloofness and sterility as the young Edmund Hooper.

In several instances, then, Hill's men are just as restricted by the patriarchy as are her women. This is similarly exposed at the end of *The Cold Country*, where Ossie, one of two remaining men in the frozen wind-swept polar land, contemplates: "We thought we were brave men. . . . It doesn't matter what goes wrong, we'll find a way out, because that is what we are like and if we don't . . . we'll face the facts squarely. . . . Bloody terrified. That's what I am. We're not like Scott's crew, are we? We've been comparing ourselves with them" (99–100). The fact is, no man was ever like Scott's crew. The fantastic tales of that legendary polar excursion were fabricated after the fact; they were part of an impossible master narrative spun by people with power and money. Hill's polar crew is trapped in the illusion of grandness wrought by that narrative, and they wonder why, as men, they are not equally as strong. Ultimately, these men—and Susan Hill with them—cannot change the structure of the story they must live, a story that always ends in death. But they can write a new "last line" that suggests a pessimistic revision of human experience: "We're not brave, we're cowards, there's nothing special about us, this is the time we haven't won" (*The Cold Country* 100).

ASSESSMENT

A brief article in a 1976 issue of *Soviet Literature* declared Susan Hill's work "to be one of the notable examples of English prose today. . . . There is something about her characters that suggests the 'little man' of the Russian literary classics. . . . [Hill's work] makes us see the capacity for the deepest feelings behind the apparent shallowness and deformity" (Sofinskaya 166–167). Though lauded in Soviet Russia, these careful depictions of the "man in each man," delivered within neat narrative structures, offer an easy target for postdeconstructionist and feminist critics. Although Hill's recent work reveals explorations of a woman's voice, she seems to belligerently refuse to pay attention to current literary and critical trends, opting instead to continue an exploration of the craft of fiction. Recent works like *The Woman in Black* and *Mrs. DeWinter*, her sequel to Daphne du Maurier's *Rebecca*, suggest that Hill intends to continue listening to her muse and trying to "tell a good story." This has not met with as much applause as her early work. Much of the current criticism runs along these lines: "In recent years, Susan Hill has taken to the literary equivalent of manufacturing reproduction furniture" (Kemp 9).

Yet is there still a place in our society for such a storyteller? In 1936 Walter Benjamin declared, "Counsel woven into the fabric of real life is wisdom. The art of storytelling is reaching its end because the epic side of truth, wisdom, is dying out." For Benjamin, the torch was handed to the novelist: "the solitary individual, who . . . is himself uncounseled and cannot counsel others. . . . through the representation of [life's] fullness, the novel gives evidence of the profound perplexity of living" (87). Susan Hill's work is rooted firmly in the tradition of the modern novel. This is not a tradition that seeks, overtly, to teach. Social lessons need to be extracted by the reader, and since Hill's better work contains such carefully constructed details, the materials for analysis abound. Hill herself offers no cues on how to begin an analysis, though, save her unwavering need to write. Therefore, perhaps the best description of how she wants her work received was also written by Walter Benjamin: "The novel is significant, therefore, not because it presents someone else's fate to us . . . but because this stranger's fate by virtue of the flame which consumes it yields us the warmth which we never draw from our own fate. What draws the reader to the novel is the hope of warming his shivering life with a death he reads about" (101).

BIBLIOGRAPHY

Primary Sources

The Enclosure. London: Hutchinson, 1961.
Do Me A Favour. London: Hutchinson, 1963.

Listening to the Orchestra. Ebrington, Gloucestershire: Long Barn, 1966.
Gentlemen and Ladies. London: Hamish Hamilton, 1968.
A Change for the Better. London: Hamish Hamilton, 1969.
I'm the King of the Castle. New York: Viking, 1970.
The Albatross and Other Stories. London: Hamish Hamilton, 1971.
Strange Meeting. London: Hamish Hamilton, 1971.
The Bird of Night. London: Hamish Hamilton, 1972.
A Bit of Singing and Dancing. London: Hamish Hamilton, 1972.
The Cold Country. BBC Radio Three, 3 March 1972.
The Custodian (short stories). London: Covent Garden Press, 1972.
In the Springtime of the Year. London: Hamish Hamilton, 1974.
Strange Meeting. Adapt. Guy Vaesen. BBC Radio Three, 22 February 1974.
"The Cold Country" (radio play). In *The Cold Country and Other Plays for Radio*. London: BBC, 1975.
The Woman in Black. London: Hamish Hamilton, 1983; London: Mandarin, 1992.
One Night at a Time. London: Hamish Hamilton, 1984.
Through the Kitchen Window. London: Hamish Hamilton, 1984.
Lanterns across the Snow. London: Joseph, 1987. New York: Potter, 1988.
The Lighting of the Lamps (essays, reviews, and plays). London: Hamish Hamilton, 1987.
Shakespeare Country. With photographs by Robert Talbot in association with Robin Whiteman. London: Joseph, 1987.
The Spirit of the Cotswolds. London: Joseph, 1988.
Air and Angels. London: Sinclair-Stevenson, 1991.
Mrs. DeWinter. London: Sinclair-Stevenson, 1994.
Letter to Mary Louise Hill, 9 February 1995.
The Service of Clouds. London: Chatto, 1998.

Secondary Sources

Beauman, Sally. "Rereading Rebecca." *New Yorker* 8 November 1993: 127–138.
Benjamin, Walter. *Illuminations*. Ed. Hannah Arendt. Trans. Harry Zohn. New York: Harcourt, Brace and World, 1968; New York: Schocken, 1969.
Billington, Rachel. "Still Dead after All These Years." *New York Times Book Review* 7 November 1993: 23.
Brookner, Anita. "The Curious Incident of the Dog." *Spectator* 24 October 1992.
———. "A Heroine Who Declines." *Spectator* 31 October 1998: 53.
Campbell, Ann Gibaldi. "Susan Hill." In *British Short-Fiction Writers, 1945–1980*. Ed. Dean Baldwin. Vol. 139 of *Dictionary of Literary Biography*. Detroit: Gale Research, 1994. 112–121.
Harris, Gale. "Dreaming of Manderley." *Belles Lettres* 9.3 (Spring 1994): 23–24.
Hofer, Ernest H. "Enclosed Structures, Disclosed Lives: The Fictions of Susan Hill." In *Contemporary British Women Writers: Narrative Strategies*. Ed. Robert E. Hosmer, Jr. New York: St. Martin's, 1993. 128–150.
Ireland, K.R. "Rite at the Center: Narrative Duplication in Susan Hill's *In the Springtime of the Year*." *Journal of Narrative Technique* 13.3 (Fall 1983): 172–180.
Jackson, Rosemary. "Cold Enclosures: The Fiction of Susan Hill." In *Twentieth Century Women Novelists*. Ed. Thomas F. Staley. London: Macmillan, 1982. 81–103.
Kemp, Peter. "Imitation Gothic." *TLS* 15 October 1993: 9.
Low, Donald A. "Telling the Story: Susan Hill and Dorothy L. Sayers." In *British Radio Drama*. Ed. John Drakakis. Cambridge: Cambridge UP, 1981. 111–138.
Moore, Charlotte. "Breaking Out in Spots." *Spectator* 26 October 1996: 46.
Muir, Kenneth. "Susan Hill's Fiction." In *The Uses of Fiction: Essays on the Modern Novel in Honour of Arnold Kettle*. Ed. Douglas Jefferson and Graham Martin. Open UP, 1982. 273–285.
Reed, Mary Jane. "Recommended: Susan Hill." *English Journal* 72.4 (April 1983): 75–76.
Schubert, Maria. "Susan Hill: Focusing on Outsiders and Losers." In *English Language and Literature: Positions and Dispositions*. Ed. James Hogg, Karl Hubmayer, and Dorothea Steiner. Salzburg: Institut für Anglistik und Amerikanistik der Universität Salzburg, 1990. 91–101.
Sofinskaya, Irina. "Susan Hill." *Soviet Literature* 11 (1976): 166–169.

Winifred Holtby
1898–1935

Patricia Rae

A new, more fully developed Winifred Holtby has recently been emerging from the shadowy portrait by which most contemporary readers know her: the loyal, self-sacrificing "best friend" whose tragically short life Vera Brittain immortalizes in *Testament of Youth* and *Testament of Friendship*. Thanks largely to the efforts of Marion Shaw, whose brilliant biography of Holtby fills in details about her range of acquaintances and preoccupations, Holtby is set to win increasing attention as one of the most gifted women of her time, an accomplished novelist, journalist, literary critic, and political activist. Shaw's well-chosen title, *The Clear Stream*, foregrounds the self-effacing character that was both Holtby's curse and her blessing: her unusual capacity for sympathetic identification with others, which made her a dutiful daughter and friend, often drew her away from her literary work, but it was also responsible for the uncommon range and depth of human portraiture in her fiction, particularly in her masterpiece, the remarkable chronicle of Yorkshire life and local government *South Riding* (1936). The evenhandedness with which that novel explores the outer and inner lives of a range of characters from across the social spectrum, struggling with economic and physical hardships, at the same time as it advocates collectivism, makes it one of the richest and most nuanced examples of "socialist realism" of the era.

BACKGROUND

The only daughter of a wealthy Yorkshire farmer, David Holtby, and a prominent local citizen and politician, Alice, Holtby was born in 1898. She entered Somerville College, Oxford, in 1917 to read modern history, but interrupted her undergraduate career to serve with the Women's Army Artillery Corps in Huchenneville, France. On returning to Somerville in 1919, she met Brittain, and on graduation in 1921 the two moved together to London, where they launched their careers as writers. Holtby credited Brittain with convincing her of the importance of feminism: her mother's prominence and academic ambitions for her daughter had made her slow to recognize the importance of the fight for women's equality. Once convinced, she campaigned for the cause with fierce energy, contributing articles on women's issues to the *Yorkshire Post*, the *Manchester Guardian*, and, most frequently, *Time and Tide*, the prominent feminist magazine of which she became a director in 1926. Her views corresponded to those of what was then known as the "Old Feminism," an egalitarian philosophy focused on women's rights and advancement in the workplace; she was slow to appreciate the merits of the "New Feminist" project of addressing problems relevant to women on the domestic front (such as birth control, maternity medicine, infant welfare, and family allowances). She eschewed "essentialist" feminism in favor of a wider humanism: "The New Feminism," she complained, "emphasises the importance of the 'woman's point of view,' where the Old Feminism believes in the primary importance of the human being" (*Testament of a Generation* 47). After a life-changing trip to South Africa in 1926 she also worked in support of the fledgling black South African trade-union movement (the Industrial and Commercial Workers' Union), promoting the leadership of its general secretary, Clements Kadalie, and facilitating links with the trade-union movement in Britain. Finally, with Brittain, she was an activist for pacifism, lecturing on behalf of the League of Nations Union and the Union of Democratic Control. While Brittain was of the school that opposed war for any reason, however, Holtby was a "pacificist," believing, with a pragmatism typical of her, that violence might be necessary in the last resort. She was not to have to test the limits of her pacifism: after a long, stoical battle with Bright's disease she died in London in 1935, before the crises of the Spanish Civil War and Hitler's incursion into Poland would force the issue.

Holtby's output as a writer was prodigious. In addition to her extensive work as a journalist and political pamphleteer, she published several plays, numerous poems and short stories, an illustrated satire of British life entitled *The Astonishing Island* (1933), a major book on women's issues called *Women and a Changing Civilisation* (1934), and five novels besides *South Riding*: *Anderby Wold* (1923), *The Crowded Street* (1924), *The Land of Green Ginger* (1927), *Poor Caroline* (1931), and *Mandoa, Mandoa!* (1933). She also made a significant contribution to literary criticism, publishing a full-length study of Virginia Woolf (the first in English) in 1932. The Woolf study offers an insight into Holtby's own aesthetic principles. Though she has effusive praise for Woolf's artistry, particularly her skills at writing from multiple points of view and at portraying the "subconscious realm in which the reason does not run" (21), she suggests that Woolf's fiction is weakened by its failure to engage adequately with "the material circumstances of life" (200–201), particularly as regards the potential of women. She traces the weakness to Woolf's own life of privilege, which has left her incapable of appreciating how, for example, the "stultifying atmosphere of provincial Philistinism" (25), or the expectations of a conventional marriage, might smother a woman's aspirations. Holtby's complaints about Woolf in some ways parallel those leveled at modernist psychological fiction by Georg Lukács, Ralph Fox, and other champions of "socialist realism" (or what Fox called "new realism") in the 1930s. Her suspicion of Woolf's idealist orientation, which was returned—Woolf wrote condescendingly of "poor, gaping Holtby" 's "photographic mind" (Shaw, *The Clear Stream* 252, 255) is well summarized by Lukács's complaint about modernist novelists whose heroes "do not develop through contact with the world" (Lukács 21). Marion Shaw classes Holtby with a group of middlebrow women novelists of the period who rejected modernist obscurity in favor of reaching a wide audience (a group including Phyllis Bottome, Doreen Wallace, Storm Jameson, Elizabeth Bowen, Lettice Cooper, and Rosamond Lehmann), and Janet Montefiore says that her tales of struggling women, drawn from her own experience and that of her friends, make her an "autobiographical novelist" similar to Vera Brittain, Naomi Mitchison, and Rebecca West. There is reason also to set her work, particularly *South Riding*, alongside the more radically materialist socialist realism of the era: James Hanley's *The Furys*, Walter Brierley's *Sandwichman*, Walter Greenwood's

Love on the Dole, and even John Steinbeck's great socialist parable *The Grapes of Wrath*.

ANALYSIS

Holtby's reservations about Woolf stemmed from a conviction that literature should motivate its readers to work for social improvement. Her achievements as a writer suggest further that, with socialist realist theorists like Lukács and Fox, she knew that mere naturalism would be insufficient to incite social change. For her (and for Fox, who envisioned the "new realism" as a reconciliation of "the old and artificial division between subjective and objective realism" [86]), material details had to be coupled with portraits of characters' inner lives in order to reveal the dialectical relationship between individuals and their environment. In exploring the inner lives of her characters, she was especially interested in what Fox called the "motive forces of human actions" (85), seeing an understanding of these as vital to any would-be reformer.

South Riding represents the perfection of the balance between "subjective and objective realism," but Holtby's earlier novels represent important steps toward what she achieves there. The novels of the 1920s are especially interesting for charting the growth of her materialist consciousness, particularly, though not exclusively, as regards the aspirations of women. *The Crowded Street* represents its heroine, a spinster named Muriel Hammond, as squandering her mathematical gifts and professional aspirations by giving herself over to service to others. After years of subordinating her own vivid dreams of participating in life's "Party" to the crises of family and friends, she discovers her lonely place on a "crowded street," unfulfilled and no longer needed by anyone. Through the helpful but unsympathetic intervention of a feminist friend (Delia, based on Vera Brittain) she finally launches herself toward personal fulfillment, working as an accountant for a feminist organization in London and rejecting a long-awaited offer of marriage from a man whose assumptions about the nurturing role of a wife finally strike her as unacceptable. In Muriel's story self-fulfillment is largely a matter of having the courage not to hide behind domestic servitude.

The Land of Green Ginger, by contrast, is more respectful of the material and social obstacles that impede a woman's self-realization. Its heroine, Joanna Leigh, shares Muriel's fantasies of a wider world—the enchanting "land of green ginger" of the book's title—but no amount of will or work is sufficient to make her dreams come true. The economic and sexual difficulties attending her marriage to a tubercular farmer, the illnesses and emotional demands of her children, and the profound disapproval provoked in her provincial community by her flirtation with a Hungarian activist present insurmountable challenges to her powerful spirit. As Joanna herself summarizes the victory of material forces over idealist ones in her story:

> She had thought her mind free to create its own enchanting world. She had refused the evidence of her eyes and ears and of her anxious heart. She had defied the knowledge of her life's disastrous circumstance, believing reality to be more than the farm at Scatterthwaite, the disheartening burden of poverty, the gloom of her husband's illness, the fear for her children's future. From these she had escaped into a lovely land of her deliverance, wandering at will along its pleasant pathways. She had climbed the sunburned hills, explored the islands, or rocked in her boat in the small, hill-girt harbours. . . . And all the time reality had imprisoned her . . . fools, to think in your vanity that you could conquer disease and poverty by a dream. (240–241)

The final blow in Joanna's life is the pregnancy ensuing from her husband's jealous rape of her, shortly before his death, and the disapproval of a community convinced that the child is the Hungarian's. The tragic pregnancy may represent Holtby's growing respect for the "New" feminist emphasis on the needs of the female body. It is also significant, though, that Holtby describes in detail the tortured consciousness of Joanna's ailing husband, Teddy, who suffers just as severely the limitations of a body: Holtby's interest in the conflict between aspirations and material impediments is not restricted by gender.

Holtby's penultimate novel, *Mandoa, Mandoa!*, takes us into the material heart of another "land of green ginger": the mythical African state of Mandoa. Inspired, like Evelyn Waugh's *Black Mischief* (1932), by the much-publicized 1930 crowning of the emperor of Abyssinia, and influenced also by Holtby's work in South Africa, this political satire anticipates *South Riding* in critiquing the weaknesses on both sides of a political argument: here, the debate over the exportation of European capitalism to Africa. The story charts the fate of a British travel company's initiative to develop a center for tourism in Mandoa and to launch it with a grand celebration of the royal wedding of the Mandoan princess. Emulating the cinematic shifts in perspective she admired in Woolf, Holtby represents the events of the story from a wide range of points of view, building a remarkably balanced picture of the pros and cons of the venture. On the one hand, the book exposes difficulties in communication and cross-cultural understanding that make a farce of the British businessmen's confidence. On the other, it demonstrates ways in which the hard-line opponents of capitalism and imperialism both idealize Mandoan culture and demonize the company. A key character in achieving this balance is Safi Talal, a Mandoan native whose own pipe dreams about European affluence make him a strong supporter of the business venture; his ethical differences from his European partners make for some inspired comic moments, while his credible insights into the potential benefits of development challenge the view, espoused by the book's most dogmatic anticapitalist, Arthur Rollett, that the Mandoans are unwitting victims of European exploitation. The satire directed against Rollett, though, and other anti-imperialist activists in the novel functions more as a reminder of the importance of respecting the differences of an alien culture than as an implicit defense of capitalism. The novel precludes a strongly procapitalist reading by developing an extended parallel between the Mandoan slave trade and the exploitation of British workers, some of whom we meet in a dole queue early in the novel.

South Riding perfects the technique of deploying multiple perspectives to convey the complexity of a politically contentious situation. In a textbook example of the "totality" required of socialist realist fiction, it offers insights into the physical and economic hardships and interconnected aspirations of characters from a variety of class backgrounds. Its protagonist is an "Old Feminist" reformer, Sarah Burton, who has returned to the town of her birth as headmistress of its school for girls. Sarah's aspirations for her students, which resemble Delia's ambitions for women in *The Crowded Street*, run aground on the realities preoccupying the "New Feminism," most notably, in the case of Sarah's star pupil, Lydia Holly, a mother's death in childbirth and the domestic obligations thus falling to the eldest daughter. Sarah comes to recognize that the interests of Old and New Feminisms are in many ways complementary, that reforms bettering the domestic lives of women will aid women in their professional aspirations. Her own ambitions therefore become entwined with the unglamorous machinations of local government: with a County Council divided over whether to raise taxes to build a new road and maternity hospital, and over a forthcoming bye-election that will shape its future direction. Again Holtby relates the story through a shifting array of characters on both sides of the debate: from the progressives Sarah and Councillor Astell and the struggling women whose interests the hospital would serve to the obstructionist landowner and councillor Carne, his loyal farmworkers, and his conservative ally Mrs. Beddows. Holtby's stated goal in telling the story is to explore "the complex tangle of motives prompting public decisions" (xi). Penetrating the "subconscious realm in which the reason does not run," her portraits expose the undercurrents of sexual desire, childhood trauma, repression, and fear that sometimes make for strange political bedfellows (or, in the case of Sarah and Carne, that make political opponents into bedfellows). The sympathetic portrait of Carne, struggling to resist changes that threaten a cherished way of life, counterbalances the claims of Lydia Holly and other characters in dire economic and physical distress. Like *Mandoa, Mandoa!*, *South Riding* ultimately resists a conservative interpretation—Carne loses his seat on the council, and the reforms proceed as they should—but it does not allow this advance to stand without itemizing the human cost. Carne, who is deeply loved by many, including, irrationally, Sarah, meets a tragic death. (Holtby was undoubtedly thinking here of her father, whose own death came not long after he abandoned farming, demoralized by a strike of farmworkers.) A final consequence of the book's roving perspective is the ironic light it casts on Sarah's initial self-importance, ambition, and condescension toward her community. She learns that her aspirations for her students can only be achieved incrementally and collectively, with tolerance for cultural difference and human frailty.

ASSESSMENT

On the face of it, the time Holtby dedicates to representing all points of view in political debates makes her fiction seem more conservative than her record as a journalist and activist would lead one to expect. Her novels communicate humanism more powerfully than they do feminism, anti-imperialism, or socialism. This discrepancy can be reconciled, I think, by viewing Holtby as a devoted champion of all these causes who was above all a pragmatist: like her contemporary, George Orwell, she recognized that social progress depended on confronting—not effacing—the murky interests, prejudices, and other human weaknesses that stood in its way, whether they resided in activists or in their opponents. The female protagonist of *Mandoa, Mandoa!*, the anti-imperialist activist Jean Stanbury, gives us an insight into how such an approach might have grown out of Holtby's personal experience as dutiful daughter: "Those of us who have been reared in the family tradition—who are always serving a small limited corporation—we can't be uncompromising about truth. I mean, you can't say what you think about Gandhi if it'll upset Uncle Algernon for weeks and be bad for Aunt Ethel's heart. . . . We get used to that sort of perpetual balance between the opportune and the ideal" (*Mandoa, Mandoa!* 125).

BIBLIOGRAPHY

Primary Sources

My Garden, and Other Poems. London: Brown, 1911.

Anderby Wold. London: Lane, 1923; London: Virago, 1981.

The Crowded Street. London: Lane, 1924; London: Virago, 1981.

The Land of Green Ginger. London: Cape, 1927; London: Virago, 1983.

Poor Caroline. London: Cape, 1931; London: Virago, 1985.

Virginia Woolf: A Critical Memoir. London: Wishart, 1932.

The Astonishing Island, Being a Veracious Record of the Experiences Undergone by Robinson Lippingtree Mackintosh from Tristan da Cunha during an Accidental Visit to Unknown Territory in the Year of Grace MCMXXX-? London: Lovat Dickson, 1933.

Mandoa, Mandoa! London: Collins, 1933; London: Virago, 1982.

Women and a Changing Civilisation. London: John Lane, 1934.

The Frozen Earth and Other Poems. London: Collins, 1935.

South Riding: An English Landscape. London: Collins, 1936; London: Virago, 1988.

Letters to a Friend. Ed. Alice Holtby and Jean McWilliam. London: Collins, 1937.

Pavements at Anderby. Ed. H.S. Reid and Vera Brittain. London: Collins, 1937.

Take Back Your Freedom (play). London: Cape, 1939.

Selected Letters of Winifred Holtby and Vera Brittain, 1920–1935. Ed. Vera Brittain and Geoffrey Handley-Taylor. London: Brown, 1960.

Testament of a Generation: The Journalism of Vera Brittain and Winifred Holtby. Ed. Paul Berry and Alan Bishop. London: Virago, 1985.

Remember, Remember! The Selected Stories of Winifred Holtby. Ed. Paul Berry and Marion Shaw. London: Virago, 1999.

Secondary Sources

Albinski, Nan Bowman. "Thomas and Peter: Society and Politics in Four British Utopian Novels." *Utopian Studies* 1 (1987): 11–22.

Baurley, George. "Winifred Holtby's *South Riding* through German Eyes." *Transactions of the Yorkshire Dialect Society* 17 (1988): 48–55.

Berry, Paul, and Mark Bostridge. *Vera Brittain: A Life.* London: Pimlico, 1996.

Brittain, Vera. *Testament of Friendship.* London: Virago, 1980.

———. *Testament of Youth.* London: Virago, 1978.

Cavaliero, Glen. *The Rural Tradition in the English Novel, 1900–1939.* London: Macmillan, 1977.

Fox, Ralph. *The Novel and the People.* New York: International, 1945.

Handley-Taylor, Geoffrey. *Winifred Holtby: A Concise and Selected Bibliography together with Some Letters.* With a foreword by Vera Brittain. London: A. Brown, 1955.

Kennard, Jean E. *Vera Brittain and Winifred Holtby: A Working Partnership.* Hanover, NH: UP of New England, 1989.

Lukács, Georg. *The Meaning of Contemporary Realism.* London: Merlin, 1963.

Montefiore, Janet. *Men and Women Writers of the 1930s: The Dangerous Flood of History.* London: Routledge, 1996.

Shaw, Marion. "'Alien Experiences': Virginia Woolf, Winifred Holtby, and Vera Brittain in the Thirties." In *Rewriting the Thirties: Modernism and After.* Ed. Keith Williams and Steven Matthew. London: Longman, 1997. 37–52.

———. *The Clear Stream: A Life of Winifred Holtby.* London: Virago, 1999.

———. "Feminism and Fiction between the Wars: Winifred Holtby and *Virginia Woolf.*" In *Women's Writing: A Challenge to Theory.* Ed. Moira Monteith. Brighton: Harvester, 1986. 175–191.

White, Evelyne. *Winifred Holtby As I Knew Her.* London: Collins, 1938.

Attia Hosain
1913–1998

Ashok Bery

Attia Hosain qualifies as a British writer by virtue of long residence in Great Britain and a British passport, but she was born in India and came to live in London only when she was in her thirties. In some ways she never felt fully at home in Britain and was conscious that leaving India had involved dislocation and loss. India pervades her writing. Her fiction is preoccupied with the cultural milieu in which she grew up as well as the turbulent political climate of the 1930s and 1940s, the years leading up to the Partition of 1947, when British rule ended and the country was divided into a predominantly Hindu India and the new Muslim state of Pakistan.

BACKGROUND

Born in 1913 in the northern Indian city of Lucknow, Attia Hosain came from a Muslim family that belonged to a feudalistic landowning class known as *taluqdars*. The tension between her privileged but circumscribed background—one in which women had a restricted role—and a striving for independence was to become an important feature of Hosain's life and fiction. Her upbringing and education drew on both Eastern and Western cultures. The family spoke Urdu at home, but she also read widely in the English classics. In a radio broadcast of 1956 she said, "I grew up with the English language but not with the culture behind it. I was always deeply rooted in my own" (qtd. in Holmström 22). When she started to write, however, she chose to do so in English, perhaps because, in her words, the English language was "a key to . . . the ideological arsenal" (qtd. in Holmström 22).

Her youth and early adulthood coincided with an important period of Indian history, when the movement against British rule, led by Mahatma Gandhi and Jawaharlal Nehru, was building up a momentum that was to prove unstoppable. Although Hosain herself—restricted by feelings of duty to her family—did not take an active part in politics, she was considerably influenced during the 1930s by friends and relatives with radical and nationalist sympathies.

In 1947 her husband went to work at the Indian High Commission in London, and she accompanied him, along with their two small children. Although she continued to make regular visits to India, she was to be based in England for the rest of her life. She had started to write when she was younger, but it was in London that she took up writing seriously, earning her living meanwhile by broadcasting for BBC Radio. Apart from articles and stories in magazines, she published two books—*Phoenix Fled*, a volume of short stories (1953), and her only novel, *Sunlight on a Broken Column* (1961). They were reissued by Virago in 1988, with introductions by the eminent Indian writer Anita Desai, and the reprints helped to revive interest in Hosain's work. She died early in 1998 at the age of eighty-four.

ANALYSIS

Certain themes recur through Hosain's work: the situation of women in a patriarchal environment; the clash between tradition and modernity; the trauma of the Partition of India, in which hundreds of thousands of people were killed and many more became refugees. The Partition dominates both the conclusion of her novel and a number of the stories in *Phoenix Fled*. The title story depicts the plight of an old Muslim woman who refuses to leave her village when the rest of her family flees from the violence of their Hindu neighbors. The story's narrative perspective provides a striking insight into the mind of the old woman, for whom the present-day realities of 1947 shade confusingly into her memories of the so-called mutiny of 1857, during which Lucknow was an important center of rebellion against the British Raj. "After the Storm," another story in the volume, evokes the "ghosts of imagined horror" (81) obliquely through the fragmentary narrative of a young servant girl who survives the violence of Partition.

Other stories, such as "The First Party" and "Time Is Unredeemable," concern the impact of modernity on traditionally brought-up Muslim women who have married Westernized men. Hosain depicts with some sympathy the women's dawning awareness of the gulf between their own ways and those of their husbands. As is evident also in *Sunlight on a Broken Column*, Hosain seems in part to see the old ways as offering a secure and ordered haven. Hosain's daughter has suggested that her mother would have resisted being labeled a "feminist." This may well be so; yet, as the stories mentioned show, it is equally true that her sympathy is usually with the vulnerable, victimized, or put-upon woman, whose perspective she espouses (Holmström 20).

The woman's perspective is central to *Sunlight on a Broken Column*, which draws heavily on autobiographical material. Narrated by its protagonist Laila, an orphan who lives with her extended family, it is a bildungsroman in which she tells her story from the age of fifteen through to her thirties. The novel charts both Laila's personal development and India's changing society between the 1930s and the early 1950s. Her expanding consciousness, her desire for independence, and her increasing frustration with the restrictions imposed on her as a girl growing up in a Muslim *taluqdar* family are depicted against the backdrop, first, of the *taluqdars*' decline as a class, and second, of the political developments that led to the independence and Partition of India.

The novel's four-part structure is designed to embody these personal and social changes. As the story opens, Laila's grandfather Baba Jan is dying, and with him, the kind of ordered, hierarchical society he represents. Depicting the ordered activities and rituals of the large joint family and the servants, this first part of the novel commemorates the last days of the traditional way of life. A particular focus is on the roles prescribed for women, who live, as was customary, in the secluded *zenana* (women's quarters), an arrangement that reflects their limited participation in public life.

In part 2, with the grandfather dead, the pace of change quickens. Laila's uncle Hamid, now the head of the family, attempts to maintain his father's heritage, but is uncomfortable with the joint-family system and prefers the "individual, Western way of living." Having "lost the leadership and authority of his father," he nurtures "ambitions for another form of leadership" beyond the "narrow confines of a tribe" (167). Laila is by now at college, her horizons increasingly expanding beyond the family, and her desires coming into conflict with her uncle's wishes. On the political front, nationalism is becoming more prominent, focused particularly by an episode in which university students demonstrate against a visit by the British viceroy.

In part 3, the core of the novel, some crucial developments take place. Laila's cousins—Hamid's sons—return from England after university, an event that is liberating for her: "My life changed. It had been restricted by invisible barriers almost as effectively as the physically restricted lives of my aunts in the zenana. . . . Now I was drawn out, made to join in, and not stand outside as a spectator" (173).

Laila's departure from tradition is embodied in her falling in love with, and marrying, Ameer Hussain, a university lecturer, against the wishes of her relations, who object to his lower status, his relative lack of wealth, and, above all, the fact that Laila follows her own desires rather than those of the family. As Laila's aunt Abida says accusingly: "You have been defiant and disobedient. You have put yourself above your duty to your family" (312). This love story and its complications are counterpointed with political developments such as the rise of the separatist Muslim League and its increasing tensions with the nationalist Congress Party.

Part 4 jumps forward fourteen years to 1952, with Laila revisiting her childhood home, Ashiana, now turned into accommodation for refugees who had left Pakistan during Partition. The narration brings us up-to-date with the fates of Laila's friends and relatives: the once-powerful and cohesive family is now scattered, some of its members dead, some living in Pakistan, others in India. Laila's husband, we learn, died in the war, and she is left to bring up their daughter. The novel ends with Laila seemingly throwing off the burdens of the past and moving into a new life as she finally reciprocates the affections of her distant cousin Asad, who has loved her for a long time.

These events are depicted with a complex mixture of attitudes. There is a sense of frustration at the restrictions the old order imposed, particularly on women. But there is also nostalgia, a feeling that the joint-family system, for all its conservatism, nevertheless nurtured a sense of belonging and identity. The title *Sunlight on a Broken Column*, borrowed from T.S. Eliot's poem "The Hollow Men," encapsulates this mixture of attitudes and draws attention to two of the important images of the novel. The broken column represents the family's ancestral home, which is not only a location for many of the events in the novel, but also a symbol, initially of the old order and then of the processes of social change. The first part of the novel, as suggested earlier, evokes clearly the structure and stability the house symbolizes. In contrast, the physical decay of the house by the end of the novel reflects the decline of the family's status and of the way of life it had once represented. Similarly, the house is used to represent Laila's increasing emancipation. In a passage quoted earlier, Laila compares the "invisible barriers" restricting her life and thinking to the physical restrictions of the *zenana*. The passage goes on to depict her slowly expanding horizons in terms of further imagery drawn from the house: "A window had opened here, a door there, a curtain had been drawn aside; but outside lay a world narrowed by one's field of vision. After my grandfather's death more windows had opened" (173). The light of the novel's title, also a recurrent image, captures the sense of a new life arising out of the ruins of the old. Laila's first meeting with her future husband, for instance, takes place against the background of the brilliant lights from a fireworks display.

Nearly all the critical commentary on Attia Hosain deals with her novel rather than the short stories. Two aspects of the novel tend to dominate discussion: one is gender, and the other is the link between Laila's personal narrative and the wider social and political forces I have described. Several studies consider the topic of *purdah* in *Sunlight on a*

Broken Column. The word *purdah*, which means "veil" or "curtain," is used both to designate the physical veil that Muslim women wear and, in a broader sense, to refer to "a social norm whereby women live in seclusion, both from men and from the sphere of civic and public action" (Parameswaran 33). In Uma Parameswaran's view, Hosain is critical of the custom of *purdah* and supports Laila's movements toward independence while also, especially at the beginning of the book, "dwelling on the general security and stability of the zenana and its environs" (43). Amina Amin also notes these two sides of *purdah*: on the one hand, "a life within the household, ordained, enclosed, warm and secure but restricted by demand[s] of modesty"; and, on the other, "a life outside, free but insecure and confusing" ("Tension" 119). Sarla Palkar, however, sees the *purdah* system in more one-sidedly critical terms as a "blatant symbol of the male-dominated culture" (109); she suggests that even some of the superficially "modern" characters in the novel give up the principle of *purdah* "in letter but not in spirit" (113). "A modern exterior," she argues, does not necessarily mean that one is free of the "metaphysical and psychological ramifications" of *purdah* (114).

Anuradha Dingwaney Needham considers the marginalization of women in relation to discourses of Indian nationalism. Drawing on Benedict Anderson and other theorists of nationalism, Needham discusses how "women's roles were constructed and mediated by nationalism's preferred self definitions" (97). Women were made into "guardian[s] of traditional values," nourishing an "essential 'Indian' identity" (98). Needham investigates whether Laila might be able to offer "a (potentially) alternative account of this nation in the act of making itself" (99) and concludes that while the "narrative possesses the potential to dismantle altogether nationalism's myth of a homogeneous, continuous, and essentialist national identity . . . this is a potential Laila seems to reject." However, "insofar as she largely attends to identifications and positions ignored or suppressed by nationalism's deliberate closures, she does provide us with alternative ways of seeing and knowing" (107).

Although they do deal with aspects of narrative form, the interest of most of the critics mentioned lies mainly in the political and gender issues the novel raises. Some interesting, if negative, evaluations of form are offered by Meenakshi Mukherjee, who sees the last part of *Sunlight* as "an orgy of sentimentality." The novel, she also feels, is beset by a "confusion of purpose" as to whether it is presenting "a picture of men and manners" or "one individual's groping towards self-realisation." She concludes that the book is flawed: as a piece of social documentation *Sunlight on a Broken Column* is competently written, but as a novel it is not satisfactory because of its stock situations, its predictable conflicts between love and loyalty, its over-indulgence in nostalgia and sentimentality, and a general weakness of structure (53) Lakshmi Holmström also singles out the last part of the novel for comment, noting that the writer herself "was never certain that the oblique approach of Part four worked; perhaps she should have written more directly about the pain and actuality of the Partition, she sometimes felt" (21).

ASSESSMENT

It is important to be wary of treating *Sunlight on a Broken Column* simply as a sociological case history of a particular class of people and to consider also how it functions as a novel. Meenakshi Mukherjee's comments suggest that it has its flaws. It is loose and episodic in structure, and this may be attributable to the division in purpose Mukherjee identifies: the attempt to be both the story of Laila's development and an account of a way of life. The latter purpose perhaps leads the author to include material that is of interest from a documentary point of view but loosens the structure of the plot. The ornateness and sentimentality of the language are also problems for some readers. The use of such language can be defended, perhaps, on the grounds that it is an influence from the Persian and Urdu literatures that Hosain learned in her youth (see Desai, "Introduction," *Sunlight* x); and it could also be argued that the language reflects Laila's idealizing and romanticizing tendencies. Nevertheless, some readers may not be entirely convinced by this defense.

There are grounds, indeed, for suggesting that the tighter discipline of the short story is better suited to Hosain's talents and helps to rein in these tendencies toward ornateness and looseness. Certainly the stories in *Phoenix Fled*, while not lacking warmth and sympathy toward most of their characters, are generally free of lapses into sentimentality. The plotting is economical, the obliqueness and conciseness that the short-story form fosters proving effective tools in Hosain's hands, as in the stories "Phoenix Fled" and "After the Storm" discussed earlier. While *Sunlight on a Broken Column* will continue to attract readers for its portrait of a vanished way of life and of a young girl striving for independence, it is the short stories that are likely to prove more interesting in their narrative techniques.

BIBLIOGRAPHY

Primary Sources

Phoenix Fled and Other Stories. 1953. London: Virago, 1988.

Sunlight on a Broken Column. 1961. London: Virago, 1988.

Secondary Sources

Amin, Amina. "Attia Hosain's *Sunlight on a Broken Column*: The Disintegration of a Family." In Dhawan 146–158.

———. "Tension between Restriction and Freedom: The Purdah Motif in Attia Hosain's *Sunlight on a Broken Column*." In Jain and Amin 119–130.

Baliga, Jaya. "Culture and Self: A Perspective of Attia Hosain's *Sunlight on a Broken Column*." In Dhawan 159–165.

Begum, Jameela. "Reconstructing Personal History: The Purdah in *Twilight in Delhi* and *Sunlight on a Broken Column*." In Jain and Amin 206–215.

Chandra, Subhash. "Androgyny in Attia Hosain's *Sunlight on a Broken Column*." In Dhawan 185–191.

Desai, Anita. Introduction to *Phoenix Fled*. London: Virago, 1988. vii–xxi.

———. Introduction to *Sunlight on a Broken Column*. London: Virago, 1988. v–xv.

Dhawan, R.K., ed. *Indian Women Novelists*. Set 3, vol. 2. New Delhi: Prestige, 1995.

Harrex, S.C. *The Fire and the Offering: The English-Language Novel of India, 1935–1970*. Vol. 1. Calcutta: Writers Workshop, 1977.

Holmström, Lakshmi. "Attia Hosain: Her Life and Work." *Indian Review of Books* 8.5 (16 February–15 March 1999): 18–22.

Jain, Jasbir, and Amina Amin, eds. *Margins of Erasure: Purdah in the Subcontinental Novel in English*. New Delhi: Sterling, 1995.

Kapadia, Novy. "Identity Crises and the Partition in Attia Hosain's *Sunlight on a Broken Column*." In Dhawan 166–184.

———. "In Search of Order: A Study of V.S. Naipaul and Attia Hosain." In Dhawan 137–145.

Khan, A.G. "Attia Hosain, Dina Mehta, and Manohar Malgonkar: Post-colonial Survey of Colonial Events." In Dhawan 129–136.

Mathur, R.K. "Socio-political Values in Attia Hosain's *Sunlight on a Broken Column*." In Dhawan 192–202.

More, D.R. "Attia Hosain's *Sunlight on a Broken Column*: A Muslim Perception of the Partition." In Dhawan 203–214.

Mukherjee, Meenakshi. *The Twice Born Fiction: Themes and Techniques of the Indian Novel in English*. New Delhi: Heinemann, 1971.

Needham, Anuradha Dingwaney. "Multiple Forms of (National) Belonging: Attia Hosain's *Sunlight on a Broken Column*." *Modern Fiction Studies* 39 (1993): 93–111.

Palkar, Sarla. "Beyond Purdah: *Sunlight on a Broken Column*." In Jain and Amin 106–118.

Parameswaran, Uma. "Purdah in Salman Rushdie, Attia Hosain, and Rama Mehta." In Jain and Amin 33–48.

Elizabeth Jane Howard
1923–

Heike Elisabeth Jüngst

Elizabeth Jane Howard is one of the most popular authors of quality fiction in England today. An inherent quality of her novels is their frequently mentioned "Englishness," which manifests itself in the choice of characters, places, and topics as well as in Howard's adherence to the English tradition of novel writing. Howard's best achievement so far is the Cazalet chronicle, a tetralogy on English family life during World War II, in which she blends personal experience and period detail into a novel of historical as well as psychological interest. Unfortunately, public interest in her private life (she was married to Kingsley Amis) has often exceeded interest in her novels.

BACKGROUND

Elizabeth Jane Howard was born on March 23, 1923, in London. She was brought up in an English upper-middle-class household, spending much of her childhood and adolescence in an extended family consisting of grandparents, aunts, uncles, siblings, and cousins. Howard was educated by a governess, later went to a domestic science school, and then trained to be an actress. She has been married three times (to Sir Peter Scott, 1942–1951, one daughter; James Douglas-Henry, 1959–1964; and Kingsley Amis, 1965–1983), each time leaving her husband when she found that the situation had turned unpleasant.

Howard has pursued several careers outside writing, including modeling, acting, and broadcasting. She was honorary artistic director of the Cheltenham Literary Festival in 1962 and co–artistic director of the Salisbury Festival in 1973. Apart from publishing eleven novels and several screenplays, Howard has coauthored a cookbook and compiled an anthology of texts about gardening. She is a fellow of the Royal Society of Literature and received the John Llewellyn Rhys Memorial Prize in 1951 (for *The Beautiful Visit*) and the Yorkshire Post Award in 1983 (for *Getting It Right*). Her first play was bought and cast when she was fourteen years old, although it was not produced due to the war ("All Her Own Work").

ANALYSIS

The novels of Elizabeth Jane Howard fall into two groups: those written before the Cazalet chronicle and the Cazalet chronicle itself (*The Light Years* [1990], *Marking Time* [1991], *Confusion* [1993], and *Casting Off* [1995]). Although the early novels are well written and interesting in their own right, it is the blend of the autobiographical and the general in the Cazalet chronicle on which Howard's reputation rests today. Her novels describe the English upper-middle class and have been dubbed novels of manners, some of them comedies of manners. This is a connection with a writing tradition that includes writers like Jane Austen. Settings like country houses provide another link with Austen, who is also frequently mentioned by characters in Howard's novels. Generally, plots center on "personal conflict, scheming, dismay, resolution against odds" (Vansittart ix). Being in the tradition of English novel writing is an important point in Howard's work that she acknowledges herself (Vansittart ix). It is also obvious from her realist style and her refusal to use experimental techniques. Hastings puts Howard firmly into a tradition of women novelists, comparing her to Jean Rhys and Rosamond Lehmann (ix).

In all her novels Howard is interested in the psychological development of her characters. Gindin speaks of an "emphasis on moral choice" (498), and Bedford mentions the themes of "the possibility of moral change" and "of choice, of limited free will" (ix). The heroes and heroines are normally young and have to make decisions that will influence their whole lives; Howard is interested in the process of growing up and finding a life of one's own. This can be funny, as in *Getting It Right*, where the young hairdresser Gavin goes through a rather grotesque process of initiation. Here Howard uses the modern everyday world for a romantic story in which Gavin has to choose among three women, a situation more typical for fairy tales. The more dramatic development of the young girl in *The Beautiful Visit* is marked by the two visits to her cousins' country house at the beginning and the end of the novel. Whereas Gavin finds his way into a normal life within society, the young girl finds herself by breaking out. In both cases the rules of society are reflected.

Frequently the moral choice is induced by an outsider who upsets an existing balance, sometimes for good (Lillian's and Emmanuel's marriage is saved by Alberta in *The Sea Change*), sometimes for bad (Anne's and Edmund's marriage is nearly destroyed by Arabella in *Odd Girl Out*), sometimes simply by forcing one of the characters to make a decision (Gavin in *Getting It Right* is disturbed in his quiet lifestyle by Minnie and Joan). Again, this is a fairly traditional kind of plot. When Howard's characters are faced with a crisis, they always emerge stronger and with a more realistic outlook on life, gaining or regaining moral integrity. *Something in Disguise* is an exception insofar as Howard concentrates on convincing social satire in a fatalistic plot and in some parts uses the conventions of the whodunit. The biggest flaw in Howard's earlier novels is that the characters sometimes lack credibility, resembling stage types and conforming to the needs of the plot. Alberta, for example, is a rather unconvincing anachronism: a vicar's daughter who seems to have sprung from a Victorian novel.

Howard's capacity for turning her observations into literature is particularly obvious in her talent for dialogue (cf. Kroll). Throughout the novels we find an often-devastating analysis of family relationships; dialogues between family members with their all-too-familiar non sequiturs and the speakers' being considerate as a basis for misunderstandings (cf. Mantel vii) are sometimes chilling. Most of the characters misjudge each others' intentions grossly out of simple good will, and even married couples who have known each other for years still make this mistake: "Hugh, who resisted an impulse to say goodbye to his wife after breakfast—not wishing to wake her again—felt relief. Sybil, lying in bed and longing for him to come up, listened to his car starting, got out of bed in time to see it disappearing down the drive" (*The Light Years* 144). Very rarely is love great enough to transcend this predicament of life in Howard's world, and very often it is the successful relationships that will not last, because one of the lovers dies in the war (*The Beautiful Visit*) or in an accident (*Something in Disguise*). There is admittedly a penchant for sentimentality in some of Howard's novels, but usually her use of irony prevents the stories from turning into kitsch (cf. Gindin 497).

The novels have clear yet intricate structures, with the chapters often finishing on well-constructed cliff-hangers. A device Howard uses in two of her novels is dividing them into sections headed by the name of the character whose point of view the reader is presented with (*The Sea Change, After Julius*; cf. Gindin 497). This is a link to the Cazalet chronicle with its concentration on two to three characters per chapter. However, the concept of a first-person narrator as used in *The Sea Change* is given up in the chronicle, except for the use of text types like diaries or letters inserted into the narrative. Howard frequently uses internal monologues and hardly ever describes actions from an omniscient point of view. But however deep her interest in her characters, and in direct contrast to the technique employed, Howard remains at a curious distance from the characters she describes ("a blend of empathy and detachment which is unique to her," Mantel vii) and is always able to ironize their actions. May in *Something in Disguise* is the victim of her evil husband, and the reader suffers with her most of the time. However, her interest in an obscure sect and her respect for its leader, Dr. Sedum, are ridiculed, and the readers suddenly find themselves not identifying with her, but laughing at her:

> "It really is a monstrous house," she thought, and recognized this to be what Dr Sedum had described in one of his "talks" as a mechanical pattern reaction—something to be avoided if one was to evolve. But later on in the same talk he had said that we were all liars because we were incapable of responding consistently to our environment, and then she did not know what to think. When she had asked Lavinia after the Time, as meetings were called in the League, Lavinia had said that one could not start at all, until one had perceived the Paradox. She had only been to one Time, and when Lavinia had said that she must not try to walk before she could fly, she realized that she had a long way to go. (*Something in Disguise* 76)

Although the novels before the Cazalet chronicle have won critical acclaim and make excellent reading, the novels of the Cazalet chronicle must be seen as Howard's best achievement so far. They also brought her back into the attention of the public as a writer after many of her books had gone out of print in the 1980s ("Casting Off the Cazalets" 30). With the Cazalet chronicle, Howard abandons characters who fit the needs of the plot but can hardly be imagined in real life. This may have to do with a change of technique. As late as 1986, Howard claimed that she did not write about people she had known or met (Gindin 497), although this is not entirely true, as autobiographical elements can be found in almost every one of her novels. In the Cazalet chronicle the characters are based on people Howard has known and go beyond the existence of mere stock types. The Cazalet chronicle takes the reader through the years 1937 to 1946, witnessing the life of an English upper-middle-class family during World War II. Awareness of the sufferings during the war is still very much alive in England today and finds frequent artistic and journalistic expression.

Howard does not describe battlefields, but the impact of the war is mirrored at the home front. Some elements of the Cazalet chronicle are foreshadowed in Howard's earliest novel, *The Beautiful Visit*, particularly in the description of family life in a country house and the impact of World War I. In the Cazalet chronicle it is the huge country house called "Home Place" where three grown-up sons and their wives and children move to live with their old parents and their unmarried sister, and where complex relationships unfold and small domestic tragedies happen along with the much bigger tragedies caused by the war. The place and characters are unmistakably English upper-middle class and provide a background whose rules and speaking manners have to be recognized by the reader from personal experience or previous reading. Howard evokes time and place in impressive detail: "The novel describes the lives of the privileged, in the late 1930s and early 40s, with the documentary exactness and passion of nostalgia—the beaded dresses, the Aertex shirts, the Tangee lipstick, the summer puddings made by the servants with fruit from the fruit garden" (Armstrong 30). These details make the novels interesting for folklore studies.

The characters on whom the tetralogy, originally planned as a trilogy ("All Her Own Work"), increasingly focuses are three young girls: Louise, Polly, and Clary. They are in Howard's age group and share her experiences. Actions are frequently presented from their point of view. The girls provide a center for the story, not only worrying about the war but also planning their futures or observing their parents (cf. Spanier). Moreover, each of the girls stands for a career choice a woman could make in those times. Instead of modeling one single heroine on herself, Howard splits up her own personality and experiences and endows each of the girls with specific components. Polly shares the author's fear of the war ("I Dreaded the War"); Louise trains as an actress, rushes into a premature and unsuccessful marriage, and leaves husband and child (the description of the marriage itself is foreshadowed with Cressy and Miles in *After Julius*); Clary is determined to become a writer. Howard's ambiguous relationship with her brothers is mirrored in various situations, as are some childhood memories she recalls in interviews ("All Her Own Work," "Life with Mr. Amis"). The "Brig" in the chronicle is a portrait of Howard's grandfather; Villy, Louise's mother, is a portrait of her own mother ("Casting Off the Cazalets" 30). The portrait that is probably most true to life is that of her governess, Miss Cobham, whom she describes in an autobiographical article ("A Dangerous Thing" 61) in exactly the words she later uses for Miss Milliment in the chronicle.

It is difficult to assess influences on Howard's writing, apart from her devotion to authors of well-written English novels. Howard wrote a small part of Kingsley Amis's *One Fat Englishman*, Amis a part of *After Julius* ("All Her Own Work"), but her fictional characters frequently mention Austen and Tolstoy as their favorite authors; if they read modern authors, they do not read Amis, but Elizabeth Taylor, someone who is as interested in family relationships as Howard herself. Howard once expresses admiration for Turgenev, another writer in a tradition of realism ("All Her Own Work"). The influence of Austen is obvious in Howard's observing and sometimes-satirical style as well as in her interest in the honesty and dishonesty of interpersonal relationships.

Praise for Howard's books usually centers on three categories: the detailed depiction of periods and places (mentioned in nearly all reviews of the Cazalet chronicle, but also by Bedford and Hastings), the psychological insight into the characters, and her sense of humor. The characters most popular with critics are the young girls she depicts (e.g., Gindin 498; Spanier), which is not surprising, as the young woman who is eager to know more about life and is just starting a life of her own is Howard's favorite heroine (cf. Gindin 497). Criticism focuses mainly on the lack of crisis and drama (e.g., Spanier).

The question of Howard's readership has not often been discussed, but has simply been taken for granted. Howard herself speaks of her readers being "women—and educated men" ("I Had to Bolt"). It is probably true that more women than men read Howard's novels, particularly as it is definitely easier for them to identify with the young heroines. Research into the actual readership might prove interesting. However, the "praise" just quoted sounds sickeningly patronizing. But then, as stated in "Casting Off the Cazalets," "the kind of fiction Howard writes will never be popular with some critics" (31).

On the whole, the reception of Howard's novels has been more favorable in Britain than in the United States, which is probably due to an abundance of detail and allusions familiar to British readers but alien to American readers. With her ability to copy speaking manners and behavior of the English upper-middle class, the detailed descriptions of their homes, her use of traditional forms, and her interest in recent English history, Howard has rightly been dubbed a "quintessentially English novelist" ("Life with Mr. Amis" 34).

ASSESSMENT

It is far easier to find comments on Elizabeth Jane Howard's marriages and childhood than serious analyses of her work. The majority of interviews center on her marriage to the writer Kingsley Amis, their lifestyle, and their subsequent breakup. It is important that the Cazalet chronicle has rewon Howard her reputation as a writer, and it is unfair to state that *Casting Off* "might not have excited such interest had it not coincided with the death of her former husband [Kingsley Amis]" ("I Had to Bolt"). There is a strong public interest in Elizabeth Jane Howard, and in the 1970s it was markedly stronger than interest in her work. Descriptions of her physical appearance abound in interviews and reviews (e.g., Howard and Amis, "Two on an Island" 64; Purves; "I Had to Bolt"). Howard is an attractive woman who has had an interesting, sometimes maybe even glamorous, life, but this should not take precedence over interest in her writing.

As with all best-selling authors, a sociological approach (including readership analysis) might offer a viable insight into Howard's novels. The Cazalet chronicle carries a historical interest, and it is interesting to see how the personal and the political are juxtaposed in a classical tradition of writing. Apart from reviews and introductions to the new editions of her novels, there is hardly any secondary literature on Howard, although there are a fair number of self-comments on her writing technique in the interviews and in Gindin. This leaves plenty of room for further research, no matter what theoretical stance is taken.

BIBLIOGRAPHY

Primary Sources

The Beautiful Visit. London: Cape, 1950; New York: Random House, 1950.

We Are for the Dark: Six Ghost Stories. With Robert Aickman. London: Cape, 1951.

The Long View. London: Cape, 1956; New York: Reynal, 1956.

Bettina: A Portrait. With Arthur Helps. London: Chatto, 1957; New York: Reynal, 1957.

The Sea Change. London: Cape, 1959; New York: Harper, 1960.

The Very Edge (screenplay). 1963.

After Julius. London: Cape, 1965; New York: Viking, 1966.

Something in Disguise. London: Cape, 1969; New York: Viking, 1970.

"A Dangerous Thing." *Daily Telegraph Magazine* 12 November 1971: 58–59, 61–62, 67–69.

Odd Girl Out. London: Cape, 1972; New York: Viking, 1972.

"The Glorious Dead" (television play). *Upstairs, Downstairs*, 1974.

Mr. Wrong: Short Stories. London: Cape, 1975; New York: Viking, 1976.

"Skittles" (television play). *Victorian Scandals*, 1976.

"Sight Unseen" (television play). *She* 1977.

The Lover's Companion: The Pleasure, Joys, and Anguish of Love. Ed. Elizabeth Jane Howard. Newton Abbot, Devon: David & Charles, 1978.

After Julius (television play). 1979.

Something in Disguise (television play). 1980.

Getting It Right. London: Hamish Hamilton, 1982; New York: Viking, 1982.

Howard and Maschler on Food. With Fay Maschler. London: Joseph, 1987.

Getting It Right (screenplay). 1989.

The Light Years. London: Macmillan, 1990; New York: Pocket, 1990.

Green Shades: An Anthology of Plants, Gardens, and Gardeners. Ed. Elizabeth Jane Howard. London: Aurum, 1991.

Marking Time. London: Macmillan, 1991; New York: Pocket, 1991.

Confusion. London: Macmillan, 1993; New York: Pocket, 1993.

Cooking for Occasions. With Fay Maschler. London: Macmillan, 1994. Rev. and exp. ed. of *Howard and Maschler on Food*.

Casting Off. London: Macmillan, 1995.

Secondary Sources

Armstrong, Isobel. "A Family Fragments: Elizabeth Jane Howard *Marking Time*." *TLS* 8 November 1991: 30.

Bayley, John. Introduction to *The Long View*. By Elizabeth Jane Howard. London: Hamish Hamilton, 1986; London: Pan, 1995. vii–xi.

Bedford, Sybille. Introduction to *The Sea Change*. By Elizabeth Jane Howard. London: Pan, 1995. ix–xiv.

Gindin, James: "Elizabeth Jane Howard." In *Contemporary Novelists*. Ed. Susan Windisch Brown. 1986. New York: St. James, 1996.

Hastings, Selina. Introduction to *After Julius*. By Elizabeth Jane Howard. London: Pan, 1995. ix–xiv.

Howard, Elizabeth Jane. "All Her Own Work." Interview with Milton Haxell. *Times* 20 March 1972: 7.

———. "Casting Off the Cazalets." Interview. *Bookseller* 3 November 1995: 30–31.

———. "A Change of Status: Janet Watts Talks to Elizabeth Jane Howard, Whose Novel 'Something in Disguise' Is Being Serialised on TV." *Observer* 4 July 1982: 25.

———. "I Dreaded the War for So Long." Interview with John Young. *Times Review Supplement* [London] 27 June 1992: 46.

———. "I Had to Bolt from Kingsley or Become an Awful Person." Interview with Valerie Grove. *Times* 3 November 1995: 17.

———. "Life with Mr. Amis and Other Tales." Interview with Naim Attalah. *Observer Magazine* 31 October 1993: 34–37, 39.

Howard, Elizabeth Jane, and Kingsley Amis. "Two on an Island: Kingsley Amis and Elizabeth Jane Howard at Home, in Conversation with Pauline Peters. Photograph: Snowdon." *Sunday Times Magazine* [London] 3 February 1974: 64–66.

"Howard, Elizabeth Jane. Long View." *Book Review Digest* 1956. New York: Wilson, 1956. 459–460.

Kroll, Steven. Rev. of *Something in Disguise*, by Elizabeth Jane Howard. *New York Times Book Review* 1 February 1970: 5.

Mantel, Hillary. Introduction to *Odd Girl Out*. By Elizabeth Jane Howard. London: Pan, 1995. vii–xii.

Purves, Libby. "Food for Thought." Rev. of *Howard and Maschler on Food*. *Times* 22 May 1987: 15.

Spanier, Muriel. "Parents Hellbent on Pleasure." Rev. of *The Light Years*, by Elizabeth Jane Howard. *New York Times Book Review* 16 September 1990: 21.

"Sweet and Sour." Rev. of *Something in Disguise*, by Elizabeth Jane Howard. *TLS* 6 November 1969: 1273.

Vansittart, Peter. Introduction to *Getting It Right*. By Elizabeth Jane Howard. London: Pan, 1996. ix–xv.

Walker, J.K.L. "Home Front Virtues." Rev. of *Confusion*, by Elizabeth Jane Howard. *TLS* 29 October, 1993: 20.

P.D. James
1920–

Tony Giffone

P.D. James, the most important contemporary mystery writer, is justifiably mentioned in the company of such "golden-age" mystery writers as Dorothy Sayers, Margery Allingham, and Agatha Christie. While upholding the conventions of the genre, she significantly adapts them, particularly in the portrayal of her principal detective, Inspector Dalgliesh, in her use of institutional settings, and in her interest in allegory and moral ambiguity rather than in creating clever puzzles. As Joyce Carol Oates has stated, "P.D. James does not 'transcend' genre; she refines, deepens, and amplifies it" (21).

BACKGROUND

P.D. James was born into a middle-class English family in Oxford, the oldest of three children. Her maternal grandfather was headmaster of the choir school in Oxford, and her father worked in the patent office. While she was still a child, James relocated with her family, first to Ludlow and then to Cambridge, where she attended the Cambridge County High School for girls. She named her principal detective, Adam Dalgliesh, after an English teacher there. After high school James went to work in the income-tax office in Ely, the beginning of a long association with the civil service.

In 1941 James married, but her husband, a doctor, suffered from schizophrenia and was in and out of asylums for most of his life. In order to support their two daughters, Claire and Jane, James went to work in 1949 for the National Health Service. Simultaneously she took evening classes at the City of London College, earning a degree in hospital administration. She stayed with the National Health Service until 1968, when she transferred to the Home Office Criminal Policy Department, working there until her retirement in 1979. Writing came late in life, as James did not publish her first novel until 1962, two years before her husband died. She has acknowledged Dorothy Sayers, Margery Allingham, Ngaio Marsh, and Josephine Tey as influences; her favorite author is Jane Austen, and she has written about Austen's *Emma* as a detective novel. She is deeply religious, and many of her titles come from the Book of Common Prayer. In addition to these literary influences, her husband's institutional confinement and her own work outside her marriage were the major influences on James's fiction. Bernard Benstock states, "Few detective writers have had a modicum of practical experience in the offices and laboratories of police bureaus, much less in the dens of iniquity they describe. . . . the necessity of supporting a family . . . provided P.D. James with a clinical environment in which she capitalized for many of her novels, realistic settings from which she derived grotesque possibilities" (104–105).

ANALYSIS

James's principal detective, Adam Dalgliesh, is a worthy successor to Sherlock Holmes, Peter Wimsey, and Hercule Poirot, but he is more humane than any of his antecedents. Dalgliesh's wife and son have both died in childbirth. He is a poet as well as a detective. As Bernard Benstock states, "It would be inaccurate to think of Dalgliesh as a detective who is also a poet . . . Dalgliesh is a poet *because* he is a detective" (119). James does not give Dalgliesh a superhuman intellect à la Holmes; his success is based more on hard work than brilliance. He comes without any comic mannerisms that mar the portrayals of Poirot or Miss Marple. His friendship with Cordelia Grey (James's other major detective) has led to some critical speculation that it would evolve into a courtship in the manner of Peter Wimsey and Harriet Vane (from Dorothy Sayers's series), especially since James is as enamored of Dalgliesh as Sayers was of Lord Peter. The romance between Dalgliesh and Deborah Riscoe that is detailed over the course of the first three Dalgliesh novels (*Cover Her Face*, *A Mind to Murder*, and *Unnatural Causes*) is doomed because Dalgliesh is not a conventional romantic hero—he is aloof, emotionally detached, a man who cannot let his emotions get in the way of his work.

James's first Dalgliesh novel, *Cover Her Face* (1962), is thoroughly in the vein of a "great-house" mystery. In these "great-house" mysteries a body is discovered in the upstairs bedroom or library, and suspicion falls on each member of the family and/or house guest until evil is expelled and order is restored. It is the violation of the family or the community that is purged by the detective hero. In each of the subsequent Dalgliesh novels James substitutes different social institutions (medical, literary, religious, and judicial) in place of the great house as their settings. If Agatha Christie's Miss Marple stories are novels of manners of village life (Trollope's Barchester with murder), then James's work provides a sociology of contemporary British institutions in the guise of a detective novel. James writes about them in a clinical, detached, third-person voice that accounts for an omniscient sense of impending doom that pervades her universe. In James's world there are omniscient forces at work that threaten to invade the individual life; the moral sanctity of the individual life is violated by the murderer, but the moral privacy of the individual life is also threatened by the police investigation.

In *A Mind to Murder* (1963), the first of the quartet of medical institution mysteries, the victim is the director of a psychiatric clinic, and the murder investigation uncovers the usual network of rivalries, affairs, and suspects. The culprit, however, turns out to be a family member written out of a will. It is as if James was still beholden to the "great-house" family mystery.

Unnatural Causes (1967) can be seen as James's killing off of the conventional detective novel. The victim is a writer of detective fiction whose body is washed ashore with the arms missing. Dalgliesh is on holiday on the Suffolk coast, and James is on holiday from her mysteries set in medical institutions. James is having fun in the novel, satirizing literary types, and there is a Dickensian relish in her choice of names: the local investigator is called Inspector Reckless; the owner of a shady London club is called Luker (lucre). But the novel is mostly of interest in James's development as a writer as a manifesto of her intent to kill off the conventional detective novel and to create an emotionally messier detective novel that would become her forte.

James hit her mark with *Shroud for a Nightingale* (1971), set in a nursing hospital, and *The Black Tower* (1975), set in a nursing home. In these novels "who done it" becomes secondary to a detailed and clinical observation of the way that institutions work. The urban hospital of *Shroud for a Nightingale* and the pastoral convalescent home of *The Black Tower* are variations on Gothic settings. The uncovering of the mystery has less to do with a clue overlooked than with the unraveling of life in a particular institution. What lingers after one has turned the last page of these novels is not the cleverness of who did it, but the deep and complex analysis of how institutions work, and since these institutions are microcosms of society, of how society works. Though some critics have found *The Black Tower* melodramatic, both of these novels won James awards from the British Crime Writers Association, the first of many awards she would receive.

Death of an Expert Witness (1977) is the last of the medical-institution mysteries and arguably the best, due to its complexity. The victim is a forensic examiner in a laboratory, and the complexity of the novel rests with the idea that the murderer acts out of a moral position, seeking justice. It is not that the victim deserves to die or that James whitewashes the moral culpability of the murderer, but that the murderer is acting on principle, just as those who bring the murderer to justice are acting on principle. Some critics have found James's treatment of the murderer in this way problematic. Commenting on a subsequent James novel that operates on the same principle, Harriet Waugh complains that "a very chilly killer is treated by the author with greater consideration than is deserved merely because he/she is intellectually attractive" (40). On the other hand, one can see James elevating the contemporary detective novel to the complexity of a Jacobean revenge drama.

With *A Taste for Death* (1986), James created one of the most structurally and morally complex of her novels. Like the subsequent Dalgliesh novels she would write (*Devices and Desires*, *Original Sin*, *A Certain Justice*, *Death in Holy Orders*) these are substantially longer than her earlier novels and rely more on allegory. In *A Taste for Death* the death of a baronet leads Dalgliesh, once again, into an investigation of the victim's family and the uncovering of family secrets. This is familiar territory, but James couples the solving of the mystery with a microscopic examination of police work; the institution under scrutiny here is the police force itself. In addition to Dalgliesh, James presents two other detectives: one male (Massingham) and one female (Kate Miskin). There is a thorough and detailed account of police work and the "taste for death" that pervades their lives. The reader's attention is deliberately diverted from the puzzle (James reveals who the killer is about a hundred pages before the conclusion) and into the details of police life, particularly the isolation and loneliness, and the conflict between career and family (which is intensified for Kate Miskin because she must care for an elderly grandmother). If plot is deemphasized, theme takes on a new importance; the novel is filled with estranged parent-child relationships, the most estranged being that between the individual and God. The victim dies in a church, thinking that he has the stigmata; by the novel's conclusion the individual who discovered the body has lost her faith. In this godless universe the only moral touchstone is Dalgliesh.

This is in keeping with James's stated belief in the validity of the mystery genre that she has chosen to work in. In an interview with Marilyn Stasio, James claimed that "[m]ysteries offer the intelligibility of the universe; the moral norm; the sanctity of life. . . . The more we live in a society where we feel our problems . . . to be literally beyond our control, it seems . . . very reassuring to read a popular form of fiction which itself has a problem at the heart of it. One which the reader knows will be solved by the end of the book and not by supernatural means or good luck, but by human intelligence, human courage, and human perseverance" (20).

If *A Taste for Death* ended with a clever manipulation of genre expectations by revealing who the murderer was before the final chapter, *Devices and Desires* (1989) begins with a similarly clever twist of genre expectations. The novel opens with the murder of a woman by a serial killer, but this is only a red herring. An executive at a nuclear power plant is murdered in the same manner as the serial killer's victims and is made to look as if she is the serial killer's next victim. However, unknown to the murderer is the fact that the serial killer had already committed suicide at the time of this murder, and suspicion falls on a narrow group of suspects who were privy to secret information about the serial killer's trademarks.

The institution that is at the center of the novel is a nuclear power plant, and the novel can be seen as an extension of the moral questions that James began to explore in *A Taste for Death.* As Christopher Lehmann-Haupt has pointed out, the novel "is pregnant with potential symbolism and significant themes. The landscape of the novel is littered with abandoned or converted religious buildings, and references to Scripture abound" (C22). If *A Taste for Death* asked how man makes meaning in a society where religion no longer holds sway, *Devices and Desires* explores a society where scientific progress has come to the point where it could mean annihilation. Poised between the novel's utilitarians and Shelleyan romantics, between its scientists and antinuclear pacifists, is James's view (via Dalgliesh) that "we're so sated now with scientific wonders that it's a bit disconcerting when we find that technology can do everything except what we want it to" (65). Commenting on the inability to trace the serial killer, Dalgliesh concludes that technology cannot discover the desires of the human heart that lead to murderous devices. If the novel has a flaw, however, it is in James's shallow characterization of political terrorists. Usually astute and insightful into the motives for violence, she is less sympathetic toward those who commit ideological murder. She understands the passions that lead to domestic murder, but not the principles that lead to political murder. She is sympathetic to the devices and desires of the human heart, but not to the political act.

Original Sin (1994) is a much more complex portrayal of literary institutions than *Unnatural Causes*, as is implied by its allegorical title. The institution is a publishing firm called Innocent House, and the victim is an associate of the firm who was planning to modernize it and change its location. The police are not the first to solve the crime; they are beaten to it by Esme Carling, a mystery writer whose latest work has been rejected by the firm. She tries to blackmail the murderer into publishing her again and winds up the next victim. James is having fun with this character, but it is unlikely that any mystery writer would be so stupid as to confront a murderer in this fashion. The playful note aside, the work is among James's darkest. There is an "original sin"—evil exists within the human heart—and sociological explanations for crime do not really apply. Crime and evil circulate through human society just as the river Thames circulates through the city of London. This is a world where crime is pervasive, justice is oblique, and the police are without the certainty of their convictions. Detective Miskin admits to believing that capital punishment deters crime—though she also admits that she would not want to go back to public hangings. This is a viewpoint similar to James's own. James has stated that she believes that capital punishment deters crime, but that she has been an opponent of capital punishment ever since reading Ernest Raymond's *We, the Accused.*

The oblique nature of justice is omnipresent in *A Certain Justice* (1997). The institution is the British law courts, and James is elegiac for moral certainty—just as one retiring lawyer misses the preautomated lighting of the lamps at the Middle Temple. The victim is a lawyer whose imminent death is reported in clinical style in the first paragraph of the novel. The title is ironic in that there is a certain type of justice at work in the novel, but not the classic type of justice that leads to confession and conviction. As Walter Goodman points out, the title's adjective "allows for contrary meanings. . . . Most commonly . . . it is a synonym for 'sure' . . . but it can also mean 'sort of' " (E10). There is a certain type of justice at work in the novel in that the victim was an expert at getting "not-guilty" verdicts for clients whom she knew were guilty. There is also a certain type of justice at work in the novel in that the housekeeper—who desecrated the victim's body and tried to ruin the lawyer's daughter's life out of personal revenge—is, in turn, murdered too. But justice is not certain. As the actual murderer states, knowing that there is not enough evidence to convict him, or even to bring his case to trial, "[A]ll human justice is necessarily imperfect" (363). Or, as another character remarks, "Sometimes the police can be sure that they've got the right man and still aren't able to take him to court" (356).

As the title implies, *Death in Holy Orders* (2001) has a religious setting. James borrows a number of motifs from *A Taste for Death*, including a lonely old woman discovering a body in the opening pages and a murder in a church. Dalgliesh even alludes to the earlier case. The plot involves multiple deaths, including the apparent suicide of a student, the apparent death by natural causes of a housekeeper, and a clear case of murder of an archbishop. The structure is in the tradition of a "weekend" murder mystery in which various guests assemble in a great house for a weekend where a murder is committed. However, the "great house" in this case is a theological college that soon may be shutting its doors. As in *A Taste for Death*, James is pondering how the spiritual life survives in the modern world. More significant than either plot or theme is Dalgliesh's character itself. In the novel, set on the Norfolk coast where he grew up, Dalgliesh revisits the scenes of his youth, recollects an adolescent crush, and becomes attracted to a guest at the college, Emma Lavenham, a literature professor at Cambridge specializing in the metaphysical poets. The final page of the novel suggests that what readers have been hoping for all along may finally come to be: the world-weary poet/detective will find love and happiness. Dalgliesh is told that he will have "to take trouble and risk failure" (413). Of course, he has been doing this every day in his professional life; the question is, will he be able to do so in his personal life as well?

While James's importance lies in her series of Dalgliesh novels, she has also written two popular novels focusing on a female detective, Cordelia Grey: *An Unsuitable Job for a Woman* (1972) and *The Skull beneath the Skin* (1982). Grey inherits a private detective agency that she works for when its cancer-ridden owner commits suicide. In the first novel Grey is hired to investigate why a famous conservationist's son committed suicide while he was at Cambridge. The most interesting thing about the novel is the kinship that Cordelia feels for the victim; both grew up essentially motherless and felt alienated from their fathers. At the end of the novel Dalgliesh is brought in to confront Cordelia Grey when she withholds some crucial evidence. Significantly, it takes Dalgliesh much less time to be able to guess the truth of the case than it took Grey, demonstrating his intellectual superiority.

In *The Skull beneath the Skin* Cordelia becomes a companion to an actress performing in an amateur production of *The Duchess of Malfi* who has been receiving death-threat notices. The villain is easy to guess if you have read your John Webster, just as Cordelia's knowledge of Blake assisted her in solving the case in the earlier novel. Dalgliesh again appears: when the police suspect Cordelia of the crime, he helps clear her reputation. Though immensely well paced and thoroughly enjoyable, the Cordelia Grey novels are mostly of interest for James's handling of a female sleuth. Grey is a professional detective only by accident and displays many of the characteristics of the amateur sleuth. James's portrayal of Kate Miskin in the more recent Dalgliesh novels is a much more insightful and realistic portrayal of a female detective.

Both the Dalgliesh and Grey novels have been adapted for television, with Roy Marsden as Dalgliesh and Helen Boxendale as Grey; in the latter case the series has created subsequent cases for Cordelia to solve, not adapted from James's actual novels, but simply based on the character she created. In both cases the series are substantially weaker than the original novels. The adaptors of the Dalgliesh series often impose a chronological order on James's much more complexly structured novels; the effect dilutes her narrative pacing, her intricate plot construction, her sense of irony, and her thematic unity. All the elements that make James the reigning queen of detective fiction are absent in the series. Those who only know James through the series don't know James.

In addition, James has written a number of works outside the Dalgliesh and Grey series. These works are primarily of interest for how they differ from her detective fiction. *The Maul and the Pear Tree* (1971), cowritten with T.A. Critchley, is a nonfiction account of the Ratcliffe Highway murder trial of 1811, a series of East End murders that were to the first decades of the nineteenth century what the Ripper murders were to the last decades. It is her attempt at a true-life crime narrative utilizing the same detailed, clinical style that she also employs in her fiction. *Innocent Blood* (1980) is a novel about an adopted young woman's attempt to remeet her biological mother, who has just been released from prison. In many ways this is James's darkest work, with all of the chilling insights into institutions of the mystery novels, but without the moral touchstone that Dalgliesh represents. With *Children of Men* (1992) James crossed genres to science fiction, contemplating not the death of an individual, but the death of the species.

ASSESSMENT

In a 1994 reader survey conducted by the *Armchair Detective*, James was ranked tenth in the list of all-time favorite mystery writers, behind such classic writers as Doyle, Christie, Chandler, Hammett, and Marsh. More significantly, she was the highest-ranking living mystery novelist. In addition, she ranked first in the category of contemporary mystery writers who would still be read fifty years from now. In general, critics have concurred with the reading public. In the first book-length study of James, Norma Siebenheller persuasively argues that "P.D. James is a novelist who happens to write in the mystery form" (ix). According to Siebenheller, what distinguishes James from mere writers of the genre is that "she stresses neither her plot (twisted though it may be), nor her detective (interesting as he is). In James' work, crime itself is the focus, not just the murder, but its effects on all who are touched by it . . . the way it shatters the lives, not only of the criminal and the victim, but also of their family, their friends, and other innocent people ensnared by its net" (6). Perhaps James's cross-over status from "genre novelist" to "contemporary novelist" is best evidenced by the fact that her novels are reviewed in the *New York Times* by its regular book critics and are not relegated to the "Crime Fiction" section—though this in turn means that her novels are held to a higher critical standard than those of other mystery writers. James is popular on both sides of the Atlantic. Among numerous honors, in 1991 she was made an honorary member of the House of Lords, accorded a life peerage and the title of Baroness James of Holland Park. In the United States she became, in 1999, the recipient of the Mystery Writers of America Grand Master Award for Lifetime Achievement.

BIBLIOGRAPHY

Primary Sources

Cover Her Face. London: Faber, 1962; Scribner's, 1966.

A Mind to Murder. London: Faber, 1963; New York; Scribner's, 1963.

Unnatural Causes. London: Faber; New York: Scribner's, 1967.

The Maul and the Pear Tree. With T.A. Critchley. London: Constable, 1971; New York: Mysterious Press, 1986.

Shroud for a Nightingale. London: Faber; New York: Scribner's, 1971.

An Unsuitable Job for a Woman. London: Faber, 1972; New York: Scribner's, 1973.

The Black Tower. London: Faber; New York: Scribner's, 1975.

Death of an Expert Witness. London: Faber; New York: Scribner's, 1977.

Innocent Blood. London: Faber; New York: Scribner's, 1980.

The Skull beneath the Skin. London: Faber; New York: Scribner's, 1982.

A Taste for Death. London: Faber; New York: Knopf, 1986.

Devices and Desires. London: Faber, 1989; New York: Knopf, 1990.

Children of Men. London: Faber, 1992; New York: Knopf, 1993.

Original Sin. London: Faber, 1994; New York: Knopf, 1995.

A Certain Justice. London: Faber; New York: Knopf, 1997.

Time to Be in Earnest. London: Faber, 1999; New York: Knopf, 2000.

Death in Holy Orders. London: Faber; New York: Knopf, 2001.

Secondary Sources

Benstock, Bernard. "The Clinical World of P.D. James." In *Twentieth-Century Women Novelists.* Ed. Thomas Staley. Totowa, NJ: Barnes and Noble, 1982. 104–129.

Gidez, Richard. *P.D. James.* Boston: Twayne, 1986.

Goodman, Walter. "Scotland Yard's Dalgliesh Swims among the Lawyers." *New York Times* 15 April 1999: E10.

Harkness, Bruce. "P.D. James." In *Art in Crime Writing: Essays on Detective Fiction.* Ed. Bernard Benstock. New York: St. Martin's, 1983. 119–141.

Joyner, Nancy Carol. "P.D. James." In *10 Women of Mystery.* Ed. Earl F. Bargainnier. Bowling Green, OH: Bowling Green State U Popular P, 1981. 107–123.

Lehmann-Haupt, Christopher. "James's Dalgliesh Tracks a Copycat Killer." *New York Times* 25 January 1990: C22.

Oates, Joyce Carol. "Inside the Locked Room." *New York Review of Books* 5 February 1998: 19–21.

Siebenheller, Norma. *P.D. James.* New York: Ungar, 1981.

Sinclair, Iain. "The Cadaver Club." *London Review of Books* 22 December 1994: 20–22.

Stasio, Marilyn. "No Gore Please—They're British: An Interview with P.D. James and Lawrence Bloch." *New York Times Book Review* 9 October 1988: 1, 18–20.

Waugh, Harriet. "The Reader Is Warned Too Much." *Spectator* 7 October 1989: 40.

Storm Jameson
1891–1986

Phyllis Lassner

Like that of many British women writers of her generation, Storm Jameson's career was shaped by the cataclysmic events of her time. As other women writers transformed their responses to World War I, the Great Depression, and World War II into a feminist modernism, Jameson created a polemicist fiction that developed out of feminist concerns but remains distinctive for dramatizing the moral consciousness of men and women caught in such political crises as fascism and colonialism.

BACKGROUND

Jameson's depiction of moral consciousness was inspired by her lifelong identification with her family's Norwegian origins and six-hundred-year residence in Whitby, Yorkshire, the combination of which she characterized in her masterful autobiography, *Journey from the North*, as willfully independent but given to emotional isolation. Drawing upon her parents' difficult marriage, Jameson centered her fiction on personal relationships in which the combination of temperamental incompatibility and ideological or political differences creates a sexual tension that is as binding as it is estranging. This bond also characterized Jameson's relationship with her mother, who encouraged her daughter's academic and writing ambitions while she was also critical of her personal life. Jameson's talents were rewarded with a scholarship to Leeds University, where in 1912 she was the first woman to earn a B.A. in English, a degree that was awarded first class. It was at Leeds that she met her first husband, Charles Douglas Clarke, whom she married in 1913 and divorced in 1915. Though she was awarded a research scholarship to University College, London, her own willful independence led her to transfer to King's College, where she felt that she would find more intellectual challenge. There she wrote an M.A. thesis on modern European drama that was accepted for publication.

At King's Jameson developed her political ideology as a Labour socialist and became the only woman member of a discussion group dedicated to the exposure of political and ethical hypocrisy and to the ideas of Freud, H.G. Wells, and the socialist A.R. Orage's magazine *New Age*. The group called themselves the Eikonoklasts, in an affected spelling that suggested a political intensity to which Jameson would always be drawn, but the full expression of which would have to wait until after struggles with an indifferent husband, poverty, and her frustrated drive to write. Uncommitted to providing either financial or emotional support, her husband was also dismissive of Jameson's talent and ambitions, and when a son was born, Jameson was left to resolve her emotional and practical conflict between her love for the child and her desire to become a writer. Her anguished decision to leave her son with her mother in Whitby is played out repeatedly in her fiction, finding its most powerful expression in her 1930s *Mirror in Darkness* trilogy. Separated from her husband and child, Jameson supported herself by working in an advertising agency and at the *New Commonwealth* magazine, all the while experimenting with her first fictions. A later position at Knopf publishers led to her meeting Guy Chapman, the historian who would become her second husband, with whom, despite their temperamental differences, she built a strong and happy marriage until his death in 1972.

Jameson's commitment to national and international politics took hold during World War I when her political views were shaped by her sense of their mediation through the experiences of the men on the battlefields. By the time of the 1926 General Strike she invested her fiction with analyses of gender inequity that were linked with the disparities of economics and power that had nearly torn the nation apart. Jameson's travels in Europe in the 1930s gave her the graphic data that would continue to inspire her political and creative imagination. Contemptuous of Western Europe's isolationism and apathy toward fascism, she began to write trenchant articles and attend political meetings to bring recognition of the crisis in Central Europe to those who she felt would rationalize away the imminent threats of Hitler and Mussolini. Her fear that political apathy could have deadly results led to her 1936 dystopia *In the Second Year*, which dramatizes a fascist takeover of Britain. Jameson had become a pacifist as a result of the horrific casualties and uneasy victory of World War I, feeling "horror at each fresh evidence of the ruin begun in the War, and finished in the Peace" (*No Time like the Present* 101). While all her writing afterwards is haunted by her younger brother's death in the war, as early as 1933, when she recognized "what Hitler planned to do to the Jews living in Germany," she began to argue that the racist persecutions and conquests of fascism and Nazism required a different response (*Journey* 1:320). As much as she loathed war, she felt that it was necessary to defeat the Third Reich before it enslaved and destroyed its innocent victims. The process of coming to this realization and facing its consequences infuses her fiction of the 1930s and 1940s. With the self-questioning that would become her hallmark, she enjoined herself: "If I believe that concentration camps, the torture of Jews and political opponents, is less vile than war, I must say so plainly, not pretend that the price is something less" (*Journey* 1:341–342).

Jameson found an activist political voice in her presidency of the English branch of PEN International from 1938 to 1945. Having always preferred friends in political rather than literary circles, she could now impose the urgency of world politics onto not only aesthetic but also professional concerns. As English delegate to the PEN Congress in Prague in 1938, she developed an attachment to the democratic spirit of the people of Czechoslovakia, embodied most powerfully in "the wit and energy" of Jan Masaryk and of Edouard Beneš, the prime minister (*Journey* 1:368). She dramatized this spirit in her 1942 dystopia *Then We Shall Hear Singing: A Fantasy in C Major*, which warns of the destruction of Central European civilization if the Nazis were to win the war, but also celebrates the resistance of Czech women. Jameson's writing during the 1930s and 1940s reflects her lifelong view that "the future is our business" (*Journey* 2:13). More than any other British writer, except perhaps for Phyllis Bottome, Jameson charted the slow, agonizing progress of World War II from fears that the Allies lacked the resolve to stop Hitler through the moral dilemmas facing those in battle and on the home front, and those in the aftermath of victory.

Throughout the war, like Phyllis Bottome, Jameson rallied tirelessly to rescue Europe's Jews. Politicizing her PEN office, she stretched every occasion to protest the lack of this rescue, which she viewed as central to the Allies' war aims. It was this urgency that led her to publish her renunciation of pacifism in the 1941 monograph *The End of This War*, in which she argued that for "pacifist and non-pacifist alike, there is a choice between two guilts, two prices. The price of surrendering to the Nazi barbarian is Auschwitz" (*Journey* 2:96). She felt a parallel surrender in Britain's internment of German Jewish refugees.

If Jameson's responses to the political crises of her time shape her fictions, they also shape the criteria by which she assessed the novelistic traditions she admired most. When world crisis was simmering in the beginnings of the Cold War, she expressed concern in an essay, "The Novelist Today: 1949," that writers "committed to a doctrine" or to "the State" lost their imaginative and critical edge (*Writer's Situation* 73). In a companion piece, "The Form of the Novel," she worried that novelists were retreating from the world into self-referential stylistic concerns. The greatest novelists for her "belong in both camps—Tolstoy, Stendhal, Proust, Dostoevsky, Murasaki" (*Writer's Situation* 56). As with her own ambitions, "writers attend . . . to their business" by looking "with a pure attention at themselves, at other selves, and human society—[to] change our lives" (*Writer's Situation* 58).

ANALYSIS

Jameson is only just beginning to receive the critical attention she deserves. Though she began publishing fiction in 1919, the form of the "chronicle," to which James Gindin attributes her most accomplished work, found expression in her Mary Hervey and Mary Hervey Russell series, begun in 1927 and, after stopping abruptly with the third volume of *The Mirror in Darkness* trilogy in 1936, ending finally in the elegaic *The Journal of Mary Hervey Russell* in 1945. In many ways autobiographical, all the Mary Hervey novels—the trilogy *The Triumph of Time*, comprising *The Lovely Ship*, *The Voyage Home*, and *A Richer Dust*; the novels *The Captain's Wife* and *That Was Yesterday; The Mirror in Darkness* trilogy, *Company Parade*, *Love in Winter*, and *None Turn Back*; and the novel *The Journal of Mary Hervey Russell*—chart the social, economic, and psychological trajectory from 1840 to 1930 of a Yorkshire shipbuilding empire headed by the matriarch, Mary Hervey, against whose power her daughter Sylvia and her granddaughter Mary Hervey Russell must construct their own sense of self. The interplay of women's psychological power over each other gains momentum with Jameson's exploration of their economic power and dependence, and it is through this relationship that she begins her development of a form I shall call the novel of women's political psychology. Because Gindin places these novels in the tradition of Arnold Bennett's *Clayhanger* trilogy and John Galsworthy's *The Forsyte Saga*, with their emphasis on the process of character development, he is unable to find a unifying thematic in which character can develop with any depth until Mary Hervey Russell takes center stage.

What this approach ignores is the way Jameson reacts against and exploits the conventions of the bildungsroman in order to situate the determinants of women's lives within social contexts that privilege the development of male characters. Critics Jennifer Birkett and Elizabeth Harvey read Jameson as assuming "a fundamental humanity common to both sexes" and having "formulated her vision of the new society in terms of equal roles and equal treatment for women and men" (29). Jameson's achievement is to invest the women of a progressive society with personal choices, assuming social responsibility, and so she makes public and private spheres, politics and psychology cohere. Consistent with Joanna Labon's observation that Jameson "is a political writer who, not surprisingly, found herself at home among the fact-hunters, socialist realists and Mass Observers of the 1930s" (36), the interwar scenes of *The Mirror in Darkness* politically historicize women's psychology by imprinting them with a 1930s view of the Great War's lingering effects. As Mary Hervey Russell traverses London's political landscape, from socialist groups to friends on the liberal left and working for the entrepreneurial and political right, her character questions both modernism's romantic despair and socialist utopianism as hallmarks of the 1930s. Birkett and Harvey find that Jameson's work is marked by ambivalence between her own "isolated cause" and sympathy "to unnumbered other women of her time who feel the stirrings of ambition but lack the scope and the experience to formulate desire and turn it into act" (68). Like Jameson herself, however, Hervey struggles to become independent and a writer while negotiating the anxieties of single motherhood in a world dominated by war-torn but ruthlessly ambitious men. The political and literary work to which Hervey commits herself, as it challenges the psychological romance of women's sublimated desires, identifies women's politicized writing in the 1930s.

Jameson's commitment to politics as text and not only as context shapes the place of European crises of the 1930s and 1940s. Her fears about worldwide fascist domination erupt in her 1936 dystopia of a fascist takeover in Britain, *In the Second Year*, and in the 1938 *No Victory for the Soldier*, about the Spanish Civil War and published under the pseudonym James Hill. By 1940, when France was overrun by the Nazi blitzkrieg, she expressed her continued suspicion of British commitment to its European allies in a stunning experimental novel, *Europe to Let: The Memoirs of an Obscure Man*. Labon, like Douglas Robillard and Gindin, assumes Jameson's political integrity and candor, and all three critics claim that she does not engage in literary experiment. Robillard goes so far as to assert that her "novels are conservative in their structure, shapely, well-expressed, careful to stay within their limits" (63–64). Similarly, Janet Montefiore finds that Jameson's career is "undermined by her contradictory attitude to the art of the realist novel to which she dedicated her talents" (39), and this attitude allows her to follow the convention of representing her narrators as "a masculine point of view" while doubting "masculine subjectivity" (103). Even a brief glance at *Europe to Let* reveals a historical epic of experimental form, as it dramatizes the doubts and political awakening of a young Englishman making his way across Central Europe from 1923 to 1938. Its unconventional action consists of polemical arguments between the dispassionate Englishman and the Europeans he meets who are fighting for the lives of their countries. Intercuts between confrontations reveal the Englishman's search for political truth as challenging the stable grounds of epic progression by questioning the viability of a paternalistic liberal progressivism and moral superiority. Even when Britain was fighting for its own life and then when it was joined by the Americans, Jameson was afraid of a Nazi victory but not of further experimentation. She depicted both in her 1942 dystopia *Then We Shall Hear Singing*, in which the men of an occupied Czech village are lobotomized as punishment, but the nation's cultural heritage and independence are kept alive by the village women as they express their political consciousness in their traditional songs, recipes, and embroidery. The power that Jameson feared from the Nazis is matched in her fiction of this period by concerns about the political weaknesses of neutrality. Her 1940 novel *Cousin Honoré*, set in Alsace, examines the self-interest of nations that justify their "malevolent blindness" by "calling up the usual words, honour, liberty, courage, and the rest" (150).

Birkett and Harvey's claim that Jameson's most powerful creation is "the authorial persona" her work "projects" is borne out by her novels' consistent voice of protest against political apathy and oppression (88). The consistency of this voice has often been noted as Jameson's habit of recycling autobiographical material and commentary into various works of fiction. Such notation, however, is incomplete without recognizing that this echo marks another of Jameson's literary experiments. Nowhere is this more apparent than in her 1945 novel *The Journal of Mary Hervey Russell*, which represents the interplay of individual consciousness and the materiality of political events as a meditation on the costs of nationalism, war, and cultural tradition on a woman's struggle for independence. The reflective movement of Hervey Russell's memory and reconstruction of the past produces an incisive interpretation of World Wars I and II through the parallels and challenging questions each event poses to the other.

Pivotal to this meditation is a political and social risk Jameson takes throughout her career. The ethical politics on which her plotting depends turn on another echoing device: her representation of Europe's Jews and its anti-semitism. From *The Mirror in Darkness* trilogy through the novels of the European World War II fronts and beyond, she portrays a disturbing confluence of attitudes that guarantee the Jew's status as outsider and then pariah. As Elaine Feinstein observes, "Few portraits of Jews owning press empires are as sympathetic as that of Marcel Cohen in *Company Parade*" (Introduction to *Company Parade* xi). Jameson's treatment of the Jew Heinrich Kalb in her postwar novel *The Black Laurel* testifies to the world's indifference to the precarious status of Europe's Jews in the 1930s, an attitude that led to complicity in denying them rescue during the Holocaust, and that would still scapegoat them after the Allied victory. Harrison Smith reviewed this novel as too pessimistic, while Nona Balakian observed that Jameson "is among the few present-day novelists who see conflict wholly in terms of moral consequences [with] a remarkable grasp of European politics" (16). Jameson certainly never failed to direct her aggressive political voice at the injustices of her own nation and in 1961 published a novel, *Last Score*, about the inglorious end of the British Empire and its roots in a racist sense of its own moral superiority. As always, she found that domestic arrangements of power ruled by ambitious and misguided men could be questioned through women's consciousness. Though they never meet, the young journalist, Sarah Leng, and her lover's mother, Sophie Ormston, dramatize the novel's political critique. Jameson's last novels explore the individual psychology of men questing for dominating power but finding that this can only produce destructive ends.

ASSESSMENT

While Storm Jameson is now receiving the serious attention she deserves, some critics remain unsure about how to place her, either in the history of the modern novel or of modern political thought. Neither modernist nor solely realist, Jameson can best be appreciated by seeing her place in British literary history as deploying realist conventions for the purpose of plotting ethical questions about the representation of the historical realities of her time. She actually theorized this combination of narrative detachment and ethical commitment in her essay "Documents," in which she insists that "emotion should spring directly from the fact" and not from the writer's sentimental "self-consciousness" with his or her own "spiritual writings" (15, 10, 11). Her commitment to representing the political perspectives of protagonists and antagonists alike leads her to the ambivalences attributed to her fictional concerns and style. While today we might see this wavering balancing act as postmodern, once she has made a political-ethical judgment, Jameson's political passions remain steadfast, as in her antifascism. Instead of portraying a destabilized world as a decentered narrative or questioning whether narrative forms can represent political chaos, Jameson develops fictional forms that dramatize a critical questioning of the motivations of her individual characters as well as those of the collective polities in which they live or to which they are exiled. In this way she leads us through a process of recognizing, along with her characters, that they are driven by a combination of unsettling internalized desires and destabilizing political events. Unlike traditional realists, Jameson offers no resolution or reconciliation as a concluding scene; instead, characters like Mary Hervey Russell and David Renn, the latter appearing first in *The Mirror in Darkness* and then in *Before the Crossing* and *The Black Laurel*, are left in the uncertain wake that characterizes and embeds individual and collective political defeat or victory in each other. If the end of *The Black Laurel* suggests hope, with David Renn adopting a child war victim, his belief in the future must find the courage to persist in the shadow of Terezín, where "forgiveness" and "justice" are overwhelmed by "anguish" (300–301).

Unlike the mythologized or figurative political landscapes of modernism, Jameson's fiction refuses to universalize historical events. If the presence of World War I is always felt as a haunting memory in her depictions of World War II, if the victory of World War II is shadowed by the injustices of colonialism, her emphasis is on the differences between these events rather than figuring one to represent the terror and tragedy of all oppression. The particularity of these depictions, rather than remaining topical and therefore destined to become outdated, achieves the kind of universality we find in moral fables. If the story of England's 1926 General Strike seems to require a historian's interest, it assumes a fresh and compelling meaning in *None Turn Back*. This is accomplished through the interweave of highly individualized characters who represent in complex forms the gendered and economically based power struggles of a society in transition from stability to world catastrophe. As Elaine Feinstein notes, "Storm Jameson always saw politics in terms of human beings; in that she was true to all the paradoxes of her inheritence" (Introduction to *Company Parade* xii).

However Jameson's narrative forms vary throughout her fiction, her quest for understanding historical change and individual inconsistency insists on the moral necessity of recognizing and representing their historical and political realities as a deeply invested subjective narrative voice, and this quest determines all her aesthetic concerns with structure and language. The forms and styles of her fictions are designed to express this quest as a process representing the material realities shaping her characters' fusion of despair and activism. In turn, what makes Jameson's novels gripping are the plots that enact this fusion as a combination of political and psychological epic and thriller. In *The Mirror in Darkness* Mary Hervey Russell discovers her sense of self by giving political meaning to her encounters and escapes from powerful men and women who are as compelling as they are often villainous. If personal and sexual relationships frequently fail or promise only sporadic fulfillment, if Mary Hervey remains not quite sure of who or what she is at the end of the unfinished *Mirror in Darkness*, what remains constant in Jameson's fiction is the slow, sometimes-sluggish, meandering, and even contradictory development of the recognition that there is no self worth having without political conscience.

If Storm Jameson's novels incorporate and replay her own passions and doubts, this only assures her strongest achievements. Her personal outrage and activist protests of economic and political oppression are written into her novels, not to be subdued by a process of creative transformation, but to infuse their plots and characters with an emotional intensity that reaches out and grabs the reader. This deep emotional connection does not, however, mean that Jameson's novels are sentimental potboilers or lose their depth in conventional forms of suspense and melodrama. Instead, her polemical voice is both heightened and chastened by a trenchant and complex political analysis that remains convincing not only for its insights into her own time, but as a basis for understanding England's and Europe's persistently complicated internal and international relations. If she is correct that she wrote too fast and too many novels, among them are more than enough to form an oeuvre that deserves fresh reading and further study.

BIBLIOGRAPHY

Primary Sources

The Pot Boils. London: Constable, 1919.

The Happy Highways. New York: Century, 1920.

Modern Drama in Europe. London: Collins, 1920.

The Clash. Boston: Little, Brown, 1922.

The Pitiful Wife. New York: Constable, 1923.

Lady Susan and Life: An Indiscretion. London: Chapman & Dodd, 1923.

Mont-Oriol. By Guy de Maupassant. Trans. Storm Jameson. New York: Knopf, 1924.

The Horla and Other Stories. By Guy de Maupassant. Trans. Storm Jameson. New York: Knopf, 1925.

Three Kingdoms. New York: Knopf, 1926.

The Lovely Ship. New York: Knopf, 1927.

Farewell to Youth. New York: Knopf, 1928.

Full Circle (one-act play). Oxford: Basil Blackwell, 1928.

The Georgian Novel and Mr. Robinson. New York: Morrow, 1929.

The Decline of Merry England. Indianapolis: Bobbs-Merrill, 1930.

Eighty-Eight Short Stories. By Guy de Maupassant. Trans. with Ernest Boyd. New York: Knopf, 1930.

The Voyage Home. New York: Knopf, 1930.

A Richer Dust. New York: Knopf, 1931.

The Single Heart. London: Benn, 1932.

That Was Yesterday. New York: Knopf, 1932.

A Day Off. London: Nicholson & Watson, 1933.

No Time like the Present. London: Cassell, 1933.

Women Against Men (A Day Off, Delicate Monster, The Single Heart). New York: Knopf, 1933; London: Virago, 1982.

Challenge to Death. Ed. Storm Jameson. London: Constable, 1934.

Company Parade. New York: Knopf, 1934; London: Virago, 1982.

Love in Winter. New York: Knopf, 1935.

The Soul of Man in the Age of Leisure. London: Nott, 1935.

In the Second Year. London: Cassell; New York: Macmillan, 1936.

None Turn Back. London: Cassell, 1936; London: Virago, 1984.

"Documents." *Fact* 4 (July 1937): 9–18

Loving Memory. As James Hill. London: Collins, 1937.

The Moon Is Making. London: Cassell, 1937.

The World Ends. As William Lamb. London: Dent, 1937.

Here Comes a Candle. London: Cassell, 1938.

The Novel in Contemporary Life. Boston: Writer, 1938.

No Victory for the Soldier. As James Hill. London: Collins, 1938.

The Captain's Wife. New York: Macmillan, 1939.

Civil Journey. London: Cassell, 1939.

Farewell, Night; Welcome, Day. London: Cassell, 1939.

Cousin Honoré. London: Cassell, 1940.

Europe to Let: The Memoirs of an Obscure Man. London: Macmillan, 1940.

The End of This War. London: Allen and Unwin, 1941.

The Fort. London: Cassell; New York: Macmillan, 1941.

London Calling. New York: Harper, 1942.

Then We Shall Hear Singing: A Fantasy in C Major. London: Cassell; New York: Macmillan, 1942.

Cloudless May. London: Macmillan, 1943.

The Journal of Mary Hervey Russell. London: Macmillan, 1945.

The Other Side. London: Macmillan, 1946.

Before the Crossing. London: Macmillan, 1947.

The Black Laurel. London: Macmillan, 1947.

The Moment of Truth. London: Macmillan, 1949.

William the Defeated (television play). In *The Book of the P.E.N.* Ed. Hermon Ould. London: Barker, 1950.

The Writer's Situation and Other Essays. London: Macmillan, 1950.

The Green Man. London: Macmillan, 1952.

The Commonplace Heart (television play). 1953.

The Hidden River. New York: Harper, 1955.

The Intruder. London: Macmillan, 1956.

A Cup of Tea for Mr. Thorgill. New York: Harper, 1957.

One Ulysses Too Many. New York: Harper, 1958.
Last Score, or, The Private Life of Sir Richard Ormston. London: Macmillan, 1961; New York: Harper, 1961.
Morley Roberts: The Last Eminent Victorian. London: Unicorn, 1961.
The Road from the Monument. New York: Harper, 1962.
A Month Soon Goes. New York: Harper, 1963.
The Blind Heart. New York: Harper, 1964.
The Early Life of Stephen Hind. New York: Harper, 1966.
The White Crow. New York: Harper, 1968.
Journey from the North: Autobiography of Storm Jameson. 2 vols. London: Collins, 1969–1970.
Parthian Words. London: Collins, 1970.
A Kind of Survivor: The Autobiography of Guy Chapman. Ed. Storm Jameson. London: Gollancz, 1975.
Speaking of Stendhal. London: Gollancz, 1979.

Secondary Sources

Balakian, Nona. "Portrait of Our Time." *New York Times Book Review* 16 May 1948: 16.
Birkett, Jennifer, and Elizabeth Harvey. *Determined Women: Studies in the Construction of the Female Subject, 1900–90*. Savage, MD: Barnes & Noble, 1991.
Feinstein, Elaine. Introduction to *Company Parade*. London: Virago, 1982. vii–xii.
———. Introduction to *None Turn Back*. London: Virago, 1984. v–vii.
Gindin, James. "Storm Jameson and the Chronicle." *Centennial Review* 22 (Fall 1978): 400–409.
Labon, Joanna. "Tracing Storm Jameson." *Women: A Cultural Review* 8.1 (Spring 1997): 33–47.
Lassner, Phyllis. *British Women Writers of World War II: Battlegrounds of Their Own*. Basingstoke: Macmillan, 1998.
———. "A Cry for Life: Storm Jameson, Stevie Smith, and the Fate of Europe's Jews." In *Visions of War: World War II in Popular Literature and Culture*. Ed. M. Paul Holsinger and Mary Anne Schofield. Bowling Green, OH: Bowling Green State U Popular P, 1992. 181–190.
Montefiore, Janet. *Men and Women Writers of the 1930s*. London: Routledge, 1996.
Robillard, Douglas. "Storm Jameson as Novelist and Critic." *Essays in Arts and Sciences* 17 (May 1988): 63–72.
Smith, Harrison. "Berlin Tragedy." *Saturday Review* 1 May 1948: 22–23.

Ann Jellicoe
1927–

Neil Novelli

BACKGROUND

Patricia Ann Jellicoe was born on July 15, 1927, in Middlesborough, Yorkshire, England. She attended the Central School of Speech and Drama in London (1943–1947) and embarked on an innovative theater career in London as actress, writer, teacher (at the Central School), director, and literary manager. She founded and directed the experimental Cockpit Theatre Club (1950–1953) (*Contemporary Authors*), which used a thrust stage without scenery like that of Shakespeare's Globe (Jellicoe, *Community Plays* 1). Her first major play, *The Sport of My Mad Mother* (1958), was wildly unconventional and drew severe criticism. *The Rising Generation*, commissioned by the Girl Guides Association and written somewhat later than *Sport*, was a bizarre misfire on both sides; exuberantly combining expressionism, science fantasy, and a critique of strident feminism, it was rejected by the Girl Guides. *The Knack* (1962), however, although in many ways unconventional, was popular with critics and audiences, was produced in New York in 1964, and was made into an American film version, *The Knack . . . and How to Get It* (1965). *Shelley; or, The Idealist* (1965) did not excite strong approval or disapproval. *The Giveaway* (1969) is a cartoonish sitcom about a family that wins a cereal contest. *3 Jelliplays* (1975) is a collection of three children's plays. Along with incidental writings, Jellicoe has translated Ibsen's *Rosmersholm* and *The Lady from the Sea*, Friedrich Kind's *Der Freischütz*, and Chekhov's *The Seagull*.

Jellicoe captured the liberated spirit of the 1960s, and so did her husband, photographer Roger Mayne, famous for his images of working-class and "swinging" London. In 1974 they moved with their two children to Lyme Regis in the West Country. Jellicoe writes, "I was dissatisfied with theatre: it's hard to say why except that perhaps it seemed totally unimportant in most people's lives" (*Community Plays* 2–3).

In the late 1970s, however, her theatrical career resumed along radically different lines when she began to produce large-scale community plays—works reflecting a community's past and involving hundreds of people, professionals as well as amateurs, in each production. She wrote and produced the first play, *The Reckoning*, in her home community in 1978 and continued to produce community plays into the 1990s, often writing the scripts, sometimes commissioning other writers. Other communities, inspired by her work, have created their own plays.

Her book *Community Plays: How to Put Them On* is a magisterial work that encompasses the whole process of putting on such plays.

Jellicoe's career in London theater cannot be understood apart from the activities of the English Stage Company at the Royal Court Theatre under the direction of George Devine during the years 1956–1965. Devine aimed to revitalize British theater by presenting the work of innovative writers. The Royal Court roster of produced authors in those ten years includes, along with Jellicoe, Bertolt Brecht, Samuel Beckett, Jean Giraudoux, Eugène Ionesco, Jean-Paul Sartre, Wole Soyinka, Harold Pinter, Shelagh Delaney, Jean Genet, and Edward Albee.

At the Royal Court Jellicoe interacted with other writers, predominantly antiestablishment, including Arnold Wesker, Evelyn Ford, Keith Johnstone, John Arden, Alison MacLeod, N.F. Simpson, and Edward Bond. In the Writers' Group Jellicoe and others explored the theories and practices of Bertolt Brecht and Antonin Artaud (Reinelt 12–14; Brown 72; Lumley 231); the focus on improvisation especially had a lasting influence on all her work. Jellicoe recalls that as a woman, she was—without being quite aware at the time—swimming against the current in her various leadership roles at the Royal Court, not only directing but serving as the first woman literary manager. "I didn't feel isolated as a woman in the earlier days at the Court. I was awfully blind . . . I didn't appreciate what tremendous disadvantages I was working under as a woman" (Findlater 155). Nevertheless, in 1984 Jellicoe was awarded the Order of the British Empire for service to drama.

ANALYSIS

In the 1950s Ann Jellicoe was one of a group of playwrights who wanted to appeal to the senses and emotions with, in her words, "Direct Theatre—a theatre of action and images." She says that her first play, *The Sport of My Mad Mother*, "was written completely intuitively, sensing along. It is an anti-intellect play . . . one hopes it will reach the audience directly through rhythm, noise and music" (*Sport* 5). She thought of her works as scores for performance, and in fact for long stretches both *Sport* and *The Knack* read like open dialogue—arbitrary words and sounds that can be given any shape the actor or director desires. She directed most of her own shows and feels that they worked best that way ("Covering" 85).

When Jellicoe's works first appeared, some critics took her at her word and described the plays as sheerly intuitional. But the apparent opposition between intellectual and instinctual is misleading. A work—for example, play, music, or dance—that directly engages an audience's emotions usually depends on considerable artistic patterning. The link between design and spontaneity, reason and emotion, preparation and execution, is complex; years of training go into a fine jazz improvisation. Although Jellicoe's plays do reach for the visceral level, they cannot help being mediated through a sophisticated, literate intelligence. Their language shows considerable rational control, perhaps, at times, interference, because an intellectual exploring the world of sheer instinct is as likely to hit wrong notes as an instinctual exploring the world of intellectuals.

The Sport of My Mad Mother, however, is Jellicoe's only play where the instinctual is obtrusively invoked. The title, according to the playbill (Jellicoe Collection), comes from a Hindu hymn and refers to Kali, goddess of creation and destruction: "All creation is the sport of my mad mother Kali" (*Sport* playbill n.p.). *Sport* depicts life among London teddy boys (street toughs) of the 1950s. Aimless, insecure, and violent, they are ruled by Greta, a menacing Australian woman with flaming red hair. At the end Greta gives birth behind a sheet, announcing, "Birth! Birth! That's the thing! Oh, I shall have hundreds of children, millions of hundreds and hundreds of millions" (*Sport* 86).

The play lengthily mirrors the randomness

and danger of street life. Characters tend to be stereotypes, and, far from being spontaneous, the play seems designed to create intellectual enigmas for the audience even while it purports to appeal only via movement and sound. *Sport* offers unusual moments of vitality, among them a wonderful passage where the toughs make a ritual chant out of the instructions on a home perm kit; but such passages bear the clear mark of a controlling rational intelligence. The character Greta gives great scope for an actress but is obviously a concocted symbol.

Sport drew bad reviews, failed at the box office, and was canceled after only fourteen performances (Findlater, Appendix 2). Critics dismissed it: "a well-acted, arty bore" (Entwisle). Kenneth Tynan, however, spoke for a few who recognized Jellicoe's talent: "[F]or all its faults, this is a play of spectacular promise." Seth Baumrin (Texas Tech University) was the producer of an all-student production at Hunter College in the 1980s. "The faculty liked it," he says, "but audiences didn't" (Interview).

It remains a mystery why, after *Sport* was produced, the Girl Guides Association chose Jellicoe to write a play for eight hundred girls and one hundred boys. The result was *The Rising Generation*, a lively, spectacle-laced work that, for obvious reasons, was rejected by the Girl Guides. It is set in the Republic of Women, a realm ruled despotically by Mother. A teacher leads the girls in rote lessons: "Shakespeare was a woman. . . . Milton was a woman," and so on through the Black Prince, Isaac Newton, and others. The lesson gets more graphic: "Men are black. Men are thick. Men are tall. Men are strong. Men will tear you, beat you, eat you." Then the boys enter. The girls repeat the chant, but now with "awe, surprise, and wonder," and the young people instantly join in a dance. As Mother sets off a hydrogen bomb, the boys and girls gather up the audience, construct a large space ship named Hope, and take off for "a new world."

If *Sport* repelled audiences and critics, *The Knack* charmed them on both sides of the Atlantic. Jellicoe says that *The Knack* was written because she became skeptical of girls' boarding-school codes ("It's not winning that matters, it's the joining in") and the Royal Court's emphasis on "the right to fail." "I now know—bitter experience has taught me—it's terribly important to be a success. Otherwise you don't get any more work. . . . I thought I'd better write something that stood some chance" ("Covering" 85–86). It opened under Jellicoe's direction at the Royal Court in 1962 and under Mike Nichols's direction in New York in 1964.

Three men share a house in London: Tolen, who likes to subjugate others, has turned seduction into an exploitive technology—a knack; Colin yearns to be sexually successful with women; and Tom sees sexuality in the context of personal relationships. Into their one-upmanship games steps Nancy, seventeen, fresh from the country. Although *The Knack* is playful in tone, it deals with a potentially damaging power struggle. Tolen threatens to dominate both Nancy and Colin; Tom tries to keep both of them free; and Nancy upsets all their schemes by mischievously shouting that she has been raped. At the end Tolen is foiled, and Colin and Nancy are together.

The play captures the spirit of the 1950s and 1960s with sensitivity and detail. Most obviously, the characters talk copiously about sex. Even more pervasive as a 1960s declaration of freedom was "doing your own thing" in room furnishings: Tom, a free soul, paints his walls in patterns of light and shadow. Among other marks of the period are verbal absurdities, plentiful whimsy, and notions of free-form education. But most fundamental to the period is the play's lighthearted blend of iconoclasm with idealism.

In connection with *The Knack*, Jellicoe speaks with shrewd good sense about the impact of audiences. In Cambridge the undergraduate audience "laughed a great deal," and she felt that the play was "quite fresh." In Bath, however, she sat with an audience that was "elderly, confused and outraged. . . . They found the play obscene." "I did not want to laugh. More than that, the play appeared obscene to me" (*Some Unconscious Influences* 4–10).

Reviewers noted that *The Knack* appealed directly to the audience's emotions. That is true to a point, but, in contrast to the potpourri of *Sport, The Knack* depends on a clear set of rational discriminations: this sexual code, not that; this partner, not that. Critics found that the New York production played up the humor at the cost of the play's "real edge of terror" ("Life as Seduction" 90). The play is occasionally produced, even though its period playfulness now seems *faux naïf* or jarring. Susan Atkinson, artistic director of the Bristol Riverside Theatre in Bristol, Pennsylvania, produced the play in 1996. "It was a good production," she says, "but the audience didn't react well. Young liberals probably found the repetitions of 'rape' offensive. For a middle-aged audience, it just didn't seem to speak to anything. It worked like gangbusters in the sixties, and it was funny then for people to say exactly what was true. But not now. People were uncomfortable with it and they walked out. Reviewers liked the production but hated the play" (Interview).

Shelley; or, The Idealist (Royal Court Theatre, 1965), a documentary-style dramatization shifting between realism and melodrama, was modestly successful. Without mitigating Shelley's immature egocentrism, the play gives him heroic stature, and Jellicoe in fact calls Shelley "this extraordinary man" ("Covering" 89). Becky Prophet (Alfred University) recalls playing Shelley's first wife Harriett (who committed suicide after he abandoned her) in a 1967 college production. "I think we all saw him as the powerful romantic poet who didn't know how to treat women he supposedly loved," she says. "I liked the challenges of the play. If any of my memories of it are even half correct, it would be a great play for students to work on. I think Shelley has to appeal to the rebel, the intellect, and artist in all of us" (E-mail).

In the late 1970s, after moving to Devon, Jellicoe launched a series of projects of incalculable effect, the community plays. Each play, drawn from a community's deepest stories, involved hundreds of people in a massive collaborative effort. Professionals wrote the scripts, dealt with specialties like costumes, and acted some roles, but the overall momentum came from townspeople. Starting with *The Reckoning* (1978) in Lyme Regis, her own community, Jellicoe has mounted more than a dozen such productions, including *Money and Land* (1988) for Holbaek, Denmark; *Under the God* for Dorchester (1989), with some participants coming from Holbaek; and *Changing Places* for Woking (1992).

Obviously, the community plays fulfill and surpass Jellicoe's earlier visions for theater: to transcend the cerebral and to involve audiences in large-scale spectacle, rhythms, movement, and emotions, and, moreover, to create theatrical experiences that remain part of audiences' lives. The plays are far from mere local boosterism; they deal with loss and conflict in highly dramatic fashion, and they focus on issues that reach across social and gender boundaries. The plays are not designed for performance outside the communities that create them, but *Entertaining Strangers* by David Edgar (Dorchester, 1985) went on to the Royal National Theatre in 1987 with Peter Hall directing and Judi Dench in the lead role of Sarah Eldridge, a hard-nosed pub keeper (Royal National Theatre Archives).

British professional actress Lindsay Ingram, who played the role of Sarah in the Dorchester production of *Entertaining Strangers*, recalls that the play did bring people from all walks of life together for the first time, and that Jellicoe had a great facility for working inclusively with all kinds of people: "I think she found that if you're not working in London, you find something to do where you are" (Interview).

In *Community Plays: How to Put Them On* Jellicoe gives an absorbing account, in sweep as well as in minute detail, of how this kind of theater evolves organically from the real life of a community, from earliest initiatives through aftermath, for example, initial talks, funding, mixing amateurs and professionals, local politics, publicity, ego problems, handling crowd scenes, refreshments, and closing the production. The book is illuminating reading for anyone interested in theater that is closely tied to a community, for example, academic or nonprofit theater.

Early on, Jellicoe created the Colway Theatre Trust as an umbrella organization for the community plays. Although she resigned as head in 1985, the trust still flourishes, and the community-play movement continues in England and elsewhere, using her productions as a model.

ASSESSMENT

Jellicoe is one of the innovative playwrights of the mid-twentieth century. A risk taker, she pushed toward new forms and new theatrical values, especially in the various dynamics that connect audience and performance. She not only depicted changing gender relationships in her plays, but as literary manager at the Royal Court she actively involved women as playwrights in London theater. Her London plays have not become staples of stage repertoire, but they are important as mirrors of their time; if they now seem dated, they and her other theatrical activities were among the innovations that changed succeeding theater. In 1999 the Royal National Theatre chose one hundred of the century's most significant plays for platform presentation; *The Knack* was one of them.

Jellicoe brings her community plays uncannily close to elemental wellsprings of theater. In creating a play, people in a community evidently open up new avenues for knowing and working with each other, and for drawing on their deepest sense of communal identity; these qualities become integral to the experience of the play and in fact seem to effect changes in the community. The scripts of community plays have little appeal for publishers, but some are finding their way into various archives.

Jellicoe's essays and talks make lively reading. A pragmatist, she always keeps in mind the real-world contexts of theater at any level, and she can be disarmingly frank and direct about herself and others.

BIBLIOGRAPHY

Citations from *The Times* (London) and the *New York Times* are from microfilm editions unless otherwise stated. Materials from the Jellicoe Collection, Lilly Library, are included courtesy of the Lilly Library, Indiana University, Bloomington, IN.

Primary Sources

Rosmersholm. By Henrik Ibsen. Trans. Ann Jellicoe. San Francisco: Chandler, 1961.

The Lady from the Sea. By Henrik Ibsen. Trans. Ann Jellicoe. San Francisco: Chandler, 1961.

The Knack and *The Sport of My Mad Mother: Two Plays by Ann Jellicoe*. New York: Dell, 1964.

Shelley; or, The Idealist. New York: Grove, 1966.

Some Unconscious Influences in the Theatre. Cambridge: Cambridge UP, 1967.

The Rising Generation. In *Playbill 2*. Ed. Alan Durband. London: Hutchinson, 1969.

The Giveaway. London: Faber, 1970.

Devon. A Shell Guide. With Roger Mayne. London: Faber, 1975.

The Seagull. By Anton Chekhov. Trans. Ann Jellicoe with Ariadne Nicolaeff. New York: Avon, 1975.

3 Jelliplays ("You'll Never Guess," "Clever Elsie, Smiling Jack, Silent Peter," and "A Good Thing and a Bad Thing"). London: Faber, 1975.

Community Plays: How to Put Them On. London: Methuen, 1987.

Secondary Sources

"Ann Jellicoe." *Contemporary Authors*. Vol. 85–88. Detroit: Gale, 1980.

"Ann Jellicoe." *Contemporary Literary Criticism*. Vol. 27. Detroit: Gale, 1984.

Ann Jellicoe Community Theatre Collection. Theatre Museum, London.

Atkinson, Susan. Telephone interview. 21 February 2000.

Baumrin, Seth. E-mail to the author. 15 February 2000.

———. Telephone interview. 16 February 2000.

Brown, John Russell. *A Short Guide to Modern British Drama*. London: Heinemann, 1983.

Clurman, Harold. "The Knack." Rev. of *The Knack*. In *The Naked Image*. New York: Macmillan, 1966: 88–89. Rpt. from *Nation*, 15 June 1964: 611–612.

Entwisle, Frank. "Slightly Lunatic London." Rev. of *The Sport of My Mad Mother*. *Daily Mirror* 26 February 1958.

Findlater, Richard, ed. *At the Royal Court*. New York: Grove, 1981.

Griffiths, Trevor R., and Margaret Llewellyn-Jones, eds. *British and Irish Women Dramatists since 1958*. Buckingham: Open UP, 1993.

Hewes, Henry. "The Resistible Rise of Barbarity." Rev. of *The Knack*. *Saturday Review* 20 June 1964: 28.

Ingram, Lindsay. Telephone interview. 6 March 2000.

Jellicoe Collection. Lilly Library, Indiana University.

"Life as Seduction." Rev. of *The Knack*. *Newsweek* 15 June 1964: 90.

Lumley, Frederick. *New Trends in 20th Century Drama*. New York: Oxford UP, 1967.

"Naive Plot with Explosive Undercurrents." Rev. of *The Knack*. *The Times* 28 March 1962: 15b. <http://www.opentheatre.co.uk/cpad/research.html>.

Oliver, Edith. "Mr. Nichols, Miss Jellicoe, and Mr. Bedford." Rev. of *The Knack*. *New Yorker* 6 June 1964: 86–88.

Oliver, Janice. "Ann Jellicoe." In *British Playwrights, 1956–1995*. Ed. William W. Demastes. Westport, CT: Greenwood, 1996.

Prophet, Becky. E-mail to the author. 24 February 2000.

Reinelt, Janelle. *After Brecht*. Ann Arbor: U of Michigan P, 1994.

Rusinko, Susan. *British Drama, 1950 to the Present: A Critical History*. Boston: Twayne, 1989.

Snyder, Laura. "Learn to Play the Game: Learning and Teaching Strategies in Ann Jellicoe's *The Knack*." *Modern Drama* 37 (1994): 451–460.

"The Sport of My Mad Mother." Playbill of production at Royal Court Theatre, 1958. Jellicoe Collection, Lilly Library, Indiana U.

Taubman, Howard. "Original 'Knack.' " Rev. of *The Knack*. *New York Times* 28 May 1964: 42:2.

Taylor, John Russell. *Anger and After*. Baltimore: Penguin, 1963. 64–71. Rpt. in *The Twentieth Century*. Ed. Robert W. Corrigan. New York: Dell, 1965.

"Towards a Theatre of Action." *The Times* 31 January 1962: 7b.

Tynan, Kenneth. "Good Sportsmanship." Rev. of *The Sport of My Mad Mother*. *Observer* [London] 2 March 1958.

Pamela Hansford Johnson
1912–1981

Chris Hopkins

Pamela Hansford Johnson's literary reputation is a curious one. She was undoubtedly seen as an important British novelist for the three decades from the 1930s till at least the 1960s. Her output was prolific (it included thirty novels), was interestingly varied in form and subject matter, was always widely and positively reviewed in serious newspapers in Britain and America, and had a broad and appreciative readership. She received recognition from several U.S. universities in the form of honorary degrees, was made a fellow of the Royal Society of Literature, and was awarded a Commander of the British Empire (CBE) in 1975. In short, she was considered a consistently successful, serious novelist whose appeal was neither simply middlebrow nor confined to a small intellectual elite. Yet her reputation has obviously not endured even into the last decades of the twentieth century and the beginning of the twenty-first. Her work has largely not made the transition from being reviewed upon publication during her lifetime to having some form of "classic" status. Thus none of her novels are now in print, and she is not studied in university literature courses in Britain or the United States. Her work is neither read by "ordinary readers" nor preserved and kept alive by the academy.

This situation is, however, not the result of any considered judgment, but an example of the vicissitudes of literary transmission and canon formation. Pamela Hansford Johnson's novels are entirely worthy of preservation for both ordinary and scholarly readerships. Her novels are original and various in form without being markedly avant-garde and still retain a vigor resulting from a balance between innovation and tradition, the readerly and the writerly. Moreover, the engagement of her novels with British intellectual and social life from the 1930s till the 1970s is profound, and several individual novels among her major works represent particular technical and cultural achievements. Thus *This Bed Thy Centre* (1935) marked a notably new frankness by a woman writer in portraying unsensationally the sexual behavior of young women and men, *The Helena Trilogy* (1940, 1947, 1948) carries out successfully, in a Proustian mode, the difficult task of adopting the focal viewpoint of a masculine protagonist, and *The Dorothy Merlin Trilogy* (1959, 1963, 1965) not only engages interestingly with the new developments of modern art, literature, and popular culture in 1960s Britain, but also contains (in *Night and Silence: Who is Here?* [1963]) an early example of what has turned out to be a vigorous novelistic genre: the campus novel.

BACKGROUND

Pamela Hansford Johnson was born on May 29, 1912, in Clapham, a respectable but far-from-smart London suburb. Her father Reginald Johnson was a relatively humble civil servant, while her mother Amy (née Howson) was an actress from a family with theatrical traditions. Reginald Johnson died when Pamela was eleven, leaving the family in impoverished circumstances. Pamela attended Clapham County Secondary School until she was seventeen. Then, after six months at a secretarial college, she followed the course—still only recently open to young women with a certain level of education—of becoming a secretary and typist at the Central Hanover Bank and Trust Company in London. She earned a living at the bank for four years while also developing her interests in writing and making some contacts in artistic circles (these contacts included Victor Neuberg, a literary journalist who worked on the middlebrow paper the *Sunday Referee*, and Dylan Thomas, to whom she was briefly engaged). Thus in 1933 she submitted a poem, "Chelsea Reach," for a prize organized by the *Sunday Referee* and won. The prize, which included publication of a volume of her poems under the title *Symphony for Full Orchestra*, together with the more substantial achievement of writing her first novel and quickly finding a major publisher for it, led her to give up her work at the bank in 1934. From then on, encouraged by the sensational success of that first novel, *This Bed Thy Centre*, brought out by Chapman and Hall in 1935, Pamela Hansford Johnson earned her living as a full-time writer and also, from 1936 on, as a regular reviewer.

In 1936 Johnson married a journalist and historian, Gordon Neil Stewart. The marriage was a happy one for some years, though it ended in divorce in 1948 (her husband had served in India for most of the war, and difficulties arose on his return home particularly because Johnson's mother was in permanent residence). There were two children, and wife and husband cowrote two thrillers together during the war under the name Nap Lombard: *Tidy Death* (1940) and *Murder's a Swine* (1943). In 1950 Johnson married the already-established novelist and scientist C.P. Snow. There was a further child from this second marriage. The couple published five jointly authored plays in the 1950s and later a joint translation. Snow died in 1980, Johnson the following year at the age of sixty-nine. Throughout her life Johnson was interested in the latest developments of contemporary thought, particularly in the fields of philosophy of art, literature, and history. She was also interested in traveling, and went to the then Soviet Union and many parts of North America, particularly in the 1950s and 1960s when she was frequently invited to universities, including Yale and York University, Toronto. She was a member of PEN and also of the Society for European Culture. When she died on June 18, 1981, many newspapers published obituaries reviewing her career.

ANALYSIS

Pamela Hansford Johnson's novels mainly fall into quite distinctive periods, with characteristic atmospheres and interests. This is true both of her subject matter and her literary style and is probably to be related to her continued openness to contemporary developments in culture and literature. Thus her work in the 1930s is mainly focused on the "ordinariness" of British middle-middle-class, lower-middle-class, and, if less substantially, working-class lives. This is in line with one of the dominant literary aesthetics in Britain in that period that, reinventing the nineteenth-century "Condition of England novel," produced many novels about "how the other half live" in a documentary mode (Johnson was a member of the Labour Party and the Left Book Club). At the same time, her work of the 1930s also deploys techniques taken from modernist traditions, particularly a use of stream of consciousness and interior monologue, though usually within a clearly realist context. Her work in the 1940s also shows a sensitivity to a more general cultural shift in moving away from the prewar aesthetic of "grim" realism toward a lusher and more romantic kind of novel. This tendency away from the socially aware novel may arise from a reaction to the war, in which a focus on the personal and emotional seemed particularly precious and important. It is surely not coincidental that both Johnson's *Helena Trilogy* and, for example, Evelyn Waugh's *Brideshead Revisited* (1945) show such interest in Proustian narratives of the prewar past and in an emphasis on the subjective and on a lyrical sensuality.

It has been pointed out that Johnson "examined ordinary people, in a wide variety of social classes" (Sheppherd 5). One may also notice, however, in Johnson's work an upward movement through time in terms of the class milieu in her novels, though bohemian and artistic and displaced characters tend to recur from the earliest novels to the latest, regardless of the general class setting. Her novels of the 1960s and 1970s seem to bear this out, with, for example, the appearance of the American millionaire Jane Merle in *The Dorothy Merlin Trilogy* and the interest in the life of staff at a prep school (a British fee-paying school with a certain social status) in *The Honours Board* (1970). Ishrat Lindblad, the author of the most substantial critical work on Johnson, argues that her later work from the 1960s onward mainly returned to "the method of the great nineteenth century novelists with an implied third-person narrator and a traditional chronological sequence of events" (177). Since Johnson was such a productive writer, this entry will, while noting all her publications, represent her career by examining in detail one of the major works from each of these three periods.

Johnson's first novel caused something of a sensation in its treatment of sexual behavior. Its title, *This Bed Thy Centre*, certainly seemed to suggest a novel focused on sexuality, given its quotation of John Donne's erotic poem "The Sun Rising" (the title was suggested by Dylan Thomas), an impression reinforced by the frankness of discussion by characters within the book: The central character, Elsie, surprises her mother by saying, "I want a man" (her mother, equally surprisingly, replies, "I can't let you say things like that. Anyway, it sounds like the films"). In a preface written in 1961 Johnson denies that the book was centered on sex, saying that its bed-centeredness seemed to her more about the aspirations and dreams of the novel's characters: "I began it with the entrance of the sun upon a new day; and when I jumped at Thomas's idea, I had the unruly sun, rather than the unruly bed, upon my mind" (1).

This comment does, though, seem a revisionist one, perhaps motivated by Johnson's disapproval of more recent changes in social and sexual behavior. Earlier reactions to the novel were surely correct to see it as centrally concerned with sex. However, Johnson's sense that some of the contemporary reaction was sensationalist is equally correct: the novel's own treatment of sexual behavior is precisely neither sensationalizing nor idealizing, but an attempt to see the centrality of sexual motivations and behavior—including ignorance—in ordinary lives. The author was particularly pleased that some reviewers at least did not respond merely to the novel's reputation for sexual content, but also noted its command of technique. The reviewer J.S. Southron, for example, praised the novel's representation of "the dumb longings and inchoate meanderings of thought that attend ordinary adolescence" (qtd. in Lindblad 30). The novel focuses on the experiences and thoughts of Elsie Cotton, a lower-middle-class young woman living in a London suburb, from her last year at school until her wedding a few years later. Though the novel is mainly narrated from Elsie's viewpoint, with much use of free indirect style, there is also considerable representation of the interiority of a range of other characters, including that of her mother, her art teacher Leda,

Mrs. Maginnis, a widow with a reputation for sexual adventure and experience, and her eventual fiancé Roly Cockerill.

The novel's interest is very much in the sexual lives of all its characters, private and public, but always within the context of the realities of other aspects of their existences. Elsie knows nothing about sex at school, though she has an intense adolescent crush on her art teacher. Her curiosity—and indeed a sense of repulsion—is aroused by such information as she can glean from her classmates. She therefore asks her mother, who, though concerned that Elsie is really too young to know, tells her the facts bluntly. We see Elsie leave school and enter employment as a secretary at the local town hall, where Roly, son of a town councillor, also works. She and he begin a relationship during which she both desires and has to fend off his sexual advances. Elsie laments quite openly, to Roly and to her mother, the stupidity of a social system that effectively forbids young women from sexual activity before marriage, through general social disapproval and by disproportionally attaching the social stigma to women. Interestingly, contraception—a solution to some at least of this problem—is not mentioned at all in the novel, despite its general frankness in describing contemporary behavior. The curious ending of the novel suggests that Elsie's problem is a key interest for the novel. As Lindblad notes, the ending does not give us the romantic closure of suggested consummation and the presumption of future married happiness: "instead of the happy ever after ending of the fairy-tale . . . the last few pages of the novel record the frightened thoughts of the young bride as she waits for her husband on her wedding night" (31). This ending is very striking, for it leaves us with a plot that has proceeded toward this one event, yet gives us no assurance of its happiness. The point may well be that Elsie's whole life has been governed and decided not by a positive experience but on the basis of a desire for something of which she has no direct experience. Sexual behavior in this novel is taken for granted, but the social results of current conventions are questioned.

Blessed above Women (1936) forms a companion piece to Johnson's first novel in also concerning itself with the effects of sexuality, this time in an older woman. Her sexual frustration leads her into desperation and finally madness. The other novels of the 1930s use techniques similar to those of *This Bed Thy Centre*, but have wider concerns. *Here Today* (1937), *World's End* (1937), and *The Monument* (1938) are, as Susan Currier says, characteristic of their period in their portrayal of "psychic deprivation and suffering, the exploitation of working-class labor, the unemployment of the 1930s, the rise of fascism, and the impending war" (qtd. in Sheppherd 6). Each of these novels gives a fully realized sense of a number of characters living in a particular community, showing how their personal lives interact and how all live within the social contexts of forces beyond their control. In these ways this group of novels is related to the main literary tendencies of their day, but the stress on what Currier aptly calls "psychic deprivation" seems especially characteristic of Johnson. Her domestication of modernist modes of showing subjectivity through application to ordinary lives and to readerly novels particularly allows her to show the production of social life through shared private lives.

Though she wrote several other novels during the 1940s, Johnson's major novels of the decade are generally agreed to be the three that later became known as *The Helena Trilogy: Too Dear for My Possessing* (1940), *An Avenue of Stone* (1947), and *A Summer to Decide* (1948). Indeed, these may be the best of all Johnson's work, as Isabel Quigly thinks, referring to her "complete assurance" in handling the characters' "public and private lives" (*Pamela* 17–18). The narrator of all three books is the art critic Claude Pickering, who recounts his life so far. However, while Claude is the main character of his own narration in the first novel, his step-mother Helena becomes increasingly important in the following two novels. The trilogy succeeds in the task of making the masculine narrator completely convincing, but there is an emphasis on his relationships to the women in his family. Indeed, the novels understand women's lives through the distancing device of Claude's narration and through the experiences that he did not understand as he lived them. In the first novel Claude tells of the relationship that he had with the woman he married (ignoring Helena's intuitions), counterpointing it with the relationship that really mattered—one that was pursued on two or three occasions, fragmentarily, with the singer Cecily Archer, who now is dead. In the second and third novels there is some reversal of roles as Claude shows insight into, but cannot intervene in, Helena and his stepsister Charmian's lives.

The Helena Trilogy is very much influenced by Proust (a writer in whom Johnson had a lifelong interest), but it is not simply derivative. The narrative, while bringing out the richness of experience recalled and exploiting a sense of the disjunction between life as experienced and life as remembered, is more plot driven than Proust's writing, producing a less aesthetic, more realistic effect. Susan Currier nicely sums up the overall strengths of the trilogy: "anger and fidelity, frustration and love . . . —these are precisely what Johnson is best at—psychological process, attached to ordinary life, in motion" (qtd. in Sheppherd 7). Similar strengths are shown in three linked novels about difficult marital situations (sometimes referred to as a trilogy) that Johnson wrote during the 1950s: *Catherine Carter* (1952), *An Impossible Marriage* (1954), and *The Last Resort* (1956).

Quite different achievements are to be seen in her most famous work of the late 1950s and 1960s, the subsequently named *The Dorothy Merlin Trilogy: The Unspeakable Skipton* (1959), *Night and Silence, Who Is Here? An American Comedy* (1963), and *Cork Street, Next to the Hatter's: A Novel in Bad Taste* (1965). Lindblad notes that contemporary reviewers regarded the first of the series as a new departure: "[It] attracted more attention than any of the books since *This Bed Thy Centre*. Critics were impressed by her ability to write a successful comic novel so different from her previous work" (141). Indeed, Susan Currier sees the trilogy as marking a "moving away from mainstream fiction." However, the novels following *The Merlin Trilogy* do not repeat this mode; Johnson returned instead to well-made fictions with a classic interaction of exterior and interior lives in particular communities. The Dorothy Merlin novels do, however, seem the most notable of Johnson's works in the last three decades of her life. While they are not entirely devoid of characters capable of inspiring sympathy in the reader, the satirical and comic edge is new. New too is the subject matter: the explicit placing of art and artists at the center of these novels (though the arty, at least, had played smaller parts in earlier books). The trilogy is concerned with the morality of modern art and artists and their associated institutions and hangers-on. Each of the novels has its own atmosphere and topic of investigation. The first contrasts the outrageously fake "arty" writer Dorothy Merlin with the thoroughly obnoxious and dishonest, yet ultimately (in fact, posthumously) significant writer Skipton (inspired by the eccentric Baron Corvo). The second explores the strange world of modern literary scholarship by following the fortunes of the amateur Matthew Prior during his scholarship at a small college in the United States (his fellow researchers display a startling variety of manias—one devotes his time to proving against the odds that Emily Dickinson and her entire poetic oeuvre were addicted to alcohol in general, and gin in particular; another loves spiders and always carries at least one on his person). The third explores what art, with a particular focus on absurdist drama, has become in 1960s Britain. The university lecturer Tom Hariot (an expert in "structural linguistics") makes a moral stand by writing a play that is grotesquely offensive and meaningless in order to show that contemporary art is a valueless sham, but it is greeted with critical acclaim, while a photographer who in his own way aims for artistic perfection achieves temporary fame through photographing the ingénue Pringle Milton in a kitten costume inside a giant coffee mug. All three novels are not only comic masterpieces, but also serious and provocative discussions of the uses of art in modern culture. Johnson's last published novel, *A Bonfire* (1981), returns to her beginnings in focusing on the sexual experiences of a girl/young woman, Emma Sheldrake, and their consequences for her life story.

ASSESSMENT

Pamela Hansford Johnson does not currently have a secure place in literary history. However, this is an omission: she has an important place as a novelist who both showed the continuing possibilities of relatively mainstream novelistic traditions and how various modernist and realist techniques could be assimilated into novels that were compelling to a broad range of readers and yet highly nuanced and sophisticated. Her novels reflect interestingly on British (and sometimes American) culture in the period from 1935 to 1981 and show the enduring flexibility of the novel as a form.

BIBLIOGRAPHY

Primary Sources

This Bed Thy Centre. London: Chapman, 1935; New York: Harcourt, 1935. Reissued with a preface. London: Macmillan, 1961.

Blessed above Women. London: Chapman, 1936; New York: Harcourt, 1936.

Symphony for Full Orchestra. London: Sunday Referee, 1936.

Here To-day. London: Chapman, 1937.

World's End. London: Chapman, 1937; New York: Carrick & Evans, 1938.

The Monument. London: Chapman, 1938; New York: Carrick & Evans, 1938.

Girdle of Venus. London: Chapman, 1939.

Tidy Death. With Neil Stewart (as Nap Lombard). London: Cassell, 1940.

Too Dear for My Possessing. London: Collins, 1940; New York: Carrick & Evans, 1940. Reissued with a preface. London: Macmillan, 1972.

The Family Pattern. London: Collins, 1942.

Murder's a Swine. With Neil Stewart (as Nap Lombard). London: Hutchinson, 1943. As *The Grinning Pig*. New York: Simon and Schuster, 1943.

Winter Quarters. London: Collins, 1943; New York: Macmillan, 1944.

The Trojan Brothers. London: Joseph, 1944; New York: Macmillan, 1945.

An Avenue of Stone. London: Joseph, 1947; New York: Macmillan, 1948. Reissued with a preface. London: Macmillan, 1973.

A Summer to Decide. London: Joseph, 1948; New York: Scribner's, 1975. Reissued with a preface. London: Macmillan, 1975.

The Philistines. London: Joseph, 1949.

I. Compton-Burnett. New York: Longman, 1951.

Catherine Carter. London: Macmillan, 1952; New York: Knopf, 1952.

An Impossible Marriage. London: Macmillan, 1954; New York: Harcourt, 1954.

The Last Resort. London: Macmillan, 1956. As *The Sea and the Wedding*. New York: Harcourt, 1957.

The Humbler Creation. London: Macmillan, 1959; New York: Harcourt, 1960.

The Unspeakable Skipton. London: Macmillan, 1959; New York: Harcourt, 1959.

An Error of Judgement. London: Macmillan, 1942; New York: Harcourt, 1962.

Night and Silence, Who Is Here? An American Comedy. London: Macmillan, 1963; New York: Scribner's, 1963.

Cork Street, Next to the Hatter's: A Novel in Bad Taste. London: Macmillan, 1965; New York: Scribner's, 1965.

The Survival of the Fittest. London: Macmillan, 1968; New York: Scribner's, 1968.

The Honours Board. London: Macmillan, 1970; New York: Scribner's, 1970.

The Holiday Friend. London: Macmillan, 1972; New York: Scribner's, 1973.

The Good Listener. London: Macmillan, 1975; New York: Scribner's, 1975.

The Good Husband. London: Macmillan, 1978; New York: Scribner's, 1978.

A Bonfire. London: Macmillan, 1981; New York: Scribner's, 1981.

Secondary Sources

Allen, Walter. *Tradition and Dream*. London: Phoenix, 1964.

Allsop, Kenneth. "Iniquity?" *Encounter* 29 (July 1967): 62.

Borowitz, A. "The Snows on the Moors: C.P. Snow and Pamela Hansford Johnson." In *Innocence and Arsenic: Studies in Crime and Literature*. New York: Harper, 1977.

Brodie, John. "First Impressions of Literary People." *Books Today* July 1947: 5.

Burgess, Anthony. *The Novel Now*. 2nd ed. London: Faber, 1971.

"Chubb Fellow." *New Yorker* 16 December 1961.

Currier, Susan. "Pamela Hansford Johnson." *British Novelists, 1930–1959*. Vol. 15, *Dictionary of Literary Biography*. Detroit: Gale, 1983.

Ferris, Paul. *Dylan Thomas*. London: Hodder, 1977.

Fitzgibbon, Constantine. *The Life of Dylan Thomas*. London: Dent, 1965.

———, ed. *Selected Letters of Dylan Thomas*. London: Dent, 1966.

Jones, Daniel. My *Friend Dylan Thomas*. London: Dent, 1977.

Karl, F.R. A *Reader's Guide to the Contemporary English Novel*. 2nd ed. London: Thames & Hudson, 1972.

Kunitz, Stanley J., and V. Colby, eds. *Twentieth Century Authors: A Biographical Dictionary of Modern Literature*. First Supp. New York: Wilson, 1955. 496–497.

Lindblad, Ishrat. *Pamela Hansford Johnson*. Boston: Twayne, 1982.

"Portrait." *Newsweek* 21 July 1952: 91.

"Portrait." *Saturday Review of Literature* 9 April 1955: 19.

"Portrait." *Saturday Review of Literature* 9 March 1957: 16.

Quigly, Isabel. *Contemporary Novelists*. Ed. James Vinson and D.L. Kirkpatrick. 2nd ed. London and New York: St. James/St. Martin's, 1976.

———. *Pamela Hansford Johnson*. Writers and Their Work Series. London: Longmans, 1968.

Raymond, John. *The Doge of Dover*. London: MacGibbon, 1960.

Sheppherd, Kenneth. "Pamela Hansford Johnson." In *Discovering Contemporary Authors*. CD-ROM. Detroit: Gale Research, 1994.

Charlotte Keatley
1960–

Regina M. Buccola

Charlotte Keatley emerged in the 1980s as one of the leading young playwrights in a burgeoning group of women writing for the stage. Her work, openly feminist and socialist in its politics, has already had a tremendous impact on drama throughout the world. Keatley's best-known work to date, *My Mother Said I Never Should*, has been performed numerous times in her native England as well as across Europe, the United States, Japan, and Australia (Keatley, Preface to *My Mother*). Keatley has repeatedly defied theatrical convention in her work both in her unabashed commitment to foregrounding women and women's issues and in her innovative approach to dramatic form. She has successfully meshed content and structure, creating theater pieces feminist in both sense and sensibility.

BACKGROUND

Charlotte Keatley was born in London in 1960. She earned her B.A. in drama at Manchester University in 1982; in the succeeding decades she has worked extensively in Britain as a writer, actor, and director in addition to teaching writing and drama in various educational institutions (Partnow 125). From the outset Keatley has sought to seize audience attention by investing her work with oddity. One of her first plays, *Dressing for Dinner*, conflates the female provinces of couture and cuisine. Keatley describes the play as "a piece of visual theatre . . . using image before word wherever possible" (Goodman 133). One of the most stunning images in the play is the dressing of a fish in aspic, suggesting the ways in which women of the 1950s were given only "horrid little bits of something in aspic . . . food that you were meant to pick at with your long fingered gloves and a thin fork, just as you were meant to pick delicately at life" (Goodman 134).

Keatley slices straight through to the pith of life and serves it to her audiences raw. She is deeply influenced both by what she has failed to see in the theater—such as no "plays about mothers and daughters, although we have hundreds of years' worth of plays about fathers and sons, or sons and mothers" (Preface to *My Mother*)—and what she has been privileged to see there. By her own admission, Keatley has "drawn strength from feeling myself to be part of a wave of about twenty-five significant women playwrights who emerged during the 1980s. Their voices are diverse, their techniques often innovative, and I know of no such flowering of women playwrights in the two thousand odd recorded years of theatre" (Preface to *My*

Mother). This group includes Caryl Churchill, Pam Gems, and the members of the Women's Theatre Group and Monstrous Regiment. Keatley professes to have learned her feminism "through living and talking with women in the North of England, in fairly depressed working-class areas" (Goodman 130). She considers her feminism "pragmatic" (130) and contends that "[T]he behaviour of mothers shapes a nation as much as governments or wars do" (Preface to *My Mother*).

ANALYSIS

Keatley relies repeatedly on images of confinement and conflated chronology in her plays to demonstrate the persistence of patriarchy and the ways in which it circumscribes women's lives (Sugarwala 295). *Underneath the Arndale* centers on six characters trapped in a nuclear fallout shelter under the shopping mall that gives the play its title. Within this confined space a West Indian woman who would be a marginal figure in the city overhead emerges as the play's central character and primary point of identification.

The title of Keatley's most celebrated work, *My Mother Said I Never Should*, suggests confinement of a different kind, specifically, the ways in which "women's lives are always hedged in by rules" (Sugarwala 297). Keatley's penchant for depicting both conflict and control across generations is apparent in this title as well, indicating the ways in which women function as agents of their own oppression. As Fatima Sugarwala notes, "Being insiders and having gone through similar experiences does not make women sympathetic towards each other. They repeat the same advice and the same admonishments" (297).

The sameness of women's experiences over the years is emphasized in the play by virtue of the fact that the adult actresses portraying four generations of British women (from the oldest, born in 1900, to the youngest, born in 1971) also interact with one another as little girls arrested in time. Keatley explores shifting social attitudes to women's issues by revealing the grand matriarch, Doris, to be the child of an unwed mother like Rosie, the youngest of the four characters. Doris grows up in poverty and is compelled to work until she marries—a job in itself. Rosie's mother Jackie, on the other hand, gives her fatherless daughter up to her own mother, Margaret, so that she can pursue her work as an independent artist. When Margaret dies of cancer, Rosie learns that she was her grandmother, not her mother, and that Jackie, whom she has idolized as a cool older sister, is actually the mother who abandoned her. When Rosie confronts Jackie with this information, she insists, "I wanted you to have opportunities I couldn't ever have given you" (48). Sounding the accusatory note that keeps many women from pursuing their life goals, Rosie retorts, "No you didn't. You wanted your own life more than you wanted mine" (48). Margaret encourages Jackie to put her own goals and ambitions before motherhood and, ironically, becomes a working mother herself to make ends meet when she adopts Rosie. The strain of her work outside of the home and having a second child to raise in middle age drives a wedge between Margaret and her husband, Ken. If Jackie cares more about her own life than she does about her daughter's, Margaret lives vicariously through Jackie.

In a brilliantly conceived scene in the first act of the play, Margaret and Doris are discussing Margaret's plans to marry Ken and move to London. Doris objects to the fact that Ken is an American and that he is taking her daughter away from their home in Manchester to the city. Throughout the conversation the two women are pulling laundry down from the clothesline as a thunderstorm brews. The weather becomes increasingly menacing as the generational conflict intensifies. Finally, Margaret runs off to meet Ken and the thundercloud unleashes on the abandoned Doris, ruining all of her laundry. Over the course of this pitched mother-daughter battle Margaret disdains domestic work, asserting, "I'll get a proper job . . . I'm not wasting my life . . . I'm going to be different! Women did so much during the war: there's nothing to stop us now" (16–17) . . . nothing save the potent force of social convention and tradition, pressures to which Margaret ultimately succumbs.

The play ends on Rosie's sixteenth birthday, in 1987. Hence Keatley spans most of the twentieth century in her representation of these four women and their lives. In addition to attitudes toward motherhood, Keatley also tracks the way in which war impacts all four generations. Doris marries Jack during the upheaval created by World War I, Margaret is put to bed under the piano with hot cocoa served in a utility mug during World War II air raids and ultimately marries an American soldier, and in the play's penultimate scene Rosie makes kites bearing protest messages about the nuclear arms race. The work that women did for the war effort during World War II, which Margaret sees as a harbinger of increased employment opportunities to come, really does not change anything since it was all done for a male-dominated war machine. Jackie, for whom the war is a story told to her about the piano and the mug from which she drinks cocoa, and Rosie, who fights her own pacifist battle against the male military complex, are the ones who really have viable options outside of the domestic sphere. Jasbir Jain notes the significance of Keatley's decision "not to locate any of the scenes in a kitchen which is considered domestic space; instead the locales are houses, living rooms, gardens, backyards, a hospital room and Margaret's office, places which are gender-neutral or strongly affected by male environment" (283). The men themselves remain outside of the play, entering only as sound effects, such as a running lawn mower or car horn. Despite their physical absence, however, men exert tremendous influence on the decisions that all of the women make about how to structure and conduct their lives (Jain 284). As Tanuja Mathur observes, "The sounds in the play—lawn mower, traffic, an ice-cream van, Ken's car horn, two male radio announcements, and four male popular songs—seem to represent the offstage world of men, intruding upon the space created by these women characters" (292). This is true of every space in the play save one: the Wasteground.

Although Keatley deliberately disrupts linear chronology throughout the play, leapfrogging through significant events in the lives of all four women with no regard to historical progression, she takes this disruption a step further with the Wasteground, an ambiguous setting that exists utterly outside the confines of time. In her stage directions Keatley variously describes the Wasteground as "a place where girls come to play" (1) and "a secret place which only girls can get to" (7). The "play" in which the girls engage is utterly shocking, including sexual exploration of one another's bodies, matricidal fantasies, and vicious infighting. Jain finds that this behavior springs from a desire "to get rid of the goodness of the female tradition" (284).

Keatley would agree with such an assessment. In her preface to the play she writes: "I have jumbled chronology because . . . the child remains inside the woman, often shouting what the adult refuses to hear. Therefore the child scenes should not be nostalgic or coy; these girls are serious, and out of the public eye they are not 'good' " (Preface to *My Mother*). Such an assessment is really a catch-22 since it is made on the basis of viewing the girls through the patriarchal lens of the public eye. What is important about the Wasteground and the interaction of four generations of girls within it is its location outside of the glare of the public eye, outside of time, beyond the reach of all rules. While casting a murderous spell in the Wasteground, Jackie says, "You can't make someone's life go backwards" (46). Yet Keatley repeatedly does this for the express purpose of suggesting new, more empowering ways for women to move forward.

ASSESSMENT

Charlotte Keatley made a greater impact on feminism and contemporary theater with a single play, *My Mother Said I Never Should*, than most thinkers and writers achieve in a lifetime. At the beginning of the twenty-first century her prominent position among feminist playwrights throughout the world has already been secured. Keatley's profound personal investments in feminism and the creation of woman-centered theatrical forms ensure that she will do much to usher feminist drama into the next millennium.

BIBLIOGRAPHY

Primary Sources

Dressing for Dinner. Prod. 1982.
Underneath the Arndale. Prod. 1982.
The Legend of Padgate. Prod. 1986.
Waiting for Martin. Prod. 1987.
My Mother Said I Never Should. Prod. 1988. With a preface by Keatley. Royal Court Writers Series. London: Methuen, 1990.
An Armenian Childhood. With Pete Brooks and Steve Schill. Prod. 1989.
Badger. Prod. 1989.
You're a Nuisance Aren't You. Prod. 1989.
The Singing Ringing Tree. Prod. 1991.

Secondary Sources

Goodman, Lizbeth. "Art Form or Platform? On Women and Playwriting." Interview with Charlotte Keatley. *New Theatre Quarterly* 6.22 (May 1990): 128–140.
Jain, Jasbir. "Feminist Drama: The Politics of the Self: Churchill and Keatley." In *Women's Writing: Text and Context*. Jaipur: Rawat, 1996. 274–287.
Mathur, Tanuja. "Metaphor of 'Space': Charlotte Keatley's Play *My Mother Said I Never Should*." In *Women's Writing: Text and Context*. Jaipur: Rawat, 1996. 288–294.
Partnow, Elaine T. "Charlotte Keatley." In *The Female Dramatist: Profiles of Women Playwrights from the Middle Ages to Contemporary Times*. New York: Facts on File, 1998. 124–125.
Sugarwala, Fatima. "Exploring Female Bonds: Keatley's *My Mother Said I Never Should*." In *Women's Writing: Text and Context*. Jaipur: Rawat, 1996. 295–303.

Rosamond Lehmann
1901–1990

Jonathan Bolton

For a novelist of considerable stature in the 1930s whose name was often mentioned in company with Virginia Woolf and Elizabeth Bowen, the reputation of Rosamond Lehmann has suffered from an unproductive middle and late career, from what some critics have deemed a lack of intensity and moral judgment, and perhaps most unfairly from her involvement, after the death of her daughter in 1958, with psychic research and mysticism. The interiority of her work, her technique of "subordinat[ing] action to reflection" (Stevenson 61), has caused many readers to find her work plodding or boring. Critics and reviewers consistently call attention to the virtuosity of her prose style, which they liken to Woolf's, but tend to denigrate the construction and plotting of her novels. In his exhaustive study *British Writers of the Thirties* Valentine Cunningham writes that Lehmann is "inexplicably ignored in all standard accounts of '30s writing" (26).

There have, however, been a few determined efforts to revive interest in her work, most notably Gillian Tindall's *Rosamond Lehmann: An Appreciation* (1985), and articles and book chapters on Lehmann are now fairly standard in studies of modern British novels by women, all of which treat her as an important writer, though certainly not of the first rank. Her technique, which incorporates shifting perspectives and multiple narrators, borrows from the innovations of modernism without advancing them or employing them in original ways. Whereas for years Lehmann's detractors have complained of the narrowness of her upper-middle-class milieu and the apparent absence of political and social commentary, recent work has focused on Lehmann's unflinching and liberal-minded treatment of difficult subjects—abortion, adultery, homosexual relations, and suicide. In addition, Judy Simons has argued that Lehmann's work does reflect a broader political context because her work is "a fiction of both personal and public disenchantment" ("Rosamond" 184) and that an instability in the private realm mirrors the political upheavals of the 1930s. In her novels the historical context is so unobtrusive that the events of the time never bear on the lives of her characters, and typically the reader can barely register the connection of which Simon speaks. However, because Lehmann's novels examine and validate a woman's perspective on issues that remain controversial today, and because she offers a glimpse into the life and thought of an emancipated, well-educated woman of the twentieth century, troubled by failed love affairs and inhibited by the expectations of motherhood and domestic economies, her work, especially *The Weather in the Streets* (1936) and *The Ballad and the Source* (1944), deserves more attention from scholars interested in sexual politics—a field in which Lehmann was, arguably, ahead of her time.

BACKGROUND

In his autobiography, *In My Own Time*, John Lehmann recalled, "Many were the vows that the Lehmann children had made to themselves at Fieldhead to find fame and honour by their deeds in the world of art, music and literature" (33). This recollection hints at the concentration of talent and ambition in the Lehmann family, and there appears to have been a strong tradition of achievement in the arts. Their father, R.C. Lehmann, belletrist, author of light verse, and an avid crewman, came from a long line of Viennese musicians. He founded *Granta* at Cambridge, held the editorship of *Punch* and the *Daily News*, and served briefly as a liberal member of Parliament. His wife, Alice Marie Chambers Lehmann, whom R.C. met during his tenure as crew coach at Harvard University, came from a Boston family and was a graduate of Radcliffe. Rosamond remembered her father as "a difficult man with a frightful temper," but this was offset by her reverence for his talent in letters, music, and sport. Gillian Tindall suggests that this competitive family environment "created an insecurity in her at the deepest level" that shows up in her novels as "complicity and rivalry, or at any rate tension, between women" (35). Rosamond's sister Beatrix became a successful actress and wrote novels, and her brother John became a poet of reputation and editor of *New Writing* (to which Rosamond contributed short stories), both of their accomplishments overshadowing the early fame Rosamond achieved from her best-selling debut, *Dusty Answer* (1927).

Two failed marriages and a doomed long-term love affair certainly contributed to Lehmann's fictional preoccupation with the ephemerality of love relationships. She married Walter Leslie Runciman shortly after leaving Cambridge in 1922; they were divorced in 1927. This was succeeded by her marriage to Wogan Philips, with whom she had two children, Hugo and Sally. They were divorced in 1942, but not before Rosamond began with C. Day Lewis (who was also married at the time) an affair that would last nine years. All of these relationships and male figures, and the complex of feelings and emotions generated by them, find their way into Lehmann's novels, but not in such a manner that readers can say with any certainty, "That character is Day Lewis," or "This one is Wogan Philips." Whereas these failed relationships inspired and supplied material for Lehmann's fiction, another heartbreak served virtually to end her career: the death of her daughter Sally from poliomyelitis in 1958. From this date on, Lehmann did not publish another novel until 1976. Her private feelings about this painful experience, however, find powerful expression in her experimental autobiography, *The Swan in the Evening* (1967), particularly in her artful description of an ecstatic experience, "self luminous and transformed by an expression of dreaming beatitude" (113), in which she communed in spirit with her daughter. Moreover, Lehmann's account of this experience renders her subsequent interest in psychical research somewhat less dubious.

ANALYSIS

Although Gillian Tindall and Margaret Crosland have both made persuasive cases for the excellence of *The Echoing Grove*—a novel most critics and readers, with good reason, find lugubrious—Lehmann's reputation rests on the merits of two exceptional novels, *The Weather in the Streets* (1936) and *The Ballad and the Source* (1944). In *The Weather in the Streets* Lehmann resumes the story of Olivia Curtis, whose young womanhood, marriage, and divorce had been traced in *In-*

vitation to the Waltz (1932). Olivia is now on her own, but suffering through the vicissitudes of genteel poverty and growing weary of the phoniness of 1930s London bohemia. She embarks on an adulterous affair with Rollo Spencer, a relationship that is carried on sporadically until Rollo's wife bears his child, suddenly transforming a barren marriage into a fertile one and signaling the end of the affair. Despite its overly simple plot, *The Weather in the Streets* is remarkable for its intricate expression of feminine consciousness undergoing a series of emotional crises. The rich interiority of Lehmann's fragmented and elliptical narrative builds on the innovations of Woolf and Joyce and broaches what were regarded as "impolite" subjects, such as abortion and feminine sexuality. Lehmann's technique, for example, is capable of registering powerfully the mental disturbances that follow emotional trauma, as when Olivia first realizes that she has become pregnant:

> Face facts tomorrow, see what to do. . . . Get hold of Rollo. But I don't want to. . . . I don't want to see or think of him. How can this be, in twenty-four hours? Is it a symptom, does it seal my fate? . . . The female, her body used, made fertile, turning, resentful, in hostile untouchability, from the male, the enemy, victorious and malignant. Like cats or bitches. Ugh! (249)

The range of emotions and flitting of the mind that Olivia experiences, or that any woman might experience, at this moment is artfully rendered, illustrating how readily recognition leads to resentment, how rational calm elides into visceral disgust, how affection or love is reinterpreted as physical abuse or conquest, and how the loftiness of love can be seen as a base, animalistic drive.

The most striking episodes in the novel, however, are certainly those pertaining to Olivia's abortion, as Lehmann unflinchingly examines the decision-making process, the fearful, surreptitious search for a qualified person to perform an abortion in 1930s Britain, and the psychological trauma resulting from such an ordeal. The particularity of detail in this painful episode, right down to having Olivia pawn a cigarette case, a precious gift from Rollo, to pay for the abortion, suggests an artist at the peak of her powers. Yet the actual abortion is brought off with the casualness of a business transaction, a routine procedure, following which Olivia hops a taxi, climbs in bed, and reads *Pride and Prejudice*. Lehmann is expert at showing how, at times, trivial events can affect one in a potent way, whereas the momentous events can affect one very little. One could also argue that Lehmann deliberately made light of the abortion, seeing it as an unfortunate necessity of women's emancipation. Critics such as Judy Simons have cautioned against reading Lehmann as a protofeminist. As Simons points out, Lehmann appears to be "suspicious of women whose political aggressiveness overrides their femininity" and reminds one that Olivia herself "loathes women who . . . hoot about sex-quality" ("Rosamond Lehmann: *The Weather*" 180). It is true that Lehmann's novels rarely disclose an advanced feminist perspective, but the extent to which her work expresses and therefore validates the predicament of modern women, especially in *The Weather in the Streets*, should be of greater interest to women's studies.

The Weather in the Streets also contains a jolting shift between the first and second parts from first- to third-person perspective, a technique that deftly reflects the self-awareness and self-consciousness that Olivia experiences upon entering a new phase of identity as Rollo's lover, as adultress, as a person in love and being loved, as a potential mother, and as a spurned lover. Gillian Tindall has called *The Weather in the Streets* a "quintessential study of unmarried womanhood" (85), an estimation that accurately, it seems, points to its lasting value. When modern women, partly emancipated by the victories of suffrage, access to public education, and economic viability, were beginning to achieve sexual independence, their experience was perhaps nowhere rendered as completely as in Lehmann's novels, particularly in *The Weather in the Streets*.

The Ballad and the Source has received the most acclaim among Lehmann's novels. Although some have found it difficult and ponderous, and as Margaret Crosland has noted, "it is as though the author had allowed technique to take over" (75), one could liken its multiple perspectives and concentric circles of influence emanating from singular events to Woolf's *The Waves*. Written during her relationship with C. Day Lewis, the novel traces the effect of an adulterous affair, illegitimate birth (suspected but never proven), and maternal abandonment on subsequent generations. The emotional failures and potentially ruinous effects of love, the novel suggests, do not necessarily end with those directly involved, and *The Ballad and the Source* can be viewed as an examination of the interior, hereditary complications of original sin. While the theme may seem conventional, the technique is not. In many ways it anticipates the postmodern treatment of the Victorian family history. A fragmentary story is pieced together via a series of monologues, presented by different narrators who relate information that they received secondhand, each of whom imperfectly understands past events. Finally, as the story of an earlier generation is revealed, with its pattern of sexual liaisons, uncertain or undisclosed parentage, and separation, an identical pattern emerges in the next. Gillian Tindall has examined the intricacy and psychological depth of *The Ballad and the Source* and situates it in a distinguished tradition that passes through Elizabeth Bowen.

ASSESSMENT

Despite being the subject of books, articles, and Ph.D. dissertations in a 1980s flurry, Rosamond Lehmann remains a marginal figure in the annals of the twentieth-century British novel, and this status is unlikely to change. Recent work has shown, however, that Lehmann's work cannot be ignored by any history or period study that claims to be complete, and her fiction should continue to serve as a window into the feminine consciousness at midcentury and as an exemplary model for what happened to women's fiction in the wake of Katherine Mansfield and Virginia Woolf. Moreover, that her work is included on university reading lists and that her novels remain in print in the United Kingdom attest to her ongoing popularity among academics, students, and lay readers.

BIBLIOGRAPHY

Primary Sources

Dusty Answer. London: Chatto, 1927.

A Note in Music. London: Chatto, 1930.

Letter to a Sister. London: Hogarth, 1931.

Invitation to the Waltz. London: Chatto, 1932.

The Weather in the Streets. London: Collins, 1936.

No More Music. London: Collins, 1939.

The Ballad and the Source. London: Collins, 1944.

The Gipsy's Baby and Other Stories. London: Collins, 1946.

The Echoing Grove. London: Collins, 1953.

A Man Seen Afar. With Wellesley Tudor Pole. London: Spearman, 1965.

The Swan in the Evening: Fragments of an Inner Life. London: Collins, 1967.

A Sea-Grape Tree. London: Collins, 1976.

Secondary Sources

Crosland, Margaret. *Beyond the Lighthouse: English Women Novelists in the Twentieth Century*. New York: Taplinger, 1981.

Cunningham, Valentine. *British Writers of the Thirties*. Oxford and New York: Oxford UP, 1988.

Dorosz, Wiktoria. *Subjective Vision and Human Relationships in the Novels of Rosamond Lehmann*. Stockholm: Almqvist, 1975.

Gindin, James. "Rosamond Lehmann: A Revaluation." *Contemporary Literature* 15 (1974): 203–211.

Lehmann, John. *In My Own Time: Memoirs of a Literary Life*. Boston: Little, Brown, 1969.

LeSturgeon, Diana E. *Rosamond Lehmann*. New York: Twayne, 1965.

Siegel, Ruth. *Rosamond Lehmann: A Thirties Writer*. New York: Peter Lang, 1989.
Simons, Judy. *Rosamond Lehmann*. Basingstoke: Macmillan, 1992.
———. "Rosamond Lehmann: *The Weather in the Streets*." In *Recharting the Thirties*. Ed. Patrick Quinn. Selinsgrove, PA: Susquehanna UP, 1996.
Stevenson, Randall. *The British Novel since the Thirties*. London: Batsford, 1986.
Tindall, Gillian. *Rosamond Lehmann: An Appreciation*. London: Chatto, 1985.

Doris Lessing
1919–

Del Ivan Janik

Doris Lessing's novels, stories, and other writings, beginning in 1950 with *The Grass Is Singing*, have appeared regularly throughout the second half of the twentieth century and beyond. Her early novels were based fairly closely on her own experiences, but in 1979 she published the first of five science-fiction novels forming the series *Canopus in Argos: Archives*. Having completed that series, she reinvented herself as a writer again in 1983 when she submitted a novel called *Diary of a Good Neighbour* under the pseudonym of "Jane Somers" to her own publisher, who rejected it; Lessing had found some support for her suspicion that star quality—a "name"—counted with publishers at least as much as literary quality. Since the *Canopus* series and the Jane Somers books, Lessing has published six novels, a play, numerous short stories, and two volumes of autobiography; she shows no signs of retiring from her calling.

BACKGROUND

Lessing was born Doris May Tayler in Kermanshah, Persia (now Iran), on October 22, 1919. Her parents, Alfred Cook Tayler and Emily McVeagh Tayler, had been born in England. Alfred met Emily, a nurse, when he was convalescing from a crippling wound received in World War I. When Doris was born, her father was working for the Imperial Bank of Persia; in 1925 the family moved to Southern Rhodesia (now Zimbabwe) to try farming. It was a rough existence—the family lived in a mud-walled and grass-roofed house whose other inhabitants included snakes, lizards, rats, a variety of insects, and occasionally a tree growing up through the dirt floor (Brewster 17)—and the farm was a financial failure.

Doris left school at the age of thirteen, and at sixteen she went to work in Salisbury, the capital, as a typist. Three years later she married Frank Wisdom, a civil servant, with whom she had two children, Jean and John. Doris and Frank were divorced in 1943, and the children stayed with their father (Barnes 161). One factor contributing to the divorce seems to have been Doris's dissatisfaction with the narrow, conservative, racist social set of which she found herself a member (Brewster 108–110). Doris had become involved in leftist politics, a fact that she believed was threatening her husband's career. It was in a Communist discussion group in Salisbury that she met her second husband, Gottfried Lessing, a German immigrant. They were married in 1945 and had a son, Peter, two years later. The Lessings were divorced in 1949; Gottfried left for East Germany and Doris, with Peter, for London, where both have lived since then.

Lessing arrived in bleak, war-damaged, still largely impoverished London with the nearly completed manuscript of *The Grass Is Singing*, which soon found a publisher, and she undertook the writing of *Martha Quest*, the first of the *Children of Violence* novels. She came to London also with a concern for the urban poor and a waning interest in communism.

> It took me four or five years from my first falling in love with Communism, or rather, ideal Communism, in 1942, to become critical enough to discuss my "Doubts" with people still inside the Communist fold. In another two or three years I discussed with other Communists facts and ideas for which in a Communist country we would have been tortured and killed. By 1954 I was no longer a Communist, but it was not until the early 1960s I ceased to feel residual tugs of loyalty, was really free. (*Under My Skin* 397)

She had been drawn to communism for the apparent alternative it offered to the smug, exclusionary imperialist society in which she had been raised; it took the end of the wartime alliance, the Soviet subjugation of Eastern Europe, and the revelation of Stalin's crimes against humanity to undermine and eventually overcome Lessing's youthful commitment. Her humanistic and humanitarian impulses remained, however, now freed from Party trappings.

In 1956 Lessing was for the first time able to revisit Southern Rhodesia. Although the family farm had reverted to nature, many elements of Rhodesian society that had repelled her remained. She returned to London to write *Going Home*, an account of her response to her contacts with Rhodesians on all levels of society and an affirmation of her commitment to individualism, liberty, and democracy, beyond party or government: "I believe in the ginger-groups, the temporarily associated minorities, the Don Quixotes, the takers-of-stands-on-principle, the do gooders and the defenders of lost causes" (*Going Home* 316).

Among Lessing's next major projects were her most outstanding and her most notorious: *The Golden Notebook* (1962), *The Four-Gated City* (1969), and the five *Canopus in Argos* novels (1979–1983). These, and for that matter her later novels, have been influenced by Lessing's readings in Sufism, or to be more exact, by the writings of Idries Shah, to whose works she came in the course of an exploration of non-Western spiritual traditions. Sufism is not a doctrine so much as a quietist Path, taken with the help of Teacher (in Lessing's case Idries Shah), toward union with God, but without a withdrawal from the everyday world.

By the 1980s Lessing was a sufficiently public figure that her pseudonymous offering of the Jane Somers novels was no mere lark but a telling, if good-humored, mark against the literary establishment, of which she herself had undeniably become a part. Along with stories and books of nonfiction, new novels continued to appear throughout the 1980s and 1990s. In the 1999 Honours List Lessing was named a Companion of Honour, a recognition that she appreciated because unlike "Dame of the British Empire," which she had declined, it carried no title and had nothing to do with a political entity that no longer existed ("Doris Lessing Retrospective").

ANALYSIS

Doris Lessing's work can best be characterized by the word "commitment." In her 1957 essay "The Small Personal Voice" she expressed admiration for the great authors of the nineteenth century who, whatever their religion or politics, had in common "a climate of ethical judgement; they shared certain values; they were humanists" (*A Small* 4–5). For Lessing, who at that time had finally renounced communism, commitment emphatically did not mean propagandism, but a recognition that as a writer she, like all of us, faced two choices: "that we force ourselves into the imagination necessary to become what we are capable of being; or that we submit to being ruled by the office boys of big business, or the socialist bureaucrats who have forgotten that socialism means a desire for goodness and compassion—and the end of submission is that we shall blow ourselves up" (9). Lessing's commitment to humanistic values has been manifested consistently from the realistically presented antiapartheid critiques of *The Grass Is Singing, African Stories*, and the early novels of the *Children of Violence* series through the feminism of *The Golden Notebook* and the fabulized Sufi wisdom of the *Canopus in Argos: Archives* apocalyptic warnings of her later novels.

The Grass Is Singing is a conventionally structured novel set in South Africa in circumstances resembling those of Lessing's parents. It begins with a newspaper report of the murder of its central character, Mary Turner, by her houseboy Moses. The bulk of the novel consists of one long flashback, to Mary's bleak childhood and her passionless and childless marriage. Her husband Dick, due partly to illness, partly to ineptitude, fails to make a go of their farm, and Mary, through an arrogance born of fear, alienates the native farmworkers and a series of houseboys. The last of these is Moses, who had received a visible scar when Mary once angrily lashed him across the face during a time when she was substituting for her sick husband as overseer. Moses, however, treats her with deference and even kindness, taking special care over her tea, solicitously helping her to bed for a nap when she is exhausted, and even doing up the buttons on her dress—tasks that a maid or a husband might perform and that are surely inappropriate for a black male servant in this racist society. Mary feels a loss of her "proper" control as a white person and discomfort at her growing awareness of a sexual attraction to Moses, which is manifested in nightmares and in daytime bouts of anxiety and disorientation. Matters are brought to a head when Dick sells his land, and as the Turners prepare to leave for the coast, the new owner, Charlie Slattery, brings in Tony Marston as manager. When Marston happens upon Moses helping with Mary's toilette, her reaction shifts from embarrassment and anger at Marston to a sudden dismissal of Moses, who goes off into the bush. The next night Mary goes out to meet what she sees as her fate. As Roberta Rubenstein points out, as well as depicting the "dehumanization of both races by the color bar" (31), *The Grass Is Singing* "anticipates many of Doris Lessing's subsequent explorations of abnormal consciousness, particularly as manifested in mental breakdown and madness," as well as issues surrounding the nexus of power and sexuality (30).

The *Children of Violence* novels are even more obviously based on Lessing's personal experiences. The first, *Martha Quest* (1952; the protagonist's surname alone places the novel firmly in the genre of the bildungsroman), recounts the life from her midteens to her early twenties of a Southern Rhodesian girl of English parentage who leaves school, rebels against her parents, and begins an independent life in the capital, becoming involved first with the high-living Sports Club crowd and through them with Douglas Knowell, a superficially iconoclastic but in fact quite conventional civil servant. In her 1957 essay "The Small Personal Voice" Lessing stated that *Children of Violence* is "a study of the individual conscience in its relations with the collective" (*A Small* 14). The "collective" in *Martha Quest* and the first part of *A Proper Marriage* (1954) is the society that centers on the Sports Club, with its eminent leaders of the white community, their irresponsible offspring, and the bourgeois young marrieds they eventually become. Martha ultimately rebels against the club's values, and the fact that she leaves not only her husband Douglas but their daughter Caroline is a testament to Martha's resolve, or perhaps an indication of how radical and personal Lessing wanted her decision to find a new life to seem. *A Ripple from the Storm* (1958) somewhat resembles *Retreat to Innocence*, a non–Martha Quest novel that Lessing had published in 1956 but later repudiated, saying, "I think a good many serious questions were far too easily, too lightly treated" (qtd. in Schlueter, *Novels* 137n). The novel accepts communism far less critically than any of Lessing's others, and it appeared in the bookstores just after she formally left the Party. *A Ripple from the Storm* treats the issues of political belief, commitment, and freedom more deeply. Martha throws herself into committee activity on behalf of the Russian ally—and eventually the avowedly Communist group that evolves from such committees, the "collective" with which Martha's "conscience" is now in most direct relation. She comes into contact with avowed Communists who apparently have attitudes toward blacks and women that make them seem no more enlightened than the Sports Club crowd, but she also meets Anton Hesse, a German Jewish refugee, with whom she has an affair and whom she eventually marries. *Landlocked* (1965), the last of the *Children of Violence* novels to take place in Africa, offers a summation as well as a farewell. Martha suffers from her estrangement from Caroline, and her new marriage offers no solace; it is poised on the edge of divorce, and she has taken a lover, Thomas Stern, a Polish Jew who at the end of the war has gone to fight for Israel. When he returns, he goes into the bush to study the working conditions of the blacks and dies of blackwater fever. At the novel's end the Left in Salisbury is in disarray, partly because of the contradictions implied in reports from Russia, partly because of a sense of impotence in the face of a general strike organized by the blacks. Martha's divorce has gone through, and she is preparing to leave for England.

The Four-Gated City (1969), the fifth and final novel of the series, was written and published after *The Golden Notebook*, and it represents a departure from the other four, not only in its locale but in its literary methods and the locus of its concerns The first four *Children of Violence* novels were essentially external and realistic in their presentation. Here Martha's quest becomes internal, perhaps reflecting Lessing's experience with Jungian analysis. The title refers to Martha's vision, in the early pages of her eponymous novel, of "a noble city, set foursquare and colonnaded along its falling, flower-bordered terraces. . . . and its citizens moved, grave and beautiful, black and white and brown together" (*Children* I:21). The vision recurs in later novels, but it is emphatically not realized in the fifth, which recounts twenty years of Martha's life in London. Visions and dreams play an increasing role in the novels of the series, and in *The Four-Gated City* psychological issues eclipse the political and even the societal; the "collective" in the earlier sense recedes into the background. The setting is not so much the city as a house—the Claridge house, presided over by the writer Mark Claridge and inhabited also by Martha, his secretary and eventually his mistress; Mark's wife Lynda, the "madwoman in the cellar"; the sensible Phoebe; and the irresponsible Jimmy Wood. If the house is a microcosm of the city—and a reflection of Martha's own condition—it is significant that, as Rubenstein points out, "a disproportionately high number of the characters . . . suffer mental breakdowns in one or the other form during the course of the narrative" (148); she quotes Lessing from a 1969 interview by Jonah Raskin: "Now, almost everyone I know has had a breakdown, is in psychoanalysis, or pops in and out of mental hospitals. Mental illness is part of the mainstream. . . . People who are called mentally ill are often those who say to the society, 'I'm not going to live according to your rules. I'm not going to conform' " (*A Small* 69). The time that Martha spends in the cellar with Lynda can be seen as a descent into her own unconscious, which ultimately frees her from her self-perceived bond to the house and makes it possible for her to proceed in life as an independent individual. However, Martha's personal achievement turns out to be rather pyrrhic. Lessing appended to the novel a kind of prophecy, told in the form of reports and letters, based on her view of the direction the world seemed to be taking in the 1960s. There has been a nuclear accident; Britain has been essentially destroyed; war has been loosed on the world, and a rigid and particularly unintelligent authoritarianism prevails; only on the island of Pharos, where Martha survives for a time, are there a few children whose superior consciousness seems to hold out hope for the future.

In a sense, Lessing wrote *The Golden Notebook* (1962) as a kind of sabbatical from the *Children of Violence* series, but this most famous of her novels pursues many of the same themes, albeit in a form that represents a significant departure from her earlier realism and reflects or, in light of its publication date, helps define the late-twentieth-century fashion of postmodernism. Anna Freeman Wilf is a mature woman born in Africa, a former Communist, living alone in London, seeking stability through Jungian analysis. The departure from Lessing's familiar materials lies in their presentation. Only a couple of years after the liberation of *Ulysses* and *Lady Chatterley's Lover* from the censors, Lessing here published a novel of unprecedented frankness about female sexuality and women's opinions of men. Rather than the linear story one might expect, she wrote it as four "notebooks," two of them retrospective, one consisting of Anna's autobiographical fiction, and one a diary. Each is divided into four parts, and each cluster is prefaced by part of a novel called "Free Women." These sequences are followed by the "GOLDEN NOTEBOOK," which recounts Anna's breakdown almost literally—the fragmentation of her personality into bits of her waking self, her dreams, the people she knows, and the characters she has created—and the beginnings of her reintegration. The novel ends with a final segment of "Free Women." Paul Schlueter has observed, "[T]he reader can either read from page 1 to the end of the book, or . . . all the parts of each notebook and 'Free Women' together" ("Doris" 280). This combination of flexibility of structure and coherence of meaning in the context of a foregrounding of the fiction as fiction makes *The Golden Notebook* one of the early successes of postmodernism.

In 1971 Lessing began a new phase in her career with the publication of *Briefing for a Descent into Hell*. Her now-familiar themes of mental illness and apocalypse are present, but Lessing moves into new realms of fantasy, blurring and never quite reconciling the borders between everyday reality, dream, and hallucination. At the book's beginning Charles Watkins (Lessing's first male protagonist), a Classics professor, is circling the Atlantic on a raft; a spaceship has abducted his companions but has left him on earth. When he arrives on a mysterious island on which a colony of apes is engaged in a bloody war against a group of cat/dog hybrids, the spaceship saves him, and he finds himself in the midst of the Olympian gods, who are plotting to send some of their number to earth as human children—the "descent into hell" of the title. The scene abruptly switches to London, where Watkins, suffering from amnesia, is admitted to a mental hospital and subjected to a variety of treatments; shock treatment finally restores him to the "real" world—but not necessarily to a satisfactory life in it. *Briefing*, like *The Four-Gated City* and *The Golden Notebook*, reflects Lessing's studies in Sufism, with its skepticism about accepted ideas and notions of reality and its emphasis on the value of openness to the irrational.

The experiences of forty-five-year-old Kate Brown, the protagonist of *The Summer before the Dark* (1973), somewhat parallel Watkins's in that (with her husband and family absent for the summer) she leaves her normal middle-class environment and attempts—voluntarily in her case—some kind of renewal. Like Watkins's, her story ends ambiguously in that her brief affair with a younger man, her friendship with Maureen, a neighbor who seems a younger version of herself, and the clarification of her feminist thinking lead only to a return to the dull life she had been leading—presumably the "dark" of the title. This novel is quite different from its predecessor, however, in that while it again pursues themes of mental illness and social displacement, it returns to the conventionally realistic mode of Lessing's early novels.

That is not the case in *The Memoirs of a Survivor* (1974), in which the background of apocalypse, the foreground of mental illness, and the modes of dream and fantasy return to prominence. Lessing's central character is a middle-aged woman living in London after a catastrophic war. For unexplained reasons she finds herself raising a girl named Emily through the crucial years from twelve to fourteen, in an extremely difficult societal context that demands radical adaptation for survival. The early part of the novel is written in a relatively realistic, if dystopian, mode, but the second half focuses on the protagonist's personal visions, which she "sees" through the "transparent" walls of her flat. They are apparently a series of metaphors for the stages of her earlier life, and they culminate in the vision of a goddess with whom she comes to identify on a mystical level—in what Lessing presents not as an escape from reality but a merging of reality and myth for the sake of psychological survival.

Lessing's fullest and most striking departure from realism, into science fiction or "space fiction" or "speculative fiction," came in 1979 with *Shikasta: Re, Colonised Planet 5* and continued through four succeeding novels: *The Marriages between Zones Three, Four, and Five* (1980), *The Sirian Experiments* (1981), *The Making of the Representative for Planet 8* (1982), and *Documents Relating to the Sentimental Agents in the Volyen Empire* (1983). The parallel that most immediately springs to mind is not literary but cinematic: George Lucas's first *Star Wars* trilogy (1977–1983), which, like Lessing's almost exactly contemporary *Canopus in Argos: Archives* series, offers analogues to earthly, especially twentieth-century, events, experiences, perplexities, and potentials from the perspective of planets far, far away. The "aliens" in Lessing's series, however, are directly concerned about earth's fate: the planet Canopus seeks to help save "Shikasta" (its name for Earth) from the degradation brought about by the evil planet Shammat, which has replaced among us the "substance-of-we-feeling" with the disease of individualism. Except for *The Marriages* and *The Making of a Representative*, the novels are presented not as conventional narratives but as a collection of documents chronicling the activities and putting forward the ideas of the "people" of the novel's planets. This in itself makes for narrative distance, and there are hardly any sympathetic "human" characters. Yet the overall theme of the series is the need for human change in the face of threats to survival. As Katherine Fishburn puts it, "[T]he pressures of a changing environment force people to evolve or die with their planet" (*Doris* 142). The idea is hardly new in Lessing; if "environment" is defined broadly and "die" is understood metaphorically as well as literally, it could be taken to apply to virtually all of her fiction. The emphasis on openness to change is directly in line with Sufism's attempt to use stories (albeit briefer than *Canopus in Argos: Archives*) to encourage receptivity to new and mind-expanding modes of awareness.

Lessing's next shift of ground was her serious joke on the publishing industry, the reviewing profession, and the reading public: *The Diary of a Good Neighbour* (1983), offered under the pseudonym "Jane Somers." As Mary Doll reports, the manuscript was rejected by British publishers Cape and Granada but accepted by Michael Joseph, where the editorial director said that it "reminded her of Doris Lessing." In America Lessing's editor at Knopf, Robert Gottlieb, reported, "I burst into laughter because it was a voice so well known to me" (Doll 287). The public, like Cape and Granada, rose to Lessing's bait. According to Gottlieb, in America the novel and its 1984 sequel *If the Old Could . . .* sold about six times as many copies in a reprint with Lessing named as the author as they did as books by Jane Somers (Doll 288). The novels themselves focus on the relationships formed by Janna (later Jane) Somers, a middle-aged magazine editor, first with Maudie, a ninety-year-old woman dying of cancer for whom Janna performs essential personal and household tasks. Through knowing, caring for, and talking with Maudie, Janna develops a sense of identity and purpose that she had found in neither her work nor her own family. In *If the Old Could . . .* Janna (now Jane) meets Richard, a married man with whom she has a romantic—but not sexual—affair that fills some of the void left by Maudie's death. The unexpected arrival of her niece Kate, who suffers from a mental illness, reverses Jane's generational position and complicates her life, but she responds to the challenge, affirming her identity and life choices with self-knowledge and confidence.

In *The Good Terrorist* (1985) Lessing returned to some of her earlier themes, but from a different perspective. Whereas she took political causes seriously in the *Children of Violence* series, here she wryly depicts the confusion and drift in the minds and lives of the young and youngish would-be terrorists who inhabit the condemned London house that her protagonist Alice Mellings tries to maintain for her fellow Communist Centre Union members. This is not a political novel so much as a novel about a certain type of politics, which Lessing depicts without any of the emotional ambivalence of the early Martha Quest novels. If not contemptible, these self-styled urban revolutionaries seem misguided and pathetic.

With her 1988 novel *The Fifth Child* Lessing began another sequence, continued in 2000 with *Ben, in the World*. *The Fifth Child* chronicles the effect on the Lovatts' conventional and stereotypically "happy" family of the arrival of a fifth child, Ben, who is mentally retarded, unusually large, extremely aggressive, and preternaturally strong. When he becomes completely unmanageable, David and Harriet Lovatt have him institutionalized, but Harriet's guilt feelings lead her to return him to the family, which promptly disintegrates, leaving her alone to cope with the destruction that Ben and his antisocial friends wreak in the formerly "ideal" Lovatt home. The book's images of futility and decay are familiar enough from many of Lessing's novels, but here they are brought down to a domestic level that makes them no less pointed and perhaps even more problematic. The sequel, *Ben, in the World*, is, although brief, something of a picaresque novel (London to France to Brazil to the Andes) in contrast to the previous situation tragedy. Ben is now eighteen, on his own, and barely surviving until he is taken in by a prostitute-with-a-heart-of-gold and then, less benevolently, by a cocaine dealer who uses him to run drugs to Nice, a filmmaker who wants to use him in a horror movie, and an unscrupulous scientist who wants to study this curious specimen after death. Ben does die at the novel's end, but with a shred of pathetic dignity, in a manner and in a place that thwart the scientist's plans. These two novels, like many of Lessing's, focus on an individual who lives on the margins of society and either exemplifies or embodies its ills—or who, like Ben, is both victimizer and victim.

In 1996, between the "Ben" novels, Lessing published *Love, Again*, an only slightly less unpleasant story in spite of the absence of literal monsters. Once again Lessing placed a cast of characters in a relatively closed setting, this time the preparation of a musical play based on the life of a nineteenth-century writer and composer, Julie Vairon. Sarah Durham, the sixty-five-year-old producer, responds to the romance of Vairon's story and music by falling in love first with Bill, an actor more than thirty years her junior, and then with Henry, the director. Meanwhile, Stephen, the play's financial backer, develops a passion for Julie herself, who has been dead for eighty years. The novel's admittedly improbable story line nevertheless again brings together several of Lessing's preoccupations: love and its ironies, the pain of aging, and the prospect of death.

After *Ben, in the World* (2000), Lessing's next novel was *Mara and Dann* (1999). Set in the far-distant future in an "Ifrik" (Africa) suffering from a new ice age, the novel recounts the adventures of a brother and sister from a royal family who must hide from their community's enemies and then, because of the dangerously unpredictable weather, join a great migration north in search of food and water. The novel is reminiscent of the *Canopus in Argos: Archives* series in its futurism and its resemblance to popular fiction, and to *The Four-Gated City* in its catastrophic conclusion.

ASSESSMENT

There is no question that Doris Lessing has been one of the most important figures on the British literary scene since 1950. If not all reviewers and critics would agree with Jeremy Brooks that she is "the best woman novelist we have," most would agree with him that she is "one of the most serious, intelligent and honest writers of the whole post-war generation" (qtd. in Schlueter, *Novels* 2). The distinction is well expressed by Florence Howe: "No one will read Doris Lessing to learn how to write a good novel or to admire a beautiful work of art. She disdains—is suspicious of—smoothness of most sorts. There is nothing subtle about her fiction; its bulk alone is formidable" (34). In this sense she is perhaps reminiscent of Thomas Hardy and D.H. Lawrence, who as novelists were above all concerned with "saying their say."

What Lessing has had to say has often accorded closely with—and perhaps to an extent shaped—some of the major public concerns of the times in which she has written. Her depiction of the dangers of apartheid—to whites as well as blacks—surely contributed to the gradual changes in racial attitudes during the second half of the twentieth century. The evolution of her protagonist's relation to communism in *Children of Violence* was part of the reevaluation of ideology and institutions that was important to leftist intellectuals in the 1950s and 1960s. Her visions of apocalypse—nuclear, as in *The Four-Gated City*, or environmental, as in *Mara and Dann*—were expressions of the ultimate fears that have haunted the postwar era. Her depictions of mental illness and madness have reflected the era's fascination with psychology and psychiatry. Above all, her novels' explorations and articulations of the problems and potentials of women in the late twentieth century—their struggle for self-awareness and self-realization—accorded with and helped give intellectual underpinning to one of the major social and intellectual shifts of her or any time.

This is not to say that Lessing has been perceived (any more than Hardy or Lawrence) as a mere didactic drudge. Betsy Draine points out that Lessing's style is far from uniform, encompassing as it does both the realism of *The Grass Is Singing* and the early *Children of Violence* volumes, the "modern perspectives" of "*The Golden Notebook*—a work that radically questions the realism and objectivity which formed the basis of the style and structure of her previous works" (xiv), and then in *The Four-Gated City* (and of course the *Canopus* novels) a "new preoccupation with the visionary," another of what Draine calls Lessing's "formal choices" (xv). How enthusiastic a reader or critic may be about any one of Lessing's novels may have to do with her or his preference for these realistic, modernist, or visionary modes, for the personal and social issues they address come out of the same humanistic sensibility.

In the 1960s and 1970s, in the wake of *The Golden Notebook* and *The Four-Gated City*, Lessing was at the forefront of the novelists writing as women about women, and her reputation as a writer soared in general. She had earned the right (which she had been exercising anyway) not to repeat herself, and so she followed her intellectual and spiritual interests with the *Canopus* series and with books as divergent as *The Diaries of Jane Somers* and *Mara and Dann.* It is safe to speculate that readers will continue to return to the *Notebook* and the *City*, and to pass through those gates to enjoy the rest of Lessing's work.

BIBLIOGRAPHY

Primary Sources

The Grass Is Singing. London: Joseph; New York: Crowell, 1950.

This Was the Old Chief's Country (stories). London: Joseph, 1951; New York: Crowell, 1952.

Martha Quest. London: Joseph, 1952.

Five: Short Novels. London: Joseph, 1953.

A Proper Marriage. London: Joseph, 1954.

Retreat to Innocence. London: Joseph, 1956.

Going Home (memoir). London: Joseph, 1957.

The Habit of Loving (stories). London: MacGibbon & Kee, 1957; New York: Crowell, 1957.

A Ripple from the Storm. London: Joseph, 1958.

"Each His Own Wilderness." In *New English Dramatists.* Ed. E. Martin Browne. Harmondsworth: Penguin, 1959.

In Pursuit of the English: A Documentary. London: MacGibbon & Kee, 1960; New York: Simon & Schuster, 1961.

The Golden Notebook. London: Joseph; New York: Simon & Schuster, 1962.

Play with a Tiger. London: Joseph, 1962.

A Man and Two Women (stories). London: MacGibbon & Kee; New York: Simon & Schuster, 1963.

African Stories. London: Joseph, 1964; New York: Simon & Schuster, 1965.

Children of Violence Vol. 1 (*Martha Quest* and *A Proper Marriage*). New York: Simon & Schuster, 1964.

Children of Violence. Vol. 2 (*A Ripple from the Storm* and *Landlocked*). New York: Simon & Schuster, 1965.

Landlocked. London: MacGibbon & Kee, 1965.

Particularly Cats. London: Joseph; New York: Simon & Schuster, 1967.

The Four-Gated City. London: MacGibbon & Kee; New York: Knopf, 1969.

Briefing for a Descent into Hell. London: Cape; New York: Knopf, 1971.

The Story of a Non-marrying Man and Other Stories. London: Cape 1972. As *The Temptation of Jack Orkney and Other Stories.* New York: Knopf, 1972.

Collected African Stories. 2 vols. London: Joseph, 1973.

The Summer before the Dark. London: Cape; New York: Knopf, 1973.

The Memoirs of a Survivor. London: Octagon, 1974.

A Small Personal Voice (essays). New York: Knopf, 1974.

Collected Stories. 2 vols. London: Cape, 1978. As *Stories.* 1 vol. New York: Knopf, 1978.

Shikasta: Re, Colonised Planet 5. London: Cape; New York: Knopf, 1979.

The Marriages between Zones Three, Four, and Five. London: Cape; New York: Knopf, 1980.

The Sirian Experiments. London: Cape; New York: Knopf, 1981.

The Making of the Representative for Planet 8. London: Cape; New York: Knopf, 1982.

The Diary of a Good Neighbour. As Jane Somers. London: Joseph; New York: Knopf, 1983.

Documents Relating to the Sentimental Agents in the Volyen Empire. London: Cape; New York: Knopf, 1983.

The Diaries of Jane Somers. London: Joseph; New York: Vintage, 1984.

If the Old Could . . . As Jane Somers. London: Joseph; New York: Knopf, 1984.

The Good Terrorist. London: Cape; New York: Knopf, 1985.

The Fifth Child. London: Cape; New York: Knopf, 1988.

The Doris Lessing Reader. New York: Knopf, 1988; London: Cape, 1989.

Particularly Cats . . . and Rufus. New York: Knopf, 1991.

African Laughter. London and New York: HarperCollins, 1992.

Canopus in Argos: Archives. New York: Vintage, 1992.

London Observed: Stories and Sketches. London: HarperCollins, 1992. As *The Real Thing: Stories and Sketches.* New York: HarperCollins, 1992.

Doris Lessing: Conversations. Ed. Earl Ingersoll. Princeton: Ontario Review P, 1994. As *Putting Questions Differently.* London: Flamingo, 1996.

Under My Skin: Volume One of My Autobiography, to 1949. London and New York: HarperCollins, 1994.

Playing the Game (graphic novel). Illus. Charlie Adlard. London: HarperCollins, 1995.

Love, Again. London: Flamingo; New York: HarperCollins, 1996.

Walking in the Shade: Volume Two of My Autobiog-

raphy, 1949–1962. London and New York: HarperCollins, 1997.

Mara and Dann, an Adventure. London: Harper Flamingo; New York: HarperCollins, 1999.

Ben, in the World. London: Flamingo; New York: HarperCollins, 2000.

The Sweetest Dream. London: Flamingo, 2001; New York: HarperCollins, 2002.

Secondary Sources

Barnes, Fiona R. "Doris Lessing." In *British Short-Fiction Writers, 1945–1980*. Ed. Dean Baldwin. Vol. 139 of *Dictionary of Literary Biography*. Detroit: Gale, 1994. 159–172.

Bertelsen, Eve. "Doris Lessing's Rhodesia: History into Fiction." *English in Africa* 11.1 (May 1984): 15–40.

Bloom, Harold, ed. *Doris Lessing*. New York: Chelsea, 1986.

Brewster, Dorothy. *Doris Lessing*. New York: Twayne, 1965.

Brooks, Ellen W. "The Image of Woman in Lessing's *The Golden Notebook*." *Critique* 15.1 (1973): 101–109.

Burkom, Selma. " 'Only Connect': Form and Content in the Works of Doris Lessing." *Critique* 11.1 (1969): 51–68.

Cederstrom, Lorelei. *Fine-Tuning the Feminine Psyche: Jungian Patterns in the Novels of Doris Lessing*. New York: Peter Lang, 1990.

Dixson, Barbara. "Structural Complexity in Doris Lessing's Canopus Novels." *Journal of the Fantastic in the Arts* 2.3 (1990): 14–22.

Doll, Mary. "Doris Lessing." In *Dictionary of Literary Biography Yearbook* 1985. Ed. Jean W. Ross. Detroit: Gale, 1986.

"Doris Lessing Number." *Modern Fiction Studies* 26.1 (1980).

"Doris Lessing Retrospective: Biography." <http://lessing.redmood.com/biography.html>.

Draine, Betsy. *Substance under Pressure: Artistic Coherence and Evolving Form in the Novels of Doris Lessing*. Madison: U of Wisconsin P, 1983.

Fahim, Shadia S. *Doris Lessing: Sufi Equilibrium and the Form of the Novel*. New York: St. Martin's, 1994.

Fishburn, Katherine. *Doris Lessing: Life, Work, and Criticism*. Fredericton, NB: York, 1987.

———. *The Unexpected Universe of Doris Lessing*. Westport, CT: Greenwood, 1985.

Galin, Muge. *Between East and West: Sufism in the Novels of Doris Lessing*. Albany: State U of New York P, 1997.

Hanley, Lynne. "Writing across the Color Bar: Apartheid and Desire." *Massachusetts Review* 32.4 (Summer 1991): 495–506.

Hardin, Nancy S. "Doris Lessing and the Sufi Way." *Contemporary Literature* 14 (Autumn 1973): 565–581.

Hite, Molly. "Doris Lessing's *The Golden Notebook* and *The Four-Gated City*: Ideology, Coherence, and Possibility." *Twentieth Century Literature* 34.1 (Spring 1988): 16–29.

Howe, Florence. "Doris Lessing's Free Women." *Nation* 200 (11 January 1965): 34–37.

Hynes, Joseph. "The Construction of *The Golden Notebook*." *Iowa Review* 4 (Summer 1973): 100–113.

Kaplan, Carey, and Ellen Cronan Rose, eds. *Approaches to Teaching Lessing's* The Golden Notebook. New York: MLA, 1989.

———, eds. *Doris Lessing: The Alchemy of Survival*. Athens: Ohio UP, 1988.

Kaplan, Sydney Janet. *Feminine Consciousness in the Modern British Novel*. Urbana: U of Illinois P, 1975. 136–172.

Karl, Frederick R. "Doris Lessing in the Sixties: The New Anatomy of Melancholy." *Contemporary Literature* 13 (Winter 1972): 15–33.

Klein, Carole. *Doris Lessing*. London: Duckworth; New York: Carroll & Graf, 2000.

Knapp, Mona. *Doris Lessing*. New York: Ungar, 1984.

Maslen, Elizabeth. *Doris Lessing*. Plymouth: Northcote, 1994.

Morgan, Ellen. "Alienation of the Woman Writer in *The Golden Notebook*." *Contemporary Literature* 14 (Autumn 1973): 471–480.

Perrakis, Phyllis Sternberg, ed. *Spiritual Exploration in the Works of Doris Lessing*. Westport, CT: Greenwood, 1999.

Pickering, Jean. "Marxism and Madness: The Two Faces of Doris Lessing's Myth." *Modern Fiction Studies* 26 (Spring 1980): 17–30.

———. *Understanding Doris Lessing*. Columbia: U of South Carolina P, 1990.

Porter, Dennis. "Realism and Failure in *The Golden Notebook*." *Modern Language Quarterly* 35 (March 1974): 56–65.

Pratt, Annis, and L.S. Dembo, eds. *Doris Lessing: Critical Studies*. Madison: U of Wisconsin P, 1974.

Rose, Ellen Cronan. *The Tree outside the Window: Doris Lessing's Children of Violence*. Hanover, NH: UP of New England, 1976.

Rowen, Norma. "Frankenstein Revisited: Doris Lessing's *The Fifth Child*." *Journal of the Fantastic in the Arts* 2.3 (1990): 41–49.

Rubenstein, Roberta. *The Novelistic Vision of Doris Lessing*. Urbana: U of Illinois P, 1979.

Sage, Lorna. *Doris Lessing*. London and New York: Methuen, 1983.

Schlueter, Paul. "Doris Lessing." In *British Novelists, 1930–1959*. Pt. 1, A–L. Ed. Bernard Oldsey. Vol. 15 of *Dictionary of Literary Biography*. Detroit: Gale, 1983. 274–298.

———. *The Novels of Doris Lessing*. Carbondale: Southern Illinois UP, 1973.

Seligman, Dee. *Doris Lessing: An Annotated Bibliography of Criticism*. Westport, CT: Greenwood, 1981.

Shah, Idries. *The Sufis*. 1964. Garden City, NY: Anchor, 1971.

———. *The Way of the Sufi*. London: Octagon, 1968.

Showalter, Elaine. *A Literature of Their Own: British Women Novelists from Brontë to Lessing*. Princeton: Princeton UP, 1977. 298–319.

Singleton, Mary Ann. *The City and the Veld: The Fiction of Doris Lessing*. Lewisburg, PA: Bucknell UP, 1977.

Sizemore, Christine. "Doris Lessing." In *Postcolonial African Writers*. Ed. Pushpa Naidu Parekh and Siga Fatima Jagne. Westport, CT: Greenwood, 1998.

———. *A Female Vision of the City: London in the Novels of Five British Women*. Knoxville: U of Tennessee P, 1989.

Sprague, Claire, ed. *In Pursuit of Doris Lessing: Nine Nations Reading*. New York: St. Martin's, 1990.

———. *Rereading Doris Lessing: Narrative Patterns of Doubling and Repetition*. Chapel Hill: U of North Carolina P, 1987.

Sprague, Claire, and Virginia Tiger, eds. *Critical Essays on Doris Lessing*. Boston: Hall, 1986.

Sukenick, Lynn. "Feeling and Reason in Doris Lessing's Fiction." *Contemporary Literature* 14 (Autumn 1973): 515–535.

Taylor, Jenny, ed. *Notebooks/Memoirs/Archives: Reading and Rereading Doris Lessing*. Boston: Routledge, 1982.

Thorpe, Michael. *Doris Lessing's Africa*. London: Evans, 1978.

Tymn, Marshall B. "Revisiting Doris Lessing: A Checklist of Critical Studies, 1962–1988." *Journal of the Fantastic in the Arts* 2.3 (1990): 50–62.

Walker, Melissa. "Doris Lessing's *The Four-Gated City*: Consciousness and Community—A Different History." *Southern Review* 17.1 (January 1981): 97–120.

Whittaker, Ruth. *Doris Lessing*. New York: St. Martin's, 1988.

Penelope Lively
1933–

Jacqueline L. Gmuca

An award-winning author in the realms of both children's literature and adult fiction, Penelope Lively is a rare phenomenon. The first eleven works of her publishing career were written for children, and then in 1977 she published her first novel for adults, *The Road to Lichfield.* From that point forward she has continued to write both children's and adult fiction, although her adult fiction has predominated since the early 1980s. Lively excels with both audiences, as witnessed by her prestigious awards: the Carnegie Medal (the highest award in Great Britain for children's literature) for *The Ghost of Thomas Kempe* in 1973; the Whitbread Award for *A Stitch in Time* (1976), her ninth book for children; the Southern Arts Literature Prize for *Nothing Missing but the Samovar, and Other Stories* (1978), her first collection of short stories; the British Arts Council's first National Book Award for her second adult novel, *Treasures of Time*; and the Booker Prize for 1987 for *Moon Tiger*, her seventh novel for adults. Whether she is writing for children or adults, her concern is the same—memories that bind together the individual's multiple selves over time, overlap personal and public history, and create the dense layering of places with people from the past, the present, and the future. In creating novels and picture books for children, Lively has worked in the genres of modern fantasy, realism, and historical realism and has developed exciting narratives, each with a clear chronological order. But it is in her work for adults that her significance is truly apparent. Lively is clearly a postmodern novelist, continuing to experiment with point of view and narrative structure. Incorporating not only shifting points of view within a narrative frame but also montagelike juxtapositions of the same event from several viewpoints, Lively has continued the experimentation of her modern predecessors, Virginia Woolf and James Joyce. Her novels explore the synchronic nature of narrative structure in which events widely separated in time coalesce in the chronological narrative.

BACKGROUND

When Lively was interviewed by Amanda Smith of *Publishers Weekly* several months after *Moon Tiger* won the Booker Prize, she detailed that the novel "was about 30 years in gestation" (48). Actually, one can trace the roots of this novel even deeper, back to Lively's early childhood in Egypt. Born in Cairo, Egypt, on March 17, 1933, to Vera Greer and Roger Low, she was often a solitary child, her mother caught up in the social whirl of British colonial society, her father occupied with his duties as a manager in the National Bank of Egypt. In her autobiography, *Oleander, Jacaranda: A Childhood Perceived* (1994), Lively relates how she felt "battered" by the "cultural confusion" of Egypt, using the most rudimentary categories of "us" and "the world at large," dress and behavior, to sort out the many cultures surrounding her, as diverse as the British and French from the Turkish and Muslim (65). One of her most memorable experiences as a child of eight or nine was a visit to an archaeological site, with British planes overhead and a skeleton thousands of years old at their feet ("Bones in the Sand" 13). Interviewed by Cathy Courtney for *Something about the Author* (1990), Lively pinpoints how this experience "of living in a very ancient land" led to her "lifelong obsession with the processes of time and of memory" (63).

She attended no formal educational institution as a child but was home schooled by her nanny, Lucy. With no training in teaching or experience as a governess, this "surrogate mother," as Lively acknowledged her (Courtney 62), followed the program designed especially for families in the British colonies by the Parents' National Education Union. Through the program's emphasis on literature, Lively was exposed to a number of masterpieces, including the Bible, Greek and Norse mythology, Dickens, and the tales of *The Arabian Nights*. The method of instruction was simple but highly influential on Lively's development as a writer: the stories were read to her, followed by her writing their plots in her own words. She told herself stories all the time, writing her first work at the age of seven, *The Flora and Fauna of the Lower Nile Valley*, in imitation of the style used by a nineteenth-century clergyman whom she had read.

With the end of World War II and the divorce of her parents, Lively's childhood in Egypt abruptly ended. She was sent to Great Britain to stay with her paternal grandmother before beginning three unhappy years in a boarding school known for its athletic rather than its academic accomplishments. In this "absolutely appalling purgatory," as she described it to interviewer Amanda Smith, Lively was chastised for reading in her spare time and was forced to hide her own writing of poetry (47). About a year after he returned to Great Britain, her father recognized that his daughter was totally unprepared for the critical exams necessary for admission to a university and subsequently enrolled her in a "crammer," a type of school known for its success in assisting students in passing exams. In 1951 she entered the "total liberation" of St. Anne's College at Oxford, quickly enjoying her social life and many new friendships. Although she was widely read in literature, Lively opted for a history degree instead, a decision she traced years later to having grown up in Egypt and "needing to place myself in time and to make some sort of interpretation of continuities" (Courtney 65). With her career choices limited after graduation, Lively followed the route taken by many female graduates at the time, enrolled in a secretarial course, and obtained a position as a research secretary at Oxford. It was there that she met her husband, Jack, and with their marriage in 1957 and the birth of her two children in 1958 and 1961, respectively, Lively dedicated herself to raising her children, determined that they would not have the same solitary childhood that she had experienced. She constantly read aloud to her daughter and son, a practice that she credits as the origin of her interest in children's books. Upon her second child's entrance to school, she gave herself six months to decide on her plans. That time gave her the leisure to delve into the history and folklore of Oxfordshire and the impetus to begin her first children's book, published in 1970 as *Astercote*. Since then Lively has been a most prolific writer, publishing ten fantasy novels for older children, over fifteen novels and picture-book stories for young children, two works of nonfiction, several collections of short stories, including an edition of children's stories, and twelve novels for adults.

ANALYSIS

Since the major concerns of Lively's fiction for adults are closely intertwined with her writing for children, it is imperative to consider two of her most popular books for children, *The Ghost of Thomas Kempe* (1973) and *A Stitch in Time* (1976). The former, her fifth book for children, was awarded the Carnegie Medal in 1974; *A Stitch in Time*, the Whitbread in 1976. Both are time fantasies in which the protagonists intersect with characters from previous centuries. In *The Ghost of Thomas Kempe* the ghost of a seventeenth-century sorcerer is released when workmen break a small bottle wedged behind an attic window frame. The reader quickly empathizes with James, the highly imaginative protagonist, when he is blamed for Thomas Kempe's noisy breaking of objects and written messages against those he sees as his rivals. Hilarious episodes underscore a quite serious theme—the presence of layers of time—as James encounters not only a ghost from the seventeenth century, but also the presence of Arnold, a Victorian boy from 1856. In reading the diary of Arnold's aunt, James discovers that the ghost of Thomas Kempe had plagued Arnold and his aunt as well. Yet another ring of time is encountered in James's next-door neighbor, Mrs. Verity. In a moment of insight James realizes that "deep within stout, elderly Mrs. Verity . . . there sheltered the memory of a little girl who had behaved outrageously in Sunday school. And that, when you stopped to think about it, was a very weird thing indeed" (80). The novel ends with a moment of epiphany in which the narrator recognizes that time is actually a continuum filled with many lives behind one as well as ahead. But that continuum does not devalue the importance of one's individual life, for "in the middle, there was James, walking home for tea" (186).

David Rees recognizes *The Ghost of Thomas Kempe* as the first novel in which the "author is completely sure of her own abilities" but ultimately deems *A Stitch in Time* her "most important and memorable book" for children (192, 195). In this novel present-day Maria intersects with Harriet Polstead, age ten, from 1865. The vehicles of their intersection, comparable to fossils of extinct forms, are Harriet's sampler and her drawings of fossils, leading Maria to experience aspects of Harriet's life. Harriet is not a tangible ghost like Thomas Kempe but a more subtle memory of a past way of life. In this work Lively affirms the importance of place as the location of memories. As Harriet tries to explain to her cat, places are like clocks "full of all the time there's ever been in them, and all the people, and all the things that have ever happened" (121). Just as James in the previously discussed novel had insight into an earlier self of Mrs. Verity, Harriet also ponders the many selves she will eventually become, and how each of these previous selves resides in a particular space and time.

Asked on a number of occasions when she would be ready to write a book for adults, Lively was vehement about the importance of works for children. In a February 1978 article for the *Horn Book* she quotes W.H. Auden that there "are no good books which are only for children" ("Children, Part I" 19), emphasizing that books read by children are just as high in quality as those for adults. In 1977, after eleven works for children and one work of nonfiction, Lively published *The Road to Lichfield*. In this novel private and public memories play a central role as Lichfield is identified as the home of Samuel Johnson. It is also the town in which the protagonist's father is approaching death. The inability to ever really know the truth of the past emerges as a central insight of the novel when Anne Linton, going over her father's financial records, finds that her father has had a long-standing extramarital affair. Her life comes to parallel his as she finds herself falling in love with David Fielding, the headmaster of a local boys' school. Anne ultimately meets the daughter of the woman her father had loved for ten years, discovering that Shirley knew all about her and her brother from the very beginning. With the advent of autumn and her father's death, her affair with David is discovered and brought to an end since no one wants a divorce. Critical reception of *The Road to Lichfield* was quite positive, as affirmed by the novel being shortlisted for the Booker Prize.

In her ensuing novels Lively continues to examine alternate viewpoints toward memory, the past, and the power of places to hold past lives. Her characters frequently confront death in one way or another, are exceedingly well developed, and struggle with diverse types of relationships. The award-winning *Treasures of Time* (1979), for example, focuses on a producer's efforts to film a documentary on Hugh Paxton, a deceased archaeologist. Private memory intersects with public memory in each character's differing views of Paxton as the plot unravels the intricate, intertwining relationships among Paxton, his wife, her sister who loved him, Paxton's daughter, and her fiancé. The opening question of this novel, whether it is possible to truthfully reconstruct another's life, is a further amplification of Anne's attempt in *The Road to Lichfield* to find out about her father's relationship to Betty Mansell and her married daughter, Shirley Barron. The novel's narrative style is characterized by shifting points of view among the major characters, a style employed in each of Lively's novels.

In *According to Mark* (1984), her sixth novel for adults, Lively approaches the same question she had posed in *Treasures of Time*, this time from the stance of a biographer gathering material on Gilbert Strong, a man of letters. When the biographer Mark Lamming finds the most unexpected collection of letters under the literary execution of Strong's granddaughter, he is overwhelmed by the fresh insights they will provide. He quickly discovers that the letters are not his only reason for making the drive from London to Dean Clos, as he has fallen in love with Strong's granddaughter, Carrie. As in *The Road to Lichfield*, the novel traces the evolution and conclusion of their affair. In the end Mark makes up with his wife, and Carrie finds herself able to begin a new relationship with a journalist. As Mark becomes more and more familiar with Strong's life, he discovers what he ultimately does not want to know, that Strong had an intense love affair with a woman who was willing to divorce her husband and marry him, but when she quite suddenly died, Strong never got over her loss. Mark's moral dilemma is clear—should such an intensely personal aspect of Strong's life be included in a biography? This is ultimately a moot point, since for the sake of truthfulness, of course it should. The novel ends with Mark feeling as if Strong is speaking to him directly in an old BBC broadcast, uniting the two characters together, writer and biographer, both involved in serious love affairs. Shortlisted for the Booker Prize, *According to Mark* was published in the same year as a collection of short stories for adults, *Corruption*, one for children, *Uninvited Ghosts and Other Stories*, and a picture-book story, *Dragon Trouble*. Throughout this time, then, Lively continued her development of short stories and novels for both children and adults.

Moon Tiger (1987) was also published the same year as two works for children, *A House Inside Out* and *Debbie and the Little Devil*. It was immediately recognized for its excellence, receiving the Booker Prize. Indeed, in her book-length study on Lively, Mary Hurley Moran considers the work to be the novelist's "most impressive display to date of her unconventional narrative methods and her characteristic themes of history, memory, evidence, and the subjective nature of reality" (111). The novel takes place over the course of a few days, the week in which a popular historian, Claudia Hampton, is dying. During this time she is visited by her sister-in-law, her daughter, her surrogate son, and Jasper, her lover for many years. The narrative structure is a complex blending of Claudia's stream of consciousness, an objective third-person point of view, and shifting third-person points of view among Claudia's family members. In addition, the novel moves synchronically in flashbacks to pivotal moments of Claudia's life, so that the moments of the novel's present time are infused by memories of the past. In inspecting these past events, yet another point of view emerges, one in which the same scene is viewed several times from the perspective of its key players. Terming this method "kaleidoscopic," Moran (1993) traces its first appearance to *The Road to Lichfield*, pointing out Lively's recognition that she derived the technique from watching the Japanese film *Rashomon* (37–38). What emerges in the novel is a highly complex view of an individual life, that of a journalist and historian who not only tackled a male-dominated field but who on her deathbed challenges a linear, cause-and-effect view of history, replacing it with her own synchronic vision. Debrah Raschke pinpoints as well Claudia's subversion of the conventional view of historiography in which the public view of history predominates, moving the personal lives of women to a secondary role (117–118). In writing a history of the world, then, Claudia is writing her own history. Such an account, which of course is never formally written down in the context of the novel, most dramatically encompasses the World War II campaign in Egypt, during which Claudia falls in love with a soldier, Tom Southern. On her deathbed she affirms his being as the essence of her core, but as Moran points out in a 1990 article for *Frontiers*, the novel extends beyond their ill-fated love affair and Tom's sudden death to reveal the many layers of Claudia's psyche as she advances in her career, has a long-lasting affair with a Russian immigrant with whom she has a daughter, raises her child, and serves as a surrogate mother to Laszlo, trapped in London when the Communists take over his native Hungary ("Penelope Lively's *Moon Tiger*" 94). Clearly, the novel is a tour de force not only in its probing of the nature of public and private history, but through its experimentation with point of view and narrative structure.

Lively's next novel for adults, *Passing On* (1989), is "a much quieter, more conventional novel" as Moran points out in her critical study (*Penelope Lively* 128). Lively shifts her focus from those involved in love affairs to the ways in which a brother and sister cope with the death of their highly abusive mother. Helen and Edward Glover, now fifty-two and forty-nine, respectively, had lived all of their adult lives with their mother. Beginning with the gathering of children at the funeral, the novel traces the expression of Helen's and Edward's sexuality, suppressed for many years by their mother. Helen falls passionately in love with their solicitor Giles, a man who continually entices women, and Edward finally displays his feelings of homosexuality, making a pass at the neighbor's boy. Throughout this whole time Helen is haunted by the presence of her mother as she encounters a number of reminders of the emotional and verbal abuse she had endured. With Edward's attempt at suicide and Helen's rejection of Giles's invitation to meet, the novel ends with their mother's presence growing dimmer and dimmer. Indeed, when Helen searches the garden for that "familiar, forbidding brown figure," she is no longer there (209). While Helen's third-person limited point of view dominates the novel, the narrative shifts to include Edward's perceptions from a third-person limited standpoint.

In *City of the Mind* (1991), Lively's next novel, she returns to a paralleling of past and present very similar to the juxtapositions in her earlier children's novels *The Ghost of Thomas Kempe* and *A Stitch in Time*. This time, however, there are only the most tenuous links between the architect who is the main focus of the story, Matthew Halland, and memories of the past juxtaposed with his experiences of London. Ruth Feingold compares the work to both Virginia Woolf's *Mrs. Dalloway* and James Joyce's *Ulysses* in its concentration on the life of a city. Indeed, place is paramount here, as a keeper of quite diverse memories, including those of the architect's ex-wife; of Jim Prothero, a fire warden during World War II; of a homeless child; of a nineteenth-century paleontologist; and then, further back in time, of the Elizabethan navigator Martin Frobisher, seeker of the Arctic. Perhaps the crux of the novel is presented at the opening of chapter 6 when the unnamed narrator, while recognizing the reader's need to see a city as part of the present, affirms its opposite nature: "It streams away into the past; it is now, then, and tomorrow" (79). The narrative traces Matthew's half-year journey in his work as an architect as well as his personal quest to accept his divorce from his wife. As Feingold points out, *City of the Mind* illustrates one of Lively's favorite concepts, a palimpsest, "the layers of experience, memory, and physical data that make up a place or a person" (164). Earlier, *The Ghost of Thomas Kempe* and *A Stitch in Time* had begun to explore the nature of such layers of time, with *Moon Tiger* further developing a narrative constructed of a palimpsest.

In Lively's next books, *Cleopatra's Sister* (1993) and *Spiderweb* (1999), seemingly separate stories are traced concerning widely different characters. In each case, setting brings the major characters of the novels together. *Cleopatra's Sister* converges two lives, that of paleontologist Howard Beamis, who is en route to view important specimens in Nairobi, and Lucy Faulkner, a travel writer. Their lives intersect when their plane makes an unexpected landing in Marsopolis, the capital of the imaginary country of Callimbia. Unexpectedly detained, the passengers soon learn the truth of their plight: they are being held hostage to ensure the release of dissidents questioning the recent presidential election in Callimbia. Quickly Howard and Lucy fall in love, establishing a rapport and closeness neither had thought possible with someone met under these circumstances. Suspense begins to build when Howard is randomly selected to be executed as an example to the British government, the novel reaching a pivotal point in the scenes where he is incarcerated and receives what he feels is his last meal. Just as he steels himself to face his own death, he is reprieved. As the translator explains, the dissidents have been taken care of, and so no harm will come to any of the passengers. After a lengthy exposition in which the experiences of Lucy and Howard and the growth of Marsopolis are juxtaposed, the second section of the novel brings all three histories together.

In *Spiderweb* (1999) the ties between characters are quite diffuse. Again, place is what brings characters together, this time two women, but their lives never truly converge. They only happen to share the same place. The main character, Stella Brentwood, a retired social anthropologist, has bought a house in the country, ostensibly to settle down. Her life is juxtaposed with that of a neighbor's, Karen Hiscox, an extremely controlling and abusive wife and mother. Stella herself recognizes the diffuseness of this community: "The truth is that this place is a web, a network. . . . All sorts of mutually exclusive groups co-existing after a fashion. And I'm in there with the rest of them. . . . Quite as alienated in my way as anyone else" (208). The novel maintains this alienation to the end, as Stella prepares to sell the cottage and Karen Hiscox packs herself, her husband, and their sons off to another community. Reviewer Rebecca Barnhouse points out that the reader assumes Stella's role; we become ethnographers "watching Stella navigate the lineage patterns and kinship structures within her new community" (144), employing a variety of documents to draw our conclusions, including letters, diary entries, newspaper articles, lists of items, and phone messages. Intertwined with the present-day narrative of her settling in this Somerset community, we encounter a number of

Stella's previous selves, giving us further insight into her well-developed character.

Throughout her career, then, Lively has explored memory and history from a number of perspectives and for two distinct audiences. Betsy Hearne affirms the close relationship between Lively's fiction for children and novels for adults, posing the larger question of what finally separates children's from adult literature. She finds the answer in narrative technique. While Lively's novels for adults subvert and transform linear narrative order, an audience of children necessitates a strong sense of story with a beginning, a middle, and an end. In "Bones in the Sand" Lively concurs, identifying "one of the fascinations of writing both for children and for adults, the subtle and sometimes half-conscious way in which you find yourself adjusting tone and mood according to the audience, although the theme may remain the same" (15). However, it is undeniable that two prominent roots of Lively's experimentation can be uncovered in her children's stories, as they can in her childhood in which myriad cultures, public and private histories, and time periods coexisted.

ASSESSMENT

During her career Penelope Lively was first recognized for her excellence in writing fiction for children and subsequently for her expertise in writing for adults. Her characters are exceedingly well developed and frequently involved in matters of both personal and public importance as they fall in love, conduct relationships with others, confront death, and ask the larger questions of life—on the importance of place, of time and events, and of the individual. But more important, both the male and female protagonists of her novels challenge preconceived notions of their time, most prominently in their subversive questioning of the linear delineation of documentaries, biographies, and histories as well as the traditional role of women. Lively's explorations of memory, history, and time coupled with her innovative approaches to point of view and narrative structure affirm her importance in terms of the development of twentieth-century literature. In 1985 she became a fellow of the Royal Society of Literature, and in 1989 she was made an officer of the Order of the British Empire in honor of her literary works. Lively has clearly emerged as a leading writer of the postmodern novel.

BIBLIOGRAPHY

Primary Sources

Astercote. London: Heinemann, 1970.

The Whispering Knights. London: Heinemann, 1971.

The Wild Hunt of Hagworthy. London: Heinemann, 1971.

The Driftway. London: Heinemann, 1972.

The Ghost of Thomas Kempe. London: Heinemann, 1973.

The House in Norham Gardens. London: Heinemann, 1974.

Boy without a Name. London: Heinemann, 1975.

Going Back. London: Heinemann, 1975.

Fanny's Sister. London: Heinemann, 1976.

The Presence of the Past: An Introduction to Landscape History. London: Collins, 1976.

The Stained Glass Window. London: Abelard-Schuman, 1976.

A Stitch in Time. London: Heinemann, 1976.

The Road to Lichfield. London: Heinemann, 1977.

"Children and the Art of Memory: Part I." *Horn Book* February 1978: 17–23.

"Children and the Art of Memory: Part II." *Horn Book* April 1978: 197–203.

Nothing Missing but the Samovar, and Other Stories. London: Heinemann, 1978.

The Voyage of QV66. London: Heinemann, 1978.

Fanny and the Monsters. London: Heinemann, 1979.

Treasures of Time. London: Heinemann, 1979.

Fanny and the Battle of Potter's Piece. London: Heinemann, 1980.

Judgement Day. London: Heinemann, 1980.

The Revenge of Samuel Stokes. London: Heinemann, 1981.

Next to Nature, Art. London: Heinemann, 1982.

Perfect Happiness. London: Heinemann, 1983.

According to Mark. London: Heinemann, 1984.

Corruption. London: Heinemann, 1984.

Dragon Trouble. London: Heinemann, 1984.

Uninvited Ghosts and Other Stories. London: Heinemann, 1984.

Pack of Cards: Stories, 1978–1986. London: Heinemann, 1986.

Debbie and the Little Devil. London: Heinemann, 1987.

A House Inside Out. London: Deutsch, 1987.

Moon Tiger. London: Deutsch, 1987.

Passing On. London: Deutsch, 1989.

City of the Mind. London: Deutsch, 1991.

Judy and the Martian. Hemel Hempstead, UK: Simon & Schuster Young Books, 1992.

Cleopatra's Sister. London: Viking Penguin, 1993.

The Cat, the Crow, and the Banyan Tree. London: Walker, 1994.

Good Night, Sleep Tight. London: Walker, 1994.

Oleander, Jacaranda: A Childhood Perceived. London: Viking, 1994.

The Disastrous Dog. Hemel Hempstead, UK: Macdonald Young Books, 1995.

A Martian Comes to Stay. Hemel Hempstead, UK: Macdonald Young Books, 1995.

Staying with Grandpa. London: Viking Penguin, 1995.

Heat Wave. London: Viking Penguin, 1996.

Beyond the Blue Mountains. London: Viking, 1997.

"Bones in the Sand." In *Innocence and Experience: Essays and Conversations on Children's Literature*. Ed. Barbara Harrison and Gregory Maguire. New York: Lothrop, 1987. 13–21.

Ghostly Ghosts. London: Heinemann, 1997.

Goldilocks and the Three Bears. Hove, UK: Macdonald Young Books, 1997.

One, Two, Three, Jump! London: Viking 1998; New York: McElderry, 1999.

Spiderweb. New York: HarperFlamingo, 1999.

A House Unlocked. London and New York: Viking, 2001.

Secondary Sources

Barnhouse, Rebecca. "About Books." Rev. of *Spiderweb*, by Penelope Lively. *English Journal* 89 (November 1999): 144–145.

Burton, Stacy. "Bakhtin, Temporality, and Modern Narrative: Writing 'the Whole Triumphant Murderous Unstoppable Chute.' " *Comparative Literature* 48 (1996): 39–64.

Courtney, Cathy. "Lively, Penelope." *Something about the Author* 60 (1990): 61–72.

Feingold, Ruth P. "Penelope Lively." In *British Novelists since 1960, Third Series. Dictionary of Literary Biography*. Vol. 207. Detroit: Gale, 1999. 163–177.

Hearne, Betsy. "Across the Ages: Penelope Lively's Fiction for Children and Adults." *Horn Book* March/April 1999: 164–175.

Jackson, Tony E. "The Consequences of Chaos: *Cleopatra's Sister* and Postmodern Historiography." *Modern Fiction Studies* 42 (Summer 1996): 397–417.

———. "The Desires of History, Old and New." *CLIO* 28 (1999): 169–187.

LeMesurier, Nicholas. "A Lesson in History: The Presence of the Past in the Novels of Penelope Lively." *New Welsh Review* 2 (Spring 1990): 36–38.

"Lively, Penelope." *Current Biography Yearbook* 1994: 338–342.

Moran, Mary Hurley. "The Novels of Penelope Lively: A Case for the Continuity of the Experimental Impulse in Postwar British Fiction." *South Atlantic Review* 62 (Winter 1997): 101–120.

———. *Penelope Lively*. New York: Twayne, 1993.

———. "Penelope Lively's *Moon Tiger*: A Feminist 'History of the World.' " *Frontiers* 11: 2–3. (1990): 89–95.

Raschke, Debrah. "Penelope Lively's 'Moon Tiger': Re-envisioning a 'History of the World.' " *ARIEL: A Review of International English Literature* 26 (October 1995): 115–132.

Rees, David. *The Marble in the Water*. Boston: Horn Book, 1988.

Smith, Amanda. "*PW* Interviews Penelope Lively." *Publishers Weekly* 223 (25 March 1988): 47–48.

Katherine Mansfield
1888–1923

Karla Alwes

The short stories of Katherine Mansfield evoke impressionistic portraits of families and individuals that, in part, constitute Mansfield's authorial response to the stasis she perceived in the better-known male writers of the time. Like the writers of the romantic period whom she admired (Keats especially), her stories create a fluid, open-ended drama in which her characters seek lasting identity through their relationships with others and with nature. Natural surroundings play a major narrative role in the stories about the search for self, as Mansfield, like the romantics before her, presents human loss as an unanswerable process and at variance with the sublimity of nature. The journey toward identity begins with Mansfield's memories of childhood but often ends with the characters' sudden recognition and tragically won acceptance of loss when the human bonds sought are discovered to be unable to sustain the epiphanic self-knowledge gained.

BACKGROUND

Katherine Mansfield, née Kathleen Beauchamp, was born in Wellington, New Zealand, in 1888. Her early years of education were spent in New Zealand, and her schooling was completed at Queen's College in London. Mansfield is known for her short stories, many of which are based on her New Zealand childhood and often involve children as the primary characters. Mansfield had no children, but suffered a miscarriage that influenced the background of her first collection of stories, *In a German Pension* (1911). In 1918 she married writer and critic John Middleton Murry and wrote for the journals he was editing, *Rhythm* and the *Blue Review*. Mansfield's best-known works are "Prelude" (1918), the collection *Bliss, and Other Stories* (1920), and the last volume to be published in her lifetime, *The Garden Party, and Other Stories* (1922). She died in 1923 of tuberculosis.

Mansfield is recognized as an experimental writer whose works are the first in English to show the influence of the Russian writer Anton Chekhov, whom she admired (Drabble 616). Her literary success provoked the envy as well as the admiration of her contemporary Virginia Woolf. Much of their relationship came from their competition as writers, but a sincere friendship emerged at times. When Woolf heard of Mansfield's death at the age of thirty-four, she felt true despair at the loss and poignantly lamented that Katherine Mansfield was no longer her rival (Lee 393).

Mansfield's stories vary in length and tone.

"Prelude" and "At the Bay" are lengthy evocations of family life (Drabble 616), while stories such as "Miss Brill" are short, sharp, and often bitterly cruel sketches of the isolated individual. Yet even the life of misery that is Miss Brill's is set on a pleasant spring day (West 678), evocative of the romantic promise of renewal.

ANALYSIS

The best of Mansfield's works create a "deliberate female aesthetic, which transformed the feminine code of self-sacrifice into an annihilation of the narrative self" (Showalter 33). In the story of the same name Miss Brill discovers such annihilation when her own identity as onlooker and imagined choreographer to the rest of her small world crumbles in the reality of loneliness. The imagined conversations she has with other people become, when overheard in reality, the onset of her destruction. A young couple on her park bench—"the hero and heroine" of Miss Brill's own fictive drama, "just arrived from his father's yacht" (*Short Stories* 553, henceforth *SS*)—are transformed by reality into two young people who cannot accept the aging woman who sits near them. The boy refers to her as "that stupid old thing at the end" (*SS* 553) of the bench and openly expresses the very question that Miss Brill has been trying so desperately to avoid through her Sunday charades in the park: "Why does she come here at all—who wants her?" (*SS* 553). Miss Brill's epiphany forces her to forgo the usual slice of honeycake at the baker's on her way home, and home, like life, has changed. It is now "a little dark room . . . like a cupboard" (*SS* 553). Both life and home have become suffocating. Miss Brill's loneliness is forced upon her in one transformative moment of acknowledgment of reality. The illusion that Mansfield's characters cling to is ultimately destroyed. Miss Brill, like others to come, has outlived her dreams (Bauermeister, Lansen, and Smith 25), and Mansfield's sympathy for such a painful awareness is made clear by her allowing Miss Brill's fur to "cry" at the story's end. It is the final voice heard.

In many of Mansfield's stories the moment of self-awareness is also the moment of self-betrayal (Showalter 246). In the story "Bliss," for example, the loneliness that will define the female character in the end is, like Miss Brill's, absent from her own self-knowledge at the beginning. Before the night of her dinner party, which is at the center of the story as well as of her transformation, Bertha Young, thirty years old and frequently "overcome, suddenly, by a feeling of bliss—absolute bliss!" (*SS* 337), saw herself as part of a couple, married to Harry. The irony of the title comes from the fact that the story involves a night that Bertha Young "for the first time in her life . . . desired her husband" (*SS* 348). At the same moment that Bertha discovers her passion for her husband, she also discovers that he is having an affair and is in love with another. Theme and feeling become the same, and, as one critic notes, Bertha is made vulnerable because of her knowledge of joy and suffering in the same instant (Beachcroft 18). The story ends with Bertha's crushing despair and the vision of her pear tree from the window, "as lovely as ever and as full of flower and as still" (*SS* 350). As with the lonely Miss Brill, the world of Bertha outside her window continues without her, oblivious to her tragedy. The small worlds both women inhabit become suffocating when the illusions disappear, as small and as still as Bertha's pear tree and Miss Brill's "cupboard" of a room.

Mansfield's stories focus on the limited worlds of the characters, constrained even more by their own insular lives. "The Daughters of the Late Colonel" portrays sisters Constantia and Josephine, following their father's death, in emotional crisis. Their past had been lived for their father. Now they are alone and too afraid to speak of the future; neither can conceive of an identity that does not include their father, even after death. The story ends in silence and forgetfulness.

The emotional lethargy that culminates at the end of Mansfield's stories of women seeking identity but finding the reality of loss instead is like Keats's own lethargy in "Ode to a Nightingale," a "numbness" that "pains," and like Keats, Mansfield permits no reprieve in the end, only the dubious satisfaction of self-awareness, at a cost.

Ellen G. Friedman writes, "[A] variation on the search for the father is the profoundly nostalgic conviction that the past has explanatory or redemptive powers" (241). Aside from the aforementioned "Daughters of the Late Colonel," Mansfield's works that explore the past in order to (re)discover her own childhood have little to do with the search for the father, at least explicitly, because the stories are peopled primarily with female characters. It is the absence of the living father through daily routine that speaks most clearly to the "search" for him. Simone de Beauvoir credits Mansfield with bestowing on her female characters "luminous moments of happiness by way of supreme recompense" (690). Such recompense is found in two well-known stories that look at the female characters' search for identity through other women, having little contact with the fathers—"Prelude" and "The Garden-Party." The characters of change are young girls and emotionally powerful women, isolated and insulated from the larger world because of emotional and physical geography in the first and wealth in the latter.

Kezia, her sister Lottie, and their family are moving at the opening of "Prelude" to a large house in the country. The women's and girls' lives will revolve around the gardens, the pastoral surroundings, and each other. Father Stanley lives for the weekends, when he may leave his job in the city to return to his newly acquired country home, when he ritualistically greets his wife with "I'm home again. Is everything all right?" (*SS* 243). This is the culmination of his own domestic identity, one not completely shared by his wife Linda, whose own identity, like that of many of the women in Mansfield's stories, is complicated by her acknowledgment of "different selves" (Lee 385). Linda's own "selves" are manifest in her feelings for Stanley: "There were all her feelings for him, sharp and defined, one as true as the other. And there was this other, this hatred, just as real as the rest. . . . She longed to hand him that last one, for a surprise" (*SS* 258).

"Prelude" had an effect on Mansfield's friend Virginia Woolf—"its fragmenting of a whole family history into intense, solipsistic moments of experience, its funny child's eye view, its brilliant tiny coloured details, its fluid movement between banal realities and inner fantasy, . . . its sexual pain—coincided with Woolf's other readings in 'modern fiction' " (Lee 385). The fragmentation of a family into "moments of experience" is first seen through the young Kezia's eyes. On the way to the new home familiarity is left behind as Kezia and Lottie travel "along new roads with high clay banks on either side, up steep, steep hills, down into bushy valleys, through wide shallow rivers. Further and further" (*SS* 225). Geographically, the new house will put as many obstacles to their past as their new lives will. Metaphorically, the wide rivers and steep hills will become the emotional obstacles to the relationship between the daughters and their mother, who "did not love her children. It was useless pretending" (*SS* 279). The events of "Prelude" are seen through many minds, corresponding to the "different selves" of the adult women, Linda and Beryl. Important to stories told through memory and reflection, the omniscient perspective allows for different viewpoints, with neither intrusion nor comment by the author. All the minds expose themselves, as a cluster of infallible narrators would, and the reader recognizes the same distancing of the narrator as time and memory are to the author (Daly 64).

In "At the Bay," the intended sequel to "Prelude," his weekend in the country over, Stanley returns to work: "Oh, the relief, the difference it made to have the man out of the house. . . . the whole perfect day was theirs" (*SS* 270). The "perfect day" becomes the definition of life itself to Linda as she rests among the flowers of her garden: "If only one had time to look at these flowers long enough, time to get over the sense of novelty and strangeness, time to know them! But as soon as one paused to part the petals, to discover the under-side of the leaf, along came Life and one was swept away. And, lying in her cane chair, Linda felt so light; she felt like a leaf. Along came Life like a wind and she was seized and shaken; she had to go . . . Was there no escape?" (*SS* 278).

"At the Bay" ends with Beryl's own answer to Linda's question of escape. Within the surrounding fuchsia and moonlight Harry Kember came through the garden "and snatched her to him" (*SS* 299). His "bright, blind, terrifying smile froze [Beryl] with horror" (*SS* 298). Beryl escaped his grasp, but not the horror of the experience and her own complication of identity:

> "Cold little devil! Cold little devil!" said the hateful voice (Harry Kember).
> "You are vile, vile," said she.
> "Then why in God's name did you come?" stammered Harry Kember.
> Nobody answered him. (*SS* 299)

Beryl is unsure of her actions and cannot answer the question. No identifiable human voice is found at the end of the story. Instead, the final paragraph of "At the Bay" focuses again, as many of Mansfield's stories about women do, on the small world of their lives, a world once more oblivious to any pain within its midst: "A cloud, small, serene, floated across the moon. In that moment of darkness the sea sounded deep, troubled. Then the cloud sailed away, and the sound of the sea was a vague murmur, as though it waked out of a dark dream. All was still" (*SS* 299). "Agreeing with Chekhov that a writer poses questions but does not answer them" (Daly 97), Mansfield the author is herself oblivious to Beryl's pain in the end. Like Bertha's pear tree after she discovers the truth about her husband, the world that surrounds Beryl is "still." Her pain cannot disturb it. Thus the final comment, and the only response to Harry Kemper's question, is given by the sea as it manifests, in the aforementioned closing paragraph, "the alternate rise and fall of emotion, negation and affirmation" (Daly 98) that is found in the many voices within the story, even those that cannot speak.

"The Garden-Party," another story of isolation of the female, but this time isolation through wealth, begins with a sentence that emits the same tenor of emotion attributable to the weather as Woolf's famous elegy *To the Lighthouse*: "And after all the weather was ideal" (Mansfield, *SS* 534); " 'Yes, of course, if it's fine tomorrow' " (Woolf, *To the Lighthouse* 9). Woolf's elegy is to her parents, Mansfield's to her childhood. Once again the natural surroundings make up the locus of the memories, creating an insular world that, as in "At the Bay," provides a "perfect day," with none of the doubt that opens Woolf's elegy: "They could not have had a more perfect day for a garden-party if they had ordered it. Windless, warm, the sky without a cloud. Only the blue was veiled with a haze of light gold" (*SS* 534). For the child of this story, Laura, the perfect day would yield her own discovery of life outside the insulated world, like Kezia. Laura's father is absent as the story opens, brushing off his hat to go to the office. It is again a world of women, and because there is "geographical juxtaposition of rich and poor" in "The Garden-Party" (Daly 122), Laura's discovery will be one that takes her from her own wealthy surroundings into the lives of those who do not share them—the poor family that lost its husband and father to death on the day of the garden party, the "perfect day."

In a conversation with her mother about the death of the workman, Laura pleads: "Of course, we can't have our party, can we? . . . The band and everybody arriving. They'd hear us, mother; they're nearly neighbors"

(*SS* 543). When she realizes that her mother does not care what happened to the "nearly neighbors" of their lives, Laura makes a final effort for compassion: "Mother, isn't it really terribly heartless of us?" (*SS* 543). "The Garden-Party" 's attempts to reconcile reality with the dream, innocence with experience, and, importantly, the levels of society (Magalaner 111) are most evident in this one plaintive cry of the young Laura. The innate recognition that yes, it is "terribly heartless of us" comes through as the obvious answer to the question posed. The meaningful choice of a garden party as the focus of the story lies behind Laura's question to her mother, in a world in which there is "little more substance than the cream puffs being served" (Magalaner 112).

The leftover cream puffs and other scraps of food from the party become the bridge of communication between Laura and the poor family when her mother insists that she take a basket of the leftover food to the grieving widow. Laura's thoughts immediately turn to the differences between her family and herself: "Again, how curious, she seemed to be different from them all. To take scraps from their party. Would the poor woman really like that?" (*SS* 545). With her basket in hand (and still wearing her party clothes and hat), Laura brings the scraps of food to the family and sees the dead workman: "He was wonderful, beautiful. While they were laughing and while the band was playing, this marvel had come to the lane. Happy . . . happy . . . All is well, said that sleeping face. This is just as it should be. I am content" (*SS* 548). The differences between Laura's own wealthy surroundings and the dead workman's are not so much greater than the differences she sees, on this "perfect day," between herself and her family.

Mansfield's garden here is a "false Eden, a dream world of artificial delight and false security" (Magalaner 117), and Laura has stepped out of it into the world of experience and reality, a fall from grace that once again proves to be a *felix culpa*. Following her visit to the poor family, Laura begins a question to her brother: " 'Isn't life,' she stammered, 'isn't life—' But what life was she couldn't explain. No matter. He quite understood. '*Isn't* it, darling?' " her brother replied (*SS* 549). Both question and answer are left unfinished as the story ends, but the reader recognizes that it is Laura who has discovered the relationship between life and death, between dream and reality, and of all her family, it is only her brother, Laurie, who realizes this. The brother and sister relationship is a close one in many of Mansfield's stories, and Laura's brother being named "Laurie" sets the two apart from the callous women of the family, creating an even closer bond between the two siblings (Magalaner 118).

ASSESSMENT

Katherine Mansfield's works look closely at the tragedy as well as the self-discovery of human lives. The knowledge gained by the characters who painfully submit to their own search for identity within the stories is at the core of who we all are. The illusions and fantasies of the characters echo those of "regular human beings"; Mansfield's best stories involve a "dreaming about alternatives and a reversal of expectations" that engage both reader and character (Hankin 466). Mansfield creates, in the small epiphanies that recur in her characters' lives, a portrait of human needs and dreams. It is finally a true statement of loss, denial, and, ultimately, the reality of life, with which one is "swept away" ("At the Bay," *SS* 278).

BIBLIOGRAPHY

Primary Sources

In a German Pension. London: Swift, 1911.
Bliss, and Other Stories. London: Constable, 1920.
The Garden Party, and Other Stories. London: Constable, 1922.
The Dove's Nest. London: Constable, 1923.
Poems. London: Constable, 1923.
"Prelude." Richmond: Hogarth Press, 1918.

The Little Girl, and Other Stories. New York: Knopf, 1924.

The Aloe. New York: Knopf, 1930.

The Letters of Katherine Mansfield. Ed. J. Middleton Murry. New York: Knopf, 1929, 1932.

The Short Stories of Katherine Mansfield. New York: Knopf, 1937.

Journal of Katherine Mansfield: Definitive Edition. Ed. J. Middleton Murry. London: Constable, 1962.

Secondary Sources

Bauermeister, Erica, Jesse Larsen, and Holly Smith. *500 Great Books by Women*. New York: Penguin, 1994.

Beachcroft, T.O. "Katherine Mansfield's Encounter with Theocritus." *English* 23 (1974): 13–19.

Beauvoir, Simone de. *The Second Sex*. Trans. H.M. Parshley. New York: Knopf, 1952.

Berkman, Sylvia. *Katherine Mansfield: A Critical Study*. New Haven: Yale UP, 1951.

Daly, Saralyn R. *Katherine Mansfield*. New York: Twayne, 1965.

Drabble, Margaret, ed. *The Oxford Companion to English Literature*. 5th ed. Oxford: Oxford UP, 1985.

Friedman, Ellen G. "Where Are the Missing Contents? (Post)Modernism, Gender, and the Canon." *PMLA* 108 (1993): 240–252.

Hankin, Cherry. "Fantasy and the Sense of an Ending in the Work of Katherine Mansfield." *Modern Fiction Studies* 24 (1978): 465–474.

Hormasji, Nariman. *Katherine Mansfield: An Appraisal*. London: Collins, 1967.

Kaplan, Sidney Janet. *Katherine Mansfield and the Origins of Modernist Fiction*. Ithaca: Cornell UP, 1991.

Kobler, Jasper F. *Katherine Mansfield: A Study of the Short Fiction*. Boston: Twayne, 1990.

Lawrence, D.H. *The Letters of D.H. Lawrence*. Ed. Aldous Huxley. London: Heinemann, 1956.

Lee, Hermione. *Virginia Woolf*. New York: Knopf, 1997. 381–396.

Magalaner, Marvin. *The Fiction of Katherine Mansfield*. Carbondale: Southern Illinois UP, 1971.

Moore, Leslie. *Katherine Mansfield: The Memories of LM*. New York: Taplinger, 1972.

Morrow, Patrick D. *Katherine Mansfield's Fiction*. Bowling Green, OH: Bowling Green State U Popular P, 1993.

Murray, Heather. *Double Lives: Women in the Stories of Katherine Mansfield*. New Zealand: U of Otago, 1990.

Murry, John Middleton. *Katherine Mansfield and Other Literary Portraits*. London: Nevill, 1949.

Parkin-Gounelas, Ruth. *Fictions of the Female Self*. London: Macmillan, 1991.

Pilditch, Jan, ed. *The Critical Response to Katherine Mansfield*. Westport, CT: Greenwood, 1996.

Ricketts, Harry, ed. *Worlds of Katherine Mansfield*. Palmerston North, New Zealand: Ngaere, 1991.

Showalter, Elaine. *A Literature of Their Own: British Women Novelists from Brontë to Lessing*. Princeton: Princeton UP, 1977.

Swinnerton, Frank. *Figures in the Foreground: Literary Reminiscences, 1917–40*. London: Hutchinson, 1963.

West, Rebecca. "The Garden Party." *New Statesman* 18 (1922): 678.

Woolf, Virginia. *To the Lighthouse*. New York: Harcourt, 1927.

———. *A Writer's Diary: Being Extracts from the Diary of Virginia Woolf*. Ed. Leonard Woolf. London: Hogarth, 1965.

Kamala Markandaya
1924–

Hena Ahmad

Kamala Markandaya's description of the freedom activist Roshan in her second novel, *Some Inner Fury*, can be seen as a fitting description of Markandaya herself: "Roshan came nearest to [Kit] in liking and sympathy for the ways of the West; but she belonged to the East too. Born in one world, educated in another, she entered both and moved in both with ease and nonchalance. It was a dual citizenship which few people had" (128). Markandaya, in fact, can be seen to resolve her loyalties to the mother country (India) and to the adopted country (Britain) by consistently criticizing both in her fiction. The formative influence of Markandaya's sociohistorical context—colonial experience, India's freedom struggle, and her diasporic location—is fundamental to understanding her work. Mapping gendered and subaltern cultural spaces, grounding her novels in Indian social concerns, Markandaya, as a diasporic cosmopolitan writer, transcends the confines of a constitutive "Indianness."

BACKGROUND

Born Kamala Purnaiya in South India into an upper-middle-class South Indian Brahmin family, Markandaya traveled to Europe at sixteen with her father. She left college without completing her degree, started a journal (espousing Gandhi's philosophy) that was banned by the British after two years, and later experimented with village living for a few months. In 1948 she finally moved to England, where she has lived ever since. She worked for the BBC as a broadcaster. Married to an Englishman, Markandaya has a daughter, to whom she dedicated *The Golden Honeycomb.*

What is important to realize about Markandaya's novels is that they emerge from the fact of her diasporic location, her Indian past, and her British present. In other words, as an expatriate/immigrant, Markandaya, in her fiction, reflects concerns that arise, variously, from the asymmetrical colonial relationship between India and Britain, from the economic poverty of India's villages, from the destruction of rural life by the invasion of industry and technology, and from Indian cultural and social traditions. Interwoven into all these concerns is the conflict between Western values, reason and rational thinking, on the one hand, and Indian values, spirituality and a lack of materialism, on the other.

Some of the other noteworthy factors that have influenced Markandaya are Hindu philosophy's emphasis on spiritualism, India's nonviolent freedom struggle led by Gandhi, and the British colonial agenda in India.

Some of the social ills that she highlights are the exploitative economic system, the disparity between the rich and the poor, the class structure, the religious perpetuation of the self-sacrificing Indian woman, and other repressive social norms and traditions in Indian culture.

The most visible artistic influence on Markandaya is that of romanticism. Susie Tharu sees the influence of nineteenth-century English literary thought on Markandaya, while Yasmine Gooneratne sees Coleridge and the romantics echoed in her works (127). The very titles of *Nectar in a Sieve* and *A Silence of Desire* are taken from Coleridge and Longfellow (Joseph 14, 35). That influence is reflected in the fact that Markandaya's novels focus on the lives of ordinary people, like the poor from the village or the city; they celebrate the beauty, harmony, peace, and spirituality that the rural landscape evokes and lament the loss of the village community by the incursion of factories, urbanization, and materialism.

Markandaya has been criticized by some Indian critics for portraying India unconvincingly or inauthentically or unfavorably in her fiction. This has been well discussed and documented by writers like Margaret Joseph and Feroza F. Jussawalla. Underlying this argument is the question of Markandaya's "Indianness." Such an argument ignores, among other things, the class, caste, and communal fissures, fractures, and fragmentations within India itself. While students of Markandaya would do well to be aware of this criticism, they should question what is supposedly authentic or inauthentic. Markandaya clearly states that she does not speak for India and does not see herself as an ambassador for India, even though she finds herself "from time to time, shoved into this . . . position" ("One Pair of Eyes" 27).

ANALYSIS

Markandaya's ten novels, broadly rooted in her country of birth, focus on Indian social and economic ills and on East/West conflicts. Her realistic, detailed depiction of ordinary human lives is pervaded by a pessimism over which, paradoxically, prevails an ultimately optimistic world view of a human identity and brotherhood. A class consciousness informs all her novels, highlighting, in different ways, injustice and exploitation of the disenfranchised subaltern. At times the stoic acceptance of poverty and suffering depicted in the novels can frustrate a postcolonial reader who wishes for more aggressive solutions for social change, instead of what can seem only a highlighting of the ills of society.

Impelled by a seeming need to justify why her novels are critical of India, Markandaya explains that India's poverty and "defects" impel her work; she argues that the only way to bring about change is to highlight its social ills. Acknowledging that "perhaps [a writer] ha[s] to be at a distance to think such thoughts," Markandaya observes that "more than most the Commonwealth writer overseas has the blessing, or bane, of duality. He, or she, has to steer carefully between justice and criticism" ("One Pair of Eyes" 28).

Markandaya's underlying concern, above all, is to demonstrate how individuals, emotionally and intellectually, can connect despite cultural, economic, political, and religious differences. Her novels establish connections between Indian and English, colonial and postcolonial, privileged and subaltern worlds. Jasbir Jain sees "two ways of life, two sets of values" in Markandaya's novels and confrontation between them leading to "a new bond of sympathy and understanding traversing both the worlds, absorbing the human . . . in both" (36). Stating that "the East-West encounter as a recurrent theme in her novels is directly related to her experience as an expatriate who inherited Indian values by birth and acquired Western values by choosing to live in England," Prem Kumar affirms that "like [Markandaya], most of her characters find themselves in situations where they must confront values rooted in opposing cultural milieus, historical processes, economic systems, political ideologies, and philosophical traditions" (84). P. Geetha "discern[s] a pattern—not a smooth progress, but a troubled swinging between tradition and modernity, between cultural exclusivism and a pluralistic cultural identity in her novels" (169).

While Markandaya maintains that the "very fact of writing in English pre-supposes an English-reading audience," she suggests that Indian words be used without "italics, or footnotes, or glossaries, or apologies" so that readers have to "work for the meaning, . . . a rewarding experience in a way that discovery by footnote could never be" ("One Pair of Eyes" 31). Keeping to standard English in her novels, Markandaya writes that she is in two minds about the use of Indian words (31). She contends that Indian words should not be employed merely to add local color, but finds it less forced to use certain Indian words rather than their English equivalents.

Markandaya's first novel, *Nectar in a Sieve* (1954), a Book-of-the-Month Club alternate selection, immediately established her reputation as a novelist and positioned her in Western eyes as a literary ambassador of India (even though she does not see herself as one). Told by Rukmani, the first-person narrator, this is a moving tale of the suffering she undergoes due to starvation. Rukmani and her husband, Nathan, who are poor tenant farmers, endure the exploitative economic system, paying the landowner even when floods and drought wreak havoc on their crops. Their family suffers calamity after calamity not only due to "Mother Nature" but also due to the urbanization that follows the building of a tannery in their village. Three of Rukmani's sons leave the village for employment; two others die, directly and indirectly, because of starvation; her daughter prostitutes herself to feed her brother; and finally, Rukmani loses her husband. In addition to depicting the social evils of child-bride practice, dowry, preference for male children, and the cultural notion that a woman's worth is defined by motherhood, the novel juxtaposes Western material values, represented by the English doctor, Kenny, with Rukmani's spiritual strength that helps her to stoically accept, endure, and survive her poverty and starvation.

Nectar in a Sieve has been criticized on the grounds that the language Rukmani uses makes her less credible as a peasant character. According to Margaret Joseph, the "literary style . . . sits strangely on an unsophisticated village woman" (22). Markandaya's powerful prose, however, overshadows any discrepancy seen in the use of cultivated prose by a peasant. What impress the reader are the imperatives for social and economic change underlying Rukmani's cultural values, spiritual strength, and stoic attitude that do help her survive the economic and social systems but at the same time keep her mired under centuries of oppression.

In *Some Inner Fury* (1955), her second novel, Markandaya shifts her focus from the underclass to the upper class and from preindependent India closer to India's struggle for independence. Describing the last years of the British Raj, this novel, unlike the first, refers to a definite time period, from a little before the beginning of World War II to the Quit India movement of 1942. While *Nectar in a Sieve* depicts a bonding between an English missionary doctor, Kenny, and Rukmani, theirs is an unequal relationship because of class and cultural differences. In the second novel Mira, an Indian, and Richard, an Englishman, belong to the same class and hence are on a more equal footing. Though they are in an intimate relationship, the two part ways for political reasons: Richard represents the colonial master, and Mira must side with her people at the end.

Some Inner Fury, like *Nectar in a Sieve*, highlights the differences between English and Indian cultural values, focusing on material/spiritual differences. We see this conflict magnified in the relationship between Mira's brother, the Anglophile Kit, and his Indian wife, Premala, who, despite trying hard, fails to adopt the style of the club-going

Westernized Indian social class to which her husband belongs. The novel thus underlines the ideological differences between Kit and Premala, Kit symbolizing the Oxford-educated Anglophile, in the service of the British colonial government, and Premala, the nonviolent Gandhian national liberation struggle.

While the focus shifts from the peasant class in *Nectar in a Sieve* to the upper class in *Some Inner Fury*, Markandaya's third novel, *A Silence of Desire* (1960), focuses on a middle-class family. Sarojini, the protagonist, who has a tumor, visits a swami for faith healing. Just as in *Nectar in a Sieve* Rukmani's spiritual strength helps her survive her tragedies, Sarojini's spiritual faith in the swami helps her bear her pain and illness. The spiritual/material dichotomy, the conflict between faith and science at the heart of this novel, causes the rift between Dandekar and his wife, Sarojini. While we see everything through the protagonists' eyes in the first two novels, Rukmani and Mira, respectively, here we have an omniscient narrator, which allows for a deeper look into the characters of both Sarojini and Dandekar.

Dandekar, a government clerk, finds that his neatly ordered domestic life is disrupted as Sarojini devotes increasingly more time to the swami. Frustrated because his wife is neglecting the house and children, Dandekar is further shocked to discover that his wife has gifted whatever valuables they possess to the swami. He asks his sympathetic boss to have the swami relocated, hoping that with the swami gone he can persuade his wife to undergo surgery for the tumor. The swami, however, before leaving, convinces Sarojini to have an operation; he drives away her fears that she might die just as her mother died under the surgeon's knife for a similar operation. Sarojini tells Dandekar: "I'm not afraid now of knives or doctors. . . . All will be well. [The Swami] said so" (246). Dandekar, filled with remorse, wishes he could bring the swami back. Markandaya's message here seems to be that human beings need both spirituality and science, faith and rational thinking.

As in *Nectar in a Sieve* and the later novels, *The Coffer Dams*, *The Golden Honeycomb*, and *Shalimar*, in Markandaya's fourth novel, *Possession* (1963), characters bond across different classes and cultures, but the differences between them emphasize their asymmetrical position/power. Again, the spiritual triumphs over the material; *Possession*, as K.S. Narayana Rao states, is a

> testimony to the supremacy of the spirit over the flesh and over the material forces. . . . The sustaining strength of the traditional roots of ancient India, the value of the ancient teaching of the Bhagavad-Gita concerning the importance of philosophic detachment in life, personal dignity in death and the absence of fear of death and finally, the affirmation of the supremacy of the spiritual powers over the temptation of material forces, especially of the West, are what constitute a major theme in this novel. ("Markandaya's" 293–294)

The first-person narrator, Anasuya, a writer, is instrumental in the meeting between Lady Caroline, a wealthy English socialite, and Valmiki, a fourteen-year-old goatherd who has a natural gift for painting. Lady Caroline, recognizing his talent, persuades Valmiki to accompany her to England, where she grooms him into a fashionable, exotic painter. Notwithstanding the fact that Valmiki's dramatic transformation from a goatherd into a wealthy painter and then back to his spiritual roots seems more like a fantasy or fairy tale, Markandaya underlines the prioritization of the spiritual over the material for Valmiki, who chooses to go back to his earlier life of poverty rather than be without spiritual sustenance.

A return to the theme of poverty, the exploitation of the poor by the rich, and the takeover of small business by big business is portrayed in Markandaya's fifth novel, *A Handful of Rice* (1966). Depicting the triumph of good over evil, where good is equal to honesty and hard work, this novel's realistic description of domestic life in a tailor's home emphasizes the strength that comes from stoic acceptance of one's lot in life, exemplified in the attitude of Nalini, the tailor's daughter. A criticism of capitalism is apparent in the fact that a big retail house squeezes the tailor out of business by drawing his clientele away.

Ravi, the son of a poor villager, moves to the city to earn a livelihood, but falls into the company of a gang of hoods. His life changes when he gets caught burgling Apu the tailor's house and falls in love with Nalini. He starts working with his future father-in-law and later takes on the responsibility of head of the household. Subsequently they start losing their tailoring customers to big retail houses and, unable to compete, cannot make ends meet. Dejected, Ravi goes to his old friend, Damodar, hoping to join his violent, illegal, Mafia-type racket, but Damodar has no use for him.

Distraught and desperate, his son having died of meningitis and his family starving, Ravi joins another mob out to loot the government-owned rice godowns but at the last moment is unable to take even a handful of rice. Later, caught up in another mob that is out to destroy the big shops, he finds himself in front of show windows behind which mannequins, dressed in glittering outfits, represent the capitalist competition that edged him out from the tailoring business. However, he finds himself unable to throw a brick at the shop window. We might read Ravi's failure to throw the brick, in one sense, as symbolic of the victory of Gandhian nonviolence even in the face of extreme poverty. The novel critiques capitalism and its dehumanization and shows that for the poor, as exemplified by Ravi's life, things are not much better in the city than in the village.

The Coffer Dams (1969), Markandaya's sixth novel, shows how the technological modernization of India has taken place at the cost of the disenfranchised tribal people. A British construction company, run by Clinton and his partner Mackendrick, is on contract with the Indian government to build a dam for which a tribal village is to be submerged under water. The clash between the political ideologies—capitalist and subaltern—is represented by the discord between Clinton and his wife Helen, who actively supports the tribals in their opposition to the dam. The novel also juxtaposes the colonial views of Millie Rawlings and her husband, who express nostalgia for the colonial master/native-servant relationship, with Helen's active interest in the tribals' cause.

Clinton's refusal to give permission to lift the boulder under which the bodies of two tribal villagers are buried and his refusal to inundate the coffer dams to save the tribals' settlement from the impending monsoon deluge expose the absolute lack of humanity engendered by capitalism in the name of technological advancement. The indifference of the Indian officers toward the plight of the tribal villagers reveals the complicity of the Indian government in uprooting the tribals from their village. The novel also juxtaposes Clinton's unfeeling attitude with the more humane attitudes of Mackendrick and Lefevre, who recognize their exploitation of the tribals. Clinton's portrayal as a ruthless capitalist is balanced with the depictions of the more humane Helen, Mackendrick, and Lefevre.

Markandaya's seventh novel, *The Nowhere Man* (1972), emerged as a response to the race riots that raged across Britain in the 1960s. This is her only novel that is set primarily in England, though the reader is taken to colonial India in flashback. In it Markandaya opens up the dilemma of the Indian immigrant faced with racial discrimination in Britain. Srinivas flees to Britain in 1918 to escape political imprisonment in British colonial India. Initially finding it difficult to belong, he eventually assimilates himself into the English culture, helped by the friendship of Mrs. Pickering. He comes to accept England as his home but is jolted when he becomes the target of bigotry: he is tarred and feathered and has his house set on fire by Fred Fletcher, a "blacks basher."

The friendship between Srinivas and Mrs. Pickering reminds us in a way of the Indian/ English bonds that form between Rukmani and Kenny in *Nectar in a Sieve*, between Mira and Richard in *Some Inner Fury*, between Valmiki and Lady Caroline in *Possession*, and between Bashiam and Helen in *The Coffer Dams*. However, the relationship between Srinivas and Mrs. Pickering is less asymmetrical than all the others, excepting that between Mira and Richard, in terms of class and power. The two stand on a more equal footing than, say, Rukmani, who is a peasant, and Kenny, who is a doctor.

Woven around Srinivas are the strands of colonial India, Indian tradition, and the Indian immigrant experience in Britain. Markandaya's nostalgia for her South Indian past is visible in the nostalgia that Srinivas experiences for the feel of teak under bare feet and mull dhotis. Though he is torn between his loyalties to India, his mother country, and to Britain, his adopted country, Srinivas learns to put his past behind him. Faced with cruel racism, he turns to his past, only to discover that alienation from India has left him with the lost identity of a "nowhere man."

In May 1974 *Two Virgins* (1973), Markandaya's eighth novel, won the first annual English-Speaking Union Award for the best work of fiction published in English by a nonnative speaker. *Two Virgins* portrays the different ways in which two sisters, Lalitha and Saroja, come to sexual awakening in a village. They go to different schools, Lalitha to a private ex–missionary school, where she learned "moral science, and how to dance around a bamboo pole which Miss Mendoza said was a maypole," and Saroja to the regular government school (14). Lalitha, the prettier of the two and her father's obvious favorite, is sent to the expensive school so that she can get a good education. Ironically, her "moral" downfall begins with her education, which teaches "moral" science.

While the two sisters are different, it is Lalitha's schooling under Miss Mendoza that exposes her to bourgeois values and encourages her to scoff at traditional ways. For example, before Miss Mendoza visits Lalitha's home for tea, Lalitha tells her mother, "Miss Mendoza has high standards . . . [she] was used to sitting in chairs at tables, and eating with forks and spoons" (58). Lalitha disparages village life and their "primitive" existence; she thinks that "it's barbaric, not having a fridge" (26). She seeks the glamor and excitement she glimpses when she goes for a week with her teacher to the city.

The novel throughout highlights Indian cultural notions about the value of a woman's reputation: "A woman's good name is her most precious possession, [Aunt Alamelu] told Saroja and Lalitha" (53). "All the rules and restrictions . . . were designed . . . to stop you becoming pregnant" until marriage (201). Lalitha brings shame upon her family in becoming pregnant by the film director, Mr. Gupta, who has no intention of marrying her. Saroja, though attracted to Devraj, the film director's assistant, rejects a relationship with him because the "only kind there could possibly be between them was the kind between Mr. Gupta and Lalitha." Their mother, Amma, tells Saroja, "Your sister wandered too far . . . she was lured outside the code of our community and is paying the penalty, that is all" (234).

K.S. Ramamurti criticizes *Two Virgins* for lacking a "well-defined central theme" (37) and finds offensive "the author's excessive preoccupation with sex in its coarsest form" (39). Jasbir Jain asks, "[W]hy is it that Lalitha . . . goes astray?" (43), and, in response, suggests that Lalitha's flight from the village to the city endorses the implications of Mr. Gupta's praise that Lalitha "is a woman with the natural desires of a woman" (*Two Virgins* 220). The novel clearly opposes the Western influence of Miss Mendoza and Mr. Gupta, who fuel Lalitha's restlessness with the restrictive village culture that provides no outlet for her sexual desires and her constant yearning for excitement. The different schooling, the novel suggests, explains why Saroja's strength, uncorrupted by bourgeois values, comes from her faith in the stability, solidity, and security represented by the village culture.

The Golden Honeycomb (1977), the ninth and longest of Markandaya's novels, is semihistorical fiction, though Markandaya refers to it as a "romantic novel" ("One Pair of Eyes" 31). Markandaya researched Indian history for this novel, and K.S. Narayana Rao informs us in his review that this work is based "partly on her own family knowledge of how princely states were maneuvered into subsidizing their own subservience to the British (for her family records may have contained some valuable information), as one of her ancestors, Dewan Purnaiya, was Dewan or Prime Minister of Mysore State" (342). Markandaya's purposes in this novel are to chronicle princely rule in India under British colonial rule, to show how the maharaja was a puppet of the British, and, what is most important in her novels, to highlight the poverty in India against the pomp and splendor of the maharaja's palace and of the British resident's mansion.

The novel focuses on Indian and British cultural and political differences, the lifestyle of a maharaja, the ways in which the British manipulated and controlled the maharajas, and how a British education fashioned the Indian maharajas into the mold of British aristocratic culture. The novel traces a maharaja's family through three generations to show how change occurs when in the third generation Rabi, the maharaja's son, takes up the cause of the people against the ruling government. Usha, the minister's daughter, and Rabi symbolize the new democratic India that is instrumental in overthrowing British colonial rule and in bringing about egalitarian reform.

Markandaya's tenth, second-longest, and last novel to date was first published under the title *Pleasure City* in Great Britain and later under the title *Shalimar* (1982) in the United States. We can draw a parallel between *Shalimar* and *Possession* at one level because both Valmiki, the goatherd, and Rikki, the fisherman in *Shalimar*, come from rural backgrounds. While Valmiki is exposed to Western culture when Lady Caroline Bell takes him to England to groom him into a fashionable, marketable painter, Rikki is exposed to some British culture through the missionary couple, the Bridies. His job at the seaside hotel resort "Shalimar" exposes him to five-star culture and the lifestyle of the wealthy. The central theme here is the somewhat intriguing bond, despite the class and cultural barriers that Tully describes as an "ocean" between them, between Rikki, an orphan son of a fisherman, and Tully, the British director of a multinational firm in charge of building the resort.

ASSESSMENT

Markandaya's novels reveal her faith in a "human brotherhood" that transcends and connects British and Indian characters in her fiction across cultural barriers, especially those of class, race, and religion. They also show a criticism of the social and economic systems in India juxtaposed with the spiritual strength that informs Indian culture. Her novels also focus on conflicting British and Indian values defined by the differences between the spiritual and the material, the spiritual and the rational, the spiritual and the scientific, the traditional and the modern: themes and attitudes that reflect her Indian heritage, colonial legacy, and diasporic sensibility. Her colonial education and exposure to the West, made possible by her privileged class and opportunities, are visible in Markandaya's Indian/Western constructions in her literary production. She seems not to have resolved the conflicts implicit in her dual-cultural background.

Situating Markandaya as a postcolonial first-generation diasporic Indian writer, we find that her novels reveal competing political ideologies that define both the British colonial legacy and an Indian national heritage from a diasporic perspective. Her dual cultural background, Indian and British, enables her to reveal, in intricate mosaics, a world view, both tragic and hopeful, complicated by the vision of an Indian immigrant writer. The Indian landscape in her fiction, connecting the individual to Earth, Nature, and God, is a source of spiritual sustenance. In the same way, the hot Indian climate, the heat and dust, the hot winds, the dry earth, the monsoons, the scorching sun, dominate her novels.

The reader needs to be wary of seeing an "essential" India in Markandaya's texts, especially because of a sense of a timeless and spaceless India, as in *Nectar in a Sieve*, which specifies no place name or time period. Along with her concern to end the exploitation of the disenfranchised subaltern, what needs to be kept in mind is that Markandaya's artistic constructions, her fictional worlds, as inspired by her diasporic sensibility, promote a vision that shows her faith in "human brotherhood" and human bonding across cultural barriers.

BIBLIOGRAPHY

Primary Sources

Nectar in a Sieve. New York: John Day, 1954.

Some Inner Fury. London: Putnam, 1955.

A Silence of Desire. London: Putnam, 1960.

Possession. London: Putnam, 1963.

"The Plan." *Illustrated Weekly of India* 24 October 1965: 9–11.

A Handful of Rice. London: Hamish Hamilton, 1966.

"Return Ticket." *Illustrated Weekly of India* 14 August 1966: 21–23.

The Coffer Dams. New York: John Day, 1969.

"Why Do We Write in English?" *Adam International Review* 36.355–360 (1971): 42–43.

The Nowhere Man. New York: John Day, 1972.

Two Virgins. New York: John Day, 1973.

"As Others See Us, Part I." *American Association of University Women* 68.3 (November 1974): 21–24.

"As Others See Us, Part II." *American Association of University Women* 68.6 (April 1975): 18–19.

"One Pair of Eyes: Some Random Reflections." In *The Commonwealth Writer Overseas: Themes of Exile and Expatriation*. Ed. Alastair Niven. Bruxelles: Librairie Marcel Didier, 1976. 23–32.

The Golden Honeycomb. New York: Crowell, 1977.

Pleasure City. London: Chatto, 1982.

Shalimar. New York: Harper, 1982.

"Reminiscences of Rural India." In *John Kenneth Galbraith Introduces India*. Ed. Frank Moraes and Edward Howe. London: Andre Deutsch, 1974. 102–113.

Secondary Sources

Geetha, P. "Images and Archetypes in Kamala Markandaya's Novels: A Study in Cultural Ambivalence." *Journal of Commonwealth Literature* 26.1 (1991): 169–178.

Gooneratne, Yasmine. "Traditional Elements in the Fiction of Kamala Markandaya, R.K. Narayan, and Ruth Prawer Jhabvala." *World Literature Written in English* 15.1 (1983): 121–134.

Jain, Jasbir. "The Novels of Kamala Markandaya." *Indian Literature* 18.2 (1975): 36–43.

Joseph, Margaret P. *Kamala Markandaya*. New Delhi: Arnold-Heinemann, 1980.

Jussawalla, Feroza F. *Family Quarrels: Towards a Criticism of Indian Writing in English*. New York: Peter Lang, 1985.

Kumar, Prem. "From Confrontation to Reconciliation: Kamala Markandaya's Evolution as a Novelist." *International Fiction Review* 14.2 (1987): 84–88.

Parameswaran, Uma. "What Price Expatriation?" In *The Commonwealth Writer Overseas: Themes of Exile and Expatriation*. Ed. Alastair Niven. Bruxelles: Librairie Marcel Didier, 1976. 41–52.

Pollard, Arthur. "Kamala Markandaya's *The Golden Honeycomb*." *Journal of Indian Writing in English* 8.1–2 (1980): 22–26.

Ramamurti, K.S. "Kamala Markandaya's *Two Virgins*—A Problem Novel." *Littcrit* 7.2 (1981): 36–45.

Rao, K.S. Narayana. "Markandaya's *Possession* and the Idea of the Triumph of the Spirit: I." *Indian P.E.N.* 36.10 (October 1970): 292–296.

———. Rev. of *The Golden Honeycomb*, by Kamala Markandaya. *World Literature Today* 52.2 (1978): 342.

Reddy, K. Venkata. *Major Indian Novelists*. New Delhi: Prestige, 1990.

Rubenstein, Roberta. "Kamala Markandaya: *Two*

Virgins." *World Literature Written in English* 13 (1974): 225–230.

Sethuraman, Ramchandran. "Writing across Cultures: Sexual/Racial 'Othering' in Kamala Markandaya's *Possession*." *ARIEL* 23.3 (July 1992): 101–120.

Srivastava, Ramesh K. "Woman as Possessor: A Reflection of Markandaya's Anti-patriarchal Rage and Divided-Consciousness in *Possession*." In *Feminism and Recent Fiction in English*. Ed. Sushila Singh. New Delhi: Prestige, 1991. 72–88.

Tharu, Susie. "Tracing Savitri's Pedigree: Victorian Racism and the Image of Women in Indo-Anglian Literature." In *Recasting Women: Essays in Colonial History*. Ed. Kumkum Sangari and Sudesh Vaid. New Delhi: Kali, 1989. 254–268.

Pauline Melville
1948–

John Thieme

Pauline Melville's fiction represents a distinctive contribution to late-twentieth-century postcolonial British writing. From the outset her writing received highly favorable reviews, and she has been the recipient of a number of literary awards: her first collection of short stories, *Shape-Shifter* (1990), won the *Guardian* Fiction Prize, the Macmillan Silver Pen Award, and the Commonwealth Writers Prize best first book award; *The Ventriloquist's Tale* (1997) won the Whitbread First Novel award.

Mainly set in London and Guyana, her fiction employs a polyphonic variety of modes to investigate issues of identity, community, and cultural belonging. Several of her short stories are written in a magic-realist mode that demonstrates an indebtedness to South American novelists such as Gabriel García Márquez and Wilson Harris, whose influence she acknowledges (Phillips, Conversation). Her fiction has, however, carved out its own highly individual terrain, alternating between fabulist and realist modes to suggest the complexities of dialogue between metropolitan and "third-world" societies and the danger of appropriation inherent in attempts to give voice to subaltern experience. Melville herself has moved between Britain and Guyana, and *The Ventriloquist's Tale*, her most significant work to date, particularly foregrounds the issue of cultural appropriation by outsider commentators.

BACKGROUND

The details of Melville's family background help to pinpoint the tension between "insider" and "outsider" perspectives that one finds in *The Ventriloquist's Tale*. The half-Amerindian McKinnon family, who are central to the narrative, appear to be based on the Melville family, who were the most prominent cattle ranchers in the remote Rupununi savannah region of Guyana (Swan 201–202). On one level, then, Melville's Guyanese fiction is derived from personal experience, and some of the more extraordinary aspects of *The Ventriloquist's Tale* appear to stem from her family background (Thieme 183ff.). So Melville has intimate inside knowledge of aspects of the cultures of Guyanese Amerindians that would be rare even among coastal Guyanese, but she has lived most of her adult life in England and despite frequent visits to Guyana can be seen to be an outside commentator, especially when it comes to describing the interior world of Guyanese Amerindian life. She describes her ancestry and affiliations by saying that her father, who married an Englishwoman, was "from a mulatto family," and that while it would be "ridiculous" for her to speak of herself as "black," she has "always been connected with that community" (Phillips, Conversation). She was born in England but at the age of nine months was sent to Guyana, where her grandmother raised her, because her mother was ill. She returned to England, where she attended school, at the age of five and went back to Guyana "for a period" when she was fourteen. Subsequently, she says, she has "been back fairly regularly" (Phillips, Conversation).

A second crucial shaping influence on her writing has been her earlier career as an actress and comedienne. Prior to the publication of *Shape-Shifter* she played a broad range of bit parts in notable British films, including *Ulysses* (1967), *Far from the Madding Crowd* (1967), *The Long Good Friday* (1980), and *Mona Lisa* (1986); she appeared in several television comedy series, including *The Young Ones*, *Blackadder*, and *The Comedy Strip Presents*, for which she cowrote and starred in the episode "Didn't You Kill My Brother?" and also had some success as a stand-up comic. Arguably, this diverse range of acting experiences lies behind her ventriloquial capacity to render a wide repertory of voices convincingly and to range, seemingly effortlessly, across a similarly broad array of fictional modes.

ANALYSIS

Despite its frequent use of fabulist elements, labeling Melville's fiction "magic realist" fails to do justice to its polyphonic variety, which is a perfect correlative of the protean transmutations of identity that have been a dominant motif of her fiction from *Shape-Shifter* onwards. This first collection is prefaced by two epigraphs that suggest the power of transformation, relating this to the practices of the Amerindian shaman, and metamorphosis is central to the whole volume. The opening three stories are set in coastal Guyana and draw not on Amerindian mythologies, but on Afro-Guyanese folklore associated with the magico-religious beliefs of obeah, posing the question of whether such magic is the preserve of tricksters or whether it contains the power to bring about genuine change. The conclusions vary: in the first story, "I Do Not Take Messages from Dead People," the folklore figure of a Diablesse is used to trick a corrupt government minister; in the third, "The Conversion of Millicent Vernon," the advice of an obeah man appears to help the eponymous Millie to secure the funds she needs to prevent losing all of her teeth, and obeah certainly strikes Millie as a more efficacious religion than that represented by the picture of an anemic Christ that hangs in the dining room of her home. At the same time, these opening stories offer social commentary on the economic impoverishment—Millie's cavities stem from the unavailability of toothpaste—and political corruption that, Melville suggests, characterize postindependence Guyanese life.

In the fourth story Melville shifts the scene to London, but her London is a city peopled by Caribbean and other migrants, so there is clear continuity. At first the London stories seem to be realistic accounts of the predicament of underdogs, mainly documenting their social exclusion. Subsequently Melville moves into different territory, and two of the most powerful stories, "The Truth Is in the Clothes" and "You Left the Door Open," insist on the intersection of parallel levels of reality. In the former the protagonist is a writer who has a magical coat of many colors made for her by a woman from Soweto, who claims that her clothes have healing qualities. Once again the story raises the issue of whether the apparent shape-shifter is a charlatan or a person with genuine shamanistic power. Initially the narrator takes the former view, but she is forced to revise her opinion when the coat ushers her into the alternative world of a Jamaican revivalist ceremony taking place on the other side of the back wall of the London flat that she has been living in for five years. This story also departs from realism through the use of a metafictive technique and ends with the protagonist sitting down to write a story called "The Truth Is in the Clothes." In "You Left the Door Open" there is a similar emphasis on surreal connections between different levels of identity as the narrator, a cabaret artist who specializes in impersonations, finds a character she has created for her act, a "vicious and predatory" small-time crook (*Shape-Shifter* 115), merging with a real-enough criminal, who has been released from a psychiatric hospital, and a nineteenth-century murderer who bore the same name, Charlie, as her creation and also worked as a cabaret artist. Behind this quasi-mystical fusion of different characters lies the sense that identity is a performance and apparently discrete roles have commonalities that cross periods, gender, race, and originary location. At the same time, the use of a performer as the narrator-protagonist opens up self-reflexive possibilities similar to those suggested by the use of a writer protagonist in "The Truth Is in the Clothes."

Shape-Shifter concludes by coming full circle: the final story, "Eat Labba and Drink Creek Water," takes its title from a Creole proverb that affirms that those who engage in these activities will always return to Guyana. Written as a series of fragments that reflect on the relationship between London and Guyana, it provides a fitting conclusion to a collection in which this dialogue has been central, even though individual stories seem to be more rooted in particular locations. From the first, then, Melville's fiction promotes a cross-cultural vision that has distinct affinities with that of Guyana's best-known novelist, Wilson Harris. However, despite her engagement with magic-realist modes, she demonstrates a concern with the material realities of particular social situations that is markedly different from Harris's abstract emphasis on the need for psychic transformation as a prelude to social change.

Initially *The Ventriloquist's Tale* gives the impression that it will be narrated by an Amerindian magic-realist narrator, but this figure identifies himself as a cultural hybrid from the outset while laying claim to the ventriloquial capacity to "do any voice: jaguar, London hoodlum, bell-bird, nineteenth-century novelist, ant-eater, epic poet, a chorus of howler monkeys, urban brutalist, a tapir" (*VT* 8). However, at the end of the Prologue this narrator dismisses any suggestion that the novel will be written in a magic-realist mode by saying, "I must put away everything fantastical that my nature and the South American continent prescribe. . . . Fancy is in the dog-house. Perhaps it has something to do with protestants or puritans and the tedious desire to bear witness that makes people prefer testimony these days" (*VT* 9), and the narrative that follows is largely written within the Puritan-derived conventions of the realist novel. The effect is to lend credence to what might otherwise seem an implausible tale of mythic incest, as it were, to endorse the seemingly far-fetched core of the narrative by couching it within a method rooted in verisimilitude.

Later on in the novel an explosive device planted by two Americans, who are surveying the Guyanese savannahs as part of their company's oil-prospecting activities, kills a child of the Wapisiana Indian family, the McKinnons, who are the novel's main protagonists. This act is the most overt of several instances in the text of Western disruption of the seemingly homogeneous world of the local Amerindian cultures. *The Ventriloquist's Tale* also depicts the interventions of a Jesuit missionary, a Czech anthropologist whose specialty is comparative mythology and whose work on incest motifs in Amerindian cultures bears a marked resemblance to that of Claude Lévi-Strauss, and a Jewish Englishwoman, Rosa Mendelson, who has come to Guyana to do research on Evelyn Waugh's visit to British Guiana in the 1930s, a visit that yielded source material for his novel *A Handful of Dust* (Lawson Welsh). The missionary very obviously sets out to change the lives of the Amerindians he encounters, but the two researchers also run the risk of "contaminating" (*VT* 79) them by their very presence among them. As the anthropologist says, "We try just to observe but our very presence alters things" (79); and in his view the ethnographical eye of the researcher is itself "a new form of colonial power" (80).

The Ventriloquist's Tale offers a complex and searching investigation of this issue, which has loomed large in recent postcolonial debates. Interestingly, it relegates the Waugh intertext to a very marginal role in its own structure. Its central action spans a period of a century and revolves around two generations of the McKinnon family, with a central focus on the incestuous relationship of the brother and sister, Danny and Beatrice McKinnon, which fairly obviously reenacts a myth noted by Lévi-Strauss and referred to in one of the novel's three epigraphs (*VT* [ix]), leaving the reader uneasy that Melville's critique of various forms of European intervention is complemented by a narrative that takes a European anthropologist's constructed version of a pan-American myth as its defining trope (Thieme, passim). Problematically, this represents a viewpoint predicated upon the essentialist view of indigenous peoples' cultures engrained in Lévi-Strauss's reading of Native American mythologies and arguably in classical structural anthropology more generally. At an opposite extreme, however, Rosa Mendelson, the figure who seems to have the most affinity with Melville herself, is a self-proclaimed "internationalist" who believes in "a mixture of the races" and is presented as an opponent of the modern trend toward ethnic and communal exclusiveness to be seen in groups such as Serbs, Muslims, and Czechs (*VT* 78). In short, *The Ventriloquist's Tale* raises a series of disturbing questions about who has the authority to speak for subaltern cultures while only partly answering them. Despite this, it succeeds brilliantly because of Melville's gift for narrative and her ability to play the role of ventriloquist as she moves across cultures, periods, and narrative modes to tell a compelling tale.

Melville's second collection of short stories, *The Migration of Ghosts* (1998), also mixes narrative modes and moves between different levels of reality, now extending the geographical range beyond London and Guyana by including stories set in several mainland European countries and, more incidentally, Nigeria. Once again the narrative modes employed blend realism and fabulation, with occasional metafictive references. Guyanese Gothic rubs shoulders with a critique of the country's postindependence government, particularly in the opening story, "The President's Exile," where several facets of the corrupt president's character bear a striking resemblance to that of Guyana's first postindependence leader, Forbes Burnham. The racial exclusivity of the president of this story is in marked contrast to Melville's cross-cultural identity politics, and the second story, "Mrs. Da Silva's Carnival," moves in an opposite direction by celebrating the irrepressibility of the matriarch of a Notting Hill Carnival band and the inclusiveness of carnival itself. Elsewhere the mood is more somber, particularly in "Lucifer's Shank," a powerful and moving story about a friend's death from cancer that invokes both Dante and Amerindian myth to provide a larger context and concludes that "each individual death is its own holocaust" (MG 84). Holocaust is also central in "Provenance of a Face," a story about a whiteface mime artist who is criticized for his repetitions of an expression that becomes known as "the Visage of Horror" (MG 175). As in several other instances, Melville employs the classic short-story formula of a concluding "twist," and here the epiphany comes when it is revealed that the "Visage" has been derived from the mime's memory of his uncle's account of what he saw as one of the first liberating troops to enter Belsen.

In the title story of the collection Melville contrasts the different value systems of a wife and husband, a Macusi Indian woman and an Englishman, in the neutral territory of post-Communist Prague, a city that is simultaneously both vividly real and surreal in Melville's depiction. The wife remains singularly unmoved by her husband's enthusiasm for sightseeing, only coming alive when she sees a figure that she identifies with a water spirit from her own culture. Unlike the marriage of two friends they visit in Prague, their "unlikely match" does not seem in "bad shape" (*VT* 193), but their relationship remains one that is founded on difference. He fails to understand her fatalism; she has no interest in his fascination with history and social change. A similar dialectic informs the finest story in the collection and Melville's most brilliant to date, "The Parrot and Descartes." This begins with an account of an aetiological tale from the Orinoco region in which at the moment of creation a parrot screams a warning. Subsequently the parrot is brought to seventeenth-century England and, after being traumatized by having to attend the first performance of *The Tempest*, a play that he comes to remember verbatim, he becomes an addition to the household of Elizabeth, daughter of James I, and Frederick, the emperor Palatine, and is taken first to Heidelberg and then to Prague. Melville's focus is on the moment in European history "when science started to split from magic" (MG 102), and the contrast between the mythic, Amerindian-centered world view of the parrot and Descartes, whom he encounters in Prague, epitomizes this schism. When he first sees the rationalist philosopher, the parrot "intuitively recognize[s] the danger" (110) and lets forth a primal scream that parallels his earlier warning at the moment of creation; his European owners have sustained the "unity of magic and science" (109), but he knows that he is encountering the "man who contributed to the rout of a certain sort of imagination" (110). This story, then, interweaves Western historiographical detail and Amerindian mythic fabulation to heal the breach between rationalism and magic that has dominated post-Cartesian Western thought. For the parrot, though, it is a tragedy, and toward the end he finds himself back in the New World, chained to a cardboard tree and chanting words from the Epilogue to *The Tempest*, along with the actor who plays Prospero, in a Guyanese performance of the play. The suggestion is that Shakespeare's final artistic testament is irrevocably implicated in the Western colonial project, and this takes on an added level of significance when the story concludes with the parrot, "wings clipped and wearing an ornamental chain on one leg" (MG 115), being taken to a new life—and, one assumes, a new form of acculturation—in America.

ASSESSMENT

Both *The Ventriloquist's Tale* and the two short-story collections demonstrate a virtuoso capacity for assuming different registers and personae that enacts Melville's belief that parallel levels of reality frequently coexist and intersect and that personality is fluid rather than fixed. At a time when discussions of globalization are being forced to evaluate the extent to which its very positive benefits are tainted by its erosion of distinctive elements in "local" cultures, her fiction to date has offered a probing, imaginative investigation of the ways in which a cross-cultural vision can exist alongside an attentiveness to the specifics of particular minority cultures.

BIBLIOGRAPHY

Primary Sources

Shape-Shifter. 1990. London: Picador, 1991.
The Ventriloquist's Tale. London: Bloomsbury, 1997.
The Migration of Ghosts. London: Bloomsbury, 1998.

Secondary Sources

Lawson Welsh, Sarah. "Imposing Narratives: European Incursions and Intertexts in Pauline Melville's *The Ventriloquist's Tale* (1997)." Proceedings of the EACLALS/ASNEL "Colonies, Missions, Cultures" Conference, Tübingen, 1999.

Phillips, Caryl. Conversation with Pauline Melville. Guardian Conversations. ICA Video, n.d.

Swan, Michael. *British Guiana: The Land of Six Peoples*. London: HMSO, 1957.

Thieme, John. "Throwing One's Voice? Narrative Agency in Pauline Melville's *The Ventriloquist's Tale*." *The Literary Criterion* 35.1–2 (2000): 170–192.

Charlotte Mew
1869–1928

Gina Wisker

The history of women's poetry in the early part of the twentieth century had been one of silence and absence until the recuperation of, among others, poets such as H.D. (Hilda Doolittle), Charlotte Mew, Gertrude Stein, Mina Loy, and Edith Sitwell in the 1980s (see Hanscombe and Smyers 1984). Charlotte Mew, born in the second half of the nineteenth century (1869), embraces both the late nineteenth and the early twentieth century in her work. She and Thomas Hardy, whose work also covers this period, had a mutual admiration for each other's poetry. Mew has been described as a Georgian poet, like Wilfred Owen, Siegfried Sassoon, and Edward Thomas, but her work is more innovative than this suggests, and she is probably better defined as one who mixes the Georgian with modernist styles. This perhaps accounts for some difficulties with her reception, since critics find such a mixture confusing, and for the same reason some editors refused to incorporate her work in their collections, notably the collections of *Georgian Poetry*, volumes 3 and 4, edited by Edward Marsh. She is also one whose position as a woman poet living in genteel poverty placed her on the outskirts of the "Bloomsbury group" of writers, artists, and thinkers, comprising Virginia Woolf, John Maynard Keynes, and Lytton Strachey, among others. Pictured as rather mannish, Charlotte Mew has recently been rediscovered as a woman writer whose sexual choices were directed at women rather than men, as often were those of other great modernist women writers including H.D., Woolf herself, Gertrude Stein, Radclyffe Hall, and Sylvia Townsend Warner. We now recognize her as both a unique individual writer and a woman poet whose mixture of subjectivity, inner feelings, and rapport with the external natural world and whose sensitivity to the complex changes and pretenses of relationships place her very definitely in the line of great, insightful, highly subjective, often-ironic women writers whose numbers include Emily Dickinson and Sylvia Plath.

Her work was rediscovered in the 1980s by feminist critics seeking foremothers, but she has not yet received the critical acclaim she deserves. Her poetry made her famous, but Charlotte Mew was also a short-story writer as well as an essayist of great variety and versatility and often a little conservatism. She was able to adopt a full range of styles to fit different publications and different ends, and in her short stories we find that she is aligned with other "daughters of decadence" as defined by Elaine Showalter: new women short-story writers of the later nineteenth and early twentieth century who spoke out and wrote against the social constructions and constraints upon women. Olive Schreiner, Charlotte Perkins Gilman, and Kate Chopin are among this number. Charlotte Mew's stories sometimes tended to be a little arch or sentimental, but her "A White Night" is troubling, an insightful critique of the compulsions and enervations of late-nineteenth-century imperialism and patriarchal attitudes.

BACKGROUND

Born in 1869 in 10 Doughty Street, Mecklenburgh Square, in the heart of London, Charlotte Mew lived most of her life with her mother and sister Anne in Gordon Square. Charlotte's father was Frederick Mew, son of a farmer from the Isle of Wight, who came to London to be an architect and worked in partnership with the renowned H.E. Kendall, whose daughter Anna he married. The family spent their time in genteel poverty, with Anna attempting to keep up appearances, believing that she had married beneath her. There were seven children, but two died after a few months, a third at age five. As adults, her brother and one of her sisters became insane and were confined to institutions. Charlotte was close to her sister Anne (1873–1927), who restored antique furniture and had artistic gifts that their impoverished condition never fully allowed to flourish, the need to earn a living always having to take precedence over the opportunity to develop her talents. In their lives the nurse Elizabeth Goodman was a dominant figure and ruled the household in an ordered fashion until she died in 1893. Of Charlotte's or "Lottie's" early life little is known, but it has been reported that she was willful and intelligent. She was lucky in finding a girls' school and a headmistress that supported her tastes and abilities. She attended Lucy Harrison's School of Girls in Gower Street and partly boarded there, but learned only what she wished: English literature and some art and music. Later she attended lectures at University College, London, played organ and piano, and read French and English. Like several other women writers, she used the open access of the British Museum reading room to read and write. Her essays "Mary Stuart in Fiction" and "Men and Trees" reveal wide reading, and she was clearly very interested in the work of George Eliot, since she died leaving an impressive list of quotes from her.

Her first recorded publication, the story "Passed" in 1894, appeared in the second edition of the *Yellow Book*, under the editorship of Henry Harland. Throughout her career Mew published stories in the *Yellow Book*, the *Egoist*, *Temple Bar*, and other little magazines and earned a living in this way to some extent. The Poetry Bookshop under Harold Monro published her poems. She was very modern, smoked, swore, visited where she wanted, and met her sister Anne's artist friends. In 1901 she first visited Brittany, and from then on, French influences appeared in her work, beginning with "Notes on a Brittany Convent" and the poem "The Little Fortress." Other visits to Brittany and Paris followed, for she was attracted to France and the Roman Catholic church. Brittany in particular offered settings for poems. Gradually Charlotte Mew started to meet others in literary London. In a letter in March 1913 she mentioned that she was now called Charlotte by "Sappho" Catherine Amy Dawson-Scott, novelist and founder of PEN. Mew got to know May Sinclair, writer, suffragette, and a central figure of literary London who introduced Ezra Pound to Ford Madox Ford. Mew sent Sinclair an admiring letter about her work, and the admiration became mutual, a friendship developing beyond literary admiration, leading to what has been viciously described (by Sinclair) as a short-lived relationship or an aborted attempt at one on Mew's part. Sinclair read much of Mew's work and admired it, bringing her poems to the attention of Edward Garnett, Austin Harrison of the *English Review*, and Pound of the *Egoist*, who enthusiastically forwarded several to *Poetry* in Chicago, which, however, rejected them. The *Egoist* printed the poem "Fete."

Alida Monro, wife of Harold, found "The Farmer's Bride" in The *Nation* in 1912 and was "electrified" (*CCP* xi). In 1916 a collection of Mew's poetry was published under the title *The Farmer's Bride* by Monro from the Poetry Bookshop. Five hundred copies were printed, but it sold badly because it was not well reviewed, although H.D. and Rebecca West responded well to it. Monro always campaigned for Mew's work and twice tried to persuade Edward Marsh to publish it with other Georgian poems in his collections of poetry, *Georgian Poetry*, volumes 3 and 4.

Hugh Walpole, poet laureate Robert Bridges, and Lady Ottoline Morrell all liked her work, the latter saying that Mew was "believed to be among the best of poets alive then" (*CCP* xi). Woolf also thought so and in 1920 found *The Farmer's Bride* very good and interesting and unlike anyone else's work. In 1924 Woolf wrote to Vita Sackville-West that she had "just met among others, Charlotte Mew (the greatest living poetess)" (*CCP* xii). Hardy thought her a fine poet, and after reading *The Farmer's Bride* he invited her to visit at Max Gate several times in 1918. A friendship sprang up between her and Florence Hardy. Mew revered Hardy, referring to him as her "King of Wessex." Mew did not write much after that time, although she expanded *The Farmer's Bride* and in 1921 wrote a few new poems that were published in *Saturday Market* in America and reviewed enthusiastically by Louis Untermeyer, who was introduced to her by Sassoon.

Mew is not described as any kind of defiant New Woman by her biographer Penelope Fitzgerald, who points out that she frequently asked men to do the speaking in professional and legal matters rather than seizing this role for herself. However, her clothes were clearly masculine, and she smoked and swore and went freely about London and Brittany. After the death of their father, Charlotte and her sister Anne remained in straitened circumstances trying to keep their mother comfortable, Anne working for the guild of decorative artists, Charlotte publishing a little, mainly for the *Temple Bar* and also for the *Academy*. Her later poems, as Fitzgerald observes, "give the essence, never the solution of an idea, a psychological study that would have made a full six shilling novel if written by a novelist" (15). Graves, loss, unfulfilled potential, suffering, and unachieved feelings are some of her favorite themes.

John Masefield and others, including Hardy and Walter de la Mare, recommended her for a civil list pension of £75 a year, but she later wished to give it up, saying that she was not writing enough after 1916. Her mother died in 1923, and Anne and Charlotte moved to a studio after the lease expired. Anne died of cancer in 1927. Charlotte was distraught and felt that she had been buried alive. She then went into a nursing home for neurasthenia on February 15, 1928, and on March 24 she killed herself by drinking half a bottle of Lysol.

ANALYSIS

Charlotte Mew's sensitive, haunting evocations of individual experience, the developments of life and relationships, and the impatience of nature are a highly original contribution to British women's poetry. Although, as noted earlier, her work was recognized by other poets during her time, it has still to be given its full critical acclaim today. Val Warner argues that Mew's "unresolved sexuality" was the basis of her work. Perhaps the vividness of her verse, compared with the vague chirrupings about nature that characterized Georgian verse, can in part be explained by the problems of her life. However, these problems cannot be understood in a purely personal context. At the time of her writing, British cultural life was being reorganized along the lines of social Darwinism. The notion of the individual was giving place to that of the citizen. New discourses of social regulation emerged that addressed the subject less as a unique person than as an object for state concern. The subject was someone to be regulated and administered according to particular forms of knowledge that took no account of the personal. Indeed, it is precisely at this moment that the personal becomes pathological, for this is the period that gives birth to psychoanalysis. Val Warner argues that Mew's "un-disclosed sexuality" underpins and informs her work, and indeed, her lesbianism has been recognized as informing the attractions and tensions between Mew and May Sinclair. It also informs her representation of herself, often, as acting a role, as artificial, as an outsider (see "Fame," discussed later). Mew established the validity of writing from a subjective viewpoint, albeit often hidden in a persona, as in "The Farmer's Bride" and "On the Road to the Sea," which adopt a male narrative voice. Although contemporary social Darwinism denied the validity of the individual as opposed to the wider social experience and although modernism sought, in poetry, to escape the emotional "slither" of the subjective by establishing its validity in tightly composed and absolutely accurate language and meter, Mew paved the way for others, most notably other women poets who sought a voice to express the hidden and silenced female self.

Mew's work can be read as an attempt to preserve the personal by rendering Georgian concerns with direct experience through modernist techniques. Of particular importance here are her experiments with line length. These are in direct contrast to the iambic pentameter, which, for example, Anthony Easthope sees as constitutive of poetic subjectivity. "Beside the Bed" opens with a thirteen-syllable line followed by one of fifteen syllables, a third of seventeen syllables, and a fourth of three:

> Someone has shut the shining eyes, straightened and folded
> The wandering hands quietly covering the unquiet breast:
> So, smoothed and silenced you lie, like a child,
> not again to be questioned or scolded.
> (*Collected Poems and Prose* [*CPP*8])

Easthope argues that the personal is best expressed through use of iambic meter, but Mew's poetry disproves this. Mew's varying line lengths and enjambments suggest a more fluid subjectivity, one that escapes the constraints of traditional verse while "preserving a sense of self from the encroachments of modernist aesthetics" (Wisker and Day 67). Her line structure is very open, enabling movement from thought to thought.

The imagery of "Madeleine in Church" acquires its resonance not from a literary tradition but from its occurrence in other poems and from its connections with events in Mew's own life. An example of this is the image of the child that appears throughout her poetry. The child also appears in the title poem of the collection *The Farmer's Bride* (1916). The poem is written from the point of view of the farmer, who describes his bride as "too young" (*CPP* 1). Their marriage has the effect of making her "afraid / Of love and me and all things human." In addition to the suggestion of the bride being more child than woman, she is also linked to the world of animals. Indeed, she flies "like a hare" and is "like a mouse." In the farmer's own words, "t'wasn't a woman." The bride will talk only to animals. "Happy enough to chat and play / With birds and rabbits and such as they." The farmer himself has "hardly heard her speak at all." Mew's own sexual orientation may be a factor in "The Farmer's Bride," for the construction of the poem allows Mew, from the position of the farmer, to express desire for the female body:

> Oh! my God! the down,
> The soft young down of her, the brown,
> The brown of her—her eyes, her hair, her hair!
> (*CPP* 2)

Hair is highly eroticized in Mew's verse: "Only the hair / Of any woman can belong to God" (*CPP* 7), while in "The Forest Road" she describes "the long sweetness of the hair that does not die" (*CPP* 21). By occupying a male subject position, that subversive female desire can be expressed. This desire can also be expressed when the speaker is also the Other who is sought: "I think it is myself I go to meet" ("The Quiet House," *CPP* 19) and "I see my soul / I hear my soul singing among the trees" ("The Forest Road," *CPP* 22). The desire for self-unification helps explain the frequent references to travel and a sense of searching for the Other in Mew's work. Titles suggest journeying and travel toward self-unity—for example, "The Forest Road," "On the Road to the Sea," and "On the Asylum Road." But in order for the self to be unified, it needs another's recognition: "There must be someone. Christ! there must, / Tell me there will be someone" ("Madeleine in Church," *CPP* 26).

However, this recognition is not forthcoming. She is an animal/natural/plant/spirit who avoids using or cannot use ordinary discourse, preferring a language she and the animals understand, the presymbolic. In "The Farmer's Bride" the farmer can only understand her as nonhuman, saying that "her smile went out, and t'wasn't a woman." A feminist reader is reminded of the madwoman in the attic. The girl's sexuality and her desire to be true to her own identity are clearly signaled in her wildness and her refusal to speak the language or behave in the established manner of "ordinary folk." Her claiming silence and a presymbolic language enables her to establish a psychological as well as a physical distance from the farmer, who, having married her rather too quickly, clearly left her terrified of the sexual encounter that followed:

> Too young maybe—but more's to do
> At harvest time than bide and woo.
>
> (*CPP* 2)

Locking her up turns her into a domestic prisoner, true only to her "wild self." But while there is invasion, trapping terror and silencing in the relationship, there is also a sense of tenderness and loss from the farmer's perspective. Mew does not merely condemn him and male force. Her poem is more balanced and sensitive than this, placing us inside the thoughts and feelings of the farmer, who longs for what he has never quite caught, and who is essentially alone. Mew enables us to sympathize with the different confusions and sufferings of both halves of this relationship.

Subjectivity in the poems is deeply fissured, the desire to identify and possess the self being set against the desire to avoid being possessed by the male. The self remains splintered, and the poetic persona remains a child: "I shall never grow up," says the speaker in "The Changeling" (*CPP* 14). The child in this poem is like the farmer's bride in that she (it?) too is associated with the animal kingdom: "The word of a bird is a thing to follow" (13). Childhood is insightful, fanciful, and linked to madness. In "Ken," a poem about a village idiot, all the children are described as belonging to him: "all the children and the deer / Whom every day he went to see / Out in the park, belonged to him" (*CPP* 15). The most important thing about Ken is that he has the capacity to use language in a positive way: "Nothing was dead: / He said 'a bird' if he picked up a broken wing" (16). That is to say, he names the whole for the part. His use of language is healing and restorative. "In psychoanalytic terms, taking the whole for the part is a reversal of metonymy, in which, Lacan says, desire is forever doomed to move forward without encountering the object that can satisfy it. Ken's reversal of metonymy recalls desire from its banishment in the signifying chain and therefore holds out the possibility of its fulfilment. So defined, Ken's madness is no longer something to be afraid of, but something to be desired" (Wisker and Day 67).

In writing tenderly but sadly of Ken's

worth and his eventual incarceration, Mew reflects her sense of loss of her brother, confined in an asylum on the Isle of Wight, where he spent his youthful and mature years and later died. She also shows some of her fears of that madness haunting herself. "Ken" characterizes the gentle otherness of the village idiot, who, like the farmer's bride, has an affinity with animals and cannot recognize death. He indicates continuity in all things living:

> Nothing was dead:
> He said "a bird" if he picked up a broken wing,
> A perished leaf or any such thing
> Was just a "rose."
>
> (15)

His naming denies the categorization of ordinary folk. Parts of things run together to suggest a continuous whole for him. He has an internal sadness, but a sense of caring and of natural ownership of all the children and of the deer. The tragedy is that Ken, who clearly disturbs some of the populace, is eventually confined behind the asylum bars, against which his waving arms often fought in his imagination, as he is taken to "that place."

Other poems by Charlotte Mew present a sense of the fairy world and English rustic color far from the cuteness and artifice of Victorian fairies. They are threatening in "The Changeling," which recalls "Goblin Market" by Christina Rossetti (and later the wry fairy tales of Stevie Smith).

"On the Road to the Sea" is at first glance a love poem concerning a chance meeting on a walk and a short-lived acquaintance in life between a man and a woman. A dramatic monologue like "The Farmer's Bride," this poem presents a picture of a man who wishes to woo and to share, conventionally, and to make the woman smile, ostensibly to brighten her days. He talks convincingly of loving her through a history of her youth, imagining her a child, loving the child in her:

> I have brushed your hand and heard
> The child in you: I like that best.
> So small, so dark, so sweet; and were you also
> then too grave and wise?
> Always, I think. Then put your far off little
> hand in mine.
>
> (29)

He talks winningly of seeing her length on sunny lawns, of picturing her set against summer days in fields or on bright roads, saying of her, "I like you best when you were small," (29) talking constantly of touching, brushing, vexing, and scaring in gentle terms. This all seems highly romantic, but the romantic dream is punctured by the other language he consistently uses and the overtones of possession and destruction in his very idolization and desire to enjoy the child in her. He says, amid noting that he wants to know what lies behind her eyes before he dies (traditional courtly convention this), "But first I want your life" and

> I want what world there is behind your eyes,
> I want your life and you will not give it me.
>
> (29)

This exposes his predatory nature, couched deceptively in romantic terms.

Writing about Charlotte Mew, one is immediately reminded of the difficulties the typesetters and printers had with printing her work. While she uses end rhyme and internal rhyme, her line lengths are deliberately irregular, and long lines, longer than alexandrines, must not be split up. The radical or innovative element is the layout, for it undercuts expectations of traditional verse forms, even as her representations of love stories and poems about nature and relationships unsettle expectations and challenge conventions. Here the young man exposes his real intentions: "I would have liked (so vile we are!) to have taught you tears" (29). One who makes women smile, who claims he asks for and frequently gets "the Moon," his phraseology turns vampirish when he says, "But I want your life before mine bleeds away" (29). His mention of cannons and bleeding suggests that he might be on his way to war, but his wild comments about dying "Reeling, —with all the cannons at your ear" (29) are directed at her dying, and he ends:

> Still I will let you keep your life a little while,
> See dear?
> I have made you smile.
>
> (29)

"Madeleine in Church" is a poem that not only caused endless problems with typesetting but also produced a rejection from the devout printers who normally printed poetry for the Monros. It is clearly blasphemous insofar as it is a very secular, very female response to the possibility of finding a way to love Christ. Madeleine is kneeling in church, and her dramatic monologue derives from the sense she has that she is more at home, more understood by plaster saints who did not actually manage many miracles than by Christ. It is in many ways a quite unconventional poem because of the role and attitude of its unconventional speaker. Madeleine is clearly either a prostitute or a woman who has had many lovers as she talks of love and money, paint and sex, comparing herself to the plaster saint, acting a role:

> And anyone can wash the paint
> Off our poor faces, his and mine!
>
> (26)

She mentions the men, younger than her now:

> But oh! These boys! The solemn way
> They take you and the things they say—
> This "I have only as long as you"
> When you remind them you are not precisely twenty-two.
>
> (26)

She acknowledges how lovely she was thought to be, how the beauty of her mother disappeared with age and pain, and how mortals must recognize their limitations. Her sacrilegious comments include such ones as "I think my body was my soul," recognizing that virtue is the smile of a husband's ownership and the trust of a child before it grows away. Her critique of woman's constricted role in the world is precise. She sees a woman as valued only for her looks, destined to be a commodity whether married or ostensibly "free." The married lot is one that is seen as tiring, denying the woman identity and self-expression, while her lot as a "loose woman" leaves her perpetually as the toy of men with less and less time to spend. The roles are artifice; women's lives are essentially very dependent, very limited. Virtuous marriage is no more than a cage:

> Oh! I know virtue, and the peace it brings!
> The temperate well-worn smile
> The one man gives you, when you are evermore his own.
>
> (27)

As she kneels in church contemplating Christ and the saints, she does not desire virtue and salvation. There is no envy of Christ and no movement toward established religion, for Christ had few lasting successes, in her secular eyes. She doubts:

> Then safe, safe are we? In the shelter of His everlasting wings
> I do not envy Him his victories, His arms are full of broken things.
>
> (27)

Madeleine's insight stretches to understanding the sensual and spiritual pleasures Mary Magdalene must have had in perceiving and relating to Christ, and to speculating on their relationship. This woman's insightful speculation is something we can also find in Michele Roberts's novel *The Wild Girl*, which even in the 1980s caused something of a sensation because of its blasphemous suggestions of sexuality and Christ in the same breath, and its understanding of how such a woman as Mary Magdalene could have felt: a mixture of "peace" and "passion" for the woman. As Charlotte Mew's Madeleine comments:

> She did not love You like the rest,
> It was in her own way, but at the worst, the best,
> She gave you something altogether new.
> (27)

And

> Surely You knew when she touched You with her hair,
> Or by the wet cheek lying there,
> And while her perfume clung to You from head to feet all through the day
> That You can change the things for which we care,
> But even You, unless You kill us, not the way.
> (27)

The essential humanity, passion, and sexuality of the woman, of humankind, are stressed. The long line referring to the clinging perfume is heavily sensual amid shorter, more speculative, simpler lines preceding it. Recalling seeing statues of Christ herself, Madeleine speculates about how alive he was to her as a child, and how she wished he would recognize and speak to her. It is a lively, insightful secular poem that moves with Madeleine's thought process, the mixture of emotion and reason as she kneels in church. The colloquial and innovative align themselves with the thought processes of Mary Magdalene herself, an outsider whom Christ preserved. Mew's own outsider status is highlighted here.

The more we read of Charlotte Mew, the less surprising is the high respect she earned from the poets of her day, particularly Hardy. Hardy's second wife, Florence, entertained her regularly and said that Charlotte Mew had true genius. In 1923 she was awarded a civil list pension on the recommendation of a group of the great poets of the day, none of them archmodernists: John Masefield, Thomas Hardy, and Walter de la Mare.

Mew's perception of the way the macabre intermingles with the everyday is very like Hardy's own, and hers is also an art that conceals art, as the simple poems are the most carefully wrought. In "Do Dreams Lie Deeper?" (39) she speculates about the thoughts of the dust of a dead man, hearing his old lover go past, speculating about her fate and that of his children. There is a postromantic sense of continuity in nature after death (also a feature in Hardy's poems) and even a sense of imprinting of the experiences of those who have existed in certain places. So in "Moorland Night" one who had died for love describes the wet moorland grass on which they have died, in detail, with a naturalist/romantic poet's perception, claiming a union with the earth and nature in death:

> My face is against the grass—the moorland grass is wet—
> My eyes are shut against the grass, against my lips there are little blades.
> (50)

At the end of the journey the "Thing" is found and left there with the speaker in a "dying world" in which s/he is at peace: "I am quiet with the earth" (50). The long run-on lines set against short final statements emphasize the mournful quality and the simplicity of the death, yet the continuity of something alive.

There are many poems of death, "Beside the Bed" and "In Nunhead Cemetery" among them, the latter recalling Hardy's "Neutral Tones" as it seems to reflect the end or staleness of a relationship embodied in the cold, wet setting of a country graveyard previously seen only from a train. One, "My Heart Is Lame," contains a fine sense of black humor and irony in describing the couple who have walked together down quiet roads, one with heart racing to keep up with the other who would hardly acknowledge her or him. They are now split, with death, when the walk has literally "Taken all my breath" and the heart, lame from running, is now actually lame, dead. She or he only comments then to the one left that perhaps "There may be something lovelier in Love's face in death / As your heart sees it," as a wry compensation.

Lost loves, deception, cemeteries, death, trickery in love, and a romantic sense of lasting after death all characterize the themes of Charlotte Mew's verse. In "Saturday Market" the gruesome is based on a kind of metaphysical wit. Literally the woman's heart has been buried alive, and those whom she shows it to at market laugh at her suffering, so she is advised to take it home and put it to rest. The naturalistic detail of the "dead-alive ducks with their legs tied down" and the sugar sticks and paraphernalia of a market, rich with rustic folk, makes the concrete metaphor the more appalling:

> See you, the shawl is wet, take out from under
> The red dead thing—. In the white of the moon
> On the flags does it stir again? Well, and no wonder!
> Best make an end of it; bury it soon.
>
> (33)

The girl told to "bury your heart" does so and is told that she will lie with a "hole in your breast" afterwards.

Charlotte Mew's poems that concentrate on nature rather than people are powerful also, notable among which are the companion pieces "The Trees Are Down" and the tiny "Domus Caedat Arborem," both of which mourn the murder of the fine plane trees, cut down at the end of the drive. "The Trees Are Down" is a dramatic and poignant poem, an elegy on the beauty of the trees that should not be cut down for natural, religious, and human sakes and because their death upsets the balance of Nature and ruins the spring like finding a dead rat in the middle of the drive on a beautiful May day.

> It is not for a moment of Spring is unmade today;
> These were great trees, it was in them from root to stem:
> When the men with the "whoops" and "whoas" have carted the whole
> Of the whispering loneliness away
> Half the Spring, for me, will have gone with them.
>
> (48)

In "Domus Caedat Arborem" it is indicated that the whole city "at night has the look of a Spirit brood crime" planning the murder of ten trees. There is an understanding of the power and beauty of living things, a celebration of their otherness, in her work, and a sense that man is one creature among other living things, one more likely to cause pain, sorrow, and destruction than the others. In "I So Liked the Spring" the joy in Spring is unchanged, but last year, with the love affair, Spring was liked through the vehicle of the lover, while now, with a natural simplicity the one who is left says:

> But I'll like the Spring because it is simply Spring
> As the thrushes do.
>
> (42)

Hardy's favorite poem by Mew, "Fin de Fete," combines the winsome qualities of these other poems with a gentle beauty recalling the thieves in children's stories who left sleeping children lying in a wood, protected with leaves by the birds. The speaker, parting with the loved one at her door, regrets that they cannot be like the children in the book, and since they must part (for decorum's and society's sake) at the door, says his farewell in simplicity and regular meter:

> Sweetheart, for such a day
> One mustn't grudge the score.
>
> (40)

The poem breaks down with a sense of regret in the last stanza:

> So you and I should have slept,—but now,
> Oh, what a lonely head!
>
> (40)

In her short stories Mew is frequently exploring forms, finding a voice or voices, and of all those that grasp the contradictory representation of women in the period and express the difficulties for women to speak out against the contradictions and how they might well deeply trouble women, "A White Night" is the best example. There Mew exposes the unpleasant line between women's sexuality and individuality and power, and the threat this poses in the imaginations of many. Her tale implies a critique of imperialism, as well as the treatment of women as objects of desire—causing terror in the one who desires because his fear of his own feelings must be destroyed. In early-twentieth-century horror by Dennis Wheatley and in much contemporary horror in fiction and film we find similar figures. The solution is to demonize and destroy them or to render them straightforwardly as sacrificial victims.

Traveling abroad, Cameron and his friend and female partner come across a dark cave, the place of a strange foreign sacrificial rite. The foreignness is suspect, the rite is suspect, the onlookers pass judgment; but then, the narrator is Cameron, whose own beliefs and prejudices litter the tale. The absence of judgment and of horror at the scene we witness with the threesome is a gap in Cameron's perceptions; he cannot see the tie in it that indicates and supports an objectification and a fetishization of women, and that his own response colludes with this. The silences and expressed wish to stop the ritual, to do something, come from the young woman, who is deeply shocked both at the ritual and the white-clad victim's collusion in it and in the response to the ritual from her male companions, who pretend they act like anthropologists not wishing to disturb a different cultural practice, but are clearly also seen as collusive in its victimization of women. The victim is in white, she is the object of a sacrifice, the moment is of great importance—this culture sacrifices women—and while the representatives of British culture watching might believe in their own superiority, they are nevertheless collusive, just as in H. Rider Haggard's *She* woman must be seen as dangerous, foreign, and to be destroyed: imperialism and sexism rule together. Mew's use of a fallible narrator and of the response and stunned silences of the woman provide critique.

ASSESSMENT

Charlotte Mew is both a short-story writer and, essentially, a very "English" poet, as is Hardy, in that her work avoids the erudite borrowings of the modernists and instead carries on a tradition of British poetry. Such poetry focuses on the countryside, on stories of ordinary people, on a relation between the romantic in terms of continuity, the life spirit of nature, and the older balladic strain that encompasses storytelling, characterization, and a hint of the macabre and the superstitious. Some poems, such as "On the Asylum Road," focus on those confined for madness and cause us to recall that her own brother and sister were in mental homes.

As a woman poet, she explores the individual self and the demands, joys, and deceptions of relationships. Although she is compared to the Georgians, her interests, her long lines, her adaptation of the personal, and her exploration and expression of women's feelings make her an exceptional modernist woman poet, a precursor of those who innovate and speak today. Charlotte Mew's work is an extraordinary omission in syllabuses that have room for both Hardy and Edward Thomas. The only explanation must be her gender, for her strengths are as great as theirs, her relation to a strain of British poetry every bit as constant, and her technical power a rewarding discovery for the student and reader alike.

BIBLIOGRAPHY

Primary Sources

The Farmer's Bride. London: Poetry Bookshop, 1916.

The Rambling Sailor. London: Poetry Bookshop, 1929.
Collected Poems. London: Duckworth, 1953.
Collected Poems and Prose. Ed. V. Warner. London: Virago, 1981.

Secondary Sources

Easthope, A. *Poetry as Discourse*. London and New York: Methuen, 1983.
Fitzgerald, Penelope. *Charlotte Mew and Her Friends*. London: Collins, 1984.
Hanscombe, G.E., and V.L. Smyers. *Writing for Their Lives: The Modernist Women, 1910–1940*. London: Women's Press, 1987.
Kerr, W. "Counting Sheep." In *Georgian Poetry*. Vol. 5. Ed. Edward Marsh. London: Poetry Bookshop, 1920–1922.
Ross, R.H. *The Georgian Revolt: Rise and Fall of a Poetic Ideal, 1910–22*. London: Faber, 1967.
Showalter, Elaine. *A Literature of Their Own: British Women Novelists from Brontë to Lessing*. Princeton: Princeton UP, 1977.
Stead, C.K. *The New Poetic: Yeats to Eliot*. London: Hutchinson, 1975.
Wisker, G., and G. Day. "Recuperating and Revaluing: Edith Sitwell and Charlotte Mew." In *British Poetry, 1900–50: Aspects of Tradition*. Ed. G. Wisker and G. Day. Basingstoke: Macmillan, 1995.

Penelope Mortimer
1918–1999

Jana L. French

As a novelist, Penelope Mortimer is best grouped with names such as Doris Lessing, Margaret Drabble, and Fay Weldon, writers who have made it their project to test women's lived experience against the promises of second-wave feminism. With a career that spanned fifty years—her first novel, *Johanna*, was published in 1947—Mortimer explored in her fiction the dramatic social changes to middle-class British women's lives during the latter half of the twentieth century, from the reliable (if repressive) conservatism of the 1950s and 1960s to the sexual permissiveness of the 1970s and the newly defined public roles for women in the 1980s, which threatened to undermine the clearly demarcated gender roles that a well-bred woman of Mortimer's generation grew up with.

BACKGROUND

"I really don't believe that there is any such thing as fiction," Mortimer once said (qtd. in "Penelope Mortimer" 27). Indeed, a cursory glance at her biography reveals a life far stranger than fiction and rich with details that would eventually make it into her novels.

Mortimer was born Penelope Ruth Fletcher in Rhyl, North Wales, the second child of an atheistic Anglican vicar married to a former missionary. As a child, she barely knew her older brother, who was sent to boarding school upon her birth, when he was four years old. In her Whitbread Prize–winning memoir *About Time: An Aspect of Autobiography* (1979) Mortimer is ironic about her privilege as a young girl. That she always "got her way" seems little recompense for being shuttled from school to school, ignored by a self-indulgent and sexually confused mother, and periodically molested by her sexually frustrated father. Mortimer describes the latter with more pathos than anger. Doubtless the kind of psychological distance she needed to cultivate in order to survive such an upbringing helped to form the sardonic point of view toward marriage and family that is evident in all her novels.

Despite this, Mortimer credits her family with influencing her development as a writer. As a curate, her father was enamored with the literary fringe of 1910 London. His brother Bertie, the family's black sheep, was not only a published novelist, but also a favorite of Mortimer's for encouraging her to freely exercise her imagination on holiday visits to his country house. This creative license—which Mortimer did not experience again until an upper-form teacher urged her to take her writing seriously—helped balance the repression that Mortimer felt at home. There, she claims, "[n]obody, except my father, ever said or wrote what they really felt; it would have been bad taste and, equally horrifying, 'inconsiderate' " (*About Time* 122).

If Arthur Fletcher was less repressed than his wife, he lacked the intellectual discipline to lead a truly unconventional life. The undereducated second son of a well-to-do family who had made their fortune in aniline, Mortimer's father was "tremendously ambitious," she writes, "without the slightest talent for success" (*About Time* 28). After dabbling in Methodism and Unitarianism as well as the doctrines of Nietzsche and H.G. Wells, he retreated to the mainstream Church of England, holding positions in Chilton and Oxfordshire and later, during World War I, in the military. Brief flirtations with theosophy, nudism, and communism left him frustrated and unhappy, as did an obsession with sexual libertinism, and he frequently told Mortimer that marriage was "the coffin of love" (*About Time* 151).

Amy Maggs, Mortimer's mother, was equally unhappy in the marriage. An attractive, independent woman, she "was too conditioned in her role of daughter and sister to strike out on her own [and] assumed that she needed a man to take care of her, although it was the last thing she wanted" (*About Time* 49). Emotionally distant and probably more attracted to women than to men, Mrs. Fletcher nevertheless modeled the emphasis on social form and manners that her daughter would later interrogate in her fiction. She tolerated her husband's affairs and may have indulged in her own (Mortimer blames her mother's close friendship with a woman named Susan for driving her father to nudism). She also shared Arthur Fletcher's spiritual eccentricity, experimenting with mysticism while maintaining her public image as the vicar's wife.

The Fletchers sent their daughter to seven schools. On her father's wishes, Mortimer left the last one—an experimental school for daughters of the clergy—at sixteen to train as a secretary in London. She soon abandoned that career path to pursue journalism and took her first job in the field as a film critic at the *Observer*. After a string of half-serious broken engagements and some early sexual experimentation, Mortimer married her first husband, Charles Dimont, in 1937.

Mortimer is brutally honest about the immaturity of her first marriage and her lack of preparation for motherhood at the age of twenty. In describing it, she reveals the inspiration for the bored housewives that populate many of her novels:

> Parts of me went off with my husband, parts of me waited for him; parts of me made an attempt to mess about in a flat, put flowers in vases; parts of me wrote, and fumed, and read the life of Rimbaud; parts of me behaved quite prettily in Salisbury Close, and parts of me still felt like ringing up Mr. Fox [an associate of her father's and adolescent crush] on an empty afternoon. This is what happened to most women in those days; and does, I believe, still. Whether it is good or bad, should be accepted or remedied, is another question: It happened, it happens, and sometimes leads to a certain lackluster, a paucity of spirit, in married people. (*About Time* 199)

This spiritual dullness, the basis for Mortimer's realism, was not for lack of interesting experiences during her marriage to Dimont. In the years leading up to World War I the couple traveled for his work as a Reuters correspondent to Vienna, Bucharest, and Prague, where Mortimer absorbed some images that would eventually find their way into her fiction.

In Vienna, for example, she observed the outrageous treatment of Jews by SS soldiers and recalls struggling with her own guilt over her relative privilege as an English citizen abroad. The Jewish Holocaust would subsequently appear as a metaphor in more than one of her novels, conflated (if, for most readers, problematically) with women's experience of self-denial and loss under patriarchy. To Mortimer, who felt torn between fulfilling the domestic script and satisfying her own intellectual and creative drive, the comparison was not strained. Indeed, her novels have been praised for honestly portraying the ambivalence that many women feel about their roles as wives and mothers. Her second novel, *A Villa in Summer* (1954), was lauded for depicting "both the ruffled surface of frustrations, worries, and temptations, and also the deep undercurrents of love and interdependence" of married life (qtd. in "Penelope Mortimer" 27).

Mortimer returned to the subjects of marriage and motherhood in most of her novels, continuing to draw her best material from life. Twice married and twice divorced, she had six children by four different men. Her second marriage, to barrister John Mortimer in 1949, was notoriously public. Indeed, the London *Daily Telegraph* recalls that the Mortimers, who frequently appeared in the society pages of that paper during the 1950s and 1960s as jet-setting literati, "seemed to represent the last word in marital chic" (Honan A14). In reality, Mortimer suffered a series of depressions during these glamorous years, and her second marriage eventually dissolved. This is recorded in the sequel to her memoir, *About Time Too: 1940–1978*, which was published in 1993, and is given fictional form in *The Home*, published in 1971.

In the last decades of her life, though she continued writing, Mortimer discovered her greatest creative outlet in gardening. Readers have identified her with Rebecca Broune in *The Handyman* (1983), a character who turns to gardening as therapy in the wake of a divorce, but finds that her publisher understands only that she is nursing a powerful case of writer's block. Mortimer adapted this novel into a teleplay for the BBC and subsequently completed two other television scripts: *A Summer Story*, based on John Galsworthy's "The Apple Tree," and *Portrait of a Marriage*, an adaptation of Nigel Nicolson's 1973 biography of his parents, Harold Nicolson and Vita Sackville-West.

ANALYSIS

The Pumpkin Eater (1962) remains Mortimer's best-known novel, in part because it was successfully adapted as a film by Harold Pinter, starring James Mason and Anne Bancroft. The novel charts the psychiatric confessions of an unnamed protagonist who defines herself through serial childbearing (the number of her children is never specified), while her husband, a successful filmmaker named Jake Armitage, engages in serial affairs. Like all of Mortimer's protagonists, Mrs. Armitage is alienated from the causes of her own suffering and happiness; focused solely on living out the prescriptive roles of wife and mother, she is unable to recognize her desire for self-fulfillment beyond them. Consequently, when Jake returns after shooting a project in Africa, she regrets that domestic pandemonium rather than champagne and flowers greets him: "He laughed, but only for a moment. I heard him thinking, weeping wife, kids, bills, joint, Saturday, nothing's changed. It did not occur to me that these were my thoughts" (114).

It is not marriage and mothering that Mortimer dismisses in her novels, but rather the promised rewards of gender-role fulfillment, particularly those that attend the domestic script. Characters who hew to this script, whether out of duty or romantic longing, are bound for disappointment when they discover the gap between the promise and the reality of their lives. What happens, Mortimer asks, when the fairy tale falls apart? Nearly all her protagonists are women who are or were married; the one exception is Muriel Rowbridge in *My Friend Says It's Bullet-Proof* (1967), a twenty-nine-year-old journalist recovering from a radical mastectomy and coming to terms with her new body as it affects her self-image and sexuality. When, on assignment in Canada, she falls in love with a man who helps her to accept these changes, she realizes that she must choose between marriage and vocation. Seen through the romantic haze of the affair, the two seem mutually exclusive to her; the security of marriage would alleviate the anxiety she feels about her body, and hence, her desire to write about it.

One wonders whether a more pragmatic, less romantic approach to marriage would enable Mortimer's heroines to have the full lives they desire. Yet the problem lies as much in their self-definition as it does in their expectations of that institution. Brigitte Salzmann-Brunner suggests as much when she writes, "[T]here is admittedly something repetitive in Mortimer's novels. All her heroines live according to a traditional conception of woman's role and nature; a conception that invariably collapses in the aftermath of a separation, divorce or the death of a spouse. The emotional terror, the stupefying effects of cultural stereotyping on the individual protagonist is an ever-present element in all her works" (55). Eleanor Strathearn, in *The Home* (1971), discovers this when she separates from her husband Graham after a twenty-five-year marriage. Urged by her adult daughters to begin dating, she takes a lover, a "Gaelic knight . . . exquisitely tired and beautiful, urbane and cruel" (8). In reality, Patrick Kilcannon fails to live up to the chivalric ideal; he does not return phone calls or show up for dates, and eventually Eleanor must own up to her naïveté. Of course, the language of chivalry belongs to romance novels, but Eleanor is willing to trade her loneliness for the slim chance that the fantasy Graham denied her might this time be borne out. A worse fate would be to subscribe to the ideals drummed into her by her mother:

> Mrs. Bennet believed in regular meals, regular bowel motions, what she called "decent" behavior, gentlemen (public schools, the law, the church, the medical profession and the Liberal party), good manners, fair play, John Galsworthy on television, and natural compost. She did not believe in sex, machinery, or the independent, unrelated existence of her daughter. While not exactly believing in God—the prospect was a little ridiculous—she was devoted to death, regarding it as the cure for all evils, by which she meant life. However, she remained indomitably alive.
>
> Eleanor had been brainwashed by this formidable good woman from the moment she had first plucked at her stern nipple and felt, perhaps, her mother's distaste. (13–14)

Mortimer's characters use language to manage the emotional turmoil that follows when they realize the gap between their expectations and the reality of their lived experience. The therapeutic value of talk enables them, quite literally, to make sense out of what has happened as they take the first tentative steps toward accessing their emotional centers. Salzmann-Brunner writes,

> [Mortimer has] an enormous belief in the power of language to uncover needs struggling for expression. . . . [I]n their plight, her heroines use language (be it soliloquy, entries into notebooks, discussion, or appointments with psychiatrists) to record their psychic experience. They do so in an attempt to explain something to themselves and to alleviate their lot. All of these novels have therefore an explicitly subjective structure, their flow of narration is necessarily tied to the consciousness of one female protagonist. (10)

To understand the radical function of talk in these novels, one must also appreciate it as a subversive tool, used to chip away at the dominant narratives that control and order women's lives. When Mortimer's characters speak of their "Virginia Woolf moments," they are asking for a privilege that men take for granted but that looks aberrant in women: the right to isolation and introspection as a route to self-discovery. Although Mortimer's novels are full of social conversations, the private forms of talk—Eleanor Strathearn's revelations to a raincoated stranger, Muriel Rowbridge's journal entries, Mrs. Armitage's confessions on the psychiatrist's couch—prove to be more productive and healing for the protagonists.

If independence from prescribed gender roles is the first step toward self-definition, it does not guarantee happiness. As newly widowed Phyllis Muspratt learns in *The Handy-*

man (1983), the freedom from domestic responsibilities that comes with life beyond marriage and children is meager compensation for loneliness. Mortimer punishes her protagonist for being unable to pick up with her life as a single woman—or, more precisely, she shows that society has no place for an unpartnered woman like Phyllis, who alternatively seeks companionship from a curmudgeonly neighbor and the woman's unstable daughter. With macabre irony, sixty-year-old Phyllis dies in a fall while decking her new cottage for Christmas and the return of her own adult children. This regression to a familiar way of life is not just about reclaiming the past, however; it is also about Phyllis's rejection of the sexual attention paid her by a sinister but attractive younger man—the handyman of the title—who might have fixed the attic stair on which she slipped. In a novel as darkly funny as it is truthful, Mortimer suggests that stripped of the safe, if stifling, rules of gender, a woman of Phyllis's generation literally has nothing to fall back on.

Mortimer does not neatly wrap up her novels. Although she seems clearly to believe that men and women cannot live together without destroying each other, she offers no consolation in the way of female communities or other support systems; her protagonists are left to fend for themselves. On the other hand, she does suggest that women have some imaginative control over their lives and that they play a significant role in replicating or redefining gender—depending on the degree of self-awareness they achieve. If this self-awareness is difficult, it ensures that the next generation of women enjoys a greater sense of freedom and self-mastery than their mothers experienced. This is the legacy of second-wave feminism.

ASSESSMENT

Like that of other female novelists, Mortimer's reputation as a serious writer has suffered because of her popular appeal. Her books are hard to find in academic libraries, and few critical commentaries on them exist. Even in the Chicago Public Library she is shelved under the unwieldy category of "fiction" rather than the more tasteful "British literature of the 1900s," where one can find a number of John Mortimer's novels.

Despite her own lukewarm reception by the academy, Mortimer has contributed a number of articles on other twentieth-century women writers to academic journals. These include pieces on Carson McCullers's novels and Elizabeth Bishop's prose.

Whether Mortimer's name will go down in the canon along with that of her second husband remains to be seen. At this writing, all of her books are out of print in the United States with the exception of *Queen Mother: An Alternative Portrait of Her Life and Times* (1995). This illustrated biography updates and expands on Mortimer's 1986 *Queen Elizabeth: A Life of the Queen Mother*, which was released to great scandal. One publisher is said to have "dropped [the book] in alarm," fearing a backlash in the press over the author's decidedly "unreverential" treatment of the royal matriarch and her early sex life ("Penelope Mortimer" 27).

Though she is currently remembered as a novelist, Mortimer's most interesting—and perhaps time will prove most enduring—work is her two-volume memoir. Captivating, funny, and painfully honest, it provides more than a key to her fiction; it offers a glimpse into the mind of a writer who lived through a century of social upheaval, learning and relearning her roles as a woman, a wife, and a mother and daring to make that the subject of her fiction.

BIBLIOGRAPHY

Primary Sources

Johanna. As Penelope Dimont. London: Secker, 1947.

A Villa in Summer. London: Joseph, 1954; New York: Harcourt, 1954.

The Bright Prison. London: Joseph, 1956; New York: Harcourt, 1957.

With Love and Lizards. With John Mortimer. London: Joseph, 1957.
Daddy's Gone A-Hunting. London: Joseph, 1958. As *Cave of Ice*. New York: Harcourt, 1959.
Saturday Lunch with the Brownings. London: Hutchinson, 1960; New York: McGraw-Hill, 1961.
The Pumpkin Eater. London: Hutchinson, 1962; New York: McGraw-Hill, 1962.
My Friend Says It's Bullet-Proof. London: Hutchinson, 1967; New York: Random House, 1968.
The Home. London: Hutchinson, 1971; New York: Random House, 1971.
Long Distance. London: Allen Lane, 1974.
About Time: An Aspect of Autobiography. London: Lane; Garden City, NY: Doubleday, 1979.
The Handyman. London: Lane, 1983; New York: St. Martin's, 1985.
Queen Elizabeth: A Life of the Queen Mother. London: Viking, 1986.
About Time Too: 1940–1978. London: Weidenfeld, 1993.
Queen Mother: An Alternative Portrait of Her Life and Times. London: Deutsch, 1995.

Secondary Sources

Honan, William. Obituary. *New York Times* 23 October 1999: A14.
"Penelope Mortimer" (obituary). *London Times* 22 October 1999: 27.
Salzmann-Brunner, Brigitte. *Amanuenses to the Present: Protagonists in the Fiction of Penelope Mortimer, Margaret Drabble, and Fay Weldon*. Berne: Peter Lang, 1988.
Stephens, E. Dolores B. "The Novel of Personal Relationships: A Study of Three Contemporary British Women Novelists." Diss. Emory U, 1976.

Iris Murdoch
1919–1999

John Louis DiGaetani

Iris Murdoch remains arguably one of the greatest British novelists since World War II. She depicts a world of artists, professors, intellectuals, and generally upper-class creative types, but she still creates fascinating characters and fascinating situations that have earned her a popular reading public on both sides of the Atlantic. She often uses the form of the thriller, and she knows how to create an exciting plot with unexpected sudden turns of event, but her novels are not just driven by plot but also ask probing questions about the nature of good, the nature of evil, the complexities of the human personality, and the realities of modern existence. Some of her novels have also become successful plays, and she has also written some poetry, but the novel remains her forte. Her life had a very sad ending once she contracted Alzheimer's disease—effectively but painfully and realistically described in her husband John Bayley's *Elegy for Iris*—but for most of her life she was a very successful Oxford professor and writer who entertained and fascinated her readers with her probing of modern life and modern mores.

BACKGROUND

Iris Murdoch was born in Dublin, Ireland, of Anglo-Irish parents, but when she was a child, the family moved to London. She attended schools in England and then went to Oxford to study philosophy; she took her degree there in 1942 and got a job for the Treasury Department. She was in London for much of the blitz, and war experiences sometimes appear in her novels. She worked for the United Nations after the war trying to help displaced persons, and while she was in Belgium, she became very interested in existentialism. She then did graduate work in philosophy at Cambridge and then Oxford, where she became a professor of philosophy. She taught existentialism and ethical philosophy, though she retired as a full-time teacher in 1963 and became a full-time writer. She continued to teach part-time after that, but her main commitment became her writing, and she soon had significant success in that field. In 1956 she married the literary critic John Bayley and remained married to him until her death. Bayley's *Elegy for Iris* (1999) describes her final years when she was struggling with the disabilities caused by Alzheimer's disease, which finally ended her life in 1999. It was tragically ironic that such a brilliant woman would be unable even to dress herself by the end of her long life.

Murdoch's background in philosophy and particularly her interest in French existentialism ensured that philosophical concerns permeated her novels, especially the search for the good philosopher and the search for the nature of good itself. Indeed, the word "good" appears often in her titles—*The Nice and the Good, The Good Apprentice*, and *The Sovereignty of Good* are examples. Increasingly, her search for good seemed to exist in a world without a God and in a suspicion of all religions, though she maintained a continued interest in them as well. In terms of literary influences, in many ways her novels continued the English tradition of the novel of manners, especially the tradition of Jane Austen's works and E.M. Forster's. Like Austen, Murdoch remained centrally concerned with plot and action and often used an omniscient but almost invisible narrator, and like E.M. Forster, she had a sense of wit and humor as well as a concern with the complex nature of her characters, family life, and goodness. Austen's novels often revolve around a few families in an English village, and that is often the case in a Murdoch novel as well, though often her characters also have flats in London. Freud can be listed as an influence on her work as well, though Freudian analysts often appear as buffoons and hypocrites in her novels. But Freud's central concerns with cycles of behavior, the repetition compulsion, the Oedipal complex, bisexuality, homosexuality, and incest recur repeatedly in Murdoch's novels, especially *A Severed Head, The Nice and the Good, The Black Prince*, and *The Good Apprentice*.

ANALYSIS

Murdoch began as an existential philosopher but soon became a novelist instead, but philosophical concerns have often appeared in her novels. The nature of good, the nature of evil, and the nature of the human condition in post–World War II Britain remained constant concerns. In addition to concerns already mentioned, sibling rivalry also recurs in her novels in that brothers and sisters remain often very wary of each other. But these complex psychological and philosophical themes are balanced with a wonderful sense of humor, so that some of her most complex theories are presented wittily and with a light touch, which has undoubtedly added to her popularity. Jane Austen said that she centered her novels around one or two families, and Murdoch often does this as well, but Murdoch, as a writer of the twentieth century, can use the themes of sexuality and complex motivation that Austen could hardly use in Regency England. In addition, Murdoch chronicles an England in which a traditionally homogeneous white society has gradually become as multinational, multiracial, and multicultural as the United States. Often Murdoch's England includes refugees from Eastern Europe, Indians and Pakistanis, blacks, and Chinese. Her Britain reflects the changes in British society since World War II. The complex social and racial forces at work in contemporary Britain often appear in her novels. Her fiction also reflects her fascination with art in the form of allusions to music, other works of literature (especially Shakespeare), and paintings. Her novels present a highly intelligent, highly cultivated view of a complex and often-brutal world. Often her most civilized characters seem the most brutal, and an obsession with power clearly balances an obsession with art.

ASSESSMENT

Iris Murdoch has remained one of the major novelists in Britain since World War II. That she is a woman has attracted many female readers, but she cannot easily be described as a feminist. She is rarely guilty of the misandry of many feminist writers who insist that men are the enemy who are always exploiting women. Some of her women are as evil and selfish as some of her male villains. In her novel *A Severed Head* the main female character, Honor Klein, is as exploitative of other people as her male counterpart Martin Lynch-Gibbon. Clearly, Murdoch does not fit easily into the framework of feminism. She does present women who are fiercely intelligent and lead liberated lives, but she does not have rigid concepts of male and female identities or of what liberation involves. Her genius, however, lives in four areas: comedy, acute characterizations, interesting ideas, and witty plots. In these areas she has been unsurpassed in her greatest novels, which include *A Severed Head, The Nice and the Good, The Black Prince, The Good Apprentice, The Green Knight,* and *The Sea, the Sea.*

Murdoch succeeds more at asking questions than offering solutions. Her moral questioning, especially about the nature of good, is provocative and intelligent. The moral universe of her novels often necessitates living in a world of confusion where questions rather than answers are the norm, but the intelligence of her questioning and the wit of her characters and situations offer provocative entertainment in her novels. Combining both humor and insight, her novels both amuse and enlighten.

BIBLIOGRAPHY

Primary Sources

Sartre, Romantic Rationalist. Cambridge: Bowes & Bowes, 1953; New Haven: Yale UP, 1953.

Under the Net. London: Chatto, 1954; New York: Viking, 1954.

The Flight from the Enchanter. London: Chatto, 1956; New York: Viking, 1956.

The Sandcastle. London: Chatto, 1957; New York: Viking, 1957.

The Bell. London: Chatto, 1958; New York: Viking, 1958.

A Severed Head. London: Chatto, 1961; New York: Viking, 1961.

An Unofficial Rose. London: Chatto, 1962; New York: Viking, 1962.

The Unicorn. London: Chatto, 1963; New York: Viking, 1963.

Women Ask Why: An Intelligent Woman's Guide to Nuclear Disarmament. With Anne Mclaren. London: Campaign for Nuclear Disarmament, 1962.

The Italian Girl. London: Chatto, 1964; New York: Viking, 1964.

A Severed Head: A Play in Three Acts. By Murdoch and J.B. Priestley. London: Chatto, 1964.

The Red and the Green. London: Chatto, 1965; New York: Viking, 1965.

The Time of the Angels. London: Chatto, 1966; New York: Viking, 1966.

The Nice and the Good. London: Chatto, 1968; New York: Viking, 1968.

Bruno's Dream. London: Chatto, 1969; New York: Viking, 1969.

A Fairly Honourable Defeat. London: Chatto, 1970; New York: Viking, 1970.

The Sovereignty of Good. London: Routledge, 1970; New York: Schocken, 1971.

An Accidental Man. London: Chatto, 1971; New York: Viking, 1971.

The Black Prince. London: Chatto, 1973; New York: Viking, 1973.

The Three Arrows and The Servants and the Snow: Plays. London: Chatto, 1973; New York: Viking, 1974.

The Sacred and Profane Love Machine. London: Chatto, 1974; New York: Viking, 1974.

A Word Child. London: Chatto, 1975; New York: Viking, 1975.

Henry and Cato. London: Chatto, 1976; New York: Viking, 1977.

The Fire and the Sun: Why Plato Banished the Artists. Oxford: Clarendon, 1977.

The Sea, the Sea. London: Chatto, 1978; New York: Viking, 1978.

Nuns and Soldiers. London: Chatto, 1980; New York: Viking, 1981.

The Philosopher's Pupil. London: Chatto/Hogarth, 1983; New York: Viking, 1983.

A Year of Birds: Poems. London: Chatto/Hogarth, 1984.

The Good Apprentice. London: Chatto, 1985; New York: Viking, 1986.

Acastos: Two Platonic Dialogues. London: Chatto, 1986; New York: Viking, 1987.

The Book and the Brotherhood. London: Chatto, 1987; New York: Viking, 1988.

The Message to the Planet. London: Chatto, 1989; New York: Viking, 1990.

Metaphysics as a Guide to Morals. London: Chatto, 1992; New York: Allen Lane/Penguin, 1993.

The Green Knight. London: Chatto, 1993; New York: Viking, 1994.

Joanna Joanna: A Play in Two Acts. London: Colophon, 1994.

Jackson's Dilemma. London: Chatto, 1995; New York: Viking, 1996.

The One Alone. London: Colophon, 1995.

Existentialists and Mystics: Writings on Philosophy and Literature. Ed. and with a preface by Peter Conradi; foreword by George Steiner. London: Chatto, 1997.

Secondary Sources

Antonaccio, Maria, and William Schweiker, eds. *Iris Murdoch and the Search for Human Goodness*. Chicago: U of Chicago P, 1996.

Bayley, John. *Elegy for Iris*. New York: St. Martin's, 1999.

———. *Iris: A Memoir of Iris Murdoch*. London: Duckworth, 1998.

Begnal, Kate. *Iris Murdoch: A Reference Guide*. Boston: G.K. Hall, 1987.

Bloom, Harold, ed. *Iris Murdoch*. New York: Chelsea House, 1986.

Bove, Cheryl Browning. *A Character Index and Guide to the Fiction of Iris Murdoch*. New York: Garland, 1986.

———. *Understanding Iris Murdoch*. Columbia: U of South Carolina P, 1993.

Byatt, A.S. *Degrees of Freedom: The Novels of Iris Murdoch*. London: Vintage, 1994.

Civin, Laraine. *Iris Murdoch: A Bibliography*. Johannesburg: U of the Witwatersrand, 1968.

Conradi, Peter. *Iris Murdoch: The Saint and the Artist*. Basingstoke: Macmillan, 1986.

———. *Iris Murdoch: A Life*. London: Harper Collins; New York: Norton, 2001.

Dipple, Elizabeth. *Iris Murdoch: Work for the Spirit*. Chicago: U of Chicago P, 1982; London: Methuen, 1982.

Fletcher, John, and Cheryl Bove. *Iris Murdoch: A Descriptive Primary and Annotated Secondary Bibliography*. New York and London: Garland, 1994.

Gordon, David J. *Iris Murdoch's Fables of Unselfing*. Columbia: U of Missouri P, 1995.

Hague, Angela. *Iris Murdoch's Comic Vision*. Selinsgrove, PA: Susquehanna UP; London: Associated University Presses, 1984.

Heusel, Barbara Stevens. *Patterned Aimlessness: Iris Murdoch's Novels of the 1970s and 1980s*. Athens: U of Georgia P, 1995.

Johnson, Deborah. *Iris Murdoch*. Bloomington: Indiana UP, 1987.

Mettler, Darlene. *Sound and Sense: Musical Allusion and Imagery in the Novels of Iris Murdoch*. New York: Peter Lang, 1991.

Ramathan, Suguna. *Iris Murdoch: Figures of Good*. New York: St. Martin's, 1990.

Spear, Hilda. *Iris Murdoch*. Basingstoke: Macmillan; New York: St. Martin's, 1995.

Stettler-Imfield, Barbara. *The Adolescent in the Novels of Iris Murdoch*. Zurich: Juris-Verlag, 1970.

Todd, Richard. *Iris Murdoch: The Shakespearean Interest*. New York: Barnes & Noble, 1979.

Tucker, Lindsey, ed. *Critical Essays on Iris Murdoch*. New York: G.K. Hall, 1992.

Turner, Jack. *Murdoch vs. Freud: A Freudian Look at an Anti-Freudian*. New York: Peter Lang, 1993.

Grace Nichols
1950–

Suzanne Scafe

Grace Nichols was born and educated in Georgetown, Guyana, but has lived in Britain, where she now works as a freelance writer, since 1977. In 1983 she won the Commonwealth Poetry Prize with her first book of poems, *i is a long memoried woman*. She has published three other volumes of poetry and one novel. Her books for children include two collections of short stories, two books of poems, and anthologies such as *A Caribbean Dozen*. She identifies the Caribbean as the source of her voice as a writer; at the same time, her cultural references are increasingly eclectic. She constructs poetic dialogues with Shakespeare, Whitman, and Edith Sodergran and with Jamaican/British poets James Berry and Jean "Binta" Breeze. Her most recent poems include meditations on objects such as a painting by Paula Rego, on places as far apart as Berlin, Brazil, and Singapore, and on gods of the Aztecs, the Greeks, and the Druids.

BACKGROUND

Nichols's work expresses a diversity of cultural experiences and influences: the experience of Caribbean migration to Britain and the ongoing negotiation of a "black" British identity; the multicultural and multiracial pasts and presents of her place of birth, Guyana, and of the Caribbean in general. All her work foregrounds what she describes as "difference, diversity, and unpredictability": she refuses to constrain and narrowly categorize the cultural and personal identities of her subjects, preferring instead to explore and reveal their contradictions and complexities. In the poem "Of Course *When They Ask for Poems about the 'Realities' of Black Women*" her challenge to the concept of an "essential" racial or gendered identity is made explicit:

> I say I can write
> no poem big enough
> to hold the essence
>
> of a black woman
> or a white woman
> or a green woman
>
> (*Lazy Thoughts* 14–19)

In her first collection of poems, *i is a long memoried woman*, she both celebrates and problematizes the strength of the African slave woman who has survived the trauma of the middle passage. In "Web of Kin" the strength of the African mother figure is represented as a "supreme burden"; the slave woman of the poem says of the silent suffering of her ancestral mothers, "I will have nothing to do with it" (20). She represents her own future in images of nature and fertility that signify, for the children that surround her, hope for the future, grounded in the belief in the regenerative possibilities of nature.

Despite the poems' depiction of the degradation of the middle passage and of slavery itself, the arrival on the slave plantation is represented as a beginning, one that combines the complex pasts of those who arrived there. The opening poem, "One Continent to Another," describes the "long memoried" woman's rebirth after the "death" of the slave ships: "she moved again / knew it was the Black Beginning / though everything said it was the end" (21–24). The subject's eroticism, sensuality, and sexual desire are foregrounded as a means of expressing female agency and of rejecting victimhood and the "silent suffering" of black women. Even where, as in "I Go to Meet Him," the meeting of their abused bodies serves as a reminder of the material reality that dominates their day-to-day experiences, the desire itself is represented as an affirmation of her humanity: "Mornings of dew / and promises . . . I must devote / some time to the / joy of living" (1–2, 7–9).

Despite the single "I" of the title, the subject of this collection of poems is complex and multi-voiced, fragmented across temporal and geographical spaces, inhabiting the cultures and histories of Africa, the Americas, and the islands of the Caribbean. The poems gather together the fragments of lives separated by time, oceans, and human brutality and piece them together without sacrificing their individual beauty and difference. Their expression of the endless creative potential of the middle-passage survivors is reflected most graphically in the contrast between the poem's prologue, which signals the subject's resilience, her feistiness, "dih pout / of mih mouth" (1–2), but ultimately, her silence, and the epilogue, in which the "long memoried woman" gives voice to the future:

> I have crossed an ocean
> I have lost my tongue
> From the root of the old
> one
> A new one has sprung
>
> (1–5)

Nichols discusses her fascination with language in an essay entitled "The Battle with Language," in which she writes: "When writing poetry, it is the challenge of trying to create or chisel out a new language that I like. I like working in both Standard English and Creole. I tend to want to fuse the two tongues because I come from a background where the two worlds, Creole and English were constantly interacting" (284). Her use of language reflects the strong influences of Caribbean poets such as Edward Kaman Brathwaite and Louise Bennett, who were among the first generation of poets to give literary expression to Creole language forms. In her own work, however, Nichols experiments with a wider range of Caribbean Creoles to represent a variety of moods and voices; at times the language is used ironically or unpredictably, as in "Body Reclining," where a single "West Indian" word, "liming," is playfully inserted into an otherwise Standard English form to suggest, as if in passing, the identity of the speaker. The poem "On Receiving a Jamaican Postcard," written entirely in Creole, comments on the humiliation of the "colourful native entertainers" who offer debased versions of historically significant cultural practices "fuh de sake of de tourist industry." The rhythmic, accessible form of the Creole used has a double function: it both contributes to and serves to undermine the picture-postcard idyll, connecting the dancers, the speaker, and the reader in a three-way "conspiracy"; the language encodes ironies that are inaccessible to the tourist audience, the only ones taken in by the "dance-prance."

ANALYSIS

Nichols's poetry exults in the sensuality of language. "My Black Triangle" remaps the African Diaspora on the female body, connecting its lost histories and its centers with the body's erotic zones. Using language more playfully, as in the first five poems of the collection *Lazy Thoughts of a Lazy Woman*, the poems liberate the constraining spaces of domesticity; full of desire for its richness, her subjects revel in the matter that accumulates: "Grease steals in like a lover / over the body of my oven" (1–2). In "Who Was It" Nichols recuperates the natural body: "let the hairline of the bikini / Be fringed with indecency" (7–8). In "Even Tho" she characteristically combines the rich succulence of nature with female sexuality and desire:

> I'm all watermelon
> and starapple and plum
> when you touch me
>
> I'm all seamoss
> and jellyfish
> and tongue
>
> (4–9)

Much of Nichols's work reflects her concern for the political and economic future of the Caribbean; its celebration of difference and diversity has a political as well as an aesthetic function. In the introduction to her latest collection of poems she describes the title poem "Sunris" as representing "a woman's journey towards self-discovery and self-naming through Carnival. . . . In this act of reclaiming herself and the various strands of her heritage, she engages with history and mythology" (5). Rather than focus on the political and cultural divisions that threaten to destroy the region, "Carnival" is used in this poem to signify "a branch of hope" for the future. In the process of dancing, physical boundaries are dissolved, as are the cultural and racial distinctions that keep people apart; through the "hummingbird" flight of the narrator's imagination, the many-colored present is connected to the diverse "strands" of the past.

Nichols's only novel, *Whole of a Morning Sky*, focuses on the political manipulation of racial and cultural difference that threatened to destroy Guyana during the period of the mid-1950s to 1960, when the novel is set. Although events in the novel are narrated from a number of different points of view, the central consciousness of the novel is that of a child, Gem, the youngest daughter of the Walcott family. Using its many voices and perspectives, the narrative balances opposing discourses: the public, usually male, voices of authority that represent traditional institutions such as the church, schools, and the government are set against feminine voices that articulate a disregard for boundaries and divisions and, like Gem's mother, Clara, nurture natural, organic disorder. Gem's father, for example, attempts to inscribe codes of regimentation and order on his female-dominated teaching staff, a "lawless bunch." Classes run into each other, animals wander into the school grounds eating children's "left-left," and the women teachers "divided their attention equally between teaching and cooking pot at home. They saw nothing wrong in putting some sums on the board and slipping home, then slipping back again" (6–7).

Scenes of political strife are interspersed with descriptions of a wedding, of the regular dances held in the yard behind the Walcotts' house, and of the Deepvali festival, attended by Indians and non-Indians alike, to suggest the importance of community and reconciliation. Despite the fires of destruction that rage in its closing pages, the novel ends with characteristic images of growth and renewal. In the Walcotts' back garden everything is blooming: "the gooseberry tree laden with fat gooseberries . . . and the bora tree climbing fresh and green as if it didn't care that the person who had planted it would be leaving" (156).

ASSESSMENT

Much of the critical attention that Nichols's writing has received locates interpretations of her work in feminist criticism that theorizes representations of the woman's body. Both Gabriele Griffin and Denise de Caires Narain focus on her representation of the body as a source of power, as the locus of physical agency. Griffin develops her argument with reference to the work of Julia Kristeva and Hélène Cixous, whose work she describes as a "cerebration" of the female body: "[T]hey invite a formalist stance: animal existence and certain kinds of physical reality are left behind in favour of metalinguistic possibilities" (21). In contrast, Nichols's work, in its focus on the body as a lived experience, represents a more physical reality where corporeal representations are used to affirm "a sense of selfhood, to support others and to subvert the structures that oppress" (28). In a detailed discussion of "The Fat Black Woman" sequence of poems, Mara Scanlon interrogates the poems' rejection of the slim ideal of a feminine body and their celebration of womanly "fat" as "regal" and as disruptive or rebellious. The Fat Black Woman refuses to be controlled or contained; her flesh signifies excess and an abundance of sensuality: "My breasts are huge, exciting / amnions of watermelon / your hands can't cup" ("Invitation," *The Fat Black Woman's Poems* 3–5). As both Griffin and Scanlon observe, however, Nichols's strategy of "situating a reclamation of identity too resolutely in the body" (Scanlon 62) is not without its dangers. It lays the writer open to accusations of biological essentialism and could be read as confirming the body/mind dichotomy that has dominated racist discourses of slavery, empire, and postimperial capitalism. Scanlon suggests, however, that "the fat black woman's manipulation of language" and "her emotional connection to the region" prevent critics from "dismissing the body here as an unthinking materialism or simple organicism" (62). In poems such as "The Fat Black Woman Remembers" the fat black woman is historicized; here she does not merely revisit and rework the Aunt Jemima figure, she questions its very existence, reminding the reader that "her Mama" was only "playing / the Jovial Jemima." Her laughter is "murderous blue," echoing the "treacherous" smile of the "long memoried woman." She refuses identifications that threaten to devour and obliterate her; she "evades . . . men who only see / a spring of children / in her thighs" ("Trap Evasions" 5, 12–14). Not only does her body, "the heritage / of my behind," represent a challenge to negative cultural and anthropological stereotypes, but as Scanlon suggests in her discussion of the last poem of the sequence, it is also used to symbolize creativity and a new beginning.

Nichols's novel *Whole of a Morning Sky* is one of a growing body of texts by women of Caribbean descent, such as Janice Shinebourne, Merle Collins, and Zee Edgell, that rewrite narratives of national and postcolonial identity. Her poetry reflects the diverse cultural currents of late-twentieth-century Britain; she is one of a number of writers whose work challenges traditional notions of Englishness, reworking racial and gendered stereotypes and reflecting its many-layered identities.

BIBLIOGRAPHY

Primary Sources

i is a long memoried woman. London: Karnak House, 1983.

The Fat Black Woman's Poems. London: Virago, 1984.

Whole of a Morning Sky. London: Virago, 1986.

Lazy Thoughts of a Lazy Woman. London: Virago, 1989.

Sunris. London: Virago, 1996.

"The Battle with Language." In *Caribbean Women Writers: Essays from the First International Confer-*

ence. Ed. Selwyn Cudjoe. Wellesley, MA: Calaloux, 1990.

Secondary Sources

Griffin, Gabriele. " 'Writing the Body': Reading Joan Riley, Grace Nichols, and Ntozake Shange." In *Black Women's Writing*. Ed. Gina Wisker. New York: St. Martin's, 1993.

Narain, Denise de Caires. "Body Language in the Work of Four Caribbean Poets." *Wasafiri* 16 (1992): 27–31.

O'Callaghan, Evelyn. *Woman Version: Theoretical Approaches to West Indian Fiction by Women*. London: Macmillan, 1993.

Scanlon, Mara. "The Divine Body in Grace Nichols's *The Fat Black Woman's Poems*." *World Literature Today* 72.1 (Winter 1998): 59–66.

Barbara Pym
1913–1980

Marlene San Miguel Groner

In 1977 Barbara Pym, then a long-neglected author of six novels, was thrust into public prominence when Philip Larkin and Lord David Cecil named her the "most underrated writer of the past 75 years" in a survey taken for the *Times Literary Supplement* ("Reputation Revisited" 67). Although Pym herself doubted that the resultant publicity would do much to revive her marketability with publishers who over the sixteen years prior had repeatedly rejected her efforts as too dated, her work and life soon became the subject of vast public interest and critical scrutiny. A seventh novel was quickly published along with reprints of the other six.

BACKGROUND

Born at Oswestry, Shropshire, to Irene (née Thomas) and solicitor Frederic Crampton Pym, Barbara Pym was educated at an Anglican boarding school, Liverpool College in Huyton, and later attended St. Hilda's College in Oxford, where she earned a degree in English literature in 1934. She was always a writer, however. Among her papers held at the Bodleian Library is an opera she wrote when she was nine years old to perform with her sister, Hilary, and her cousins. Her first novel, *Young Men in Fancy Dress*, influenced by Aldous Huxley's *Crome Yellow*, was written when she was sixteen, and in addition to her diaries, notebooks, letters, and drafts of her completed works, among her papers are many drafts of other incomplete or unrevised works, most of which were ultimately edited, revised, and published after her death by her friend and literary executor, Hazel Holt. During her final year at St. Hilda's Pym began what was to become her first published work, *Some Tame Gazelle*, published in 1950.

Having completed her degree, Pym returned home to write, although she made frequent trips back to Oxford and to the Continent to meet with her university friends. In 1938 she completed *Civil to Strangers*, which was published posthumously, and in addition briefly served as a governess in Poland until worsening political conditions made it necessary for her to return to England to help her family prepare for war. In Oswestry she made blackout curtains, helped with the evacuees, and even worked in the canteen at a local military camp until she had to register for war service in 1941. Although she was queried about a political intelligence job in the country, she ultimately was assigned to the Censorship Office in Bristol, censoring civilian letters to Southern Ireland until she entered the Women's Royal Naval Service (WRNS) in 1943. During the early war years she continued to write, revising existing works and even starting what she called her "spy novel." However, once she was in the service, she found little time to write, although she certainly continued to observe and to gather material that would ultimately be incorporated into her later works.

After World War II and the death of her mother in 1945, Pym moved to London to live with her sister and to work at the International Institute of African Languages and Cultures under Professor Daryll Forde as an assistant and later assistant editor of the journal *Africa*, a position she held until her retirement in 1974. Even though Pym had little interest in Africa or its many languages, she was fascinated by the world of anthropology she encountered at the institute, and anthropologists figure prominently in several of her later novels. By 1949 she completed her final revision of *Some Tame Gazelle* and by 1961 had published five other novels: *Excellent Women* (1952), *Jane and Prudence* (1953), *Less than Angels* (1955), *A Glass of Blessings* (1958), and *No Fond Return of Love* (1961).

ANALYSIS

The most literary of Pym's novels, *Some Tame Gazelle* portrays two spinsters living together, Belinda and Harriet Bode. In ironic contrast to her next novel, *Excellent Women*, it presents, as Diana Benet points out, "an unmarriage plot" (15), and its heroines remind us of Jane Austen characters turned upside down. Instead of young women looking for husbands, Pym presents two middle-aged women who seek "something to love" but who ultimately reject the burdens of marriage for the joys of singleness while maintaining all of their very necessary romantic fantasies: Harriet continues to be entranced by each successive curate, while Belinda sustains her thirty-year illusions of her lost love, Henry Hoccleve. Each, then, is content with her role in life.

Pym's next novel, *Excellent Women*, remains one of her most popular. Its heroine, Mildred Lathbury, a seemingly self-deprecating, almost archetypal, plain but good woman is a contemporary Jane Eyre despite her claims otherwise. She moves through the world seemingly in self-abnegation, limited by her interest in others and in church service, while she is in fact determined to find some role other than lonely spinster to play. Pym's third novel, *Jane and Prudence*, is her most staunchly feminist, providing reoccurring portrayals of the foibles of men, the disappointments of marriage, and the aimlessness of women who find themselves unable or unwilling to make use of their abilities and educations because they are ultimately happy with the roles they have assumed for themselves. Following *Jane and Prudence, Less than Angels* is a diffuse, unfocused work that is filled with unconvincing and unnecessary plot manipulation and detail. Indeed, one of its major characters is killed almost as an aside. Yet, with its focus on lonely people who feel trapped by the limits of their particular societies, this novel again presents characters establishing satisfying roles to play.

Wilmet, in *A Glass of Blessings*, is one of Pym's few married protagonists. Bored, she tries to cast everyone she meets into roles that allow her to see herself as a sensitive, vital woman, only to discover by the novel's end that her conceptions of everyone else are completely mistaken. The novel is, then, a rite-of-passage novel. Its heroine moves from self-centered ignorance and insensitivity to self-awareness, knowledge, and understanding. In contrast, *No Fond Return of Love* presents a protagonist whose ability to transform a vain, silly man into a "rare person" enables her to escape a lonely spinsterhood. Common to all of these six novels, besides gentle humor and irony, are protagonists particularly gifted in imagining and sometimes placing themselves and others in more satisfying roles without substantially changing either their world or their positions in it.

After six novels Pym was dismayed when her publisher, Jonathan Cape, in 1963 rejected *An Unsuitable Attachment* outright, "giving their reason for rejecting it as their fear that with the present cost of book production . . . they doubted whether they could sell enough copies to make a profit" (*A Very Private Eye* 216). Repeated efforts to place the novel elsewhere failed, even with the endorsement of Philip Larkin. Reviewers labeled the work well written but commercially risky. The novel, published posthumously, explores Ianthe Broome's decision to marry a younger, less refined young man than she and the resultant public reaction to that decision. Pym herself was unsatisfied with the work. Writing to Philip Larkin, she noted, "You are quite right about Ianthe and John. Ianthe is very stiff and John had been intended to be much worse—almost the kind of man who would bigamously marry a spinster, older than himself, for the sake of £50 in the P.O. Savings Bank! And some of the other people are too much like those in earlier books" (*A Very Private Eye* 222). Despite being unable to find a new publisher, Pym continued writing, completing *The Sweet Dove Died* (1963–1969) and *Quartet in Autumn* (1973–1977) as well as writing an uncompleted academic novel that was, like *An Unsuitable Attachment*, revised and published posthumously by her literary executor. Second only to *Quartet in Autumn* in critical acclaim, *The Sweet Dove Died*, Pym's personal favorite, is a remarkable study of narcissism, and it is unusual in that it contains little of the humor of Pym's earlier works. All of its major characters parallel each other in their efforts to manipulate reality to ensure admiration and dominance.

As the only living author to be named to the *Times Literary Supplement*'s most-underrated-author list in January 1977, virtually overnight Pym saw her work once again in demand. Macmillan published *Quartet in Autumn*, and in November 1977 it was shortlisted for the Booker Prize. The most unified of Pym's works, it is also the bleakest, presenting the story of how four elderly people cope with retirement and the subsequent loss of the identity employment provides. Inexorably, it demonstrates what happens to ordinary people when they become unable to see life's possibilities. The four central characters not only become isolates but also become isolates unable to imagine more than loneliness and despair and the resultant anger and madness that these generate. *Quartet in Autumn* remains among Pym's most critically acclaimed works, although it is also her most atypical. The following year Macmillan published *The Sweet Dove Died*, and the BBC made a television program about her life and work. Her final work, *A Few Green Leaves*, was finished shortly before her death from cancer on January 8, 1980.

ASSESSMENT

Repeatedly Pym has been labeled an "old-fashioned" novelist, compared to Jane Austen, a comparison Pym herself considered "mildly blasphemous" (*A Very Private Eye* xv). Certainly, many of her novels do concern themselves with life in small towns and the interactions of characters who themselves could be thought of as stock figures from nineteenth-century literature: spinsters, clergymen, curates, unmarried sisters. However, Pym has a deeper fascination with everyday life than most modernists. Her novels, filled with elaborately detailed descriptions of food, clothing, bric-a-brac, garden fêtes, and jumble sales, display a passion for the mundane, the prosaic, and the trivial. At the same time, Pym's characters exhibit one of the modernists' leading attributes: they see themselves as characters in their own lives and actively participate in the shaping and reshaping of the reality they perceive.

For Pym, detail is paramount, and this is why her novels often appear episodic and weakly plotted. Her characters, at first glance seemingly weak and ineffectual, often revel in and are entranced by the mundane details of their lives or of those around them because the stories they are a part of, the lives they actually must lead, are in many ways unfulfilling. The larger picture, the plot, is not as important to them as the immediate, the small around them. Repeatedly her characters engage in an almost obsessive search for the most trivial snippets of information, often setting out like detectives to observe and flesh out background detail for those who have caught their interest. They use their observations as fodder for their imaginations. Since they often see themselves or others as characters in their lives and actively participate in the shaping and reshaping of the reality they perceive, they order and reorder the atomic, the minutiae that surround them to create a different reality, almost a different story, than the one encasing them. Thus Prudence in *Jane and Prudence* out of very little evidence transforms a coworker into a poor-boy orphan who is good to maiden aunts and happily decides that they will have a doomed relationship. There is, of course, no impediment to the relationship but Prudence's imagination. Pym's characters consciously and unconsciously mimic novelists, and thus it is no surprise that most of her major characters either contrast themselves to characters in other works or question whether they should become novelists.

Naomi Schor in *Reading in Detail* notes that "detail does not occupy a conceptual space beyond the laws of sexual difference"; detail and the preoccupation with detail are feminine. Furthermore, if one is to retell a story from the perspective of detail, one "inevitably . . . tell[s] *another* story" (4). What stories, then, do Pym's novels tell? Her plots are usually quite simple and quite the same—a character or characters' ordinary routine is interrupted by the intrusion of the outside world (people or events), and by the end the characters, usually female, have either changed and grown, even if only minimally, or failed to change and stagnated. What strikes us most, following the plots, is that these characters seem to live "like mice in the wainscoting of life, never invited to the table, contenting themselves with crumbs" (Duchêne 96). But if the detail tells another story, and as important as detail is to Pym, it must, then we must find the other story and interpret it as a distinctly feminine story.

The details of Pym's novels reoccur from work to work. We are given repeated information about her women's detachment and withdrawal into silence or digression and their awareness of literature and of food, to name just a few items. Looked at as details, they show us women who are creating or trying to create a different reality than the one they are in, one that they control by the imaginative manipulation or organization of that which surrounds them. Imagination is, as Patricia Mayer Spacks explains, "a slippery term, designating power that penetrates the inner meaning of reality but also a power that creates substitutes for reality" (4). For Pym's protagonists, it is more: It is a form of subversion, salvation, and, when misused, isolation or self-destruction. It enables them to conceal their motivations and escape from empty reality, as well as revise the stories of their lives. It gives them the ability to create and re-create themselves as characters in what Elaine Showalter calls a "double-voiced discourse, containing a 'dominant' and 'muted' story" (266).

In short, Pym's women ignore the larger picture because they cannot control it, but they can control, and thus have power over, the small. On one level they are making do with what is around them, while on another level they are triumphing over their limitations. For them, power is not measured by the dynamics of plot or even of theme but by detail observed and ordered by their active imaginations.

BIBLIOGRAPHY

Primary Sources

Some Tame Gazelle. London: Cape, 1950; New York: Dutton, 1983.

Excellent Women. London: Cape, 1952; New York: Dutton, 1978.

Jane and Prudence. London: Cape, 1953; New York: Dutton, 1981.

Less than Angels. London: Cape, 1955; New York: Dutton, 1980.
A Glass of Blessings. London: Cape, 1958; New York: Dutton, 1980.
No Fond Return of Love. London: Cape, 1961; New York: Dutton, 1982.
Quartet in Autumn. London: Macmillan, 1977; New York: Dutton, 1978.
The Sweet Dove Died. London: Macmillan, 1978; New York: Dutton, 1979.
A Few Green Leaves. London: Macmillan, 1980; New York: Dutton, 1980.
An Unsuitable Attachment. London: Macmillan, 1982; New York: Dutton, 1982.
A Very Private Eye: An Autobiography in Diaries and Letters. Ed. Hazel Holt and Hilary Walton. London: Macmillan, 1984; New York: Dutton, 1984.
Crampton Hodnet. London: Macmillan, 1985; New York: Dutton, 1985.
An Academic Question. London: Macmillan, 1986; New York: Dutton, 1986.
Civil to Strangers and Other Writings. London: Macmillan, 1987; New York: Dutton, 1988.

Secondary Sources

Benet, Diana. *Something to Love*. Columbia: U of Missouri P, 1986.
Brothers, Barbara. "Women Victimised by Fiction: Living and Loving in the Novels by Barbara Pym." In *Twentieth Century Women Novelists*. Ed. Thomas F. Staley. New York: Barnes & Noble, 1982. 61–80.
Burkhart, Charles. *The Pleasure of Miss Pym*. Austin: U of Texas P, 1987.
Duchêne, Anne. "Brave Are the Lonely." *TLS* 30 September 1977: 96.
Glendinning, Victoria. "The Best of High Comedy: *Excellent Women* and *Quartet in Autumn*." *New Times* 24 December 1978: C8.
Holt, Hazel. *A Lot to Ask*. London: Abacus, 1990.
Larkin, Philip. "The World of Barbara Pym." *TLS* 11 March 1977: 260–264.
"Reputations Revisited." *TLS* 21 January 1977: 66–67.
Rossen, Janice. *The World of Barbara Pym*. New York: St. Martin's, 1987.
Salwak, Dale, ed. *The Life and Work of Barbara Pym*. Iowa City: U of Iowa P, 1987.
Schor, Naomi. *Reading in Detail*. New York: Methuen, 1987.
Showalter, Elaine. "Feminist Criticism in the Wilderness." In *The New Feminist Criticism: Essays on Women, Literature, Theory*. Ed. Elaine Showalter. New York: Pantheon, 1985. 243–270.
Spacks, Patricia Meyer. *The Female Imagination*. New York: Avon, 1976.

Jean Rhys
1890–1979

Joy Castro

Though the early work of Jean Rhys was embraced by only a discriminating few when it was published in the 1920s and 1930s, her insights seem particularly germane to us now, for they occupy a nexus of concerns—modernism, postmodernism, feminism, and postcolonialism—that pervade the inquiry of scholars and critics at the beginning of the twenty-first century. Because of her complicated and layered interrogations of class, race, colonialism, and gender, Rhys has been a difficult writer for many critics to evaluate. Her own subject position was multiply indeterminate and multiply conflicted, and her literary observations grew from her contested location in the world. Rhys's graceful, melancholy fiction, with its complex explorations of identity, structural innovations, and stylistic experiments, was so far ahead of its time that many of her accomplishments were initially ignored by the mainstream literary establishment. Only in 1966, with the publication of her masterpiece *Wide Sargasso Sea*, did she begin to receive—at the age of seventy-six—the literary acclaim that was her due. The novel, which famously retells Charlotte Brontë's *Jane Eyre* to uncover the linked discourses of imperialism and patriarchal power at its center, was wildly successful with readers and critics alike and has since prompted a serious reevaluation of her earlier corpus.

BACKGROUND

While Rhys is often considered a British writer, her Caribbean upbringing and her early adulthood in major European cities are key factors in understanding the semiautobiographical protagonists who populate her work. Ella Gwendoline Rees Williams was born in 1890 in Roseau, Dominica, to a Creole mother and a doctor father who had immigrated from Wales in 1881. Rhys's mother's family had lived in Dominica since 1824, when a Scottish forefather arrived and settled on a large working plantation ten years prior to the emancipation of slaves. In 1844 freed blacks burned down the mansion, and it was replaced with a smaller, less grand version, where Rhys lived as a child and which also later burned.

Rhys's family had black servants, whom Rhys admired for what seemed to her their more direct, sensual way of life, though she also feared the African-Caribbean practice of obeah—witchcraft—and the open hostility toward whites. This ambivalence and anxiety about race would permeate much of her fiction. In her semiautobiographical novel *Voyage in the Dark*, for example, the white West

Indian protagonist reflects, "I wanted to be black, I always wanted to be black. . . . Being black is warm and gay, being white is cold and sad" (31). In *Wide Sargasso Sea* the white West Indian girl Antoinette is wounded when her best friend, a young African-Caribbean girl, hurls a rock at her face during the political unrest of Emancipation.

Rhys's early sexual experiences were difficult. As a young adolescent, she was molested by a retired military officer, a respected friend of the family. Though the connection was severed by her family when suspicions were roused, the trauma of that early experience would inform her late story "Good-bye Marcus, Good-bye Rose." Rhys's first consensual sexual experience occurred a few years later, during an adolescent romance with a young man of mixed race. The families briskly separated the two, and Rhys was sent to England the following year at the age of seventeen.

The transition to the strict British social structure and the cold, dreary climate was traumatic for her; she never felt at home in England. She first attended the Pearse School for Girls, Cambridge, and then the Academy of Dramatic Art, but was left without an income when her father died in 1910. Alone in a strange country, incompletely educated, and with no money of her own, Rhys used her beauty and slender figure to support herself as a chorus girl, a profession then considered akin to prostitution. Indeed, after the end of a love affair left her emotionally devastated, she became a demimondaine. In 1913 a late-term abortion nearly resulted in her death. After this trauma she began compulsively to write, but she showed her work to no one.

Rhys worked as a model during the years of World War I. In 1919 she met and married Dutch writer, journalist, and spy Jean Lenglet, and together—propelled by Lenglet's suspect financial dealings, of which Rhys was unaware—they lived in the great cities of Europe: Vienna, Budapest, Paris. In 1919 a son was born to them, but he died in infancy; a daughter, Maryvonne, was born in 1922, but Rhys, who never recovered from her son's death, was unable to form a bond with the little girl. As the Lenglets' life became increasingly precarious—Lenglet was arrested and deported for theft in 1925—Maryvonne fell under the care of the state.

In 1924 Rhys met Ford Madox Ford in Paris, and this led to her brief immersion in the whirlwind that was the Lost Generation. Amazed by her writing talent, Ford appointed himself her literary mentor. He suggested that she use a pseudonym, and so Ella Lenglet chose the masculine Jean Rhys, a combination of her husband's first name and a variant of her father's name Rees. Ford published her fiction in his avant-garde journal the *Transatlantic Review* and introduced her to the expatriate literary community—Hemingway, Stein, Joyce. Ford, then in his fifties, also pressed Rhys into an affair; with Lenglet's 1925 arrest, Rhys was alone in Paris without money, family, or social position, and she acceded to the affair, which transpired with the knowledge of Ford's common-law wife Stella Bowen. Rhys's relationship with Ford, which ended badly, would form the basis for her first novel, *Postures* (1928). Following their hostile break, Rhys dropped out of the Paris literary scene completely.

She met Leslie Tilden Smith, a British literary agent and World War I pilot, in London in 1927, and they began a relationship that would last nearly two decades. Oxford educated and gentle, Tilden Smith nurtured Rhys and encouraged her literary talent. They married in 1934 after her divorce. During their relationship Rhys published three novels in addition to *Quartet: After Leaving Mr. Mackenzie* (1931), *Voyage in the Dark* (1934), and *Good Morning, Midnight* (1939). In spite of financial difficulties and Rhys's developing alcoholism, the marriage lasted until Tilden Smith's death in 1945.

Two years later Rhys married Tilden Smith's cousin, Max Hamer, a solicitor who shared Rhys's problems with alcohol; he also had his own difficulties with legally suspect activities. Made increasingly paranoid by poverty and alcoholism, Rhys took to quarreling violently with her neighbors. Arrested and incarcerated for psychiatric evaluation in 1949, Rhys was released on probation but continued her destructive pattern of heavy drinking and assault. When Hamer was arrested for larceny in 1950, Rhys sold all their belongings to make his bail, and while he spent the next two years in prison, Rhys, impoverished and alone in her sixties, moved from one rented room to another.

Rhys's career took an abrupt turn for the better in 1956, when the British Broadcasting Corporation aired a radio production of *Good Morning, Midnight* organized by actress Selma Vaz Dias. The public interest in Rhys's life and work rekindled her desire to write, and she began to work in earnest on her long-considered project, a subversive reimagination of *Jane Eyre*. Published in 1966, *Wide Sargasso Sea* made Rhys an overnight literary celebrity. She lived to see the recuperation of her work, publish two additional collections of short fiction, and enjoy her final years free from the poverty that had plagued her throughout her life. Jean Rhys died in 1979.

ANALYSIS

Rhys's first book, *The Left Bank and Other Stories* (1927), was published with the help of Ford Madox Ford and includes his lengthy, self-congratulatory introduction. Ford notes two of the qualities that characterize much of the critical appreciation of Rhys's work: her depiction of life on the margins from the subject position of the marginalized, her "terrific—an almost lurid!—passion for stating the case of the underdog," in Ford's phrase; and what he early recognized as Rhys's "singular instinct for form" (24), an assessment with which Rhys herself concurs in her autobiography: "[A] novel has to have a shape," she comments, "and life doesn't have any" (*Smile Please* 10). Now reprinted in *The Collected Short Stories* (1987), the *Left Bank* stories ring with a wit and an economy that resemble Colette's, blending formal influences drawn from Rhys's self-directed reading of Maupassant, Flaubert, and other continental writers with a focus on traditionally feminine subjects such as women's clothing and appearance. This first book offers sketches of life on the bohemian fringes of European society, frequently focusing on female characters who suffer a variety of troubles caused by the men in their lives. In this, the stories would form the pattern for the novels that followed.

Rhys published four novels before the outbreak of World War II. The first, *Quartet* (originally published as *Postures* in 1928), fictionalizes Rhys's relationship with Ford. The most traditionally structured of her novels, *Quartet* follows the decline and fall of Marya Zelli, a young and lovely British orphan who supports herself as a chorus girl before marriage. When her husband is imprisoned for the purveyance of stolen goods, she turns to a British couple sojourning in Paris for support. They take her in, and she becomes involved in an exploitative affair with the man, Heidler. When she confesses the affair to her husband upon his release from prison, he attacks her, leaving her for dead in a borrowed apartment. *Quartet* explores the unexamined class privilege of the bourgeois Heidlers and their easy commodification of Marya while limning her vulnerability as a woman alone in a predatory environment without money, family, or class position.

Rhys's second novel, *After Leaving Mr. Mackenzie* (1931), examines a similar decline. The protagonist, Julia Martin, is a fragile dreamer, a thirty-six-year-old kept woman in Paris who sees her beauty rapidly fading. Dropped by Mr. Mackenzie, the lover who has been supporting her, she gallantly repudiates him in a restaurant. Returning to her mother's deathbed in England, she again confronts rejection, this time by the members of her struggling lower-class family who, while condemning her lax morality, are themselves complicitous in her choices, for they have refused to help her financially. While attending her mother, she becomes involved with a kind and gentle man (patterned on Tilden Smith) who admires her, but she destroys the relationship with her paranoia after her mother dies. Without familial or romantic love, she returns to Paris a broken woman. In this novel Rhys examines the complex of male money and power that prevents Julia from supporting herself independently, as well as the self-destructive character traits that keep her from forming constructive relationships.

Rhys's third novel, *Voyage in the Dark*, is based upon the painful early manuscript about her affair and abortion that she wrote upon her recovery and carried in a suitcase for two decades before its revision for publication in 1934. Anna Morgan, the white West Indian narrator, supports herself as a chorus girl with a traveling company in England. Eighteen years old and innocent when the novel begins, she is nonetheless viewed as a woman of easy virtue by the men who pursue her, and—again, alone and without means—she eventually assents to a relationship. When it ends, leaving her emotionally devastated, she slides gradually into the life of a kept woman and finally prostitutes herself openly, declining into self-destructive anger and alcohol abuse. When she finds herself pregnant, she begs her first lover for money for an illegal abortion. Hemorrhaging in her rented room, Anna flashes back to her West Indian girlhood and yearns for oblivion; the novel's harrowing finale originally closed with her death. Rhys was pressed by her publisher, however, to change the conclusion to one less dismal, and the novel ends instead with the cynical pronouncement of the doctor who attends Anna that she will be "[r]eady to start all over again in no time" (187). (Rhys's original ending has since been published in *The Gender of Modernism* [1990].) With this novel Rhys continues to examine issues of class and gender while beginning an exploration into postcolonial concerns. Exploring Anna's doubled marginality, Rhys depicts such alienation as profoundly problematic. Using language that connects Anna's sexual commodification by the bourgeois white men of England with the slave records of her family in the islands, Rhys offers a complex portrayal of race, class, and gender concerns.

Good Morning, Midnight, set in 1937 and published in 1939, also depicts the fall of a woman, from the first-person point of view. Exploring, like *After Leaving Mr. Mackenzie*, the plight of an older woman facing the decline of her looks, *Good Morning, Midnight* slides back and forth between the present—the terrifying descent toward fascism and war—and the protagonist Sasha Jensen's painful, unstable past. Though it focuses on a single individual, *Good Morning, Midnight* also anticipates and critiques European fascism; critic Helen Carr predicts that it will eventually be seen as "one of the great anti-fascist novels of the thirties" (20). Sasha is one of the outcasts, unable to function in a society that requires complete conformity, a hard, attractive surface that, for Rhys, thinly masks the inhumanity below. After a brief respite of hopefulness in Paris the much-rejected narrator allows into her bed her hostile neighbor, who is depicted throughout the novel as a figure of death. Haunted and terrified by hallucinations of a fascist future, Sasha resigns herself to obliteration.

Wide Sargasso Sea, Rhys's most famous work, functions as a prequel to *Jane Eyre* and is narrated by Rochester's first wife—depicted as a sane, sensual woman driven mad by Rochester's attempts to suppress and rename her—and by Rochester himself, who, despite his destructive actions, is rendered sympathetically. Threatened to his Cartesian core by the open warmth of the island culture and his uninhibited young wife, Rochester responds the only way he can: by controlling everything that endangers his carefully constructed rational ego. The motif of the burning manor unites the action of *Wide Sargasso Sea*, in which the protagonist Antoinette's destruction of Rochester's British mansion mirrors the burning of her childhood home by hostile freed slaves. Race relations are central to the text: while Rochester is terrified by an insinuation that Antoinette's racial purity may have been compromised, he nonetheless helps himself to sex with a black household servant. With its multiple narrators, elegant tripartite structure, and layered interrogation of imperialism and patriarchy, *Wide Sargasso Sea* was immediately recognized as a masterpiece.

ASSESSMENT

Postcolonial theory and postmodernism, as well as the proliferation of a variety of feminist theories, have greatly aided our understanding of Rhys's work and contributed to her now-solid reputation, though her fiction initially met with considerable resistance. Interested in liberating sexuality and creativity from repressive Victorian constraints and in criticizing what they saw as a spiritually deadened society, modernist writers such as Rhys, Joyce, Lawrence, and Faulkner were all variously dismissed as sordid, overly sexual, and gratuitously violent by mainstream critics in their own time. Moreover, modernist experimentation was initially viewed by the reading public as willfully bizarre, rather than as a serious interrogation of the possibilities of language. While the New Critics did a great deal in later decades to vindicate the experimentation of some modernists, the reputations of many modernist women, such as Virginia Woolf and H.D. (Hilda Doolittle), had to await the birth of feminist scholarship in the 1970s and afterward to enjoy their own renaissance.

Since the critical methodology of many early feminist readings focused primarily on analyses of female characters, Rhys's passive, self-destructive heroines were rejected as constituting negative role models, with the result that Rhys herself was initially rejected as an antifeminist writer. More recent feminist critics, however, have noted the sophisticated, subtle brand of gender analysis that emerges in Rhys's exposure and examination of legal and political systems, constrained educational and professional opportunities, and structures of inherited wealth that have historically privileged men and disenfranchised women. Complicating her critique of gender politics with an analysis of race, class, and colonial inequalities, Rhys follows her generous, intelligent women through the labyrinth formed by such structures, amply demonstrating the tremendous waste of human potential they cause. Rather than dismissing Rhys because of her characters, feminist critics now perceive her work as taking an entire culture to task. Critic Molly Hite, for example, argues that by centering her texts on the subjectivities of characters usually objectified and silenced in canonical works—the chorus girl, the mannequin, the demimondaine—Rhys restructures narrative itself.

Rhys's reputation has benefited from such recuperation, not only by feminists but by postmodern and postcolonial theorists as well. For the recognition of Rhys as a major twentieth-century author, the timing of *Wide Sargasso Sea*'s 1966 publication could not have been more ideal. Postmodernists concerned with indeterminacy, multiplicity, and intertextuality were quick to embrace the experimental shifts of Rhys's narratives, and postcolonial theorists and writers, just beginning to gain a voice in and out of the academy, eagerly welcomed Rhys's critique of imperialist assumptions and complicated exploration of doubled marginality.

Wide Sargasso Sea restored Rhys to critical view and led to the reprinting of all her previous work. Her final two books of short stories, *Tigers Are Better-Looking* and *Sleep It Off, Lady*, were published in 1968 and 1976, and the *New York Times Book Review* called her "The Best Living English Novelist" in 1974 (Alvarez 6). She was made a fellow of the Royal Society of Literature and honored with the W.H. Smith Award. In 1978, the year before she died, she was awarded commander, Order of the British Empire, for her contributions to literature.

In 1979 a short, unfinished autobiography, *Smile Please*, was published posthumously, and her selected letters appeared in 1984. Two of Rhys's novels have been produced as films: in 1981 *Quartet* was adapted for the screen by James Ivory and Ruth Prawer Jhabvala, and a cinematic version of *Wide Sargasso Sea* appeared in 1993. All of Rhys's work is currently in print, and critical interest continues to grow.

BIBLIOGRAPHY

Primary Sources

The Left Bank and Other Stories. London: Cape; New York: Harper, 1927.

Postures. London: Chatto, 1928. As *Quartet*. New York: Simon & Schuster, 1929.

After Leaving Mr. Mackenzie. London: Cape; New York: Knopf, 1931.

Voyage in the Dark. London: Constable, 1934; New York: Morrow, 1935.

Good Morning, Midnight. Harper, 1939.

Wide Sargasso Sea. London: Deutsch, 1966; New York: Norton, 1967.

Tigers Are Better-Looking. London: Deutsch, 1968; New York: Harper, 1974.

Sleep It Off, Lady. London: Deutsch; New York: Harper, 1976.

Smile Please: An Unfinished Autobiography. London: Deutsch, 1979; New York: Harper, 1979.

Letters, 1931–1966. Ed. Francis Wyndham and Diana Melly. London: Deutsch, 1984.

The Collected Short Stories. New York: Norton, 1987.

"Voyage in the Dark: Part IV (Original Version)." In *The Gender of Modernism*. Ed. Bonnie Kime Scott. Bloomington: Indiana UP, 1990. 381–389.

Secondary Sources

Alvarez, Alfred. "The Best Living English Novelist." *New York Times Book Review* 17 March 1974: 6–7.

Angier, Carole. *Jean Rhys*. London: Deutsch, 1990.

Carr, Helen. *Jean Rhys*. Plymouth: Northcote House, 1996.

Emery, Mary Lou. *Jean Rhys at "World's End": Novels of Colonial and Sexual Exile*. Austin: U of Texas P, 1990.

Hite, Molly. *The Other Side of the Story: Structures and Strategies of Contemporary Feminist Narrative*. Ithaca: Cornell UP, 1989.

Howells, Coral Ann. *Jean Rhys*. London: Harvester Wheatsheaf, 1991.

Naipaul, V.S. "Without a Dog's Chance." In *Critical Perspectives on Jean Rhys*. Ed. Pierrette Frickey. Washington, DC: Three Continents, 1990. 54–58.

O'Connor, Teresa. *Jean Rhys: The West Indian Novels*. New York: New York UP, 1986.

Sternlicht, Sanford. *Jean Rhys*. New York: Twayne, 1997.

Dorothy Richardson
1873–1957

Laura Frost

Most contemporary readers consider Virginia Woolf and James Joyce to be the most important early contributors to experimental modern British literature. However, a look at literary journals and reviews in the crucial years around 1914 to 1922 reveals the presence of another, equally important figure: Dorothy Richardson. Richardson's major work is a thirteen-volume, two-thousand-page novel, *Pilgrimage* (published between 1915 and 1938, with the last volume published posthumously in 1967), which chronicles the life of one woman, Miriam Henderson, from 1893 to 1912. When the first volume of *Pilgrimage* appeared, Richardson was hailed as one of the creators of what is known as "high modernist" style: fragmented syntax, stream of consciousness, multiple narrative viewpoints, nonlinearity, and unconventional plot development. Richardson's method is sometimes called "feminine impressionism," and *Pilgrimage* has been termed "an imagist novel." Richardson undertook all of these effects very determinedly in response to what she felt to be the limitations of conventional realist writing. In a 1940 letter, for example, Richardson remarked, "Plot, nowadays, save the cosmic plot, is inexcusable. Lollipops for children" (*Journey* 139). In addition to revolutionizing narrative and the novel genre, Richardson also broke new ground on the level of the sentence. In 1923 Virginia Woolf wrote that Richardson had "invented, or if she has not invented, developed and applied to her own uses, a sentence which we might call the psychological sentence of the feminine gender. It is of more elastic fibre than the old, capable of stretching to the extreme, of suspending the frailest particles, of enveloping the vaguest shapes." For Woolf, this was "a woman's sentence, but only in the sense that it is used to describe a woman's mind by a writer who is neither proud nor afraid of anything she may discover in the psychology of her sex" (229).

In the first part of the twentieth century Richardson was often mentioned as a literary pioneer alongside Proust, Woolf, Joyce, and Stein, yet by the time Richardson died in 1957, her name had become obscure (her death was unmarked by a ceremony). While her work is well known among literary scholars today, her writing remains largely unread outside academia: indeed, her most important work, *Pilgrimage*, is out of print in America. The reasons for Richardson's fading popularity are related to the very factors that made her work innovative and explosive when it first appeared: it is suggestive, allusive, demanding, and uncompromising in its quest to chart the minute vicissitudes of one woman's consciousness over many years.

BACKGROUND

Pilgrimage is a loosely autobiographical novel, in the sense that Proust's and Joyce's novels might also be called autobiographical. (Interestingly, although critics now read the outlines of Richardson's life in *Pilgrimage*, her contemporary readers, for the most part, did not see the novel as an autobiography.) The main events in Richardson's novels basically correspond to her own life, and many characters are based on Richardson's acquaintances. Like Miriam Henderson, Richardson grew up in a comfortable upper-middle-class home in a London suburb. At the age of seventeen she took a job as an instructor at a German school for a number of months—a daring endeavor for the time. The most formative arc of Richardson's also appears as Miriam's: in 1895 Richardson's family was destroyed when her father, an idealistic intellectual dreamer, went bankrupt, and her mother committed suicide. Suddenly Richardson was on her own, and she moved to London (into a boardinghouse in Bloomsbury) and took a job as a secretary for a dentist's office. The ensuing challenges of independence as a young woman alone in the city—a city alive with anarchists, socialists, and suffragettes—defined Richardson's life and craft.

In 1896 Richardson met H.G. Wells, whose novel *The Time Machine* had recently appeared to great acclaim. Wells, a formidable and intellectually stubborn man, introduced Richardson to important social, political, and artistic circles, including the Fabian Socialists. Wells was the inspiration for the character Hypo in *Pilgrimage*, who coaxes Miriam into an uninspiring affair (like Wells, Hypo is an advocate of free love) and, more significantly, encourages her to write. Richardson's letters and Gloria Fromm's biography give the impression that Richardson kept herself distant from people—even those with whom she had her primary relationships. She led her closest woman friend (and possible erotic interest) to marry a man with whom Richardson herself had been involved. In 1917 Richardson married Alan Odle, a flamboyant artist whose work was compared to that of Beardsley, when he was tubercular, and Richardson thought that he did not have more than six months to live. He survived well beyond this, and the couple lived in Cornwall and London as Richardson continued to add to *Pilgrimage*. The last chapters of Richardson's biography are very sad, as she died in poverty in a nursing home in 1957, with her work largely forgotten.

More interesting than the dramas of Richardson's personal life was her development as a writer. In the absence of any clear model, how did she arrive at her groundbreaking techniques? Her early publications include an eclectic range of essays on literature, socialism, and health issues for journals ranging from the anarchist journal *Ye Crank* to more prestigious magazines such as *Saturday Review* and the *Freewoman*. She had a long-running column in an unlikely forum, the *Dental Record*, and later contributed short stories to various literary magazines and essays to *Vanity Fair* and wrote a regular column for one of the earliest film journals, *Close Up*. (Many of Richardson's essays are collected in Bonnie Kime Scott's *Gender of Modernism*, and her short stories have been reprinted in *Journey to Paradise*.) In 1914 Richardson published her first book, a study of Quakers. Around that time she ensconced herself in a friend's Cornwall cottage to begin a novel that would become the first volume of *Pilgrimage*.

In her foreword to the 1938 edition of *Pilgrimage* Richardson wrote that she was attempting "a feminine equivalent of the current masculine realism," by which she meant the novels of Wells, Arnold Bennett, and Balzac, for example. Richardson thought that these writers' representations of reality were limited by their conventional narrative designs. One literary influence Richardson acknowledged was Henry James, whose novels explored complex points of view and renderings of consciousness. Richardson had a great deal of time to plan her literary contribution: her first novel was published relatively late in her life, when she was forty-two. Most remarkably, Richardson already envisioned her debut novel as a mere beginning in the vast epic *Pilgrimage*.

ANALYSIS

"Miriam left the gaslit hall and went slowly upstairs. The March twilight lay upon the landings, but the staircase was almost dark. The top landing was quite dark and silent. There was no one about. It would be quiet in her room." The first sentences of *Pointed Roofs* introduce the primary features of *Pilgrimage*: an intense, richly atmospheric focus on the movement and experiences—physical and psychological—of one woman. The concentrated description of the play of light in space is characteristic of Richardson's intimate and evocative method of narration. Miriam Henderson is seventeen years old when she is first introduced; *Pointed Roofs* covers the period from Thursday, March 2, 1893, to July 1893 (for a careful account of the chronology in *Pilgrimage*, see Thomson's *A Reader's Guide*). *Pilgrimage* is a female bildungsroman (novel of development) and, more precisely, a *Künstlerroman* (novel about an artist's development). However, Miriam betrays no optimism about her life's trajectory in the opening pages of the novel. At the ripe old age of seventeen she thinks, "There was nothing to look forward to now but governessing and old age" (4).

The opening sentence of *Pointed Roofs* deceptively suggests a straightforward, realistic narrative. Instead, the narrative moves from a third-person narrator carefully recording Miriam's sensations to the intuitions of Miriam herself ("It would be quiet in her room"). More radically, the narrative constantly switches back and forth between the present and Miriam's memories. These shifts are disconcerting, as Richardson changes the time frame without signaling or explaining it to her reader. We only figure out gradually that these shifts in time and narrative perspective are determined by Miriam's patterns of thinking.

Early in *Pointed Roofs* a curious configuration of ellipses appears as Miriam meditates on English grammar and teaching. "It was a fool's errand. . . . To undertake to go to the German school and teach . . . to be going there . . . with nothing to give" (26). The passage continues in this style for several pages, the ellipses calling attention both to the language on the page and to the subjective quality of the ideas. Jean Radford suggests that Richardson's ellipses, a device she uses throughout *Pilgrimage*, represent "the unconscious forces working within and through" the narrator's consciousness, and that the gaps serve as "printed silences to register the activities of the unconscious which neither speech nor writing can reach" (69–70). Other narrative devices surface in *Pointed Roofs*: a sentence three pages long communicates Miriam's free associations as she is thinking "sleepily" (31). She has a number of intense experiences that have the quality of epiphanies. As she contemplates "a featureless freedom," a room fills with brightness: "She felt that she was looking at nothing and yet was aware of the whole room like a picture in a dream" (52).

The narrator's perspective in relation to Miriam's consciousness changes over the course of *Pilgrimage*. In *Pointed Roofs* Miriam's interior monologues are not fully internal, as Miriam is still referred to in the third person. In this stage of *Pilgrimage* the narrator reveals details the significance of which Miriam may not completely grasp. Later the first person is more common and Miriam becomes more aware of herself as she grows into her consciousness.

The main event in *Pointed Roofs* is Miriam's trip to and teaching experiences in

Germany, which provoke humiliation, strong feelings about patriotism and national identity, and misanthropy, all of which shed light on Miriam's character. A visit to an English church provokes her religious skepticism, which will continue throughout *Pilgrimage* as Miriam attempts to find an acceptable theological framework. She gets along with her pupils and attracts the interest of a pastor, but the disapproving and jealous headmistress dismisses her and sends her home. A characteristic that might puzzle a reader seeking a feminist heroine in Miriam is her harsh criticism of and negative identification with other women. She thinks, "I don't like men and I loathe women. I am a misanthrope" (31). Bourgeois values also irritate Miriam, and she begins a search to define her life in another way.

The first review of *Pointed Roofs* generally praised it, but also observed that "[t]he book somehow reads as if the reader did not exist . . . no allusion explained or incoherence apologized for" (qtd. in Fromm, *Dorothy Richardson* 70). This would come to be a general feature of modernism, but readers were getting their first taste of it. In 1944 Richardson admitted that the reader of *Pilgrimage* would be greatly helped by a précis or guide along the lines of the annotated reader's guides for *Ulysses*. If Richardson jettisons traditional elements of realistic storytelling and novelistic plotting—linearity, an omniscient narrator, straightforward presentation of characters, chronological development, and a decisive conclusion—there are compensations. In the place of plot Richardson substitutes detailed descriptions of sensations, light, spaces, clothes, and sounds. The level of detail with which Richardson describes the most mundane or minute element is almost unrivaled. Jean Radford suggests that *Pilgrimage* "uses physical description, descriptive detail, repeatedly and at great length not to ensure the 'reality effect' but to produce a resistance to meaning . . . to delay or impede meaning construction, to slow up the reading and 'hold up the development of the whole' [*Pilgrimage* I: 11], which Richardson thought desirable in the novel" (18–19). It does have this effect, but it also draws the reader deeply into Miriam's subjective experiences.

It would be impossible to cover, or even adequately summarize, all thirteen volumes of *Pilgrimage* (with over eight hundred characters). Instead, I will focus on the fourth, *The Tunnel*, which is one of the most accomplished and is a richly suggestive portrait of the Edwardian period and its excitements. It also demonstrates the idiosyncrasies with which Richardson structures (or deconstructs) her novels. Miriam returns to England in *Backwater* (set from August 28, 1893, to December 1894, a period in which she comes increasingly into her independence. *The Tunnel* begins as she is moving into a London boardinghouse: "Twenty-one and only one room to hold the richly renewed consciousness, and a living to earn" (6). She has a job in a dentist's office (described by Richardson in queasy detail). Unlike the dejected Miriam of *Pointed Roofs* who believes that she has limited options, she is now exhilarated by the freedom of youth, her independence, and glorious London. "Tansley Street was a soft gray gloaming after the darkness. When she rattled her key into the keyhole of number seven she felt that her day was beginning. It would be perpetually beginning now. Nights and days were all one day; all hers, unlimited" (22).

A major thread in *The Tunnel* is Miriam's meditations on science and the discourse of scientific progress in relation to religion and individual experience. In the beginning of *The Tunnel* she is reading Darwin's *Voyage of the Beagle* (7); later she considers scientific discourse about women (presented discouragingly as "undeveloped" men). Inevitably, the new scientific discoveries raise questions about theology, and as Gloria Fromm has pointed out, there are echoes of Dante's *Divine Comedy* throughout *The Tunnel*. The novel has thirty-three parts (a structure shared by Dante's canticles); there are many evocations of circular forms (like the rings of Dante's *Inferno*); and in the middle chapter Miriam goes to a lecture on Dante (Fromm,

Dorothy 128). Unlike Dante's journey, which ends with a reunion with the beloved Beatrice and a glimpse of the Creator, Miriam's quest remains unconcluded. As its title indicates, *Pilgrimage* is in dialogue with Bunyan's *Pilgrim's Progress*, a prototypical narrative of spiritual development. However, Richardson is not interested in bringing her protagonist to the Promised Land.

In the subsequent volumes of *Pilgrimage* Miriam begins to define herself as a writer. The last volumes take a decidedly philosophical turn and, as several critics have remarked, increasingly explore the linguistic power of silence. The posthumous and unfinished thirteenth volume, *March Moonlight*, ends with a question: "If Jean's marriage with Joe Davenport brought her a child, should I feel, in holding it, that same sense of fulfillment?" While some critics have suggested that Richardson planned another sequence of novels, and others see a ring-composition closure in *March Moonlight* based on the fact that Miriam begins writing her first novel (*Pilgrimage* itself), these ideas would seem to contradict the principles Richardson follows in the extant volumes. In fact, the open-ended question about fulfillment and desire, with its questioning of the classic novelistic ending—marriage—is very much in keeping with Richardson's literary ambitions. Richardson found closure contrived and false to experience; in 1952 she said of *Pilgrimage*, "It dealt directly with reality. Hence the absence of either 'plot,' 'climax,' or 'conclusion' " (Thomson 56).

Pilgrimage raises a multiplicity of formal and thematic questions that are too vast to cover here. Issues that have been of particular interest to contemporary critics include the status of feminism and eroticism in *Pilgrimage*. The question of whether *Pilgrimage* can be legitimately claimed as feminist begins with the fact that neither Richardson's work nor her political statements are feminist in any explicit sense. Richardson did not publicly identify herself as a feminist; she maintained that men and women should not aspire to equality because they were completely different creatures. Moreover, she opined that women's novels to date had "too much set upon exploiting the sex motif" and sought to distinguish herself (Hanscombe and Smyers 62). However, as Kristin Bluemel acutely suggests, *Pilgrimage* can be read as a feminist text insofar as it "wants to critique the false conditions imposed by a gender-conscious society while simultaneously wanting to affirm the separate truths her experience of womanhood brings" (24).

A related question is the evasive manner in which Richardson treats Miriam's sexual experiences. Her loss of virginity to Hypo has been cited ironically as one of the most elusive sex scenes ever written. In one of the later volumes Miriam thinks that she may be pregnant (there is a possible miscarriage); in general, her libidinal life is neither exciting nor rewarding. Many critics complained about Miriam's prudery and lack of interest in sex, despite declarations such as "I'm a free-lover. Of course I'm a free-lover" (*Dawn's Left Hand* 254). Some recent critics (including Bluemel and Carol Watts) have examined Miriam's relationship with Annabel as lesbian eroticism.

As early as 1918 writers were imitating Richardson's style, and the publisher Alfred Knopf even referred to a rash of imitations as "Richardsonitis" (Fromm, *Dorothy Richardson* 119). After 1922, however, the signature style of high modernism was more likely to be termed "Joycean." In 1918, in a remarkable moment of synchronicity, portions of the fifth volume of *Pilgrimage*, *Interim*, appeared in serialized form in the *Little Review* along with an excerpt from Joyce's *Ulysses*. Richardson wrote in a letter of 1919, "I had read none of the moderns when my first book was published & have read very little since. In James Joyce I recognise one who uses the same method as I, more strictly beautifully & perhaps to a wider end—that I don't know. I have not read Ulysses" (*Windows on Modernism* 26–27). Richardson's speculation that *Ulysses* aspired toward "a wider end" than *Pilgrimage* is significant and strangely prophetic.

While *Pilgrimage* takes us more deeply into a single consciousness than perhaps any other modern text, Joyce diffuses that concentration in *Ulysses* across a city, a series of characters, and language itself. *Ulysses* is tremendously challenging, but it is manageable: it can be read in a week or two, along with one of the many guides to decoding the novel. *Ulysses* dwells on one day, but it never stays in one consciousness for more than forty pages. *Pilgrimage* demands a kind of sustained attention that very few readers are willing to extend or capable of extending to a text. One could say that Richardson's novels simply did not stand the test of time, or one could say that she was the most uncompromising modernist of all.

ASSESSMENT

In part, Richardson is not read much today because her major contribution is lengthy and challenging. Unlike Woolf or Joyce, whose novels can be (and are) taught in survey courses on modernism, Richardson is harder to excerpt—although the same could be said of Proust and his twelve-volume *A la recherche du temps perdu*, and this has not hindered his longevity. The more complex reason for Richardson's relative obscurity outside of academia is that *Pilgrimage*'s effect is cumulative: a slow and systematic disruption of its reader's usual apparatus of reading. Richardson's subtle, disorienting, and often-opaque writing steadily undermines all realist conventions, but the rewards are substantial: luminous, concentrated prose that offers nothing short of a theory of consciousness. Any account of twentieth-century experimental writing is incomplete without an acknowledgment of Richardson's groundbreaking contributions.

BIBLIOGRAPHY

Primary Sources

The Quakers, Past and Present. London: Constable, 1914.

Pointed Roofs. London: Duckworth, 1915.

Backwater. London: Duckworth, 1916.

Honeycomb. London: Duckworth, 1917.

"The Reality of Feminism." 1917. Rpt. in Scott, *The Gender of Modernism* 401–407.

Interim. London: Duckworth, 1919.

The Tunnel. London: Duckworth, 1919.

Deadlock. London: Duckworth, 1921.

Revolving Lights. London: Duckworth, 1923.

"Talent and Genius." 1923. Rpt. in Scott, *The Gender of Modernism* 407–411.

"About Punctuation." 1924. Rpt. in Scott, *The Gender of Modernism* 414–418.

"Women and the Future." 1924. Rpt. in Scott, *The Gender of Modernism* 411–414.

The Trap. London: Duckworth, 1925.

"Women in the Arts." 1925. Rpt. in Scott, *The Gender of Modernism* 419–423.

Oberland. London: Duckworth, 1927.

Dawn's Left Hand. London: Duckworth, 1931.

Clear Horizon. London: J.M. Dent and Cresset Press, 1935.

"Novels." 1948. Rpt. in Scott, *The Gender of Modernism* 432–435.

Pilgrimage. Incl. *March Moonlight*. 4 vols. London: Virago, 1979.

Journey to Paradise: Short Stories and Autobiographical Sketches of Dorothy Richardson. London: Virago, 1989.

Windows on Modernism: Selected Letters of Dorothy Richardson. Athens: U of Georgia P, 1995.

"Continuous Performance" columns. Rpt. in Donald, Friedberg, and Marcus, *Close Up*.

Secondary Sources

Bluemel, Kristin. *Experimenting on the Borders of Modernism: Dorothy Richardson's Pilgrimage*. Athens: U of Georgia P, 1997.

Donald, James, Anne Friedberg, and Laura Marcus, eds. *Close Up, 1927–1933: Cinema and Modernism*. Princeton: Princeton UP, 1998.

Fromm, Gloria G. "Dorothy M. Richardson." In *British Novelists, 1890–1929: Modernists*. Detroit: Gale, 1985. 203–220.

———. *Dorothy Richardson: A Biography*. Urbana: U of Illinois P, 1977.

Gevirtz, Susan. *Narrative's Journey: The Fiction and Film Writing of Dorothy Richardson*. New York: Peter Lang, 1996.

Hanscombe, Gillian E. *The Art of Life: Dorothy Richardson and the Development of Feminist Consciousness*. London: Peter Owen, 1982.

———, and Virginia L. Smyers. *Writing for their*

Lives: The Modernist Women, 1910–1940. London: Women's P, 1987.

Henke, Suzette. "Male and Female Consciousness in Dorothy Richardson's *Pilgrimage*." *Journal of Women's Studies in Literature* 1 (1979): 51–60.

Marcus, Laura. "Introduction to Continuous Performance: Dorothy Richardson." In Donald, Friedberg, and Marcus 150–159.

Powys, John Cowper. *Dorothy M. Richardson*. London: Joiner & Steele, 1931.

Radford, Jean. *Dorothy Richardson*. New York: Harvester, 1991.

Scott, Bonnie Kime, ed. *The Gender of Modernism*. Bloomington: Indiana UP, 1990.

Showalter, Elaine. *A Literature of Their Own: British Women Novelists from Brontë to Lessing*. Princeton: Princeton UP, 1977.

Sinclair, May. "The Novels of Dorothy Richardson." In *British Novelists, 1890–1929: Modernists*. Detroit: Gale, 1985. 319–323.

Thomson, George H. *A Reader's Guide to Dorothy Richardson's* Pilgrimage. Greensboro, NC: ELT, 1996.

Watts, Carol. *Dorothy Richardson*. Plymouth, UK: Northcote House, 1995.

Woolf, Virginia. "Romance and the Heart." *Nation and Athenaeum Literary Supplement* 19 May 1923: 229.

Vita Sackville-West
1892–1962

Peter F. Naccarato

Insight into the literary and cultural life of early-twentieth-century England can come from both the artistic and the biographical writings of its prominent figures. While some of the women discussed in this reference volume made significant contributions to the development of modern and postmodern English literature, Vita Sackville-West, an accomplished poet and novelist, is remembered less for her writing and more for her fascinating life. Although she began writing at the young age of twelve and continued to write throughout her life, she did not make significant contributions to the growing modernist canon. While her life story reflects the dramatic changes in English culture as it moved from its Victorian past into the twentieth century, her writing remained traditional during a time of equally radical literary change. In other words, it is her own life, rather than her literary work, that offers the most dramatic representation of this evolving society.

BACKGROUND

Vita Sackville-West in many ways personifies the complicated society in which she lived. With one foot grounded firmly in her family's distinguished lineage, she enjoyed all of the advantages that wealth afforded. Much of her youth was spent either at Knole, the estate her family had owned since the mid-sixteenth century, or in Scotland, Paris, and Italy. By the age of eighteen she was well educated, well traveled, and ready to emerge onto the English social scene. By that time she had already refused one marriage proposal—from Marchese Orazio Pucci, an Italian aristocrat who had fallen madly in love with her during one of her visits to Florence—and she was prepared to assume her role as "the daughter of Knole [who] went to parties, sometimes to four balls a week and luncheons every day" (Nicolson 83). It was at one of these parties, during the summer of 1910, that she met her future husband, Harold Nicolson. After a long engagement Harold and Vita were married in 1913, had two sons—Ben and Nigel (between them, another son died at birth)—and remained married until Vita's death in 1962. During their many years together Harold and Vita traveled extensively, and she continued to play the pseudoaristocratic role that her family's distinguished history made available to her. In addition, a review of the bibliography for this entry makes clear that throughout her life she not only wrote fiction and poetry, but also published biographies, family histories, travel narratives, and gardening books. As England made the transition from a Victorian to an Edwardian culture, Vita emerged as one of its finest creations. Decades later, as the political and cultural landscape around her shifted, she remained an emblem of this bygone era.

At the same time, Vita embodies the fundamental contradictions of the very era that produced her. If at first glance her life seems traditional by Edwardian standards, with her extravagant homes, her long marriage, and her two sons, behind this facade lies another side of Vita's complex identity. If, as already suggested, Vita had one foot firmly grounded in the British upper class, her other foot rested on a much less secure grounding. In her own autobiographical writings Vita separates the two sides of her personality by drawing a distinction between her traditional British roots and the Spanish blood and spirit she inherited from her grandmother, Josepha Durán, referred to familiarly as Pepita. A long relationship between Pepita and Vita's grandfather, Lionel Sackville-West, was never solidified by marriage; thus Vita's family tree connects the traditional with the scandalous in ways that would anticipate her own contributions to this family history.

Throughout her life Vita balanced her desire for a solid family, grounded in her deep love for Harold Nicolson and her two children, with her strong feelings for women. Nigel Nicolson's *Portrait of a Marriage*, published in 1973, includes Vita's own autobiographical account of her relationship with Violet Trefusis, a childhood friend. Throughout this moving account Vita shares the complexity of this relationship and the depth of her feelings for Violet. At the same time, she recounts many of their escapades, including Vita's cross-dressing during their travels across Europe, and the threat this relationship posed to her own marriage. Although her marriage survived this affair, Vita continued to pursue intimate and complex relationships with women throughout her life, including one with Virginia Woolf, who immortalized Vita in her novel *Orlando*. With its portrait of a strong, gender-bending hero/heroine who lives across centuries, it is this novel, perhaps, that provides the most complete portrait of this immensely complex woman.

ANALYSIS

While Vita Sackville-West published extensively throughout her career and enjoyed popular successes with several of her novels and much of her poetry, she has not emerged as a major figure in the literary history of modernism. Perhaps Sackville-West herself most clearly articulated one reason for this fact in a letter she wrote to Harold Nicolson in October 1945: "What worries me a bit, is being so out of touch with poetry as it is being written today. I get so many volumes sent to me by the *Observer* and also by would-be poets, and I see the influence of Tom Eliot and the Stephen Spender–Auden school is paramount—yet I can't get into gear with it. It is just something left out of my makeup" (Glendinning 341). As a poet, Sackville-West found herself at odds with contemporary trends; similarly, as a novelist, despite her associations with prominent Bloomsbury writers, she never achieved their level of critical acclaim or notoriety. Despite this, however, her writing does provide unique insight into both her personal story and the complexities of British history and culture.

In her first published novel, *Heritage* (1919), Sackville-West begins to build the bridge between her biography and her fiction as she introduces two characters, Rawdon Westmacott and his lover, Ruth, who are both of mixed ancestry. By mirroring her own mixed Spanish/British heritage in her characters, Sackville-West is able to explore her own sense of duality through her fictionalization of it. A second feature of this novel that would reappear in much of her fiction is what Victoria Glendinning calls the Vita Sackville-West hero: "Malory was the traveler with no dependents, no address; he was the man she would have liked to have been, and her ideal man, from her woman's point of view" (89). Thus from the beginning fiction provided a space for Sackville-West to think through the complexity of her own identity as she created characters who struggled with their own dualities, whether cultural or sexual.

At the same time, Sackville-West incorporated into her writing her own thoughts on a wide variety of social issues. *Family History* (1932), for example, uses the romance between Evelyn and Miles Van-Merrick (fifteen years her junior) to raise questions concerning marriage and love. For Glendinning, this novel, with a relationship whose "age-gap perhaps replace[s] homosexuality as a focus for the world's disapproval," offers a justification for the type of open marriage that Vita and Harold practiced while also condemning "claustrophobic possessive love" (252). In *All Passion Spent* (1931) Sackville-West uses the meditations of Lady Slane, her eighty-eight-year-old heroine, "to express her own ungentle feelings about the distorting effects marriage and the expectations of society have on the individual" (Glendinning 236). Such social criticism is also at the center of one of Sackville-West's most successful novels, *The Edwardians* (1930), a period piece in which she re-creates the world of her childhood. As the novel moves from the late Victorian period through the Edwardian period, ending with the coronation of George V in 1910, it explores the social values and assumptions of the British upper classes. In one of her most political novels, *Grand Canyon* (1942), Sackville-West offers a cautionary tale in which Germany has won the war in Europe and, as the result of a treaty, has taken over the United States. After being rejected by the Hogarth Press because Leonard Woolf was concerned with both its vision of Hitler's victory as the war still raged on and its implicit criticism of the U.S. failure to become involved in the war, and then being rejected by Heinemann, the book was finally published by Michael Joseph.

From the social and political realities fictionalized in *The Edwardians* and *Grand Canyon*, Sackville-West returned to a more personal kind of writing in her final two novels. As in her first novel, Sackville-West fictionalizes her own sense of duality in *The Easter Party* (1953) as she tells the story of Sir Walter Mortimer and his wife, Rose. For Glendinning, "[T]he novel sets romanticism against rationalism, revelation against reason." Although she admits that it is not a good novel, she does suggest that "for the student of Vita's life and nature it is a moving book to read" (376). The line from Mortimer and Rose, with their unconsummated marriage and their battling temperaments, to Sackville-West, with "her own unresolved duality, as well as the enigma of her sexless love for Harold" (376), is a fairly easy one to draw. This sense of duality, which followed Sackville-West throughout her writing and her life, was also at the center of her final novel, *No Signposts in the Sea* (1961). The story of a terminally ill man who takes a sea voyage, this book is the first in which "Vita envisaged . . . a synthesis between love and lust, mind and heart, love and 'in love'—a complete union, too late for her doomed hero Edmund" (Glendinning 399). It is also in this novel that Sackville-West explicitly writes about lesbianism—a theme that she had explored with more depth and complexity in much of her poetry—through the character of Laura. In her final novel Sackville-West continues to struggle for synthesis but, in the end, can offer "the if-onlys and what-ifs of [her] divided life, divided love, divided nature, which had made total commitment and the luxury of faithfulness impossible" (400).

ASSESSMENT

In her biography of Vita Sackville-West Victoria Glendinning "sees Vita's life as a dramatic human adventure" (jacket). It is this life, in the end, that proves more fascinating than the impressive list of Sackville-West's published writings. Though these works provide important insight into British history and her own family's genealogy, they remain secondary to the woman herself. In other words, if her fiction and poetry do not capture the rich literary changes that occurred in the first half of the twentieth century, they do offer significant insight into this complicated woman and her complex times. Rather than looking to her writing for examples of an evolving modernist style, one can look to her own life to discover a glimpse into England's complex evolution from a Victorian to a modern society.

BIBLIOGRAPHY

Primary Sources

Poems of West and East. London and New York: John Lane, 1917.
Heritage. London: Collins, 1919.
The Dragon in Shallow Waters. London: Collins, 1921.
Orchard and Vineyard. London and New York: John Lane, 1921.
The Heir. London: Heinemann, 1922.
Knole and the Sackvilles. London: Heinemann, 1922.
Challenge. New York: Doran, 1923.
The Diary of the Lady Anne Clifford. Ed. Vita Sackville-West. London: Heinemann, 1923.
Grey Wethers. London: Heinemann, 1923.
Seducers in Ecuador. London: Hogarth, 1924.
The Land. London: Heinemann, 1926.
Passenger to Teheran. London: Hogarth, 1926.
Aphra Behn. London: Gerald Howe, 1927.
Twelve Days. London: Hogarth, 1928.
Andrew Marvell. The Poets on the Poets. London: Faber, 1929.
King's Daughter. London: Hogarth, 1929.
The Edwardians. London: Hogarth, 1930.
All Passion Spent. London: Hogarth, 1931.
Invitation to Cast Out Care. London: Faber, 1931.
Sissinghurst. London: Hogarth, 1931.
The Death of Noble Godavary and Gottfried Künstler. London: Benn, 1932.
Family History. London: Hogarth, 1932.
Thirty Clocks Strike the Hour. Garden City, NY: Doubleday, 1932.
Collected Poems. Vol. 1. London: Hogarth, 1933.
The Dark Island. London: Hogarth, 1934.
Saint Joan of Arc. London: Cobden-Sanderson, 1936.
Pepita. London: Hogarth, 1937.
Some Flowers. London: Cobden-Sanderson, 1937.
Solitude. London: Hogarth, 1938.
Country Notes. London: Joseph, 1939.
Country Notes in Wartime. London: Hogarth, 1940.
English Country Houses. Britain in Pictures. London: Collins, 1941.
Selected Poems. London: Hogarth, 1941.
Grand Canyon. London: Joseph, 1942.
The Eagle and the Dove. London: Joseph, 1943.
The Women's Land Army. London: Joseph, 1944.
Another World Than This (anthology). With Harold George Nicolson. London: Joseph, 1945.
The Garden. London: Joseph, 1946.
Devil at Westease. Garden City, NY: Doubleday, 1947.
Nursery Rhymes. London: Dropmore, 1947.
In Your Garden. London: Joseph, 1951.
The Easter Party. London: Joseph, 1953.
In Your Garden Again. London: Joseph, 1953.
More for Your Garden. London: Joseph, 1955.
Even More for Your Garden. London: Joseph, 1958.
A Joy of Gardening. New York: Harper, 1958.
Daughter of France. London: Joseph, 1959.
Faces: Profiles of Dogs. London: Harvill, 1961.
No Signposts in the Sea. London: Joseph, 1961.
V. Sackville-West's Garden Book. Ed. Philipa Nicolson. London: Joseph, 1968.
Dearest Andrew (letters to Andrew Reiber, 1951–1962). Ed. Nancy MacKnight. London: Michael Joseph, 1979.
The Letters of Vita Sackville-West to Virginia Woolf. Ed. Louise DeSalvo and Mitchell A. Leaska. New York: Morrow, 1985.
Vita and Harold: The Letters of Vita Sackville-West and Harold Nicolson. Ed. Nigel Nicolson. New York: Putnam, 1992.

Secondary Sources

Brown, Jane. *Vita's Other World: A Gardening Biography of V. Sackville-West*. Harmondsworth and New York: Viking, 1985.
Glendinning, Victoria. *Vita: The Life of V. Sackville-West*. New York: Knopf, 1983.
Nicolson, Nigel. *Portrait of a Marriage*. London: Weidenfeld & Nicolson, 1973.
Philippe, Julian, and John Phillips. *The Other Woman: A Life of Violet Trefusis, Including Previously Unpublished Correspondence with Vita Sackville-West*. Boston: Houghton Mifflin, 1976.
Souhami, Diana. *Mrs. Keppel and Her Daughter*. New York: St. Martin's, 1997.

Stevens, Michael. *V. Sackville-West: A Critical Biography*. New York: Scribner's, 1974.

Trefusis, Violet Keppel. *Violet to Vita: The Letters of Violet Trefusis to Vita Sackville-West, 1910–21*. Ed. Mitchell A. Leaska and John Phillips. New York: Viking, 1990.

Watson, Sara Ruth. *V. Sackville-West*. Boston: Twayne, 1972.

Dorothy L. Sayers
1893–1957

Edmund Miller

While it is argued whether Dorothy L. Sayers was a fine prose stylist who happened to write detective stories or an ingenious hack who merely made a pretense of fine writing, it is generally agreed that her practice of the detective genre and her advocacy of it made literary critics first begin to take detective stories seriously. In addition, the philosophical vision that informs her translations and religious dramas also informs her fiction, in particular with regard to the place of women in society and the importance of work to women as well as men, yet she denied that there is a "woman's point of view," writing in *Unpopular Opinions*, "Every woman is a human being . . . and a human being *must* have occupation. . . . [And] a job should be done by the person who does it best. . . . What is repugnant to every human being is to be reckoned always as a member of a class and not as an individual person" (110–113).

BACKGROUND

Having taken a first in modern languages at Somerville College, Oxford, Sayers began a career as a writer, publishing devotional verse but earning a living as an advertising copywriter. Armed with the tricks of advertising, she began the first Lord Peter Wimsey mystery, *Whose Body?* (1923). Then finding herself pregnant out of wedlock, she turned in earnest to writing mysteries to be able to keep the child. After eight years of fame as a writer she quit advertising, but she never settled for popularity and developed themes she felt passionately. As a result, her mysteries always illustrate fine writing, characteristically raise serious ethical issues, and often use her knowledge of other languages.

The novels of Wilkie Collins were archetypes of detective fiction for Sayers because they combine elaborate plotting with social satire, but Collins does not have Sayers's charm and offers no theological insights. More generally, her mysteries are in the tradition of the Victorian novel, where secrets create a structural framework for moral edification. *The Documents in the Case* (1930), in particular, is part of the tradition of the epistolary novel, but most of her novels include some correspondence and documents. Specifically within the tradition of the mystery, Sayers writes puzzles, the point of which is ingenious complications. Consequently, murder is typically premeditated (Merry 21). When it is not, as in *The Five Red Herrings* (1931), then the time of death is manipulated to rig an alibi. *The Unpleasantness at the Bellona Club* (1928) has both devices as two characters work at cross-purposes.

Ultimately any literary detective owes something to Sherlock Holmes. In the case of Wimsey, the debt is parodic and also owes something to P.G. Wodehouse's Bertie Wooster. Wimsey, like Wooster, frequently finds himself the butt of a joke, but he often creates such situations to disarm suspects. He plays the parody aristocrat just because he has serious work to do. Yet he is believably human—from the shell shock he suffers in *Whose Body?* to his compassionate courtship of Harriet Vane.

Like the novels, the plays use traditional forms. *The Zeal of Thy House* (1937) and *The Devil to Pay* (1939) are morality plays. *He That Should Come* (1939) is a medieval mystery play, dramatizing a biblical story for edification. *The Man Born to Be King* (1943) is an entire cycle of such mystery plays. *The Emperor Constantine* (1951) is an Elizabethan chronicle play. The play version of *Busman's Honeymoon* (1937) is both a "well-made play" and a comedy of manners, as is *Love All* (published in 1984). In later life Sayers turned explicitly to theology for subject matter in plays, essays, and translations. Although these works are scholarly, they address ordinary people through colloquial language.

ANALYSIS

Trying consciously to make the detective story more like mainstream fiction, Sayers succeeded so well that it is still debated whether *Gaudy Night* (1935) is a detective story. In addition, she influenced other mystery writers of the golden age and deepened the genre, by example but also as an anthologist and apologist and as a founder of the writers' circle called the Detection Club. She was one of the first to predict the movement of the detective story toward psychological realism.

The first novel, *Whose Body?*, unravels the procedure of a murder without much mystery about the identity of the culprit, a callous, self-absorbed villain. The book had trouble getting published because of perceived "coarseness" until Sayers changed the section in which Lord Peter noted that the naked corpse in the bathtub is not the missing Jewish financier Sir Reuben Levy since it is uncircumcised. This telling detail is replaced by bad teeth and flea bites. Sayers's descriptions of how Jews are regarded by Lord Peter's social circle have led to criticism for anti-Semitism, but as she pointed out, her Jewish characters are among her nicest and most morally upright.

With a duke as the accused, *Clouds of Witness* (1926) more explicitly than any of the other novels focuses on the aristocracy, but it also seriously explores the nature of work and responsibility. This time the social milieu led to criticisms of snobbism, although, again, Sayers's characters merely illustrate values of the time. Martin Green called her the "Fanny Hill of *class* distinctions" (461). Although her lower-class characters have mental limitations while her professional men are often insensitive, she distributes ethical awareness evenhandedly. Denis Cathcart, the victim in *Clouds of Witness*, is thoroughly amoral, and the Duke of Denver, Lord Peter's brother, is a slow-witted adulterer willing to lie to the House of Lords while on trial for murder rather than compromise the honor of a farmer's wife. But these elitist values are not the point of the book. They are aids to values clarification in a world that needs morals. Indeed, the snobbishness is never at the expense of the reader, who is treated as a knowledgeable insider. Sayers's technique subtly redefines social classes, including the reader in an intellectual elite. She is writing for Oxbridge graduates, not younger sons of peers.

Contrasts among the suitors of Lady Mary nicely illustrate the dignity of human life regardless of class. Lady Mary is engaged to Denis Cathcart, a decadent aristocrat seeking a marriage of convenience to keep his mistress in more lavish style. He may be the victim, but when his motives are disclosed, he becomes completely unsympathetic. With some relief, the reader learns that Lady Mary—disillusioned by Cathcart's lack of passion—has planned an elopement with another suitor on the very night of Cathcart's death. George Goyles, the alternative suitor, turns out to be less satisfactory and less ethical than Cathcart. A knee-jerk socialist who gives beautiful speeches about human rights, he has no compassion for actual people. Cathcart at least has the passion to die for love, and if he intends to marry Lady Mary without love, he is doing so with her knowledge and without pretense. While Goyles, by contrast, professes to love Lady Mary, the problem is not simply intellectual dishonesty, for overweening self-love leads him to abandon his intended when he discovers the corpse of her fiancé at their appointed rendezvous. Run to earth, Goyles assumes, erroneously, that she has identified him. Lady Mary's third and successful suitor is Inspector Charles Parker, friend and detective colleague of her brother Lord Peter. Parker has old-fashioned, middle-class values that neither Cathcart nor Goyles appreciates, but his distinguishing characteristic is that he works—and takes work seriously. Thus he makes moral judgments Goyles does not have the right to and Cathcart does not understand the need for. The rejected lovers take too cheap a view of life. They may be willing to kill (Goyles takes a shot at Lord Peter, and Cathcart is finally shown to have committed suicide), but only the due process of law and religion can ever justify the taking of life.

Cathcart's suicide allows the book to suggest the harmony of existing society. There is no murderer to bring to justice. When the Duke is acquitted, the farmer Grimethorpe tries to kill him anyway, only to be dealt with by fate as a passing taxicab runs him over in the confusion he creates. Thus Grimethorpe himself liberates his wife, the Duke's mistress. Free, she refuses the Duke's offer of financial support and, what is more important, makes no emotional claim. Recognizing her affair as a morally transgressive reaction to domestic unhappiness and not an expression of true feeling, she terminates it when she is a free agent. Strength of character keeps traditional society stable.

As in many detective stories, the detective/observer here is more interesting and more fully developed than the characters of the plot. Lord Peter is especially engaging as the brother of two suspects. While we understand his emotional involvement, we also enjoy the lighthearted enthusiasm with which he pursues the investigation even in the face of danger (not only is he shot at, he almost disappears in a peat bog while seeking to discover where his brother was the night Cathcart died).

Longer and more elaborate than most mysteries, *Clouds of Witness* develops many characters fully as part of Sayers's program of deepening the scope of such works. Among fully rounded characters who reappear in later novels are Lady Mary, Inspector Charles Parker (not a lively character but a believable one in his restrained admiration of Lady Mary, his dogged pursuit of evidence, and his warm friendship with Lord Peter), and the Dowager Duchess, whose native good sense is combined with happy incoherence. Even minor figures in this book like the Grimethorpes are sensitively characterized.

As in many detective stories, the point of view in *Clouds of Witness* is omniscient narrative with a good deal of dialogue. But there are also letters, floor plans, newspaper clippings, footnotes, literary quotations, epigraphs, and trial transcripts. A major exculpating clue is embedded in a long letter in French. It has been objected that in this early novel Lord Peter spends less time pursuing clues than in thinking about them, but this is an inherent characteristic of detective stories. The puzzle is rewarding and plausible.

Unnatural Death (1927) is another novel of complication. The focus is the ingenious method of murder, but the characterization is even more interesting since lesbianism motivates several characters. This subject was quite daring for the time. The book is a serious discussion of how women can control their destiny. Some do so selfishly, but other women-only societies work for the general good. There are evil, manipulative women living in worlds that exclude men, but there are also good women beloved by all despite having no sexual interest in men. Among these latter is the new continuing character Alexandra Climpson, who works in the Cattery, a combination secretarial service and detective bureau founded by Lord Peter but staffed by unmarried women. Lord Peter's idea is to make use of these underappreciated resources of humanity. Miss Climpson has intense religious scruples but keen skill in insinuating herself into situations where she can uncover information. Her epistolary reports are full of exaggerations and enthusiasms that make them hilarious but somehow still endearing.

The Unpleasantness at the Bellona Club is another puzzle novel, this time concerning the time of death. Social satire addresses medical fads and men's clubs. Having identified the murderer, Lord Peter allows him to take the gentlemanly way out and shoot himself. While this is artistically more satisfying than the denouement of *Whose Body?* at which the police capture the guilty party just as he is about to commit suicide, it involves a pagan view of nobility at odds with Sayers's own views. Deferring discussion of the Harriet Vane novels, the following novel, *The Five Red Herrings*, is something of a mechanical exercise, but the incidents are ingeniously complicated. The main interest is the presentation of alternative solutions by five detectives, each accusing a different suspect. Lord Peter then triumphantly reenacts the crime, breaking an unbreakable alibi and clearing all five serious suspects.

Murder Must Advertise (1933), the first mature novel, is as complicated as any in the series. The identity of the murderer is established early on, but there are many related mysteries concerning the drug trade. These complications are not unraveled convincingly. It strains credulity to depend on even the British postal service to attempt delivery every week of a letter to the same wrong address on a particular day and not just to begin chucking each new letter directly into the dead-letter office. The plan is particularly absurd since, like the small distributors, the drug lords could simply look in the newspaper for the information. On the other hand, decadent society is well presented, and the scenes in the advertising agency Pym's Publicity are brilliant satire. The denouement steers a middle course between the ending of *Whose Body?* and the classical way out of *The Unpleasantness at the Bellona Club*. Sayers allows the murderer in *Murder Must Advertise* to put himself in the way of assassins. This means that he can take responsibility for his crime with the possibility of achieving Christian redemption while he avoids embarrassing innocent parties, as a trial would have required. *Murder Must Advertise* also includes a different author self-portrait than the more famous Harriet Vane. Miss Meteyard, a university woman working at Pym's Publicity, has the detective skill to penetrate Lord Peter's disguise and also the sangfroid to look the other way at a murder because the victim is a dirty little blackmailer who deserves what he gets. Murder is not quite the thing to do, but then neither is telling.

Edmund Wilson has objected that *The Nine Tailors* (1934) is boring in its obsession with details of the ringing of church bells (258–259). Most readers of detective stories, however, have high praise for the book. Although the puzzle is introduced into the story late, it is genuinely intriguing. Yet the mystery is less important than ethical questions raised when the gruesome death turns out to be an accident caused by the ringing of a peal of bells in which Lord Peter participated, thus putting him in the position of murderer. The irony and attendant discussion of human responsibility give the book its stature as a major work. As Aaron Elkins has pointed out, *The Nine Tailors* is also remarkable as the first major example of a novel that presents "a thoroughly researched, coherent body of information about an entire field of knowledge . . . that is integral, absorbing, and a necessary part of the mystery" (107).

In the middle of the sequence of Lord Peter novels chronologically, Sayers began a subsidiary series coupling Lord Peter and Harriet Vane. Sayers believed that Harriet was such a powerful character in *Strong Poison* (1930) that the book could not end with her marriage to Lord Peter as originally intended. Sayers said that she wrote the solo Lord Peter works that followed *Strong Poison* to deepen Lord Peter's character to make him worthy of her. Many critics agree with Sayers. Indeed, Alzina Stone Dale states that no critic could disagree (Introduction, *Love All* xx). But Sayers was deluding herself. It is Harriet who deepens in the novels in which she appears between her trial for murder in *Strong Poison* and her hectic *Busman's Honeymoon*. Sayers used her experience with the novelist John Cournos in writing *Strong Poison*, which introduces Harriet Vane. Insisting that he had conscientious scruples opposing marriage, Cournos had convinced Sayers to live with him unmarried. His eventual proposal of marriage revealed that he merely believed in trial marriage and did not believe in full disclosure. Sayers has a kind of eternal revenge, having modeled the victim in *Strong Poison* on Cournos (he wrote his own revenge novel, *The Devil Is an English Gentleman*).

In *Strong Poison* Harriet Vane is on trial for murdering her lover. A hung jury is created by Miss Climpson, who is genuinely unconvinced by the evidence. She then aids Lord Peter in clearing Harriet. Harriet, despite her bohemian lifestyle, is priggish and rigid, and while it is easy enough to see why Lord Peter appreciates her scruples and believes in her innocence, it is harder to understand his romantic interest. Yet he loves her completely and immediately, although expecting (and receiving) no thanks for the time and money he spends disinterestedly establishing her innocence. Clearly Harriet needs to unbend. Lord Peter not only respects the need for Harriet to continue her work but loves her because she values this independence. She must learn that letting herself like him will not diminish her independence. To illustrate the importance of this issue, the book includes episodes involving other characters, as, for example, when Miss Murcheson is having a short course in lockpicking to help her in some Cattery detective work and the convention-minded wife of the safecracker/tutor fails to see why it is important to learn "artistic" lockpicking.

By leaving Harriet on her own for much of *Have His Carcase*, Sayers allows her to begin unbending. When later she works with Lord Peter to unravel the conspiracy at the root of the murder, Harriet realizes how unfair she has been to him. The book is successful both as mystery and as mainstream fiction. That the victim is afflicted with hemophilia will become clear early on to contemporary readers, but there are many other complications, including improbable multiple impersonations by several villains. There is also a cipher, probable in relation to the plot and decoded plausibly. The real strength of *Have His Carcase* is the interplay between Lord Peter and Harriet. The fact that the relationship does not eventuate in marriage by the end of the book shows restraint by Sayers and makes the love story more realistic. Harriet comes to realize that although a woman should not define herself in relation to men, she can work with men and enjoy their company. Early in the book, a typical career woman, she sneers at women with domestic lives. Surveying prospects for help at the murder scene, she reasons that in the fishermen's houses along the road "she would find nobody at home but women and children, who would be useless in the emergency." She finds Mrs. Weldon's love for the young gigolo Paul Alexis pathetic even as Dorothy Sayers reports accurately and sympathetically Harriet's realization that the professional dancers are doing a job with at least as much honor and happiness as most jobs. By the end of the book Harriet's understanding is as deep as the author's.

A mainstream novel of intellectual life with detective interruptions, *Gaudy Night* is a controversial mystery. In an essay also called "Gaudy Night" Sayers describes plotting so that Harriet learns that her intellectual integrity makes her equal to Peter despite his wealth and station: "By choosing a plot that should exhibit intellectual integrity as the one great permanent value . . . I . . . found a universal theme . . . integral both to the detective plot and to the 'love interest' " ("Gaudy Night" 82). In *Gaudy Night* the mystery concerns malicious mischief being done at Harriet's alma mater, Shrewsbury College, Oxford. The theme explores the importance of work, particularly for women. Sayers supports the intellectual life for women but is aware of the difficulties. However, the major intellectual dishonesty at the root of the mystery is a man's. As she attempts to understand what is going on, Harriet comes to see that intellectuality requires neither the sexlessness of a women's college nor the sentimentality of domesticity. When she learns to balance mind and passion rather than set them in opposition, she can accept Lord Peter's proposal. She realizes that marriage need not circumscribe life and that marriage with Peter will instead enlarge her life. Feminists have objected to the form of Lord Peter's proposal: he provides the sestet to a sonnet Harriet has been unable to finish. For such limited readers, the implication is that the male acts because the female is inadequate, but Sayers shows male and female as complementary, working better together than either works alone. Harriet and Peter work together to create a unified sonnet symbolic of their newly synchronized intellectual lives. Harriet then accepts Peter's proposal in a Latin phrase used by a schoolmaster to indicate that a student is acceptable to show the joint willingness of this man and this woman to function within traditional patterns.

Gaudy Night is a great novel for the realistic Oxford atmosphere and the intellectually interesting moral dilemma. Readers are sometimes disappointed that it evades the expectation of a suspicious death. But if the book is not a detective story because it does not focus on a mysterious death, apparent murders in some detective stories do turn out to be accident or suicide; indeed, Sayers has novels where an apparent murder is resolved in each of these ways. Adding a murder puzzle would neither enlarge the book to a detective story nor diminish it to one. But in a sense *Gaudy Night* does have a murder puzzle: the very first of the poison-pen letters lays an accusation of murder, and ultimately the motivation for the outrages at Shrewsbury College is explained by taking that charge of murder seriously. The charge of murder is resolved as Miss de Vine sits "frowning" at the denouement, "dispassionately considering her claim to have done murder." She had exposed something the man did, and this led to the man's suicide. The entire Senior Commons Room agrees that she has done right in exposing intellectual dishonesty and yet is not accountable for the man's death. But Sayers is astute enough to show that a saintly person (Miss Lydgate is the example) might have thought beyond duty and sought to help the man and his family after having exposed the intellectual fraud.

The last complete novel, *Busman's Honeymoon* in 1937, began conceptually as a play in collaboration with Muriel St. Clare Byrne. Inexperienced as a playwright, Sayers nevertheless had the clearly defined goal of creating a work that plays fair with the audience about clues and provides a murder device "visible from the back of the gallery" (*Love All*, x) used in a thrilling reenactment of the crime. She generated more material than could be used on stage and subsequently included this in the novelization while also extending the time frame. The stage version is a well-made play that justifies the subtitle *A Love Story with Detective Interruptions* far better than the novel. While less philosophical than *The Nine Tailors* and *Gaudy Night*, *Bus-*

man's Honeymoon in either version is profoundly concerned with the partnership of man and woman. The delay of the marriage of Harriet Vane to Lord Peter through three novels allows Sayers to illustrate gender equality. Critics who object that Harriet defers to Lord Peter or fails to act independently miss Sayers's point. At the beginning of the series of Harriet Vane books in *Strong Poison*, Harriet is a man-rejecting feminist. Woman's independence for Sayers is independence within a social fabric of mutual respect between the sexes and with awareness of the different abilities of individuals. In *Busman's Honeymoon* Harriet points out to Peter the damage done to woman's nature when husbands please wives by doing things contrary to their own needs. Of course, Sayers argues, women should not give up meaningful work when they marry (a point Harriet already knows in *Strong Poison*), but it is equally true that men must not give up their convictions (something Harriet only comes to understand in a key scene in *Busman's Honeymoon*).

In addition to this important presentation of the interaction of men and women, *Busman's Honeymoon* continues Sayers's affectionate description of British social-class distinctions. In the novel version there is also a substantial coda after the murder is solved. In this coda Lord Peter grapples with his scruples about having played God in exposing the murderer. Lord Peter hires the best barrister possible for him and yet feels complicit when the man is executed. Epithalamion chapters at the end describe a visit of the newlyweds to Lord Peter's ancestral home. There Harriet encounters a family ghost and recognizes the apparition as an illustration of the Wimsey heritage to which marriage joins her permanently.

Among the minor characters in *Busman's Honeymoon* are several lively additions to the Sayers portrait gallery. Most interesting biographically is the brooding Frank Crutchley, the crude but plausible villain. He is in part a portrait of the motor mechanic Bill White, the father of Sayers's child. Her letters during pregnancy show more sympathy for the unpaternal feelings of a "superior man," as Miss Twitterton repeatedly calls Crutchley, who has been brought up without social advantages or the opportunity to do meaningful work, as White had been. Although the novel *Busman's Honeymoon* was composed together with the play, it is remarkable for technical variety. The basic structure is omniscient narration, but there are dialogue scenes, an occasional interior monologue, and an epistolary prothalamion. The main narrative is interlaced with quotations, epigraphs, Latin tags, and snippets of French (including pillow talk on the wedding night). Inspector Kirk's penchant for literary quotation shows that Sayers can allow an intellectual life to her lower-class characters. On the other hand, Kirk's quotations elicited from some original reviewers of both play and novel the objection that the story is weighted down with literary allusions. But what is new here is neither the frequency nor the intensity of literary allusion. It is just that the game playing is explicit. All the Lord Peter detective works are filled with literary allusions, but here the characters make a game of identifying them.

The posthumous short stories of *Striding Folly* (published in 1972) provide details of the later married life of Peter and Harriet. More interesting than the mystery of stolen peaches in the last of the stories, "Talboys," is the revelation that the three sons of Lord Peter are being raised by different sets of rules in light of their different characters and prospects (the eldest son being heir to a large entailed estate). While many readers prefer the novels, some admirers of more traditional detective stories find Sayers at her best in these short stories just because they are simpler in structure and thus do not dilute the pure detective genre with techniques of mainstream fiction. While there are also Lord Peter short stories in three earlier collections, eleven stories feature Montague Egg, a commercial traveler, as detective, including one set at Oxford that would have been more plausibly handled by Lord Peter.

The one Sayers novel not featuring Lord Peter is an epistolary novel—or more precisely a documentary novel, for various sorts of writing, not just letters, are included. The novel was officially coauthored with Robert Eustace, but the writing was done by Sayers while Eustace provided scientific information. Mary Brian Durkin (50) calls this work a turning point in Sayers's career for adding depth of character to the fundamental mystery puzzle. But character development in the earlier novels is shrewder than it is sometimes given credit for being. This novel does treat at length some of the issues of artistic and moral value that figure more and more prominently later.

Love All, the only secular play apart from the play version of *Busman's Honeymoon*, is centrally concerned with woman's work. The heroine gains control of her life by turning herself into a writer. In the process she neglects the duty thrust upon her of being muse to a male writer (and is so busy as a working playwright that she simply forgets to obtain the divorce she has agreed to). The play is a witty drawing-room comedy but suffers perhaps by allowing the three successfully emancipated female characters to triumph too emphatically over the male protagonist. Since the first act is set in Venice and the dialogue includes some Italian, the play looks forward in a way to Sayers's later work with Dante (editor Dale suggests that there are numerous errors in the Italian, but except for two places where English-speaking characters plausibly confuse French with Italian, the mistakes are simply correct Venetian dialect).

Later works by Sayers focus on theology. *The Mind of the Maker* (1941), a book of what is now called critical theory, lucidly expounds the thesis that creative art is a metaphor for understanding the Trinity. Artistic creation requires an idea, a physical embodiment of that idea, and an emanation of that embodied idea. These three elements are analogous to the idea of creation in the Mind of God the Father, the energy of creation as performed by God the Son, and the power of creation as experienced through the Holy Ghost. This is consonant with tradition, but no one else has worked out so specifically the analogy with the work of the creative artist. Her discussion of the nature of evil is particularly illuminating in this context of literary creation. By creating good, God creates evil in the limited sense that a great literary work like *Hamlet* creates a void by comparison: "The act of creation enriches the world with a new category of Being, namely: *Hamlet*. But simultaneously it enriches the world with a new category of Non-Being, namely: Not-Hamlet" (101). In the same way, evil has not existed until the creation of good has made it possible in distinction. This book grew as Sayers worked on her first religious play, *The Zeal of Thy House*, which was first performed at Canterbury Cathedral and later had a run in the West End. The play illustrates Sayers's theoretical position that artists do God's work by creating to the best of their abilities. The central incident is a fall sustained in the cathedral in 1179 by the architect William of Sens while repairing the roof. Sayers presents an inspired tragic understanding of what brought about this fall. William of Sens has been carrying on an affair with a woman patron of the restoration, but he is not punished for that. Instead, his affair momentarily distracts him from the work and also distracts the workers who are supposed to be examining the rope that fails him. He is hurt as a consequence of not putting the work first.

The Man Born to Be King (1943) is a sequence of twelve one-act radio plays on the life of Christ. The plan was to illustrate Christian Incarnation theology dramatically in everyday language to make the story real for ordinary people. Despite the difficulty of keeping the large cast of characters distinct in listeners' minds without visual cues and the difficulty of identifying appropriate moments of climax in a long-form drama that must have some closure in each episode, the dramatization is expertly managed. While it was necessary to invent characters and dialogue, at no point does Sayers find "artistic truth and theological truth at variance" (19). Some of the dramatic condensation is inspired, in particular the placing of Judas Iscariot as a disciple of John the Baptist to motivate his betrayal: a spiritual zealot, Judas becomes convinced that Jesus intends to divert His mission into restoring a merely temporal kingdom. On the other hand, the realistic language ran afoul of adverse publicity. The objections raised were not, however, to episodes of truly groundbreaking realism, for example, having the bad thief curse the crowd after he loses a tooth to a stone thrown at him or having Mary Magdalen flirt with old acquaintances among the Roman soldiers to get permission for the chief mourners to pass through to their stations at the foot of the Cross. The outcry was against deviating from the language of the King James Bible, as if the translation itself had the authority of a sacred text. However, after the broadcasts began, the overwhelming response was strongly positive, and the production was widely appreciated for helping people understand the stories in real-world contexts. Nowadays the realistic language seems completely decorous.

The Just Vengeance (1946) is a miracle play in the medieval sense of a play on a theological but not biblical story. A World War I airman learns to leave his destiny to the Incarnation. A pageant in which the airman encounters many historical and allegorical figures, the play is remarkable for its variety of poetic forms but is Sayers's least original. *The Emperor Constantine* (1951) also deals with the Incarnation. In form a chronicle history with a huge cast, the play retells the complex story of Constantine and his times. Written for performance at Colchester Cathedral, it naturally makes use of the local tradition that Constantine's mother, St. Helen, was the daughter of Old King Coel of Colchester. The play also gives considerable attention to the Council of Nicaea, which ended the Arian heresy. This knotty abstract theology is effectively dramatized by showing Constantine being made to see that mental reservations about the full Godhead of the Second Person of the Trinity would be analogous to mental reservations about the full authority of Constantine as Augustus. The focus on Constantine enables Sayers to dramatize the historic moment when Christianity ceased to be "the cult of a minority" and when "the power of purse and sword" came to the church, as it had to if the gospel was to be preached worldwide (5).

The Devil to Pay (1939) is a Faust play dramatizing the existence of evil. Sayers's Faust can dismiss Mephistopheles in the end with "Mock me not, nothingness" (118), having learned that evil only exists as that which is by definition not good. Her Mephistopheles (like Goethe's) is cheated of Faust's soul when he comes to judgment, but not because Faust illustrates eternal striving to create, as Goethe's Faust does. Sayers's Faust sells his soul to escape into fantasy, thereby enacting Christ's injunction that we should become as little children: "Undo the sin of Adam, turn the years back to their primal innocence" (67). Although the heavenly Judge informs Mephistopheles that Faust's soul was never his to sell, Faust discovers that he has been cheated as well since he has not fully experienced the prelapsarian innocence he bargained for. As a consequence, he is destined for Limbo, not Hell: the souls there neither see God nor understand their loss. Under the circumstances, Faust opts for Hell but finds a promise of redemption. This Hell is apparently only Purgatory since, although Mephistopheles takes Faust away, it is with the divine proviso "Thou has claimed thy own, / It is thine. Burn it. Touch not my good grain, / I shall require it at my hand some day" (118–119).

Besides numerous volumes of cultural criticism about women, work, and religion, Sayers spent time in later years translating epic poetry. Her *Divine Comedy* intended to make Dante accessible as a great storyteller, but she went beyond this by copying his difficult terza stanza. The work is brilliant and illuminates many points missed by other translators. But because Sayers's translation mirrors Dante's range of styles from slang to Latinate diction, it is not as accessible as she supposed. She also translated Thomas the Troubadour's *Tristan in Brittany* and *The Song of Roland*.

ASSESSMENT

Sayers is most famous for mysteries featuring Lord Peter Wimsey. In addition to attractive puzzle plots, these works have literate style and incorporate serious thinking about Christian justice and the nature of work—particularly women's work. These themes are also explored in the dramatic works she wrote during the second stage of her career, and the concern with Christian theology is evident in the translation of Dante's *Divine Comedy* that occupied her last years.

BIBLIOGRAPHY

Primary Sources

Op. I. Oxford: Blackwell, 1916.

Catholic Tales and Christian Songs. Oxford: Blackwell, 1918.

Whose Body? London: Unwin, 1923.

Clouds of Witness. London: Gollancz, 1926.

Unnatural Death. London: Benn, 1927.

Lord Peter Views the Body. London: Gollancz, 1928.

The Unpleasantness at the Bellona Club. London: Benn, 1928.

Tristan in Brittany by Thomas the Troubadour. Trans. Dorothy L. Sayers. London: Benn, 1929.

The Documents in the Case. With Robert Eustace. London: Benn, 1930.

Strong Poison. London: Gollancz, 1930.

The Five Red Herrings. London: Gollancz, 1931.

Have His Carcase. London: Gollancz, 1932.

Hangman's Holiday. London: Gollancz, 1933.

Murder Must Advertise. London: Gollancz, 1933.

The Nine Tailors. London: Gollancz, 1934.

Gaudy Night. London: Gollancz, 1935.

Busman's Honeymoon: Detective Comedy in Three Acts. With M[uriel] St. Clare Byrne. London: Gollancz, 1937.

Busman's Honeymoon: A Love Story with Detective Interruptions. London: Gollancz, 1937.

"Gaudy Night." *Titles to Fame.* Ed. Denys Kilham. London: Nelson, 1937.

The Zeal of Thy House (play). London: Gollancz, 1937.

The Greatest Drama Ever Staged. London: Hodder, 1938.

The Devil to Pay, Being the Famous Play of John Faustus. Canterbury: Goulden, 1939.

He That Should Come: A Nativity Play. London: Gollancz, 1939.

In the Teeth of the Evidence. London: Gollancz, 1939.

Strong Meat. London: Hodder, 1939.

Begin Here: A War-Time Essay. London: Gollancz, 1940.

Creed or Chaos? London: Hodder, 1940.

The Mind of the Maker. London: Methuen, 1941.

The Mysterious English. London: Macmillan, 1941.

Why Work? London: Methuen, 1942.

The Man Born to Be King: A Play-Cycle on the Life of Our Lord and Saviour Jesus Christ. London: Gollancz, 1943.

The Just Vengeance (play). London: Gollancz, 1946.

Unpopular Opinions. London: Gollancz, 1946.

The Lost Tools of Learning. London: Methuen, 1948.

Hell. By Dante. Trans. Dorothy L. Sayers. Harmondsworth: Penguin, 1949.

The Emperor Constantine: A Chronicle (play). London: Gollancz, 1951.

The Days of Christ's Coming. London: Hamilton; New York: Harper, 1960.

Introductory Papers on Dante. London: Methuen, 1954.

Purgatory. By Dante. Trans. Dorothy L. Sayers. Harmondsworth: Penguin, 1955.

Further Papers on Dante. London: Methuen, 1957.

The Song of Roland. Harmondsworth: Penguin, 1957.

Paradise. By Dante. Trans. Dorothy L. Sayers with Barbara Reynolds. Harmondsworth: Penguin, 1962.

The Poetry of Search and the Poetry of Statement. London: Gollancz, 1963.

Christian Letters to a Post-Christian World. Grand Rapids: Eerdmans, 1969.

Are Women Human? Grand Rapids: Eerdmans, 1971.

Striding Folly. Alyesbury: New English Library, 1972.

A Matter of Eternity. Grand Rapids: Eerdmans, 1973.

Wilkie Collins. Ed. E.R. Gregory. Toledo: Friends of U of Toledo Libraries, 1977.

The Whimsical Christian. New York: Macmillan, 1978.

Love All: A Comedy of Manners *by Dorothy L. Sayers; and,* Busman's Honeymoon: A Detective Comedy *by Dorothy L. Sayers and Muriel St. Clare Byrne*. Ed. Alzina Stone Dale. Kent: Kent State UP, 1984.

The Letters of Dorothy L. Sayers, Vol. 1. *1899–1936: The Making of a Detective Novelist*. Ed. Barbara Reynolds. New York: St. Martin's, 1996.

The Letters of Dorothy L. Sayers, Vol. 2. *1937–1943: From Novelist to Playwright*. Ed. Barbara Reynolds. New York: St. Martin's, 1996.

Thrones, Dominations. With Jill Paton Walsh. London: Hodder, 1998.

The Letters of Dorothy L. Sayers, Vol. 3. *1944–1950: A Noble Daring*. Ed. Barbara Reynolds. Cambridge: Dorothy L. Sayers Society, 1999.

The Letters of Dorothy L. Sayers, Vol. 4. *1951–1957: In the Midst of Life*. Ed. Barbara Reynolds. Cambridge: Dorothy L. Sayers Society, 2000.

Secondary Sources

Brabazon, James. *Dorothy L. Sayers: The Life of a Courageous Woman*. London: Gollancz, 1981. As *Dorothy L. Sayers: A Life*. New York: Scribner's, 1981.

Brunsdale, Mitzi. *Dorothy L. Sayers: Solving the Mystery of Wickedness*. Providence: Berg, 1991.

Clarke, Stephan. *The Lord Peter Wimsey Companion*. New York: Mysterious, 1985.

Coomes, David. *Dorothy L. Sayers: A Careless Rage for Life*. Batavia, NY: Lion, 1992.

Cournos, John. *The Devil Is an English Gentleman*. New York: Farrar, 1932.

Dale, Alzina Stone, ed. *Dorothy L. Sayers: The Centenary Celebration*. New York: Walker, 1993.

Drake, Dan. *An Annotated Wimsey*. 22 August 2001 <http://www.dandrake.com/wimsey/>.

Durkin, Mary Brian. *Dorothy L. Sayers*. Boston: Twayne, 1980.

Elkins, Aaron. "The Art of Framing Lies: Dorothy L. Sayers on Mystery Fiction." In Dale 99–107.

Gaillard, Dawson. *Dorothy L. Sayers*. New York: Ungar, 1981.

Gilbert, Colleen B. *A Bibliography of the Works of Dorothy L. Sayers*. Hamden, CT: Archon, 1978.

Hall, Trevor H. *Dorothy L. Sayers: Nine Literary Studies*. London: Duckworth, 1980.

Hannay, Margaret P., ed. *As Her Whimsey Took Her: Critical Essays on the Work of Dorothy L. Sayers*. Kent: Kent State UP, 1979.

Harmon, Robert B., and Margaret A. Burger. *An Annotated Guide to the Works of Dorothy L. Sayers*. New York: Garland, 1977.

Hitchman, Janet. *Such a Strange Lady: A Biography of Dorothy L. Sayers*. New York: Harper, 1975.

Hone, Ralph E. *Dorothy L. Sayers: A Literary Biography*. Kent: Kent State UP, 1979.

Kenney, Catherine. *The Remarkable Case of Dorothy L. Sayers*. Kent: Kent State UP, 1990.

Lewis, Terrance L. *Dorothy L. Sayers' Wimsey and Interwar British Society*. Lewiston, NY: Edwin Mellen, 1994.

McGregor, Robert Kuhn, and Ethan Lewis. *Conundrums for the Long Week-End: England, Dorothy L. Sayers, and Lord Peter Wimsey*. Kent: Kent State UP, 2000.

Merry, Bruce. "Dorothy L. Sayers: Mystery and Demystification." In *Art in Crime Writing: Essays on Detective Fiction*. Ed. Bernard Benstock. New York: St. Martin's, 1983. 18–32.

Reynolds, Barbara. *Dorothy L. Sayers: Her Life and Soul*. New York: St. Martin's, 1993.

———. *The Passionate Intellect: Dorothy L. Sayers' Encounter with Dante*. Kent: Kent State UP, 1989.

Scott-Giles, C. W[ilfrid]. *The Wimsey Family*. London: Gollancz, 1977.

Seven: An Anglo-American Review. Home page. 23 August 2001 <http://www.sayers.org.uk/seven.html>.

Thurmer, John. *A Detection of the Trinity*. Exeter: Paternoster, 1984.

Walsh, Jill Paton. "Thrones, Dominations." *Mystery Scene* 60 (1998): 30–32.

Wilson, Edmund. "Who Cares Who Killed Roger Ackroyd?" In *Classics and Commercials*. New York: Vintage, 1962. 257–265.

Youngberg, Ruth Tanis. *Dorothy L. Sayers: A Reference Guide*. Boston: Hall, 1982.

May Sinclair
1863–1946

Melinda Harvey

BACKGROUND

May Sinclair—novelist, literary critic, philosopher, biographer, poet, translator, and short-story writer—was born in Rock Ferry, Cheshire, the youngest child and only surviving daughter of Belfast-born Amelia Hind and Liverpudlian shipowner William Sinclair (a sister, Gertrude, died in infancy in 1854). Like that of so many offspring of the Victorian mercantile middle class, her prosperous and comfortable childhood was shattered by her father's bankruptcy in or about 1870. While Sinclair was herself infamously evasive about the time prior to the 1897 publication of her first novel, *Audrey Craven*, it is certain that a prolonged period of familial estrangement, financial insecurity and residential itinerancy ensued.

Two key sequences of events or "motifs" from these years emerge from both documentary evidence and her own writings as significant, despite Sinclair's reticence. The first of these relates directly to the fortunes of the Sinclair family: by 1897 four of the five Sinclair men were dead—all more or less due to the bad brew of heart disease and alcoholism—leaving May the lone companion and carer of her difficult and demanding mother. The last surviving brother, Joseph, had immigrated to Canada in 1885 and ultimately succumbed to the "family curse" of mitral valve disease in 1905, aged fifty. This notoriously fraught mother-daughter relationship not only provided the inspiration and dramatic impetus for a large number of Sinclair's writings (*Nakiketas and Other Poems*, *Mary Olivier*, *Life and Death of Harriett Frean*), it was also the battlefield upon which Sinclair played out her most important religious, political, and philosophical struggles. Intellectual pursuits were a welcome refuge from, as well as an antidote to, Amelia's compelling call to rigid Protestantism and docile femininity: wrangles with the likes of Euripides, Sophocles, Shakespeare, Milton, Hume, Pope, and Shelley offered the earnest and inquisitive Sinclair a pleasurable and profitable alternative form of confrontation.

Though Sinclair's assiduity for knowledge was evident in the extent of her self-tutoring—by the age of eighteen, for example, Sinclair was proficient in French, German, and Greek—her intellectual and artistic development was in no small part fostered and framed by her year at Cheltenham Ladies' College in 1881 and her relationship with its principal, Dorothea Beale, the second key "motif" in Sinclair's early life. Impressed by Sinclair's candor, clarity, and conscientiousness following a disputation over a written task on God (which Sinclair, due to a profound agnosticism, refused to complete), Beale encouraged Sinclair's tendency toward philosophical speculation, with the aim of shoring up her religious faith: as well as introducing her to the idealism of Plato, Hegel, Kant, and T.H. Green, Beale also enjoined Sinclair to write tracts out of her crisis of faith, publishing her first article, "Descartes," in the school's reputable *Cheltenham Ladies' College Magazine*.

Despite a lifelong interest and investment in philosophy—Sinclair would go on to write two defenses of idealist philosophy against Russellian neorealism and was elected as a member of the Aristotelian Society for the Systematic Study of Philosophy in 1917—her fame and modest fortune were found as a prolific professional novelist. Averaging close to a new novel every year (the last six novels were published within three years), Sinclair became a literary luminary upon the publication of her first best-seller, *The Divine Fire*, a phenomenon that led to a whirlwind two-month publicity tour of the United States, a meeting with President Theodore Roosevelt, and dinner with Mark Twain, who, it is said, thanked her derisively at the end of the evening for "a remarkably interesting silence." Sinclair's status as the shy woman of English letters was not assuaged by the typically impassive, starched nature of her relations with literary contemporaries such as Thomas Hardy, Henry James, Arnold Bennett, Edith Wharton, H.G. Wells, John Galsworthy, Sinclair Lewis, Violet Hunt, Cicely Hamilton, Dorothy Richardson, Virginia Woolf, Rose Macaulay, Ford Madox Ford, Wyndham Lewis, T.S. Eliot, Ezra Pound, Richard Aldington, H.D., and Winifred Bryher. In 1927 Sinclair retired entirely from the literary scene, living out her last nineteen years with her companion of thirty years, Florence Bartrop, in the Buckinghamshire countryside.

ANALYSIS

Apart from offering a compelling portrait of the shift from Victorian to modernist sensibilities in both her life and her novels, it is perhaps as a reader, interpreter, and critic, as Diane Gillespie has suggested, that Sinclair offers her most lasting literary bequest. In the first instance, Sinclair was an exceptionally well read and lissome proponent of literary modernism, stalwartly defending its aesthetic experimentation against the charges of formlessness, narcissism, obscurity, and inconsequence. Although one could diagnose Sinclair's own poetry in terms of the literary public as distinctly unresonant and unsuccessful, she was, because of her ardent early-career poetic forays, able to act as a keen and lucid arbiter between other verse innovators and their contemporary readership. Alongside Ezra Pound, Sinclair was a sincere and indefatigable voice of T.S. Eliot's incipient vanguard: in one of the first reviews of *Prufrock and Other Observations*, published in Margaret Anderson's *Little Review*, she exults in the abstruseness, discomfiture, and sordidness of Eliotian verse, celebrating poems such as "Preludes" and "La Figlia Che Piange" for their reality and their potentialities for "writerly" pleasure. Sinclair found the consonance between form and content in Eliot's poems especially laudable, an imagist trait she was, time and again, to celebrate in her reviews of the likes of H.D., Pound, and F.S. Flint. In their poems presentation, not representation—a "direct, naked contact with reality" as opposed to a distant, composed bout of "spectacular reflection"—was, with the concomitant crispness and precision, singled out for exegesis and then commendation.

Sinclair's celebration of the writer as delicate sensorium—her belief in the writer's duty to delineate an unmediated, immediate connection with the world of things for the reader—underlies two of her greatest literary achievements, one critical, one creative. The first of these is her April 1918 review for the *Egoist* entitled "The Novels of Dorothy Richardson," which introduced, borrowing from William James's *Principles of Psychology* (1890), the term "stream of consciousness" into literary discourse. Though it has been and remains a much-debated, even maligned phrase, signifying as much a free-associative and unpunctuated written style as a meticulously dredged confessional narrative of psychological content, "stream of consciousness" continues to meaningfully refer to a large body of post–World War I novels produced under the influence of Freud and his attendant analysts and sexologists. It registers a move in prose fiction away from the omnipresent, omniscient narrator of nineteenth-century naturalism who frames, judges, and intervenes in human drama and toward a focus on the delimited, instantaneous feelings, thoughts, and sensations of an acting, involved central consciousness—from, in Sinclair's own terms, the "analytic" to the "synthetic" psychological novel.

Indeed, one can understand Sinclair's own novelistic output to be charting this aforesaid trajectory: in the novels published prior to 1914 narratorial intrusion is maintained, for the most part, as a cry for social, sexual, and spiritual autonomy in the "marriage-plot" novels (*The Divine Fire*, *Kitty Tailleur*, *The Combined Maze*) or as a comic device marking the incongruity between things as they are and things as they appear to the main protagonist (as in *The Helpmate* and *The Creators*). The later novels, however, endeavor to speak as entirely from the position of character—and never as the wise, all-knowing author—as possible and offer an exposé of unconscious desires and unacknowledged emotions rather than an exploration of socioeconomic conditions and constraints.

This move toward extended interior monologue saw many notable critics, including Frank Swinnerton, Walter Allen, and Catherine Dawson Scott, herald Sinclair as the pioneer of the psychological novel, her second great literary contribution. Certainly, from about 1913, when Sinclair became a founding member and financial benefactor of the Medico-Psychological Clinic of London, her novels began to bear the mark of a keen and active engagement with the new psychology. Arguably, this interest was spawned by Sinclair's obsession with what she saw, after Gissing, Hardy, and Meredith, as the twin oppressors in the religious, sexual, and intellectual development of the individual, heredity and environment. While the earlier works revealed the repressive and destructive effects of the parent-child bond to be the fault of Victorian values or a deterministic world view, novels such as *Arnold Waterlow*, *The Three Sisters*, *Mary Olivier*, and *Life and Death of Harriett Frean* offer a psychoanalytic account of familial conflict and the struggle for self-determination beyond the crush of societal expectations, the latter three, alongside the phenomenally successful *The Divine Fire*, unanimously considered by critics past and present—including Walter Allen, Hrisey Zegger, and Kenneth Robb—to be her finest achievements.

The Three Sisters stands as a transitional text in Sinclair's move from the analytic to the synthetic psychological narrative. Part Victorianesque family saga, part case study of the evils of sexual sublimation, the novel tells the story of sisters Gwenda, Mary, and Alice and the repercussions of their uneventful, unfulfilling lives under the rule of a bellicose father. Here, as elsewhere in her oeuvre, Sinclair gestures toward the Brontë sisters as an apt and compelling archetype for the female condition—as exemplars par excellence of the distance between women's inner and outer lives. Indeed, the Brontës' lives and writings were, for Sinclair, a lifelong obsession—by the time of her retirement from the literary scene in 1927, she had produced seven short introductions to Dent's Everyman's Library Series editions of key texts by or about the Brontës (*Jane Eyre*, *Shirley*, *Villette*, *The Professor*, *The Tenant of Wildfell Hall*, *Wuthering Heights*, and *The Life of Charlotte Brontë*) as well as a book-length appreciation, *The Three Brontës*. With the exception of her 1919 novel *Mary Olivier*, in her musings on Charlotte Brontë in particular—the frustrations of the fiercely passionate and intellectually ambitious woman trapped in an isolated domestic scene; the complicity of sexuality, creativity, and sacrifice, to name two such themes of contemplation—Sinclair comes as close to autobiography as she ever did anywhere in her vast body of work.

The subsequent novels, *Mary Olivier* and *Life and Death of Harriett Frean*, highly praised on publication by the likes of E.M. Forster, Wells, and Eliot, read like psychoanalytic investigations of the frigid, self-forfeiting Victorian ideal of femininity and the claims of marriage and motherhood. *Mary Olivier* is in many ways a modernist rewriting of George Eliot's *The Mill on the Floss*, Mary bearing a strong likeness to Maggie Tulliver in her oscillations from raw sensuousness to strident asceticism and her struggle for intellectual and artistic development as a female child. *Life and Death of Harriett Frean* ploughs a similar thematic field—the stultifying, infantilizing effects of the mother-daughter bond and religious conformism and repression—but is far more extravagantly experimental in form and style. At just over one hundred pages, *Life and Death of Harriett Frean* is a taut, understated but entirely relentless piece of stream-of-consciousness virtuosity, not to mention a caustic attack on the so-called feminine virtues of compliance, renunciation, and "behaving beautifully." Its compressed limited-perspective narrative, heavily imagistic representations of sexuality squandered, and imbrication of storytelling, psychoanalysis, metaphysics, and social critique assure Sinclair's recognition as a modernist innovator, as her first modern and best-versed critic, Theophilus Boll, has argued.

But it has been for this conjoining of science and literature that Sinclair has been criticized: for as Katherine Mansfield, the desire for an accurate rendition of the human mind ran counter to the telling of a good tale. Slowly but surely, however, Sinclair's contemporary critics found it more and more difficult to muster anything approaching excitement or praise: a new novel meant the eruption of a poignant and inevitable nostalgia for *The Divine Fire* followed just as inevitably by a sour recognition that the author had not daringly or meaningfully strayed from her overploughed and barren field.

ASSESSMENT

Virtually forgotten altogether after her withdrawal from the literary scene at the onset of Parkinson's disease, Sinclair is indebted for her current renown to two biocritical studies from the 1970s (Boll, Zegger) and the reissue, synchronous with the retrieval project of second-wave feminism, of *The Three Sisters, Mary Olivier*, and *Life and Death of Harriett Frean* by Virago Press. Despite the flurry of feminist short pieces in journals during the 1990s, Sinclair remains a seldom-read, but often-mentioned British author—the stuff of the contextual name drop or the anecdotal aside, overshadowed not only by the big men of modernism but a set of newly anointed interwar women writers who seem to make the grade as often for their sexual exploits and voguish lifestyles as the quality of their literary output. Suzanne Raitt's recent work on Sinclair, especially her biography, *May Sinclair: A Modern Victorian*, and a new concentration on Sinclair's World War I writings are suggestive of a new and fruitful line of inquiry previously overshadowed by the themes of technical innovation and first-wave feminism.

BIBLIOGRAPHY

Primary Sources

Nakiketas and Other Poems. As Julian Sinclair. London: Kegan Paul, 1886.

Essays in Verse. London: Kegan Paul, 1891.

Audrey Craven. London: Blackwood, 1897; New York: Holt, 1906.

Mr. and Mrs. Nevill Tyson. London: Blackwood, 1898. As *The Tysons*. New York: B.W. Dodge, 1906.

Two Sides of a Question (stories). London: Hutchinson, 1900. As *Superseded*. New York: Holt, 1906.

The Divine Fire. London: Constable; New York: Holt, 1904.
The Helpmate. London: Constable; New York: Holt, 1907.
Kitty Tailleur. London: Constable, 1908. As *The Immortal Moment: The Story of Kitty Tailleur*. New York: Doubleday, 1908.
The Creators: A Comedy. London: Constable; New York: Century, 1910.
Feminism. London: Women Writers' Suffrage League, 1912.
The Flaw in the Crystal. New York: E.P. Dutton, 1912.
The Three Brontës. London: Hutchinson; Boston and New York: Houghton Mifflin, 1912.
The Combined Maze. London: Hutchinson; New York: Harper, 1913.
The Judgment of Eve and Other Stories. London: Hutchinson, 1914.
The Three Sisters. London: Hutchinson, 1914; London: Virago, 1982; New York: Dial, 1985.
America's Part in the War. New York: Commission for Relief in Belgium, 1915.
A Journal of Impressons in Belgium. London: Hutchinson; New York, Macmillan, 1915.
Tasker Jevons: The Real Story. London: Hutchinson, 1916. As *The Belfry*. New York: Macmillan, 1916.
A Defence of Idealism: Some Questions and Conclusions. London and New York: Macmillan, 1917.
The Tree of Heaven. London: Cassell, 1917; New York: Macmillan, 1917.
Mary Olivier: A Life. 1919. London: J. Lehmann, 1949; London: Virago, 1980.
The Romantic. London: Collins; New York: Macmillan, 1920.
Mr. Waddington of Wyck. London: Cassell; New York: Macmillan, 1921.
Anne Severn and the Fieldings. London: Hutchinson; New York: Macmillan, 1922.
Life and Death of Harriett Frean. London: W. Collins, 1922; London: Virago, 1980.
The New Idealism. London and New York: Macmillan, 1922.
Uncanny Stories. London: Hutchinson, 1923.
Arnold Waterlow: A Life. London: Hutchinson; New York: Macmillan, 1924.
A Cure of Souls. London: Hutchinson; New York: Macmillan, 1924.
The Dark Night (poems). London: Cape; New York: Macmillan, 1924.
The Rector of Wyck. London: Hutchinson; New York: Macmillan, 1925.
Far End. London: Hutchinson; New York: Macmillan, 1926.
The Allinghams. London: Hutchinson; New York: Macmillan, 1927.
The History of Anthony Waring. London: Hutchinson; New York: Macmillan, 1927.
Fame. London: Elkin Mathews, 1929.
Tales Told by Simpson (stories). London: Hutchinson; New York: Macmillan, 1930.
The Intercessor and Other Stories. London: Hutchinson, 1931; New York: Macmillan, 1932.

Secondary Sources

Boll, T.E.M. *Miss May Sinclair, Novelist: A Biographical and Critical Introduction*. Rutherford, NJ: Fairleigh Dickinson UP, 1973.
Eliot, T.S. "London Letter." *Dial* 73 (September 1922): 329–331.
Gillespie, Diane F. "May Sinclair." In *The Gender of Modernism: A Critical Anthology*. Ed. Bonnie Kime Scott. Bloomington: Indiana UP, 1990. 436–442.
———. "May Sinclair and the Stream of Consciousness: Metaphors and Metaphysics." *English Literature in Transition, 1880–1920* 21.2 (1978): 134–142.
———. "The Muddle of the Middle: May Sinclair on Women." *Tulsa Studies in Women's Literature* 4.2 (Fall 1985): 235–251.
Harris, Janice H. "Challenging the Script of the Heterosexual Couple: Three Marriage Novels by May Sinclair." *Papers on Language and Literature* 29.4 (Fall 1993): 436–458.
Kaplan, Sydney. " 'Featureless Freedom' or Ironic Submission: Dorothy Richardson and May Sinclair." *College English* 32 (1971): 914–917.
Mansfield, Katherine. "Ask No Questions." *Athenaeum* 4721 (22 October 1920): 522.
———. "The New Infancy." *Athenaeum* 4651 (20 June 1919): 494.
Miller, Jane Eldridge. "New Wine, New Bottles: H.G. Wells and May Sinclair." In *Rebel Women: Feminism, Modernism, and the Edwardian Novel*. London: Virago, 1994. 163–202.
Mumford, Laura Stempel. "May Sinclair's *The Tree of Heaven*: The Vortex of Feminism, the Community of War." In *Arms and the Woman: War, Gender, and Literary Representation*. Ed. Helen M. Cooper, Adrienne Auslander Munich, and Susan Merrill Squier. Chapel Hill: U of North Carolina P, 1989. 168–183.
Neff, Rebecca Kinnamon. "May Sinclair's *Uncanny Stories* as Metaphysical Quest." *English Literature in Transition, 1880–1920* 26.3 (1983): 187–191.

———. "New Mysticism in the Writings of May Sinclair and T.S. Eliot." *Twentieth Century Literature* 26 (1980): 82–108.

Phillips, Terry. "Battling with the Angel: May Sinclair's Powerful Mothers." In *Image and Power: Women in Fiction in the Twentieth Century*. Ed. Sarah Sceats and Gail Cunningham. London: Longman, 1996. 128–138.

Raitt Suzanne. "Charlotte Mew and May Sinclair: A Love-Song." *Critical Quarterly* 37.3 (Fall 1995): 3–17.

———. " 'Contagious Ecstasy': May Sinclair's War Journals." In *Women's Fiction and the Great War*. Ed. Suzanne Raitt and Trudi Tate. Oxford: Oxford UP, 1997.

———. *May Sinclair: A Modern Victorian*. Oxford: Clarendon, 2000.

Robb, Kenneth A. "May Sinclair." *English Literature in Transition, 1880–1920* 18 (1975): 72–73.

———. "May Sinclair: An Annotated Bibliography of Writings about Her." *English Literature in Transition, 1880–1920* 16.3 (1973): 177–231.

Scott, C.A. Dawson. "May Sinclair." *Bookman* 52 (November 1920): 246–249.

Zegger, Hrisey D. *May Sinclair*. Boston: Twayne, 1976.

Edith Sitwell
1887–1964

Gina Wisker

Edith Sitwell, daughter of Sir George Sitwell and his wife, Ida, whose parents the earl and countess of Londesborough owned most of Scarborough in the north of England, has a mixed reputation and has certainly never received the critical appraisal her work deserves. Ostensibly one of the "bright young things" of the 1920s generation, she was actually more of a critic of the frivolous worldliness of her parents' world. Her status as minor aristocracy hides the lack of money she and her brothers Osbert and Sacheverell often suffered. Indeed, politically, they were not extremely right-wing, but intellectual. One stood for Parliament as a Liberal, rather than a Conservative, but failed to gain a seat. Edith was a critic of the Victorians, such as Tennyson and Matthew Arnold, and the Georgians, such as Alfred Noyes and Edward Thomas, and aligned her own work with that of the modernists, such as T.S. Eliot and Ezra Pound. Her work is experimental, musical, fantastic, critical of the constructedness of the world around her, filled with the sense of decay and disorientation that permeates much of Eliot, but preferring the musical phrase and the fantastic image. She was also a woman, and we are still developing critique of the modernist women poets, who received shockingly less attention than did their male counterparts. Much of her work focuses on expressions of subjects and feelings deemed irrelevant by the modernists and overlooked or criticized in contemporary criticism.

BACKGROUND

Edith Sitwell was brought up more by her grandparents than her parents and was a formidably precocious child who preferred the company of adults rather than of children. Her rather silly mother, who had Edith when she was only seventeen, clearly disliked and ignored her, although her family stories lived on in Edith's retelling of them to her younger brothers Osbert and Sacheverell. Young Edith, apparently developing a devotion to a peacock (who deserted her for a female peacock), found solace and creative opportunities in the world of the nursery and the garden. She identified with spirits and ghosts:

> I was always a little outside life—
> And so the things we touch could comfort me;
> I loved the shy dreams we could hear and see—
> For I was like one dead, like a small ghost,
> A little cold air, wandering and lost.
> ("Colonel Fantock," *Collected Poems* [*CP*] 174)

Her governess Helen Rootham was a friend and guide, teaching her about French poetry.

From 1919 Rootham and Edith Sitwell shared a house in Bayswater. Rootham, who was clearly a great influence on Sitwell's writing, died after a long illness in 1938, and Edith Sitwell's work of this period reflects her tremendous sense of loss. Her periodical *Wheels* set out to provide an opposition to the "Englishness" of the Georgians and largely published poetry that was international, often experimental, and eclectic.

Virginia Woolf describes the adult Sitwell as quite eccentric but striking: "Edith Sitwell is a very tall young woman, wearing a perpetually startled expression and . . . a high green silk head dress concealing her hair so that it is not known whether she has any" (qtd. in Glendinning 3). On the 1960s BBC *Monitor* program Sitwell's face was sharp, intelligent, her dialogue witty, a turban balanced precariously on her head, her nose long and aristocratic. This rather startling appearance matched her incisive, witty critiques of her contemporaries. For example, she wrote that the Georgians "seem obsessed by the predilection for sheep," and she satirizes a hangover of despondency from the late Victorian days as a kind of "wandering among gardens with tall walls, and much complaining and woe" (qtd. in Ross 195). Although she seems to have flamboyantly advertised her own work, she was extremely secretive about her rather sad private life. Her unfulfilled love for the Russian artist Pavel Tchelitchew, which runs through much of her poetry, gave her a mixture of joy and sadness in her life. We know few intimate details of their relationship, but group holidays are recorded, and he painted her several times. Her biographers John Pearson, Geoffrey Elborn, and Victoria Glendinning provide insights into her life and some critique of her surprising imagery and the musicality of her poetry. Her own autobiography *Taken Care Of* provides a mix of fabrication and truth. She was a woman of imagination when it came to her own life as well as her poetry. She was also a cruel critic of some of the less imaginative, less modernist, narrative verse of the period and attacked Noyes and Laurence Binyon, comparing their poetry to rolls of cheap linoleum. However, she was active in promoting good writing. Her editorship of *Wheels* (1916–1921) with her brothers and Nancy Cunard enabled the publication of the work of many young writers and artists, notably Wilfred Owen. Edith Sitwell's letters to Owen's mother are lively, supportive, and celebratory of his talent. She labored over editing his work to produce the exactly right edition of the poems and dedicated herself to publishing him, among other talented young writers, when others might have overlooked their work.

ANALYSIS

Sitwell found both the Victorians and the Georgians tedious and trivial. Her sympathies and talents lay mainly with modernism. However, while critics have recognized the experiments of such writers as T.S. Eliot and Pound, they have overlooked those of Sitwell. For example, Julian Symons refers to her as "the arch-nurse of empty phrases" (qtd. in Glendinning 64). Much of the critique of Sitwell, where it exists, arises from a certain ignorance and undervaluing of women's writing per se, mistaking a concern with subjectivity, emotion, and engagement for lack of rigor and precision in imagery. Aldous Huxley, for example, claims that though her poetry is "exquisite," it is also limited, confined to "the immediacies of consciousness [rather than reaching] towards the universal" (qtd. in Glendinning 89). While contemporary critics, informed by poststructuralism, might celebrate her recognition of constructions and surfaces, nonetheless they also seem to overlook her talents. It is certainly time that Sitwell was accorded the celebration she is due.

Edith Sitwell's influences on women's poetry are still to be fully traced. Her nursery and fairy world remind us of Stevie Smith, delicate, dangerous, witty, and critical. Her record of a certain bohemian life is, it seems, unique. Sitwell's poetry is one of dazzling surfaces, artifice, fantasy, dream, and nightmare. It is sensual, filled with sounds, rhymes, and rhythms that often seem to substitute for a decipherable sense; as Day and Wisker have termed it, it "alerts us to the primacy of the signified in the constitution of meaning" (67). This gives her work a radical edge, "its brilliant coruscations are a refusal of the consolations of modernism's myths" (66). Surfaces and sounds predominate over meaning. This is writing for and to music, sound appearing to take over from sense, rhyme, and rhythm, with witty, dreamlike comment dominating the whole. Indeed, *Facade*, a group of poems reveling in word play and the sound of words together, set to music by William Walton in 1922, is the piece for which she is best known. Another poem, "The Sleeping Beauty," captures happy experiences from her rather unhappy childhood. In maturity she was friends with Robert Graves and his wife Nancy, impressed Virginia Woolf, and admired T.S. Eliot's imagery. Her book *Alexander Pope* (1930) caused something of a revival of his work. Sitwell was photographed by Cecil Beaton and counted artists and poets, photographers and novelists among her friends. Her novel *I Live under a Black Sun* (1937) was well received by the novelist Evelyn Waugh and the poet Edwin Muir, among others, although Sitwell insisted that it met with a poor reception. In it she founds relationships upon the life of Jonathan Swift but sets it in her own circle, so it tends to be realistic and autobiographical.

It is on her poetry that her reputation mainly rests, and she was a prolific writer of it. Some of her best poems are fantastic, musical as well as witty. "When Sir Beelzebub" comments on the hellish nature of contemporary cosmopolitanism, pokes fun at the steadiness of late Victorians, and edges toward surrealism in the drifting and floating of the barmaid and temporary residents of Brighton, who are seemingly on the verge of being washed out to sea. The layout and the repetition of and variation on word sounds produce a hypnotic effect:

> When
> Sir
> Beelzebub called for his syllabub in the hotel in
>   Hell
>   Where Proserpine first fell,
>
> Blue as the gendarmerie
> (Rocking and shocking the barmaid).
> (*CP* 158)

The situation is absurd, surreal. Emphasis on the alliteration of the *l* and *ll* ties the poem tightly together, as does the rhyme scheme that, while mimicking the forced conformity of rhyme and meter of Victorian poetry, similarly satirizes the restraint and stuffiness of the poets themselves. So Tennyson is seen (after one of his own poems, "Crossing the Bar")

> crossing the bar laid
> with cold deputations
> (*CP* 158)

Victorian culture is pompous, she seems to indicate, too heavily reliant upon the order first of religion, then of Darwinism.

Sitwell's mischievous references to Tennyson where the poet crosses the bar in "classical metres" carrying workers' deputations all signed "In Memoriam" lead into further satires on Victorians in "The White Owl." In a rather surreal pastoral scene Hardyesque maids walk by walls in cherry-tree-laden gardens, and the bustling "Mother Bunch" represents Victoria and Victorianism. Sitwell parodies Matthew Arnold's angst in "Dover Beach":

> If once I begin to howl, I am sure that my sobs
>   would drown the seas
> With my "oh's" and my "ah's" and my "oh dear
>   me's!"
> (*CP* 38)

Religion comes under attack in "Four in the Morning," which is reputed to be the time of Christ's betrayal. The dramatic moment is robbed of its significance and is only the substance of a hangover for " 'Mr. Belaker / the allegro Negro cocktail shaker" (*CP* 123). His dreamlike world of bars and seedy hotels is peopled with the rootless and aimless with faces "flattened like the moon" (*CP* 124). Senses are shaken together to make a cocktail producing a state of synaesthetic inebriation. Vague, surrealist images and a repetitive rhyme scheme emphasize a disorganized, confused, unreal sense of being. Here Sitwell recalls Edward Lear's Victorian nonsense poetry. Like him, she deploys rhinos and hippos in her poems, their flattened browns and greys staring out oddly in a fantastic, bizarre nursery/dream world of confusion and disorientation. She also looks forward to the surrealism of David Gascoyne and Dylan Thomas, the one emphasizing strange metaphors and images, the other sounds to evoke emotions. Her lyrics recall dance forms and are influenced by a variety of music. Her satirical "Gold Coast Customs" (1929) compares African Ashanti rituals to those in Mayfair, using jazz rhythms.

As a woman writer, while she cannot be called a feminist, we see her exploring the superficial and dowdy lives of a variety of women. These range from the frivolous, dilettante subaristocracy who party their lives away to governesses confined with young girls, teaching them how to conform, and barmaids in Brighton. Her later poems testify to an acute observation of how women construct themselves with cosmetics and clothes, presenting an increasingly cracked, aging, hysterical figure. Women are not the only ones she critiques, however. As a woman poet, Sitwell refuses the confines of the modernist order, the authoritarian domination of absolutely accurate rendition of the moment, the perfectly selected word and image pared to its essentials, as is found in Ezra Pound's poetry or Eliot's *The Waste Land*. Like Virginia Woolf, she attempts to escape a masculine sentence structure emphasizing logic, clarity, and orderly progression. Julia Kristeva's notion of "semanalysis" is helpful here. Semanalysis focuses upon the tension between the symbolic and the semiotic orders in the construction of subjectivity. The symbolic order, considered "masculine" by some feminists, is the source of rules and structures that might confine and constrain expression into certain acceptable forms, but also enables the subject to be in a shared language with shared meanings. The semiotic, Kristeva argues, is more specifically the realm of women's expression and enables a politicized articulation of sense, emotion, feeling, and individual experience in the face of the constraints of the symbolic order. It runs the risk of not being communicated, however, because of its subversive expression. Sitwell's seemingly nonsensical, singsong, nursery-image verse seems to belong to Kristeva's semiotic order.

Such a fantastic setting and concentration on sound and rhythm instead of absolutely accurate sense did not preclude political comment, however, although many critics would have it that the two are incompatible. Sitwell was highly articulate in her criticism of the insane waste of World War I and expresses this in "The Dancers." She uses vampiric images to characterize the waste of young lives and points out the guilt of those of the older generation who send young men to die in the trenches while they carry on normally, observing from a distance. Likening their inanity to a giddy whirling 1920s dance, she uses vampiric imagery to indicate how those of the older generation feed as "carrion" on the energies and losses of the younger. The party continues, oblivious: "the floors are slippery with blood" (Reilly 100), a concrete metaphor emphasizing the culpability of the revelers in the deaths of the soldiers, for an increasingly dubious national glory.

Sitwell's collection *Street Songs* (1942) is filled with reflections and comments on

World War II. "Still Falls the Rain" was described by Geoffrey Thurley as being one of "the finest and most serious statements about war in our time" (136):

> The last faint spark
> In the self-murdered heart, the wounds of the sad uncomprehending dark,
> The wounds of the baited bear,—
> The blind and weeping bear whom the keepers beat
> On his helpless flesh . . . the tears of the hunted hare.
>
> (*CP* 273)

Notice that even here imagery of the zoo and circus reappears. Sitwell seeks order, and a more ordered poetic expression follows. A modernist reflection of chaos and confusion runs throughout "Myself in the Merry-Go-Round," which expresses a desire for order in a world that "shake[s] the body's equipoise" and where "words [are] set all awry" (*CP* 170). The giddy procession of images, like painted horses on a roundabout, indicts the artifice, excess, and riot of the social circle of postwar "bright young things." Her images are those of the circus, carnivalesque, critical, absurd. In the harsh, Gothic "Lo, this is she that was the world's desire" (*CP* 322) Sitwell takes the figure of Helen of Troy to stand for representations of women and berates the painted superficial construction of women, using nightmarish images to represent the decay of old age and its ravages, which are both physical and psychological. Noting the time "when the appalling lion-claws of age" rip the pretense and beauty apart and beauty is revealed as transient so that "Venus now, grown blackened, noseless old!" (*CP* 322) stands for human decay and the vanity of human wishes, Sitwell dramatizes and critiques the superficial character of her age and the superficial roles accorded to women. Words such as "giddy" and "swirling" emphasize a world breaking apart under the force of its own momentum. Sitwell seems to accelerate the process of dissolution by piling rhymes on top of one another, "Daisy and Lily / Lazy and silly" ("Waltz," *CP* 144), so that meaning is lost in an acceleration of sound. Nonetheless, some order is sought, and here she allies herself with the other modernists such as Eliot and D.H. Lawrence, who also seek order, although Eliot's resides in conventional religion, and Lawrence's in versions of relationships and older religions. There is nevertheless a desire for some sort of stability to repair the "frayed ends" ("Myself in the Merry-Go-Round," *CP* 171) of sense that have been frayed precisely by the friction of movement. This desire to reach beyond the glittering cascade of the bon vivants finally becomes an appeal to traditional religious morality. In "Gold Coast Customs" London is seen as "Gomorrah" (*CP* 251), and Africa is depicted as a swamp, "mud and murk" from which "arises everything" (*CP* 240). Only through an act outside of history, "God shall wash the mud" (*CP* 252), can redemption be imagined.

Sitwell's emphasis on the constructed nature of poetry becomes a comment on the constructed nature of subjectivity. Sounds, rather than sense, of the words predominate. The overall impression is one of flexibility, metamorphosis, an organic buildup of sounds into a feeling or argument sensed rather than logically constructed, her system of imagery mythic, contemporary, Gothic, personal. Unlike Eliot, who uses symbols to reach outwards to an ultimately Christian order, and Yeats, whose symbol system develops and builds up cohesively through his oeuvre, Sitwell's is often simultaneously epic and taken from the world of fairy, political and personal. As she comments on the constructed nature of woman, of human beliefs in different ages, including the deceptions of wars, she emphasizes the ways in which poetry too is constructed, in image and wordplay, sound and rhythm fired by emotion and mood. In this she is unlike the other modernists. The self-conscious aspects of her poetry indicate a different and often-profound understanding of the implications of modernity, for example, that it recognizes dissolution, chaos, a potentially dangerous freedom that could be "mere anarchy." Unlike the modernists, she was prepared to embrace this freedom, and her verse is a testament to the contingent nature of meaning rather than an expression of nostalgia for a lost essentialism.

Technically, too, her work is unconventional. Sitwell's poetry uses a four-stress accentual meter, as in "Great Snoring and Norwich / A dish of pease porridge" ("One o'Clock," *CP* 132), giving the fantastic or bitter verse a nursery-rhyme lilt. It is a light touch increasingly set against the absurd, the destructive, entrapping the reader in the repetitions of sound, the use of couplets, internal rhyme, and the pace of the meter.

Sitwell might have been largely ignored by feminist critics because she does not deal directly with suffrage and often, unlike her contemporary H.D., seems to reinforce and recycle myths that place women in negative roles, such as those of Helen of Troy or Medusa. However, she does also expose the suffering, loneliness, and sense of loss felt by many women who have historically depended upon conventional roles, the construction of beauty, the search for romance as woman's driving force, and undying love. In "Dido's Song" she explores the feelings of the lover whom Aeneas left behind, suffering a "Sun of death," and how even Medusa, once beautiful, feels spring burned away from her, numbed: "But now there is neither honey nor bee for me— / Neither the sting nor the sweetness" (*CP* 346). She is preoccupied with the lies told women, which they internalize, and the loneliness of lack in old age. In several of her poems she deals with historical or mythological incidents where women's role has traditionally been relegated to that of an extra: "Anne Boleyn's Song" (*CP* 303) and "Eurydice" (*CP* 267) both give women a voice. In the former her lover compares her to spring, new life, but she is blamed for "the primal Fall"; she grows cold and death becomes her King. Eurydice also is returned to death when Orpheus, having recognized and rescued her, brought her back to the world with his golden mouth. We know the story's end, the loss, but Eurydice speaks of her own awakening here in a tale normally only heard from the point of view of the faithful husband whose folly, turning back to look at the wife he has rescued from hell, returns her there.

ASSESSMENT

Unlike later women poets whose feminist impetus causes them to go further than to represent the silent and hidden women of myth and history and to turn the stories around, revaluing the women positively, Sitwell does not provide alternative roles of women, but regenerates those whose voices have been lost. She examines and deplores the constructedness of women's lives and roles. She is a victim of lost romance herself, caught up in the artifice she critiques. Sitwell has no doubts about the powers of poetry, though she does not, like Eliot and many other modernists, ultimately discover and insist on an orthodoxy to bring a sense of unity and wholeness to all that has been exploded and exposed. The insights a poet brings are highlighted in her "Elegy for Dylan Thomas," one of her last poems. She likens his powers to those of Blake and asserts that Sisyphus who rolls the stone perpetually up a mountain only to see it roll down again (emphasizing the ultimate pointlessness of man's endeavors) is reassured to continue by the power and insight of Thomas's poetry, part of which is, like her own work, a revelation of our shortcomings in this world of flawed, constrained words, and part of which aims, through the image and the fantasy, the rhythm and the sound, to enlighten through such revelation:

> to the Minotaur in the city office
> Crying to the dunghill in the soul "See, it is morning!"
>
> (*CP* 424)

In her later years Sitwell enjoyed a revival as a poetry icon, had a successful lecture tour of America in 1948, was made Dame in 1954, converted to Roman Catholicism in 1955, and became a friend to Marilyn Monroe. Her fascination with publicity dominates her reputation, and indeed there is a mixture of good work still to be sorted from the myth and the lesser work, for she wrote so much. But it is well worth this sorting out. Her contribution in poetry to the fantastic, the musical, and the commentary upon artifice and constructedness has yet fully to be recognized.

BIBLIOGRAPHY

Primary Sources

The Mother. Oxford: Blackwell, 1915.

Twentieth Century Harlequinade. With Osbert Sitwell. Oxford: Blackwell, 1916.

Wheels. Ed. Edith Sitwell. Oxford: Blackwell, 1916, 1917, 1918, 1919; London: Parsons, 1920. London: Daniel, 1921.

Clowns' Houses. Oxford: Blackwell, 1918.

The Wooden Pegasus. Oxford: Blackwell, 1920.

Facade. London: Favil, 1922.

Bucolic Comedies. London: Duckworth, 1923.

The Sleeping Beauty. London: Duckworth, 1924; New York: Knopf, 1924.

Poetry and Criticism. London: Hogarth, 1925.

Troy Park. London: Duckworth, 1925; New York: Knopf, 1925.

Elegy on Dead Fashion. London: Duckworth, 1926.

Rustic Elegies. London: Duckworth, 1927; New York: Knopf, 1927.

Gold Coast Customs. London: Duckworth, 1929; Boston and New York: Houghton Mifflin, 1929.

Alexander Pope. London: Faber, 1930; New York: Cosmopolitan, 1930.

Collected Poems. London: Duckworth, 1930. The 1954/1957 edition is the one cited in the text.

The Pleasures of Poetry. 3 vols. London: Duckworth, 1930–1932.

The English Eccentrics. London: Faber, 1933; Boston and New York: Houghton Mifflin, 1933.

Aspects of Modern Poetry. London: Duckworth, 1934.

Victoria of England. London: Faber, 1936; Boston: Houghton Mifflin, 1936.

I Live under a Black Sun. London: Gollancz, 1937; Garden City, NY: Doubleday, 1938.

Edith Sitwell's Anthology. London: Gollancz, 1940.

Street Songs. London: Macmillan, 1942.

Green Song and Other Poems. London: Macmillan, 1944; New York: Vanguard, 1946.

The Song of the Cold. London: Macmillan, 1945; New York: Vanguard, 1948.

Fanfare for Elizabeth. London and New York: Macmillan, 1946.

Canticle of the Rose: Poems: 1917–1949. New York: Vanguard, 1949. As *The Canticle of the Rose: Selected Poems: 1920–1947*. London: Macmillan, 1949; London: Macmillan, 1950. New York: Vanguard, 1949.

Gardeners and Astronomers. London: Macmillan, 1953; New York: Vanguard, 1953.

Collected Poems. New York: Vanguard, 1954; London: Macmillan, 1957. This edition is cited in the text.

The Queens and the Hive. London: Macmillan, 1962; Boston: Little Brown, 1962.

Selected Poems. London: Macmillan, 1965.

Taken Care Of. London: Hutchinson, 1965; New York: Atheneum, 1965.

Selected Letters. Ed. Richard Green. London: Virago, 1998.

Secondary Sources

Day, Gary, and Gina Wisker. "Recuperating and Revaluing: Edith Sitwell and Charlotte Mew." In *British Poetry, 1900–50: Aspects of Tradition*. Ed. Gary Day and Brian Docherty. Basingstoke: Macmillan, 1995. 65–80.

Elborn, G. *Edith Sitwell: A Biography*. London: Sheldon, 1981.

Glendinning, V. *Edith Sitwell: A Unicorn among Lions*. Oxford: Oxford UP, 1983.

Kristeva, J. "The System and the Speaking Subject." *TLS* 12 October 1973: 1249–1250.

Pearson, John. *Facades: Edith, Osbert and Sacheverell Sitwell*. London: Macmillan, 1978.

Reilly, Catherine. *The Virago Book of Women's War Poetry and Verse*. London: Virago, 1977.

Ross, R.H. *The Georgian Revolt: Rise and Fall of a Poetic Ideal, 1910–22*. London: Faber, 1967.

Thurley, G. *The Ironic Harvest: English Poetry in the Twentieth Century*. London: Edward Arnold, 1974.

Stevie Smith
1902–1971

Julie Sims Steward

One of the most original poets of the twentieth century, Stevie Smith described herself as "well on edge" (*Stevie Smith: A Selection* 186). With a glance at the bizarre drawings she placed with her poems and an attuned ear to the multiple voices in her work who speak of topics as vast as love and death or as specific as Christian hymns or her personal muse, few would disagree. Far from "marginal," Smith is a writer whose challenges to patriarchal authority and, specifically, to traditional conceptions of gender place her in the center of modern women's writing, and yet her work always maintains a kind of edge or bite that vacillates between humor and deadpan seriousness. Skeptical about marriage, domestic bliss, and the rewards of motherhood, Smith reads as a woman ahead of her time whose critiques of rigid constructions of gender make her as contemporary and significant as she is eccentric and difficult to categorize. A performer of her own poems at public readings, Smith emphasizes as well the performativity of gender in her work. She reveals how gender identities are assigned and can be challenged as she paints a broad canvas of characters who employ strategies of masquerade, parody, and multivocality in order to refashion themselves in new and liberating ways. As she writes in *Novel on Yellow Paper*, "[I]n this world of catch-as-catch-can we are so often being in the place that is certainly *not* our place at all, and so being unhappy" (183). That her work does not offer a site free from gender trouble may be her greatest value. The complexity of her novels and poetry points to answers, raises more questions, encourages debate, and ultimately requires the reader, in the words of her first novel's subtitle, to "work it out for yourself."

BACKGROUND

Stevie Smith was born on September 20, 1902, in Hull, Yorkshire, the second daughter of Charles Ward Smith and Ethel Spear Smith. Her efforts to break free from the limitations assigned her as a woman in Edwardian England are nowhere more evident than in her name change. Born Florence Margaret Smith but also called Peggy, she adopted the name Stevie after riding horseback past a group of taunting young boys who called her Steve, referring to the well-known jockey Steve Smith. In 1906 her father abandoned Stevie, her older sister Molly, and her mother, leaving the Smith women to find a home in the London suburb of Palmer's Green with Ethel's sister Margaret Annie Spear. After her mother's early death in 1919, Smith continued to live with her beloved "Lion Aunt" until the aunt's death in 1968. While her father's neglect spurred in Smith resentment and suspicion of marital happiness, growing up only with women fostered pride in female independence and self-reliance. Smith never married, though she recorded two of her love affairs in her first novel, one with a Swiss-German graduate student, Karl Eckinger, whose German nationalism mirrored pre–World War II politics and strained their relationship, and one with Eric Armitage, to whom she was briefly engaged but for whom she could not bear to take on the traditional role of wife.

When she was only five years old, Smith contracted tubercular peritonitis and was sent to a convalescent home off and on for three years. This early brush with death provided her with a fascination with suicide. Specifically, she was enthralled with the idea of control and agency, of being able to take one's own life instead of passively waiting to die. In 1953, torn between her writing and secretarial work, her creative ambition and the drudgery of mindless labor, she cut her wrists in her office at Newnes, Pearson, the publishing firm specializing in women's magazines where she had worked since 1923. The suicide attempt failed, and she retired, living on a pension and money earned through book reviews.

Smith's secretarial career was preceded by her graduation in 1917 from Palmer's Green High, where she enjoyed performing in plays and received a prize for literature. She advanced to North London Collegiate School for Girls and then to Mrs. Hoster's Secretarial Training College before taking the position of private secretary for Sir Neville Pearson. She took time at the office to maintain a reading journal, studying classics from Spinoza to Woolf, and to write poems in her spare time. She tried to publish her first volume of poetry in 1934, but women's poetry was not easily published at the time, and she was advised to prove her worth by writing a novel instead. In six weeks she produced her heavily autobiographical *Novel on Yellow Paper*, typed on the yellow paper used for carbon copies. Jonathan Cape published it in 1936, and her first volume of poetry, *A Good Time Was Had by All*, followed in 1937.

Fame and success followed her first two publications, and Smith went on to publish seven more volumes of poetry, several short stories, and two more novels. Although she received the Cholmondeley Award for Poetry in 1966 and the Queen's Gold Medal for Poetry in 1969, her popularity was not always assured. Her volume *Harold's Leap* (1950) sold poorly, and her eccentric poetry readings, in which she often dressed like a young girl and sang her poems off key, did not always meet with audience approval. Likewise, editors were hesitant to publish her poems with their attendant drawings of such things as dancing cats and swinging monkeys. In a time when New Criticism and the Movement were holding sway, Smith's quirky, humorous verse challenged critical and popular standards of what "poetry" should be. However, by the early 1960s, with a new interest in the absurd and the popularity of poetry readings, critics again found her work to be a refreshing example of original voice. In 1959 her radio play *A Turn Outside* was produced by the BBC, and her work drew praise from such poets as Sylvia Plath, Robert Lowell, and Philip Larkin.

In 1971 doctors discovered that Smith had an inoperable brain tumor. In her last months Smith composed "Come Death (2)," a poem in which she praises death as an obliging servant. She performed the poem on her sickbed for visitors, enacting her courage in the face of her illness. On March 7, 1971, she died, leaving behind a life that would be memorialized in Hugh Whitemore's 1977 West End play *Stevie: A Play from the Life and Work of Stevie Smith* and a film version of the play a year later starring Glenda Jackson.

ANALYSIS

Stevie Smith's work provides textual evidence of her commitment to challenging culturally determined gender roles and to uncovering possibilities of constructing gender identity. Smith's writing takes an antiessentialist position as its inaugural point and then launches into regions only her distinctive imagination could conjure. From *Novel on Yellow Paper*'s secretarial pool and the no-man's-land of *Over the Frontier* to palace walls and desert islands, Smith immerses her readers in a world where characters' assertions of autonomy result in either rewarded independence or ambivalence. Much of what is at stake in her work involves exploring the limits of agency in redefining gender identities against established cultural signification.

Smith published three novels, all of which are largely autobiographical. Sanford Sternlicht identifies them as "gender documents testifying to the discomfiture, disappointment, and discrimination experienced by Western women in the interbellum years" (*In Search* 51). Virago Modern Classics reissued the novels beginning in 1979, and *Novel on Yellow Paper* was rereleased by New Directions in 1994, printed on yellow paper. The novels read like extended monologues and establish the brassy, witty voice that Smith continued to develop in her essays, reviews, and BBC talks.

Her first published book, *Novel on Yellow Paper* (1936), presents female subjectivity as a site of competing literary and cultural discourses and can best be understood in the context of autobiographical fiction, a genre that maintains that identities are always to some extent fictional and, therefore, subject to self-invention. Smith challenges the notion of a fixed female essence by employing different narrating voices that allow the protagonist, Pompey, to change her identity at whim, thus escaping the imposition of marriage and domesticity her culture prescribes.

In the sequel, *Over the Frontier* (1938), Pompey enters an allegorical battle of the sexes in order to deconstruct the stability and exclusivity of the combatants' genders. Smith complicates Pompey's mercurial ability to reconfigure her identity in the first novel by disclosing in the second an attending guilt for resisting traditional feminine roles. Self-construction carries the potential for self-destruction. Cast as an exile, Pompey crosses the frontier, a figure for the outer limits of conventional gender roles, into the warfront, a space gendered male, but provisionally so. As Pompey is forced to don a male soldier's uniform, Smith reveals the failure of androgyny as a solution to the woes of femininity and shows that a woman impersonating a man exposes the category "man" as a subject position inhabitable by either sex.

Smith's favorite novel, *The Holiday*, was published in 1949, although she wrote it during World War II. The difficulty she had publishing it arose, in part, from the frustration of her editors and readers with her experimental form. Yet, as Laura Severin argues, the novel should be read as a "break [with] patriarchal forms, particularly the romance plot, [in order] to envision new ones" ("Recovering" 462). To this degree the novel places Smith in the company of other modernist innovators like Dorothy Richardson and Virginia Woolf. Smith revisits the themes of failed love and escape from her first two novels. Celia, a new protagonist, praises female friendship and despairs at the impossibility of a romance with her cousin Casmilus. She resists domestic ideology as Pompey did in *Novel on Yellow Paper* and similarly flirts with the possibility of death in her attempt to drown herself. Through her discussions of British politics and Indian independence, *The Holiday* also opens the door to consider Smith's critique of imperialism and to explore connections between patriarchy and colonialism.

Smith never considered herself a novelist, but it was through fiction that she first achieved the literary fame that enabled her to publish her poems. Her fascination with frontiers in the novels serves as a useful location and locution in considering her poetry in that it underscores the importance of position, the unknown, and undecidability in terms of her thinking about gender. The poems reassert her claim from *Novel on Yellow Paper* that "the thing that really counts is what is making you all the time" (183). In the poems Smith examines the social and familial forces shaping women's roles and urges women to rethink their gender identity in unconventional ways.

One image that recurs in Smith's poetry is the hat; her hat poems serve as clear examples of the risks and possibilities of refashioning gender. For Smith, hats serve as vestimentary signs that either reify or reformulate traditional identities. Her characters "wear different hats" to emphasize the importance for women of being able to occupy different subject positions. Whereas hats in the novels recuperate the wearer into an identity that culture deems intelligible and acceptable, in the poems women most often use hats as masquerade to redefine the terms within which their culture confines them. In "Magna Est Veritas," for instance, the speaker dons an unusual hat that allows her to escape the terms "simple" and "fast" within which she is perceived. In "The Queen and the Young Princess" the mother, a recurring figure of socialization in Smith's work, passes on to her daughter a crown that signifies not political power but the "headache" of remaining a marginal figure in relation to her husband's authority. However, the poem "My Hat" serves as a kind of response from the princess. The daughter in this poem accepts a hat that her mother hoped would help her attract suitors and instead uses it to escape domesticity by fleeing to a desert island.

Beneath Smith's hats are bodies, individual forms that, in their differences, bear the marks of socialization. Smith's own stylized, childish performances at her poetry readings embody the contradictions she maintains as crucial and reactionary in the formation of identity. In her poetry she tropes the female body as a prison; in order to escape essentialist definitions associated with these bodies, she revises fairy tales to imagine physical transformations that transport women out of inevitable acculturation to social roles. For example, while the title character of "This Englishwoman" is trapped in a body that defines class status by a lack of weight and female attributes, the character Saffron, in the poem of the same name, is praised for her ability to transform her body in a kind of Puckian fashion.

Smith's interest in the fantastic is exemplified as well in the drawings that accompany her poems. Her sketches subvert poetic statements that appear to endorse "proper" feminine concerns and traditional masculine values. The drawings' marginality, a term referring to their placement on the margins of the text as well as to their status as "other" to the text, vies for centrality with the poems' content and encourages the reader always to look at the margins where women, too, are commonly relegated. They work in tandem with the multivocality in Smith's work, but visually, in order to destabilize any identity a poem may claim as stable or essential.

Smith's drawings most clearly mark her singularity as a poet and point to the excesses that permeate her writing. She is, after all, a poet who thinks that it would be "marvelous" to be dead, who just as easily writes about drugs, drowning, or the devouring of Christians by lions as about more traditional topics, and who would rather sing her poems than read them to audiences. The mysterious, even unreal, quality of much of her writing calls to mind literature of the time like Djuna Barnes's *Nightwood* or contemporary texts like Angela Carter's *Nights at the Circus*. In the end, Smith can be understood through romanticism, modernist experimentation, or the cultural revolutions of the 1960s, to name a few possible contexts. The endless play of construction and deconstruction in her work asserts her difference from the literary tradition she inherits and extends. Readers must simultaneously take into account her cultural critique and her "larking." She is much further out than we think, and not drowning, but waving.

ASSESSMENT

Smith's eccentric ingenuity—her "childish" verse, darkly humorous themes, and attending drawings—coupled with the rise of feminist theory has made her an increasingly popular author to study and a provocative but challenging writer to categorize. She has steadily gained critical attention since the publication of two biographies in the 1980s, and readers can now turn to journals like *Contemporary Literature, Twentieth Century Literature*, and *Journal of Modern Literature* to find appraisals of her work. Most critics resort to biographical moves, reading backwards through her speakers' contradictory statements to the writer herself in an effort to apprehend the "real" Stevie Smith. Sanford Sternlicht entitled his collection of Smith criticism *In Search of Stevie Smith*, and Arthur Rankin's study *The Poetry of Stevie Smith: Little Girl Lost* suggests that she can be contextualized best in the romantic tradition. However, recent critics like Romana Huk reread Smith's "shifty, polyvocal works precisely as prescient critiques of such conceptions of unmediated subjectivity" (241). Huk views her revision of fairy tales, hymns, Greek tragedies, and traditional poetic forms as "problematized representations of, and negotiations with, the competing/collusive languages/voices that construct Smith's English selfhood and womanhood" (242). Similarly, Sheryl Stevenson describes Smith as a vocal dramatist whose work emphasizes dialogue as a means of exploring multiple points of view.

Smith did not identify herself as a feminist, nor would she subscribe to a kind of cultural feminist surge to rehabilitate and celebrate femininity. As her poem "Girls" asserts, she prefers to be seen more broadly as human, not specifically as female. A typical move in her work is to disaffiliate her self from woman as a category, but to do so necessitates a definition of the term first, and then a redefinition of the self apart from that term, to whatever degree possible. She often directly addresses women, writing as a woman to women, but her emphasis is always on the "as." To write as a woman is to formulate a provisional definition of the term, and one that can be changed. For instance, she takes pains to distinguish between Englishwomen in general and "This Englishwoman" in particular, as one poem is titled.

There are, to be sure, no easy alternatives to the discourses, narratives, and cultural imperatives that define gender, and Smith offers no easy solutions. At best her work produces various paradoxes and comic incongruities. Muriel Spark describes her work as dominated by a central paradox: although life is terrible, it must be praised. Barbera sees her drawings as playful juxtapositions to much of the sadness in her work and as subversive acts that challenge New Critical ideals of poems as self-enclosed icons. Paradoxes and incongruity, in fact, appear throughout her work. The death plot offers salvation in *Novel on Yellow Paper*. The possibilities of self-fashioning can lead to self-destruction, as *Over the Frontier* evinces. In her most famous poem, "Not Waving but Drowning," the dead can still speak, and a gesture of despair is easily misread as greeting. While Huk argues that Smith's work "disrupts [dominant perspectives] without redefining" (248), Martin Pumphrey reads her sense of paradox and childlike play as a method of cultural subversion, challenging the notion of "serious" literature and the authoritative persona. Acknowledging her "mask of oddness and triviality," Pumphrey views her struggle with gender roles as one that negotiates between "inner desires and outer restraint" and one that "contemplate[s] the allure and danger of transgression" (*In Search* 100).

Underscoring Smith's emphasis on gender construction, recurring tropes of home and frontier figure prominently in her work. In *Novel on Yellow Paper* Pompey flees from her home, the suburbs, and their attending domestication. In *Over the Frontier* Smith grafts gender onto the division of home front and war front to show how each location is infected by the other's oppressive ideologies. Likewise, the poems emphasize the value of mobility through disavowals of home and domestic scenes. The woman in "Wretched Woman," for example, is trapped in her kitchen, but the daughter in "My Hat" finds freedom on a deserted island. Similar locales remote from civilization—fairy worlds, the sea, forests—serve as frequent destinations for her self-constructing heroines, but just as often she casts them in an illusory light that undercuts the practicality and viability of escape. Smith's ability to cross boundaries and to defy categorization recalls the title of one of her poems, "No Categories!" and its insistence on resisting hierarchies and easy classification. While she presents herself and her work as a puzzle to her critics, she invites us to continue our search, if not for her, then for the rich complexities of her writing.

BIBLIOGRAPHY

Primary Sources

Novel on Yellow Paper. 1936. London: Virago, 1980.
A Good Time Was Had by All. London: Cape, 1937.
Over the Frontier. 1938. London: Virago, 1980.
Tender Only to One. London: Cape, 1938.
Mother, What Is Man? London: Cape, 1942.
The Holiday. 1949. London: Virago, 1979.
Harold's Leap. London: Chapman & Hall, 1950.
Not Waving but Drowning. London: Deutsch, 1957.
Some Are More Human Than Others: Sketchbook by Stevie Smith. London: Gaberbocchus, 1958; New York: New Directions, 1989.
A Turn Outside. Radio Play. BBC, 1959.
Selected Poems. London: Longmans, 1962.
Two in One: Selected Poems and The Frog Prince and Other Poems. London: Longman, 1971.
Scorpion and Other Poems. London: Longman, 1972.
The Collected Poems of Stevie Smith. Ed. James MacGibbon. London: Allen Lane, 1975.
Me Again: Uncollected Writings of Stevie Smith. Ed. Jack Barbera and William McBrien. New York: Farrar, 1982.
Stevie Smith: A Selection. Ed. Hermione Lee. London: Faber, 1983.

Secondary Sources

Barbera, Jack. "The Relevance of Stevie Smith's Drawings." *Journal of Modern Literature* 12.2 (1985): 221–236.
Barbera, Jack, and William McBrien. *Stevie: A Biography of Stevie Smith*. Oxford: Oxford UP, 1987.
Barbera, Jack, William McBrien, and Helen Bajan. *Stevie Smith: A Bibliography*. Westport, CT: Meckler, 1987.
Civello, Catherine A. "Stevie Smith's *Ecriture Féminine*: Pre-Oedipal Desires and Wartime Realities." *Mosaic* 28.2 (June 1995): 109–122.
Dick, Kay. *Ivy and Stevie: Ivy Compton-Burnett and Stevie Smith*. London: Alison & Busby, 1983.
Huk, Romana. "Eccentric Concentrism: Traditional Poetic Forms and Refracted Discourse in Stevie Smith's Poetry." *Contemporary Literature* 34 (1993): 240–265.
Rankin, Arthur C. *The Poetry of Stevie Smith: Little Girl Lost*. Totowa, NJ: Barnes, 1985.
Ricks, Christopher. *The Force of Poetry*. Oxford: Clarendon, 1984.
Severin, Laura. "Recovering the Serious Antics of Stevie Smith's Novels." *Twentieth Century Literature* 40.4 (1994): 461–476.
———. *Stevie Smith's Resistant Antics*. Madison: U of Wisconsin P, 1997.
Spalding, Frances. *Stevie Smith: A Biography*. New York: Norton, 1989.
Spark, Muriel. "Melancholy Humor." *Observer* 3 (1957): 16. Rpt. in Sternlicht, *In Search of Stevie Smith* 73–74.
Sternlicht, Sanford, ed. *In Search of Stevie Smith*. Syracuse: Syracuse UP, 1991.
———. *Stevie Smith*. Boston: Twayne, 1990.
Stevenson, Sheryl. "Stevie Smith's Voices." *Contemporary Literature* 33 (1992): 24–45.
Steward, Julie Sims. "Ceci N'est Pas un Hat: Stevie Smith and the Refashioning of Gender." *South Central Review* 15.2 (1998): 16–33.
———. "Pandora's Playbox: Stevie Smith's Drawings and the Construction of Gender." *Journal of Modern Literature* 22.1 (1998): 70–91.
Storey, Mark. "Why Stevie Smith Matters." *Critical Quarterly* (Summer 1979): 41–55.
Thaddeus, Janice. "Stevie Smith and the Gleeful Macabre." *Contemporary Poetry* 3.4 (1978): 36–49.
Upton, Lee. "Stevie Smith and the Anxiety of Intimacy." *CEA Critic* 53.2 (Winter 1991): 22–31.

Muriel Spark
1918–

Frank Kelly

Muriel Spark has produced a substantial body of work—twenty novels, plus stories, poetry, drama, literary criticism, and biography—in which she considers, in lean, gemlike, ironic prose and plots of surpassing ingenuity, the social interaction of people and through them the moral and cultural concerns of the twentieth century. Though many of her works are set in Great Britain, other novels and stories focus on political and ethical dilemmas in South Africa and Europe, particularly Italy, as well. A realist who includes spirituality, even religion, in her reality, she often experiments with the literary forms in which she is working.

BACKGROUND

In a personal interview poet John Masefield told Muriel Spark, then thirty-two years old, "All experience is good for an artist" (*Curriculum Vitae* [CV] 197). Spark's eminence among twentieth-century British writers may be traced in part to the unusual variety of social, cultural, and religious experiences that have informed her life and work.

She was born Muriel Uezzell Camberg in the Morningside district of Edinburgh, Scotland, on February 1, 1918. Her father Bernard was a Scottish-Jewish engineer who had refused to change his name to Camber, as the rest of his family had done. Her mother Sarah was English. The small but telling differences between her mother's speech, dress, and manner and those of her Edinburgh neighbors were among Spark's most vivid childhood observations.

She felt an early affinity with fellow Edinburgher Robert Louis Stevenson, whose *A Child's Garden of Verses* was among the first books she owned. She spent twelve years at James Gillespie's High School for Girls, the basis for the Marcia Blaine School in Spark's most famous work, *The Prime of Miss Jean Brodie*. Spark was a Jew in a school whose official religion was Presbyterian, but other Jews, Catholics, and girls of mixed faith attended as well. "In my day Tolerance was decidedly the prevailing religion, always with a puritanical slant" (CV 53). At Gillespie's Spark encountered the teacher Miss Christina Kay, the model for Jean Brodie, and immediately began to write about her. Kay's enthusiasm for foreign locales and culture in many forms also shows up in Spark's life and work. She saw John Masefield read aloud; twenty years later she wrote a book about him. She memorized the Border ballads; her own poetry brought her prizes while she was still in school. The fact that Spark's maternal grandmother lived with her family for the last four years of her life may have honed Spark's extraordinary skill in presenting the habits and concerns of the aged, particularly in her novel *Memento Mori* (1959).

She enrolled at the Heriot-Watt College with the expressed purpose of mastering "economical prose," certainly a distinctive feature of her work (CV 102). In the late 1930s the first of many Penguin paperback books she purchased was André Maurois's *Ariel*, a biography of Shelley. The first version of Spark's own critical biography of Mary Shelley appeared in 1951.

In August 1937 she set out for Southern Rhodesia (now Zimbabwe), there to marry Sydney Oswald Spark, "a disastrous choice. Unbeknownst to us, the poor man had mental problems, not obvious at the time" (CV 116). In the colony where she settled initially, there were fifty-five thousand whites to one and a half million blacks. The clashes she observed in South Africa informed her stories "The Curtain Blown by the Breeze," "The Seraph and the Zambesi," "The Portobello Road," and "The Pawnbroker's Wife."

Refusing to have an abortion as her husband suggested, Spark gave birth to her son Robin in 1938. Moving from place to place gave her full knowledge of the country even as her marriage became intolerable. She read Shakespeare, the Bible, T.S. Eliot, and Ivy Compton-Burnett, whose work she considered, in opposition to major opinion at the time, "basically surrealistic" (CV 146). After a protracted divorce proceeding she retained her husband's name so that it would be the same as her son's.

In the bombed-out London she returned to in 1944, she registered as required for war service and lived at the Helena Club, the basis for the May of Teck Club in *The Girls of Slender Means* (1963). She found work in the Political Intelligence Division of the Foreign Office, where she was trained in disinformation or "black" propaganda, delivering to Germany "detailed truth with believable lies" (CV 148). The intrigue and subterfuge associated with this work shows up notably in the tone and plots of many of her novels, especially in the form of blackmail. In her novel *The Hothouse by the East River* (1973) she used an incident involving a colleague who had a romance with one of the POWs who worked at the job. Also, her story "The House of the Famous Poet" is based on an actual visit to the home of Louis MacNeice while he was away, as is her essay "The Poet's House."

She was employed as a researcher, copy editor, and writer for *Argentos*, a quarterly that dealt with the history of jewelry and allied crafts. At twenty-nine she became the editor of the journal of the Poetry Society, *Poetry Review*, which had twice awarded her prizes for poems. Her first editorial, which barely hinted at the upheaval to come, began, "Cannot we cease railing against the moderns?" by which she meant Eliot, Auden, and Pound (CV 169). After two years of disputes she chose to be fired rather than resign so she could collect severance pay. Her experiences at *Poetry Review* were translated later into her novel *Loitering with Intent* (1981). They also led her to the habit of maintaining complete documentary evidence of her life and work.

Spark began a literary partnership with critic and poet Derek Stanford, with whom she shared a voluminous correspondence. Spark and Stanford coedited a volume, *Tribute to Wordsworth*, to mark the centenary of the poet's death in 1850, and a selection of Mary Shelley's letters. At about this time Spark also published her first book of poems, *The Fanfarlo and Other Verse* (1952), and edited a volume of Emily Bronte's poetry. The plot device of incriminating letters that appears in several of her novels, including *Memento Mori*, may be traced to her later experience when certain of her letters to Stanford were offered to her for sale. In her autobiography *Curriculum Vitae* (1993), which covers her life up to the late 1950s,

Spark complains vigorously and in great detail of the inaccuracies that plague both Stanford's book about her and his later volume about the 1940s.

Spark's initial dedication to lyrical poetry turned to an increasing interest in narrative verse that was reflected in her book *John Masefield* (1953). Her job as a secretary at Falcon Press was the source for some portions of her novel *A Far Cry from Kensington* (1988). Spark identifies 1951 as a turning point in her professional life when she won a short-story competition sponsored by the *Observer* with "The Seraph and the Zambesi."

Influenced by the writings of John Henry Newman, Spark first converted to the Church of England and then, in May 1954, to Roman Catholicism. Her reason was that it "corresponded to what I had always felt and known and believed" (CV 202). This was a pivotal event in her life, and faith is often a subject in her writings. Indeed, she coedited with Stanford a selection of Newman's letters, published in 1957. Her fascination with the Book of Job was later the focus of her novel *The Only Problem* (1984).

Shortly after she began writing a study of Eliot, a combination of malnourishment and medication produced hallucinations. She recovered while living with two groups of Carmelite nuns (a convent is the setting of her 1974 Watergate fable *The Abbess of Crewe*). In 1954, when she was commissioned by Macmillan to write a novel, she produced *The Comforters*, the title of which she derived from Job's comforters, who were, "in fact, like modern interrogators who come to interview and mock the victim in shifts" (*CV* 203). The novel dealt with a character who heard voices; the book was published in 1957 just before Evelyn Waugh's *The Ordeal of Gilbert Pinfold*, on a similar theme. Waugh declared her approach to be the better one.

Spark was named a commander of the Order of the British Empire in 1967. She resided in New York City during the 1960s, but thereafter lived in Italy.

ANALYSIS

Muriel Spark once commented that the word "nevertheless" has a great deal of significance to her. It implies that the acknowledged existence of one set of facts or "realities" does not negate another set that exists as well. The contradictions between these two realities may be acknowledged or explained, or they may not be. The ironies inherent in these juxtapositions may not always be pointed to. They are simply there. It may be useful to remember "nevertheless" in trying to assess Spark's works, for she has confounded attempts to be classified according to the major tides of twentieth-century fiction. She writes lean, economical "literary" prose; nevertheless, she has enjoyed persistent "popular" success. Her plots are thought too well developed for the more ruminative strains of twentieth-century literature (some are even described as whodunits), yet her spiritual and moral preoccupations distinguish her work from the mainstream of genre fiction.

The assumptions of the realist tradition in literature are twofold: realism is the novel's sole legitimate domain, and this domain is necessarily secular. In its meticulous accumulation of detail, Spark's work could hardly be described as anything but realistic. The problem is that she routinely presents phenomena that are extraordinary but nevertheless actual. The fact that this involves issues of spirituality and, worse, religion only exacerbates the realists' problem with Spark's works. Of course, for many of Spark's readers, her brand of realism is all the more realistic for these inclusions.

If her "realities" are more broadly based than many others in the tradition, nevertheless there is a self-consciousness in many of her works—an awareness of their being artistic constructs—that aligns her with the more experimental writers of the century. She has often explored form qua form: the novel as novel (*The Comforters*), the play as play (*Doctors of Philosophy*). Some critics have complained that her refusal to subscribe fully to any particular literary tradition or approach limits her achievement as an artist. However, this may be a failure of their critical systems rather than of Spark's vision of art.

ASSESSMENT

Muriel Spark cuts a very distinctive profile in twentieth-century English literature. A few would argue that she is an exquisite miniaturist, but the weight of the themes she considers makes this classification seem confining and dismissive. Wherever she has turned her gaze, whether the classroom or the office, the Scottish or the Italian countryside, wartime London or premillennial Rome, her clarity, wit, and questing spirit have produced a substantial oeuvre whose weight is belied by its gemlike precision and luster. Readers looking for a clear-eyed yet passionate consideration of the major moral and cultural concerns of the twentieth century could do no better than to make Muriel Spark their guide. Though she is often concerned with problems of faith and with Roman Catholicism in particular, the breadth of her interests and the depth of her vision require that she be labeled catholic with a small *c*.

BIBLIOGRAPHY

Primary Sources

Tribute to Wordsworth: A Miscellany of Opinion for the Centenary of the Poet's Death. Ed. with Derek Stanford. London: Wingate, 1950.

Child of Light: A Reassessment of Mary Wollstonecraft Shelley. Hadley, UK: Tower Bridge, 1951. Rev. as *Mary Shelley*. New York: Dutton, 1987.

The Fanfarlo and Other Verse. Adlington, UK: Hand & Flower, 1952.

A Selection of Poems by Emily Brontë. Ed. with an introduction by Muriel Spark. London: Grey Walls, 1952.

The Letters of the Brontës: A Selection. Ed. with an introduction by Muriel Spark. London: Peter Nevill, 1954; Norman: U of Oklahoma P, 1954.

Emily Brontë: Her Life and Work. With Derek Stanford. London: Peter Owen, 1953; New York: Coward, McCann, 1966.

John Masefield. London: Peter Nevill, 1953. Rev. ed. London: Hutchinson, 1992.

My Best Mary: The Selected Letters of Mary Wollstonecraft Shelley. Ed. with Derek Stanford. London: Wingate, 1953.

The Comforters. London: Macmillan, 1957; Philadelphia: Lippincott, 1957.

Letters of John Henry Newman. Ed. with Derek Stanford. London: Peter Owen, 1957.

The Go-Away Bird with Other Stories. London: Macmillan, 1958; Philadelphia: Lippincott, 1960.

Robinson. London: Macmillan; Philadelphia: Lippincott, 1958.

Memento Mori. London: Macmillan; Philadelphia: Lippincott, 1959.

The Bachelors. London: Macmillan, 1960; Philadelphia: Lippincott, 1961.

The Ballad of Peckham Rye. London: Macmillan; Philadelphia: Lippincott, 1960.

The Prime of Miss Jean Brodie. First published in the *New Yorker*, 14 October 1961. London: Macmillan, 1961; Philadelphia: Lippincott, 1962.

Voices at Play. London: Macmillan; Philadelphia: Lippincott, 1962.

Doctors of Philosophy: A Play. London: Macmillan, 1963; New York: Knopf, 1966.

The Girls of Slender Means. London: Macmillan; New York: Knopf, 1963.

The Mandelbaum Gate. London: Macmillan; New York: Knopf, 1965.

Collected Poems 1. London: Macmillan, 1967; New York: Knopf, 1968.

Collected Stories 1. London: Macmillan, 1967; New York: Knopf, 1968.

The Public Image. London: Macmillan; New York: Knopf, 1968.

The Very Fine Clock (children's book). New York: Knopf, 1968; London: Macmillan, 1969.

The Driver's Seat. London: Macmillan; New York: Knopf, 1970.

Not to Disturb. London: Macmillan, 1971; New York: Viking, 1972.

The Hothouse by the East River. London: Macmillan; New York: Viking, 1973.

The Abbess of Crewe. London: Macmillan; New York: Viking, 1974.

The Takeover. London: Macmillan; New York: Viking, 1976.

Territorial Rights. London: Macmillan; New York: Coward, McCann, 1979.

Loitering with Intent. London: Bodley Head; New York: Coward, McCann, 1981.

The Only Problem. London: Bodley Head; New York: Putnam, 1984.

The Stories of Muriel Spark. New York: Dutton, 1985.

A Far Cry from Kensington. London: Constable; Boston: Houghton Mifflin, 1988.

Symposium. London: Constable; Boston: Houghton Mifflin, 1990.

Curriculum Vitae: Autobiography. London: Constable, 1992; Boston: Houghton Mifflin, 1993.

Reality and Dreams. London: Constable, 1996; Boston: Houghton Mifflin, 1997.

Open to the Public: New and Collected Stories. New York: New Directions, 1997.

Secondary Sources

Adler, Renata. "Muriel Spark." In *On Contemporary Literature*. Ed. Richard Kostelanetz. Expanded ed. New York: Avon, 1969. 591–596.

Auerbach, Nina. *Communities of Women: An Idea in Fiction*. Cambridge, MA: Harvard UP, 1978.

Baldanza, Frank. "Muriel Spark and the Occult." *Wisconsin Studies in Contemporary Literature* 6 (Summer 1965): 190–203.

Bold, Alan. *Muriel Spark*. Contemporary Writers. London and New York: Methuen, 1986.

———, ed. *Muriel Spark: An Odd Capacity for Vision*. London: Vision, 1984.

D'Erasmo, Stacey. "Grand Dame: Interview with Author Muriel Spark." *Artforum* 36 (November 1997): 21.

Dobie, Ann B., and Carl Wooton. "Spark and Waugh: Similarities by Coincidence." *Midwest Quarterly* 13 (1972): 423–434.

Edgecombe, Rodney Stenning. *Vocation and Identity in the Fiction of Muriel Spark*. Columbia: U of Missouri P, 1990.

Frankel, Sara. "An Interview with Muriel Spark." *Partisan Review* 54 (1987): 443–457.

Halio, Jay L. "Muriel Spark: the Novelist's Sense of Wonder." In *British Novelists since 1900*. Ed. Jack I. Biles. New York: ASM, 1987. 267–277.

Harrison, Bernard. "Muriel Spark and Jane Austen." In *The Modern English Novel: The Reader, the Writer, and the Work*. Ed. Gabriel Josipovici. London: Open Books, 1976. 11, 48–49.

Heptonstall, Geoffrey. "Muriel Spark." *Contemporary Review* 269 (November 1996): 185–188.

Holloway, John. "Narrative Structure and Text Structure: Isherwood's *A Meeting by the River* and Muriel Spark's *The Prime of Miss Jean Brodie*." *Critical Inquiry* 1 (1975): 581–604.

Hoyt, Charles Alva. "Muriel Spark: The Surrealist Jane Austen." In *Contemporary British Novelists*. Ed. Charles Shapiro. Carbondale and Edwardsville: Southern Illinois UP, 1965. 125–143.

Hynes, Joseph. *The Art of the Real: Muriel Spark's Novels*. Rutherford, NJ: Fairleigh Dickinson UP, 1988.

———, ed. *Critical Essays on Muriel Spark*. New York: G.K. Hall, 1992.

Kelleher, V.M.K. "The Religious Artistry of Muriel Spark." *Critical Review* 18 (1976): 79–92.

Kemp, Peter. *Muriel Spark*. Novelists and Their World. London: Paul Elek, 1974.

Kermode, Frank. *Continuities*. London: Routledge, 1968.

Keyser, Barbara. "Muriel Spark, Watergate, and the Mass Media." *Arizona Quarterly* 32 (1976): 146–153.

Little, Judy. *Comedy and the Woman Writer: Woolf, Spark, and Feminism*. Lincoln: U of Nebraska P, 1983.

Lodge, David. "The Uses and Abuses of Omniscience: Method and Meaning in Muriel Spark's *The Prime of Miss Jean Brodie*." *Critical Quarterly* 12 (1970): 235–257.

Malkoff, Karl. *Muriel Spark*. Columbia Essays on Modern Writers, no. 36. New York: Columbia UP, 1968.

Massie, Allan. *Muriel Spark*. Edinburgh: Ramsay Head, 1979.

Monterrey, Tomas. "Old and New Elements in Muriel Spark's *Symposium*." *Studies in Scottish Literature* 27 (1992): 175–188.

Page, Norman. *Muriel Spark*. Modern Novelists. Basingstoke: Macmillan, 1990.

Parrinder, Patrick. "Muriel Spark and Her Critics." *Critical Quarterly* 25 (1983): 23–31.

Pearlman, Mickey. *Re-inventing Reality: Patterns and Characters in the Novels of Muriel Spark*. Studies in Romantic and Modern Literature. New York: Peter Lang, 1996.

Reid, Alexander. "The Novels of Muriel Spark." *Scotland's Magazine* April 1961.

Richmond, Velma Bourgeois. *Muriel Spark*. New York: Ungar, 1984.

Rose, Jacqueline. *States of Fantasy*. Oxford: Clarendon; New York: Oxford UP, 1998.

"A Sinister Affair." *Economist* 321.7734 (1991): 102.

Snow, Lotus. "Muriel Spark's Use of Mythology."

Research Studies of Washington State University 45 (1977): 38–44.

Sproxton, Judy. *The Women of Muriel Spark*. New York: St. Martin's, 1992.

Stanford, Derek. *Inside the Forties: Literary Memoirs, 1937–1957*. London: Sidgwick & Jackson, 1977.

———. *Muriel Spark: A Biographical and Critical Study*. With a Bibliography by Bernard Stone. Fontwell, England: Centaur, 1963.

Stubbs, Patricia. *Muriel Spark*. Writers and Their Work. Harlow, UK: Longman, 1973.

Tominaga, Thomas T., and Wilma Schneidermeyer. *Iris Murdoch and Muriel Spark: A Bibliography*. Scarecrow Author Bibliographies, no. 27. Metuchen, NJ: Scarecrow, 1976.

Walker, Dorothea. *Muriel Spark*. Boston: Twayne, 1988.

Whiteley, Patrick J. "The Social Framework of Knowledge: Muriel Spark's *The Prime of Miss Jean Brodie*." *Mosaic* 29.4 (1996): 79–100.

Whittaker, Ruth. *The Faith and Fiction of Muriel Spark*. New York: St. Martin's, 1982.

Wilce, Gillian. "Her Life in Fiction." *New Edinburgh Review* 55 (1981): 13–14.

Lisa St. Aubin de Terán
1953–

Elizabeth Hoffman Nelson

Lisa St. Aubin de Terán is at her best when she writes about place. She has traveled widely, has an obsession with the railway, and possesses a keen sense of how place transforms people and lives. This love of place imbues her entire body of work—fiction, poem, or memoir.

BACKGROUND

Lisa St. Aubin de Terán was born in London in 1953. At the age of sixteen she married an aristocratic Venezuelan sugar-plantation owner and wanted bank robber, Jaime Terán. After several years riding the rails through Europe with her eccentric husband and his two comrades (all three in exile), St. Aubin de Terán moved to Venezuela. There she became "la Doña" of the Terán "hacienda" and developed a close relationship with "la gente"—the laborers and their families. In South America her husband's eccentricities blossomed into a terrifying and often-violent insanity. After seven years and the birth of her daughter, Iseult, St. Aubin de Terán fled Venezuela, returning to her home in England. In the early 1980s she briefly married Scottish poet George MacBeth, with whom she had a son, Alexander. In 1985, while separated from MacBeth, she fell in love with Scottish painter Robbie Duff Scott. They moved to Venice in 1986 and have since married and added a daughter, Florence, to their family. Lisa St. Aubin de Terán now divides her time between homes in Italy and England.

The influences on Lisa St. Aubin de Terán's work are largely nonacademic. What shapes her writing is her life, her homes, her families—and the importance of place. Her fiction, memoirs, and poetry mirror the choices she has made. She chose to marry an outlaw with hereditary insanity, and her writing about life in Venezuela is a product of that choice. Her writing takes different forms—autobiographical memoirs, loosely fictionalized histories of her husband's family, short stories, and poetry. Later, after returning to Europe, she chose to live both in Italy and in England, an arrangement that necessitated constant travel via the railroad—a motif that mimics this means of transport, crisscrossing all of her writing.

The political and social influences on Lisa St. Aubin de Terán's work stem directly from her migratory and unstable marriage to Jaime Terán. She kept company with Venezuelan political exiles who were often arrested and/or escaping to new hideouts. St. Aubin de Terán learned little of the political reasons for the exile—she could not speak Spanish very well, she was only a teenager, and she was female.

Once she settled on the sugar and avocado plantation in Venezuela, she got a firsthand look at how politics and socioeconomics function in the daily lives of "la gente." Her predicament was odd: she married a Terán, and therefore she was a "Doña," a person of rank and title, but St. Aubin de Terán was also a young girl, European, and not fluent in Spanish. Despite her nominal title of "Doña Terán" and her outsider status, she found herself drawn to "the other" ("la gente"), those who, like herself, are looked down on by the powerful. She saw firsthand the poverty, the malnutrition, the deaths of these laborers and their families, and also their spirit and perseverance. Lisa St. Aubin de Terán acknowledges the importance of this in the final paragraph of her memoir *The Hacienda*: "The people of Hacienda Santa Rita have been the greatest influence on my life and work" (342). The stories she tells of "la gente" are some of her finest.

The other place that engages her imagination is Italy. This place, with its rich land, history, food, and people, captures her heart. Several of her books highlight the beauty of Venice and Umbria and St. Aubin de Terán's love of all things Italian. There are hardships in all of the places she chooses to live, but the reader is fully aware of the joy, however odd or hard won, that the varied landscapes give her.

ANALYSIS

Lisa St. Aubin de Terán writes in three genres: fiction (novels and short stories), memoir, and poetry. She began writing during her seven years in the Venezuelan Andes and published her first novel, *Keepers of the House*, in 1982. (It was published in the United States under the title *The Long Way Home*.) It is a fictionalized account of her time on the sugar plantation and of the history of her husband's family, and it was awarded the Somerset Maugham Award, given to promising young British writers. It is with this first novel that her readers are given a sense of place—of destructive droughts and plagues of locusts—and how the tragedies test yet strengthen "la gente."

The Slow Train to Milan, Lisa St. Aubin de Terán's second novel, published the next year, returns to familiar territory. It is a fictionalized autobiographical tale of the years after she married her husband, when they traveled across Europe, often accompanied by Terán's two comrades in exile, Otto and Elías. This novel also won a prestigious literary award, the John Llewellyn Rhys Memorial Prize, for a memorable work by a British writer under the age of thirty. St. Aubin de Terán tells her readers on the first page of this novel that there are actually five protagonists, the final one being the train itself: "And the slow train was the slide rule of our existence, often our raison d'être" (7). This statement is misleading. The train functions in the novel as the means to change locales (often fleeing poverty, hunger, angry landlords, or suspicious police), but it is not a central figure. Only a few pages are devoted to loving descriptions of St. Aubin de Terán's obsession with the rails, a passion that began in early childhood and continues today. At the end of their long and often-difficult journey she finally describes how the train's movements and sounds were important to her and her companions: "The train itself divided like vertebrae, linked shapes like planed coffins flick-tailing along the tracks, and the old lump in my throat had come to tell me that I would never return to this slow train" (223). The people in the story are linked like vertebrae as well. They are an odd contingent, especially this teenaged wife dressed to excess in Edwardian clothes and her mentally unbalanced husband. Add two angry, intellectual political exiles to the mix, and the result is an odd but intriguing story of friendship and love and the sights, tastes, and sounds of France and Italy.

After writing two award-winning and successful novels, Lisa St. Aubin de Terán continued to concentrate on fiction during the mid-1980s, with one exception, a collection of poems. The work written between 1984 and 1987 does not measure up to her early writing in terms of plot, characterization, or focus. In the novels especially there is a trend toward the dark, the violent, and the gruesome.

The Tiger, published in 1984, also has roots in South America—it is the story of an aristocratic plantation-owning family with an ancestry of violence. The title refers primarily to Misia (short for "Mi Señora"), a vicious woman who has killed her husband and many others, and who rides the back of her grandson, Lucien, like "el tigre." Lucien is obsessed with Misia, and the violence becomes generational. St. Aubin de Terán gives no justification for the brutality of this old woman—the deaths and abuses operate in a vacuum. She does, however, continue what she does best: she describes the land, the daily lives of the peasants, the food, the labor. But even lovely detail is not enough to justify the unreasoned cruelty of many of her characters. With this piece of fiction, Lisa St. Aubin de Terán begins two motifs that will continue throughout her work: With Misia, she begins a long line of female characters who marry very badly. Is this autobiographical? Second and more annoying, she begins to use an affected style of sporadic unexplained naming. Lucien's father is "el Patrón," the head of the plantation; we are not told his given name. What was Misia's real name? This affectation tends to produce disdain for the characters. If the author does not name them, why should the reader care about them at all?

In 1985 Lisa St. Aubin de Terán published her only collection of poetry, *The High Place*. The poems are about "la gente"—stories from Venezuela. There are prologue and epilogue poems that frame the individual synoptic poems. The poems are undistinguished and prosaic. Her prose stories on the villagers are far superior to her poems.

The next novel, *The Bay of Silence* (1986), tends toward the gruesome. It is a reworking of her short story "I Never Eat Crabmeat Now," which was anthologized in 1985 in *Foreign Exchange*, a collection of travel fiction—an odd choice considering that the nightmarish plot overshadows any sense of place. The novel's structure consists of chapters narrated alternately by William Walsh and his movie-star wife, Rosalind. The author immediately (and ineffectively) hints at the horrible truth—an awful smell. We learn that Rosalind is mad, and their baby boy dies while on holiday in Sestri Levante, the Italian coast. The details of Amadeo's death and the aftermath are ghastly. In expanding the short story, St. Aubin de Terán fills the pages with predictable characterizations (Rosalind had been sexually abused by her uncle) and plot devices (the boy's death might have been due to a nearby nuclear power plant). Character traits are oversimplified. For example, William explains, "It may be naïve of me to say so now, but I didn't know that you were schizophrenic when I married you" (12). This line produces giggles, not sympathy or understanding. This is a disturbing book, largely lacking redeeming power.

Black Idol (1987) is a fictionalized account of the life and death of Harry Crosby, the godson of J.P. Morgan. This novel is very oddly constructed. It begins with a highly detailed chronology whose purpose—to highlight life events—is diminished by the detail. The chronology ends suddenly in 1929, and the novel begins with an unnamed narrator who tells the story of Harry Crosby. (The reader eventually learns that the narrator is Crosby's mistress, Josephine.) The narrative style is maddening—Josephine talks to someone (herself? Harry?) in a very conversational way while filling in the gaps of Harry's biography. There is a lot of badly written, florid sex talk ("Your fork rose like a mound in your black trunks with excitement" [22]). "Black idol," or opium, drives these shallow characters to the depths of drunkenness and orgies. In a flawed ending, Harry shoots Josephine, then himself. Our narrator is dead, but she keeps narrating. It is St. Aubin de Terán's worst book.

The Marble Mountain and Other Stories, a short-story collection, was released in 1989. It is a step above *Black Idol*, but many of the stories continue to focus, without much value, on the violent and the repulsive. "The Lady Gardener" is about a hit woman who poses as a gardener. "Diamond Jim" (also anthologized in *The Virago Book of Ghost Stories*) revolves around a lynching. The one story whose horror redeems the rest is "The Green Boy," about El Capino, a little Venezuelan boy who was accidentally poisoned by his father, and who literally turns green before dying. Like all her Venezuelan stories here and elsewhere, it captures the often-tragic lives of "la gente" and St. Aubin de Terán's powerlessness, even as "la Doña."

Off the Rails: Memoirs of a Train Addict, also published in 1989, focuses on trains and travel. In this first of three memoirs Lisa St. Aubin de Terán gives the reader a look at her life through the window of a train. We are introduced to her family—she gets her travel obsession from her father, who traveled continually. She tells us of her loves and losses, all in relation to the rails, and returns to her great skill, place description. The reader is treated to a vivid painting of train stops throughout the world.

By this time Italy had become home for the author, and her focus shifted in that direction, to writing about the land, people, and history. In 1989 she wrote the commentary for John Ferro Sims's collection of photographs, *Landscape in Italy*. The writing is good—we see the landscape by train as she writes. The photographs of the Italian countryside are also lovely.

In 1990 the author returned to something she knows—family. In *Joanna* St. Aubin de Terán writes a fictionalized look at an odd trinity: her mother (Joanna), her grandmother, and her great-grandmother. This family drama is powerful and often painful. Her grandmother physically and psychologically abuses Joanna. The novel is full of rage and depression. It is not an easy book to read, but the characterizations are tightly crafted.

Nocturne, published in 1992, takes place in Italy, and once more, pain and grief figure largely in the novel. There is also love, unconsumated, between Alessandro and Valentina—a crippling war wound prevents their union. The author focuses on the villagers and their unity, in war and in peace. There is fine description of place and custom as well.

In the same year Lisa St. Aubin de Terán collaborated on another book of photographs of Italy. This time she wrote seasonal descriptions for *Venice: The Four Seasons*, with photos by Mick Lindberg. This is a very personal account of her life in Venice. The photographs are a delightful complement to the lavish descriptions of the seasonal changes in food, weather, and custom. Occasionally the prose is a bit florid, verging on the precious: "In the summer I lie like a lizard on a cushion of thick marsh grass and vetch listening to the pattern of waves sucking and gulping at the edge of this flat breast of an island with its sculpted nipple of a church" (35). However, most of her narrative is accessible and rich.

A Valley in Italy: The Many Seasons of a Villa in Umbria (1994) details the joys and pitfalls of restoring a crumbling palazzo, la Villa Orsola, in Umbria. Alongside the detailed discussions of the slow, laborious process of making this castle livable are vivid impressions of the fecund land, the villagers, gardens, festivals, and daily family life. Community is very important there. Big life changes happen at the villa, including the birth of her daughter, Florence, and the wedding of her eldest daughter. Again the author reverts to an odd, affected style of naming. She refers to her daughter as "the child Iseult," even though the girl is a teenager. Born in Venezuela, Iseult was called "la niña

Iseult" by the villagers, but without this information, the reader is lost. She also hires two Irish au pairs and only calls them "the Irish Beauties." Is this affectation a protective urge? Carelessness? Whimsy? It often seems intrusive or opaque. Beyond that, the memoir is a delightful introduction to the people and customs of Umbria.

In 1997 Lisa St. Aubin de Terán published *The Hacienda*, a memoir of her seven years in Venezuela. The book operates on many levels. It is a sad tale of a doomed marriage. It is a fitting tribute to "la gente" she loved and respected. It is an adventure story filled with struggles with the land, animals, and cultural isolation. Her husband, Jaime Terán, leaves her alone, penniless and hungry, and when he does return home, his madness causes violent episodes. While he is gone, she learns to run the plantation and gain the respect of the peasants who work for her. She lives with two dogs, a vulture named Napoleon, and several maid-cooks who rotate through her employ. As Jaime's insanity worsened, she began to fear for her life and the life of her daughter, Iseult. Escape was difficult because Iseult was Venezuelan and needed her father's permission to go abroad. In 1979 mother and daughter fled the country and returned home to England. As St. Aubin de Terán feared, the hacienda fell apart after she left—most of "la gente" have since left or died.

St. Aubin de Terán leaves a lot out of her memoir. What happened to her and Iseult? What happened to Jaime? There are emotional gaps as well. We learn next to nothing about her marriage. The author is blessed with a child, one she was told she could never have, but we get no sense of the close mother-daughter bond; we learn more about Iseult's relationship with the servants. The strengths of this memoir are the fine descriptions of the people and the land.

The Palace, Lisa St. Aubin de Terán's latest novel, was published in Britain in 1997 and in the United States in 1999. The novel takes place in nineteenth-century Italy and tells the story of Gabriele del Campo, a prisoner of war who struggles to become successful enough to build an outrageously opulent palace for Donatella, his unrequited love. The novel is, once again, full of rich descriptions of the land and the building.

Lisa St. Aubin de Terán has also edited two collections of travel essays. *Indiscreet Journeys: Stories of Women on the Road* (1990) tells the stories of women who explore and escape through travel. *The Virago Book of Wanderlust and Dreams* (1998) is dedicated to "the women who have had the courage to say 'yes' to life."

ASSESSMENT

There is little significant criticism about the work of Lisa St. Aubin de Terán. Why? I believe that it is her accessibility. Her novels and memoirs focus on basic things—family, home, love, and work. Does this mean that her work is too simple to be scrutinized by academics? No. The themes are basic, but there are many areas where critical attention could be paid—feminist theory, Marxist theory, and more. Lisa St. Aubin de Terán's writing is fundamentally about place. She gives us a sugar plantation, a ruined castle in Umbria, a slow train to Milan, a flat in Venice. These are places we may go and stay a while. During our visits we learn about "la gente," or the Orsolani stonemason, or the Venezuelan bank robber, or the gondolier. Lisa St. Aubin de Terán gives us history and language and politics and economics and much more.

BIBLIOGRAPHY

Primary Sources

Keepers of the House. London: Cape, 1982. As *The Long Way Home*. New York: Harper, 1982.
The Slow Train to Milan. New York: Harper, 1983.
The Tiger. London: Cape, 1984.
The High Place. London: Cape, 1985.
"I Never Eat Crabmeat Now." In *Foreign Exchange*.

Ed. Julian Evans. London: Hamish Hamilton, 1985. 97–111.
The Bay of Silence. London: Cape, 1986.
Black Idol. London: Cape, 1987.
"Diamond Jim." In *The Virago Book of Ghost Stories: The Twentieth Century*. Ed. Richard Dalby. London: Virago, 1987. 318–323.
"Commentary." In *Landscape in Italy*. Photographs by John Ferro Sims. Boston: Bullfinch Press, 1989.
Indiscreet Journeys: Stories of Women on the Road. Ed. Lisa St. Aubin de Terán. Boston: Faber, 1990.
The Marble Mountain and Other Stories. London: Cape, 1989.
Off the Rails: Memoirs of a Train Addict. London: Bloomsbury, 1989.
Joanna. London: Virago, 1990; New York: Carroll & Graf, 1990.
Nocturne. New York: St. Martin's, 1992.
Venice: The Four Seasons. London: Hamish Hamilton, 1992; New York: Clarkson Potter, 1993.
A Valley in Italy: The Many Seasons of a Villa in Umbria. New York: Harper Collins, 1994.
The Hacienda: A Memoir. Boston: Little, Brown, 1997.
The Palace. London: Macmillan, 1997; New York: Ecco, 1999.
The Virago Book of Wanderlust and Dreams. Ed. Lisa St. Aubin de Terán. London: Virago, 1998.

Secondary Sources

Duchêne, Anne. "In a Den of Vice in Umbria." Rev. of *The Palace*. *TLS* 27 June 1997: 23.
Gornick, Vivian. "Out of Venezuela." Rev. of *The Hacienda: A Memoir*. *Women's Review of Books* May 1998: 9–10.
McCullough, David Willis. "L'Uomo about Town." Rev. of *The Palace*. *New York Times Book Review* 1 August 1999: 8.
Upchurch, Michael. "The Robber's Bride." Rev. of *The Hacienda: A Memoir*. *New York Times Book Review* 12 April 1998: 19.

Elizabeth Coles Taylor
1912–1975

Robert Ellis Hosmer, Jr.

Elizabeth Taylor came to prominence in post–World War II England, a world she chronicled in twelve novels and several dozen short stories. Because Taylor excelled at writing deft comedies of manners, with limited scope and without pretense, she has often been compared to Jane Austen, but that comparison has restricted relevance and limited value, since Taylor's work departs from Austen's in several crucial respects, although the resemblance is often striking. Yet Taylor's most interesting work lies in two novels in which she departed from her characteristic concerns and explored the role of the artist, producing an interesting, unsuccessful novel in the first instance and an engaging, very successful novel in the second.

BACKGROUND

In an autobiographical sketch published in the *New York Herald Tribune* (October 11, 1953) Elizabeth Taylor wrote that "nothing sensational, thank heavens, has ever happened" (23), and indeed, though her life spans a period of history (1912–1975) marked by wars, the Great Depression, the Holocaust, and the Cold War, her fiction reflects virtually nothing of it, filled as it is with the ordinary, understated events of everyday life. Born on July 3, 1912, in Reading, Berkshire, Elizabeth Coles attended the Abbey School, leaving in 1930 to become a governess, then a librarian, in Buckinghamshire. She liked teaching children, and the fiction she would later write exhibits a notable ability to depict children authentically. In the 1930s Coles was an active Communist, and though she later severed her Party connections, she maintained her left-wing sympathies and voted Labour her whole life.

In 1936 she married John William Kendall Taylor, and they settled in Penn, Buckinghamshire; by him she had two children, and with the exception of five years at Scarborough, Yorkshire (1940–1945), for her husband's RAF service, Taylor spent almost all her time in Buckinghamshire. She remained a deeply "English" writer, and village life in the Thames Valley would be the subject of nearly all her fiction. After her first novel, *At Mrs. Lippincote's* (1945), which draws upon those years at Scarborough, Taylor, in a manner recalling Jane Austen's concern with three or four families in a village, rarely left the precincts of Buckinghamshire, either in person or in her fiction. When she did, if she strayed farther than London, as she did in her last novel, *Blaming* (1976), she did so at her peril.

Taylor was an avid reader (Austen, the Brontës, Hardy, James) and writer from childhood on. Sure of her vocation as a writer, she wrote stories, plays, and poems; one poem, rejected for publication with the observation "too stormy" attached, evidently persuaded her to concentrate on fiction. Her first publication, a short story, appeared in 1942, followed by her first novel in 1945. Throughout her career Taylor wrote and published in both genres, producing four volumes of short stories, a children's book (*Mossy Trotter*), and twelve novels.

At Mrs. Lippincote's (1945) launched Taylor's career as a novelist, attracting favorable attention from L.P. Hartley; her second novel, *Palladian* (1946), garnered praise from Elizabeth Bowen and Rosamond Lehmann. Ten more novels followed in the course of the next thirty years, ending with the posthumously published *Blaming* (1976).

ANALYSIS

Some readers and critics have lamented the widespread critical neglect of this mid-twentieth-century British writer whose works—both bought and borrowed—were very popular in their time. It has been mostly fellow writers (Kingsley Amis, Paul Bailey, Elizabeth Bowen, L.P. Hartley, Rosamond Lehmann) who have risen to speak; critics have generally ignored her work, though in Arthur Mizener, who deemed her "the modern man's Jane Austen," and William H. Pritchard, who qualifies that judgment somewhat in his essay "Almost Austen," she has found two articulate partisans.

True, Taylor's novels do give what Pritchard has called "a sense of the real, of life going on" (160); sometimes in scenes rather more than in sum, they are poised comedies of manners, distinguished by sharp psychological probing, a keen ear for inflections of thought and speech, a shrewd eye for what she called "background" and "illuminating details" ("Choosing Details" 15). Drawing upon the middle class for characters and confining her canvas almost exclusively to England, Taylor created a series of lantern slides of post–World War II English life. Novels like *A View of the Harbour*, *A Game of Hide-and-Seek*, and *The Soul of Kindness* display an "almost Austen" quality, but none achieves the full distinction. Here there is no universal moral truth revealed; indeed, Taylor would shun such a task. Here there are no heroes and rarely anything approaching heroic resolve or action (in a later novel, *Mrs. Palfrey at the Claremont*, Taylor seems to deliberately undercut the very considerable potential heroism of the title character). Here there may be wit, a good deal of ironic understatement, and a random comic touch, but rampant pessimism and gloom have driven out the festivity and joy of, say, *Pride and Prejudice*.

It is better, perhaps, to leave aside Austen as much as possible for the moment and acknowledge that in her own right Taylor, who admitted a certain kinship not only with Austen but with a number of other writers as diverse as Ivy Compton-Burnett, Anton Chekhov, and Virginia Woolf, wrote a dozen novels that are characterized by what Angus Wilson called her "warm heart, sharp claws and exceptional powers of formal balance" ("Sense and Sensitivity" 22), nearly every one a pleasing, insightful comedy of manners. Yet far more interesting and intriguing are the novels in which she took greater risks by dealing at length with a theme that reverberates in every novel: the role of the artist and the work of art. Most often (and accurately) considered a writer who chose not to deal, at least explicitly, with big ideas or philosophical propositions (indeed, she consistently satirizes one of the great philosophical propositions, belief in God, in nearly every novel), Taylor focused on aesthetic matters in two novels, one a notable failure on those terms (and paradoxically a best-seller), the other arguably her best novel and also a popular success.

"Elizabeth Taylor wrote about people who are comfortably off and who feel uncomfortable" (Clapp vi). In every one of her novels Taylor narrowed her focus to a small group of people, in a very specified setting, and detailed their ordinary lives; rarely are men central figures in the generally unoriginal plots. Plot is simply not crucial: character, setting, and mood are. In Taylor's fictional world people are sad, lonely, isolated, driven, often self-deceiving, and largely unaware. Every novel concerns itself with a complex of human relationships—sibling rivalry in many, marriage in all but one, mothers and children in all.

Taylor's first six novels, published between 1945 and 1953, can be seen as a group; each is a richly detailed and carefully contextualized account of rather ordinary middle-class life. In each, secondary characters nearly displace primary characters, while setting sometimes threatens to overwhelm everything. In *At Mrs. Lippincote's*, the only Taylor novel set during World War II itself, Julia Davenant accompanies her son, her husband, Wing Commander Roddy Davenant, and his cousin to Scarborough. Julia tries to fulfill her role as wife and mother, unable to practice the hypocrisy displayed around her. She strikes up friendships with the base commander and renews previous acquaintance with Mr. Taylor, former maître d' at a stylish London restaurant frequented by the Davenants before the war. Julia stands out from the others for her compassion, humor, and honesty: neither delusional nor self-deceived, she struggles to adapt to a private world not of her own making in a public world not of anyone's making. At the novel's end the artificial life imposed by wartime life dissipates, the household disperses, but Julia carries on, curiously and perhaps permanently isolated from her husband and child.

Palladian (1946) seems to be very much in the tradition of the Brontës and Daphne du Maurier, a reworking of the young governess/older lord of the manor story. Taylor provides enough of the clichéd romance plot and Gothic apparatus to raise such expectations, and, at least in the technical sense, she does not disappoint: Cassandra Dashwood marries Marion Vanburgh and returns to Cropthorne Manor, a gloomy aged pile menaced by the presence of a superannuated nanny and a spiteful charwoman. Yet Taylor's eye, which catches a number of local village characters, most particularly Mrs. Veal, the Rubenesque publican's wife, is on another relationship, that between Marion and his cousin Tom, a sad alcoholic, mysteriously tied to the small world of the manor and its environs. This study of mutual dependence and self-destructive behavior eclipses the main plot line. Working the narrow two inches of ivory she carves, Taylor reveals a world of resented dependencies, not-always-repressed aggression, and cruelty, and she does it deftly.

Taylor's third novel is really not a view of the harbor at all; rather, it is a view of the small, decaying coastal town of Newby just after World War II. With a variegated canvas of characters, predominantly female, *A View of the Harbour* would seem to foreground the story of Beth Cazabon, successful minor novelist, and Tory Foyle, a friend of Beth's from schoolgirl days, now recently divorced and living next door. The condition of the Old Town district of Newby, where these two women live, is an obvious metaphor for personal relationships, most prominently Beth's with Tory: unbeknownst to Beth, her husband Robert and Tory are having an affair. Given the ostensible centrality of Beth the writer figure, one might expect her story to be *the* story, but it is not; rather, a half-dozen secondary characters displace central characters. Of these, the coarse, crippled Mrs. Bracey, confined to home at the back of the shop she shares with her two daughters, dominates. Mrs. Bracey, with her Rabelaisian stories, her pessimistic view of life, and her superior attitude toward others, displaces Beth (and nearly everyone else) as the central, if flawed, intelligence of a novel that minutely documents life in a small town. Typically, Taylor's concern is not with action but with perception; here the relativity and instability of perception, hence the title's indefinite, rather than definite, pronoun. Taylor is not after big effects or grand statements, only the painful truths of lives lived in a world of compromise, a world without compensation or sustaining transcendence. *A View of the Harbour* is the novel that Taylor would write and rewrite for the rest of her career.

These first several novels were followed in rapid succession by *A Wreath of Roses* (1949), *A Game of Hide-and-Seek* (1951), and *The Sleeping Beauty* (1953). All three follow, more or less, the patterns and concerns established by the earlier novels, though with a greater economy, reflecting particularly the more tightly plotted structure of *A View of the Harbour* and an enhanced stylistic elegance. *A Wreath of Roses* benefits from compression; fifty pages shorter than *A View,* it sets a triangle of women at its center: Camilla and Liz, friends from school days in Switzerland, and Frances Rutherford, Liz's former governess. The "girls," now in their twenties, return for their annual summer's visit to Frances. Liz's life has been complicated by marriage to a dull vicar and the birth of a child, Camilla's by a fateful meeting with a young man en route to Frances's country cottage. Female friendship, marriage, and the little hurts and larger disappointments of an often-random existence flesh out this novel. The concern with disillusionment is amplified in *A Game of Hide-and-Seek,* the story of Harriet Claridge's late adolescent infatuation with Vesey Macmillan, an unstable, self-absorbed young man. After that summer experience their lives take different trajectories: Harriet's into a respectable marriage and motherhood, Vesey's into a rather aimless life of little accomplishment. Years later Harriet remains in love with Vesey, but his predictable reappearance comes to naught; as Elizabeth Janeway noted, "In the beginning they are too young, in the end too old to be able to make anything of their love" (5).

The Sleeping Beauty may be one of Taylor's best novels for its greater psychological complexity, its diversity of believable personalities, and its narrative assurance. It rises well above the comedy-of-manners genre so well practiced by Elizabeth Taylor up to this point. What has arguably been Taylor's central concern, love in some of its permutations and combinations, is her sole concern here: "love," however conceived or defined—between man and woman (or, to be more precise, man and women here), between parent and child, between siblings. The love story of Vinny Tumulty, fiftyish married man, and Emily Kelsey, wounded single woman charged with the care of her sister's damaged daughter, is told with extraordinary delicacy and the sharpest intuition. Its resolution—in a world of exquisitely drawn secondary characters, nearly all of them women—is an act of magical suspension. The perception of one secondary character gives acute insight not only into this novel but into each novel Taylor wrote: "Behind the facades of other people lay a labyrinth of mystery, a vast terrain of secrecy, which resulted in unaccountable behaviour" (140).

Of these three novels, *A Wreath of Roses* is the signal failure, but in that failure lies something of very considerable importance in Taylor's literary career. For the first time Taylor attempted something larger in a novel, and the reader is alerted to that from the novel's epigraph, a passage taken from *The Waves* by Virginia Woolf, arguably her most difficult—and greatest—achievement in the genre. The story of Liz and Camilla sometimes obscures *A Wreath of Roses*'s central concern with the shape and structure of the work of art, the relationship of artist and audience, and the role of art. In the construction of Frances Rutherford, the retired governess turned painter, Taylor has attempted to address these issues. She deliberately took a risk in doing so: the result is a largely unsuccessful novel, but an intriguing, brave book nonetheless.

The Frances Rutherford whom we meet in the novel has moved away from her earlier mode of realistic representation into one that might loosely be termed expressionistic. In her dissatisfaction not only with painting but with life itself, Rutherford struggles for meaning and means of representation. Without the foundation and reference points of religious belief (agnosticism, if not atheism, is a given perspective for the thinking people in Taylor's fiction), Frances's view of life is dark and gloomy; so, too, are these paintings done in the newer style. Like Woolf, Frances struggles to capture and hold fugitive moments of being: " 'Life persists in the vulnerable, the sensitive,' she said. 'They carry it on. The invulnerable, the too-heavily armored perish. Fearful, ill-adapted, cumbersome, impersonal. Dinosaurs and men in tanks. But the stream of life flows differently, through the unarmed, the emotional, the highly personal' " (77).

About halfway through the novel Frances stands in a dark garden and contemplates the night sky. Taylor gives her a dramatic soliloquy that expounds upon Frances's perception of the emptiness and futility of all human accomplishment, however great, in a world decaying into dust that will be carried off into the abyss. Even a longtime admirer of Rutherford's earlier painting, a film director named Morland Beddoes, cannot move her; one of their exchanges prompts her to declare, "Life's not simplicity. . . . Not long kindness either. It's darkness and the terrible things we do to one another, to ourselves. The sooner we are out of it the better. And paintings don't matter. They are like making daisy chains in the shadow of the volcano. Pathetic and childish" (170). These are but two of a half-dozen such moments in the novel, and while they are certainly thought-provoking in themselves, when they are put together, they damage the narrative texture of the work to such an extent that it may seem as though Taylor wrote two novels simultaneously. Nonetheless, *A Wreath of Roses* is perhaps the most engaging, intellectually stimulating novel Taylor ever wrote.

Taylor's next novel, *Angel* (1957), is arguably her finest, and its achievement represents not only the high point of Taylor's career but a fusion of early sharply observed studies of loneliness and self-deception with the aesthetic preoccupations that surfaced prominently in *A Wreath of Roses*. *Angel* came as a mild surprise to a number of readers and critics, yet it should not have; it represents Taylor's most ambitious and daring involvement with themes of art and the artist's life. In *Angel* Taylor seems largely to ignore a number of her earlier concerns with mores and manners in order to focus on the creative artist. Angelica ("Angel") Deverell is a scarcely educated young woman whose overactive imagination eventually severs her completely from all reality; "a sort of Edwardian Marie Corelli, she misconceives the world and her part in it almost to the point of genius" (Amis 784). Fifteen years old at the novel's opening, Angelica lives above the shop with her widowed mother. Longing to escape a dreary backstreet existence, Angel retreats into a world of extraordinary fantasy, spinning elaborate tales about her own life and writing torrents of purple prose; for her, "experience was a makeshift for imagination" (49). Against the odds, her first novel is bought, published, and greatly successful; her career launched, Angel proceeds to write novel after novel, each one more successful than the last.

Angel Deverell is Taylor's most sharply edged and affecting portrait of self-deception and disillusionment. Childish, naïve, terribly vulnerable, and deluded, Angel sees the world as she wills, believing that it can be molded just as much as the novels she writes. Angel Deverell's fall is a painful study in the diseased imagination, and though *Angel* is a fictionalized account, it derives undeniable autobiographical resonance from Taylor's authentic knowledge of the life of the creative artist. At one level it must be read as a cautionary tale: without moralizing, and without sentimentality, Taylor exposes the insidious dangers of the imagination: when Angel's husband comments, "I think that the secret of your power over people is that you communicate with yourself, not with your readers," she responds, "Yes, that is true" (133–134).

Taylor explores the issues that have figured, at least peripherally, in her earlier novels and that will continue to figure in her later novels, but nowhere is the result of Taylor's musing as deeply disturbing as it is here in *Angel*; that Taylor resists the temptation to mock or judge or satirize Angelica Deverell speaks volumes. Nowhere else does she focus so brilliantly on these concerns, nowhere else does she weave traditional elements of narrative with larger philosophical concerns so seamlessly.

In its focus on female character and its thematic concerns with self-deception, isolation, and vulnerability, *Angel* does not represent a substantive departure for Taylor. In her selfishness, cruelty, and detachment from real connection with others, Angel represents Taylor's most elaborate, sustained variation on the monstrous personality. Rather, in its choice of time period (Angel's story begins in 1900 and ends just after World War II) and its central, rather than marginal, concern with matters artistic, *Angel* represented a considerable risk for Taylor, whose works had been steadily growing in popularity. Yet *Angel*'s near-best-seller status did not prompt Taylor to follow suit in the five novels she wrote in the last twenty years or so of her life. Rather, with the exception of *The Wedding Group* (1968), which touches marginally on aesthetic concerns with its lightly fictionalized use of Eric Gill's commune at Pigotts, the novels that follow rework standard Taylor themes in carefully constructed fictions grounded in typically cool, elegant prose.

In a Summer Season (1961) puts Taylor back in familiar territory: a large house in the Thames Valley with members of three generations resident. The narrative focuses on Kate Heron, a wealthy, attractive, middle-aged widow who remarries a charming Irishman ten years her junior. Here Taylor displays her characteristically deft abilities with irony and understatement, arranging a study of love and marriage in the modern world, a fiction much in the Jamesian mode, though its moral point is made without the master's subtlety. *The Soul of Kindness* (1964) takes as dramatis personae a rather more upper-middle-class group than usual. Flora Quartermaine believes herself to be "the soul of kindness," but of course she is not. Her mother, husband, and friends conspire to insulate her and promote the delusion. Like Angel Deverell, Flora is self-deceived and disconnected from reality. Only Liz Corbett, a feisty, sharp-eyed realist (and painter), does not participate in the conspiracy; however, though she may be a rather heavy-handed counterbalance, a symbol of truth and goodness in direct contrast to Flora, Liz is a figure of significantly less appeal and therefore unable to carry the weight Taylor assigns to her in this narrative. Ultimately, *The Soul of Kindness* leaves its characters adrift and isolated, unable to connect in a world typically more tragic than comic, despite Taylor's efforts to deploy her wit and humor to the contrary.

The *Wedding Group* (1968) has the distinction of presenting Midge Little, the third in the trio of "characters with monstrous aspects" cited by Elizabeth Jane Howard in her introduction to the Virago Press reprint of the novel. At the novel's center are Midge Little, her son David, village residents, and Cressida McPhail, granddaughter of Harry Bretton, artist and patriarch of a commune just outside the village. In the marriage of David and Cressy the two worlds, one secular and materialist, the other spiritual and artistic, are evidently meant to merge, but the novel, like the marriage, lacks the vitality of creative tension between opposing forces. *The Wedding Group* deflects so much attention to Midge that the narrative thread is all but broken, most damagingly at the end.

Mrs. Palfrey at the Claremont (1971) charts the remaining days of the recently widowed Mrs. Palfrey, who moves into the Claremont Hotel, a residence for a number of engaging, comical eccentrics. This is familiar fictional territory, though not for Taylor. Typically, Taylor touches upon the artist theme in the person of young Ludovic Myers, who befriends Mrs. Palfrey, but subordinates it. Mrs. Palfrey suffers the indignities of old age and the neglect of family; Ludo comes to the rescue as a surrogate grandson to fill some of the void in her life, but in the end this dignified, stoic, independent woman of charm and substance goes under. All the while, Taylor stubbornly resists allowing Mrs. Palfrey to assume heroic dimension. Taylor's pessimistic vision of human life admitted of no heroes. Her study of old age stands in sharp and uncomfortable contrast to those made by Barbara Pym (*Quartet in Autumn*) and Muriel Spark (*Memento Mori*).

Taylor's last novel, *Blaming* (1976), published the year after her death by her husband, is a bittersweet delineation of a recently widowed woman's attempts to fashion a life for herself. It delicately reworks the major themes of her fiction—love, loss, friendship between women, codes of behavior. It is the only novel to set some of the scene—and not altogether convincingly—outside England. Early on, the central relationship lies between Nick Henderson, a middle-aged English painter, and his wife Amy; with the death of Nick, the relationship between Amy and Martha, an American writer, moves to the center. Taylor populates Amy's world with her son, his wife, and their daughter as well as a doctor of long acquaintance and a quite unbelievable servant aptly named Ernie Pounce as she sketches the new life Amy must create for herself. *Blaming* shows no signs of incompleteness or need for revision, but it is an unsatisfying novel. Taylor's portrait of Amy Henderson is a convincing study of the psychological dynamics of the grieving process, yet her presentation of Martha, especially at the end, is a hasty sketch, not a finished portrait. *Blaming* is a dignified close to Taylor's career, but it is not her best work; in the words of Rosemary Dinnage, "*Blaming* . . . brings to a quiet conclusion a most honourable literary career" (1096).

ASSESSMENT

Taylor's literary success was remarkable, and for at least two major reasons. First, her novels and stories are very much against the grain, appearing in a post–World War II Britain dominated by the likes of Amis, Sillitoe, Wain, and Osborne, on the one hand, and Waugh and Powell on the other. In the decades that followed, her writing stands quite apart from the dominant female voices of Spark, Murdoch, and Lessing as well. Second, Taylor writes primarily about and for women at a time when the means of production and the venues of criticism were certainly dominated by men, and so it seems a wonder that she ever had the opportunity to achieve considerable popularity. The rise of feminist literary scholarship did bring her a new audience in the 1980s, much helped by Virago Press's reprinting of a number of her works, but at present she is little known and scarcely read.

BIBLIOGRAPHY

Primary Sources

At Mrs. Lippincote's. London: Peter Davies, 1945; London: Virago, 1988.

Palladian. London: Peter Davies, 1946; New York: Knopf, 1947; London: Virago, 1985.

A View of the Harbour. London: Peter Davies, 1947; New York: Knopf, 1947; London: Virago, 1987.

A Wreath of Roses. London: Peter Davies, 1949; New York: Knopf, 1949.

A Game of Hide-and-Seek. London: Peter Davies, 1951; New York: Knopf, 1951; London: Virago, 1986.

"Elizabeth Taylor." *New York Herald Tribune* 11 October 1953: 23–25.

The Sleeping Beauty. London: Peter Davies, 1953; New York: Viking, 1953; London: Virago, 1982.

Hester Lilly, and Twelve Short Stories. London: Peter Davies, 1954; New York: Viking, 1954; London: Virago, 1990.

Angel. London: Peter Davies, 1957; New York: Viking, 1957; London: Virago, 1984.

The Blush and Other Stories. London: Peter Davies, 1958; New York: Viking, 1958; London: Virago, 1986.

In a Summer Season. London: Peter Davies, 1961; New York: Dial Press, 1983.

The Soul of Kindness. London: Chatto & Windus, 1964; New York: Viking, 1964; London: Virago, 1983.

A Dedicated Man and Other Stories. London: Chatto & Windus, 1965; New York: Viking, 1965; London: Virago, 1993.

"Setting a Scene." *Cornhill Magazine* 1045 (Autumn 1965): 68–72.

Mossy Trotter. London: Chatto & Windus, 1967; New York: Harcourt, 1967.

The Wedding Group. London: Chatto & Windus, 1968; New York: Viking, 1968; London: Virago, 1985.

"England." *Kenyon Review* 31.4 (1969): 469–473.

"Some Notes on Writing Stories." *London Magazine* 9.12 (March 1970): 8–10.

Mrs. Palfrey at the Claremont. London: Chatto & Windus, 1971; London: Virago, 1982.

The Devastating Boys and Other Stories. London: Chatto & Windus, 1972; New York: Viking, 1972.

Blaming. London: Chatto & Windus, 1976; New York: Viking, 1976.

"Choosing Details That Count." *Writer* 83.1 (January 1970): 15–16.

Dangerous Calm: The Selected Stories of Elizabeth Taylor. Ed. Lynn Knight. London: Virago, 1995.

Secondary Sources

Amis, Kingsley. "At Mrs. Taylor's." *Spectator* 14 June 1957: 784, 786.

Austen, Richard. "The Novels of Elizabeth Taylor." *Commonweal* 10 June 1955: 258–259.

Bailey, Paul. "Brave Face." *New Statesman* 17 September 1956: 380.

Bowen, Elizabeth. "*Palladian*." *Tatler* 25 February 1946: 23.

Brickner, Richard. "Killing with Kindness." *New Republic* 22 August 1964: 30, 32.

Brown, Catherine Meredith. "Ruffled English Retreat." *Saturday Review of Literature* 32 (26 March 1949): 12.

Clapp, Susannah. Introduction to *The Sleeping Beauty*. London: Virago, 1982. v–xiv.

Dinnage, Rosemary. "The Tick of Blood in the Wrist." *TLS* 10 September 1976: 1096.

Gillette, Jane Brown. " 'Oh, What a Something Web We Weave': The Novels of Elizabeth Taylor." *Twentieth Century Literature* 35.1 (Spring 1989): 94–112.

Groberg, Nancy. "Strange, Amazing People." *Saturday Review of Literature* 29 (20 April 1946): 15.

Grove, Robin. "From the Island: Elizabeth Taylor's Novels." *Studies in the Literary Imagination* 11.2 (Fall 1978): 79–95.

Hicks, Granville. "Amour on the Thames." *Saturday Review* 21 January 1961: 62.

Howard, Elizabeth Jane. Introduction to *The Wedding Group*. London: Virago, 1985. v–x.

Janeway, Elizabeth. "How Things Work Out." *New York Times Book Review* 22 January 1961: 5, 26.

———. "Love Is a Sad Game." *New York Times Book Review* 4 March 1951: 5.

Leclercq, Florence. *Elizabeth Taylor*. Boston: Twayne, 1985.

Liddell, Robert. *Elizabeth and Ivy*. London: Peter Owen, 1986.

———. "The Novels of Elizabeth Taylor." *Review of English Literature* 1 (April 1960): 54–61.

Macheski, Cecilia. ". . . Elizabeth Taylor (the Novelist, of Course) . . ." *Barbara Pym Newsletter* June 1988: 5–7.

Mizener, Arthur. "In the Austen Vein." *New Republic* 2 November 1953: 25.

Pritchard, William H. "Almost Austen." In *Playing It by Ear: Literary Essays and Reviews*. Amherst: U of Massachusetts P, 1994. 155–160.

Rosenthal, Lucy. "*Mrs Palfrey at the Claremont*." *Saturday Review* 31 July 1971: 25–26.

Saxon, Alice. "Novel about a Juvenile Novelist." *Commonweal* 25 October 1957: 102–103.

Sayre, Nora. "Violence Is Primary." *New York Times Book Review* 31 March 1968: 40.

Wilson, Angus. "In the Jane Austen Tradition." Rev. of *The Wedding Group*. *Observer* 28 April 1968: 28.

———. "Sense and Sensitivity." Rev. of *A Dedicated Man*. *Observer Weekend Review* 27 June 1965: 22.

Wyatt-Brown, Anne M. "The Loathly Lady and the Edwardian Statue: Life in Pensioner Hotels." *Gerontologist* 26.2 (1986): 207–210.

Angela Thirkell
1890–1961

Mitchell R. Lewis

Angela Margaret Thirkell was a popular writer of novels, short stories, historical fiction, and children's stories. She also wrote a biography, an autobiography, and numerous newspaper and magazine articles. Thirkell is widely known for her Barsetshire series, a well-received cycle of realistic novels depicting English country life before, during, and after World War II. Modeled primarily on Victorian fiction, each of the novels takes place in the fictional county of Barsetshire, the name and topography of which Thirkell borrowed from the pastoral imagination of Anthony Trollope, the nineteenth-century novelist. As critics have often noted, Thirkell's overall intention in the Barsetshire series is to document the transformations in the class structure of English society that followed in the wake of the two world wars, profoundly altering the social habits of rural England. Thirkell documents these transformations from the perspectives of the titled nobility of England and the sympathetic professional and upper-middle classes. Consequently, the customary opinion of Thirkell, developed first in the contemporaneous reviews of her work, is that she can be best understood as a nostalgic, conservative, sometimes even reactionary social historian. Such a view is certainly warranted, particularly because some of Thirkell's most prominent themes include the tragic demise of the nobility, the unfortunate mixing of the classes, the breakdown of traditional values, and the disastrous rise of the Labour Party. In addition to this commonplace view, however, Thirkell can also be seen as a writer who was very much preoccupied with pointing out some of the dissatisfying social roles available to middle- and upper-class English women, even if she was by no means a progressive feminist.

BACKGROUND

Born in London on January 30, 1890, and baptized Angela Margaret Mackail, Thirkell was raised in the twilight of a late Victorian middle-class world in which the arts were highly esteemed, often drawing the patronage and the respect of the upper classes. It was a world of highbrow culture that shaped her sensibilities and of which, in later years, she would always speak fondly, as if it were a bygone golden age. Thirkell's father, Dr. John William Mackail, was a brilliant Dante scholar, a classicist, and an Oxford professor of poetry. Having graduated from the University of Edinburgh at the age of sixteen, he later worked for the Ministry of Education and, throughout his life, produced a steady stream of respected criticism, translations, and biographies. As a promising young scholar, Mackail was introduced to the celebrated Victorian painter Edward Burne-Jones, who enjoyed the patronage of such notable English peers as William Graham, Percy Scawen Wyndham, and Arthur Balfour, who occupied the office of prime minister for a brief term. As a result, Mackail was admitted to Burne-Jones's distinguished circle of painters, musicians, writers, and actors, among whom were William Morris, Henry James, George Eliot, Sarah Bernhardt, Oscar Wilde, John Ruskin, and Dante Gabriel Rossetti.

In the presence of this society of towering Victorian dignitaries, the young Thirkell found herself. Her mother, Margaret Mackail, was the only daughter of Burne-Jones. Among Mrs. Mackail's cousins were the popular author Rudyard Kipling and the statesman Stanley Baldwin, who served several terms as prime minister. Mrs. Mackail herself played the piano and the harp with distinction and sang as well. She was often a model for her father's rather ethereal but highly sought-after paintings, as was her mother Georgiana. Figuratively and literally speaking, Burne-Jones placed both his wife and daughter on a pedestal, worshipping them in a romantic manner typical of the Pre-Raphaelite painters. Because of her devotion to her father, Mrs. Mackail named Thirkell after Burne-Jones, who was known as "Angelo," after the Italian painter Fra Angelico. Burne-Jones doted on Thirkell as he did on his wife and daughter. Many times, at public occasions, Burne-Jones saw to it that Thirkell sat at his right hand, thus sharing, in effect, the homage of his many visitors. As an impressionable child, Thirkell was deeply affected by her grandfather's lifestyle, as well as by his dream world, which he depicted in his paintings. For Thirkell, however, the sun soon began to set on this golden age, Burne-Jones having died when she was only eight years old. Brief though this time was, it left an indelible mark on her memory, becoming not only a kind of touchstone by which she would measure her subsequent experiences, but also a fruitful source for many of her books.

Educated at home by a series of French and German governesses, Thirkell later attended the Anglican Froebel Institute in Kensington and the St. Paul's Girls' School in Hammersmith. As a young adult, Thirkell developed her proficiency at the piano, acquiring a taste for Beethoven, Schumann, Schubert, Wagner, and Brahms. She also read a great deal of literature, including the works of Charles Dickens, George Eliot, Anthony Trollope, and Elizabeth Gaskell, but she was particularly taken with the novels of Henry Kingsley. From her reading Thirkell developed vague aspirations to be a writer, even going so far as to buy a typewriter on which to type her first modest attempts at fiction, but her parents discouraged her, hoping that she would make a fashionable marriage.

In 1911 Thirkell disappointed her parents by hastily marrying James Campbell McInnes, a working-class concert baritone who earned a reputation not only for singing country airs, but also for sexual promiscuity. Thirkell had two children by him, Graham and Colin McInnes, the latter of whom would grow up to be a novelist himself. Following the decline of her husband's career during the war and his precipitous descent into drinking, debt, spousal abuse, and extramarital affairs, Thirkell successfully divorced him in 1917 on the grounds of cruelty and adultery. In 1918, however, Thirkell made yet another hasty marriage, this time to George Lancelot Allnut Thirkell, a Tasmanian engineer serving in the Australian Imperial Forces. They left England for Australia in 1920 on a troopship full of riotous soldiers, deserters, and convicts, the traumatic experience of which became the basis of her *Trooper to the Southern Cross* (1934), a novel that Thirkell published under the pseudonym Leslie Parker. In Australia Thirkell began to write for newspapers, magazines, and radio stations, garnering a respectable literary reputation, even as she was waiting hand and foot on her husband, as local customs dictated. Thirkell also gave birth to another child, Lance Thirkell, but she grew increasingly dissatisfied with Australia and her financially strapped husband and returned to England with Lance in 1929. Thirkell never divorced her second husband, keeping his last name for the rest of her life, but she also never saw him again. Through with married life, Thirkell reportedly said, "It's very peaceful with no husbands" (qtd. in Strickland, *Angela* 164).

Without a means of support, Thirkell turned to her parents, who were displeased to have their daughter's troubles among them again. Determined to make her living as a writer, Thirkell first tried her hand at journalism, contributing articles on literary subjects to *Fortnightly Review* and *Cornhill*. The income meager but encouraging, Thirkell then wrote her autobiographical *Three Houses* (1931), a chronicle of her childhood memories of the Burne-Jones's household. It was published by Oxford. The critical praise of the memoir led to a meeting between Thirkell and James Hamilton of the publisher Hamish Hamilton. For nearly three decades Hamilton published most of Thirkell's books, marketing them as escapist entertainment for middlebrow tastes. Throughout the 1930s Thirkell's popularity increased, extending abroad to America, where she eventually made several visits at the requests of such universities as Yale, Princeton, Harvard, and Columbia. Writing two books a year, Thirkell tried her hand at a variety of genres. Some of her most notable books at this time include *High Rising* (1933), Thirkell's first Barsetshire novel; *The Demon in the House* (1934), a selection of short stories centering on the popular Barsetshire character Tony Morland; *The Grateful Sparrow and Other Stories* (1935), a collection of children's stories; *The Fortunes of Harriette* (1936), a biography of Harriette Wilson, the eighteenth-century Regency courtesan; and *Coronation Summer* (1937), a historical novel focusing on Queen Victoria's coronation festivities in 1837.

After the successes of the 1930s Thirkell's popularity began to wane, largely due to her audience's dissatisfaction with Thirkell's growing bitterness over the postwar transformations of English society. In her novels Thirkell expressed her displeasure with the policies of the Labour government, which she always referred to as "Them," but many of her fans were not interested because they read her books primarily for relief from the pressures of reality. By the 1950s it was apparent that Thirkell's abilities as a writer were diminishing as well. Criticism was commonly directed at Thirkell's decreasing sense of plot. Nonetheless, publishing at least one book a year since 1940, Thirkell had achieved her independence, shirking traditional roles for women and accruing a considerable amount of money in the process. In her final years Thirkell became increasingly critical of her own life, except for the Burne-Jones years. Of her childhood Thirkell wrote, "I haven't a single complaint or criticism to make of my early years" (qtd. in Strickland, *Angela* 173). In 1961 Thirkell died of aplastic anemia, a rare blood disease.

ANALYSIS

Thirkell's lifelong conservative sensibilities are clearly manifested in such individual works as *Three Houses* and *Coronation Summer*. The former dwells lovingly on detailed portraits of the Victorian notables Thirkell knew as a child, while the latter revels in the advent of the Victorian period. In this regard Thirkell's Australian novel *Trooper to the Southern Cross* is also symptomatic because it expresses considerable anxiety over the "ungovernable" lower classes, but it is the long-running Barsetshire series that most fully develops Thirkell's views. The series presents a broad canvas, for it consists of over two dozen novels written between 1933 and 1961, with which period of time the events of the novels as a whole are roughly contemporaneous. Individually, the Barsetshire novels are similar to Jane Austen's novels in terms of technique and theme, as has been most recently noted by Rachel R. Mather (65). As a result, each novel is typically concerned with courtship and marriage and is generally conveyed with a certain wit and charm that many readers still find endearing. Collectively, however, the Barsetshire novels move beyond the nineteenth-century comedy of manners in that they attempt to create what Laura Roberts Collins calls a microcosm of twentieth-century English rural society. Aspiring to the status of social history, they are particularly concerned with chronicling and evaluating the demise of the English nobility, charting during their course a recognizable progression in which the values of the peerage are gradually displaced by labor interests, to the detriment of the world in which Thirkell grew up.

A typical situation for the nobility in the early Barsetshire novels is the disheartening one in which the aging seventh Earl of Pomfret finds himself. One of the oldest and most respected families in Barsetshire county, Lord Pomfret's venerable family can trace its lineage back to the twelfth-century noble Giles de Pomfret, but the family line is about to come to an end because Lord Pomfret's only son and heir to the family estate, Lord Mellings, died in India after World War I. In *Pomfret Towers* (1938) it is determined that the estate will eventually fall to the outside heir, Gillie Foster, who has the blessing of Lord Pomfret, even though Foster is clearly not of his class. Until his death Lord Pomfret commands considerable respect as a paternal figure, in spite of his gruff manner. He spends much of his time preserving the rural character of the county by warding off encroaching commercial interests. In *Before Lunch* (1939), for instance, Lord Pomfret successfully deters Sir Ogilvie Hibberd, a new peer recently dubbed by the Labour government, from purchasing a piece of land known as Pooker's Piece, which Hibberd intends to develop into a subdivision. In spite of his achievements, however, the overall sense of Lord Pomfret is that he is part of a dying way of life.

With the precarious position of the nobility established, later novels underscore the progression of changes that are taking place in Barsetshire. Important in this regard is the emergence of Sam Adams and his daughter Heather, who are introduced in *The Headmistress* (1944). Mr. Adams is a rich ironmaster from Hogglestock, the mill town in east Barsetshire, and the novels following his introduction chronicle his steady rise in influence. In spite of the fact that he and his daughter are juxtaposed unfavorably with the conservative order in *Miss Bunting* (1946), Mr. Adams becomes a member of Parliament on the Labour ticket in *Peace Breaks Out* (1947), buys an old Barsetshire mansion in *The Old Bank House* (1949), and engages the daughter of a respectable Barsetshire family in *County Chronicle* (1950). As a result, Mr. Adams gains a certain measure of respect from the nobility, but the unpromising prospects for the future are clearly apparent in his daughter's marriage to Ted Pilward, owner of Pilward Brewery in Hogglestock. The Pilwards, it is understood, will never have the approval of the nobility. All of this is generally conveyed with humor, but noticeable to most readers is a general shift in tone over the course of the Barsetshire novels, one in which a lighthearted sense of irony, similar in effect to the novels of Jane Austen, is increasingly displaced by an acerbic sense of scorn, contempt, and even anger. Prompted by contemporaneous social changes documented in the Barsetshire novels, this emerging new tone unmistakably reveals Thirkell's conservatism.

In addition to developing conservative political views, the Barsetshire series also dwells on the dissatisfying social roles available to women, especially in marriage. It is certainly true that naïve, lovesick young women abound in Thirkell's novels, but it is also true that alongside them there are many older, more experienced women who ruminate on their largely unhappy marriages. In *Pomfret Towers*, for instance, several older women retreat from their marriages in some manner, providing a stark contrast with the young, moonstruck Alice Barton. Lady Pomfret, who is described often as a sad broken beauty, maintains a nearly permanent exile from her husband in Italy, mourning the death of her only child, while Mrs. Hermione Rivers escapes into the writing of her popular romance novels, which are thinly veiled stories of her own unfulfilled desires and fantasies. Similarly, Mrs. Susan Barton cuts herself off from her husband by completely absorbing herself in the research for her highbrow historical fiction, leaving Mr. Barton to feel on occasion that something is wanting in their relationship. Because these types of unsuitable marriages are maintained, the young distraught Phoebe Rivers is prompted to see in them a form of masochism. This theme is continued in *Before Lunch*, where Mrs. Catherine Middleton silently puts up with her older husband, longing for greater fulfillment. Only the often-recurring Mrs. Laura Morland, who is introduced in *High Rising*, seems to be the exception to the rule. Slightly eccentric, she separates from her husband, makes a living as a popular novelist, and never remarries, in spite of the proposals that she receives. Not surprisingly, as critics have often noted, Mrs. Morland is really a portrait of Thirkell herself.

Some of Thirkell's non-Barsetshire novels also maintain this focus on troubled marriages. In *Ankle Deep* (1933) the heroine, Aurea, leaves her husband and children in a British dominion to visit her parents in London, where she has an affair with the hero, Valentine Ensor. The similarity between Aurea's and Thirkell's situations has prompted critics to see this novel as at least partly autobiographical. In another autobiographical (Crosland 89; Strickland, *Angela* 69) novel, *O, These Men, These Men!* (1935), the central focus is on a woman who fears the return of her drunken husband, from whom she has separated. Thirkell's biographer has noted that the villain, who is named James, is a portrait of Thirkell's first husband, James McInnes (Strickland, *Angela* 92). The point is that in addition to being concerned with social history, Thirkell was also very much preoccupied with writing about women's experiences, as Penelope Joan Fritzer has confirmed. The fact that Thirkell often criticized marriage and did not remarry herself may account for her interest in Harriett Wilson, the intellectually liberated courtesan. For all this, however, it must be emphasized that Thirkell did not consider herself a feminist, as Margot Strickland has indicated (*Angela* 21).

ASSESSMENT

Thirkell is largely neglected by critics, who have often noted that she shunned the modernist experimentation of writers like Dorothy Richardson and Virginia Woolf, choosing to write instead what may be considered conventional realistic novels, inspired in large part by such nineteenth-century authors as Austen, Dickens, Eliot, Gaskell, and Trollope. This fact, conjoined with Thirkell's conservatism and her popularity, has prompted many critics to dismiss Thirkell's work right off the bat. Clearly they have missed out on the opportunity to investigate an interesting cultural phenomenon, which geared up again in the 1990s with the Moyer-Bell reprinting of Thirkell's novels and the rise of Thirkell reading groups. The few critics who have taken Thirkell seriously have usefully categorized her as either a social historian or a comic writer. Some have even done groundbreaking work on gender and ethnicity in relationship to the Barsetshire novels, but most of these critics have remained on the elementary level of personal response and appreciation. As a result, Thirkell really has not received the kind of detailed attention she deserves. In spite of this oversight or shortcoming, Thirkell's work remains important because it speaks to contemporaneous social developments in England. Her work clearly participates in many of the significant dialogues, conversations, and debates in the English society of her time, the full extent of which has yet to be determined. Because of its popularity, Thirkell's work deserves the attention of the social or literary historian. Thirkell's work also remains important because it is part of a recognizable tradition of British women authors who value and write about women's experiences. Neglected until the 1970s, this tradition includes not only Austen and Eliot, but also the many women novelists of the eighteenth century who paved the way for them. Thirkell's work joins this tradition as a significant record of women's lives and opinions.

BIBLIOGRAPHY

Primary Sources

Three Houses. London: Oxford UP, 1931.

Ankle Deep. London: Hamish Hamilton, 1933.

High Rising. London: Hamish Hamilton, 1933.

The Demon in the House. London: Hamish Hamilton, 1934.

Wild Strawberries. London: Hamish Hamilton, 1934.

The Grateful Sparrow and Other Stories. London: Hamish Hamilton, 1935.

O, These Men, These Men! London: Hamish Hamilton, 1935.

Trooper to the Southern Cross. As Leslie Parker. London: Faber, 1934.

August Folly. London: Hamish Hamilton, 1936.

The Fortunes of Harriette. London: Hamish Hamilton, 1936.

Coronation Summer. London: Oxford UP, 1937.

Summer Half. London: Hamish Hamilton, 1937.

Pomfret Towers. London: Hamish Hamilton, 1938.

Before Lunch. London: Hamish Hamilton, 1939.

The Brandons. London: Hamish Hamilton, 1939.

Cheerfulness Breaks In. London: Hamish Hamilton, 1940.

Northbridge Rectory. London: Hamish Hamilton, 1941.

Marling Hall. London: Hamish Hamilton, 1942.

Growing Up. London: Hamish Hamilton, 1943.

The Headmistress. London: Hamish Hamilton, 1944.

Miss Bunting. London: Hamish Hamilton, 1946.

Peace Breaks Out. London: Hamish Hamilton, 1947.

Private Enterprise. London: Hamish Hamilton, 1947.

Love among the Ruins. London: Hamish Hamilton, 1948.

The Old Bank House. London: Hamish Hamilton, 1949.

County Chronicle. London: Hamish Hamilton, 1950.

The Duke's Daughter. London: Hamish Hamilton, 1951.

Happy Returns. London: Hamish Hamilton, 1952.

Jutland Cottage. London: Hamish Hamilton, 1953.

What Did It Mean? London: Hamish Hamilton, 1954.

Enter Sir Robert. London: Hamish Hamilton, 1955.

Never Too Late. London: Hamish Hamilton, 1956.

A Double Affair. London: Hamish Hamilton, 1957.

Close Quarters. London: Hamish Hamilton, 1958.

Love at All Ages. London: Hamish Hamilton, 1959.

Three Score and Ten. With Caroline A. Lejeune. London: Hamish Hamilton, 1961.

Secondary Sources

Collins, Laura Roberts. *English Country Life in the Barsetshire Novels of Angela Thirkell*. Westport, CT: Greenwood, 1994.

Crosland, Margaret. *Beyond the Lighthouse: English Women Novelists in the Twentieth Century*. New York: Taplinger, 1981.

Fritzer, Penelope Joan. *Ethnicity and Gender in the Barsetshire Novels of Angela Thirkell*. Westport, CT: Greenwood, 1999.

Kenny, Virginia. "A Refined Look at Australia: Angela Thirkell as Trooper to the Southern Cross." In *Aspects of Australian Fiction*. Ed. Alan Brissenden. Nedlands: U of Western Australia P, 1990.

Lee, Hermione. "A Critic at Large: The Novels of Angela Thirkell." *New Yorker* 7 October 1996: 90.

Mather, Rachel R. *The Heirs of Jane Austen: Twentieth-Century Writers of the Comedy of Manners*. New York: Peter Lang, 1996.

McInnes, Graham. *The Road to Gundagai*. London: Hamish Hamilton, 1965.

McIntyre, Clare F. "Mrs. Thirkell's Barsetshire." *College English* 17.7 (1956): 398–401.

Strickland, Margot. *Angela Thirkell: Portrait of a Lady Novelist*. London: Duckworth, 1977.

———. "George Eliot and Angela Thirkell." *George Eliot Fellowship Review* 13 (1982): 37–39.

Sylvia Townsend Warner
1893–1978

Chris Hopkins

Sylvia Townsend Warner had a reputation during most of her career as an ever-inventive, idiosyncratic, and subtle writer, noted mainly for her novels and short stories (though she also wrote poetry). This sense of her talent often led to descriptions of her work in the following kinds of terms: "simply and charmingly written" (*New Republic*, 1926, qtd. in Wiloch 4) and "written with a most tranquil grace and a dainty humour" (Christopher Morley, *Saturday Review of Literature*, 1927, qtd. in Wiloch 4). However, where some reviewers and critics summarized Warner's work as coming from a tradition of English delicacy and whimsy, others detected sharper undertones. Benedict Kiely, writing in the *New York Times Book Review* in 1982, thought that there was always an underlying quality of irony and "ruthless coolness" (qtd. in Wiloch 6), while Melvin Maddocks observed acutely that "the too-casual reader . . . who thinks he is strolling down the garden-path of English whimsy will soon find his heels being nipped by demons" (*Time*, 1982, qtd. in Wiloch 7). The two qualities—elegance of style and critical distance—are certainly both to be found in Warner's writing. Emphasis on the first quality has often led to characterization of Warner as a "minor artist" (Michiko Kakutani, *New York Times Book Review*, 1984, qtd. in Wiloch 7). However, her critical reputation has risen over the last two decades as both new editions (particularly those from Virago Press) and new critical work have been published. Many now stress rather the critique playing against the surface. Sylvia Townsend Warner was often compared to Jane Austen, and indeed, her critical reputation has certain parallels. From "gentle Jane" we now have a more radical Austen, and similarly a more subversive Warner, as Claire Harman notes: "Reviewers mistook both writers as essentially genteel, but there was more to the comparison than they may have intended. . . . Sylvia's view [in her short pamphlet] of Jane Austen was of a worldly writer with a subversively satiric purpose" (*Biography* 244). Even now, some characterizations of Warner's work miss her critical concerns, the interplay between surfaces and depths. However, it seems clear that her writing across her career is engaged, very much in its own ways, with a range of social, sexual, gender, and political issues, as well as with equally important and linked ideas about style, language, and storytelling.

BACKGROUND

Sylvia Townsend Warner was born at Harrow-on-the-Hill, Middlesex, on December 6, 1893, to George Townsend Warner, an assistant master (junior teacher) at Harrow School, and his wife, Nora Hudleston Warner, who was the daughter of an Indian army colonel and was born in Madras. Sylvia was to be their only child, and she was brought up in comfortable circumstances in a cultured household where reading was the main pursuit. By this period girls of Sylvia's class might normally expect some degree of formal education, usually at a school. However, Sylvia never attended a school (after a brief and unsuccessful term at a kindergarten). Instead, she was educated at home, at first mainly by her mother, later by her father. "I wasn't educated—I was very lucky," she later said (*Collected Poems* xiv).

In later life Warner recalled what she regarded as a fact: her mother did not love her as much after the age of seven: "[F]or the first seven years of my life I interested her heart . . . but nothing compensated for my sex . . . and later still she was jealous and I could do nothing right" (*Letters* 251). Nora had wanted a son; failing this, a conventionally attractive daughter. But she had decided that Sylvia was not to be that. Thereafter, Nora did what Sylvia called her "duty" to her daughter, "and doing one's duty by inevitably hardens the heart against" (*Letters* 251). Sylvia's father (by now a housemaster), however, took an increasing interest in her education: the two often had free-ranging and extensive conversations about history or literature. Claire Harman records that she was known by some at this period as "the cleverest boy at Harrow" (*Biography* 20). Additionally, at the age of sixteen Sylvia began studying music with great commitment. Neither of her parents was at all accomplished in music, but it was arranged that she should take lessons from the Harrow music master, Dr. Percy Buck. She studied piano, organ, composition, theory, and the history of music. This was to have a considerable impact on her life.

At eighteen, Warner was—as convention dictated—expected by her mother to attend "coming-out" balls (a public acknowledgment of her being ready to be sought in marriage). However, Warner did not cooperate, talking about theology at one such occasion and generally showing no enthusiasm. She did, though, soon enter a relationship, but not one of which her mother could have approved, had she known of it. In 1913 Warner began, at the age of nineteen, a secret affair with her music teacher and close friend, Percy Buck. He was forty-two, was married, and had two children. The relationship continued until 1930.

More public events soon intervened with the outbreak of the 1914–1918 war. In 1915 Warner joined in a scheme through which women from "the leisured classes" could contribute to the war effort by working for a period in munitions factories, which were now working round the clock. She went to live in lodgings in order to work at a Vickers factory, machining shell cases. In 1916 her father, for his part, was summoned to the Foreign Office to undertake work of national importance (its exact nature is still unclear). This presumably was a result of some influential articles he had written earlier in the war, based on historical analysis, about how Britain might win the war.

However, George Warner was showing some signs of ill health. In September 1916 he died suddenly, probably as a result of a burst stomach ulcer. Both Nora and Sylvia were bereft. Nora blamed her daughter, making it clear that she could have spared Sylvia, but not her husband. Sylvia for her part was grief stricken and unsupported in any way by her mother: "[I]t was as though I had been crippled, and at the same time realised that I must make my journey alone" (*Letters* 251). To make all worse, as a consequence of George Warner's death, they also had to move out of their home, since it was owned by Harrow and was needed for the new housemaster who must replace him. Tension between mother and daughter was unbearable, especially since the terms of George's will made Sylvia dependent on Nora. But

Percy Buck came to the rescue. He had been appointed to a committee charged with organizing an edition of the body of Tudor church music, which at this time existed only in the original manuscripts. He suggested that Sylvia be added to the editorial team, with a salary of three pounds per week. This gave her not only an acceptable reason for parting company with her mother, but also the means (just) to afford it. Thus in 1917 Sylvia Townsend Warner moved to a flat in Bayswater and began her independent life.

At first this was a life centered on her work as an editor and historian of early music. She worked hard and meticulously with Buck and the other editors and became expert in the subject. The project was originally envisaged as taking five years; in fact, it took twelve years, not coming to completion until 1929. It was not until 1922 that Warner began to write—poetry. Soon she developed the habit of writing one poem every week, using waste pages from the church music drafts. In 1923 she began writing a novel, *Lolly Willowes*. Toward the end of that year Warner went to meet the editor Charles Prentice at Chatto and Windus to discuss possible publication of a volume of her poems; he accepted for publication both poems and novel. When *Lolly Willowes* came out in 1926, it was a great success, both in Britain and in the United States, where it sold over ten thousand copies within months. Though she continued work on Tudor church music until the project was completed, her career as a writer was launched.

Warner wrote steadily and prolifically from then until her death, producing seven novels, twelve volumes of short stories, five poetry collections, and a smaller number of editions, translations, and literary biographies. Her long relationship with Percy Buck petered out in 1930, but in the same year she began an even more enduring one: she met and fell in love with Valentine Ackland, the woman she was to live and work with until Ackland's death in 1969. Valentine Ackland was a poet and was to share intimately in Sylvia's literary, intellectual, and political life. The two women moved into a small cottage in Chaldon, Dorset. Their relationship had many complexities (Ackland was tormented by various demons, including alcoholism), but was a source of much (if not always straightforward) strength.

After 1933 Ackland became increasingly concerned at the rise to power of the Nazi movement in Germany, as well as with social conditions in Britain. Warner, reviewing her own class attitudes, joined Ackland in her leftist views. In 1935 they joined the Communist Party of Great Britain and became politically active, both through writing and other contributions to the work of the Party. Each was invited to the International Congress in Defence of Culture held by the Republican government in embattled Spain in July 1937. After 1940, depressed by Britain's failure to help the Spanish Republic, the two contributed variously to what was now a national struggle against fascism.

After the war Ackland's commitment to communism began to weaken, and she found herself moving back toward Christian belief. In 1955, to Warner's disquiet, Ackland became a Catholic. Warner feared that this would mean the end of their long relationship. Ackland's religious commitment was allied to a shift in her political convictions. Unlike many European intellectuals in this period, Warner for her part remained sympathetic to communism and continued to admire Stalin and the Soviet Union despite evidence of the purges in the 1930s and despite the Soviet invasion of Hungary in 1956. Warner's belief in communism was, in fact, long lived. Also, Ackland developed a less positive sense of the permissibility of their sexual relationship. Though Warner was saddened by these points of departure from their long shared experience, the two continued to live together. Toward the end of her life Ackland became disillusioned with the Catholic church and attended Quaker meetings. In 1967 Ackland was diagnosed as having breast cancer. After several operations and much illness she died in 1969. Warner felt that she had lost her main reasons for living. She took, however, what pleasure she could from life, continuing to write (particularly short articles for the *New Yorker*) and to work on a number of literary projects. She was surprised and pleased that a number of her works were reprinted during the 1970s and that a volume of her *Collected Poems* was planned. She died, aged eighty-four, on May 1, 1978.

ANALYSIS

Though her poetry has its admirers, Sylvia Townsend Warner is best remembered for her prose, both in short-story and novel form. This account will concentrate on the novels as her major achievement (the short-story collections, though quite individual, share many themes and a wide stylistic range with the novels). Her first novel, *Lolly Willowes; or, The Loving Huntsman* remained her most successful in terms of immediate publicity and commercial gain. It concerns Laura Willowes, a middle-class woman whose beloved father dies when she is twenty-eight. Her brothers and their wives instantly take control of her life and look after her so thoroughly for the next twenty years that she is hardly ever able to make a decision for herself until, at the age of forty-seven, she decides to move into a cottage of her own in the village of Great Mop. There she does exactly what she wants, but is drawn toward an unavoidable destiny, provoked by the arrival of her demanding nephew Titus. The Devil (curiously lacking in malice in this world) or "loving huntsman" seeks her out, and both agree that she is irrevocably "a witch now" (232). It is clear to Laura that she is not the only witch in Great Mop. Witches are those who escape the stultifying and trivial oppression of routine life:

> The night was at her disposal. She might walk back to Great Mop and arrive very late: or she might sleep out and not trouble to arrive till to-morrow. Whichever she did Mrs. Leask would not mind. That was the advantage of dealing with witches; they do not mind if you are a little odd in your ways, frown if you are late for meals, fret if you are out all night, pry and commiserate when at length you return. Lovely to be with people who prefer their thoughts to yours. (246)

Most reviewers found the novel amusing, but some saw the potential of its witty ideas about witches to make a serious point about the bonds of the routine and delivery from them. More recent feminist criticism has reinforced and developed this approach to the novel (see Brothers, "Flying").

Warner's next novel, *Mr. Fortune's Maggot*, has been said to represent a move from "fantasy to realism" (Thomas Lask, *New York Times*, 1929, qtd. in Wiloch 4). However, its themes can certainly be related to those of *Lolly Willowes*: in both novels the norms of "ordinary" life are seen as having both little real power and little potential for happiness. The Reverend Timothy Fortune goes to a South Sea island to convert the "natives." But he falls in love with one of the young men, Lueli, and, anyway, finds the people happy as they are—happier than conversion could make them. At the end of the novel Reverend Fortune decides that he will make no attempt to convert his lover and leaves the islanders to lead their own lives. He returns to a European world of much lesser promise. This novel was also a success in both Britain and the United States. Warner's next novel, *The True Heart*, was less successful; readers were probably unsure what to make of it. The story was, as Claire Harman points out, a retelling of the classical story of Cupid and Psyche, set in nineteenth-century England. The heroine, Sukey Bond, an orphaned servant girl, falls in love with a simpleton, Eric Seaborn, and must win him from his parents, a rector and his wife, who will not let him go, not from love but from shame. As in the previous two novels, real feeling is opposed to convention: "Sukey had seen all her scruples and vanities of obligation vanish like a handful of dust" (227). It is a deliberately simple story—indeed, it is about simplicity, as the contemporary reviewer in the *Times Literary Supplement* noted: it "does not belong to the actual world at all, but to the ever-imagined youth of the world when a true and innocent heart could go unscathed through every danger" (qtd. in Wiloch 5).

Warner did not publish her next novel for some seven years, though she published prolifically: seven volumes of short stories and one of poems. *Summer Will Show*, published in 1936, marked a new interest in the historical novel, which she sustained throughout the remainder of her novel-writing career. It is these historical novels that Wendy Mulford argues are Warner's major works (104). The choice of genre was partly due to her interest in politics and public events at this period: the historical novel was a genre that a number of leftist writers explored during the 1930s. Historical novels had considerable approval among leftist critics and commentators because they were argued to have a capacity for representing authentically how individual lives were formed through historical change, and also how individuals could contribute to the "dialectic of history" by realizing the reality of their own situations. Equally, it could be argued that it was a genre that developed from the Victorian setting of *The True Heart*, and into which Warner's readers would be prepared to follow her, for the historical novel had a more "genteel" reputation, as well as its leftist one. Indeed, the first three of these historical novels may particularly explore how discontents among "the bourgeoisie" might find their way to the possibility of revolution.

This seems especially true of *Summer Will Show*. It is set in the revolutionary year of 1848, mainly in Paris. There are two protagonists: the genteel Englishwoman Sophia Willougby and the exotic Minna Lemuel, a Jew who has escaped from a pogrom in Lithuania. These characters undoubtedly have, as Claire Harman suggests, some of their origin in the relationship between Warner and Ackland (*Biography* 149). However, they also continue earlier novelistic concerns in showing how marginal figures—and particularly marginal women—can leave behind the safety of normality for a fuller life. The landowning Sophia has been abandoned by her husband, Frederick. Her two children die of smallpox, and she seeks out Frederick in Paris. There she meets his mistress, Minna, and the two become involved in the revolutionary cause. Claire Harman argues that the novel, started before Warner joined the Communist Party, does not wholly succeed in making its political message central (*Biography* 149). However, it could be said that the evolution of Warner's commitment in parallel with that of the actual text of the novel lends the novel considerable conviction. Terry Castle takes a different approach, arguing that the apparently realist surface of the novel is itself often subverted by a vein of fantasy, which both connects with Warner's earlier work and is also an aspect of lesbian writing more generally (145). However, strangely, the new political content may not have been noticed by all of Warner's readers.

Her next novel, *After the Death of Don Juan* (1938), was equally engaged with politics. It is a historical novel, but one that adopts the form of allegory as well. While it is a markedly idiosyncratic novel with a curious, detached narrative tone throughout, this generic inflection also had some parallel with leftist literary interests in the period (a number of leftist allegorical or parable works, such as W.H. Auden and Christopher Isherwood's play *The Ascent of F6* and Rex Warner's *The Wild Goose Chase*, had been published). The novel is set in eighteenth-century Spain and is a retelling of the Don Juan story. In this version the reprobate is only allegedly killed by the Commendador. He turns up at his father Don Saturnino's estate. The novel pursues what happens next, and also what attracts women (including Donna Anna) to such a figure. In this allegory Don Juan is clearly a fascist figure who, utterly ruthless and calculating himself, illustrates through his sexual appeal the hysterical power of fascist leadership. Thus Donna Anna does not much care that Don Juan has killed her father, and makes blatant use of religion to regain her lover. The novel also charts the (possible) history of European politics. Don Saturnino is a liberal, interested in progressive ideas and new inventions. The villagers are peasants, living in poverty and constant hard labor. For years Don Saturnino has talked of improving the land through an irrigation system, but has never quite got around to it. He has never had the energy, the means, or the decisiveness. Don Juan is unlike his father: he can make radical decisions. But when he irrigates the land, he plans to dispossess the peasants and exploit it mercilessly. The peasants, shown as early revolutionaries, rebel at the end of the novel and are shot down by the army, which Don Juan has called in. Don Saturnino disapproves, but, imprisoned by his son, he is powerless and ineffectual, as usual. Clearly this is a parable about liberalism and fascism. The peasants are a kind of collective hero, who die hoping that one day there will be a successful revolution and a better life for the people. The novel is by no means either simplistic or didactic, however, but is ironic, witty, and subtle. There is complex characterization, and much is left for readers to work out for themselves. Above all, it is an exploration of myth and reality, apparent and actual meanings. Claire Harman writes that this is the least known of Warner's novels; Warner said that it was "swamped by 1938–9 events"—that is, by a version of the events of which it warned (*Biography* 173).

It was ten years before Warner's next novel was published, though it had been started in 1941: *The Corner That Held Them* (1948) was another historical novel. Warner later said that it was begun "on the purest Marxian principles, because I was convinced that if you were going to give an accurate picture of the monastic life, you'd have to put in all their finances" (*Biography* 216). However, it was less classically a leftist novel than either of her previous two books. Where they contain, respectively, enactment of liberation and an explanatory or even predictive framework, *The Corner That Held Them* portrays and imagines the texture of life in a medieval nunnery. It analyzes what life is like there and shows how interactions of larger historical narratives and individual ones produce it. But it does not show positive development. It is thus a more classically naturalist novel than her others. Claire Harman notes the connection between this naturalism and the unconventional narrative of the novel: "She abandoned many conventional elements of novel-writing, such as the use of a protagonist or plot, and set out . . . a long . . . well-imagined chronicle. And there is no overall pattern to the book, except that of time passing" (*Biography* 216). This was Warner's own favorite novel, and many readers have concurred. Warner wrote one further novel, *The Flint Anchor* (1954), a family novel set in East Anglia in the nineteenth century. It concerns the Barnard family, particularly the father, John, who, though he is a righteous man, is caught up in a chain of bad deeds. It was fairly well reviewed, but Warner felt that it had not gained as much attention as it merited. Though Warner's literary career continued until the end of her life, she did not write any further novels, but continued to write short stories, which, like her novels, were of a great variety and inventiveness.

ASSESSMENT

Sylvia Townsend Warner was an especially individual writer. She was, of course, influenced by literary models and by historical events, but she had, as has been observed by several critics, a great capacity to develop her work in her own, often not obviously fashionable ways. Claire Harman notes that her writing did not settle into easy patterns: "It . . . seemed that Sylvia was incapable of producing any two books the same. There is remarkably little consistency—except in a prevailing intelligence—between one of her novels and the next, a fact which explains why she has escaped the attention of literary critics. She was not interested in developing a 'presence' as a novelist; the individual book was what absorbed her" (*Biography* 175). Terry Castle has argued that this refusal of categorization is characteristic of lesbian writing: "such a fiction will be, both in the ordinary sense and in a more elaborate sense, non-canonical" (146).

However, certain characteristics recur, though they are ones that are indeed hard to summarize easily. Her writing offers a degree of emotional engagement, yet is always nuanced, ironic, and entertaining; equally, there is usually a sharply critical sense of the failings of routine and habit and of the more imaginative possibilities that lie beyond. Gillian Beer describes these qualities as "misfitting, discontinuous, eccentric, imperturbable," and Sylvia Townsend Warner as a writer who "relishes experience that will not fit neatly, improvises pleasure for the reader" (86).

BIBLIOGRAPHY

Primary Sources

The Espalier. London: Chatto; New York: Dial, 1925.
Lolly Willowes. London: Chatto; New York: Viking, 1926.
Mr. Fortune's Maggot. London: Chatto; New York: Viking, 1927.
Time Importuned. London: Chatto; New York: Viking, 1928.
Some World Far from Ours. London: E. Matthews and Marrot, 1929.
The True Heart. London: Chatto; New York: Viking, 1929.
Elinor Barley. London: Cresset, 1930.
A Moral Ending and Other Stories. London: Jackson, 1931.
Opus 7. London: Chatto; New York: Viking, 1931.
The Rainbow. New York: Knopf, 1932.
The Salutation. London: Chatto; New York: Viking, 1932.
Whether a Dove or a Seagull. With Valentine Ackland. New York: Viking, 1933; London: Chatto, 1934.
More Joy in Heaven. London: Cresset, 1935.
Summer Will Show. London: Chatto; New York: Viking, 1936.
After the Death of Don Juan. London: Chatto, 1938; New York: Viking, 1939.
The Cat's Cradle-Book. New York: Viking, 1940; London: Chatto, 1960.
A Garland of Straw. London: Chatto; New York: Viking, 1943.
Museum of Cheats. London: Chatto, 1947.
The Corner That Held Them. London: Chatto; New York: Viking, 1948.
Somerset. London: Paul Elek, 1949.
Jane Austen. London: Longmans, 1951.
The Flint Anchor. London: Chatto; New York: Viking, 1954.
Winter in the Air. London: Chatto, 1955; New York: Viking, 1956.
Boxwood. London: Monotype, 1957. Enlarged edition. London: Chatto, 1960.
A Spirit Rises. London: Chatto; New York: Viking, 1962.
A Place of Shipwreck. Trans. of *La Côte Sauvage*, by Jean-René Huguenin. London: Chatto, 1963.
A Stranger with a Bag. London: Chatto, 1966. As *Swans on an Autumn River*. New York: Viking, 1966.
T.H. White. London: Jonathan Cape and Chatto & Windus; New York: Viking, 1967.
King Duffus and Other Poems. Wells and London: Clare, 1968.
The Innocent and the Guilty. London: Chatto; New York: Viking, 1971.
Kingdoms of Elfin. London: Chatto; New York: Viking, 1977.
Azrael and Other Poems. Newbury: Libanus, 1978.
Twelve Poems. London: Chatto, 1980.
Scenes of Childhood and Other Stories. London Chatto. As *Scenes of Childhood*. New York: Viking, 1981.
Collected Poems. Ed. Claire Harman. Manchester: Carcenet, 1982; New York: Viking, 1982.
Letters. Ed. William Maxwell. London: Chatto; New York: Viking, 1983.
One Thing Leading to Another. Ed. Susanna Pinney. London: Chatto; New York: Viking, 1984.
Selected Poems. Manchester: Carcanet; New York: Viking, 1985.

Selected Stories. London: Chatto; New York: Viking, 1988.

The Diaries of Sylvia Townsend Warner. Ed. Claire Harman. London: Chatto, 1994.

Secondary Sources

Beer, Gillian. "Sylvia Townsend Warner: 'The Centrifugal Kick.' " In *Women Writers of the 1930s: Gender, Politics, and History*. Ed. Maroula Joannou. Edinburgh: Edinburgh UP, 1999. 76–86.

Brothers, Barbara. "Flying the Nets at Forty: *Lolly Willowes* as Female Bildungsroman." In *Old Maids to Radical Spinsters: Unmarried Women in the Twentieth-Century Novel*. Ed. Laura L. Doan. Urbana: U of Illinois P, 1991.

———. "*Summer Will Show*: The Historical Novel as Social Criticism." In *Women in History, Literature, and the Arts: A Festschrift for Hildegard Schnuttegen in Honor of Her Thirty Years of Outstanding Service*. Ed. Lorrayne Y. Baird-Lange and Thomas A. Copeland. Youngstown, OH: Youngstown State U, 1989.

———. "Writing against the Grain: Sylvia Townsend Warner and the Spanish Civil War." In *Women's Writing in Exile*. Ed. Mary Broe and Angela Ingram. Chapel Hill: U of North Carolina P, 1989.

Castle, Terry. "Sylvia Townsend Warner and the Counterpoint of Lesbian Fiction." In *Sexual Sameness: Textual Differences in Lesbian and Gay Writing*. Ed. Joseph Bristow. London: Routledge, 1992. 128–147.

Foster, Thomas. " 'Dream Made Flesh': Sexual Difference and Narratives of Revolution in Sylvia Townsend Warner's *Summer Will Show*." *Modern Fiction Studies* 41:3–4 (Fall–Winter 1995): 531–562.

Harman, Claire. *Sylvia Townsend Warner: A Biography*. London: Chatto, 1989.

———, ed. "Sylvia Townsend Warner, 1893–1978: A Celebration." *PN Review* 23 (1981).

Hopkins, Chris. "Sylvia Townsend Warner and the Marxist Historical Novel." *Literature and History*, 3rd ser., 4.1 (Spring 1995): 50–64.

Knoll, Bruce. " 'An Existence Doled Out': Passive Resistance as a Dead End in Sylvia Townsend Warner's *Lolly Willowes*." *Twentieth Century Literature* 39.3 (Fall 1993): 344–363.

Marcus, Jane. "A Wilderness of One's Own: Feminist Fantasy Novels of the Twenties: Rebecca West and Sylvia Townsend Warner." In *Women Writers and the City*. Ed. Susan Squier. Knoxville: U of Tennessee P, 1984.

Montefiore, Janet. "Listening to Minna: Realism, Feminism, and the Politics of Reading." *Paragraph: A Journal of Modern Critical Theory* 14.3 (November 1991): 197–216.

Mulford, Wendy. *This Narrow Place: Sylvia Townsend Warner and Valentine Ackland: Life, Letters, and Politics, 1930–1951*. London: Pandora, 1988.

Trodd, Anthea. *Women's Writing in English: Britain, 1900–1945*. London and New York: Longman, 1998. 204–210.

Wiloch, Thomas. "Sylvia Townsend Warner." In *Discovering Contemporary Authors*. CD-ROM. Detroit: Gale Research, 1994.

Fay Weldon
1931–

Kathleen Ellis

Since the publication of her first novel in 1967, Fay Weldon has been one of the most popular writers dealing with women's liberation. She is known for her wicked wit, relentless critique of the patriarchy, and wonderfully flawed but indomitable women who, through their calamitous lives, reveal the hypocrisies and absurdities at the heart of our relationships with each other and with ourselves. If the purpose of much of feminist theory and literature has been to promote equality for marginalized groups, to subvert the understanding that the world is based on binary oppositions forever privileging one side at the expense of the other, Weldon answers that the conflict will never be resolved. "Sometimes I think there is simply a body of human suffering in the world," Weldon said in an interview, ". . . and the sum of it never alters: it just gets handed round from this group to that" ("Changing" 197). The central question for Weldon, then, is how to live in a world where contradiction and paradox reign, where there is no justice, and where imperfect women and men, trying to get along the best they can, usually make a muddle of things. A grim message. But Weldon's resilient protagonists never give up, and their struggles to construct their own identities and to determine their own economic, sexual, and reproductive rights demand courage and tremendous sacrifice and offer some hope for the evolution of humanity. Weldon's vision, in her own idiosyncratic, postmodern manner, is intensely moral. Our job, according to Sonia, the convicted arsonist and heroine of *The Heart of the Country*, is "to be scavengers: to pick up the dregs and dust of creation and save what's possible and render it back to the Almighty, not to hang about carelessly, adding to the mud, the trouble and confusion" (14).

BACKGROUND

Weldon's work reflects very powerfully the early philosophy of the feminist movement, that "the personal is political." Her fiction focuses primarily on the everyday lives of women, and political action often happens in kitchens, on playgrounds, or at suburban dinner parties—wherever women spend their lives. It is also evident from several interviews Weldon has given that she draws heavily on her own life in creating her fictional world. She has, however, refused to clarify a number of conflicting or ambiguous biographical details. In answer to a query on the online Weldon discussion list Weldon said, "I am a writer of fiction; you cannot expect me to provide true or reliable information.

You must learn what you can from the internal evidence of my novels or from websites, which indeed get everything wrong" ("Thank"). I must also point out that Weldon is very helpful to students requesting explication of her work, always urging them not to overanalyze and to trust their own interpretations. The following summary of Weldon's life, taken mainly from Lana Faulks's excellent critical analysis of her work, reflects the most current research.

Born Franklin Birkinshaw in Alvechurch, a village in Worcestershire, England, in 1931, Weldon emigrated with her family to New Zealand when she was around five years old. Weldon's parents divorced when she was still quite young, and the impact on her work can be seen in the recurring theme of men who abandon their wives and children. Weldon returned to England with her mother and sister when she was fourteen. For most of her life Weldon was raised in relative poverty and in a household of women—mother, sister, and grandmother—which profoundly influenced her writing. "I believed the world was female," Weldon has said (Faulks 1).

In 1949 Weldon entered St. Andrews University in Scotland, where she received an M.A. degree in economics and psychology. Her first son was born in 1955 during a brief marriage. She spent the next few years as a struggling single parent, working at a number of jobs: on the problem page of the *Daily Mirror* and as a copywriter for the Foreign Office. In 1960 she married Ron Weldon, an antique dealer, with whom she had three more sons (1963–1977). During the 1960s she had a successful career in advertising, starting as a copywriter for Ogilvy, Benson and Mather, London. Her most famous slogan is "Go to work on an egg." The mid-1960s marked the beginning of her prolific career as a screenwriter and novelist. Her first television play for the BBC aired in 1966 and was followed by one almost every year through 1977. Her three episodes for *Masterpiece Theatre*'s series *Upstairs Downstairs* (1971–1973), one of which won the Society of Film and Television Arts award, and her adaptation of the BBC's production of Jane Austen's *Pride and Prejudice* (1985) are probably her most noted television works. Her first novel, *The Fat Woman's Joke* (called *And the Wife Ran Away* in the United States) was published in 1967. She has written twenty-four novels, six short-story collections, four nonfiction works (the fourth, *Godless in Eden*, has at this writing not yet been released in the United States), and numerous radio, stage, and television plays. She and Ron Weldon divorced in 1994, and she is currently married to Nicholas Fox and living in London.

The influence of Weldon's early training in economics and psychology is evident in the major thrust of her work: the effects of post–World War II British political and economic systems on women's lives, especially as concerns the development of the feminist movement. Weldon's relentless critique of the hypocrisy, greed, and evil that too often masquerade beneath the latest "theory" or "ism" begins with Britain's experiment in bureaucratic socialism of the 1950s and 1960s and continues through the 1970s—the "me" decade of privatization and welfare cutting, policies honed by Margaret Thatcher in the 1980s—to the most recent millennial new liberalism of Tony Blair.

British scholar Janet Todd points out that along with Marxism, British feminism has been influenced by postmodern theories of deconstruction and psychoanalysis (87); but Weldon's fiction continually questions the existence of any foundational truths that privilege one idea or ideology over another. According to Regina Barreca, Weldon's official biographer, "A structuring principle for all Weldon's fiction is an un-evasive acknowledgment of the mutability of perception and definition. Only the worst are full of unconsidered conviction" ("It's the End" 176). However, Weldon's work does not give way to a postmodern ennui or debilitating inaction, but presents a more existential construction of self reflective philosophers like

Heidegger and Sartre, incorporating a Nietzschean call for transgressive action. According to Patricia Waugh, "The Nietzschean subject must create its own order out of itself, for there is no Divine I AM, no blueprint to be discovered. . . . divinity has to be relocated in a self which must aesthetically construct its own ground in a transformation of the body through body" (21).

For Weldon, too, sexuality, the body, is the site of transformation. She seems particularly to share some of the ideas of French feminists like Hélène Cixous who reject the phallocentric psychology of both Freud and his more radical interpreter, Lacan, and who posit a woman-centered psychology—one based on difference as powerful to women rather than as subjugating, one that delights in female desire. A passage from Cixous's "The Laugh of the Medusa" (1991) mirrors what Weldon attempts in her fiction: "A feminine text cannot fail to be more than subversive. It is volcanic; as it is written it brings about an upheaval of the old property crust, carrier of masculine investments; there's no other way. There's no room for her if she's not a he. If she's a her-she, it's in order to smash everything, to shatter the framework of institutions, to blow up the law, to break up the 'truth' with laughter" (344). Weldon's novel *The Lives and Loves of a She-Devil*, for example, clearly reflects this subversive intent, reversing gender roles, shattering our concept of the feminine, and illustrating the enormous price paid for the illusion of romantic love.

Although Weldon writes in great detail about the oppressive, often tragic lives of women in a patriarchal society, satire is the literary device she most often uses to present the all-too-familiar failings of both men and women that create these situations. This satiric style has a long tradition in British fiction, and Weldon has been compared most often with Evelyn Waugh and Muriel Spark. Critic Karen Karbo points out that "Ms. Weldon's earlier books are hysterical, fierce and gleefully mean in a way that only British novelists seem to be able to get away with." Her prolific nonfiction work, which includes numerous magazine and newspaper articles and speeches as well as books, presents an ongoing, razor-sharp commentary on the often-failed liberal orthodoxy and the "paralysis of the well-intentioned." In a 2000 editorial in the *New York Times* Weldon takes British prime minister Tony Blair to task regarding his hesitation to take paternity leave: "It is the [same decision] that faces all forward-looking leaders who preach non-elitism but find its practice difficult when it comes to themselves" ("New").

ANALYSIS

Weldon's universe is created as much by her style as by her message, a lesson she learned in her advertising career. As critic Olga Kenyon summarizes, "She has developed a dramatic style of the novel, dealing with essentials only, in media language, easy to relate to" (*Women Novelists Today* 108). Sensationalism—outrageous plots that heap one calamity after the other on her female characters, snappy one-liners reminiscent of marketing slogans, and sound-bite paragraphs separated by extra spacing—both shocks readers out of complacency and appeals to a diverse audience:

> I take off my clothes. I stand naked. I look. I want to be changed.
>
> Nothing is impossible, not for she-devils.
>
> Peel away the wife, the mother, find the woman, and there the she-devil is.
>
> Excellent!
>
> Glitter-glitter. Are those my eyes? They're so bright they light up the room.
>
> (*The Life and Loves of a She-Devil* 44)

A pastiche of genres and styles—fairy tale, allegory, biblical allusion, pop culture, journalism, nineteenth-century romance novel, stand-up comedy—helps, as critic Agate Nesaule Krouse comments, to "distance many of the horrors, make them comically absurd, and hence either funny or at least endurable for both characters and readers" (6). Multiple narrators present a dizzying array of contradictory statements, switching from first person to third in a technique that while creating abundant opportunities for satirical comment and postmodern self-reflexivity sometimes seems abrupt or manipulative.

Both critics and the public have generally received Weldon's work enthusiastically. Jenny Newman argues that her experimental style "makes Weldon one of the most innovative and popular writers in Britain today" (205). However, many critics do agree that her work can be uneven, citing heavy-handed polemic, lack of characterization, and overuse of advertising techniques. Kenyon says, "Weldon is a variable writer, too episodic in *Down Among the Women*, too far-fetched in *The Life and Loves of a She-Devil*" (*Women Novelists Today* 124). Victoria Glendinning, reviewing *Female Friends* (1976) in the *Times Literary Supplement*, presents a fairly typical criticism: "The characters are real, in that one knows the most intimate things about them; and yet they are schematic, reduced, as are people known only through an informant—or through the television screen" (565).

Novels that are more naturalistic, with more fully developed, nuanced characters, received the most praise: *Praxis* (1978) was shortlisted for the Booker Prize; *The Heart of the Country* (1987) won the Los Angeles Times Book Award for 1989; and *Worst Fears* (1996) was nominated for the Whitbread Prize. Reviewing Weldon's 1997 collection of short stories *Wicked Women*, Deborah Mason says that Weldon has become "one of the most cunning moral satirists of our time." In her most sophisticated work Weldon juxtaposes her breezy media style with longer, more lyrical sentences, creating a more complicated inner life and a deeper emotional impact:

> That God was not good. That the earth you stood upon shifted, and chasms yawned; that people, falling, clutched one another for help and none was forthcoming. That the basis of all things was evil. That the beauty of the evening, now settling in a yellow glow on the stone of The Cottage barns, the swallows dipping and soaring, a sudden host of butterflies in the long grasses in the foreground, was the lie: a deceitful sheen on which hopeful visions flitted momentarily, and that long, long ago evil had won against good, death over life. (*Worst Fears* 94)

Weldon's fiction generally follows a similar plot structure: the female protagonist(s), caught in the illusions and deceptions created by the patriarchal culture, suffers a series of traumatic events, realizes her predicament, rebels, and must then deal with the consequences of her actions. Some of Weldon's most damning narrative depicts how the attributes idealized in a patriarchal culture—reason, the scientific method, survival of the fittest, monotheism—are illusions responsible for much of the evil in the world: the repetitive cycle of poverty and victim consciousness of the powerless, war, the increasing devastation of the planet's resources. In *The Cloning of Joanna May*, set during the aftermath of the Chernobyl disaster, the evil Carl May creates four clones of his wife, an attempt to use science to create the perfect wife, one who will love him unconditionally. In *The Heart of the Country* (1987) a collusion of male real estate developers and businessmen sell illegal toxic chemicals to farmers. *Wicked Women* chronicles the privatization of the 1980s and 1990s and the havoc wreaked by greedy businessmen, corrupt politicians, and hypocritical new-age practitioners.

Weldon also describes with scathing humor how the patriarchy creates and maintains the illusion that women are weak, irrational, unstable creatures equipped only for mothering and marriage. Most of the female characters begin in ignorance, dutifully living through the men in their lives; they typify "the embryonic woman," as Deborah Mason says, "who grows up by default and becomes shrewd by suffering." In discussing why the women in Weldon's fiction betray other women and demean themselves in their competition for male approval and economic support, Faulks points to "the sadomasochistic urge that exists in the division of power . . . Women are sexual and domestic servants in return for economic solvency" (68).

When the illusion is broken—arrogant, heartless husbands run off with their mistresses, leaving their wives and children penniless and at the mercy of humiliating and inept government institutions—the disillusioned protagonist begins her descent into the bleak world described powerfully in Weldon's second book, *Down among the Women* (1971): "The tower block where I live is full of women who were once girls . . . now off to bingo, desperate, with their children left locked up; pale, worried and aging badly; without the spirit any more even to tuck a free-gift plastic daffodil behind the ear" (120). The British welfare state has failed not only because it has not provided economic and political equality, but because the myth of romantic love and female subordination has left women unable to act, blaming themselves for their failure and filled with anger and hatred at their circumstances. Women then pass on this legacy of delusion, guilt, and degradation to their children. Looking back at her terrible childhood, Praxis, the beleaguered protagonist in *Praxis*, says, "Children who have been hurt, grow up to hurt . . . the shrieks of generations growing louder, not softer, as the decades pass" (21).

Extreme measures are needed, Weldon suggests, to break free from this deadly cycle: her female characters burn down buildings, give away their children, have affairs, prostitute themselves, and commit incest. By breaking sexual taboos, by reclaiming their sexuality, and by creating alternative lifestyles conducive to their own goals and desires, women refuse to be bound by traditional roles of virgin/mother or whore. Sex, as Weldon most clearly defines it in *Life Force*, "is the energy not so much of sexual desire as of sexual discontent: the urge to find someone better out in the world, and thereby something better in the self." However, because sex is also "irrational, uncontrolled, universal, shameful," it must be reconciled with its opposite aspect that "yearns for a moral shape to the universe" (15–16). It is a seemingly impossible task, Weldon suggests, leaving us to balance eros and instinct, on the one hand, with responsibility and consequences, on the other.

Praxis, one of Weldon's richest and most sophisticated novels, presents perhaps the most outrageous transgression. Praxis smothers her friend Mary's infant, born with Down syndrome, in an attempt to release both Mary and her baby from an existence of poverty and hopelessness. Faulks believes that "[b]y killing the baby, Praxis has enacted a symbolic turning point for all women, freeing them to pursue independent, self-fulfilling lives" (41). The act has even deeper significance, however, and ties the quest for women's liberation, for some recourse against the pervasive suffering in the world, with a complex interaction of love, compassion, and sacrifice. "And there is perhaps a force abroad—or in ourselves—" Praxis muses, "which demands that sacrifice is a part of faith. That Abraham must sacrifice Isaac, to prove that God exists" (262). Praxis spends some years in prison, and after getting out, destitute and in ill health, she looks back at her struggles and wonders if the sacrifice was worth it:

> Then what we feel is the pain of the female Lucifer, tumbling down from heaven, having dared to defy the male deity, cast out for ever, but likewise never able to forget, tormented always by the memory of what we threw away. Or else, and on this supposition my mind rests most contentedly, we are in the grip of some evolutionary force which hurts as it works, and which I fear has already found its fruition

> in that new race of young women which I encountered . . . dewy fresh from their lovers' arms and determined to please no one but themselves. (13)

This is Weldon at her best, reversing traditional roles, combining hope and despair in powerfully lyric prose.

The development of the feminist movement as a crucial aspect of this evolutionary force is one of Weldon's most important themes. Beginning with her earliest novels, Weldon criticizes feminists who oppress other women by their dogmatic adherence to theory and their unwillingness to look at the hypocrisy of their own actions. *Big Girls Don't Cry* (1997), Weldon's most comprehensive commentary on the history of the movement, follows the lives of Nancy, Layla, Alice, and Stephanie, who in 1971 start Medusa, a feminist publishing company, for all the right and all the wrong reasons. While they are publishing liberationist articles and books, starting women's studies programs, and protesting nuclear weapons, they also sleep with their friends' husbands, ignore their children, fight among themselves for power and men, and sell out for money. Nancy, desperately trying to convince herself that giving up her life to work for the movement, being underpaid and alone, is making her happy, argues, "Truth can never be too big a price to pay for social change. If you only believe hard enough, what is not true can become true" (105).

And what of the next generation? Saffron, the young, liberated 1990s woman, is cold and calculating, embodying a consumer mentality that argues for profit and pragmatism over politics and "love . . . that old thing" (341). In a wonderfully humorous scene Saffron and Layla stage a hostile takeover of Medusa, the old generation and the new converging in a postfeminist version of the patriarchy. Has the feminist movement failed, then? Weldon's answer is as complicated and contradictory as the history of feminism. In the end, however, Weldon's sympathy is always with "big women," who, despite their failings, are not afraid to try to change the world. "They had got things wrong, personally and politically," the narrator says, "but who ever got everything right?" (338).

Understand and forgive, Weldon enjoins over and over again, and get on with it. Numerous short stories describe both men and women who have come to terms with their painful childhoods, dysfunctional mothers, and absent or abusive boyfriends and husbands and decide, against all the odds, that life is worth living. In *Puffball* (1980), Weldon's favorite novel, pregnancy becomes a redemptive act that leads Liffey to face the dangers of the patriarchy. Motherhood (freely chosen, of course), caring for another person, and individual acts of kindness come the closest to an unselfish love, one not based on sexual or romantic illusions. In the short story "Down the Clinical Disco" two characters meet in the Broadmoor institute for the criminally insane, victims of society's often-absurd and convenient definitions of sane/insane, normal/abnormal, and find refuge in each other: "I reckon love's a talisman. If we hold on to that we'll be okay," the narrator says (79).

However, some of Weldon's most beautifully written and complex stories are the most pessimistic, refusing the tacked-on happy ending that is common in her work. "Wasted Lives," set in the crass, post-Communist world of Sarajevo after the war, juxtaposes the British narrator, a wealthy businessman, with Milena, his pregnant mistress, who, moved by poverty and desperation, commits suicide (we are never certain whether or not she succeeds) when the narrator refuses to marry her. One of the few male protagonists in Weldon's work, the narrator tells his story with a terrible sadness, a grim recognition of his inability to love the weak, the pitiful, the "other." "The powerful are indeed whimsical," he says, "they leave their elegant droppings where they choose—be they Milena's baby, Benetton, the Marlboro ads which now dominate the city: no end even now to the wheezing, the coughing, the death rattling along the river" (*Wicked Women* 101).

Even in the most hopeless situations, however, Weldon interjects the concept of the "frivolous" or the "wicked," especially in her later work. As John Glavin explains, "Historically, the frivolous has meant everything the good bourgeois is not" (135). Weldon's women break the rules, reject self-righteousness, and face life with a remarkable exuberance and determination to enjoy themselves. For example, as the many complications in *Life Force* resolve into a Weldonesque "happy" ending, Nora contemplates her life: "Perhaps now I would be able to give up smoking. The thought prompted me to open a new pack. There had to be some source of pleasure in life, even though it kills you" (219). In her 1991 essay "On the Reading of Frivolous Fiction" Weldon urges us to "read the bad good books while you gather strength for the good good books" (qtd. in Barreca, *Fay* 228). Being wicked, indulging in frivolity, then, is a survival tactic that can help us maintain a sense of humor and keep us from the sin of overzealousness.

ASSESSMENT

Weldon addresses the inequities and devastation created by the power struggles central to all relationships, whether between people or countries. Her answer to the central question "Is change possible?" is both grim and hopeful, reflecting Weldon's refusal to indulge in easy answers and her insistence on acknowledging paradox as the underlying force and meaning in the world. By refusing primacy to any religion, movement, philosophy, or political system, she leaves moral decisions up to the individual, based on, as Barreca argues, a philosophy of situational ethics ("It's the End" 181). However, Weldon's recognition of flawed human nature leads her to explore the painful consequences that result from the struggle to gain the economic and political equality necessary to create an authentic self, free from the oppressive manipulation of the patriarchy. Her most successful characters, having been dealt a tough hand to play, grow up: they use their suffering to learn something about themselves and the world, they try to make the world a more just place, and, most important, they try to, as E.M. Forster urged, "only connect."

BIBLIOGRAPHY

Primary Sources

The Fat Woman's Joke. London: MacGibbon, 1967. As *And the Wife Ran Away*. New York: McKay, 1968.

Mixed Doubles (play). Prod. London, 1969, as *Permanence*. London: Samuel French, 1970.

Down among the Women. London: Heinemann, 1971; New York: St. Martin's, 1972.

Time Hurries On (play). In *Scene Scripts*. Ed. M. Marland. London: Longman, 1972.

Words of Advice (play). Prod. London, 1974. London: Samuel French, 1974.

Female Friends. London: Heinemann, 1974; New York: St. Martin's, 1974.

Friends (play). Prod. Richmond, Surrey, 1975.

Moving House (play). Prod. Farnham, Surrey, 1976.

Remember Me. London: Hodder; New York: Random House, 1976.

Words of Advice. New York, Random House, 1977. As *Little Sisters*. London: Hodder, 1978.

Action Replay (play). Prod. Birmingham, 1978; prod. Vancouver, 1982, as *Life among the Women*. London and New York: Samuel French, 1980.

Mr. Director (play). Prod. Richmond, Surrey, 1978. London: Samuel French, 1984.

Praxis. London: Hodder; New York: Summit, 1978.

Polaris (play). London: Eyre Methuen, 1979.

Puffball. London: Hodder; New York: Summit, 1980.

Simple Steps to Public Life. With Pamela Anderson and Mary Stott. London: Virago, 1980.

After the Prize (play). Prod. New York, 1981; prod. Newbury, Berkshire, 1984, as *Word Worm*.

Watching Me, Watching You. London: Hodder and Stoughton; New York: Summit, 1981.

I Love My Love (play). Prod. Richmond, Surrey, 1982. London and New York: Samuel French, 1984.

The President's Child. London: Hodder, 1982; Garden City, NY: Doubleday, 1983.

The Life and Loves of a She-Devil. London: Hodder, 1983; New York: Pantheon, 1984.

Letters to Alice on First Reading Jane Austen. London: Michael Joseph, 1984; New York: Taplinger, 1985.

Polaris and Other Stories. London: Hodder and Stoughton, 1985; New York: Penguin, 1989.

Rebecca West. Hamondsworth: Penguin, 1985; New York: Viking, 1985.

Jane Eyre (adaptation for the stage). Prod. Birmingham, 1986.

The Shrapnel Academy. London: Hodder, 1986; New York: Viking, 1987.

The Heart of the Country. London: Hutchinson, 1987; New York: Viking, 1988.

The Hearts and Lives of Men. London: Heinemann, 1987; New York: Viking, 1988.

The Hole in the Top of the World (play). Prod. Richmond, Surrey, 1987.

The Rules of Life. London: Hutchinson, 1987.

Leader of the Band. London: Hodder, 1988; New York: Viking, 1989.

Wolf the Mechanical Dog. With Pat Layshun. London: Collins, 1988.

The Cloning of Joanna May. London: Collins, 1989; New York: Viking, 1990.

Party Puddle. With Carol Wright. London: Collins, 1989.

Sacred Cows. London: Chatto, 1989.

Darcy's Utopia. London: Collins, 1990; New York: Viking, 1991.

Someone like You (play). Prod. London, 1990.

Moon over Minneapolis. London: HarperCollins, 1991; New York: Penguin, 1992.

Growing Rich. London: HarperCollins, 1992.

Life Force. London: HarperCollins; New York: Viking, 1992.

Affliction. London: HarperCollins, 1993. As *Trouble*. New York: Viking, 1994.

"The Changing Face of Fiction." In Barreca, *Fay Weldon's Wicked Fictions* 188–197. See "Secondary Sources."

Angel, All Innocence, and Other Stories. London: Bloomsbury, 1995.

The Lady Is a Tramp: Portraits of Catherine Bailey. Photos by David Bailey. New York and London: Thames, 1995.

Splitting. New York: Atlantic Monthly, 1995.

Worst Fears. New York: Atlantic Monthly, 1996.

Big Women. London: Flamingo, 1997. As *Big Girls Don't Cry*. New York: Atlantic Monthly, 1997.

Nobody Likes Me! London: Bodley Head, 1997.

Wicked Women. London: Flamingo, 1995; New York: Atlantic Monthly, 1997.

A Hard Time to Be a Father. London: Flamingo, 1998.

The Four Alice Bakers (play). Prod. Birmingham, 1999.

Godless in Eden. London: Flamingo, 1999.

"Thank you for your help." Online posting. 16 March 2000. Fay Weldon Discussion List. 1 April 2000 <http://clio.lyris.net/cgi-bin/lyris.pl?visit=weldon-discuss&id=113113030>.

"New Labor's New Dad." *New York Times* 31 March 2000. *New York Times Online*. 4 April 2000 <http://nytimes.qpass.com/qpass-archives?Q . . . rs2-oc!+10+wAAA+Fay%20Weldon>.

Rhode Island Blues. London: Flamingo; New York: Atlantic Monthly, 2000.

The Bulgari Connection. London: Flamingo; New York: Atlantic Monthly, 2001.

Secondary Sources

Barreca, Regina, ed. *Fay Weldon's Wicked Fictions*. Hanover, NH: UP of New England, 1994.

———. "It's the End of the World As We Know It: Bringing Down the House in Fay Weldon's Fiction." In *Fay Weldon's Wicked Fictions* 172–187.

Brain, John. "A Natural Novelist." *Books and Bookmen* January 1977: 28.

Cixous, Hélène. "The Laugh of the Medusa." In *Feminisms: An Anthology of Literary Theory and Criticism*. Ed. Robyn R. Warhol and Diane Price Herndl. New Brunswick, NJ: Rutgers UP, 1991. 335–349.

Dowling, Finula. *Fay Weldon's Fiction*. Madison, NJ: Fairleigh Dickinson UP, 1998.

Faulks, Lana. *Fay Weldon*. New York: Twayne, 1998.

Glavin, John. "Fay Weldon, Leader of the Frivolous Band." In Barreca, *Fay Weldon's Wicked Fictions* 133–151.

Glendinning, Victoria. "The Muswell Hill Mob." *TLS* 24 September 1976. Rpt. in *Contemporary Literary Criticism* 11. Ed. Dedria Bryfonski. Detroit: Gale, 1981. 565.

Haffenden, John. *Novelists in Interview*. New York: Methuen, 1985.

Hebert, Ann Marie. "Rewriting the Feminine Script: Fay Weldon's Wicked Laughter." *Critical Matrix* 7.1 (1993): 21–40.

Hosmer, Robert E., Jr. *Contemporary British Women Writers: Narrative Strategies*. New York: St. Martin's, 1993.

Karbo, Karen. "Love Fails Again." *New York Times*

Online. 1 January 2000 <http://www.nytimes.com/books/search/bi . . . ook-rev+bookrev-arch+19699+12+wAAA+Weldon>.

Kenyon, Olga. *Women Novelists Talk*. New York: Carroll & Graf, 1989.

———. *Women Novelists Today*. New York: St. Martin's, 1988.

Krouse, Agate Nesaule. "Feminism and Art in Fay Weldon's Novels." *Critique: Studies in Modern Fiction* 202 (1978): 5–20.

Lodge, David. *The Art of Fiction*. New York: Viking, 1993.

Mason, Deborah. "Divine Justice." *New York Times Online* 29 June 1997. <http://www.nytimes.com./books/97/06/29/reviews/970629.mason.html>.

Newman, Jenny. " 'See Me as Sisyphus, but Having a Good Time': The Fiction of Fay Weldon." In *Contemporary British Women Writers*. Ed. Robert E. Hosmer, Jr. New York: St. Martin's, 1993. 188–211.

Palmer, Paulina. "Contemporary Lesbian Feminist Fiction." In *Plotting Change: Contemporary Women's Fiction*. Ed. Linda Anderson. London: Edward Arnold, 1990.

Sinfield, Alan. *Society and Literature, 1945–1970*. New York: Holmes & Meier, 1983. 51–86.

Todd, Janet. *Feminist Literary History*. New York: Routledge, 1988.

Waugh, Patricia. *Practising Postmodernism, Reading Modernism*. London: Edward Arnold, 1992.

Timberlake Wertenbaker 1944(?)–

John H. Lutterbie

Whether or not Timberlake Wertenbaker belongs in a book on British writers is open to question. She was born in America, was educated in France, and only then decided to settle in Britain and write plays. Why she chose Britain rather than the United States or France remains a mystery. It might have been serendipity—Soho Polytechnic commissioned a play from her (Cantacuzino C49). Or perhaps she thought that her work was more likely to be produced in England, at venues like the Royal Court Theatre. Wertenbaker's plays have a political edge that has been popular in Britain since the early 1970s, with writers such as Edward Bond, Howard Brenton, Howard Barker, and others. Moreover, her plays bear a closer resemblance to the work of Caryl Churchill or Pam Gems than to that of American counterparts Marie Irene Fornes, Wendy Wasserstein, or Marsha Norman. Her time in Europe may have led to the development of an aesthetic that is not encouraged in the United States, where there is virtually no federal support of the arts, where psychological realism remains the dominant paradigm, and where politics is preferred on television and in the newspaper rather than on stage.

The politics represented in Wertenbaker's plays reflects the feminist claim that the personal is political. Her characters are individual and drawn with dimension, finding themselves in conflict with institutions and their representatives rather than with the internecine tensions of familial relationships. When families are the center of her drama, as in *The Break of Day* or *The Love of the Nightingale*, the problems the characters encounter reflect the pressures placed on them by contradictions within society, rather than personal relationships. Wertenbaker seems to enjoy exploring the effects of ideology on her characters, particularly when they push the boundaries of respectability in an effort to resist the limitations placed on their freedom. Perhaps it is her own experience crossing between cultures, albeit primarily white and European, and the tensions and possibilities that presented themselves that kindle her interest in characters who find themselves caught in the space between social structures. It is in the spaces that define the peripheries of institutions and the play that life within these margins allows that one can locate the politics of Timberlake Wertenbaker.

BACKGROUND

Timberlake Wertenbaker maintains an aura of mystery about her past. When asked whether she perceives of herself as being American, French, or British, she responded: "I feel I am an American but not completely. I grew up in Europe so I am not an expatriate. Really, that's just narrow nationalism, and I don't know why people can't accept that you can have several cultures. The whole thing about being a writer is that you can have a floating identity anyway" (de Vries, "This Angry" H10). A "floating identity" is surely appropriate for a writer who must inhabit the different worlds and perspectives of her characters, but it also indicates a resistance to having herself defined by critics who wish to see her plays as a reflection of her earlier life. According to one reporter, she "refuses to reveal her age and believes personal details to be irrelevant and unimportant" (Cantacuzino C49). As a result, much of what is "known" about her life is uncertain.

It is believed that she was born in New York in 1944 (McDonough 406) as Lael Louisiana Wertenbaker (Chaillet 553). Her father was Charles Wertenbaker, a foreign correspondent for *Time* magazine, but there is no available information about her mother. Wertenbaker was raised in the Basque region of France and educated "at schools near St. Jean-de-Luz" (Chaillet 553). She returned to the United States for college, graduating from St. John's in Annapolis, Maryland, after which she worked as a writer for Time-Life Books in New York (McDonough 406). In the 1970s she took a position teaching English and French in Greece, where she formed a small company and began writing plays for Greek children before moving to England (McDonough 406). Her first play, *Case to Answer* (1980), was commissioned (or simply produced) by Soho Poly in 1980. Wertenbaker's early and unpublished works were performed by the Women's Theatre Group and the Shared Experience Company: *This Is No Place for Tallulah Bankhead* (1978), *Second Sentence* (1980), and *Breaking Through* (1980). *New Anatomies*, Wertenbaker's first original script to be published, was performed at the Edinburgh Festival in 1981 by the Women's Theatre Group (McDonough 406–407), but her breakthrough was a production of *The Third*, which won Wertenbaker the All London Playwrights Award in 1983.

After *The Third* she became a writer-in-residence during 1984–1985 at the Royal Court Theatre, the company that has produced much of her work since. In 1984 it presented *Abel's Sister* (1984) and in 1985 *The Grace of Mary Traverse*. The latter play garnered for Wertenbaker the *Plays and Players* Award for most promising playwright (McDonough 409). The artistic director of the Royal Court, Max Stafford-Clark, encouraged her to write a play about the first theatrical production to be performed in Australia. In response, Wertenbaker wrote her most noted play, *Our Country's Good*, based on Thomas Keneally's novel *The Playmaker*. The production was the first of her plays toured to the United States and received the Olivier Award for best play of 1988, the *Evening Standard* Award for best play of the year, and the New York Drama Critics Circle Award for best foreign play. The Royal Shakespeare Company produced her next play, *The Love of the Nightingale*, also in 1988, a reworking of the Philomela and Procne myth. She returned to the Royal Court in 1992 with *Three Birds Alighting on a Field*, which earned her another Olivier Award nomination and won her the Susan Smith Blackburn Prize for playwriting, and in 1995, with *The Break of Day*.

In addition to writing original plays, Wertenbaker has translated plays from French and Greek into English and has written for the cinema. Two plays by Pierre Marivaux, *Successful Strategies* and *False Admissions*, were the best received according to Carla J. McDonough, although she has also translated works by Anouilh, Maeterlinck, and Euripides and Ariane Mnouchkine's play *Mephisto*. Three of Sophocles' tragedies, *Oedipus Rex*, *Oedipus at Colonus*, and *Antigone*, were translated and produced under the title of

The Thebans. Wertenbaker also has two screenplays to her credit, *The Children* (1989), based on a novel by Edith Wharton, and a film entitled *Do Not Disturb* (1990) for BBC 2.

Timberlake Wertenbaker decided to work in the theater because of the challenge and potential it offers. "The theatre is a difficult place, it requires an audience to use its imagination. You must accept that and not try to make it easy for them" (Chaillet 554). Her plays are difficult because she believes that the theater confronts problems and encourages her audiences to find solutions. "But I do think you can make people change, just a little, by forcing them to question something, or by intriguing them, or giving them an image that remains with them. And that little change can lead to bigger changes. That's all you can hope for" (Chaillet 554). This is undoubtedly why Timberlake Wertenbaker remains secretive about her life. Focusing on her past would distract from the larger issues she is dealing with in her plays.

ANALYSIS

As secretive as Timberlake Wertenbaker is about her early life, she is equally willing to give significant clues about the concerns addressed in her plays: "My plays often start with a very ordinary question: If women had power, would they behave the same way as men? Why do we seem to want to destroy ourselves? Is the personal more important than the political? If someone has behaved badly all of their lives, can they redeem themselves?" (Chaillet 553). Unlike that in mainstream American drama, the focus is not on individual psychology but on more global questions that take the play out of the living room. "I do not like naturalism. I find it boring. My plays are an attempt to get away from the smallness of naturalism, from enclosed rooms to open spaces, and also to get ideas away from the restraints of closed spaces to something wider" (Chaillet 553). She uses ordinary situations to open the imagination of the audience and make its members aware of the precarious state of the world. "The bubble has burst and people are in terrible trouble, and I want to write something about values—what is of value, what is the price of something" (de Vries, "Of Convicts" 339). The price about which she speaks is the cost incurred through human interaction and its effects on the relationship between the individual and the community.

The body of critical writing that is beginning to develop around the works of Timberlake Wertenbaker focuses on the intersection of her characters and the institutions with which they come into conflict. Within these tensions a few themes have been identified. Perhaps the most predominant is human agency, specifically the ability of women to define an identity for themselves and to enact their lives based on this construct. Implicit in this thematic is a second theme, a belief in the possibility of change, or, as Hilary de Vries writes, "the human ability to transcend circumstances" (de Vries, "This Angry" H10). The third idea that resonates in most of her plays is the power of language and its significance in allowing men and women to express their identities and, conversely, how people are silenced.

Language, in the plays of Timberlake Wertenbaker, creates a paradox. On the one hand, language is linked to society's attempt to control the individual by limiting the characters' ability to express who they are. Reading *The Grace of Mary Traverse*, David Ian Rabey writes that "prescriptive imperialistic definition attempts to restrict and elicit responses which accord only with its own ideological terms" (527). On the other hand, language is the only means available for engaging in a process of self-definition or transcending the limits imposed by culture, "demonstrating the compulsion to question these restrictive terms in a process of 'recreation' " (Rabey 527). It is in the interstices of these two potentials in language that feminists address the question of subjectivity and agency. Ann Wilson finds in Wertenbaker's

Mary Traverse a desire in the female characters to create a language of women, an *écriture féminine*. Bordering on cultural feminism, Wilson believes that "Sophie [Mary's servant] evokes through her song the true maternal, so strikingly absent from the play. Wertenbaker suggests that it is difficult, if not virtually impossible to sustain the maternal in a world which is overdetermined by the patriarchy" ("Forgiving History" 153). In discussions of *The Love of the Nightingale*, Philomela's ability to communicate the violence done to her without language (her tongue has been cut out) suggests that women can find a means of communicating their experiences through forms of representation other than the language of patriarchy. The difference between men and women and the factors that limit their ability to express themselves are also explored in Joe Winston's examination of morality in Wertenbaker's *The Love of the Nightingale*. Winston argues that Wertenbaker uses the myth of Philomela in contrast with the myth of Phaedra to explore "hidden attitudes and values with regard to male and female sexuality which need to be exposed and challenged, for they distort social reality at the same time as they help shape social assumptions" (511). He believes that Wertenbaker engages the concepts of shame and guilt and the moral imperatives that attempt to impose limits on human sexuality. Winston does not see a resolution to the dialectic he finds in the play, but values Wertenbaker's decision to focus on the continual necessity to question the assumptions and proscriptions of morality. Wertenbaker clearly believes that language provides a means for women to transcend the limits of their existence and define their own identity.

Most critics applaud Wertenbaker's exploration of the lives of women and the positive ability of women to reconstruct their lives in the face of social and cultural resistance. Mary Karen Dahl sees this idea in *The Grace of Mary Traverse*: "[T]he play questions the processes through which men and women may effect changes in the existing power structures" (151). For Dahl, Mary Traverse refuses to be seduced by the reactionary forces that seek to define her as a subject because she rejects the image of herself presented to her by society and therefore the values that society is trying to impose upon her. Instead, Wertenbaker's play suggests for this critic "the possibility of a resistant, mobile subjectivity" (Dahl 156). Martha Ritchie also perceives Mary Traverse as an exemplar of postmodern subjectivity, "a role playing heroine whose identity continually shifts and changes, depending upon her circumstances" (405). Ritchie ultimately believes that Wertenbaker embraces a kind of cultural feminism that believes that there is an essential quality that defines a difference between men and women. In her reading of the play she privileges Mary's servant Sophie, who represents "women's capacity for love, particularly maternal love" (413).

Wertenbaker is accused of conflating the specificity of women's experience under the rubric of "woman," a move Ann Wilson sees as maintaining the hierarchy between men and women, where "man is the first element with woman understood only in relation to him" (Wilson, "Forgiving History" 160). Wertenbaker's tendency to universalize the construct of woman causes the critic to question whether these plays can be said to suggest a way forward, a means of instigating change. Christine Dymkowski takes a more positive view toward the endings of Wertenbaker's plays. She believes that a dialectic is established in the plays that does not allow the audience closure. "Paradoxically, in turning this kind of mirror onto itself, each play impels its audience to engage dynamically with political and social realities, thereby returning the word 'theatre' to its radical meaning as a place of seeing" (132). A similar questioning, with somewhat different conclusions, is carried out by Esther Beth Sullivan. Looking at a broader range of plays, Sullivan questions the endings of the plays, which she frequently finds unsatisfactory.

While Wilson focuses on language, Sullivan is interested in the possibility of actions that can contest the interpellation of the individual into complicity with the dominant value structures of gender, race, and class. She sees in Wertenbaker's plays a political value:

> They take us vicariously through the invigorating, colorful, and passionate process of coming into consciousness. As such, they function to keep the *process* of consciousness-raising central and vital. In light of the not-new, not-old, not-progressive, but necessarily permanent state of contestation, they can serve to redeploy critical engagement and to reinvigorate tired consciences with the fantasy of starting anew. (153)

It is the element of fantasy that Sullivan questions, particularly with endings that seem to subvert the radical questioning that is taking place throughout the plays.

Charlotte Canning presents a very different reading of Timberlake Wertenbaker's plays, perhaps because she is focusing on a more recent play, *The Break of Day*. For Canning, it is the relationship between the past and the present and the difficulties in charting a course for the future that are important because in this effort she traces a history of feminism and its discontents. Wertenbaker, according to Canning, embraces feminism and through her play enters into a dialogue with women, "evoking the experiences, memories, and pasts of those audiences." Wertenbaker seldom, if ever, takes a simplistic view of these themes. The uses of language and silence, of creating an identity, and the value of transcending circumstances are perceived as complex and complicated processes that never lead to completely comfortable conclusions.

The arguments these critics make for the importance of resisting the seductive forces of dominant ideologies and the very real structures that silence women's voices are convincing, but less attention has been paid to the conditions and the locations in which this resistance takes place. Ann Wilson comes closest to addressing this issue when she writes, "Wertenbaker critiques the cohesiveness of the ideological apparatus which supports hegemony, implying that the fissures which such a critique exposes might effectively be used as the sites of social change" ("Forgiving History" 146). The emphasis on the incoherence of ideology and the implication that it is a fabric with gaps in which contradictions can be recognized and exploited in the name of change provide access to a significant aspect of this writer's plays.

In each of her plays the main characters either find themselves in or seek a place that is on the margins of society, most often in spaces that are defined by institutions that exist in tension with each other. In *New Anatomies* Isabelle Eberhardt attempts to escape an oppressive European culture by living a nomadic existence in the deserts of northern Africa. Instead of finding the freedom she seeks, she is caught between the accepting nomads, who, like herself, love to roam the desert, and the French colonial government, which resists allowing a woman dressed as a man free movement in the arid wastes. A similar structure exists in *The Grace of Mary Traverse*, in which Mary rebels against the rigidities of gender difference in eighteenth-century England by leaving her father's home in favor of the streets of London. There she experiences the vagaries of male existence, its cruelties and its power, in a search for an identity that will resemble her sense of herself and that will quench her thirst for knowledge. The prisoners do not actively seek free spaces in *Our Country's Good*, but find themselves transported to Australia for crimes and misdemeanors. Rehearsing a production of *The Recruiting Officer* by George Farquhar, they encounter each other in a collaborative activity and begin to perceive the world through the eyes of each other. In Wertenbaker's more recent plays the spaces in which the characters move are more difficult to identify. In *The Break of Day* the women find themselves caught between values they had as young feminists and the realities of aging and their desire to have children. One of the women, in her determination to have children, encounters the medical establishment, while another becomes engaged in the bureaucracy of adoption. Both of these women are, at the same time, confronting the stresses these encounters create in their marriages and the workplace.

The institutions that define the limits of the characters' ability to act espouse values and expect certain modes of behavior. The most obvious example is the incarceration and transportation of the criminals in *Our Country's Good.* The prisoners are expected to behave in certain ways, and failure to do so results in corporal punishment, in this case either flogging or hanging. In *The Break of Day* Tess must either continue to pay for the medical interventions that hold out diminishing hopes that she will become pregnant or surrender the hope of having a child. In both cases, and in the other plays as well, there is a degree of coercion and surveillance that attempts to control the lives of and determine the values of the characters. By locating her stories between institutions that have competing values and less authority over the decisions and discoveries made by the characters, Wertenbaker provides a locale in which her people can experiment with choices and exercise a greater degree of free will.

By using spaces that exist on the margins of institutional authority, Wertenbaker gives her characters the opportunity to try out new identities, to resist ideologies imposed on them as they grew up, and to create a subjectivity for themselves. These are not utopian spaces, however, for they are fraught with dangers. Mary Traverse experiences disease and penury and causes the death of hundreds when she dons the cloak of masculinity in *The Grace of Mary Traverse*, while in *The Love of the Nightingale* Philomela has her tongue cut out for speaking out against her rape. Tess loses everything—her marriage, her house, her money—in the futile quest to become pregnant. For others, the ability to find a space in which to play with the possibilities of being is a positive experience that gives them a sense of agency and the ability to recognize their potential. Isabelle Eberhardt finds satisfaction roaming with her Arab friends, and the prisoners in *Our Country's Good* encounter a new way of living together through the process of creating theater. There is no guarantee for Wertenbaker's people as they move in the liminal space that exists at the interstices of ideology, but there is potential for self-definition if the right choices are made. The meaning of her plays seems to lie in the values that determine the choices the characters make, whether they choose to fit into the outlines of an existing identity or locate a way of being that fits the contours of their own desires.

ASSESSMENT

It is difficult to assess the work of someone who is in midcareer. Timberlake Wertenbaker continues to be productive as a playwright and appears to be moving in new directions as the themes of her plays become more sophisticated and complex. What does seem clear is that she remains committed to exploring the complex lives of women who struggle to express themselves and their experiences. Her playing out of these conflicts between individuals and the institutions that obstruct her characters' efforts to establish their own identity raise issues of moral and ethical dimensions that seem likely to resonate beyond the limited perspective of the present time. Whether or not she is right in believing in the power of theater to transform is an open question. What is less open to question is the power and individuality of Wertenbaker's voice and her commitment to exploring the struggles of women against a society that seems determined to limit their ability to experience and express themselves. As long as she is able to pursue these issues with the same passion and intelligence, with the love of language and belief in her characters, Timberlake Wertenbaker will be a significant voice in the theater and in literature.

BIBLIOGRAPHY

Primary Sources

Case to Answer. Kentucky: University of Kentucky Library, 1980.

Abel's Sister. Kentucky: University of Kentucky Library, 1984.

New Anatomies. London: Faber, 1984.

Leocadia. In *Five Plays*, by Jean Anouilh. Trans. Timberlake Wertenbaker. London: Methuen, 1987.

Our Country's Good. London: Methuen, 1988.

The Children. Kentucky: University of Kentucky Library, 1989.

False Admission, Successful Strategies, La Dispute: Three Plays by Marivaux. Trans. Timberlake Wertenbaker. Bath: Absolute Classics, 1989.

The Love of the Nightingale and The Grace of Mary Traverse. London and Boston: Faber, 1989.

Do Not Disturb. Kentucky: University of Kentucky Library, 1990.

Interview with John L. DiGaetani. In *A Search for a Postmodern Theater: Interviews with Contemporary Playwrights*. Ed. John L. DiGaetani. New York: Greenwood, 1991. 270–271.

The Thebans: Oedipus Tyrannos, Oedipus at Colonus, and Antigone. London: Faber, 1992.

Three Birds Alighting on a Field. London: Faber, 1992.

The Break of Day. London: Faber, 1995.

Plays One. London: Faber, 1996.

After Darwin. London: Faber, 1998.

The Ash Girl. London: Faber, 2000.

Credible Witness. London: Faber, 2001.

Plays Two. London: Faber, 2002.

Secondary Sources

Aston, Elaine. "Geographies of Oppression: The Cross-Border Politics of (M)othering: *The Break of Day* and *A Yearning*." *Theatre Research International* 24.3 (Autumn 1999): 247–253.

Baker, Russell. "Makes You Think." *New York Times* 18 May 1991: 1:23.

Bimberg, Christiane. "Caryl Churchill's *Top Girls* and Timberlake Wertenbaker's *Our Country's Good* as Contributions to a Definition of Culture." *Connotations* 7.3 (1997–1998): 399–416.

Brustein, Robert. "Robert Brustein on Theater: Dress-up Plays." *New Republic* 19 June 1991: 29–30.

Canning, Charlotte. "Feminists Perform Their Past: Constructing History in *The Heidi Chronicles* and *The Break of Day*." Unpublished manuscript.

Cantacuzino, Marina. "Why Writing Came Second." *Sunday Times* 6 April 1986: C49.

Carlson, Susan. "Issues of Identity, Nationality, and Performance: The Reception of Two Plays by Timberlake Wertenbaker." *New Theatre Quarterly* 35 (August 1993): 267–289.

———. "Self and Sexuality: Contemporary British Women Playwrights and the Problems of Sexual Identity." *Journal of Dramatic Theory and Criticism* 3.2 (1989): 157–178.

———. *Women and Comedy: Rewriting the British Theatrical Tradition*. Ann Arbor: U of Michigan P 1991.

Cartledge, Paul. "Colonus in Colour." *TLS* 22 November 1991: 18.

Case, Sue Ellen. "The Power of Sex: English Plays by Women, 1958–1988." *New Theatre Quarterly* 7 (1991): 238–245.

Chaillet, Ned. "Timberlake Wertenbaker." In *Contemporary Dramatists*. Ed. D.L. Kirkpatrick. 4th ed. Chicago: St. James, 1988. 553–555.

Collings, Matthew. Rev. of *Three Birds Alighting on a Field*. *City Limits* 19 September 1991.

Cook, Rena. Rev. of *The Love of the Nightingale*. *Theatre Journal* 45 (October 1993): 381–382.

Cousin, Geraldine. "Revisiting the Prozorovs." *Modern Drama* 40 (Fall 1997): 325–336.

Crew, Robert. "Don't Ask Wertenbaker Why They Named Her Timberlake." *Toronto Star* 19 December 1986: 20.

Cropper, Martin. "London Theatre: Open and Closet." *The Times* 24 October 1985: 17.

Dahl, Mary Karen. "Constructing the Subject: Timberlake Wertenbaker's *The Grace of Mary Traverse*." *Journal of Dramatic Theory and Criticism* 7 (Spring 1993): 149–159.

Davis, Jim. "Festive Irony: Aspects of British Theatre in the 1980s." *Critical Survey* 3.3 (1991): 339–350.

———. "A Play for England: The Royal Court Adapts *The Playmaker*." In *Novel Images: Literature in Performance*. Ed. Peter Reynolds. London: Routledge, 1993. 175–190.

De Vries, Hilary. "Of Convicts, Brutality, and the Power of Theater." *New York Times* 30 September 1990: 339–350.

———. "This Angry Young Man Is a Woman." *Los Angeles Times/Calendar* 10 September 1989: H10.

Dymkowski, Christine. " 'The Play's the Thing': The Metatheatre of Timberlake Wertenbaker." In *Drama on Drama*. Ed. Nicole Boireau. New York: St. Martin's, 1997. 121–135.

Fenton, James. "Marriage by Design." *Sunday Times* 13 November 1983: 38.

Fitzsimmons, Linda. "The Use and Interrogation of Myth and Myth-Making in the Work of Timberlake Wertenbaker." Paper presented at "Breaking the Surface," November 1991, Calgary, Alberta.

Foster, Verna N. "Conflicts, Characters, and Conventions of Acting in Timberlake Wertenbaker's *Our Country's Good.*" *Connotations* 7.3 (1997–1998): 417–432.

Gardner, Lynn. Rev. of *The Grace of Mary Traverse. Plays and Players* 387 (December 1985): 24.

Gussow, Mel. "Of Convicts, the Stage, and Australia's Beginnings." *New York Times* 21 October 1990: 1, 59.

———. "A Sexual Cover-up in 'New Anatomies.' " *New York Times* 22 February 1990: C19.

Hewison, Robert. "An Affair of the Heart." *Sunday Times* 12 August 1984: G37.

Hornby, Richard. "*Our Country's Good.*" *Hudson Review* 44 (Autumn 1991): 455–456.

Inverso, Mary Beth. "*Der Straf-block*: Performance and Execution in Barnes, Griffiths, and Wertenbaker." *Modern Drama* 36 (1993): 420–430.

Irwin, Robert. "The Game of Camels." *TLS* 16 March 1990: 284.

James, John. "Laughing through Tears." *TLS* 16 September 1988: 36.

Kennedy, Douglas. "Hey Big Spender." *New Statesman and Society* 8 December 1989: 44–45.

Kingston, Jeremy. "Masterpiece Alight with Truth." *The Times* 12 September 1991: 20.

———. "Tedious and Trivial Pursuit." *The Times* 10 June 1992: Life and Times 3.

Kramer, Mimi. "Our Culture's Good." *New Yorker* 20 May 1991: 94–95.

LaRue, Michele. "*Our Country's Good*: Three Approaches to a Play about Theatre and Australian History." *Theatre Crafts* 25.3 (1991): 40–43, 61, 63, 65–70.

MacCarthy, Fiona. Rev. of *Three Birds Alighting on a Field. TLS* 20 September 1991: 18.

Mackay, Shena. Rev. of *The Break of Day. TLS* 22 December 1995: 18.

Martin, Mick. "Sloane Square Savages." *Guardian* 31 August 1988.

Mason, John Hope. "Formality and Abandon." *TLS* 25 November 1983: 1323.

Masters, Anthony. "Theatre: *Successful Strategies.*" *The Times* 16 November 1983: D10.

McDonough, Carla J. "Timberlake Wertenbaker." In *British Playwrights, 1956–1995: A Research and Production Sourcebook.* Ed. William W. Demastes. Westport, CT: Greenwood, 1996. 406–415.

Mcmurray, Emily J. "Timberlake Wertenbaker." In *Contemporary Theatre, Film, and Television.* Vol. 10. Detroit: Gale, 1993: 435–436.

Morley, Sheridan. "Gender Is Not the Case." *The Times* 7 November 1988: 20.

Neill, Heather. "Theban Marathon Enters Stratford." *Sunday Times* 17 October 1991: 6:9.

Nokes, David. "Stage Struck on the Fatal Shore." *TLS* 23 September 1988: 1049.

Patrick, Tony. "Mysterious, Beautiful Silence." *The Times* 24 August 1989: 16.

Peter, John. "The Moving Lessons That History Can Teach Us." *Sunday Times* 18 September 1988: C11.

———. "Political Realism Crushed by Paranoia." *Sunday Times* 11 March 1990: E4.

———. "The Shock of the New." *Sunday Times* 27 October 1985: D43.

Rabey, David Ian. "Defining Difference: Timberlake Wertenbaker's Drama of Language, Dispossession, and Discovery." *Modern Drama* 33.4 (December 1990): 518–528.

Radin, Victoria. "Sex for Sale." *New Statesman* 8 November 1985: 32.

Richards, David. "In the Language of Lockjaw, Subtext Is All." *New York Times* 19 May 1991: H28.

Ritchie, Martha. " 'Almost Better to Be Nobody': Feminist Subjectivity, the Thatcher Years, and Timberlake Wertenbaker's *The Grace of Mary Traverse.*" *Modern Drama* 39 (1996): 404–420.

Rubik, Margarete. "The Silencing of Women in Feminist British Drama." In *Semantics of Silences in Linguistics and Literature.* Ed. Gudrun M. Grabher and Ulrike Jessner. Heidelberg: Universitätsverlag C. Winter, 1996. 177–190.

Seibert, Gary. "Theatre: Under the London Sun." *America* 9 September 1989: 145.

Simon, John. "Shows within Shows." *New York* 13 May 1991: 88, 90.

Stafford-Clark, Max. *Letters to George: The Account of a Rehearsal.* London: Nick Hern, 1989.

Stephenson, Heide, and Natasha Langridge, eds. *Rage and Reason: Women Playwrights on Playwriting.* London: Methuen, 1997.

Sullivan, Esther Beth. "Hailing Ideology, Acting in the Horizon, and Reading between Plays by Timberlake Wertenbaker." *Theatre Journal* 42.5 (March 1993): 139–154.

Taylor, Val. "Mothers of Invention: Female Characters in *Our Country's Good* and *The Playmaker.*" *Critical Survey* 3.3 (1991): 331–338.

Wagner, Jennifer A. "Formal Parody and the Metamorphosis of the Audience in Timberlake Wertenbaker's *The Love of the Nightingale.*" *Papers on Language and Literature* (Summer 1995): 227–254.

Wilson, Ann. "The English Stage Company Visits the Canadian Stage Company." *Queen's Quarterly* 97 (Spring 1990): 140–153.

———. "Forgiving History and Making New Worlds: Timberlake Wertenbaker's Recent Drama." In *British and Irish Drama since 1960*. Ed. James Acheson. New York: St. Martin's, 1993. 146–161.

———. "*Our Country's Good*: Theatre, Colony, and Nation in Wertenbaker's Adaptation of *The Playmaker*." *Modern Drama* 34.1 (March 1991): 23–34.

Winston, Joe. "Re-casting the Phaedra Syndrome: Myth and Morality in Timberlake Wertenbaker's *The Love of the Nightingale*." *Modern Drama* 38 (1995): 510–519.

Wolf, Matt. "Love Returns to Court." *The Times* 9 September 1991: Arts 11.

Wright, Michael. "New Anatomies." *The Times* 9 March 1990: 16.

Young, Stuart. "Fin-de-Siècle Reflections and Revision: Wertenbaker Challenges British Chekhov Tradition in *The Break of Day*." *Modern Drama* 41.3 (Fall 1998): 442–460.

Mary Wesley
1912–

Beverly E. Schneller

Mary Wesley published her first novel at seventy, in 1982. By 1999 she had issued eleven more, and two children's books. She concentrates her stories largely on women in the society, constructing plots with wit and sensitivity. Her fiction explores the complexities of family life and family loyalty, and she uses irony, humor, and realistic detail to draw insightful portraits of human nature. The tone with which she writes is key to the absence of moralism, as her works are not didactic. They possess intellectual and structural depths sufficient to raise them above romantic ephemera. Wesley's heroines are typically at odds with social conventions in some fashion, only modestly radical in their behaviors, successful in their endeavors. They seek to mold society to match their emerging characters and personal aspirations. While some of the books end in marriage, others end with the heroine's suicide or decision to return to single life.

BACKGROUND

Wesley was born on June 24, 1912, in Englefield Green, Berkshire, England. She presently resides in Devon, and many of her novels are set in the countryside of England. Her parents were Colonel Mynors and Violet Dalby Farmer. She attended Queen's College (1928–1929) and the London School of Economics (1931). Because her father was in the military, she moved around as a child, and she described herself in an interview with a British magazine after her first novel was published as not very well educated, saying that she was deficient in classical languages and history. In 1937 she married Lord Swinfen, and during World War II she worked in the War Office in London (1939–1941). Her first marriage ended in divorce in 1950, and she married Eric Siepman, a journalist, in 1951. After his death from Parkinson's disease in 1970, Wesley turned to novel writing, initially as a way to restore structure in her life. In 1995 Wesley was honored with the CBE. In addition to eleven novels, she also has published two children's books, and four of her novels have been filmed: *The Camomile Lawn*, *Harnessing Peacocks*, *Jumping the Queue*, and *Not That Sort of Girl*. She is the mother of three sons.

ANALYSIS

Wesley's novels are family dramas. In most she develops multilayered plots over many years to provide a comprehensive style of character development. Readers can easily see the heroine as a product of a family and a specific social environment. Wesley employs dialogue, such description as is necessary to create settings or physical traits in the characters, irony, humor, and limited symbolism. Usually the title of the novel is taken from the dialogue. The novels are set in the twentieth century and feature precise geographical detail, including road names and English train timetable information. Her novels are predominantly told in the third person, and she uses linear and nonlinear plots depending on the story. While Wesley's novels have recurring thematic elements and similarly structured plots, each female protagonist is distinctive and captures the readers' interest.

The novels can be compared to those of Jane Austen (1775–1817), George Eliot (1819–1880), Ivy Compton-Burnett (1884–1969), and Elizabeth Bowen (1899–1973). All five of these novelists convey the individual woman's need to find a suitable place in society, which is already full-blown and uncompromising. Wesley is like Elizabeth Bowen, whose novels also focus on "history and generations, with the changes in the transmissions of ethical values from one generation to another. . . . morality involves relationships, the quality of interchange between one person and another, and cannot be developed in isolation" (Gindin 30). Calypso Grant, who is first introduced in *The Camomile Lawn* (1984) and reappears in *The Vacillations of Poppy Carew* (1986), *Second Fiddle* (1988), and *A Dubious Legacy* (1992), bridges the multiple generations of social change and stagnation, first coming on the scene as a young woman in the 1940s and appearing as the older, experienced aunt in later novels. She is something of a bellwether. Sensuous and sexual, Calypso is admired by both sexes; yet, unlike the nymph of Ogygia, her attractiveness to men is not harmful. That her marriage to an older man is stable and lasts until his death in no way compromises Calypso's own dignity and integrity, for Wesley's Calypso embodies the endurance of passion with love. She is as striking as the calypso orchid and as vibrant, in Wesley's quiet landscapes, as the improvised calypso songs of Trinidad. Compared to the other characters in the novels, she is exotic and challenging, to both their opinions and their patterns of living. How the characters react to her sexual reputation is an indication of their own senses of ethical values and morality in relationships. From *Jumping the Queue* to *Part of the Furniture*, Wesley shows a repeated attraction to subjects that people sometimes have difficulty talking about or accepting; or, as Aruna Vasudevan has expressed, "[S]he deals with seemingly taboo subjects" (1040). A survey of her novels will show how she has developed unity in her style, and how she has established a specific voice in her fiction.

In *Jumping the Queue* (1983) Wesley brings Mathilda Poliport, a widow in her fifties, and Hugh Warner, in his thirties, together in an unlikely situation—they are both trying to commit suicide. She has developed an elaborate plan involving an apparent accidental drowning, while he is about to jump off a bridge when Poliport stops him. Her interference strikes up a relationship over a period of weeks, in which she learns the truth behind Warner's so-called matricide and reveals that her husband was a drug smuggler and spy; how untrustworthy her "friends" really are; and how much zest for life she really has. She takes up with Warner for the adventure of hiding a wanted man, and when he leaves, she completes her planned suicide.

The primary technique of the story's telling is dialogue in which irony plays a central role. The story, as it unfolds, shatters the veneer of the Poliports' family unity. The descriptions are specific, and the psychological development is carried forward within the plot. The primary themes involve honesty, love, fidelity, and problems with parent-child relationships. Mathilda's children betray her love by neglect, and in the end she is more attached to the memories of her dead pets, who loved her unconditionally, and to her affection for Warner than to her own offspring. Mathilda, in preventing Warner's death, may have done him a disservice, however, as he will be the bearer of sorrow for both his own mother's and Mathilda's deaths.

Harnessing Peacocks (1985) is the story of Hebe Rutter, who defies her grandparents and at seventeen gives birth to a son, Silas. This story confronts prejudice, prostitution, and illegitimacy as Hebe insists on a place in society for herself and her son as a single-parent family. The plot is centered on a week in the Christmas season when Silas accepts an invitation to visit the Scillies with a school chum, Michael Reeves. Silas cannot stand the quarreling between the two parents and runs home after a boating accident in which he, who cannot swim, is nearly drowned. Hebe, who works as a cook for elderly ladies (and a prostitute in a syndicate she operates), does not get the message about Silas's returning home and is frantic that he has become lost. A subplot involves Bernard Quigley and Jim Huxtable, both antique dealers who are friends. Huxtable wants to know Hebe better, but she fends him off. Huxtable finds Silas at Hebe's home and takes him to Quigley's, where he is reunited with his mother. Huxtable is Silas's father, and as the novel closes, Hebe and Huxtable, aware of this now, agree to get to know one another better, with marriage as the likely result.

The construction of this family drama is similar to those of Ivy Compton-Burnett; in fact, there is an allusion to Hebe's respecting her "elders and betters," the title of one of Compton-Burnett's novels. Hebe is open about her prostitution; Hannah, Hebe's neighbor, is involved with a black man, Terry, who wears women's underwear; and abortion, adultery, and vulgar talk are bandied about. While Compton-Burnett's style was more prim, both authors expose the flaws of civilization with wit and compassion. Hebe is another orphaned female in literature, made to find her own way using her wits, and showing a willingness to defy convention by deliberately compromising her sexual reputation. If she becomes involved with Jim Huxtable, she has given up her chance at independence, but Silas's happiness and success are her central concerns. The potential marriage is not self-destructive, however, as it will replace her precarious economic existence. *A Part of the Furniture* (1997) is similar in plot and overall style to *Harnessing Peacocks*.

The Vacillations of Poppy Carew (1986), like *A Sensible Life* (1990), establishes several sexual relationships for the heroine and ends with an apparently successful marriage. Both novels use physical violence in their telling and are set in locations other than England. Poppy Carew finds herself in North Africa, while some of *A Sensible Life* occurs in India. Poppy Carew has some humorous incidents in her life, while Flora Trevelyan does not. Also, like *A Dubious Legacy* (1992), *Poppy Carew* has a complex, multilayered plot that includes Calypso Grant in a small role. Carew has ended a tempestuous affair with Edmund Platt at the start of the novel. Her father dies, and she engages Furnival's Fun Funerals at Bob Carew's request to handle the burial. It is supposed to be Furnival's Fine Funerals, but there was a rather significant typo, which turned out to be good for business after all. The people of Furnival's provide a full-blown subplot featuring Fergus Furnival, mother and son, Mary and Barnaby, and Victor Lucas, Fergus's cousin. Fergus is Barnaby's father, but he does not know this until the end of the novel. When news of Bob Carew's death hits the papers, Platt decides to try to reconcile with Poppy, even though he is involved with another woman. After the funeral Carew and Platt travel to North Africa, where on the third day of business, which is not going well, he gets drunk and beats her badly. She breaks his leg with a chair and goes to the airport. Meanwhile, Will Guthrie, Calypso Grant's nephew, has met and fallen in love with Carew. She was fleeing her feelings for him when she left England with Pratt. Grant finds out where

Carew is and sends Guthrie to intercept her, which he does. Later, as she and Guthrie are driving to his farm in the country, they are forced off the road by fog, and she is pinned under a lorry. She decides that she wants to remain with Guthrie while she is waiting for help to arrive: a wicked way to end her vacillations.

A Sensible Life (1990) takes up the abandoned female, love, marriage, duty, and honor as its themes. It is similar to *Second Fiddle* (1988) in that Flora Trevelyan, like Laura Thornby, chooses a single life, but Flora abandons it for marriage to Cosmo Leigh, whom she has known since her childhood. Flora is an unwanted daughter of a military couple posted to India, and late in the story she is revealed not to be Denis Trevelyan's child, but the product of her mother's affair with another man. Flora is in a love triangle for much of the story, which follows her into late middle age, when she has established herself in a village on the English coast. Cosmo finds her there, and they agree to marry, mainly so they will not grow old alone. *A Sensible Life* can be successfully approached from the perspective of myth criticism as Flora provides an opportunity to examine the woman-in-the-green-world pattern. She retreats into nature to find herself and to experience a "bridge to the wider universe" (Pratt 131) of self-determinacy and transforming isolation. When Flora elects to marry, she joins the other heroines who have given up the ideal of a perfect mate and allows herself to be led back into the normative patterns of male-female relations. Even so, as with Poppy Carew, the reader is led to accept her "anti-normative point of view" (Pratt 113) as acceptable and desirable. Ultimately, Wesley's novels reject the patterns of social development in which "the authors conceive of growing up as a female as a choice between auxiliary or secondary personhood, sacrificial victimization, madness, and death" (Pratt 36). Instead, her novels offer a blend of selfhood and social integration that provides realism in her fiction.

A Dubious Legacy (1992) is a family novel of the sort that Wesley wrote in *The Camomile Lawn* and *An Imaginative Experience* (1994). Using the multilayering of *A Sensible Life*, this is the story of Henry Tillotson from his youth as a soldier in 1944 to his death in 1990. The title refers to his wife, Margaret, his two illegitimate daughters, and the legacy of his father, do-gooder and man-about-the-village. Margaret is a focal character, with her agoraphobia and violent temper. Henry married her in Egypt as a favor to his father. The plot addresses the consequences of Henry's affairs with the fiancées of two of his friends, and the two children, Hillarie and Clio, who are produced. These two are Henry's loyal caretakers at his death. Margaret drowns in the lake when Susan, another child, tries to teach her to swim. Or, at least, that is how it seems. The major themes in this novel are deception, lying, pride, and family loyalty. Henry is surrounded by women in this novel, which covers forty-six years and several generations of different families. In its chronology it is the most ambitious of Wesley's couples novels and employs several different examples of marriages, including that of Calypso and Hector Grant.

ASSESSMENT

Mary Wesley presents female characters who eventually gain control of their environments and achieve the ends they seek for themselves. Choices, challenges, decision making, and responsibility are part of each character from Mathilda Poliport to Juno Marlowe. Aruna Vasudevan describes Wesley's heroines as "misfits," which to some degree they are (1040). However, Wesley's characters seem more like the "talented heroines" Susan Siefert studies in the fiction of Jane Austen, the Brontës, and George Eliot. What Siefert writes of Eliot's heroines is applicable to Wesley's as well: "None of these heroines exhibits an extreme or uncompromising stance with relation to her social world. While each of them dwells in a society which has stereotyped expectations for young ladies, no one heroine aspires to or is capable of completely fulfilling these social demands" (7). Avoiding feminist stereotyping of characters as reactors to patriarchal oppression, Wesley offers characters who work within society, making modest adjustments within themselves and with those who are susceptible to change. Belonging to a community or electing to strike out on one's own is repeatedly shown as the thoughtful outcome of each woman's effort at individuation.

The tensions in Wesley's novels do not result from the destruction of the heroine, though she may be attached to more than one man in the course of the story. Wesley's woman, while finding herself in situations similar to Thomas Hardy's Tess or Virginia Woolf's Mrs. Dalloway, does not fail "to reconcile opposing forces within herself" (Daleski 4). Yet, like the "divided heroines" Daleski studies, Wesley's protagonists are self-divided and pulled in opposing directions. But because they do not all self-destruct, Wesley's novels return to the novel-of-manners style, in which the heroine's choices lead to a better, more productive environment for herself and her circle.

Wesley's characters expose how social conventions suppress individuality, but like Austen, Fanny Burney, and Eliot, Wesley makes her characters understand themselves more clearly through integration into, not rejection of, societal strictures. All the characters in her landscapes are fully aware of society and family as "shaping forces . . . through which [they] read themselves and others" (Bowers and Brothers 13). Wesley's tone, like Bowen's and Compton-Burnett's, remains key to her novels' successes. She approaches human nature from a nonjudgmental stance and leaves the evaluation of the characters' lives, actions, and outcomes in the hands of the readers.

BIBLIOGRAPHY

Primary Sources

The Sixth Seal. London: Macdonald, 1969.
Speaking Terms. London: Faber, 1969.
Haphazard House. London: Dent, 1983.
Jumping the Queue. London: Macmillan, 1983.
The Camomile Lawn. London: Macmillan, 1984.
Harnessing Peacocks. London: Macmillan, 1985.
The Vacillations of Poppy Carew. London: Macmillan, 1986.
Not That Sort of Girl. London: Macmillan, 1987.
Second Fiddle. London: Macmillan, 1988.
A Sensible Life. London: Bantam, 1990.
A Dubious Legacy. London: Bantam, 1992.
An Imaginative Experience. London: Bantam, 1994.
Part of the Furniture. London: Bantam, 1997.

Secondary Sources

Bowers, Bege K., and Barbara Brothers. *Reading and Writing Women's Lives: A Study of the Novel of Manners*. Ann Arbor: UMI, 1990.
Daleski, H.M. *The Divided Heroine: A Recurrent Pattern in Six English Novels*. New York: Holmes & Meier, 1984.
Gindin, James. "Ethical Structures in John Galsworthy, Elizabeth Bowen, and Iris Murdoch." In *Forms of Modern British Fiction*. Ed. Alan Warren Friedman. Austin: U of Texas P, 1975. 15–41.
"Mary Wesley." *Something about the Author* 66 (1991): 227–228.
Pratt, Annis. *Archetypal Patterns in Women's Fiction*. Bloomington: Indiana UP, 1981.
Siefert, Susan E. *The Dilemma of the Talented Heroine*. St. Albans, VT: Eden, 1977.
Vasudevan, Aruna. "Mary Wesley." In *Contemporary Novelists*. 6th ed. Ed. Susan W. Brown. Detroit: St. James, 1996. 1040–1041.

Rebecca West
1892–1983

Sarah Miles Watts

Rebecca West, Dame of the British Empire, revealed her rebellious individualism for almost a century in her wide-ranging works, most memorably journalism. As her pseudonym eclipsed her genteel given name and embraced Ibsen's heroine in *Rosmersholm* (in which she appeared during her short theatrical career), so did her writing reach beyond daily journalism to probing moral absolutism about literature as art; government and responsibility; and humans' lust for death. At West's memorial service the paradox of her work surfaced. Edward Crankshaw said that West had not reached the first rank of novelists because "she was too much concerned with tearing open the pretenses and disguises with which her characters covered themselves." Yet, he concluded, she hewed closely to the truth because her vision transcended her shortcomings (Rollyson 429).

Influenced by her family, fellow writers, and political ideas, she nevertheless upheld her individualism. In her masterpiece, *Black Lamb and Grey Falcon*, she explained that she wrote "to discover for my own edification what I knew about various subjects which I found to be important to me" (Orel 1).

BACKGROUND

Rebecca West was born Cicily Isabel Fairfield in 1892 to Scotch-Irish parents, both of whom were to appear as characters in her fiction. Her mother, Isabella, was a pianist of strong character who West believed could understand anything; her father, Charles, was a military man and journalist, but a deserter, unable to provide his family financial security, whom West came to consider brilliant but flawed (West, *Fountain* 218; Glendinning 23).

Tuberculosis interrupted West's formal education and led to her and her two sisters' solitary activities, confirming their faith in music and thinking as the important things in life (Ray 4). West finished George Watson's Ladies College and went to study acting at the Royal Academy of Dramatic Arts until dismissal for having "no personality" (Orel 6; Deakin, *Rebecca West* 31; Rollyson 32). West plunged into journalism, where her work in the *Freewoman*, the *Clarion*, and the *New Freewoman* made "not so much a splash, as a hole in the world" (Glendinning 40). Far beyond a "beat" reporter, she studied life from the angle of the suffrage movement and Fabian Socialism. Her oft-quoted September 29, 1912, *Freewoman* attack on H.G. Wells's style and ideas of sex in his novel *Marriage* aroused his interest for years. She called him "the old maid among novelists; [with a] sex obsession that lay clotted" (Ray 2, Orel 6, Weldon 34). Although he was married, he invited her to his home, and they soon became lovers, naming their battling selves "Panther" (West) and "Jaguar" (Wells) (Ray 36).

West became pregnant, never considered abortion, and wrote prodigiously, moving from feminist periodicals to Fleet Street's *Daily News and Leader* (Rollyson 51). Her son's birth, on August 4, 1914, when England declared war on Germany, signaled their lifelong quarrels and began another battle with Wells over the child's upbringing and Wells's continual infidelities. "In all my life," he says in his experiment in autobiography, "I do not know if I loved Rebecca West, though I was certainly in love with her toward the latter part of our liaison" (Wells 96).

He encouraged her writing, secured jobs for her (*New Republic*), shared his literary agent J.B. Pinker for the publication of *Henry James*, and noted their differences in approach: "She writes like a loom producing her broad rich fabric with hardly a thought of how it will make up into shape, while I write to cover a frame of ideas. We did harm to each other as writers" (Wells 102). Yet they wove each other into their work, such as West's *Return of the Soldier*, inspired by Wells's two wives, Isabel and Jane, and Wells's *World of William Clissold* and *The Research Magnificent* with characters suggestive of her (Ray 160). Entwined as West was with Wells and involved as she was with other literary figures such as Ford Madox Ford, Ezra Pound, and Wyndham Lewis, she never became part of a literary circle. Furthermore, West rejected earlier beliefs in communism, siding with Emma Goldman's radical rejection of Bolshevist Russia as tyrannical.

As she changed her politics, so did she change her literary outlets, reflecting her individualism in all ways. After World War I she became book critic for the *New Statesman and Nation* and also contributed articles to *Time and Tide* and *Leader* (Packer xi). In 1923 West began a long-deferred American tour intended to ensure the end of her relationship with Wells. Preceded by her literary reputation as a journalist and novelist (*The Return of the Soldier* and *The Judge*), she became literary contributor to the *Herald Tribune*, *Bookman*, and the Hearst organization (Glendinning 96). She collected her literary essays in *The Strange Necessity* and *Ending in Earnest* and published her favorite novel, *Harriet Hume*.

West's numerous liaisons led to psychoanalytic therapy in 1927 to discover why she seemed to emasculate men (Rollyson 114) and to learn about dark interests in Eros and Thanatos (Hall 77). She married Henry Maxwell Andrews in 1930, as English as she was exotic (former mistress, staunch feminist), which made a "trying yet enduring marriage" (Rollyson 143). While her Edwardian upbringing stressed the necessity for a man in the house, her father's desertion and her husband's sexual abstinence contributed to her ambivalence toward men (Hall 76), whom she called "congenitally flawed lunatics."

West's considerable income in the 1930s came from her journalism on both sides of the Atlantic, a new exclusive arrangement with the *Daily Telegraph* until 1982, and short stories that became books like *The Harsh Voice*. Her interest in study of the religious mind led to the *St. Augustine* biography, and her moral conscience took her to Germany, where she wrote about her fear of the apocalypse in the *New York American*. Her continued interest in socialism took her again to the United States in 1935 for a series of articles on the New Deal for British and American journals (Rollyson 170).

Her only funny novel, *The Thinking Reed*, was her last novel for twenty years as she turned to nonfiction about the war, *The*

Meaning of Treason, *The New Meaning of Treason*, and *Black Lamb and Grey Falcon*. After World War II she explained her change of position from her younger rebellious self to her current anti-Communist critique of the Left for not combating tyranny (Rollyson 284). Unmoved by accusations of shifting to the Right, she suffered charges of pro-McCarthyism for her moral anti-Communist stance (Rollyson 291). The magnitude of her position appeared in a 1953 series of articles in the London *Sunday Times*, reprinted in *U.S. News and World Report* (Rollyson 287).

Nothing daunted her individualistic spirit, not even operations, infections, and chronic medical complaints (Glendinning 179). She always held a moral view, as she did at Yale in her lectures on literature's social significance, compiled into *The Court and the Castle*. This coincided with the first of her family trilogy, *The Fountain Overflows*, her best-selling and best-loved novel (Glendinning 209), followed by several posthumous publications.

More journalism ensued, including a *Sunday Times* series that continued her moral position against apartheid. Calling journalism "an ability to meet the challenge of filling the space," she prided herself on deadline writing and suffered only one lost defamation suit, that of a judge of the South African Supreme Court, in 1958 (Orel 25). After her husband's death in 1968 and a robbery at Ibstone House, she took a flat in Kensington, where she observed the literary and political scene.

West started many ambitious projects in her later years, such as *The Only Poet*, a novel probing the male psyche, and constantly rewrote them (Rollyson 385). She contributed to Warren Beatty's film *Reds* (1981), the BBC adaptation of *The Birds Fall Down*, and the film of *The Return of the Soldier*. She gave an interview to Bill Moyers for American television and continued reviews for the *Telegraph* and the *Sunday Telegraph* until 1982 (Orel 28). If she had to do it all over again, she said, she would have concentrated on fiction (Orel 29). In interviews her bleak and brutal remarks may account for critics' restraint in summations of her career (Orel 30). She never ceased her quarrels with her son (Rollyson 398). All her life she rebelled, her passionate nature surfacing in her prose, heightened by individualistic moral vision (Hall 79).

ANALYSIS

West has not received due attention from scholarly critics (Packer xviii) because of varied interests and shifting politics. Scholarly efforts to name a controlling principle range from her treatment of human dignity to the Manichaean doctrine of good and evil. But her work is best seen as a dark vision of humanity in search of moral order and justice. It stemmed from almost a century of living through two world wars, terrorism, social uprootedness, communism, fascism, and Nazism—and her personal grievances—that convinced her that all human beings yearned for death. As Leslie Garis said, "She perceives man's nature as divided between a lust for death and suffering, on the one hand, and a redeeming, life-sustaining faith in justice and art on the other" (30).

Starting with her first sentence for *Freewoman* (November 30, 1911), "There are two kinds of imperialists—imperialists and bloody imperialists" (*The Young Rebecca* 12), she lambasted class structure, male prerogatives, and literary pretense, considering herself a left-wing journalist from the start (Orel 7). Fierce and funny and Celtic, and substantial, say the critics. West's early journalism rings with her youthful cries for suffrage, just wages, and improved working conditions for women, and her scathing criticism of books and officials. She was a modernist, says Margaret D. Stetz, at every stage of her career, "expressing . . . interest in the individual writer's relation to artistic tradition" (50).

At first her writing style resembled that of Henry James, although the writer she would have liked to imitate was Mark Twain (Orel 22). Besides her talent for astute perception and relatedness beyond the facts to morality, she understood that journalism was storytelling, soaring to elegiac heights and stooping to acerbic blows. She also wrote poetically and wittily, often being quoted as saying there is no reason for the existence of the male sex except that one sometimes needs help with moving the piano. Such epigrams still appear frequently.

Critic after critic characterizes her writing by its lofty moral tone and implacable belief in her own judgments. These judgments culminate in *Black Lamb and Grey Falcon*, reporting raised to literary art. She said that she wrote it as "the past comprehended in the presence of that which still exists but yet is part of that past" (Deakin 94). *Black Lamb and Grey Falcon* ranks as her magnum opus. It describes a journey to the Balkans in 1937 with a moral plot on the spiritual and lyrical greatness of the Serbs as contrasted to the half-Germanized and legalistic Slav Croats and Turkified Slav Muslims. It becomes a history of Yugoslavia's past and present, its archaeology and history, art, people, and politics, and an attempt to locate West's personal perspective at a particular time where political and moral history converge. The physical evidence of past thought and action—the statue, the church, the battlefield, the memorial plaque—is comprehended in the presence of what still exists but yet is past (Deakin, *Rebacca West* 93–94). The reality and the history of the Yugoslavian spirit West found were couched in death and the two dominant symbols, black lamb and grey falcon.

The *New York Times Book Review* (October 26, 1941) critic Katherine Woods hailed *Lamb* as "the apotheosis" of the travel book. The *New Yorker* (October 25, 1941) critic Clifton Fadiman called it "one of the great books of spiritual revolt" (Rollyson 212). John Gunther said, "[T]he conflict between love of life and love of death, applied to every sort of human problem" (Glendenning 166). But its political stance and absence of feminism elicited some negative criticism (Glendinning 214). Loretta Stec traces, through the nostalgia that grips Yugoslavia, West's conclusion that despite seeming masochism women must heroically submit to male domination in the fight for national security. *Lamb* still remains a book to consult on the Balkans, as scores of current newspapers and periodicals indicate.

With the same individualistic spirit she first exhibited against the government that denied female rights, she turned on traitors to the government, seeking to know why and to probe her goal of civilization—personal liberty—in her next most important works, *The Meaning of Treason* and the revised and expanded *The New Meaning of Treason*. Skilled as a novelist, she precedes, as fellow experimenter Truman Capote said, the movement of journalism as literature. She reports the event and the person who illuminates the fact. The first book earned recognition by *Time* magazine (December 8, 1948) as "No. 1 Woman Writer" (Rollyson 260).

A Train of Powder, a companion study to *Treason*, also is based on court trials, and it too has its origins in the search for a new moral order that followed World War II. It contains six essays written between 1946 and 1954. West's religious belief also sees God's grace as surpassing even human breakdown. She recounts trials that elicit no meaning or pattern but still affirm life's continuance (Wolfe 69). Her sense of the meaning and value of history as "an act of discovery" (Deakin, *Rebecca West* 80) appears also in *St. Augustine*. In it she finds history a collection of biographies of great men, demonstrating that man thinking is more important than man doing (Deakin, *Rebecca West* 87). Of her extensive literary criticism, Frank Kermode extols her *Court and the Castle*, a lifetime's thinking about the social significance of literature (Rollyson 310).

West's novels do not read like her journalism. They are intricate, stylized, constructed, conceptual, and argumentative (Deakin, *Rebecca West* 130). While most critics agree that her literary ability is not basically fictive, some stress a guiding vision: morality (Orlich) and mastering reality (Redd). West's dark vision surfaces in *The Judge* in its theme of the inability of love and parenthood to redeem humanity. Frank Overton praised it indiscriminately, and Patrick Braybrooke gave special praise but noted her "liability" of polemicism (Deakin, *Rebecca West* 135). Of her other novels, *The Return of the Soldier*, considered "one of the defining works of World War I," contains the "antithesis that continues throughout her work, between the will-to-die . . . and the will-to-live" (Rollyson 11).

ASSESSMENT

Upon West's death, William Shawn, then editor of the *New Yorker*, said that she was one of the giants and will have a lasting place in English literature. True, but not a high place. Her writing generally was discussed only in reviews of her books. Starting with *Henry James* she gained a reputation as a superior reporter and a second-rate novelist—though George Bernard Shaw responded, "Rebecca can handle a pen as brilliantly as ever I could, and much more savagely" (Redd 30). Other early critics saw her potential; as Patrick Braybrooke said, "[S]he has every chance of a most distinguished career in the world of letters" (*Novelists* 141), and he later added that she "is an eminent example of that school of modern women writers who are reformers first and novelists afterwards" (*Philosophies* 77). Before she was thirty, she had produced a series of reviews that Frank Swinnerton described as a model of excellence. Peter Wolfe, whose 1971 study is one of the first book-length assessments of West's work, contends that the "superior reporter" term did her an injustice considering her wide scope (vii). As for West's novels, Rollyson, her biographer, notes how West "personalized and psychologized virtually everything" (171). Her novels' mixed reviews, he asserted, were "symptomatic of West's problematic place as a novelist" (175).

West's best critic, G.E. Hutchinson, sees her in the tradition of British empiricism and as both tragic and comic in books of the delights of the mind and a connoisseur's appreciation of human individuality (Hutchinson, "Dome" 248; Wolfe 7). Samuel Hynes, whose important essay for the *Times Literary Supplement* (December 21, 1973) appears revised as the introduction to *Rebecca West: A Celebration*, suggests that West's worth is the whole of her work, the mind of Rebecca West (Orel x).

Contemporary scholars like Bonnie Kime Scott see West as a political thinker and outspoken polemicist, qualities that set her apart from traditional definitions of modernism and the nonauthoritarian style embraced by feminists and postmodernists. Although West's concern with heterosexual relations and her authoritative and masculine writing tone undermine her position with feminists today, West's binary forces of spirit and matter elevate her standing, says Scott (124).

While Victoria Glendinning in her commissioned short biography defensively and sensitively views West's private life but glosses over her literary one, and Carl Rollyson piles fact upon fact in his psychological analysis from his access to West's letters and diaries, the definitive biography of West's life and letters remains to be written. She requested a "full" one by Stanley Olson, who died. Her final place in history hinges on her complexities. As she herself said, her work as a whole could not fuse to make a portrait of a writer, since the interstices were too wide. Still, she springs from every line.

BIBLIOGRAPHY

Primary Sources

Henry James. London: Nisbet; New York: Holt, 1916.

The Return of the Soldier. London: Nisbet, 1918; New York: Popular Library, 1960.

The Judge. London: Hutchinson; New York: Doran, 1922.

Lions and Lambs. With David Low. London: Cape, 1928; New York: Harcourt, 1929.

The Strange Necessity. London: Cape; Garden City, NY: Doubleday, 1928.

Harriet Hume. London: Hutchinson, 1929; New York: Popular Library, 1957.

D.H. Lawrence. London: Secker, 1930.

Arnold Bennett Himself. New York: John Day, 1931.

Ending in Earnest: A Literary Log. Garden City, NY: Doubleday, 1931; Freeport, NY: Books for Libraries, 1967.

St. Augustine. London: Peter Davies; New York: Appleton, 1933.

The Modern "Rake's Progress." With David Low. London: Hutchinson, 1934.

The Harsh Voice: Four Short Novels. London: Jonathan Cape, 1935; Garden City, NY: Doubleday, 1936.

The Thinking Reed. London: Hutchinson, 1936; New York: Viking, 1936.

Black Lamb and Grey Falcon. New York: Viking, 1941; London: Macmillan, 1942.

The Meaning of Treason. New York: Viking, 1947; London: Macmillan, 1949.

A Train of Powder. London: Macmillan; New York: Viking, 1955.

The Fountain Overflows. New York: Viking, 1956; London: Macmillan, 1957.

The Court and the Castle: Some Treatments of a Recurrent Theme. New Haven: Yale UP, 1957. As *The Court and the Castle: A Study of the Interactions of Political and Religious Ideas in Imaginative Literature*. London: Macmillan, 1958.

The New Meaning of Treason. New York: Viking, 1964.

The Birds Fall Down. London: Macmillan; New York: Viking, 1966.

Rebecca West: A Celebration: Selected from Her Writings. New York: Viking, 1977.

1900. London: Weidenfeld, 1982; New York: Viking, 1982.

The Young Rebecca: Writings of Rebecca West, 1911–17. New York: Viking, 1982.

This Real Night. London: Macmillan, 1984; New York: Viking, 1985.

Cousin Rosamund. London: Macmillan, 1985; New York: Viking, 1986.

Sunflower. London: Virago, 1986; New York: Viking, 1987.

Family Memories. London: Virago, 1987; New York: Viking, 1988.

Secondary Sources

Braybrooke, Patrick. *Novelists We Are Seven*. 1926. Freeport, NY: Books for Libraries, 1966.

———. *Philosophies in Modern Fiction*. 1929. Freeport, NY: Books for Libraries, 1965.

Charlton, Linda. "Dame Rebecca West Dies in London." *New York Times* March 16, 1983: 7.

Deakin, Motley F. *Rebecca West*. Boston: Twayne, 1980.

———. "Rebecca West: A Supplement to Hutchinson's Preliminary List." *Bulletin of Bibliography* 39 (June 1982): 52–58.

Garis, Leslie. "Rebecca West." *New York Times Magazine* 4 April 1982: 30–36, 98–101.

Glendinning, Victoria. *Rebecca West: A Life*. New York: Knopf, 1987.

Hall, Brian. "Life and Letters: Rebecca West's War." *New Yorker* 15 April 1996: 74–83.

Hutchinson, G. Evelyn. "The Dome." In *The Itinerant Ivory Tower: Scientific and Literary Essays*. New Haven: Yale UP, 1953.

———. *A Preliminary List of the Writings of Rebecca West, 1912–1951*. New Haven: Yale U Library, 1957.

Orel, Harold. *The Literary Achievement of Rebecca West*. New York: St. Martin's, 1986.

Orlich, Sister Mary Margarita, C.S.J. *The Novels of Rebecca West: A Complex Unity*. Diss. U of Notre Dame, 1966. Ann Arbor: UMI, 1967.

Packer, Joan Garrett. *Rebecca West: An Annotated Bibliography*. New York: Garland, 1991.

Ray, Gordon N. *H.G. Wells and Rebecca West*. New Haven: Yale UP, 1974.

Redd, Tony Neil. "Rebecca West: Master of Reality." Diss. U of South Carolina, 1972.

Rollyson, Carl. *Rebecca West: A Life*. New York: Scribner's, 1996.

Scott, Bonnie Kime. *Readings of Woolf, West, and Barnes*. Bloomington: Indiana UP, 1995.

Stec, Loretta. "Female Sacrifice: Gender and Nostalgic Nationalism in Rebecca West's *Black Lamb and Grey Falcon*." *Ariel* 1997: 138–158.

Stetz, Margaret D. "Rebecca West's Criticism: Alliance, Tradition, and Modernism." In *New Directions in Feminist Criticism*. New York: Garland, 1994.

Weldon, Fay. *Rebecca West*. London: Viking, 1985.

Wells, G.P., ed. *H.G. Wells in Love: Postscript to an Experiment in Autobiography*. Boston: Little, Brown, 1984.

West, Anthony. *Heritage*. New York: Random House, 1955.

———. *H.G. Wells: Aspects of a Life*. New York: Random House, 1984.

Wolfe, Peter. *Rebecca West, Artist and Thinker*. Carbondale: Southern Illinois UP, 1971.

Jeanette Winterson
1959–

Maria Koundoura

Why is it that in the last years of the twentieth century and the beginning of the twenty-first, after all the transformations of the novel and after postmodernism has shown the "real" to be a discursive effect, realism is still at the heart of evaluations of Jeanette Winterson's work? The answer lies in the tension between Winterson's use of the fictions of her life and the fictions of her characters' lives. Despite her use of "fictional nobodies" as her protagonists, Winterson's novels always have an extratextual reference to somebody; in her instance it is always the author. It is a figure that Winterson cultivates both in her work and in her interviews about her work. It is this tension between fact and fiction that ties Winterson's work to the realist tradition and not only to postmodernism.

BACKGROUND

The story of Jeanette Winterson's life is as well known as her fictions. She was born in 1959 in Manchester, England, was adopted by John William Winterson, a factory worker, and his wife Constance Brownrigg, and grew up in Accrington, a mill town in northern England. Her adopted parents were Pentecostal Evangelists and deeply committed to God. They raised Winterson for evangelical service, to be a missionary and to spread the word of God among the heathen. At the age of eight she was already writing sermons. Her reputation as a preacher spread, and believers came to Accrington just to hear her preach. She learned to read by slowly plodding through the Fifth Book of Moses, the Deuterotnomy. Her interest in reading was not shared by her parents, who owned only six books between them, three of them Bibles. Books that Winterson used to sneak in at home during her adolescence and hide under her mattress were all found and burned by her mother. She left home, or was more or less thrown out, when at fifteen, after she had her first lesbian relationship, she told her parents about it. She had a number of odd jobs after she left home, including makeup artist at a funeral parlor and assistant at Calderstones Mental Hospital. Eventually she moved to Oxford, where in 1981 she graduated with an M.A. in English. She then moved to London and worked at the Roundhouse Theatre and then at Pandora Press. She became a full-time writer in 1987. She was awarded the Whitbread Award for best first novel in 1985 for *Oranges are not the only fruit*, the John Llewellyn Rhys Memorial Prize in 1987 for *The Passion*, and the E.M. Forster Award from the American Academy of Arts and Letters in 1989 for *Sexing the*

Cherry. Winterson is an avid book collector, a passion that she describes in detail in the essay "The Psychometry of Books" in *Art Objects*. Her collection mainly contains the work of the English and American modernists in signed first editions: Virginia Woolf, Marianne Moore, Gertrude Stein, T.S. Eliot, Ezra Pound, W.B. Yeats, and many more.

Interestingly, these are the authors that she herself tells us have influenced her work as a writer. "Modernism" is a term used to describe the early-twentieth-century literary and cultural movement that tried to convey an increasingly sharp sense of historical relativism through stylistic experimentation. The term, as Matei Calinescu states in *Five Faces of Modernity: Modernism, Avant-Garde, Decadence, Kitsch, Postmodernism*, was first used by the South American writer and critical commentator Rubén Darío in the early 1890s to designate a movement of aesthetic renovation, but also of cultural independence from Spain (69). Its English and American application was consolidated in the 1920s under Ezra Pound's motto "Make it new." After the destruction and chaos of World War I, writers lost faith in the eternal and the immutable, so they turned to language to make sense of the chaos around them. They believed in the restorative power of art; hence their desire to make life like art, not lifelike art, as was the goal of Victorian realism. Modernism is the tradition that informs Winterson's individual talent, to paraphrase the title of her favorite modernist's essay, T.S. Eliot's "Tradition and the Individual Talent." It is also the tradition that, according to her, should inform all contemporary writers. "To assume that Modernism has no real relevance to the way that we need to be developing fiction now," she writes in *Art Objects*, "is to condemn writers and readers to a dingy Victorian twilight" (176). Exemplifying the "Make it new" motto of her "ancestors," she continues, "[W]e can only look for writers who know what tradition is, who understand Modernism within that tradition, and who are committed to a fresh development of language and to new forms of writing" (177).

"Modernism" as a term needs to be distinguished from the general concept of "modernity." Modernity, according to Peter Osborne in *The Politics of Time*, is a category of historical consciousness, a distinctive way of temporalizing history as a radical break with tradition characterized by self-consciousness (ix, 9–13). It is also the name for the period of time that began in the eighteenth century with the Enlightenment and with colonial expansion. While most literary and cultural historians echo Osborne's definition and agree on modernity's origins, few agree on when it ends. Only the theorists of postmodernity celebrate the end of modernity; most others argue that since modernity is about breaking with tradition, our consciousness of that break makes modernity a continuous present. Postmodernists point to this ultimately self-defeating character of modern time consciousness, in which the new is an "invariant" and thus the "ever same," and attempt to overcome this pessimism by celebrating its end. Unlike their earlier counterparts, the modernists, whose work was informed by an anxiety over the fragmented nature of experience and by a desire to unify it, postmodernists celebrate the fragmentation, the anxiety, and the impasse. Thus, according to Fredric Jameson, whose *Postmodernism; or, The Cultural Logic of Late Capitalism* was instrumental in both defining and criticizing the term, the characteristic feature of postmodern art is "the random cannibalization of all the styles of the past" (18).

This is certainly a characteristic of Winterson's fiction. She, like the writers she describes in *Art Objects*, uses modernism but makes it new, postmodern: she uses allegory, myth, symbolism, fairy tales, mysticism, and history. She references romanticism, the Renaissance, the seventeenth century, and the ancient world. She admittedly uses "history as a device" in order to "create an imaginative reality sufficiently at odds with our daily reality to startle us out of it" (*Art Objects* 188). Jameson finds this problematic because if one's relation to the past is a matter of randomly retrieving various styles, then one loses the impetus to find out what actually happened in that past. Postmodernism's skepticism about how much we can know from the past, he tells us, has resulted in nostalgia for the "look" of the past: "the past as historical referent finds itself gradually bracketed, and then effaced altogether, leaving us with nothing but texts" (18). Textuality is certainly central in Winterson's work. Her narratives from *Oranges are not the only fruit* get progressively more antilinear; chronological order and nature are willed away, and everything is about style, that is, textuality itself. "Style," she writes in *Art Objects*, proving Jameson's point, "refuses history as documentary and recognizes that history is as much in the reconstruction as in the moment" (187).

The fluidity of styles and the lack of desire to control meaning that characterize Winterson's texts and make them postmodern also link them to the tradition of feminist writing exemplified by Virginia Woolf (an author whom Winterson consciously strives to emulate). Like Woolf, in *The Waves*, Winterson also wants to recapture "some little language such as lovers use, broken words, inarticulate words" in her work (161). Also like Woolf's, her efforts at recapturing these fragments can be seen as part of the woman writer's attempt to find "a room of her own," a voice that is not controlled by the male-dominated Western tradition. Feminist literary critics argue that this tradition codes woman and her body as negative, threatening, a body so excessive in its functions and sexuality that it must be controlled either through violence or silence. In *Art and Lies* Winterson expresses this through the figure of Sappho, the most famous writer of the Greek island of Lesbos. "Her body is an apocrypha," she writes, "she has become a book of tall stories, none of them written by herself. Her name has passed into history. Her work has not. Her island is known to millions now, her work is not" (69). Winterson makes that work known not through her own (like Sappho's) sexual preference for women, as most commentators are quick to argue, but through her efforts in her writing to change traditional narrative structures. As Teresa de Lauretis has insightfully shown in *Technologies of Gender: Essays on Theory, Film, and Fiction*, the traditional narrative structure is the movement of a mobile figure, marked male, through a boundary or passive space, marked female (43). In this scheme only one gender has agency or subjectivity, and this gender also has the ability to conquer and control its opposite. Western thought, feminists like de Lauretis argue, constructs these gendered distinctions in narrative as a way of establishing and confirming a number of oppositional values: pure/impure, order/disorder, natural/unnatural. What seems most important in this ideology is the maintenance of boundaries. Winterson's work is part of that tradition of writing—made up primarily but not exclusively by women—that blurs these boundaries by upsetting the reader's sense of them and leaving them "abject." In *Powers of Horror* the prominent feminist theorist Julia Kristeva introduces and explains the term "abject." She defines it as that which we are repulsed by, not as an innate quality, but because it "disturbs identity, system order" (4). Winterson's work consciously disturbs identity, system, and order, not only as part of a postmodernist self-consciousness, but also, which is more important, as part of a conscious political practice that seeks to decode the "apocryphal" body of woman and her writing.

ANALYSIS

"It seems that if you tell people that what they are reading is 'real,' they will believe you, even when they are being trailed in the wake of a highly experimental odyssey" (*Art Objects* 53). Certainly reading a Jeanette Winterson novel is like being trailed in a highly experimental odyssey. From *Oranges are not the only fruit* to *The Passion*, *Art and Lies*, and *Gut Symmetries* she has gotten progressively more and more experimental. For example, *Oranges are not the only fruit* has a traditional story line: it is a first-person narrative of a young girl's coming into her own despite all the allegorical fairy tales that are woven into it and the fact that it is a novel about storytelling. *Gut Symmetries*, on the other hand, although beguilingly simple in its story line—it is about how Alice, the main character, meets Jove, a married man, and starts an affair with him and then meets his wife Stella and starts an affair with her—has nothing traditional about it. The story is told through a wide spectrum of philosophical discussions, Jewish mysticism, tarot, quantum physics, and fairy tales: a mishmash of things all striving in different directions. "What I am seeking to do in my work," Winterson writes, explaining this gradual shift to experimentalism, "is to make a form that answers to the twenty-first-century needs" (*Art Objects* 191). This is why, she tells us in classic postmodernist self-conscious fashion, she uses "stories within stories within stories within stories" (*Art Objects* 189). It is also why again as a classic postmodernist she focuses on style. "Style," she writes, "makes a nonsense of conventional boundaries between fiction and fact" (*Art Objects* 187). "Through the development of style," she continues, "imagination is allowed full play. The writer is not restricted to what she has experienced or to what she knows, she is let loose outside of her own dimensions. This is why art can speak to so many different kinds of people regardless of time and space. It is why it is so foolish to try to reconstruct the writer from the work" (187).

This is advice that has clearly not been heeded by most Winterson critics, positive and negative, who constantly try to reconstruct her from her work. Exasperated with these efforts, she said in a June 1997 interview in The *Advocate*: "It is fine here in *The Advocate* to be talking about myself as a lesbian. But to be constantly forced back to this in the mainstream press is not good for me, because it diminishes my work. That's why I say that I'm not a lesbian writer but a writer who is a lesbian." It does not especially help the critics from the popular press that all of her books are centered around lesbian characters, that *Oranges are not the only fruit* is strikingly similar to her own biography, and that she, as she admits in the *Advocate* interview, cultivated a wild image early on in her career. Despite her eloquent explorations of the process of writing and reading in *Art Objects*, her insistence on style in her writing on writing, and her exemplification of style in her writing itself, it appears that her style does not make "a nonsense of conventional boundaries between fact and fiction." In fact, as is seen in the merger of her life and her work, quite the opposite: her style with its mixture of fact and fiction, the "real" and the "fanciful," seems to reinforce these boundaries. This is why one could argue that Winterson is not a postmodernist but a realist writer, that she is not making a new "form that answers to twenty-first-century needs" but is revisiting the old form of the novel at its origin. This claim goes against every article that has been written about Winterson, against Winterson's own claims, and against what the reader sees with her own eyes when reading her novels.

Such a contrary evaluation of her work is supported by the tension between fact and fiction in Winterson's work and by the fact that, as we saw earlier, Winterson is not only aware of this tension but actively plays with it. "I'm telling you stories. Trust me," she writes in *Art Objects* to muddy the waters of her realist game (189). This is an old poetic trick reminiscent of Sir Philip Sidney's "the poet never lies because he never tells the truth" and of the claims of writers at the novel's origin, a form that she tells us "is finished" (*Art Objects* 191). Winterson is aware of the history of the novel and of its early practitioners' use of the fact/fiction dichotomy to consolidate its form. Her direct use of Daniel Defoe's *Robinson Crusoe* and its author's preface that tells you that what you are reading is a fact when you know it is a fiction by the fact that you are reading what the author tells you is his autobiography of Robinson Crusoe shows her knowledge of this history. *Robinson Crusoe* has been uniformly declared by critics working on the origin of the novel as not only the first English novel but also the first realist novel. Winterson uses this example to defend attacks on Gertrude Stein's *Autobiography of Alice B. Toklas* and to deflect readings of *Oranges are not the only fruit* as autobiographical (*Art Objects* 53–54). Considering the extent to which the fact/fiction debate is central in readings of her work, it is important to look at its critical history.

In *Nobody's Story*, the most important work on the novel since Ian Watt's *The Rise of the Novel*, Catherine Gallagher has shown how the real was a highly charged term in the mid-eighteenth century. "A massive reorientation of textual referentiality took place" at that time, she tells us, and the unmapped and unarticulated "wild space" of fiction became the "preferred form of narrative" and the novel the preferred form of fiction (xvi, 164). The new category of fiction, she continues, renounced claims of historical truth and replaced them with mimetic ones whose "truth" rested not on any extratextual references but on their lack of referentiality (165). Thus, contrary to Ian Watt's argument that "formal realism" was a way of trying to disguise or hide fictionality, Gallagher suggests that "realism was the code of the fictional" (174). The "wealth of circumstantial and physical detail" in novels, she argues, that referred to nothing and "nobody in particular" (174) should be viewed as "a confirmation, rather than an obfuscation, of fiction" (173). Fictionality, for Gallagher, "simultaneously, if somewhat paradoxically, allowed both the author and the reader to 'be acquisitive without impertinence.' That the story was nobody's made it entirely the author's; that it was nobody's also left it open to the reader's sentimental appropriation," that is, to his or her emotional identification and "ownership" of the novel (174–175). Unlike "true" characters (like the ones in scandal, for example), "fictional nobodies" were "a species of utopian common property, potential objects of universal identification" that everyone could have a sentimental "interest" in without paying any of the penalties (172). This is the main point of Gallagher's book, whose purpose is to examine the affective force of fiction. "Eighteenth-century readers identified with the characters in novels *because* of the characters' fictiveness and not in spite of it," she tells us. "Moreover, these readers had to be taught how to read fiction, and as they learned this skill (it did not come naturally), new emotional dispositions were created" that formed the basis for the modern "self" (xvii). The primary one of these is one that is still in use today: it is the ability to invest and divest emotionally with characters we know are not "real."

This explains the popularity of Winterson's novels: readers emotionally invest in her characters they know are not real, for who could argue that Jordan the sexually ambivalent character from *Sexing the Cherry* is real, or Dog Woman the grotesque giant from the same novel, or Villanelle the web-footed Venetian woman of *The Passion*, or Handel, Picasso, and Sappho from *Art and Lies*? The fact/fiction debate described by Gallagher also explains the confusion of Winterson's fiction with her life. Her use of "fictional nobodies"—characters loaded with circumstantial and physical detail like Jeanette of *Oranges are not the only fruit*, or the storyteller of *Written on the Body*, or Alice of *Gut Symmetries*, or herself in all of her interviews and in *Art Objects*—makes Winterson's characters entirely her own. It also leaves them open to the reader's sentimental appropriation: the popularity of her novels testifies to this. It is because these fictional nobodies are her own and because she consciously stages herself as one of them—"I prefer myself as a character in my own fiction," she tells us in *Art Objects* (53)—that

Winterson's novels have been read as autobiographical and critics continuously attempt to reconstruct her life from her work. "I'm telling you stories. Trust me," she insists throughout *Art Objects* (189). But nobody seems to believe her, even though what they are reading is a fact and not a fiction; after all, she is indeed telling us stories. They are "real" stories, that is, that is why they are fictional.

ASSESSMENT

Winterson is one of the most contradictory of contemporary British women writers. A realist despite her use of myth, fairy tale, tarot, mysticism, and postmodern styles, political despite her repeated attempts to hide it all as fiction, traditional despite her repeated disavowals and her deconstruction of tradition, she is truly modern in the epochal sense of the term. In other words, her work is a self-conscious radical break with a tradition that it is an example of, the tradition, that is, sometimes called realism, by others modernism, and by others still postmodernism, in which writers attempted to represent the eternal in the light of the ephemeral. These attempts have resulted in her offering examples of both lifelike art (realist fictions) and of life like art (factual fictions). This is her originality.

BIBLIOGRAPHY

Primary Sources

Boating for Beginners. London: Methuen, 1985.

Oranges are not the only fruit. London: Pandora, 1985; New York: Atlantic Monthly, 1987.

The Passion. London: Bloomsbury, 1987; New York: Vintage Books, 1989.

Sexing the Cherry. London: Bloomsbury, 1989; New York: Atlantic Monthly, 1990.

Written on the Body. London: Cape, 1992; New York: Vintage, 1994.

Art and Lies: A Piece for Three Voices and a Band. London: Cape, 1994; New York: Knopf, 1995.

Great Moments in Aviation; and, Oranges are not the only fruit: Two Filmscripts. London: Vintage, 1994.

Art Objects: Essays on Ecstasy and Effrontery. London: Cape, 1995; New York: Knopf, 1996.

Gut Symmetries. London: Granta; New York: Knopf, 1997.

Interview. *The Advocate*. June 1997.

The World and Other Places (short stories). London: Cape, 1998; New York: Knopf, 1999.

The Powerbook. London; Vintage, 2001. As *The Power Book*. New York: Vintage, 2001.

Secondary Sources

Calinescu, Matei. *Five Faces of Modernity: Modernism, Avant-Garde, Decadence, Kitsch, Postmodernism*. Durham, NC: Duke UP, 1987.

de Lauretis, Teresa. *Technologies of Gender: Essays on Theory, Film, and Fiction*. Bloomington: Indiana UP, 1987.

Gallagher, Catherine. *Nobody's Story: The Vanishing Acts of Women Writers in the Marketplace, 1670–1820*. Berkeley: U of California P, 1994.

Jameson, Fredric. *Postmodernism; or, The Cultural Logic of Late Capitalism*. Durham, NC: Duke UP, 1991.

Kristeva, Julia. *Powers of Horror: An Essay on Abjection*. Trans. Leon Roudiez. New York: Columbia UP, 1982.

Osborne, Peter. *The Politics of Time: Modernity and Avant-Garde*. London: Verso, 1995.

Watt, Ian. *The Rise of the Novel: Studies in Defoe, Richardson, and Fielding*. Berkeley: U of California P, 1957.

Woolf, Virginia. *The Waves*. 1931. London: Granada, 1977.

Virginia Woolf
1882–1941

Peter F. Naccarato

In recent decades Virginia Woolf's place within the canon of English literature has been secured. Her most familiar novels, *Mrs. Dalloway* and *To the Lighthouse*, have become standard texts in the literature classroom. At the same time, her most famous essay, *A Room of One's Own*, has become an essential part of most women's studies courses. While her literary innovations, including her stream-of-consciousness method, have profoundly influenced the development of literature throughout the twentieth century, her feminist ideas have had an equally strong intellectual and cultural impact. The vast and ever-growing amount of scholarship that has been produced about Woolf and her literary work confirms her prominent position within twentieth-century literary and social history. At the same time, it underscores a number of unanswered questions, including the relationship between Woolf's literary work, her social and political concerns, and her personal life. Although much of Woolf scholarship can be divided into these three categories, the most productive exploration of Virginia Woolf begins by acknowledging the complex intersections between them.

BACKGROUND

To begin to understand why Woolf has emerged as such an important figure at the end of the twentieth century, one might first consider the historical moments that her own lifetime bridged. Virginia Stephen, born in 1882, grew up in one of England's many prestigious Victorian families; its patriarch, Sir Leslie Stephen, was editor of the *Dictionary of National Biography*, an encyclopedia that chronicled the lives of England's most important citizens. Although her early childhood was strongly influenced by staunchly conservative Victorian codes and mores, it was also marked by personal tragedy, including the death of her mother and sexual abuse. After this oppressive childhood, however, Woolf found liberation in a highly unusual and much-criticized lifestyle. With the death of her father, Woolf and her sister, Vanessa, lived together and began hosting weekly meetings that included their brother, Thoby, and his Cambridge friends. This eclectic assortment of philosophers, historians, economists, writers, and artists eventually became known as the Bloomsbury Group. Their uninhibited and often-raucous meetings—in which Virginia and Vanessa began as observers but eventually became participants—provided a space in which these young intellectuals could challenge the traditions and expectations of their Victorian predecessors. Within this context Woolf was free to develop her artistic vision, to challenge accepted literary conventions, and to form her own social and political beliefs.

In addition to these biographical details, it is important to recognize the connection between Woolf's work and the larger social and political conditions in England during these decades. Scholars have long explored the relationship between the political circumstances of the late nineteenth and early twentieth centuries and the birth of modernism. In England growing social crises, including labor unrest, campaigns for Irish independence, women's suffrage, and the death of King Edward VII in 1910, produced a society "more anarchic, more uncontrolled, more 'modern' " (Stansky 4). Modernism continued to mature against a backdrop of social crises, including the two world wars. From the grieving women and shell-shocked veterans who populate her novels to her increasingly pacifist politics, Woolf's life, both personally and artistically, was deeply impacted by the wars. For Woolf and her contemporaries, there was an essential link between the social and the intellectual, the political and the artistic.

In addition to this historical perspective, it is also important to recognize how intellectual developments in a variety of fields also contributed to Woolf's artistic vision. From Darwinian evolution to Freudian psychoanalysis, the intellectual climate in which Woolf lived and worked was one in which the very nature of the self was being investigated. While biology and psychology were attempting to answer complex questions concerning the origins, growth, and development of human beings, Woolf was not only interested in learning about this work, but wanted to participate in it by undertaking her own explorations in her fiction. Thus Woolf's literary achievements should be placed in line with the work produced in other disciplines whose major focus was understanding the nature of the self. At the same time, Woolf was also strongly influenced by innumerable developments in science and technology that led to reevaluations of the universe and our place within it. For example, what is the link between Woolf's literary experimentation and the theories of relativity that changed basic perceptions of time and space? How do inventions like the radio, automobile, or airplane change not only the landscape in which Woolf's characters live, but also the very nature of these characters themselves? In many ways questions concerning the nature of the universe and the place of human beings within it that were being explored across the intellectual spectrum invited the kind of personal exploration of self and society that fills Woolf's novels.

ANALYSIS

During the early decades of the twentieth century Woolf contributed to an almost complete reevaluation of the social, political, and literary conventions that had dominated England throughout the nineteenth century. While her first two novels, *The Voyage Out* (1915) and *Night and Day* (1919), offer fairly conventional prose, her short stories provided a space in which she could begin to challenge literary standards and conventions. As Woolf explored familiar issues of love, marriage, class, and family in these early novels, she experimented with both form and content in "The Mark on the Wall" (1917) and "Kew Gardens" (1919). In both of these stories one finds the roots of what would eventually develop into Woolf's hallmark. In the former the reader is taken on an extended mental journey through the thoughts and memories of the narrator as she ponders an insignificant mark on her wall. Absent a traditional plot or character development, the story almost completely abandons the outside world in favor of mapping the inner landscape of the narrator's mind. Similarly, in "Kew Gardens" Woolf experiments with point of view and subjective narration as the story is told through the restricted eyes of a snail in a flowerbed. From this limited position the reader is offered momentary glimpses into the thoughts and conversations of passersby. Four disconnected and seemingly random groups wander across our narrator's line of vision, and as they do so, we are offered random and incomplete access to their lives. Essentially plotless, these two stories mark the beginning of Woolf's literary experimentation as she refuses the conventions provided by her predecessors and works to redefine the process and the purpose of writing fiction.

Woolf's work in these early short stories culminated in *Jacob's Room* (1922), her first full-length experimental novel. Two years prior to its publication Woolf wrote about the Unwritten Novel in her diary, linking it to the experiments in form and style she was already producing in her short stories:

> Suppose one thing should open out of another—as in An Unwritten novel—only not for 10 pages but 200 or so—doesn't that give the looseness and lightness I want; doesn't that get closer and yet keep form and speed, and enclose everything, everything? My doubt is how far it will enclose the human heart—Am I sufficiently mistress of my dialogue to net it there? For me figure that the approach will be entirely different this time: no scaffolding; scarcely a brick to be seen; all crepuscular, but the heart, the passion, humor, everything as bright as fire in the mist. (*Diary*, II 13)

Published in 1922, the same year as James Joyce's *Ulysses* and T.S. Eliot's *The Waste Land*, *Jacob's Room* marks not only a crucial stage in Woolf's development as a writer, but also a significant moment in the history of modern fiction. The extent to which Woolf challenges the formal literary conventions of her predecessors and dismisses the fundamental narrative structures that had become standard in the novel makes *Jacob's Room* a difficult and, for many readers, a baffling novel to tackle. As the excerpt from Woolf's diary suggests, she was initially concerned with questions of form and style. While modern readers had come to expect coherent plots, elaborately developed characters, and trustworthy narrators to guide them through their reading, *Jacob's Room* offers none of these support systems. Emulating the style she introduced in her short stories, Woolf offers her readers disconnected thoughts, subjective ruminations, incoherent reflections, and random memories. As Alex Zwerdling suggests, this experimental style presents its readers with a unique challenge:

> Scenes are swiftly and allusively outlined, not filled in, the essential relationships between characters intimated in brief but typical vignettes chosen seemingly at random from their daily lives. . . . No incident is decisive or fully developed. Nothing is explained or given special significance. The narrative unit is generally two or three pages long and not obviously connected to the one before or after it. The effect is extremely economical and suggestive but at the same time frustrating for an audience trained to read in larger units and to look for meaning and coherence. (63)

While reactions to *Jacob's Room* were varied, from those who celebrated its experimental style and praised Woolf for her innovations to those who dismissed it as a failure, its publication initiated the most productive and celebrated phase of Woolf's literary career.

In the years following *Jacob's Room* Woolf published several important essays in which she outlined her thoughts about fiction, in general, and modern fiction, in particular. For the student of Woolf, these essays provide invaluable insight into her theories about fiction and the goals she set for her own writing. Both "Mr. Bennett and Mrs.

Brown" (1924) and "Modern Fiction" (1925) are essential companions to the novels that Woolf would write in subsequent years. In both essays she distinguishes between the fiction she and her contemporaries were writing and the novels produced by their immediate predecessors. She argues that in the early decades of the twentieth century something crucial changed that made it possible for the art of fiction to develop in sharply different directions. In "Mr. Bennett and Mrs. Brown" Woolf answers the criticisms waged against contemporary novelists by author and critic Arnold Bennett. As Woolf reports, based on his contention that "the foundation of good fiction is character-creating and nothing else," Bennett concludes that "we have no young novelists of first-rate importance at the present moment, because they are unable to create characters that are real, true, and convincing" ("Captain's Death Bed" 95). This criticism becomes the focus of Woolf's essay, in which her primary strategy is to interrogate the notion of "character" to which Bennett and his contemporaries subscribe and to consider how it has changed in recent decades. In doing so, she outlines the fundamental differences between her Edwardian predecessors and her Georgian contemporaries and, in the process, theorizes the radically different kind of fiction that would become her hallmark.

Although Woolf agrees with Bennett's assertion that "all novels . . . deal with character and that it is to express character . . . that the form of the novel . . . has been evolved" (102), she has very different ideas concerning why characters are so crucial and how they are best created. In other words, while Woolf does not disagree with Bennett's argument that good fiction depends upon characters who are "real, true, and convincing," she does believe that the criteria by which characters are created and judged are historically specific and, by the early decades of the twentieth century, had undergone a radical change. Specifically, she juxtaposes the standard conventions employed by her predecessors for creating characters with the new strategies she was developing in her experimental fiction. Woolf begins by perusing one of Bennett's own novels to discover his strategy, realizing that he "tr[ies] to make us imagine for him; he tr[ies] to hypnotize us into the belief that, because he has made a house, there must be a person living there" (109). This, Woolf concludes, is the Edwardian approach to creating characters who are "real, true, and convincing." In attempting to create a bridge between their characters and their readers, Woolf asserts, her Edwardian predecessors relied on familiar external objects, thereby "lay[ing] enormous stress upon the fabric of things" (112). The fundamental change that Woolf explains in her essays and enacts in her fiction is to relocate this focus away from the external details of her characters' lives and toward an exploration of their inner selves.

At the same time that Woolf was articulating her theories of fiction in her essays, she was also enacting them in her novels. The stream-of-consciousness method that she first experimented with in her short stories, developed in *Jacob's Room*, and explained in her essays reaches its peak in three canonical Woolf novels: *Mrs. Dalloway* (1925), *To the Lighthouse* (1927), and *The Waves* (1931). In each, Woolf relies on her newly developed theories and methods to offer a substantially new kind of fiction. Without a central narrator to direct the action and impose order, the reader follows a continuous and often-confusing stream of thoughts and ideas as characters act and react in the present, allow their minds to wander into the past, and offer speculations about the future. The deceptively simple plot of *Mrs. Dalloway*, for example, which begins with the title character preparing for a party that will occur at the end of the novel, masks an intricate web of characters, thoughts, associations, connections, memories, and feelings. As we delve deeper into characters' minds, the rigid details of the external world recede into the background. For example, the familiar clock that readers would expect to rigidly mark time as the plot moves forward is replaced by a much less formal and structured attitude toward time:

> For having lived in Westminster—how many years now? over twenty,—one feels even in the midst of the traffic, or waking at night, Clarissa was positive, a particular hush, or solemnity; an indescribable pause; a suspense (but that might be her heart, affected, they said, by influenza) before Big Ben strikes. There! Out it boomed. First a warning, musical; then the hour, irrevocable. The leaden circles dissolved in the air. Such fools we are, she thought, crossing Victoria Street. (4)

Big Ben, like all external objects, is less significant for its function in the outside world than for the insight it provides into a character's thoughts and feelings. In all three novels it is the seemingly random and often-chaotic flow of these subjective mental associations that guides the prose. Like Big Ben's leaden circles, familiar conventions of plot, character, time, and structure dissolve in the air as Woolf pushes her literary experiments further and fine-tunes her evolving methodology.

Although the majority of Woolf scholarship and criticism focuses on these three central novels in which she best employed her stream-of-consciousness method, Woolf did push her fictional experiments in other directions. *Orlando* (1928), her fanciful tribute to Vita Sackville-West, for example, is conventional in style, while its plot is highly untraditional. Written as a biography of its title character, the novel moves chronologically through the major events, both personal and historical, that mark Orlando's life. Using criteria that would be familiar and acceptable to any nineteenth-century reader (including Arnold Bennett), the narrator describes the external world that Orlando inhabits, including people, places, clothes, and houses. Each transition in Orlando's life is given detailed exploration, and the central character provides a stable foundation upon which the entire novel rests. If the novel's style and form are familiar and traditional, however, its plot breaks past these boundaries. While time, for example, provides chronological structure to the novel, Orlando's life spans several centuries, thus undermining this stability and familiarity. Similarly, while Orlando serves consistently as the center upon which the entire novel is organized and the lens through which the world is experienced and understood, a crucial ambiguity in Orlando's character undermines the possibility of such certainty. Having been introduced as a man, Orlando unceremoniously wakes up one day as a woman and, without hesitation, proceeds through the rest of her life. As Woolf challenges standard notions of time and identity, she experiments less with style and more with content as she raises crucial questions about the relationship between the individual and society that continue to echo for the most contemporary reader.

While her stream-of-consciousness method has become Woolf's most significant contribution to modern and postmodern fiction, her experiments with form, plot, character, and structure complement her most familiar stylistic developments. Two of her later novels, *The Years* (1937) and *Between the Acts* (published posthumously in 1941), exemplify the complementary relationship between Woolf's finely tuned stream-of-consciousness method and her simultaneous interest in pushing the boundaries of plot and genre. *The Years*, which Woolf initially began as an essay-novel in which she would alternate fiction and nonfiction chapters, exemplifies her interest in genre and the connection between fiction and social criticism. Rather than abandoning the outside world in favor of an exploration of her characters' inner selves, Woolf worked to merge the two as she offered a multigenerational chronicle of the Pargiter family. Highly traditional in that its chapters are arranged chronologically from "1880" to "Present Day," the novel offers an intricate inquiry into the personal lives of its many characters, a consideration of major historical events and social crises, and a thoughtful investigation of the complex relationship between them. Similarly, *Between the Acts* can be read as a novel concerned with synthesis and balance. Set at Pointz Hall, a British country house, in the summer of 1939, the novel employs a "play-within-a-play" technique as Miss LaTrobe offers a pageant to her audience. This plot provides a framework through which Woolf can explore questions concerning the nature of art and artistic production, as well as its social value and its connection to individuals and society at large. As it moves between LaTrobe's play, the interactions between the myriad of people gathered on this particular day, and the highly personal thoughts and feelings of individual characters, the novel brings together the various strands that had developed throughout Woolf's career. When these later novels are read in relation to the more familiar or canonical Woolf texts, the complexity of her contribution to modern fiction is evident. In addition to the irrefutable significance of her stream-of-consciousness method, these later novels demonstrate her deep interest in connecting this initial experiment in style with complementary experiments in form and content.

Another valuable consequence of considering the complete Woolf oeuvre is that rather than seeing Woolf as abandoning any concern with the outside world in favor of her overwhelming interest in the deep self, we can consider how her fiction provides a new way of thinking about the connection between the individual and society. If at the center of *Mrs. Dalloway*, for example, are the thoughts, feelings, and emotions of its protagonist and if much time in this novel is spent inside her mind as we share her thoughts, the reader, at the same time, finds important commentary concerning the world in which Clarissa lived. Although there is no overt political commentary in the pages of this novel, Woolf uses her stream-of-consciousness method to explore the impact of contemporary events on the feelings and thoughts of her characters. From the postwar trauma suffered by Septimus Warren Smith to his strong reaction against the doctors who claim to offer relief, Woolf uses her new literary method not to privilege the internal self at the expense of the external world, but rather to explore the intricate relationship between them. While many scholars have discussed the overt social and political commentary found in Woolf's essays, especially *A Room of One's Own* and *Three Guineas*, they have often discounted the equally strong criticisms woven throughout her fiction. The distinction between Woolf, the literary figure whose theories of fiction and experimental methods contributed to the birth and maturity of modernism, and Woolf, the political activist who actively critiqued British society at the beginning of the twentieth century, is a false one. Unfortunately, the directions in which Woolf scholarship has developed through the twentieth century have often validated rather than challenged this false dichotomy.

While her novels, short stories, and essays were widely read during her lifetime, in the decades following her death Woolf not only assumed a significant position within the traditional canon of English literature, but also assumed an increasingly important role for scholars whose work challenged it. For some scholars, Woolf became the preeminent female representative of modernism. Her stream-of-consciousness method and the novels in which she most successfully employed it became part of this modernist canon. Much Woolf scholarship substantiated this identity by either reading Woolf's novels through the lens of modernist aesthetics or situating Woolf in relation to other modern authors. At the same time, scholars who worked from a more feminist perspective resisted containing Woolf within this traditional framework. For them, Woolf was not only an important author whose work contributed to the evolving modernist tradition; she was, at the same time, a critical feminist thinker whose social and political commentary had a vital impact on their movement. Rather than maintaining this and other divisions in their approaches to Woolf studies, however, scholars have increasingly worked to understand the complex connections between these supposedly separate identities.

Perhaps an accurate metaphor for this kind of scholarship comes from Virginia Woolf herself. In *Mrs. Dalloway*, as the title character reflects on her image in a mirror, she considers the relationship between the face that confronts her and her "self." As she purses her lips, she comments, "That was her self—pointed; dartlike; definite. That was her self when some effort, some call on her to be her self, drew the parts together, she alone knew how different, how incompatible and composed so for the world only into one centre, one diamond, one woman who sat in her drawing-room and . . . had tried to be the same always, never showing a sign of all the other sides of her" (55). This metaphor of Clarissa Dalloway as a multifaceted diamond who must pull her separate parts together into one coherent self at the demand of the outside world also provides a productive approach for reading and studying Woolf. While much Woolf criticism has been concerned with highlighting or privileging one particular facet of this complex figure, the most complete scholarship recognizes her multifacetedness. At its foundation is the conclusion that Clarissa Dalloway recognizes as she looks in the mirror, namely, that any attempt to present a coherent self is always incomplete and must always yield to the pressures of the outside world. Thus while some scholarship—most notably, biographical studies—aims for a total and complete representation of Virginia Woolf, much contemporary work aims to bring together multiple facets of this complex figure while acknowledging that any such attempt must remain incomplete.

In the decades following her death most of Woolf's personal writing, including her diaries and letters, was published. The Hogarth Press published five volumes of Woolf's diaries between 1977 and 1984 and six volumes of letters between 1975 and 1980. This material, added to the highly personal essays and autobiographical sketches that had already been published, provided much information not only about Woolf's professional career and public persona, but also about her private life. Her diaries and letters offered unique insights into personal thoughts and reflections on everything from her writing to her most intimate relationships. Access to this writing has had a profound impact on Woolf scholarship. For some, it became the basis for extensive biographical study of an important historical and literary figure. In addition to this material, the publication of *Virginia Woolf: A Biography* (1972) by Woolf's nephew, Quentin Bell, offered an inside perspective on her life. While Bell's is perhaps the most personal Woolf biography, it is certainly not the only one. Others include Aileen Pippett's *Moth and the Star* (1953), Lyndall Gordon's *Virginia Woolf: A Writer's Life* (1984), Alma Bond's *Who Killed Virginia Woolf? A Psychobiography* (1989), John Mepham's *Virginia Woolf: A Literary Life* (1991), James King's *Virginia Woolf* (1994), Hermione Lee's *Virginia Woolf* (1996), and Panthea Reid's *Art and Affection: A Life of Virginia Woolf* (1996).

This wealth of biographical information has not only generated tremendous interest in Woolf's life, but has also had important consequences on the development of Woolf studies. For many critics, her letters and diaries, in conjunction with her own autobiographical writing and that of her friends and associates, have served as the foundation for both biographical and literary studies of Woolf and her work. In the decades since her death Woolf scholars have constructed and, for the most part, maintained a bridge between Woolf's life experiences and her writing as they employ biographical details to explicate her fiction. From details of sexual abuse found in Woolf's autobiographical writing to her well-known bouts with mental illness, from the ambiguous sexual identity that emerges from her letters and diaries to her suicide in 1941, the details of Woolf's personal life have often provided a starting point for literary scholarship. In some cases Woolf's own reflections have contributed to this approach. Many critics, for example, use Woolf's contention that in *To the Lighthouse* she was exorcising the ghost of her mother as the foundation for their explorations of this novel. Whether the protagonist, Mrs. Ramsay, is the representative of Woolf's mother, or the struggling artist, Lily Briscoe, is read as Woolf's stand-in, the biographical becomes the starting point for literary scholarship. In other cases scholars use specific details from Woolf's life as a lens for reading most, if not all, of her writing. Works like Stephen Trombley's *All That Summer She Was Mad: Virginia Woolf, Female Victim of Male Medicine* (1982), Louise DeSalvo's *Virginia Woolf: The Impact of Childhood Sexual Abuse on Her Life and Work* (1989), and Thomas Caramagno's *The Flight of the Mind: Virginia Woolf's Art and Manic-Depressive Illness* (1992) depend on a link between the biographical and the literary that has in many ways become a hallmark of Woolf scholarship.

This link between Woolf's life and her art has provided other directions for scholars as they not only draw connections between biographical details and fictional characters or moments, but also consider how other intellectual developments have influenced both Woolf's writing and their critical readings. For example, feminist scholars have explored extensively the intersection of Woolf's feminist politics and her art. Whether it is employing feminist literary theory in a discussion of Woolf's novels or emphasizing the often-subtle political commentary embedded in their pages, feminist scholarship has had a tremendous impact on Woolf studies. Consider, for example, Jane Marcus's *Virginia Woolf and the Languages of Patriarchy* (1987), Makiko Minow-Pinkney's *Virginia Woolf and the Problem of the Subject: Feminine Writing in the Major Novels* (1987), Ellen Bayuk Rosenman's *A Room of One's Own: Women Writers and the Politics of Creativity* (1995), Rachel Bowlby's *Feminist Destinations and Further Essays on Virginia Woolf* (1997), J.R. Maze's *Virginia Woolf: Feminism, Creativity, and the Unconscious* (1997), and Jane Goldman's *The Feminist Aesthetics of Virginia Woolf: Modernism, Post-Impressionism, and the Politics of the Visual* (1998).

In addition to this feminist perspective, two other intellectual developments that have had strong influences on Woolf studies are psychoanalytic literary criticism and postmodernism. As previously noted, Woolf lived and worked during decades when Freud's writing was widely circulated throughout Europe and America. In fact, the Hogarth Press, founded and managed by Leonard and Virginia Woolf, published the first English translations of Freud's work. While some scholars attempt to make direct connections between Freud's psychoanalytic theories and Woolf's fiction, others have considered the more subtle relationship between the simultaneously emerging discourses of psychoanalysis and modernist aesthetics. From using psychoanalytic theories as a lens for reading and analyzing Woolf's characters to exploring how Woolf's writing augments or even challenges Freudian paradigms, much Woolf scholarship relies heavily on this connection. At the same time, Woolf studies have developed within the larger context of literary history, not only following the transition from modernism to postmodernism, but, in many cases, arguing that Woolf is a central figure in this transition. While some scholars have explored Woolf's place within the history of modernism, including Ulysses D'Aquila's *Bloomsbury and Modernism* (1989), N. Takei Da Silva's *Modernism and Virginia Woolf* (1990), and Bonnie Kime Scott's *Refiguring Modernism* (1995), others have argued that she fits more comfortably within the boundaries of postmodernism. For some scholars, Woolf's experimental style, her literary innovations, and her theories of fiction situate her at its forefront. Two such works are Patricia Waugh's *Feminine Fictions: Revisiting the Postmodern* (1989) and Pamela Caughie's *Virginia Woolf and Postmodernism: Literature in Quest and Question of Itself* (1991).

ASSESSMENT

What the preceding pages have demonstrated is that there are multiple and varied approaches to reading and analyzing Virginia Woolf and her writing. Rather than maintaining rigid divisions between these separate directions, however, much recent scholarship has moved toward exploring the intersections between them. No longer confined by one particular approach, Woolf scholars increasingly work to connect the biographical, the historical, the political, and the literary facets of Woolf's writing. For some scholars, this work is performed under the rubric of cultural studies as they assume a more inclusive perspective aimed not at limiting their approaches to Virginia Woolf but rather expanding the possibilities. Like Clarissa Dalloway, recognizing her own multifacetedness, contemporary students of Woolf are best served by an early recognition of Woolf's complexity and the diversity of scholarship that precedes them. It is not, in other words, a matter of deciding whether Virginia Woolf belongs among great modernist authors or early feminist thinkers; it is not about choosing between biographical details or theoretical perspectives before engaging in critical reading; instead, the most productive Woolf scholarship confronts the question of how the many voices of Virginia Woolf herself and of the chorus that has swelled in the decades following her death can best be brought into harmony.

BIBLIOGRAPHY

Primary Sources

The Voyage Out. London: Hogarth, 1915.
"The Mark on the Wall." London: Hogarth, 1917.
"Kew Gardens." London: Hogarth, 1919.
Night and Day. London: Hogarth, 1919.
Monday or Tuesday. London: Hogarth, 1921.
Jacob's Room. London: Hogarth, 1922.
"Mr. Bennett and Mrs. Brown." London: Hogarth, 1924.
The Common Reader. London: Hogarth, 1925.
Mrs. Dalloway. London: Hogarth, 1925.
To the Lighthouse. London: Hogarth, 1927.
Orlando: A Biography. London: Hogarth, 1928.
A Room of One's Own. London: Hogarth, 1929.
The Waves. London: Hogarth, 1931.
The Common Reader: Second Series. London: Hogarth, 1932.
Letter to a Young Poet. London: Hogarth, 1932.
Flush: A Biography. London: Hogarth, 1933.
Walter Sickert: A Conversation. London: Hogarth, 1934.
The Years. London: Hogarth, 1937.
Three Guineas. London: Hogarth, 1938.
Roger Fry: A Biography. London: Hogarth, 1940.
Between the Acts. London: Hogarth, 1941.
The Death of the Moth and Other Essays. London: Hogarth, 1942.
A Haunted House and Other Short Stories. London: Hogarth, 1943.
The Moment and Other Essays. London: Hogarth, 1947.
The Captain's Death Bed and Other Essays. London: Hogarth, 1950.
A Writer's Diary: Being Extracts from the Diary of Virginia Woolf. Ed. Leonard Woolf. New York: Harcourt, 1954.
Hours in a Library. New York: Harcourt, 1957.
Granite and Rainbow. London: Hogarth, 1958.
Contemporary Writers. London: Hogarth, 1965.
Collected Essays. 4 vols. London: Hogarth, 1966–1967.
The Letters of Virginia Woolf. 6 vols. Ed. Nigel Nicolson. New York: Harcourt, 1975–1980.
Freshwater: A Comedy. Ed. Lucio P. Ruotolo. New York: Harcourt, 1976.
Moments of Being: Unpublished Autobiographical Writings. Ed. Jeanne Schulkind. New York: Harcourt, 1976.
Books and Portraits: Some Further Selections from the Literary and Biographical Writings of Virginia Woolf. Ed. Mary Lyon. London: Hogarth, 1977; New York: Harcourt, 1981.
The Diary of Virginia Woolf. 5 vols. Ed. Anne Olivier Bell. London: Hogarth, 1977–1984.
The Complete Shorter Fiction of Virginia Woolf. Ed. Susan Dick. London: Hogarth, 1985.
The Essays of Virginia Woolf. 4 vols. Ed. Andrew McNeillie. San Diego: Harcourt, 1987–1994.

Congenial Spirits: The Selected Letters of Virginia Woolf. Ed. Joanne Trautmann Banks. San Diego: Harcourt, 1990.

A Passionate Apprentice: The Early Journals, 1897–1909. Ed. Mitchell A. Leaska. London: Hogarth, 1990.

Secondary Sources

Abel, Elizabeth. *Virginia Woolf and the Fictions of Psychoanalysis*. Chicago: U of Chicago P, 1989.

Barrett, Eileen, and Patricia Cramer, eds. *Virginia Woolf: Lesbian Readings*. New York: New York UP, 1997.

Bell, Quentin. *Virginia Woolf: A Biography*. New York: Harcourt, 1972.

Bishop, Edward. *A Virginia Woolf Chronology*. Basingstoke: Macmillan, 1989.

Bond, Alma Halbert. *Who Killed Virginia Woolf? A Psychobiography*. New York: Human Sciences, 1989.

Bowlby, Rachel. *Feminist Destinations and Further Essays on Virginia Woolf*. Edinburgh: Edinburgh UP, 1997.

Caramagno, Thomas C. *The Flight of the Mind: Virginia Woolf's Art and Manic-Depressive Illness*. Berkeley: U of California P, 1992.

Caughie, Pamela L. *Virginia Woolf and Postmodernism: Literature in Quest and Question of Itself*. Urbana: U of Illinois P, 1991.

D'Aquila, Ulysses L. *Bloomsbury and Modernism*. New York: Peter Lang, 1989.

Da Silva, N. Takei. *Modernism and Virginia Woolf*. Windsor: Windsor, 1990.

DeSalvo, Louise A. *Virginia Woolf: The Impact of Childhood Sexual Abuse on Her Life and Work*. Boston: Beacon, 1989.

Dunn, Jane. *A Very Close Conspiracy: Vanessa Bell and Virginia Woolf*. London: Cape, 1990.

Ferrer, Daniel. *Virginia Woolf and the Madness of Language*. London and New York: Routledge, 1990.

Gillespie, Diane F. *The Sisters' Arts: The Writing and Painting of Virginia Woolf and Vanessa Bell*. Syracuse: Syracuse UP, 1988.

Goldman, Jane. *The Feminist Aesthetics of Virginia Woolf: Modernism, Post-Impressionism, and the Politics of the Visual*. Cambridge and New York: Cambridge UP, 1998.

Goldman, Mark. *The Reader's Art: Virginia Woolf as Literary Critic*. The Hague: Mouton, 1976.

Gordon, Lyndall. *Virginia Woolf: A Writer's Life*. New York: Norton, 1984.

Hussey, Mark. *The Singing of the Real World: The Philosophy of Virginia Woolf's Fiction*. Columbus: Ohio State UP, 1986.

———, ed. *Virginia Woolf and War: Fiction, Reality, and Myth*. Syracuse: Syracuse UP, 1991.

King, James. *Virginia Woolf*. London: Hamish Hamilton, 1994.

Laurence, Patricia Ondek. *The Reading of Silence: Virginia Woolf in the English Tradition*. Stanford: Stanford UP, 1991.

Lee, Hermione. *Virginia Woolf*. London: Chatto, 1996.

Levenback, Karen L. *Virginia Woolf and the Great War*. Syracuse: Syracuse UP, 1999.

Marcus, Jane. *Virginia Woolf and the Languages of Patriarchy*. Bloomington: Indiana UP, 1987.

Maze, J.R. *Virginia Woolf: Feminism, Creativity, and the Unconscious*. Westport, CT: Greenwood, 1997.

McNichol, Stella. *Virginia Woolf and the Poetry of Fiction*. London and New York: Routledge, 1990.

Mepham, John. *Virginia Woolf: A Literary Life*. New York: St. Martin's, 1991.

Minow-Pinkney, Makiko. *Virginia Woolf and the Problem of the Subject: Feminine Writing in the Major Novels*. New Brunswick, NJ: Rutgers UP, 1987.

Moore, Madeline. *The Short Season between Two Silences: The Mystical and the Political in the Novels of Virginia Woolf*. Boston: Allen & Unwin, 1984.

Panken, Shirley. *Virginia Woolf and the "Lust of Creation": A Psychoanalytic Exploration*. Albany: State U of New York P, 1987.

Pippett, Aileen. *Moth and the Star*. New York: Viking, 1953.

Poresky, Louise A. *The Elusive Self: Psyche and Spirit in Virginia Woolf's Novels*. Newark: U of Delaware P, 1981.

Raitt, Suzanne. *Vita and Virginia: The Work and Friendship of V. Sackville-West and Virginia Woolf*. Oxford: Clarendon Press; New York: Oxford UP, 1993.

Reese, Judy S. *Recasting Social Values in the Work of Virginia Woolf*. Selinsgrove, PA: Susquehanna UP, 1996.

Reid, Panthea. *Art and Affection: A Life of Virginia Woolf*. New York: Oxford UP, 1996.

Roe, Sue. *Writing and Gender: Virginia Woolf's Writing Practice*. New York: St. Martin's, 1990.

Rosenman, Ellen Bayuk. *The Invisible Presence: Virginia Woolf and the Mother-Daughter Relationship*. Baton Rouge: Louisiana State UP, 1986.

———. *A Room of One's Own: Women Writers and the Politics of Creativity*. New York: Twayne, 1995.

Ruotolo, Lucio P. *The Interrupted Moment: A View of Virginia Woolf's Novels*. Stanford: Stanford UP, 1986.

Scott, Bonnie Kime. *Refiguring Modernism*. 2 vols. Bloomington: Indiana UP, 1995.

Silver, Brenda R. *Virginia Woolf's Reading Notebooks*. Princeton: Princeton UP, 1983.

Smith, Patricia Juliana. *Lesbian Panic: Homoeroticism in Modern British Women's Fiction*. New York: Columbia UP, 1997.

Squier, Susan M. *Virginia Woolf and London: The Sexual Politics of the City*. Chapel Hill: U of North Carolina P, 1985.

Stansky, Peter. *On or about December 1910: Early Bloomsbury and Its Intimate World*. Cambridge, MA: Harvard UP, 1996.

Transue, Pamela J. *Virginia Woolf and the Politics of Style*. Albany: State U of New York P, 1986.

Trombley, Stephen. *All That Summer She Was Mad: Virginia Woolf, Female Victim of Male Medicine*. New York: Continuum, 1982.

Waugh, Patricia. *Feminine Fictions: Revisiting the Postmodern*. London and New York: Routledge, 1989.

Wussow, Helen. *The Nightmare of History: The Fictions of Virginia Woolf and D.H. Lawrence*. Bethlehem, PA: Lehigh UP, 1998.

Zwerdling, Alex. *Virginia Woolf and the Real World*. Berkeley: U of California P, 1986.

E.H. Young
1880–1949

Stella Deen

E.H. Young's modern, witty novels both invoke and depart from traditional generic forms to portray change and tension in English middle-class life. She especially examined the influence of conventional morality and social practice on female self-definition. Young sympathized with the questioners and rebels she portrayed—those gifted with an imaginative, moral vision reaching beyond social law—but she explored the border where right and wrong shade into one another and the hazy region where truth is confounded with self-deception. In her fiction the disruptive power of love and sexual desire clashes with middle-class standards of sexual propriety. Love and desire are themselves half compounded of pride and romantic idealism; Young suggested that the daydreams and fantasies of her protagonists could both liberate and entrap them. As one character realizes, "She had made [her life] narrower than it need have been, a little enclosure for her thoughts, her memories, her dreams of what things would have been if they had all been different" (*Celia* 373).

BACKGROUND

Emily Hilda Young was born on March 21, 1880, one of seven children of a Northumberland shipowner. She was educated at Gateshead High School and Penrhos College, Wales. In 1902 she married John A.H. Daniell, a Bristol solicitor. Very little is known about her marriage to Daniell, who was killed in World War I in 1917. Young herself worked during wartime, first as a stables groom and then in munitions production. During these years of young adulthood she continued her education by reading classical and modern philosophy, and in preparation for her vocation, she wrote fortnightly essays. She also pursued her passionate interest in rock climbing, returning frequently to vacation in Wales. By 1915 she was recognized as an expert and daring climber, having established a route on a cliff that male predecessors had pronounced impossible (Henderson).

Through her husband Young met Ralph Henderson, headmaster of Alleyn's School in London, and he was to become her lover and lifelong companion. In an unusual arrangement Young moved to London in 1918 to live with Henderson, in the same house with his wife (who was wife in name only). Apparently the ménage à trois was acceptable to all three parties, lasting until Henderson's retirement in 1940, when Emily and Ralph moved to Wiltshire (Gotch). Henderson and Young (known in private life as Mrs. Daniell) could not publicly acknowledge the nature of their association, but as Sally Beauman notes, in her novels Young dealt openly with "the duality of her name, of her life, of her nature" (Introduction to *The Misses Mallett* xii).

Between 1910 and 1947 E.H. Young published eleven novels, several short stories, and two children's books. Although she lived in Bristol for only sixteen years, its physical and social topography clearly took hold of her imagination, becoming an integral part of nine of her eleven novels. Ralph Henderson supported and encouraged Young's writing, calling it "my privilege—and fearful joy—to watch the growth of her works from the first word written to the last word printed" (Henderson). The privacy characterizing Young's personal life also marked her career as a novelist. In an era when writers were increasingly aware of the value of professional status, Young did not participate in any literary circles or contribute to the journal of any "avant-garde" movement. She disliked public attention and insisted that her books must stand or fall on their own merits. The privacy of Young's personal and professional life undoubtedly contributed to her relative obscurity in the years following her death.

During her lifetime and in the years following her death Young's books enjoyed both popular and critical success. *Miss Mole* won the James Tait Black Memorial Prize when it was published in 1930, and *William*, Young's most popular novel, was reprinted twenty times between 1925 and 1948. (Virginia Woolf read *William* and, thinking Young a very good novelist, wondered at her not being better known.) Radio adaptations of several of Young's novels—*Miss Mole*, *The Curate's Wife*, *William*, and *Chatterton Square*—as well as a few short stories were read for BBC broadcasts by Young's sister, the actress Gladys Young (BBC). Contemporary readers appreciated Young's "rich fund of subtle and delicately astringent humour" ("Miss E.H. Young"); they emphasized her sympathy, tact, and subtle, meticulous treatment of character; and they applauded the quiet vein in which she treated potentially explosive subjects. Some reviewers compared Young to Jane Austen, especially for her sparkling wit and irony. Others saw that for a standard of truth, she looked beyond society toward Plato's Form of the Good (Memorial).

Although she traveled to France, Spain, Greece, Turkey, and Italy, Young remained deeply devoted to England. During World War II she worked in Air Raid Precautions. Young felt deeply the disgrace of the Munich Pact and was not able to write about the events leading up to the war until afterwards, in *Chatterton Square* (1947). Two years later she died of lung cancer.

Emily Young, loved and admired by those who knew her, is said to have had a transforming influence on those she met even casually (Memorial). Her life and work reflect her belief that more than the movements of public and political bodies, our everyday lives are a rich source of the passions and perplexing mysteries of human life.

ANALYSIS

Emily Hilda Young's invocation of traditional forms emphasizes her affiliation with English novel traditions at the same time that it affords her an ironic indicator of modern instability and tension. In courtship novels and in studies of marriage Young queries and stretches the assumptions and conclusions of her literary predecessors. For example, the domestic novel *William*, alluding to *Pride and Prejudice* (Trodd 98), dramatizes the lack of moral consensus in modern society. *Miss Mole* highlights the courtship novel's damaging emphasis on female youth and chastity. If Young's protagonists suffer from the effects of gender and social prejudice, their spirited, intelligent, and imaginative natures direct them toward growth rather than self-defeat.

All the novels explore the distinction between a conventional and a true morality, and the conflict between them elicits Young's satirical humor. She is "a sharp and funny writer with a brilliant eye for moral fudging and verbal hypocrisy" (Beauman, Introduction to *Miss Mole* ix). One of her favorite scenarios is the encounter between the clergyman or the prosperous middle-class citizen and the perturbing individual who cannot be readily classified. Thus the minister in *Miss Mole* is silenced when he learns that his housekeeper owns property. He senses that Hannah Mole's education makes her his equal, but this threat to his notion of class boundaries leads him to conceal this fear as disapproval: "The alert bearing of her head, her quick step, seemed to him unsuitable in a housekeeper, and arrogant in a woman who had no pretensions to good looks" (160). Characteristic of Young's novels are witty sentences mimicking the contortions of characters whose desires conflict with their beliefs. Thus Maurice Roper struggles before the vivacity and beauty of his cousin's wife: "this approach justified, but unfortunately, it increased the attraction for which he had been blaming himself" (*The Vicar's Daughter* 215). Kate Nesbitt, believing that one's husband should never be openly criticized, "could still think bitterly that her own husband was often wrong, but where she triumphed was in never saying so" (*William* 140). The narrator of *The Curate's Wife* summarizes the curate's attitude toward his bride: "She was beautiful and gay and independent, she was like light in a dark place to Cecil Sproat and his fear of what she might ultimately make him see was at present submerged in his desire for her" (15).

In several of the novels, including *William*, *Miss Mole*, and *The Curate's Wife*, a woman's search for truth apart from social or religious doctrine leads to an unconventional sexual liaison. Louisa Grimshaw of *The Curate's Wife*, once guilty of adultery, is unacceptable to Upper Radstowe society, yet she embodies the vitality and natural wisdom that can help her well-married daughter through her own marital difficulties. In *William* one of the five Nesbitt children leaves her husband for another man. Lydia's decision estranges her from her mother, who finds safety in a fixed moral code, but it earns the sympathy of her father, for whom Lydia's action is an instance of moral courage. *William* illustrates how the modern novel engaged in the social debates of its day: by making Lydia's father the center of sympathetic perception, Young defuses the modern woman's restlessness of the misogynist tone with which it was often treated in the press. For William, "this affair had not the faintest colouring of immorality. He saw it, stripped of all falseness, all habits of mind and all accepted safeguards, as a painful attempt after truth and beauty" (183).

To explore the conflict between a morality based in social and religious codes and an intuitive, natural morality, Young turned to the beloved landscape of Bristol and Clifton (which she rechristened "Radstowe" and "Upper Radstowe"). As early as *The Misses Mallett*, originally titled *The Bridge Dividing*, she drew on the dramatic contrast between the town on one side of the Avon and the untamed Somerset country on the other to express the dual nature of her characters. The steep Avon gorge mirrors the gulf within them; the Brunel suspension bridge and their travel across it suggest the possibility of negotiating the divide between their societally shaped and their natural, instinctive, or passionate selves. Both Glen Cavaliero and Sally Beauman have discussed this dimension of Young's fiction. Lydia Nesbitt of *William* escapes from her marriage and from London into this country with her lover. In *The Misses Mallett* Rose Mallett's susceptibility to the wild beauty of the country awakens her passion for Francis Sales, whose suit she had earlier rejected. At first the landscape is merely a vehicle for her wistful emotions, but as she matures, she recognizes that the country, with its "secrets kept for countless centuries by the earth which was rich and fecund and alive," has a meaningful and separate heritage (57). As Cavaliero points out, although Young shares some features of rural novelists, she does not attempt to recapture a way of life lived in a rural society. The topography to which she returns again and again in her novels is used, instead, as an index of characters' responses to the pressures of social change in the first half of the century. William Nesbitt, for example, delights in the "happy, haphazard intertwining of countryside and city" (*William* 5), perhaps aware that the "aged city had tried to conquer the country and had failed, for the spirit of woods and open spaces, of water and trees and wind, survived among the very roofs" (*The Misses Mallett* 76–77). Many of Young's characters, though they may have been transplanted to the city, retain their country heritage in the form of an essential wisdom, a vitality free of prudery, and a confidence underlying personal misfortune. These qualities enable them to cut through the rigid lines governing social transactions in the city.

The competing claims of individual and society—a staple of English fiction—recur in all the novels, but are informed, in tone and technique, by modern psychology. Young was especially interested in romantic fantasy and explored the fine line between consolatory daydreaming and harmful self-deception. The elder Misses Mallett construct romantic pasts both to conceal and compensate for the emptiness of their lives. Both *Miss Mole* and *Celia* portray women who use imagination to escape from constricted domestic roles, though the atmosphere of *Celia* is considerably more claustrophobic. At the outset of the novel Celia must "teach herself with difficulty that the mind need not be bounded by walls" (17). But these two novels also portray the egotistical, isolating side of the imagination. Each woman makes an imaginative excursion into the past, where each reconstructs a past love affair as an "inviolably safe" treasure (*Celia* 280). For both women, this private fantasy is an unacknowledged retreat from the more challenging relationships of the present. The self-deception they at last uncover, and its basis in egotism, brings out a humbling resemblance to those they had regarded as moral or imaginative inferiors.

Increasingly in the later novels—*The Curate's Wife*, *Celia*, and *Chatterton Square*—Young studied the effects of such egotism within marriage. While Hannah Mole and Celia each take shelter in romantic fantasy, the education of the men in these novels has made them more liable to an inflated self-image. Young therefore did not rely on the eventual self-examination of the women to bring about the reform of the men. Instead, she drew parodically on the conventions of Gothic fiction. Both John Fellows (*Celia*) and Herbert Blackett (*Chatterton Square*) use domestic space as a mirror for an aggrandized self-image, but their environment becomes phantasmagoric when they are forced to confront the horror of their own self-representation.

Miss Mole illustrates Emily Young's concerns and her gifts at their best. Although it is still little known, it is a masterpiece of twentieth-century fiction. Young's protagonist—a forty-year-old unmarried woman, by birth a countrywoman, by education a gentlewoman—had hardly before been given a central place in fiction. If the society of Upper Radstowe has difficulty placing Hannah Mole, the reader glimpses her rich life experience in the background of present events and understands its decisive influence on her nature. Hannah's self-perception is characterized by a pervasive doubleness, for "[s]he could see herself clearly enough with other people's eyes" (37). That duality informs the structure of the novel and the shape of its characteristic sentences. A distinctly and memorably individual character, Hannah nonetheless embodies a female experience of modernity. A chance encounter with her well-to-do cousin brings out Hannah's wit and irreverence, along with an evasiveness born of self-protection. But alone, and aware that she is about to be dismissed from yet another job offering no scope for her faculties, Hannah's thoughts darken. As she walks behind the cart transporting her trunk to a new post, she sees the procession as "a detachment of an army of women like herself who went from house to house behind their boxes, a sad multitude of women with carefully pleasant faces, hiding their ailments, lowering their ages and thankfully accepting less than they earned" (51). Throughout the novel a dark undertone beneath a spirited, witty surface captures Hannah Mole's duality as well as E.H. Young's vision.

Miss Mole's form and characteristic sentence shapes—including circumlocution, elision of events in the plot, and ruptures in the narrative line—reflect both the underlying confidence of its protagonist and her evasion of painful memory. This invention of techniques to represent competing layers of the protagonist's consciousness aligns Young with the innovations of modernism. For example, the characteristic circumlocution of the sentences, by keeping painful material subordinated to self-congratulation, implies Hannah's position at the margins of her society and suggests itself as a vehicle for her defensive posture. (Hannah is also defensive in ways that are less immediately apparent to the reader.)

As in other Young novels, the protagonist's wide outlook has a foil in the narrower vision of an insider, in this case, a minister. The antagonism between Hannah Mole and Robert Corder illustrates the countrywoman's perception of herself as one piece of a natural design in friction with the patriarch's vision of himself at the center of the world. But the protagonist's moral vision is tested in the course of the novel. Hannah's intelligence and life experience make her a sharp critic of patriarchal double standards; she voices the feminist argument only half articulated by younger, less experienced Young heroines. Without undermining that argument, Young meticulously illuminates the moral complexity of the conflict. There is a fine line between Hannah's harmless imaginative excursions and her harmful tale telling, and in crossing the line she begins to resemble the self-important Robert Corder, whose need for a flattering role she had secretly mocked. This self-confrontation, this grotesque parody of herself in her opponent, sets self-reform in motion.

ASSESSMENT

The early twentieth century saw rapid expansion and diversification of the novel-reading public. Such expansion brought with it the proliferation of terms used to categorize works of fiction. Novels deemed modernist have been valued as works of high culture and incorporated into academic literary canons. Other novels, maintaining high literary standards and reaching a large audience of middle-class readers, engaged with urgent social questions and performed important cultural work. Among such novelists E.H. Young is prominent. Her eleven novels, written in a distinctive, modern, witty voice, are evidence of high literary achievement. Young made strategic use of generic expectations, maintaining English novel traditions even as she adapted them for the experiences of modernity. Her novels probed central questions of morality and sexuality; she specialized in what one reviewer termed "the contact of differing outlooks" ("Old and New Fashions") to explore how individuals in modern society may find fulfillment.

BIBLIOGRAPHY

Primary Sources

A Corn of Wheat. London: Heinemann, 1910.
Yonder. 1912. London: Heinemann; New York: Doran, 1913.
Moor Fires. 1916. London: Murray; New York: Harcourt, 1927.
The Misses Mallett. First pub. as *The Bridge Dividing*. 1922. Garden City, NY: Dial-Doubleday, 1984.
William. 1925. London: Virago, 1988.
The Vicar's Daughter. 1928. London: Virago, 1992.
Miss Mole. 1930. Garden City, NY: Dial-Doubleday, 1985.

Jenny Wren. 1932. London: Virago, 1985.

"The Stream." In *Twelve Best Stories from Good Housekeeping*. Ed. Alice M. Head. London: Ivor Nicholson & Watson, 1932.

The Curate's Wife. 1934. London: Virago, 1985.

Celia. 1937. London: Virago, 1990.

Caravan Island. Illus. H.J. Haley. London: Black, 1940; New York: Harcourt, 1940.

River Holiday. London: Black, 1942.

Chatterton Square. 1947. London: Virago, 1987; New York: Penguin, 1987.

"The Grey Mare." Adapt. and narr. Richard West. *Mid-Morning Story*. BBC. 17 February 1948.

"A Cow's Tail." Narr. Gladys Young. BBC. 20 September 1950.

Secondary Sources

Bayley, John. Introduction to *William*. By E.H. Young. London and New York: Virago, 1988. v–xv.

Beauman, Sally. Introduction to *The Curate's Wife*. By E.H. Young. London: Virago, 1985. v–xv.

———. Introduction to *Jenny Wren*. By E.H. Young. New York: Penguin, 1985. v–xv.

———. Introduction to *The Misses Mallett*. By E.H. Young. London: Virago, 1984. vii–xvi.

———. Introduction to *Miss Mole*. By E.H. Young. London: Virago, 1984. vii–xiii.

BBC Written Archives Centre. Programme Index. Reading, England.

Cavaliero, Glen. *The Rural Tradition in the English Novel, 1900–1939*. Totowa, NJ: Rowman, 1977.

Gotch, David. Letter to the author, 19 October 1990.

Henderson, Ralph. Letter to Jonathan Cape. N.d. Jonathan Cape Archive, University of Reading.

Knight, Lynn. Introduction to *Celia*. By E.H. Young. London: Virago, 1990. i–vi.

Mais, S.P.B. *Some Modern Authors*. New York: Dodd, 1923.

Memorial essay, ts. Papers of E.H. Young and Ralph Henderson. London.

"Miss E.H. Young." Obituary. *Times* 10 August 1949: 7e.

Mooney, Bel. Afterword to *Chatterton Square*. By E.H. Young. 1987. 369–378.

"Old and New Fashions." Rev. of *William*. *Spectator* 134 (30 May 1925): 896.

Trodd, Anthea. *Women's Writing in English: Britain, 1900–1945*. London: Longman, 1998.

Woolf, Virginia. "To Lady Ottoline Morrell." 19 February 1938. In *Leave the Letters Till We're Dead: The Letters of Virginia Woolf*. Ed. Nigel Nicolson. Vol. 6. London: Hogarth, 1994: 215–216.

Selected Bibliography

Abel, Elizabeth. *Virginia Woolf and the Fictions of Psychoanalysis*. Chicago: U of Chicago P, 1989.

———, Marianne Hirsch, and Elizabeth Langland, eds. *The Voyage In: Fictions of Female Development*. Hanover: UP of New England, 1983.

Alexander, Flora. *Contemporary Women Novelists*. London: Edward Arnold, 1989.

Allan, Tuzyline Jita. *Womanist and Feminist Aesthetics: A Comparative Review*. Athens: Ohio UP, 1995.

Anderson, Linda, ed. *Plotting Change: Contemporary Women's Fiction*. London: Edward Arnold, 1990.

Angier, Carole. *Jean Rhys*. London: Deutsch, 1990.

Antonaccio, Maria, and William Schweiker, eds. *Iris Murdoch and the Search for Human Goodness*. Chicago: U of Chicago P, 1996.

Aston, Elaine. *Caryl Churchill*. Plymouth, UK: Northcote, 1997.

———, and Janelle Reinelt, eds. *The Cambridge Companion to Modern British Women Playwrights*. Cambridge: Cambridge UP, 2000.

Auerbach, Nina. *Communities of Women: An Idea in Fiction*. Cambridge, MA: Harvard UP, 1978.

Austin, Allan E. *Elizabeth Bowen*. Rev. ed. Boston: Twayne, 1989.

Bailey, Hilary. *Vera Brittain*. New York: Penguin, 1987; Oxford: Isis, 1988.

Baldanza, Frank. *Ivy Compton-Burnett*. New York: Twayne, 1964.

Barbera, Jack, and William McBrien. *Stevie: A Biography of Stevie Smith*. Oxford: Oxford UP, 1987.

Bargainnier, Earl F. *The Gentle Art of Murder: The Detective Fiction of Agatha Christie*. Bowling Green, OH: Bowling Green U Popular P, 1980.

———, ed. *Ten Women of Mystery*. Bowling Green, OH: Bowling Green State U Popular P, 1981.

Barreca, Regina, ed. *Fay Weldon's Wicked Fictions*. Hanover, NH: UP of New England, 1994.

Barrett, Eileen, and Patricia Cramer, eds. *Virginia Woolf: Lesbian Readings*. New York: New York UP, 1997.

Bayley, John. *Elegy for Iris*. New York: St. Martin's, 1999.

———. *Iris: A Memoir of Iris Murdoch*. London: Duckworth, 1998.

Beauman, Nicola. *A Very Great Profession: The Woman's Novel 1914–39*. London: Virago, 1983.

Beauvoir, Simone de. *The Second Sex*. Trans. H.M. Parshley. New York: Knopf, 1952.

Bell, Quentin. *Virginia Woolf: A Biography*. New York: Harcourt, 1972.

Belsey, Catherine. "Constructing the Subject: Deconstructing the Text." In *Feminist Criticism and Social Change*. Ed. Judith Newton and Deborah Rosenfelt. London: Methuen, 1985. 45–64.

Berkman, Sylvia. *Katherine Mansfield: A Critical Study*. New Haven: Yale UP, 1951.

Berney, K.A., ed. *Contemporary Women Dramatists*. London: St. James, 1994.

Berry, Paul, and Mark Bostridge. *Vera Brittain: A Life*. London: Chatto, 1995.

Biles, Jack I., ed. *British Novelists since 1900*. New York: AMS, 1987.

Blain, Virginia, Patricia Clements, and Isabel Grundy, eds. *Feminist Companion to Literature in English*. New Haven and London: Yale UP, 1990.

Bloom, Harold, ed. *Iris Murdoch*. New York: Chelsea House, 1986.

———, ed. *Elizabeth Bowen*. Modern Critical Views. New York: Chelsea, 1987.

Bluemel, Kristin. *Experimenting on the Borders of Modernism: Dorothy Richardson's Pilgrimage*. Athens: U of Georgia P, 1997.

Bokat, Nicole Suzanne. *The Novels of Margaret Drabble: This Freudian Family Nexus*. New York: Lang, 1998.

Bold, Alan. *Muriel Spark*. Contemporary Writers. London and New York: Methuen, 1986.

———, ed. *Muriel Spark: An Odd Capacity for Vision*. London: Vision, 1984.

Boll, T.E.M. *Miss May Sinclair, Novelist: A Biographical and Critical Introduction*. Rutherford, NJ: Fairleigh Dickinson UP, 1973.

Bowers, Bege K., and Barbara Brothers. *Reading and Writing Women's Lives: A Study of the Novel of Manners*. Ann Arbor: UMI, 1990.

Bowlby, Rachel. *Feminist Destinations and Further Essays on Virginia Woolf*. Edinburgh: Edinburgh UP, 1997.

Brabazon, James. *Dorothy L. Sayers: The Life of a Courageous Woman*. London: Gallancz, 1981. As *Dorothy L. Sayers: A Life*, New York: Scribner's, 1981.

Brater, Enoch, ed. *Feminine Focus: The New Women Playwrights*. Oxford: Oxford UP, 1989.

Bristow, Joseph, ed. *Sexual Sameness: Textual Differences in Lesbian and Gay Writing*. London: Routledge, 1992.

Brittain, Vera. *Testament of Friendship: The Story of Winifred Holtby*. 1940. London: Virago, 1980.

Brittain, Vera. *Testament of Youth: An Autobiographical Study of the Years 1900–1925*. London: Virago, 1978.

Brothers, Barbara. "*Summer Will Show*: The Historical Novel as Social Criticism." In *Women in History, Literature and the Arts: A Festschrift for Hildegard Schnuttegen in Honor of Her Thirty Years of Outstanding Service*. Ed. Baird Lange and Thomas A. Copeland. Youngstown, OH: Youngstown State U, 1989.

Brownley, Martine Watson. *Deferrals of Domain: Contemporary Women Novelists and the State*. New York: St. Martin's, 2000.

Brunsdale, Mitzi. *Dorothy L. Sayers: Solving the Mystery of Wickedness*. Providence: Berg, 1991.

Burkhart, Charles. *The Pleasure of Miss Pym*. Austin: U of Texas P, 1987.

———, ed. *The Art of I. Compton-Burnett: A Collection of Critical Essays*. London: Gollancz, 1972.

———, ed. *I. Compton-Burnett*. London: Gollancz, 1965.

———, ed. *Twentieth Century Literature* [Ivy Compton-Burnett issue] 25.2 (1979).

Byatt, A.S. *Degrees of Freedom: The Novels of Iris Murdoch*. London: Vintage, 1994.

———. *Iris Murdoch*. London: Longman, 1976.

Calinescu, Matei. *Five Faces of Modernity: Modernism, Avant-Garde, Decadence, Kitsch, Postmodernism*. Durham, NC: Duke UP, 1987.

Carlson, Susan. *Women and Comedy: Rewriting the British Theatrical Tradition*. Ann Arbor: U of Michigan P, 1991.

Cavaliero, Glen. *The Rural Tradition in the English Novel, 1900–1939*. Totowa, NJ: Rowman, 1977.

Cederstrom, Lorelei. *Fine-Tuning the Feminine Psyche: Jungian Patterns in the Novels of Doris Lessing*. New York: Peter Lang, 1990.

Christensen, Philip Harlan. "Penelope Fitzgerald." In *British Novelists since 1960, Second Series*. Vol. 194 of *Dictionary of Literary Biography*. Detroit: Gale, 1998. 120–127.

Collins, Laura Roberts. *English Country Life in the Barsetshire Novels of Angela Thirkell*. Westport, CT: Greenwood, 1994.

Coomes, David. *Dorothy L. Sayers: A Careless Rage for Life*. Batavia, NY: Lion, 1992.

Creighton, Joanne V. *Margaret Drabble*. London: Methuen, 1985.

Crosland, Margaret. *Beyond the Lighthouse: English Women Novelists in the Twentieth Century*. New York: Taplinger, 1981.

Cunningham, Valentine. *British Writers of the Thirties*. Oxford and New York: Oxford UP, 1988.

Dale, Alzina Stone, ed. *Dorothy L. Sayers: The Centenary Celebration*. New York: Walker, 1993.

Daleski, H.M. *The Divided Heroine: A Recurrent Pattern in Six English Novels*. New York: Holmes & Meier, 1984.

Daly, Saralyn R. *Katherine Mansfield*. New York: Twayne, 1965.

Day, G., and G. Wisker. *British Poetry: 1900–50 Aspects of Tradition*. London: Macmillan, 1995.

de Lauretis, Teresa. *Technologies of Gender: Essays on Theory, Film, and Fiction*. Bloomington: Indiana UP, 1987.

Deakin, Motley F. *Rebecca West*. Boston: Twayne, 1980.

Demastes, William W., ed. *British Playwrights, 1956–1995*. Westport, CT: Greenwood, 1996.

Dhawan, R.K, ed. *Indian Women Novelists*. Set 3, vol. 2. New Delhi: Prestige, 1995.

Dick, Kay. *Ivy and Stevie: Ivy Compton-Burnett and Stevie Smith, Conversations and Reflections*. London: Duckworth, 1971.

———. *Ivy and Stevie: Ivy Compton-Burnett and Stevie Smith*. London: Alison & Busby, 1983.
Dipple, Elizabeth. *Iris Murdoch: Work for the Spirit*. Chicago: U of Chicago P, 1982; London: Methuen, 1982.
Doan, Laura, L., ed. *Old Maids to Radical Spinsters: Unmarried Women in the Twentieth Century*. Urbana: U of Illinois P, 1991.
Dock, Leslie A. "Brigid Brophy: Artist in the Baroque." Diss. U of Wisconsin at Madison, 1976.
Dorosz, Wiktoria. *Subjective Vision and Human Relationships in the Novels of Rosamond Lehmann*. Stockholm: Almqvist, 1975.
Dowling, Finula. *Fay Weldon's Fiction*. Madison, NJ: Fairleigh Dickinson UP, 1998.
Draine, Betsy. *Substance under Pressure: Artistic Coherence and Evolving Form in the Novels of Doris Lessing*. Madison: U of Wisconsin P, 1983.
Durkin, Mary Brian. *Dorothy L. Sayers*. Boston: Twayne, 1980.
Edgecombe, Rodney Stenning. *Vocation and Identity in the Fiction of Muriel Spark*. Columbia: U of Missouri P, 1990.
Emery, Mary Lou. *Jean Rhys at "World's End": Novels of Colonial and Sexual Exile*. Austin: U of Texas P, 1990.
Faderman, Lillian. *Surpassing the Love of Men: Romantic Friendship and Love between Women from the Renaissance to the Present*. 1981. London: Women's Press, 1985.
Faulks, Lana. *Fay Weldon*. New York: Twayne, 1998.
Ferrer, Daniel. *Virginia Woolf and the Madness of Language*. London and New York: Routledge, 1990.
Fishburn, Katherine. *Doris Lessing: Life, Work, and Criticism*. Fredericton, NB: York, 1987.
———. *Reading Buchi Emecheta: Cross-Cultural Conversations*. Westport, CT: Greenwood, 1995.
Fisher-Wirth, Anne. " 'Hunger Art:' The Novels of Anita Brookner." *Twentieth Century Literature* 41 (Spring 1995): 1–15.
Friedman, Alan Warren, ed. *Forms of Modern British Fiction*. Austin: U of Texas P, 1975.
Fritzer, Penelope Joan. *Ethnicity and Gender in the Barsetshire Novels of Angela Thirkell*. Westport, CT: Greenwood, 1999.
Fromm, Gloria G. *Dorothy Richardson: A Biography*. Urbana: U of Illinois P, 1977.
Gaillard, Dawson. *Dorothy L. Sayers*. New York: Ungar, 1981.
Galin, Muge. *Between East and West: Sufism in the Novels of Doris Lessing*. Albany: State U of New York P, 1997.
Gentile, Kathy Justice. *Ivy Compton-Burnett*. New York: St. Martin's, 1991.
Gevirtz, Susan. *Narrative's Journey: The Fiction and Film Writing of Dorothy Richardson*. New York: Peter Lang, 1996.
Gidez, Richard. *P.D. James*. Boston: Twayne, 1986.
Gilbert, Sandra M. "Soldier's Heart: Literary Men, Literary Women, and the Great War." *Signs* 8.3 (1983): 422–450.
Gill, Gillian. *Agatha Christie: The Woman and Her Mysteries*. New York: Free Press, 1990.
Gillette, Jane Brown. " 'Oh, What a Something Web We Weave': The Novels of Elizabeth Taylor." *Twentieth Century Literature* 35.1 (Spring 1989): 94–112.
Gindin, James: "Elizabeth Jane Howard." In *Contemporary Novelists*. Ed. Susan Windisch Brown. 1986. New York: St. James, 1996.
Glendinning, Victoria. *Edith Sitwell: A Unicorn among Lions*. Oxford: Oxford UP, 1983.
———. *Elizabeth Bowen*. 1977. New York: Knopf, 1978.
———. *Rebecca West. A Life*. New York: Knopf, 1987.
———. *Vita: The Life of V. Sackville-West*. New York: Knopf, 1983.
Goldman, Jane. *The Feminist Aesthetics of Virginia Woolf: Modernism, Post-Impressionism, and the Politics of the Visual*. Cambridge and New York: Cambridge UP, 1998.
Gorham, Deborah. *Vera Brittain: A Feminist Life*. Oxford: Blackwell, 1996.
Griffiths, Trevor R., and Margaret Llewellyn-Jones, eds. *British and Irish Women Dramatists since 1958*. Buckingham: Open UP, 1993.
Hannay, John. *The Intertextuality of Fate: A Study of Margaret Drabble*. Columbia: U of Missouri P, 1986.
Hannay, Margaret P., ed. *As Her Whimsey Took Her: Critical Essays on the Work of Dorothy L. Sayers*. Kent: Kent State UP, 1979.
Hanscombe, Gillian E. *The Art of Life: Dorothy Richardson and the Development of Feminist Consciousness*. London: Peter Owen, 1982.
———, and Virginia L. Smyers. *Writing for Their Lives: The Modernist Women, 1910–1940*. London: Women's Press, 1987.
Harkness, Bruce. "P.D. James." In *Art in Crime Writing: Essays on Detective Fiction*. Ed. Bernard Benstock. New York: St. Martin's, 1983. 119–141.
Harman, Claire. *Sylvia Townsend Warner: A Biography*. London: Chatto, 1989.
Harrex, S.C. *The Fire and the Offering: The English-Language Novel of India, 1935–1970*. Vol. 1. Calcutta: Writers Workshop, 1977.
Harris, Greg. "Compulsory Masculinity, Britain, and

the Great War: The Literary-Historical Work of Pat Barker." *Critique* 39.4 (Summer 1998): 290–304.

Heusel, Barbara Stevens. *Patterned Aimlessness: Iris Murdoch's Novels of the 1970s and 1980s*. Athens: U of Georgia P, 1995.

Hite, Molly. *The Other Side of the Story: Structures and Strategies of Contemporary Feminist Narrative*. Ithaca: Cornell UP, 1989.

Holtby, Winifred. *Letters to a Friend*. Ed. Alice Holtby and Jean McWilliam. 1937. Bath: Chivers, 1971.

Hone, Ralph E. *Dorothy L. Sayers: A Literary Biography*. Kent: Kent State UP, 1979.

Hopkins, Chris. "The Neglect of Brigid Brophy." *Review of Contemporary Fiction* 15.3 (Fall 1995): 12–17.

Hosmer, Robert E., Jr., ed. *Contemporary British Women Writers: Narrative Strategies*. New York: St. Martin's, 1993.

Howells, Coral Ann. *Jean Rhys*. London: Harvester Wheatsheaf, 1991.

Humm, Maggie. *Border Traffic: Strategies of Contemporary Women Writers*. Manchester and New York: Manchester UP, 1991.

Hutcheon, Linda. *A Poetics of Postmodernism: History, Theory, Fiction*. London: Routledge, 1988.

Hynes, Joseph. *The Art of the Real: Muriel Spark's Novels*. Rutherford, NJ: Fairleigh Dickinson UP, 1988.

———, ed. *Critical Essays on Muriel Spark*. New York: G.K. Hall, 1992.

Itzin, Catherine. *Stages in the Revolution: Political Theatre in Britain since 1968*. London: Methuen, 1986.

Jain, Jasbir. "Feminist Drama: The Politics of the Self: Churchill and Keatley." In *Women's Writing: Text and Context*. Jaipur: Rawat, 1996. 274–287.

Jain, Jasbir, and Amina Amin, eds. *Margins of Erasure: Purdah in the Subcontinental Novel in English*. New Delhi: Sterling, 1995.

Jameson, Fredric. *Postmodernism, or, the Cultural Logic of Late Capitalism*. Durham, NC: Duke UP, 1991.

Jordan, Heather Bryant. *How Will the Heart Endure? Elizabeth Bowen and the Landscape of War*. Ann Arbor: U of Michigan P, 1992.

Joseph, Margaret P. *Kamala Markandaya*. New Delhi: Arnold-Heinemann, 1980.

Kaplan, Sydney Janet. *Feminine Consciousness in the Modern British Novel*. Urbana: U of Illinois P, 1975.

———. *Katherine Mansfield and the Origins of Modernist Fiction*. Ithaca: Cornell UP, 1991.

Kennard, Jean E. *Vera Brittain and Winifred Holtby: A Working Partnership*. Hanover, NH: UP of New England, 1989.

Kenney, Catherine. *The Remarkable Case of Dorothy L. Sayers*. Kent: Kent State UP, 1990.

Kenyon, Olga. *Women Novelists Talk*. New York: Carroll & Graf, 1989.

———. *Writing Women: Contemporary Women Novelists*. London and Concord, MA: Pluto, 1991.

———, ed. *Women Novelists Today: A Survey of English Writing in the Seventies and Eighties*. Brighton: Harvester, 1988.

Keyssar, Helene. *Feminist Theatre: An Introduction to Plays of Contemporary British and American Women*. Basingstoke: Macmillan, 1984.

———, ed. *Feminist Theatre and Theory*. New York: St. Martin's, 1996.

Khan, Nosheen. *Women's Poetry of the First World War*. New York: Harvester, 1988.

Klein, Carole. *Doris Lessing*. London: Duckworth; New York: Carroll & Graf, 2000.

Klein, Kathleen Gregory. *The Woman Detective: Gender and Genre*. 2nd ed. Urbana: U of Illinois P, 1995.

Knapp, Mona. *Doris Lessing*. New York: Ungar, 1984.

Kobler, Jasper F. *Katherine Mansfield: A Study of the Short Fiction*. Boston: Twayne, 1990.

Kristeva, Julia. *Powers of Horror: An Essay on Abjection*. Trans. Leon Roudiez. New York: Columbia UP, 1982.

Lassner, Phyllis. *British Women Writers of World War II: Battlegrounds of Their Own*. Basingstoke: Macmillan, 1998.

———. *Elizabeth Bowen*. Women Writers. Basingstoke: Macmillan, 1990.

———. *Elizabeth Bowen: A Study of the Short Fiction*. Twayne's Studies in Short Fiction 27. New York: Twayne, 1991.

———. "Fiction as Historical Critique: The Retrospective World War II Novels of Beryl Bainbridge and Maureen Duffy." *Phoebe* 3.2 (Fall 1991): 12–24.

Laurence, Patricia Ondek. *The Reading of Silence: Virginia Woolf in the English Tradition*. Stanford: Stanford UP, 1991.

Leclercq, Florence. *Elizabeth Taylor*. Boston: Twayne, 1985.

Lee, Hermione. *Virginia Woolf*. London: Chatto, 1996.

LeSturgeon, Diana E. *Rosamond Lehmann*. New York: Twayne, 1965.

Levenback, Karen L. *Virginia Woolf and the Great War*. Syracuse: Syracuse UP, 1999.

Liddell, Robert. *Elizabeth and Ivy*. London: Peter Owen, 1986.

Light, Alison. *Forever England: Femininity, Literature and Conservatism Between the Wars*. London: Routledge, 1991.

Lilly, Mark, ed. *Lesbian and Gay Writing: An Anthology of Critical Essays*. London: Macmillan, 1990.

Lindblad, Ishrat. *Pamela Hansford Johnson*. Boston: Twayne, 1982.

Little, Judy. *Comedy and the Woman Writer: Woolf, Spark, and Feminism*. Lincoln: U of Nebraska P, 1983.

Maida, Patricia D, and Nicholas B. Spornick. *Murder She Wrote: A Study of Agatha Christie's Detective Fiction*. Bowling Green, OH: Bowling Green State U Popular P, 1982.

Malkoff, Karl. *Muriel Spark*. Columbia Essays on Modern Writers, no. 36. New York: Columbia UP, 1968.

Marcus, Jane. *Virginia Woolf and the Languages of Patriarchy*. Bloomington: Indiana UP, 1987.

———. "A Wilderness of One's Own: Feminist Fantasy Novels of the Twenties: Sylvia Townsend Warner and Rebecca West." In *Women Writers and the City*. Ed. Susan Squier. Knoxville: U of Tennessee P, 1984.

Maroula, Joannou, ed. *Women Writers of the 1930s: Gender, Politics and History*. Edinburgh: Edinburgh UP, 1999.

Massie, Allan. *Muriel Spark*. Edinburgh: Ramsay Head, 1979.

Mather, Rachel R. *The Heirs of Jane Austen: Twentieth-Century Writers of the Comedy of Manners*. New York: Peter Lang, 1996.

Mathur, Tanuja. "Metaphor of 'Space': Charlotte Keatley's Play My *Mother Said I Never Should*." In *Women's Writing: Text and Context*. Jaipur: Rawat, 1996. 288–294.

Michael, Magali Cornier. *Feminism and the Postmodern Impulse*. Albany: State U of New York P, 1996.

Montefiore, Janet. *Men and Women Writers of the 1930s: The Dangerous Flood of History*. London: Routledge, 1996.

Monteith, Moira, ed. *Women's Writing: A Challenge to Theory*. Sussex: Harvester, 1986.

Moran, Mary Hurley. *Penelope Lively*. New York: Twayne, 1993.

Morrow, Patrick D. *Katherine Mansfield's Fiction*. Bowling Green, OH: Bowling Green State U Popular P, 1993.

Muir, Kenneth. "Susan Hill's Fiction." In *The Uses of Fiction: Essays on the Modern Novel in Honour of Arnold Kettle*. Ed. Douglas Jefferson and Graham Martin. Open UP, 1982. 273–285.

Mukherjee, Meenakshi. *The Twice Born Fiction: Themes and Techniques of the Indian Novel in English*. New Delhi: Heinemann, 1971.

Munt, Sally R. *Murder by the Book? Feminism and the Crime Novel*. New York: Routledge, 1994.

Murray, Heather. *Double Lives: Women in the Stories of Katherine Mansfield*. New Zealand: U of Otago, 1990.

Murry, John Middleton. *Katherine Mansfield and Other Literary Portraits*. London: Nevill, 1949.

Newton, Judith, and Deborah Rosenfelt, eds. *Feminist Criticism and Social Change*. London: Methuen, 1985.

Nicolson, Nigel. *Portrait of a Marriage*. London: Weidenfeld & Nicolson, 1973.

O'Callaghan, Evelyn. *Woman Version: Theoretical Approaches to West Indian Fiction by Women*. London: Macmillan, 1993.

O'Connor, Teresa. *Jean Rhys: The West Indian Novels*. New York: New York UP, 1986.

Orel, Harold. *The Literary Achievement of Rebecca West*. New York: St. Martin's, 1986.

Parkin-Gounelas, Ruth. *Fictions of the Female Self*. London: Macmillan, 1991.

Pilditch, Jan, ed. *The Critical Response to Katherine Mansfield*. Westport, CT: Greenwood, 1996.

Pratt, Annis. *Archetypal Patterns in Women's Fiction*. Bloomington: Indiana UP, 1981.

Quigly, Isabel. *Contemporary Novelists*. Ed. James Vinson and D.L. Kirkpatrick. 2nd ed. London and New York: St. James/St. Martin's, 1976.

———. *Pamela Hansford Johnson*. Writers and Their Work. London: Longman, 1968.

Rabey, David Ian. "Defining Difference: Timberlake Wertenbaker's Drama of Language, Dispossession, and Discovery." *Modern Drama* 33.4 (December 1990): 518–528.

Radford, Jean. *Dorothy Richardson*. New York: Harvester, 1991.

Raitt, Suzanne. *Vita and Virginia: The Work and Friendship of V. Sackville-West and Virginia Woolf*. Oxford: Clarendon Press; New York: Oxford UP, 1993.

Randall, Phyllis, ed. *Caryl Churchill: A Casebook*. New York: Garland, 1988.

Rankin, Arthur C. *The Poetry of Stevie Smith: Little Girl Lost*. Totowa, NJ: Barnes, 1985.

Reddy, K. Venkata. *Major Indian Novelists*. New Delhi: Prestige, 1990.

Reynolds, Barbara. *Dorothy L. Sayers: Her Life and Soul*. New York: St. Martin's, 1993.

Rollyson, Carl. *Rebecca West: A Life*. New York: Scribner's, 1996.

Rose, Ellen Cronan. *The Novels of Margaret Drabble: Equivocal Figures* London: Macmillan, 1980; Tocown, NJ: Barnes & Noble, 1980.

———, ed. *Critical Essays on Margaret Drabble*. Boston: G.K. Hall, 1985.
Rosenman, Ellen Bayuk. *The Invisible Presence: Virginia Woolf and the Mother-Daughter Relationship*. Baton Rouge: Louisiana State UP, 1986.
———. *A Room of One's Own: Women Writers and the Politics of Creativity*. New York: Twayne, 1995.
Rossen, Janice. *The World of Barbara Pym*. New York: St. Martin's, 1987.
Ruddick, Bill. " 'A Clear Channel Flowing': The Poetry of Fleur Adcock." *Critical Quarterly* 26.4 (1983): 61–66.
Rule, Jane. *Lesbian Images*. London: Peter Davies, 1976.
Rusinko, Susan. *British Drama, 1950 to the Present: A Critical History*. Boston: Twayne, 1989.
Sadler, Lynn Veach. *Anita Brookner*. Boston: Twayne, 1990.
———. *Margaret Drabble*. Boston: Twayne, 1986.
Sage, Lorna. *Angela Carter*. Plymouth, UK: Northcote, 1994.
Salwak, Dale, ed. *The Life and Work of Barbara Pym*. Iowa City: U of Iowa P, 1987.
Salzmann-Brunner, Brigitte. *Amanuenses to the Present: Protagonists in the Fiction of Penelope Mortimer, Margaret Drabble, and Fay Weldon*. Berne: Peter Lang, 1988.
Sceats, Sarah, and Gail Cunningham, eds. *Image and Power: Women in Fiction in the Twentieth Century*. London: Longman, 1996.
Scott, Bonnie Kime, ed. *The Gender of Modernism*. Bloomington: Indiana UP, 1990.
———. *Readings of Woolf, West, and Barnes*. Bloomington: Indiana UP, 1995.
Severin, Laura. *Stevie Smith's Resistant Antics*. Madison: U of Wisconsin P, 1997.
Shaw, Marion. *The Clear Stream: A Life of Winifred Holtby*. London: Virago, 1999.
———, and Sabine Vanacker. *Reflecting on Miss Marple*. New York: Routledge, 1991.
Showalter, Elaine. *A Literature of Their Own: British Women Novelists from Brontë to Lessing*. Princeton: Princeton UP, 1977.
Siebenheller, Norma. *P.D. James*. New York: Ungar, 1981.
Siefert, Susan E. *The Dilemma of the Talented Heroine*. St. Albans, VT: Eden, 1977.
Siegel, Ruth. *Rosamond Lehmann: A Thirties Writer*. New York: Peter Lang, 1989.
Simons, Judy. *Rosamond Lehmann*. Basingstoke: Macmillan, 1992.
Sinfield, Alan. *Society and Literature, 1945–1970*. New York: Holmes & Meier, 1983.
Sizemore, Christine. *A Female Vision of the City: London in the Novels of Five British Women*. Knoxville: U of Tennessee P, 1989.
Skinner, John. *The Fictions of Anita Brookner: Illusions of Romance*. Basingstoke: Macmillan; New York: St. Martin's, 1992.
Smith, Patricia Juliana. *Lesbian Panic: Homoeroticism in Modern British Women's Fiction*. New York: Columbia UP, 1997.
Soule, George. *Four British Women Novelists: Anita Brookner, Margaret Drabble, Iris Murdoch, and Barbara Pym*. Pasadena, CA: Salem, 1998.
Spacks, Patricia Meyer. *The Female Imagination*. New York: Avon, 1976.
Spalding, Frances. *Stevie Smith: A Biography*. New York: Norton, 1989.
Spear, Hilda. *Iris Murdoch*. Basingstoke, Macmillan; New York: St. Martin's, 1995.
Spender, Dale. *Women of Ideas and What Men Have Done to Them: From Aphra Behn to Adrienne Rich*. London: Routledge, 1982.
Sproxton, Judy. *The Women of Muriel Spark*. New York: St. Martin's, 1992.
Spurling, Hilary. *Ivy: The Life of Ivy Compton-Burnett*. New York: Knopf, 1984.
Squier, Susan M. *Virginia Woolf and London: The Sexual Politics of the City*. Chapel Hill: U of North Carolina P, 1985.
———, ed. *Women Writers and the City*. Knoxville: U of Tennessee P, 1984.
Staley, Thomas F., ed. *Twentieth Century Women Novelists*. London: Macmillan, 1982.
Stannard, Julian. *Fleur Adcock in Context: From Movement to Martians*. Lewiston, NY: E. Mellen, 1997.
Stephenson, Heide, and Natasha Langridge, eds. *Rage and Reason: Women Playwrights on Playwriting*. London: Methuen, 1997.
Sternlicht, Sanford. *Jean Rhys*. New York: Twayne, 1997.
———. *Stevie Smith*. Boston: Twayne, 1990.
Stetz, Margaret D. "Rebecca West's Criticism: Alliance, Tradition, and Modernism." In *New Directions in Feminist Criticism*. New York: Garland, 1994.
Stevens, Michael. *Vita Sackville-West: A Critical Biography*. New York: Scribner's, 1974.
Stevenson, Randall. *The British Novel since the Thirties: An Introduction*. London: Batsford, 1986.
Stovel, Nora Foster. *Margaret Drabble: Symbolic Moralist*. Mercer Island, WA: Starmont House, 1989.
Strickland, Margot. *Angela Thirkell: Portrait of a Lady Novelist*. London: Duckworth, 1977.
Todd, Janet. *Feminist Literary History*. New York: Routledge, 1988.

———, ed. *Dictionary of British Women Writers*. London: Routledge, 1989.

Trodd, Anthea. *Women's Writing in English: Britain, 1900–1945*. London and New York: Longmans, 1998.

Tucker, Lindsey, ed. *Critical Essays on Iris Murdoch*. New York: G.K. Hall, 1992.

Umeh, Marie, ed. *Emerging Perspectives on Buchi Emecheta*. Trenton, NJ: African World Press, 1996.

Wagoner, Mary S. *Agatha Christie*. Boston: Twayne, 1986.

Walker, Dorothea. *Muriel Spark*. Boston: Twayne, 1988.

Watson, Sara Ruth. *V. Sackville-West*. Boston: Twayne, 1972.

Waugh, Patricia. *Feminine Fictions: Revisiting the Postmodern*. London and New York: Routledge, 1989.

———. *Metafiction: The Theory and Practice of Self-Conscious Fiction*. London: Methuen, 1984.

———. *Practising Postmodernism, Reading Modernism*. London: Edward Arnold, 1992.

Weldon, Fay. *Rebecca West*. London: Viking, 1985.

Wennö, Elisabeth. *Ironic Formula in the Novels of Beryl Bainbridge*. Göteborg, Sweden: Acta Universitatis Gothoburgensis, 1993.

Werlock, Abby H.P., ed. *British Women Writing Fiction*. Tuscaloosa: U of Alabama P, 2000.

Whitehead, Anne. "Open to Suggestion: Hypnosis and History in Pat Barker's *Regeneration*." *Modern Fiction Studies* 44.3 (Fall 1998): 674–694.

Wisker, Gina, ed. *Black Women's Writing*. New York: St. Martin's, 1993.

———, and G. Day. "Recuperating and Revaluing: Edith Sitwell and Charlotte Mew." In *British Poetry, 1900–50: Aspects of Tradition*. Ed. G. Wisker and G. Day. Basingstoke: Macmillan, 1995.

Women's Writing: Text and Context. Jaipur: Rawat, 1996.

Woolf, Virginia. "Modern Fiction." In *Collected Essays*, vol. 2. London: Hogarth, 1966.

———. *Mr. Bennett and Mrs. Brown*, London: Hogarth, 1924

———. *A Room of One's Own*. 1929. New York: Harcourt, 1981.

———. *Three Guineas*. London: Hogarth, 1938.

Zangen, Britta. *A Life of Her Own: Feminism in Vera Brittain's Theory, Fiction, and Biography*. Frankfurt: Lang, 1996.

Zegger, Hrisey D. *May Sinclair*. Boston: Twayne, 1976.

Zwerdling, Alex. *Virginia Woolf and the Real World*. Berkeley: U of California P, 1986.

Index

Page numbers in **bold** refer to main entries.

3 Jelliplays (Jellicoe), 174
4:50 from Paddington (Christie), 75–76

Abbess of Crewe, The (Spark), 317
A.B.C. Murders, The (Christie), 75–77
Abel's Sister (Wertenbaker), 359
Abortive (Churchill), 81
About Time: An Aspect of Autobiography (Mortimer), 247
About Time Too: 1940–1978 (Mortimer), 249
Absent in the Spring (Christie), 75
According to Mark (Lively), 210
Account Rendered (Bowen), 36
Adcock, Fleur, **1–8**
Adventures of God in His Search for the Black Girl, The (Brophy), 47, 49
African Stories (Lessing), 198
After Easter (Devlin), 95–96
After Julius (Howard), 155–156
After Leaving Mr. Mackenzie (Rhys), 268, 270
After the Death of Don Juan (Warner), 345
Afterthought (Bowen), 29
Albatross, The (Hill), 136
Aldous Huxley: A Biography (Bedford), 22
Alexander, Flora, xv
Alexander Pope (Sitwell), 304
All Passion Spent (Sackville-West), 282
Amis, Kingsley, 153, 156–157
Anderby Wold (Holtby), 143
Angel (Taylor), 331–332
Angels and Insects, (Byatt), 57, 59
Anglo-Irish, 27, 30, 96
Anglo-Irish writers, 28
animal rights, 48, 106, 108, 110
Ankle Deep (Thirkell), 339
Another World (Barker), 19
antiapartheid, 198
anti-Communist, 374
antifascism, 171
anti-Imperialism, 146
anti-modernism, xi–xiii
anti-Semitism, 170, 286
Arnold Waterlow (Sinclair), 298
Art and Lies (Winterson), 381–383
Art Objects (Winterson), 380–384
As It Was: Pleasures, Landscapes, and Justice (Bedford), 22
Astercote (Lively), 208
Astonishing Island, The (Holtby), 143
At Bertram's Hotel (Christie), 75
At Freddie's (Fitzgerald), 125
At Mrs. Lippincote's (Taylor), 328–329
atheisim, 47
Audrey Craven (Sinclair), 296
Avenue of Stone, An (Johnson), 183
Awfully Big Adventure, An (Bainbridge), 9–10, 13

Babel Tower (Byatt), 57, 60
Backwater (Richardson), 276
Bainbridge, Beryl, **9–15**
Ballad and the Source, The (Lehmann), 192, 194
Barker, Pat, **16–20**
Baroque-'n'-Roll (Brophy), 49–50
Barsetshire series (Thirkell), 335, 338–339
Bay of Angels, The (Brookner), 43
Bay of Silence, The (St. Aubin de Terán), 323

Bayley, John, 253
Beautiful Visit, The (Howard), 153–155
Bedford, Sybille, **21–26**
Before Lunch (Thirkell), 338–339
Before the Crossing (Jameson), 171
Beginning of Spring, The (Fitzgerald), 123, 125
Belsey, Catherine, 57, 60
Ben, in the World (Lessing), 202–203
Benes, Edouard, 167
Bennett, Arnold, 387–389
Bertolt Brecht, 82–83, 86
Best We Can Do, The (Bedford), 22–23
Between the Acts (Woolf), 389–390
Big Girls Don't Cry (Weldon), 354
Big Mother, 113, 116
Bird of Night, The (Hill), 136
Birds Fall Down, The (West), 374
Birthday Boys, The (Bainbridge), 11–12, 14
Black Idol (St. Aubin de Terán), 323
Black Lamb and Grey Falcon (West), 372, 374–375
Black Laurel, The (Jameson), 170–171
Black Prince, The (Murdoch), 253, 255
Black Venus U.S title, *Saints and Strangers* [Carter]), 63
Blaming (Taylor), 327–328, 333
Blessed above Women (Johnson), 183
Bliss, and Other Stories (Mansfield), 215
Bloody Chamber, The (Carter), 63, 66
Bloomsbury group, 236, 281, 385
Blow Your House Down (Barker), 16–18
Blue Flower, The (Fitzgerald), 123, 126–127
Body in the Library, The (Christie), 75
Bonfire, A (Johnson), 185
Booker Prize, 9, 16, 19, 23, 41, 44, 56, 123, 207, 210, 352
Bookshop, The (Fitzgerald), 123–125, 127
Born (Bowen), 36
Bottle Factory Outing, The (Bainbridge), 9, 14
Bowen, Elizabeth, **27–34**, 191, 194, 368, 371
Bowen's Court (Bowen), 29, 33
Break of Day, The (Wertenbaker), 358, 362–363
Bride Price, The (Emecheta), 113, 115, 117, 119
Brief Lives (Brookner), 43
Briefing for a Descent into Hell (Lessing), 200
British Anti-Vivisection Society, 49
Brittain, Vera, **35–40**, 142
Brookner, Anita, **41–46**
Brophy, Brigid, **47–55**
Burglar, The (Brophy), 48–49, 52
Burne-Jones, Edward, 124, 336
Busman's Honeymoon (Sayers), 286, 289–291
Byatt, A.S., **56–62**, 99–100
Camomile Lawn, The (Wesley), 367–368, 370
Canopus in Argos: Archives (Lessing), 196–198, 201, 203–204
Capital (Duffy), 109
Captain's Wife, The (Jameson), 168
Caribbean Dozen, A (Nichols), 257
Carnegie Medal, 207, 209
Carter, Angela, xv, 16, **63–71**, 312
Case to Answer (Wertenbaker), 359
Casting Off (Howard), 153
Catherine Carter (Johnson), 184
Cazalet chronicle (Howard), 153–157
Celia (Young), 399
Century's Daughter, The (Barker), 16, 18–19
Changing Places (Jellicoe), 177
Charlotte Mew and Her Friends (Fitzgerald), 124
Chatterton Square (Young), 397, 399
chi, 114
Children of Violence (Lessing), 197–200, 202–203
Children, The (Wertenbaker), 360
Christie, Agatha, **72–80**
Churchill, Caryl, **81–87**, 97, 188, 358
City of the Mind (Lively), 211–212
Civil to Strangers (Pym), 262
Cixous, Hélène, 57, 351
Cleopatra's Sister (Lively), 212
Clocks, The (Christie), 76
Cloning of Joanna May, The (Weldon), 352
Closed Eye, A (Brookner), 42–43
Cloud Nine (Churchill), 81–85
Clouds of Witness (Sayers), 286–287
Coffer Dams, The (Markandaya), 224–226
Cold Country The (Hill), 136, 140
Collected Impressions (Bowen), 29
Collected Poems (Duffy), 106–107
Collected Poems (Sitwell), 302
Collected Poems (Warner), 342, 344
Collected Poems and Prose (Mew), 239
Collected Short Stories, The (Rhys), 269
Collected Stories (Bowen), 28, 30, 33
Collins, Wilkie, 285
colonialism, 166, 171, 267
Combined Maze, The (Sinclair), 298
Come, Tell Me How You Live (Christie), 75
comedies of manners, 328
Comforters, The (Spark), 317
Commonwealth Poetry Prize, 257
Communist, 196, 199–200, 327
Communism, 197, 199, 373
Communist Party, 343, 345
Community Plays: How to Put Them On (Jellicoe), 175, 178
Company Parade (Jameson), 168, 170

Compass Error, A (Bedford), 22, 24–25
Compton-Burnett, Ivy, **88–92**, 316, 328, 368–369, 371
Confusion (Howard), 153
Cork Street, Next to the Hatter's: A Novel in Bad Taste (Johnson), 184
Corner That Held Them, The (Warner), 345
Coronation Summer (Thirkell), 337
Corruption (Lively), 210
Country Chronicle (Thirkell), 338
Court and the Castle, The (West), 374–375
Cousin Honoré (Jameson), 169
Creators, The (Sinclair), 298
Crooked House (Christie), 76
Crowded Street, The (Holtby), 143–145
Crown Princess The (Brophy), 48, 50
Curate's Wife, The (Young), 397–399
Curriculum Vitae (Spark), 315–316
Curtain (Christie), 74–75

Dark Tide, The (Bowen), 36
Dawn's Left Hand (Richardson), 277
Dead Man's Folly (Christie), 76
Death Comes as the End (Christie), 75
Death in the Clouds (Christie), 75
Death of the Heart, The (Bowen), 31
Death on the Nile (Christie), 75, 77
Debbie and the Little Devil (Lively), 210
Deconstruction, 68, 350
Demon in the House, The (Thirkell), 337
Demon Lover and Other Stories, The (Bowen), 29
Desai, Anita, 149, 152
Destination Biafra (Emecheta), 120
Devil to Pay, The (Sayers), 286, 293
Devlin, Anne, **93–98**
dialogue novel, 90
Diaries of Jane Somers, The (Lessing), 204
Diary of a Good Neighbour, The (Lessing), 196, 201
Divine Comedy, The (trans. Sayers), 293–294
Divine Fire, The (Sinclair), 297–299
Djinn in the Nightingale's Eye, The (Byatt), 59
Do Not Disturb (Wertenbaker), 360
Doctors of Philosophy (Spark), 318
Documents in the Case, The (Sayers), 285
Documents Relating to the Sentimental Agents in the Volyen Empire (Lessing), 201
Don't Never Forget (Brophy), 47–49
Dorothy Merlin Trilogy, The (Johnson), 180, 182, 184
Double Yoke (Emecheta), 117
Down Among the Women (Weldon), 352–353
Downstairs (Churchill), 81
Drabble, Margaret, 56, **99–105**
Dragon Trouble (Lively), 210
Dressing for Dinner (Keatley), 187
Dressmaker, The (U.S. title, *The Secret Glass* [Bainbridge]), 9–10, 13–14
Dubious Legacy, A (Wesley), 368–370
Duffy, Maureen, 49, **106–112**
Dusa, Fish Stas, and Vi (Gems), 129–130, 132–134
Dusty Answer (Lehmann), 192

Early Death (Churchill), 81
Easter Party, The (Sackville-West), 282
Echoing Grove, The (Lehmann), 192
Edwardians, The (Sackville-West), 282
Efuru (Nwapa), 116
Elegy for Iris, An (Bayley), 253
Elementals: Stories of Fire and Ice (Byatt), 60
Elephants Can Remember (Christie), 76
Eliot, T.S., 2, 58, 107, 150, 297, 302–303, 305, 316, 380
Emecheta, Buchi, **113–122**
Emperor Constantine, The (Sayers), 286, 293
Enclosure, The (Hill), 136
Encounters (Bowen), 28
End of This War, The (Jameson), 168
Ending in Earnest (West), 373
English Stage Company, 175
Erotic World of Faery, The (Duffy), 108
Europe to Let: The Memoirs of an Obscure Man (Jameson), 169
Eva Trout (Bowen), 28, 32
Every Man for Himself (Bainbridge), 9, 12, 14
Evesong (Duffy), 107
Excellent Women (Pym), 263
existentialism, 253–254
expressionist, 96
Eye in the Door, The (Barker), 16, 18
Eye of the Hurricane, The (Adcock), 3

Faber Book of Modern Short Stories, The; "Preface" (Bowen), 29–30
Faber Book of Twentieth Century Women's Poetry, The (Adcock, ed.), 4–5
Fabian Socialism, 373
Fabian Socialists, 274
fabulist mode, 230
Facade (Sitwell), 304
Faces of Justice, The (Bedford), 22–23
Falling Slowly (Brookner), 44
False Admissions (Wertenbaker, trans.), 359
Family and a Fortune, A (Compton-Burnett), 89–91
Family and Friends (Brookner), 41, 43
Family History (Sackville-West), 282

Family, The (Emecheta), 120
Fanfarlo and Other Verses, The (Spark), 316
Far Cry from Kensington, A (Spark), 317
Farmer's Bride, The (Mew), 238–239
fascism, 166–167, 169; German, 35
Fat Black Woman's Poems, The (Nichols), 260
Fat Women's Joke, The (U.S. title, *And the Wife Ran Away* [Weldon]), 350
Father and His Fate, A (Compton-Burnett), 89
Favourite of the Gods, A (Bedford), 22, 24–25
Female Friends (Weldon), 352
feminine: impressionism, 273; writing, 57
femininity, 63, 66
feminism, 35–37, 44, 47, 81, 100–101, 103, 142–143, 146, 187–188, 190, 198, 247, 251, 253, 267, 299, 350, 354, 362; cultural, 361; literary, 56–57; New, 143–145; Old, 143, 145
feminist, xv, 35, 56, 103, 106, 149, 376; African, 116; criticism, 82, 260; critics, 236; drama, 190; equality, 37; ideals, 35; ideas, 385; issues, 129; modernism, 166; movement, xiii, 129, 130, 354; novel, 263; perspective, 193; politics, 390; theory, 313, 349; thinkers, 393; tract, 66
féminité, 57
Fen (Churchill), 81, 83
Few Green Leaves, A (Pym), 264
Fifth Child, The (Lessing), 202
Fifty Works of English and American Literature We Could Do Without (Brophy), 49
Finishing Touch, The (Brophy), 48, 51
Firbank, Ronald, 48–49, 52–53
Fireworks: Nine Profane Pieces (Carter), 65
Fitzgerald, Penelope, **123–128**, 238
Five Notes After a Visit (Devlin), 93
Five Red Herrings, The (Sayers), 285
Flesh: A Novel of Indolent Passion (Brophy), 48, 51–52
Flint Anchor, The (Warner), 345
Ford, Ford Madox, 268–269
Fortunes of Harriette, The (Thirkell), 337
Fountain Overflows, The (West), 374
Four-Gated City, The (Lessing), 197, 199–200, 203–204
Fraud (Brookner), 43
Friend from England, A (Brookner), 41–43

Game of Hide and Seek, A (Taylor), 328, 330
Game, The (Byatt), 58–59, 100
Garden Party, and Other Stories, The (Mansfield), 215
Garrick Year, The (Drabble), 100
Gate of Angels, The (Fitzgerald), 123, 126–127
Gates of Ivory, The (Drabble), 100–101, 103
Gaudy Night (Sayers), 286, 290
gay rights, 47
Gems, Pam, **129–135**, 188, 358
gender studies, 53
Getting It Right (Howard), 153–154
Ghost of Thomas Kempe, The (Lively), 207, 209, 211–212
Ghost Road, The (Barker), 16, 19
Girls of Slender Means, The (Spark), 316
Giveaway, The (Jellicoe), 174
Glass of Blessings, A (Pym), 263
Godless in Eden (Weldon), 350
Going Home (Lessing), 197
Golden Child, The (Fitzgerald), 123–125
Golden Honeycomb, The (Markandaya), 221, 224, 227
Golden Notebook, The (Lessing), 197–200, 203–204
Good Apprentice, The (Murdoch), 253, 255
Good Morning, Midnight (Rhys), 268, 270
Good Terrorist, The (Lessing), 202
Good Time Was Had by All, A (Smith), 310
Grace of Mary Traverse, The (Wertenbaker), 359–363
Grand Canyon (Sackville-West), 282
Grass Is Singing, The (Lessing), 196–198, 203
Grateful Sparrow and Other Stories, The (Thirkell), 337
Green Knight, The (Murdoch), 255
griotte, 113, 121
Gut Symmetries (Winterson), 382–383

Hacienda, The (St. Aubin de Terán), 322, 325
Hackenfeller's Ape (Brophy), 48, 50
Handful of Rice, A (Markandaya), 224
Handyman, The (Mortimer), 249–251
Harnassing Peacocks (Wesley), 367, 369
Harold's Leap (Smith), 310
Harriet Hume (West), 373
Harriet Said (Bainbridge), 9–10, 14
Harsh Voice, The (West), 373
Have His Carcase (Sayers), 289
Having a Wonderful Time (Churchill), 81
He That Should Come (Sayers), 286
Head Above Water (Emecheta), 113–114
Headmistress, The (Thirkell), 338
Heart of the Country, The (Weldon), 349, 352
Heartlanders (Devlin), 94
Heat of the Day, The (Bowen), 28, 31–32
Helena Trilogy, The (Johnson), 180, 182–184
Helpmate, The (Sinclair), 298
Henry James (West), 373, 376
Here Today (Johnson), 183
Heritage (Sackville-West), 281
Heroes and Villains (Carter), 63, 65

High Place, The (St. Aubin de Terán), 323
High Rising (Thirkell), 337, 339
Hill, James (pseud. of Storm Jameson), 169
Hill, Susan Elizabeth, **136–141**
historicism, 58
Hogarth Press, 391
Holiday, The (Smith), 311
Hollow, The (Christie), 75
Holtby, Winifred, 35, **142–147**
Home The (Mortimer), 249–250
Honourable Estate (Bowen), 36
Honour's Board, The (Johnson), 182
Hosain, Attia, **148–152**
Hotel du Lac (Brookner), 41–44
Hotel, The (Bowen), 30
Hothouse of the East River, The (Spark), 316
House and Its Head, A (Compton-Burnett), 90–91
House in Paris, The (Bowen), 31–32
House Inside Out, A (Lively), 210
Howard, Elizabeth Jane, **153–158**, 332
Human Voices (Fitzgerald), 125
Humm, Maggie, xiv–xv
Huxley, Aldous, 21–24, 262

i is a long memoried woman (Nichols), 257
I Live Under a Black Sun (Sitwell), 304
Ice Age, The (Drabble), 100
Identical Twins (Churchill), 81
If the Old Could . . . (Lessing), 202
ifo, 113
Igbo Women's War, 116
Imaginative Experience, An (Wesley), 370
imagist novel, 273
imperialism, 97, 237
imperialist, 197
Impossible Marriage, An (Johnson), 184
I'm the King of the Castle (Hill), 136, 138–139
In a German Pension (Mansfield), 215
In a Summer Season (Taylor), 332
In the Ditch (Emecheta), 114–115, 119
In the Second Year (Jameson), 167, 169
In the Springtime of the Year (Hill), 136
In Transit (Brophy), 47, 49, 52–53
Incident Book, The (Adcock), 5–6
Incidents in the Rue Laugier (Brookner), 43–44
Indiscreet Journeys: Stories of Women on the Road (St. Aubin de Terán, ed.), 325
Infernal Desire Machines of Doctor Hoffman, The (U.S. title, *The War of Dreams* [Carter]) 63, 65
Injury Time (Bainbridge), 9–11, 14
Innocence (Fitzgerald), 125, 127
Interim (Richardson), 277
intertextuality, 42, 60

Invitation to the Waltz (Lehmann), 192–193
IRA (Irish Republican Army), 94
Irigaray, Luce, 57

Jacob's Room (Woolf), 387–388
James, P.D., **159–165**
Jameson, Storm, **166–173**
Jane and Prudence (Pym), 263, 265
Jellicoe, Ann, 106, **174–179**
Jerusalem the Golden (Drabble), 100
Jigsaw: An Unsentimental Education: A Biographical Novel (Bedford), 22–23, 25
Joanna (St. Aubin de Terán), 324
Johanna (Mortimer), 247
John Llewellyn Rhys Memorial Prize, 63, 101, 153, 379
John Masefield (Spark), 317
Johnson, Pamela Hansford, **180–186**
Joint Stock, 81
Journal of Mary Hervey Russell, The (Jameson), 168, 170
Journey from the North (Jameson), 166
Joys of Motherhood, The (Emecheta), 114, 116–119
Judge, The (West), 373
Jumping the Queue (Wesley), 367–368
Just Vengeance, The (Sayers), 293

Kaplan, Sydney Janet, xiv–xv
Keatley, Charlotte, **187–190**
Keepers of the House (St. Aubin de Terán), 322
Kenyon, Olga, xv, 41, 44
King of a Rainy Country, The (Brophy), 47–48, 50–51
Kitty Tailleur (Sinclair), 298
Knack, The (Jellicoe), 174–178
Knox Brothers, The (Fitzgerald), 124
Kristeva, Julia, 57, 381

la gente, 321–322
Labour government, 337
Labour Party, 49, 99,181, 327, 335
Labour socialist, 166
Land of Green Ginger, The (Holtby), 143–144
Landlocked (Lessing), 199
Landscape in Italy (St. Aubin de Terán), 324
language, disintegration of, 52
Lanterns across the Snow (Hill), 137
Last Resort, The (Johnson), 184
Last Score (Jameson), 170
Last September, The (Bowen), 30–31
Latecomers (Brookner), 43
Lazy Thoughts of a Lazy Woman (Nichols), 259
Left Bank and Other Stories (Rhys), 269
Left Book Club, 181

Legacy, A (Bedford), 22, 24–25
Lehmann, Rosamond, **191–195**
lesbian: feminist poet, 106–107; literature, 51; sexuality, 108; students, 51; themes, 53; writing, 345
Lesbian Body, The (Wittig), 57
lesbianism, 48, 282
Less Than Angels (Pym), 263
Lessing, Doris, xiv–xv, 103, **196–206**
Letters (Warner), 342
Letters from Darkness: Poems (Adcock), 3
Lévi-Strauss, Claude, 232–233
Lewis Percy (Brookner), 43
Life and Death of Harriett Frean (Sinclair), 296, 298–299
Life Force (Weldon), 353
Light Shining in Buchinghamshire (Churchill), 82
Light Years, The (Howard), 153–154
Literature of Their Own, A: British Women Novelists from Brontë to Lessing (Showalter), xiv, 68
Little Girls, The (Bowen) 28, 32
Lively, Penelope, **207–214**
Lives and Loves of a She-Devil, The (Weldon), 351–352
Lives of the Great Poisoners (Churchill), 81
Lodge, David, xi
Loitering with Intent (Spark), 316
Lolly Willowes (Warner), 343–344
Lombard, Nap (pseud. of Pamela Hansford Johnson and Gordon Neil Stewart), 181
Londoners (Duffy), 109
Long March, The (Devlin), 93–94
Long Way Home, The (St. Aubin de Terán), 322
Look at All Those Roses (Bowen), 30
Look at Me (Brookner), 42
Looking Back (Adcock), 3
Love (Carter), 63–65
Love, Again (Lessing), 202
Love All (Sayers), 286, 292
Love Child (Duffy), 109
Love in Winter (Jameson), 168
Love of the Nightingale, The (Werterbaker), 358–359, 361, 363
Lovely Ship, The (Jameson), 168
Lovesick (Churchill), 81
Loving Women (Gems), 132–133

Mad Forest (Churchill), 81, 86
magic realism, 65
Magic Toyshop The (Carter), 63–64
Making of the Representative for Planet 8, The (Lessing), 201
Man Born to Be King, The (Sayers), 286, 292
Man Who Wasn't There, The (Barker), 16, 18
Mandoa, Mandoa! (Holtby), 143, 145–146
Manservant and Maidservant (Compton-Burnett), 91
Mansfield, Katherine, 194, **215–220**, 299
Mara and Dann (Lessing), 203–204
Marble Mountain and Other Stories, The (St. Aubin de Terán), 324
March Moonlight (Richardson), 277
Markandaya, Kamala, **221–229**
Marking Time (Howard), 153
Marlene (Gems), 131–132
Marriages between Zones Three, Four, and Five, The (Lessing), 201
Martha Quest (Lessing), 197–199
Marxism, 350
Mary Olivier (Sinclair), 296, 298–299
Masaryk, Jan, 167
Master Georgie (Bainbridge), 9, 12–13
Matisse Stories, The (Byatt), 59
Meaning of Treason, The (West), 373–375
Melville, Pauline, **230–235**
Memento Mori (Spark), 316
Memoirs of a Survivor, The (Lessing), 201
Memorials of the Quick and the Dead (Duffy), 107
Men and Wives (Compton-Burnett), 89
Mephisto (trans. Wertenbaker), 359
metafiction, 58, 60; self-reflexive, 60
metahistoriography, 58
Mew, Charlotte, **236–246**
Microcosm, The (Duffy), 108–110
Middle Ground, The (Drabble), 100
Migration of Ghosts, The (Melville), 233
Millstone The (Drabble), 100–101
mimetic, 60, 63
Mind of the Maker, The (Sayers), 292
Mirror in Darkness, The (Jameson), 167–171
Miss Bunting (Thirkell), 338
Miss Mole (Young), 397–400
Misalliance, A (Brookner), 42–43
Misses Mallett, The (Young), 397–399
modern, the, xi
modernism, xi–xiii, xv, 33, 53, 169, 171, 191, 239, 267, 278, 281, 297, 299, 304, 376, 380, 384, 386, 390
modernist, 88, 103, 170, 185, 203, 264, 278, 374, 393; autonomy, 58; experimentation, 270; high, 273, 277; modes, 183; standards, 33; style, 283; traditions, 181
Money and Land (Jellicoe), 177
Monstrous Regiment, 81, 188
Monument, The (Johnson), 183
Moon Tiger (Lively), 207, 210–212
Mortimer, Penelope, **247–252**
Mossy Trotter (Taylor), 328
Mousetrap, The (Christie), 74

Mouthful of Birds (Churchill), 81
Movement, The, 310
Movement poetry, 6
Moving Finger, The (Christie), 76
Mozart the Dramatist: A New View of Mozart, His Operas, and His Age (Brophy), 48
Mozart, Wolfgang Amadeus, 48, 50–53
Mr. Fortune's Maggot (Warner), 344
Mrs. DeWinter (Hill), 140
Mrs. Dalloway (Woolf), xii, 385, 388–391
Mrs. Jordan's Profession (Devlin), 96
Mrs. Palfrey at the Claremont (Taylor), 328, 332
Mulberry Tree, The (Bowen), 28, 30–31
Murder Is Announced, A (Christie), 74, 76–77
Murder Must Advertise (Sayers), 288
Murder of Roger Ackroyd, The (Christie), 72–75
Murder on the Orient Express (Christie), 75
Murder's a Swine (Johnson and Stewart), 181
Murdoch, Iris, 61, **253–256**
Murry, John Middleton, 215
My Friend Says It's Bulletproof (Mortimer), 249
My Mother Said I Never Should (Keatley), 187–190
Mysterious Affair at Styles, The (Christie), 73, 76–77
myth criticism, 370

Nakiketas and Other Poems (Sinclair), 296
National Book Award, 207
nationalism, 96
Natural Curiosity, A (Drabble), 100, 102
naturalism, 65, 103, 298, 360
Nazism, 167, 169
Nectar in a Sieve (Markandaya), 222–224, 226–227
Needle's Eye, The (Drabble), 100–101, 103
Nemesis (Christie), 74, 76
New Criticism, 310
New Meaning of Treason, The (West), 374–375
Nice and the Good, The (Murdoch), 253, 255
Nichols, Grace, **257–261**
Nicholson, Nigel, 281
Night and Day (Woolf), 386
Night and Silence: Who Is Here? (Johnson), 180, 184
Nightingale in Bloomsbury Square, A (Duffy), 108–110
Nights at the Circus (Carter), 63, 66–67
Nine Tailors, The (Sayers), 288, 290
No Fond Return of Love (Pym), 263
No Signposts in the Sea (Sackville-West), 282
No Time Like the Present (Jameson), 167
No Victory for the Soldier (Jameson), 169
Nocturne (St. Aubin de Terán), 324
None Turn Back (Jameson), 168, 171
Not That Sort of Girl (Wesley), 367
Not without Honour (Bowen), 36
Nothing Missing but the Samovar, and Other Stories (Lively), 207
Nothing Sacred (Carter), 65
Novel on Yellow Paper (Smith), 309–311, 313
novel-of-manners style, 371
Nowhere Man, The (Markandaya), 225
Nwapa, Flora, 116

Odd Girl Out (Howard), 154
Off the Rails: Memoirs of a Train Addict (St. Aubin de Terán), 324
Offshore (Fitzgerald), 123, 125, 127
Old Bank House, The (Thirkell), 338
Oleander, Jacaranda: A Childhood Perceived (Lively), 208
Olivier Award, 82, 359
One, Two, Buckle My Shoe (Christie), 75–76
Only Poet, The (West), 374
Only Problem, The (Spark), 317
Oranges are not the only fruit (Winterson), 379, 381–383
Ordeal by Innocence (Christie), 76
Orlando (Woolf), 389
Osborne, Charles, 49
O, These Men, These Men! (Thirkell), 339
Our Country's Good (Wertenbaker), 359, 362–363
Ourselves Alone (Devlin), 94, 95
Over the Frontier (Smith), 311–312
Oxford Companion to English Literature, The (ed. Drabble), 101

pacifism, 35–37, 47, 143, 189
Palace, The (St. Aubin de Terán), 325
Palace without Chairs (Brophy), 49, 52–53
Palladian (Taylor), 328–329
Parker, Leslie (pseud. of Angela Thirkell), 336
Part of the Furniture (Wesley), 368–369
Partition of India, 148–151
Partners in Crime (Christie), 74
Passenger to Frankfurt (Christie), 76
Passing On (Lively), 211
Passion of New Eve, The (Carter), 63, 65–66
Passion, The (Winterson), 379, 382–383
Passions of the Mind (Byatt), 59–60
Peace Breaks Out (Thirkell), 338
Peace Pledge Union, 35
PEN (Poets, Playwrights, Editors, Essayists, and Novelists), 23, 167–168, 181, 237
Perfect Happiness (Churchill), 81
Peril at End House (Christie), 75
Phoenix Fled (Hosain), 149, 152
Piaf, Edith, 130
Piaf (Gems), 131–132

Pictures and Conversations (Bowen), 27
Pilgrimage (Richardson), 273–278
Pleasure City (U.S. title, *Shalimar* [Markandaya]), 224, 227
Pocket Full of Rye, A (Christie), 76
Pointed Roofs (Richardson), 275–276
Pomfret Towers (Thirkell), 338–339
Poor Caroline (Holtby), 143
Portrait of a Marriage (Mortimer), 249
Portrait of a Marriage (Nicholson), 281
Possession (Byatt), 56, 58–61
Possession (Markandaya), 224, 226–227
postcolonial theory, 271
postcolonialism, 267
Postern of Fate (Christie), 76
postmodern: era, 68; feminism, 103; metafiction, 58; novel, 213; novelist, 207; querying of language, 32; theories, 350; work, 17; writer, 58
postmodernism, xii–xiii, 53, 200, 267, 271, 379, 382, 384, 391
postmodernist, 42, 103, 376; metafiction, 59
postmodernists, 380
post-Movement poetry, 6
Postures (U.S. title, *Quartet* [Rhys]), 268–269, 272
Prancing Novelist: A Defence of Fiction in the Form of a Critical Biography in Praise of Ronald Firbank (Brophy), 48
Praxis (Weldon), 352–353
Pride and Prejudice (Weldon, television adaptation), 350
Prime of Miss Jean Brodie, The (Spark), 315
Private View A (Brookner), 42–43
privatization, 350
Proper Marriage, A (Lessing), 198
protection of: animals, 47; authors' rights, 47
Providence (Brookner), 42
psychological novel, 298
Public Lending Right Bill, 49
Puffball (Weldon), 354
Pumpkin Eater, The (Mortimer), 249
purdah, 150–151
Pym, Barbara, **262–266**, 333

Quakers, 99–100
Quartet in Autumn (Pym), 264
Queen Elizabeth: A Life of the Queen Mother (Mortimer), 251
Quiet Life, A (Bainbridge), 9–10, 14
Queen Mother: An Alternative Portrait of Her Life and Times (Mortimer), 251

Radiant Way, The (Drabble), 100, 102
Rainbow, The (Devlin, television adaptation), 95
rape motif, 119
Rape of Shavi, The (Emecheta), 120
Reads (Brophy), 49
realism, xi–xii, 32, 57–59, 63, 103, 182, 201, 203, 247, 317, 318, 379, 382, 384; new, 143, 144
realist, 170, 185; fiction, 60; mimetic, 60; mode, 230; naturalist, 96
Realms of Gold, The (Drabble), 100–101, 103
Reckoning, The (Jellicoe), 174, 177
Reds (West, contributor), 374
Regeneration (Barker), 16, 18–19
Retreat to Innocence (Lessing), 199
Return of the Soldier, The (West), 373, 376
Rhys, Jean, **267–272**
Richardson, Dorothy, **273–279**, 339
Richer Dust, A (Jameson), 168
Ripple from the Storm, A (Lessing), 199
Rising Generation, The (Jellicoe), 174, 176
Rites (Duffy), 109–110
Road to Litchfield, The (Lively), 207, 209–210
romance, 63; novel, 42
romanticism, 222
Room of One's Own, A (Woolf), 390
Royal Court Theatre, 81, 93–94, 97, 175–178, 358–359
Royal Court writers' group, 106
Royal National Theatre, 177–178
Royal Shakespeare Company, 100, 129–130, 359

Sackville-West, Vita, 238, 249, **280–284**, 389
Sadeian Woman, The (Carter), 63, 66
Sayers, Dorothy L., **285–295**
Scenic Route, The (Adcock), 1, 5
Schreber's Nervous Illness (Churchill), 81
science fiction, 201
Sea Change, The (Howard), 154–155
Second Fiddle (Wesley), 368, 370
Second Sentence (Wertenbaker, 359
Second Virago Book of Fairy Tales, The (Carter, ed.), 66
Second-Class Citizen (Emecheta), 114, 116, 119
Secret Adversary, The (Christie), 873
See, the Sea, The (Murdoch), 255
Selected Poems (Adcock), 4–5
Sensible Life, A (Wesley), 370
Serious Money (Churchill), 81, 86
Service of Clouds, The (Hill), 136
Several Perceptions (Carter), 63–64
Severed Head, A (Murdoch), 253, 255
Sexing the Cherry (Winterson), 379, 383
Shadow Dance (Carter), 63–64
Shadow of the Sun, The (Byatt), 58
Shape Shifter (Melville), 230–232

Shared Experience Company, 359
Shelley; or, the Idealist (Jellicoe), 174, 177
Shikasta: Re, Colonised Planet 5 (Lessing), 201
Showalter, Elaine, xiv–xv, 68, 236
Silence of Desire, A (Markandaya), 222, 224
Sinclair, May, 237, 239, **296–301**
Sirian Experiments, The (Lessing), 201
Sitwell, Edith, 236, **302–308**
Skinner, John, 44
Skriker, The (Churchill), 82
Slave Girl, The (Emecheta), 114, 119
slavery, 119
Sleep It Off, Lady (Rhys), 271
Sleeping Beauty and Other Favourite Fairy Tales (Carter), 66
Sleeping Beauty, The (Taylor), 330
Sleeping Murder (Christie), 74
Slow Train to Milan, The (St. Aubin de Terán), 322
Small Personal Voice, A (Lessing), 197–198
Smile Please (Rhys), 269, 272
Smith, Stevie, 303, **309–314**
Snow Ball, The (Brophy), 48, 52
Snow, C.P., 181
social realist tradition, 63
socialism, 146, 187, 198, 350
socialist realism, 142, 143
socialist realists, 169
Some Inner Fury (Markandaya), 221, 223, 226
Some Tame Gazelle (Pym), 262–263
Some Unconscious Influences in the Theatre (Jellicoe), 177
Somers, Jane (pseud. of Doris Lessing), 196–197, 201
Something in Disguise (Howard), 154–155
Song of Roland, The (Sayers, trans.), 294
Soul of Kindness, The (Taylor), 332
South Riding (Holtby), 142, 144–146
Sovereignty of Good, The (Murdoch), 253
Spark, Muriel, **315–320**, 333, 351
Spider's Web (Christie), 74
Spiderweb (Lively), 212
Sport of My Mad Mother, The (Jellicoe), 174–177
St. Aubin de Terán, Lisa, **321–326**
St. Augustine (West), 373, 375
Stanley (Gems), 131, 133
Start in Life, A (Brookner), 42, 44
Stevie Smith: A Collection (Smith), 309
Stewart, Gordon Neil, 181
Still Life, (Byatt), 56, 59–60
Stitch in Time, A (Lively), 209, 211–212
Strange Meeting (Hill), 136–137, 139
Strange Necessity, The (West), 373
stream of consciousness, 297–298, 385, 388–390
Street Songs (Sitwell), 305
Striding Folly (Sayers), 291
Strong Poison (Sayers), 289, 291
Successful Strategies (Wertenbaker, trans.), 359
Sudden View, The: A Mexican Journey (Bedford), 22–23
Sufism, 197, 200–201
suffrage, xiii, 193, 374, 386
suffrage movement, 372
suffragettes, 35
Sugar and Other Stories (Byatt), 59
Summer Before the Dark, The (Lessing), 200
Summer Bird-cage, A (Drabble), 99–100, 103
Summer Story, A (Mortimer), 249
Summer to Decide, A (Johnson), 183
Summer Will Show (Warner), 345
Sunlight on a Broken Column (Hosain), 149–152
Swan in the Evening, The (Lehmann), 192
Sweet Dove Died, The (Pym), 264
Sweet William (Bainbridge), 11, 14
Symphony for Full Orchestra (Johnson), 181

Taken at the Flood (Christie), 75
Taken Care Of (Sitwell), 303
taluqdars, 148–149
Taylor, Elizabeth Coles, **327–334**
Ten Little Niggers (Christie), 75
Testament of a Generation (Brittain), 37, 143
Testament of Friendship (Brittain), 142
Testament of Youth (Brittain), 35–37, 142
That Was Yesterday (Jameson), 168
That's How It Was (Duffy), 106–108
Thebans, The: Oedipus Tyrannos, Oedipus at Colonus, and Antigone (Wertenbaker, trans.), 360
Then We Shall Hear Singing: A Fantasy in C Major (Jameson), 167, 169
Thinking Reed, The (West), 373
Third Girl (Christie), 76
Third, The (Wertenbaker), 359
Thirkell, Angela, **335–340**
This Bed Thy Centre (Johnson), 180–184
This Is No Place for Tallulah Bankhead (Wertenbaker), 359
Thomas, Dylan, 181–182, 307
Three Brontës, The (Sinclair), 298
Three Guineas (Woolf), 390
Three Houses (Thirkell), 337
Three Sisters, The (Sinclair), 298–299
Tidy Death (Johnson and Stewart), 181
Tiger, The (St. Aubin de Terán), 323
Tigers (Adcock), 3–4
Tigers Are Better-Looking (Rhys), 271

Time Zones (Adcock), 7
Titanic Town (Devlin, screenplay adaptation), 96
To the Lighthouse (Woolf), xii, 385, 388, 392
To the North (Bowen), 30
Too Dear for My Possessing (Johnson), 183
Top Girls (Churchill), 81–85
Towards Zero (Christie), 75
traditionalism, xii–xiii
Train of Powder, A (West), 375
Treasures of Time (Lively), 207, 210
Tribute to Wordsworth (Spark), 316
Tristan in Brittany (Sayers, trans.), 294
Triumph of Time, The (Jameson), 168
Trodd, Anthea, xv
Trooper to the Southern Cross (Thirkell), 336, 338
True Heart, The (Warner), 344–345
Tunnel, The (Richardson), 276
Turn Outside, A (Smith), 310
Two Virgins (Markandaya), 226

Under My Skin (Lessing), 197
Under the God (Jellicoe), 177
Underneath the Arndale (Keatley), 188
Undue Influence (Brookner), 44
Uninvited Ghosts and Other Stories (Lively), 210
Union Street (Barker), 16–18
Unnatural Death (Sayers), 287
Unpleasantness at the Bellona Club, The (Sayers), 285, 288
Unpopular Opinions (Sayers), 285
Unspeakable Skipton, The (Johnson), 184
Unsuitable Attachment, An (Pym), 264
Upstairs, Downstairs (Weldon), 350

Vacillations of Poppy Carew, The (Wesley), 368–369
Valley in Italy: The Many Seasons of a Villa in Umbria, A (St. Aubin de Terán), 324
vegetarianism, 47
Venice: The Four Seasons (St. Aubin de Terán), 324
Ventriloquist's Tale, The (Melville), 230, 232–233
Venus Touch, The (Duffy), 107
Very Private Eye, A (Pym), 264
Vicar's Daughter, The (Young), 398
View of the Harbour, A (Taylor), 328–330
Vigo (Devlin), 96
Villa in Summer, A (Mortimer), 249
Vinegar Tom (Churchill), 81–83
Virago Book of Fairy Tales, The (Carter, ed.), 66
Virago Book of Wanderlust and Dreams, The (St. Aubin de Terán, ed.), 325
Virago Modern Classics, 110, 311
Virago Press, xiii, 16, 18, 149, 299, 332–333, 341
Virgin and the Nightingale, The (Adcock), 3
Virgin in the Garden, The (Byatt), 59–60
Voyage Home, The (Jameson), 168
Voyage in the Dark (Rhys), 268, 270
Voyage Out, The (Woolf), 386

Warner, Sylvia Townsend, 236, **341–348**
Waterfall, The (Drabble), 100
Watson's Apology (Bainbridge), 12
Waves, The (Woolf), 388
Way-Paver, The (Devlin), 93, 97
Wayward Girls and Wicked Women (Carter, ed.), 66
Weather in the Streets, The (Lehmann), 192–194
Wedding Group, The (Taylor), 332
Weekend with Claude, A (Bainbridge), 9
Weldon, Fay, **349–357**
Wells, H. G., 274, 372–373
Wertenbaker, Timberlake, **358–366**
Wesley, Mary, **367–371**
West, Rebecca, 238, **372–378**
Wheels (Sitwell), 303
Whitbread Award, 9, 136, 207, 209, 247, 352, 379
Whitbread First Novel Award, 230
Whole of a Morning Sky (Nichols), 259–260
Whose Body? (Sayers), 285–287
Wicked Women (Weldon), 352
Wide Sargasso Sea (Rhys), 267–272
William (Young), 397–399
Winterson, Jeanette, **379–384**
Wise Children (Carter), 63, 66–67
Witch of Exmoor, The (Drabble), 99, 101–102
Witness for the Prosecution (Christie), 74
Wittig, Monique, 56–57
Woman Calling, A (Devlin), 93–94, 97
Woman in Black, The (Hill), 136–138, 140
Women and a Changing Civilisation (Holtby), 143
women's: liberation movement, 103, 130, 349; literature, xiii; movement, 35; oppression, 119;
writer, 102–103;
writing, xiv–xv
Women's Company, 129–130
Women's Playhouse Trust, 129
Women's Theatre Festival, 130
Women's Theatre Group, 129–130, 188, 359
Woolf, Leonard, 391
Woolf, Virginia, xii–xiv, 28, 42, 88, 108, 110, 143–144, 191, 193–194, 207, 212, 215, 217–218, 236, 238, 250, 271, 273, 281, 305, 310, 328, 330–331, 339, 381, **385–395**, 397
Working with Structuralism (Lodge), xi
World of Love, A (Bowen), 32
World's End (Johnson), 183
Worst Fears (Weldon), 352

Wounds (Duffy), 109
Wreath of Roses, A (Taylor), 330–331
Writers' Action Group, 49
Writers' Group, 175
Written on the Body (Winterson), 383
Wuthering Heights (Devlin, screenplay adaptation), 95, 97

Years, The (Woolf), 389
Young Adolf (Bainbridge), 12
Young Men (Pym), 262
Young, E.H., **396–401**

Zeal of Thy House, The (Sayers), 286, 292
zenana, 149–150

About the Editors and Contributors

HENA AHMAD received her Ph.D. from the University of Massachusetts at Amherst in 1998. She is now an assistant professor of English at Truman State University, Missouri, where she teaches courses in anglophone postcolonial literatures.

KARLA ALWES is Professor of English at the State University of New York at Cortland. She is the author of *Imagination Transformed: The Evolution of the Female Character in Keats's Poetry* and several articles on poetry and gender.

ASHOK BERY is a senior lecturer in English at the University of North London, where he teaches courses on postcolonial literatures and modern poetry. He is the coeditor of *Comparing Postcolonial Literatures* (1999) and has published articles on the novels of R.K. Narayan and on other aspects of Indian literature.

JONATHAN BOLTON is an assistant professor of English at Auburn University. He is the author of *Personal Landscapes: British Poets in Egypt during the Second World War* and has published a number of articles on twentieth-century British and Irish literature.

REGINA M. BUCCOLA has taught in the English Department and the Women's Studies Program at the University of Illinois at Chicago, where she currently serves as the assistant to the director of Undergraduate Studies in English. She has published review articles and essays on twentieth-century poetry and drama and is a published poet herself. She has written, directed, and performed in a number of performance pieces in Chicago.

JOY CASTRO teaches fiction writing and twentieth-century literature at Wabash College in Indiana. Her work has appeared in such journals as *Quarterly West*, *Chelsea*, *Review of Contemporary Fiction*, *North Carolina Literary Review*, and *South Central Review*. She is currently finishing a collection of short stories and a critical study of American modernist Margery Latimer.

DOUGLAS CLAYTON is Director of the M.A. program in writing and publishing at Emerson College and the former editor-in-chief at the University of Nebraska Press. He has published articles on American and British literature, modern cultural criticism, and the history of public intellectuals. He is the author of *Floyd Dell: The Life and Times of an American Rebel.*

ANDRÉ L. DECUIR is an assistant professor of English at Muskingum College in New Concord, Ohio. He has published and presented papers on Charlotte Brontë, Elizabeth Gaskell, Mary Shelley, George Eliot, Thomas Hardy, and recently on Stephen King, as he is interested in the aesthetics of horror fiction, Victorian and modern.

STELLA DEEN, Assistant Professor of English at the State University of New York at New Paltz, has written about novelists E.H. Young, Enid Bagnold, and Molly Keane. She is currently working on a study of Emily Hilda Young's novels. Additionally, she is a founding member of The Space Between, a society for the study of literature and culture between the wars.

JOHN LOUIS DIGAETANI is professor of English at Hofstra University. His extensive publications include books ranging from *The Handbook of Executive Communication* to *Richard Wagner and the Modern British Novel*, *A Search for a Postmodern Theater*, and *Money: Lure, Lore, and Literature*. He is the director of Hofstra's London Program.

KATHLEEN ELLIS has taught English at several universities in the Northeast. Currently she consults with businesses and corporations on the role of communication in business performance.

JERILYN FISHER is an assistant professor of English at Hostos Community College of the City University of New York. She is coeditor of *Analyzing the Different Voice: Feminist Psychological Theory and Literary Texts* and coauthor of "Fairy Tales, Feminist Theory, and the Lives of Women and Girls," a chapter in that volume. She is also coediting *Women and Literature: Evaluating Fiction for Gender Bias*, forthcoming from Greenwood Press.

JANA L. FRENCH studies contemporary fiction, postmodernism, and women's traditions in the novel. Most recently she has taught literature and humanities in Christ College, the honors college of Valparaiso University.

LAURA FROST is an assistant professor of English at Yale University, where she teaches twentieth-century British and comparative literature. She is currently working on a book on fascism and sexuality in modern and contemporary culture.

TONY GIFFONE is an associate professor of English and humanities at the State University of New York at Farmingdale. His previous articles on detective fiction include an investigation of the representation of the Chinese in contemporary detective fiction, a study of contemporary detective fiction that utilizes Victorian settings, and a reading of "*Twin Peaks* as Post-Modernist Parody: David Lynch's Subversion of the British Detective Novel."

JACQUELINE L. GMUCA is currently an assistant professor of English at the University of Texas at El Paso, where she also serves as Director of the West Texas Writing Project. Her scholarship includes presentations and publications on F. Anstey, Brendan Behan, and William Butler Yeats. She is currently working on a book manuscript entitled *The Irish Renaissance and Childhood.*

MARLENE SAN MIGUEL GRONER is an associate professor of English and humanities at the State University of New York College at Farmingdale. She is coauthor of *A Blueprint for Writing and a Glossary of Usage* and of numerous articles on twentieth-century British literature, women's studies, and philosophy. She is a recipient of the State University Chancellor's Award for Excellence in Teaching.

MELINDA HARVEY is completing a Ph.D. on Dorothy Richardson in the Department of English at the University of Sydney, Australia. She is interested in interwar women's writing—in particular, Katherine Mansfield, Virginia Woolf, Elizabeth Bowen, and Jean Rhys—and in modernism's engagement with travel, art, psychoanalysis, film, and the city.

MARY LOUISE HILL holds a Ph.D. from New York University's Department of Performance Studies. She first encountered Susan Hill's work while researching her dissertation, "When the Voice Must Be the Body: Feminism and Radio Drama." Her articles have appeared in *TDR: The Drama Review, Theatre Journal*, and *Women and Performance*, and she has also written and published fiction, poetry, and drama. She is not related to Susan Hill.

SUSANNA HOENESS-KRUPSAW is an assistant professor of English at the University of Southern Indiana, Evansville. She has written "The Role of the Family in the Novels of E.L. Doctorow" (unpublished dissertation, Southern Illinois University, Carbondale, 1992), "Colette" and "Simone de Beauvoir" in *Feminist Writers*, and "Elaine Showalter" in *Gay and Lesbian Writers*.

CHRIS HOPKINS is a senior lecturer in English studies at Sheffield Hallam University. He has published on the British novel in the 1930s and on Anglo-Welsh writing in numerous journals, including *Critical Survey, Literature and History, Journal of Gender Studies, Review of Contemporary Fiction*, and *Style*. He recently published *Thinking about Texts: An Introduction to English Studies*.

ROBERT ELLIS HOSMER, JR., has been a member of the Department of English Language and Literature at Smith College since 1990; he teaches courses in fiction, poetry, world literature, and twentieth-century women novelists. His publications include *Contemporary British Women Writers: Texts and Strategies* (1993) and articles in *America, Cross Currents*, and *Southern Review*.

DEL IVAN JANIK, coeditor, Professor of English at the State University of New York College at Cortland, holds an M.A. from the University of Michigan and a Ph.D. from Northwestern University. He has written on British, Irish, and American writers, including D.H. Lawrence, Flann O'Brien, Gary Snyder, and, most recently, Graham Swift, A.S. Byatt, and other contemporary English novelists, an interest he developed while he was an exchange lecturer at the University of North London.

VICKI K. JANIK, coeditor, is Associate Professor of English at the State University of New York College at Farmingdale, where she teaches Shakespeare and technical writing and recently received a Chancellor's Award for Excellence in Teaching. She holds degrees from Vanderbilt, DePaul, and the State University of New York at Stony Brook. Her publications include an edition of John Heywood's *The Play of the Wether* and *Fools and Jesters in Literature, Art, and History* (Greenwood, 1998). Her latest project is a book on *The Merchant of Venice*.

HEIKE ELISABETH JÜNGST was trained at Germersheim University, Germany, as a translator. She holds a Ph.D. on women characters in modern English drama. She has taught English and German at the Universities of Mainz, Germersheim, and Cambridge. Her main research interests are graphic novels, women cartoonists, women's novels, technical writing, and translation.

ANNA KATSAVOS is an associate professor at Nassau Community College, where she teaches English, women's studies, and multidisciplinary courses. She received her Ph.D. in English from the City University of New York Graduate School and University Center. She is coauthor of *Complements*, a freshman composition textbook, and has just completed a critical study of the works of Angela Carter.

FRANK KELLY is Professor of English and humanities at the State University of New York College at Farmingdale; he studied at the University of Scranton and the University of Kansas, where he received a Ph.D. in theater and drama. He is coauthor of the musical comedy *Pageant*, which played Off-Broadway and subsequently throughout the United States and in Japan, Australia, and London's West End.

MARIA KOUNDOURA holds an M.A. from the University of Melbourne and a Ph.D. from Stanford. Her most recent publications are essays on aspects of multiculturalism and of popular culture. She has just completed a book on the use of Greece as a locating topos in Western modernity.

PHYLLIS LASSNER teaches women's studies, Holocaust studies, and writing at Northwestern University. She is the author of two books on Elizabeth Bowen, articles on American women writers and British women writers of the interwar and World War II eras, and, most recently, the book *British Women Writers of World War II: Battlegrounds of Their Own*.

MITCHELL R. LEWIS teaches at the University of Oklahoma, where he is also completing a dissertation on modernism and science and assisting Vincent B. Leitch with *The Norton Anthology of Theory and Criticism* (2001). His article on György Lukács appears in *The Edinburgh Encyclopaedia of Modern Criticism and Theory*, edited by Julian Wolfreys.

ALAN LUTKUS, former host of College FM's *The Radio Detectives*, is Associate Professor of English at the State University College at Geneseo, New York, where he teaches linguistics and detective fiction.

JOHN H. LUTTERBIE is the chair of the Theatre Arts Department at the State University of New York at Stony Brook and the author of *Hearing Voices: Modern Drama and the Problem of Subjectivity*, an investigation of ethics and intersubjectivity. He is currently working on a phenomenology of performance.

EDMUND MILLER is the chair of the English Department at the C.W. Post Campus of Long Island University. He is the author of *Drudgerie Divine: The Rhetoric of God and Man in George Herbert* and other works about seventeenth-century British literature. He has written on Dorothy L. Sayers before and on other mystery novelists and religious writers.

PETER F. NACCARATO earned his Ph.D. from the State University of New York at Stony Brook in 1997. He is currently Assistant Professor of English at Manhattan Marymount College. He is coeditor, with Susan Squier, of the Shakespeare Head Press edition of Virginia Woolf's *The Years*.

ELIZABETH HOFFMAN NELSON is a lecturer in English at the State University of New York College at Fredonia. She is a coeditor of Peter Lang's American Indian Studies Series. Her most recent publication was in *Leslie Marmon Silko: A Collection of Critical Essays*. She also published two entries in Greenwood Press's *Fools and Jesters in Literature, Art, and History*.

NEIL NOVELLI is Professor of English at LeMoyne College, Syracuse, New York. He has produced plays by Shakespeare and performed in various theatrical productions, including the medieval drama festivals at the University of Toronto. He is a drama critic and columnist for the *Syracuse Herald-Journal* and the *Post-Standard*.

JOSÉ RAMÓN PRADO PÉREZ is Lecturer in English Literature at Universidad Jaume 1 de Castellón, Spain. He specializes in contemporary British alternative theater. His areas of research include popular culture, literature in its social and cultural context, and film adaptations of Shakespeare's works.

PATRICIA RAE is an associate professor of English at Queen's University, Canada. She is the author of *The Practical Muse: Pragmatist Poetics in Hulme, Pound, and Stevens* and of numerous articles on English and American modernist literature in journals including *Comparative Literature*, *ELH*, *Twentieth Century Literature*, and *English Studies in Canada*.

SUZANNE SCAFE is a senior lecturer at South Bank University, London. Her publications include *The Heart of the Race: Black Women's Lives in Britain; Teaching Black Literature*; and *"Quiet As It's Kept": Reading Black Women Writers*. She has also written a number of articles on contemporary Caribbean writers.

BEVERLY E. SCHNELLER is the author of articles on British women writers, British publishing history, Irish cultural history, and American poets and poetry. A graduate of the Catholic University of America, she teaches at Millersville University. She has been teaching Mary Wesley's fiction at the undergraduate and graduate levels since 1991.

The late ROBERTA M. SCHREYER taught writing and courses in women and literature, psychology and literature, and folklore and myth at the State University of New York College at Potsdam.

JOEL SHATZKY is Professor of English at the State University of New York College at Cortland. He is the editor of *Theresienstadt: Hitler's "Gift" to the Jews* by Norbert Troller and (with Michael Taub) of two books for Greenwood Press: *Contemporary Jewish-American Novelists* and *Contemporary Jewish-American Dramatists and Poets*.

KARL L. STENGER attended the University of Bonn and passed the state examination in English and German. He received an M.A. and Ph.D. from Ohio State University. He has taught at Ohio Wesleyan, the State University of New York at Potsdam, and the University of Alabama at Birmingham and is currently Associate Professor at the University of South Carolina at Aiken. He has published on nineteenth- and twentieth-century German literature and the detective novel.

JULIE SIMS STEWARD is an assistant professor of English at Samford University, where she teaches literary theory and modern poetry. Her publications have appeared in *Journal of Modern Literature* and *South Central Review*. A playwright and poet, she is currently at work on a book on Stevie Smith and gender construction.

JOHN THIEME is Professor of English studies at South Bank University and has taught previously at the Universities of Guyana, North London, and Hull. His books include *The Web of Tradition: Uses of Allusion in V.S. Naipaul's Fiction* (1987), *The Arnold Anthology of Post-Colonial Literatures in English* (1996), *Derek Walcott* (1999), and *Post-Colonial Con-Texts: Writing Back to the Canon* (2001).

SARAH MILES WATTS is coauthor of *The Press and the Presidency*, which won the Frank Luther Mott 1986 Research Award of the School of Journalism, University of Missouri, and was nominated for the Pulitzer Prize. Now teaching at the State University of New York College at Geneseo, she has also written *The Art of Belgian Cooking* and much theater criticism.

GINA WISKER is head of Women's Studies at Anglia Polytechnic University in

Cambridge, where she also teaches English and is Director of Learning and Teaching Development. Her interests are in twentieth- and twenty-first-century U.S., United Kingdom, and postcolonial women's writing. She has recently published books on romance in contemporary literature, postcolonial and African American women's writing, and Virginia Woolf.

BRITTA ZANGEN worked as a fashion designer, a teacher of English, and chief librarian before returning to education as a mature student. In 1995 she finished a Ph.D. on Vera Brittain at Heinrich-Heine-Universität Düsseldorf, where she is now a lecturer in English literature. She has published several articles and is currently working on her Habilitation, which is on feminism and Victorianism.

JOSEPH ZEPPETELLO is the Writing Program director at Marist College. He has published a book on composition theory as well as articles in various journals including the *Writing Lab Newsletter*.